The Economic Causes of the English Civil War

This is a coordinated presentation of the economic basis of revolutionary change in sixteenth- and early seventeenth-century England, addressing a crucial but neglected phase of historical development. It traces a transformation in the agrarian economy and substantiates the decisive scale on which this took place, showing how the new forms of occupation and practice on the land related to seminal changes in the general dynamics of commercial activity. An integrated, self-regulating national market generated new imperatives, particularly a demand for a right of freedom of trade from arbitrary exactions and restraints. This took political force through the special status that rights of consent had acquired in England, based on the rise of sovereign representative law following the Break with Rome. These associations were reflected in a distinctive merchant-gentry alliance, seeking to establish freedom of trade and representative control of public finance, through parliament. This produced a persistent challenge to royal prerogatives such as impositions from 1610 onwards. Parliamentary provision, especially legislation, came to be seen as essential to good government. These ambitions led to the first revolutionary measures of the Long Parliament in early 1641, establishing automatic parliaments and the normative force of freedom of trade.

George Yerby took his degree at Birkbeck College, London University in 1986, and has since worked as an historical researcher. He specialises in the economic and political history of the sixteenth and seventeenth centuries. He is the author of *People and Parliament: Representative Rights and the English Revolution*, published in 2008, and *The English Revolution and the Roots of Environmental Change*, published in 2016.

Routledge Research in Early Modern History

Social and Cultural Relations in the Grand Duchy of Lithuania
Microhistories
Edited by Richard Butterwick and Wioletta Pawlikowska

Spain, Rumor, and Anti-Catholicism in Mid-Jacobean England
The Palatine Match, Cleves, and the Armada Scares of 1612–1613 and 1614
Calvin F. Senning

Firsting in the Early-Modern Atlantic World
Edited by Lauren Beck

Early Modern English Noblewomen and Self-Starvation
The Skull Beneath the Skin
Sasha Garwood

Maurits of Nassau and the Survival of the Dutch Revolt
Comparative Insurgences
Nick Ridley

The Economic Causes of the English Civil War
Freedom of Trade and the English Revolution
George Yerby

Edwin Sandys and the Reform of English Religion
Sarah L. Bastow

For more information about this series, please visit: www.routledge.com/Routledge-Research-in-Early-Modern-History/book-series/RREMH

The Economic Causes of the English Civil War

Freedom of Trade and the English Revolution

George Yerby

Routledge
Taylor & Francis Group
NEW YORK AND LONDON

First published 2020
by Routledge
52 Vanderbilt Avenue, New York, NY 10017

and by Routledge
2 Park Square, Milton Park, Abingdon, Oxon, OX14 4RN

Routledge is an imprint of the Taylor & Francis Group, an informa business

Library of Congress Cataloging-in-Publication Data
A catalog record for this book has been requested

ISBN: 978-0-367-18923-5 (hbk)
ISBN: 978-0-429-32555-7 (ebk)

Typeset in Sabon
by Apex CoVantage, LLC

MIX
Paper from responsible sources
FSC® C013056

Printed and bound in Great Britain by
TJ International Ltd, Padstow, Cornwall

In memory of my grandparents

Contents

Figures

Acknowledgements

Thanks are due to David Parker, Neil Davidson, Colin Mooers, John Rees and Michael Hunter for reading and commenting on this book in various aspects, and at various stages of development. I also remain grateful to Colin Richmond for his advice, and his kind and encouraging words about the importance of these themes, summed up in his guiding tenet that the cabbages are as significant as the kings. Illustrations are integral to the study, and in this respect I have to thank Chris Reynolds for his timely and invaluable photograph capturing the reappearance of the open field strips at Wilstone, and the Oxfordshire History Centre for permission to add their photo of a similar re-emergence at Marston. I am also grateful to the Parish of St. Mary's, Putney for allowing me to include Nicholas Lane's map of Putney in 1636. As regards architectural history, I am greatly in debt to Hugo Butterworth for expertly conveying the significance of the new style of manor house that arose in Elizabethan times. Last, but by no means least, I would like to thank my editor Max Novick for his support.

Abbreviations

Add. Ms.	Additional Manuscript, British Library
Agrarian History	*The Agrarian History of England and Wales 1500-1640* ed. J. Thirsk, (Cambridge 1967)
APC	*Acts of the Privy Council*
BL	British Library
CJ	*Commons Journal*
CSP	*Calendar of State Papers*
EETS	Early English Text Society
Gardiner	S. R. Gardiner, *History of England 1603-1642*, (London 1880s)
HA	Hertfordshire Archives
HMC	Historical Manuscripts Commission
Hutchinson	Lucy Hutchinson, *Memoirs of the Life of Colonel Hutchinson,* ed. J. Hutchinson, (London 1846)
LJ	Lords Journal
NA	Nottinghamshire Archives
Procs in Parl.	Proceedings in Parliament
DRO	Devon Record Office
SP	State Papers
TED	*Tudor Economic Documents*, ed. R. Tawney and E. Power
Discourse	*A Discourse of the Commonweal* (1549) ed. M. Dewar, (Virginia 1969)
TNA	The National Archives
TRHS	Transactions of the Royal Historical Society
VCH	Victoria County History
Woodhouse	A. S. P. Woodhouse ed. *Puritanism and Liberty*, (London 1938)

Introduction

Recovering the Economic Context of History

This volume attempts a broad, but coordinated view of the economic context of the English Civil War and Revolution of the mid-seventeenth century. It seeks to substantiate the economic causes that were fundamental to the contest between king and parliament for command of the emergent English state. It affirms this perspective in the face of the uneven treatment that it has received from historians. Some have taken the force of economic factors as read, but presented it in a somewhat generalised form, which has enabled others, inherently unsympathetic to economic interpretations, to regard it as unproven, and set it aside. The answer offered here provides an inclusive and detailed picture of the seminal changes in the social, agricultural and commercial fields in sixteenth- and early seventeenth-century England, identifying the new imperatives that came into being, and drawing out the specific connections between economic developments and the momentous political overturning of the 1640s.

Contemporary commentators writing before, or at the time of the Civil War were in no doubt that a great socio-economic transition had taken place in England. It was generally observed that there had been a transfer of property power from the king and the high nobility to "the people", or the middle ranks. This thesis was propounded most notably by James Harrington in the 1650s, but similarly held by all "the best thinkers among his predecessors and contemporaries"—including Walter Raleigh, Sir Francis Bacon, James I, John Selden, Sir Henry Wotton, Sir Thomas Wislon, Spelman Bishop, Francis Quarles, Godfrey Goodman, Henry Parker, Henry Ireton, Gerrard Winstanley and Thomas Hobbes.[1] Many of them believed that the change in the balance of landowning and wealth created a platform for the parliamentary challenge to the crown. The best-known statement of this perception is in the writings of James Harrington. But we can find another, equally cogent, in the work of Lucy Hutchinson, who also noted a rise of "the people" at the expense of the old elite.

> When the nobility shrank into empty names the crown lost its supporters . . . when the full body of the people came rolling in upon it . . . the interest of the people, which had been many years growing,

> made an extraordinary progress in the reign of Henry VIII, who returning the vast revenues of the church into the body of the people, cast the balance clear on their side.[2]

This was consistent with her first-hand identification of the "middle sort" of yeomen and merchants as the distinctive and substantial core of parliamentarian support, when battle was joined. Of particular interest is her comment that this access of economic strength "left them now only to expect an opportunity to resume their power". She seems to have perceived that as a result of socio-economic change in favour of "the people" there had arisen a specific popular demand for some kind of political change.

Modern historical writing may be taken as beginning two hundred years after the Civil War, with the work of Thomas Macaulay. He inaugurated the "Whig" interpretation, which was the basis of the dominant academic tradition for another hundred years. The "Whigs" acknowledged the events of the Civil War period as revolutionary, but defined them almost exclusively in terms of constitutional disputes and developments. In essence they were describing the rise of parliament. Macaulay is not usually included in the ranks of the scholarly, but he offered some of the most incisive observations of the political aims of parliamentarians. "They were resolved to place the King in such a situation that he must . . . conduct his administration in conformity with the wishes of his parliament".[3] This was a precise description of the kind of power that parliament was seeking, but it was only half the story. Like most "Whig" historians, Macaulay seemed happy to suppose that the constitutional ambitions of parliament were held just for their own sake, or in the pursuit of a general notion of "liberty". This paid scant attention to the possibility that there may also have been other, more material motivations for enhancing the authority of parliament. It is interesting however that like most "Whig" historians, Macaulay does mention in passing some of the socio-economic factors that were seen as significant at the time. He notes, for instance, that, "The main strength of the opposition lay among the small freeholders in the country, and among the merchants and shopkeepers of the towns".[4]

The "Whig" thesis was sustained in Samuel Gardiner's magisterial study of the years between 1603 and the Civil War. Although it was written in the later nineteenth century, it remains the most balanced and comprehensive treatment of the political and constitutional history of the period. But it was compiled essentially from an exhaustive study of the State Papers, and for ten volumes there appears to be no significant awareness of the socio-economic context. It is of interest once again, however, that there is eventually a fleeting reference to the contrasting economic and geographical situations of the two sides. "England was divided by an undulating line, which left only the less wealthy and thickly populated districts of the north and west to Charles". Gardiner noted that this gave parliament a substantial advantage in terms of the depth of financial resources.[5] The idea of an economic and geographical divide was to be revived some seventy years later by a committed social historian, who felt that it was a better guide to Civil War allegiances than just analysing political differences.[6] But to Gardiner it was a way of describing the Civil War rather than explaining it.

The Whig historian who attained the widest readership was George Trevelyan. He is an interesting case because he was a very acute observer of the social scene in itself. His general history of England under the Stuarts begins with an extended survey of social relations, but when he comes to define the central confrontation between king and parliament, it is treated as a separate, political and constitutional issue. Since, however, he was a social historian as well, he made more passing references to the significant, seminal socio-economic changes than did his Whig predecessors. He noted the disappearance of the open fields, and the associated rise of the yeoman farmer, which was one of the most crucial and distinctive developments of the period. He was aware that in other ways too English society was moving in a different direction from other European kingdoms. He observed the critical distinction that, unlike their later French counterparts, the English revolutionaries were not needy people, but "prosperous men". In the end, however, he thought that none of this should be regarded as causative. The contesting parties were "enamoured of liberty, or of loyalty, for their own sakes".[7]

The next generation of "Whig" historians were similarly focused on the constitutional perspective. The two most prominent figures continued to deal essentially with the rise of parliament, as it sought new areas of political initiative and independence. John Neale's in-depth study of the parliaments of Elizabeth I made him the most notable successor to Gardiner. And Wallace Notestein repeated the exercise in relation to the parliaments of James I. Yet, while still not advancing any idea of economic causation, they did not fail to note, in passing, some further aspects of significant change in the economic sphere. Neale recorded the appropriation of the borough seats in the House of Commons by gentleman landowners, an important development by which the socio-economic expansion of the gentry acquired a national-political focus.[8] Notestein, for his part, faithfully reflected the coordinated radical thrust of the free trade movement in the Commons in the first parliament of James I.[9] This was a particularly important contribution, since the demand for freedom of trade became a vital foundation of parliamentarian aims. Notestein did a great service in highlighting a crucial factor that has been generally ignored by historians of all persuasions in more recent times.

The Whig interpretation has often been criticised as the product of "hindsight" or "predetermination"—that is to say, reading history backwards. It must be said, however, that accusations of "hindsight" have no actual verifiable force—they are allegations that can never be proved. There is no reason to suppose that it cannot be perfectly valid to see signs in the past of the way that history was to develop. In fact, as E. H. Carr pointed out, charges of "pre-conception" are really just devices by which unsympathetic historians seek to pre-exclude the evidence for radical change that they prefer not to recognise.[10] In fact, the Whigs were not preconceiving a process of constitutional development, they were reflecting and describing it. Macaulay was writing in the wake of the Great Reform Act of 1832, Gardiner in the light of two further extensions of the franchise in 1867 and 1884. The lifetimes of Neale and Notestein saw the struggle and success of women's suffrage. It is a simple and important truth that the history of the English polity since 1604 has been characterised by a process of constitutional change. The flaw in the Whig thesis was not pre-determination. The true limitation of Whig history was their assumption that constitutional development was undertaken just for its own sake, and that it owed nothing to the underlying socio-economic context of the place in which it occurred. They presented it as an abstract notion of national liberty, divorced from the real life of the community.

In the critical circumstances of the 1930s and 40s, constitutional process no longer seemed adequate to balance the affairs of the nation. The situation of the generality of people, in terms of what they required to survive, became a matter of greater political concern. The history of social relations acquired a new currency. Socially aware historians began to focus on the significance of the economic factors that had been identified by Civil War contemporaries, and sometimes noted in passing in the traditional Whig thesis. Richard Tawney led the way in elaborating the effects of economic change. He highlighted the plight of the peasant smallholders who, from the end of the fifteenth century, were increasingly losing their place on the commons and open fields in the face of market pressures, rising rents, and the enclosure or "engrossing" of holdings by larger commercial farms.[11] Less securely, Tawney went on to suggest a link between the work ethic of Reformed religion, and the emergence of a more capitalist economy.[12] But perhaps his most important thesis was "The Rise of the Gentry". In a variation on James Harrington's theme from three hundred years before, founding the Civil War on a transfer of economic strength to "the people", Tawney posited a redistribution of landed power from the higher nobility to the middle-ranking gentry, through a great increase in their numbers and their property holdings.[13] This, like most of Tawney's interpretations carried an essential truth, though it was not always to be measured precisely as he proposed.

Tawney's principal successor in publicising the case of economic history was the more explicitly socialist figure of Christopher Hill, who noted that the great changes in mid-seventeenth-century England fulfilled most of the conditions for the bourgeois stage of Marx's idea of a sequence of revolutions, beginning with the transition from a medieval to a capitalist form of exchange and production. This was true enough, but once again, Hill did not really elaborate the precise form in which it was taking place. There was more clarity in his focus on another general observation of Civil War contemporaries—that the "middle sort" of people were at the heart of the parliamentary cause. He also gave centre stage to the geographical divide noted by Gardiner, outlining a Royalist north and west against a Parliamentarian south and east. Hill characterised the latter not just as richer, but economically "advanced". He was implying in effect that the force of commercialisation, by "the industrious sort of people" was the essential basis of parliamentary allegiance.[14] This may well have been the case, but again we were left without a definitive view of specific motivations, or a clear indication of how these economic developments were related to the political revolution at the centre of the state.

These omissions left the interpretations vulnerable to criticism, or to simply being set aside by historians who were inherently unsympathetic to the economic case. In the later twentieth century, notwithstanding the emerging environmental crisis that was demonstrating the contrary, there was a general tendency among historians to reject the significance of economic factors. There were various circumstances that encouraged, or enabled academics to turn a blind eye in that direction. Information technology was becoming the dominant force in society, and post-modern thought was propounding the conceit of the indeterminacy of language. Many philosophers and historians became trapped in the notion that linguistic form was a law unto itself, determined only by its own structures, incapable of being used with meaningful reference to independently definable realties beyond. Political events also implied a retreat from material certainties. The uprising in Paris in 1968, forceful as it was, appeared to be led by students and intellectuals with little connection to labour in any respect. At the same time the leading examples of materialist theory as a governing system were being discredited. The destruction of the Prague Spring exposed the Marxist inspired regimes of Eastern Europe as incorrigibly repressive and structurally unsustainable. All in all, even leftward-inclined figures like Michel Foucault concluded that it was no longer helpful to postulate a beneficial process of history from an economic base, and that the forces of domination were rather to be targeted as a "discourse-power" axis.[15]

Those of a rightward leaning seized on the failings of the Eastern European regimes as proof positive that Marxism was nothing more than a threat to liberty, in principle and in practice. They concluded that Marxist theory could now be discounted in every aspect. It should be recalled, however, that conservatives also had to deal with a real and flourishing manifestation of freedom that had arisen closer to home, especially in Britain and the United States. In the 1960s, Western society saw the emergence of a fully-fledged counter culture that denied the validity of power structures per se. This could be seen from certain angles as the better side of Marxist theory, leaning towards direct democracy. It posed a fundamental challenge to the ruling system, and it had all the best tunes.

In reaction to these opportunities and challenges arose the New Right, or neo-liberalism, conceived to defend and reaffirm the hegemony of the capitalist system against all threats of subversion. In political terms, like it or not, this could at least be seen as a rational response. But in the field of history it was much less so. In fact, it led to some fundamental distortions of the historical discipline. In the 1970s there emerged a "revisionist" generation of historians, which can be seen as the academic wing of neo-lilberalism. Their contribution was to reject any concept that promoted or encouraged the idea of radical change. Fallacies arose when this present aim was superimposed upon the past. Interpretations of history that perceived a process of social, or constitutional, advance were henceforth to be disallowed in advance. The revisionists were rejecting Marxism as a theory, and were therefore driven to discount it in every aspect, irrespective of actual historical status. If Marx said that history was moving in a particular direction, then the revisionists must deny the very idea of consecutive change in history. If Marx said that economic factors were at the core of historical development, then the revisionists must dismiss any possibility of economic motivation.

They promoted an "empirical" methodology that could appear to justify their rejection of the idea of history as a process of development. They proposed instead an analysis of the past based on an account of isolated particulars, divorced in place and time.[16] They asserted that any perception of consecutive change was to be avoided, and that the past could and should be studied in dissected and dissociated form "in its own right".[17] This had the tactical advantage of sounding unexceptionable when stated glibly as a scientific axiom. But further consideration reveals it to be inapplicable to the discipline of history, and in fact a direct denial of the nature of chronological form. To assert a specific capacity to treat history empirically is a contradiction of our true relationship with the past. As a more authentic empirical theorist A. J. Ayer pointed out, to look at the past literally as it was "would require of the observer that he should occupy a position which ex hypothesi he does not".[18] Roland Barthes expressed the same thought in the abstract terms of post-modernism, and captured the character of historical pseudo-empiricism as a polemical device. It was, he said, "a sleight of hand, whereby something is aimed for outside the discourse, without it ever being possible to attain it outside the discourse".[19]

But to identify revisionist-empiricism as an illusion does not fully expose its negative effects. Far from looking at the past "as it was", it contradicts the nature of chronological form as continuous movement, and contrives to conceal the most powerful historical evidences. It depends on a variety of tactical sleights of hand. Since the revisionist preconception was of something that did *not* happen it was easier to present it as not a preconception at all. And although it was impossible in actuality to see the past "in its own right", there was a means by which that impression could be created, by the simple expedient of refusing to recognise anything that seemed to prefigure the future. Revisionists could be heard to assert in tones of utter seriousness that to note any sign of forward development was to fail to see the past "as it was". This injunction had the effect of silencing the evidences that would reveal the strongest and most characteristic desires of the time—that is to say, the preferences and perceptions that were in the process of changing. We had been led into a kind of never-never land, where nothing ever changed. We were clinically divorced from the past, as if it had never existed.

It was the prospect of economic causation that provoked the most glaring and debilitating pattern of avoidance. The idea was dismissed by revisionism as a preconceived theory, "reducing" history to an economic explanation. This served to discount it in advance, and had the effect of concealing many of the most genuine and pertinent of historical evidences. This is graphically illustrated by some exchanges between two eminent historians, centring on David Underdown's study of Civil War allegiance in the near West Country.[20] Ironically, Underdown was unusual in the revisionist generation in that he could not ignore the logical probability that there was some kind of radical popular motivation behind the Civil War, but he shared the basic revisionist prejudice against economic causes. When challenged by the more thoroughgoing revisionist John Morrill to demonstrate the reality of popular sentiment, Underdown sought to find it in the notion of religio-cultural independence. There was an important truth in the idea of a motivating spirit of independent-mindedness, but Underdown had not presented it in the most relevant or cogent form. Morrill was in any case unconvinced, but his response was surprising. Focusing simply on rebutting Underdown's theory of popular culture, and no doubt assuming that in a revisionist world economic factors could not possibly be regarded as significant, he said that the only thing shown by Underdown's evidence was a general link between parliamentarian support and the commercial and manufacturing centres. Underdown expressed surprise that Morrill had even mentioned that correlation, and replied that he could not acknowledge it himself, because it would have been economically reductionist to do so.[21] The two professors had tripped up over their own prejudices, and tumbled together into the vale of self-contradiction. The only thing demonstrated was that the revisionist determination to ignore the force of economic motivation and causative development resulted in the specific concealment of the most crucial and conspicuous kinds of evidence.

Meanwhile, back in the real history of the seventeenth century, and not far away from Underdown's West Country, John Corbet was observing the issue at first hand, as chaplain to the parliamentary garrison in another thriving commercial and manufacturing centre—the market town of Gloucester. Corbet made a balanced and precise assessment of the character of the personnel who formed the backbone of the parliamentarian movement, and identified their principles and beliefs. He noted that the cause depended principally on "a generation of men truly laborious, jealous of their properties, whose principal aim is liberty and plenty".[22]

The capacity of a generation of revisionist historians to discount such statements, and to indulge in the deliberate avoidance of economic causation, is one of the most distorting and debilitating academic tendencies of our time. It is graphically demonstrated once again in a recent publication misleadingly described as a *Handbook of the English Revolution*.[23] The general thrust of the contributions is in fact to deny the idea of a developing revolution, largely by concealing the distinctively English character of the English Civil War. This agenda produces the bizarre situation where the editors begin by disowning the title of their book. Michael Braddick calls it "problematic". Peter Lake prefers to talk of "the events formerly known as the English revolution".[24] They would rather have called it "The War(s) of the Three Kingdoms", but as Braddick admits, this concept has little currency outside academia. Perhaps the commissioning publisher perceived that such a title was simply not intelligible, either in itself or as a reflection of the revolutionary nature of the event. All possibility of coherence vanishes into the unbridgeable gap between singular and plural. It demonstrates again the lengths to which revisionist historians are prepared to go in order to avoid the force of economic causes, for it is much easier to set aside the seminal socio-economic changes that were noted by contemporary commentators, and were distinctive to the English kingdom, if you transpose the Civil War into an imaginary and amorphous "British" dimension.

"The War(s) of the Three Kingdoms" is an artificial construct, exaggerating the significance of the part played by Scotland and Ireland in a Civil War that was essentially English in character. The supposed "British" dimension seems to consist of seeking out any reference to Scottish and Irish contributions, however incidental or contingent they may be, and gathering them together as if this automatically converts them into one and the same occurrence.[25] The interpretation presents nothing in the way of reasoned association or logical sequence of a sort that might indicate a common movement among the peoples of the three lands. It is difficult to imagine indeed what form such a development could take. Ireland was not in any case an English kingdom. It was a land of many Irish sub-kings, and only partly colonised by the Anglo-Normans. The lack of any pretence of a unitary structure meant that Ireland could not possibly have played a direct part in the English Civil War. We shall see ahead that the part played by the Scottish Covenanters was also indirect. They were involved only briefly, until they found that their essentially religious agenda was in fact foreign to the aims of the English Parliamentarians.

Further resisting a more substantial explanation for the English Civil War, leading contributors to the *Handbook* seek to avoid the whole category of causes. Peter Lake sets the tone for the denial of historical cause with an article on "Post-Reformation Politics, or On Not Looking for the Long-Term Causes of the English Civil War". Lake attempts to address some of the great seminal changes in the century before the Civil War, while precluding the possibility that these things might have contributed to the causes of the struggle itself. He has taken on a difficult task, since the English Reformation was a change so dramatic, so undeniably long-term, so distinctively laicised and English in character that it is difficult to believe that it did not have some effect on the political balance. So lest his readers may stumble into that logical assumption, he begins by issuing an injunction that the developments that he records are not to be taken as causes of the Civil War, though they might have influenced the form of it once it had occurred. He then makes a careful selection of "influences" that relate to the fringes rather than the substance of affairs, and are least likely to be regarded as causative. He deals with the peripheral and superficial, like variations in the platitudes of church supremacy, and the flurries of invective that arose at the religious extremes between the Puritan and Catholic camps, which he describes as the political discourse of the period. He treats the Reformation as a struggle for control between crown and Papacy. He ignores the truly distinctive features of the English Reformation, like the great reversal of socio-economic potential that was completed by the laicisation of the church lands, which contemporaries like James Harrington and Lucy Hutchinson regarded as the platform for the challenge to the crown. He takes no account of the unique concept of sovereign representative law that emerged from the destruction of the independent jurisdiction of the church, giving parliament a defining share in legislative sovereignty, which established the radical proposition that the crown could not exercise such sovereign powers by its own authority, and provided a model upon which other prerogatives of the crown could and would be challenged, as was done quite specifically in the dispute over impositions. Nor does Lake perceive that statute law had thereby acquired a unique nationally binding force that gave it broad public appeal and made it the basis of an alternative concept of good government. And he does not recognise that the Reformation did much to create a set of national priorities, and a view of foreign policy definable without reference to the interests of the crown—a perspective that the House of Commons pursued independently in the 1620s, by refusing to pay for anything else. All these matters were aspects of what I have called the growing tension between the governmental claims of "patent" or "parliament", and this was the real political discourse in the early seventeenth century.

After a long journey in which he manages to overlook these major issues, Lake arrives at an extraordinary passage that attempts to make the concept of cause actually disappear. He notes that there was a heightening of tensions in establishment circles and in the exchanges of invective between the "Puritan" and "Catholic" sides in the late 1620s, then goes on: "But, of course, since the civil war did not start in the 1620s, we are still not talking about the causes of said civil war".[26] He seems to be saying that the Civil War could not have been caused until it had actually started. He is supposing in effect that the Civil War was caused by itself, and that the guns were set firing by spontaneous combustion. A further chapter in the present volume will describe a parliamentarian zone in the English Civil War. The people of the area joined forces to sustain an independent military position in the face of Royalist opposition in the county, over the course of several years. They established a series of garrisons across the region by a considerable communal effort of organisation and supply. They expended substantial amounts of money and resources, losing many men, and setting up nursing centres for the wounded, year after year, "in the public service". It does scant justice to the obvious commitment and sacrifice of these people to suggest that the deep conflict in England was the result of a series of accidental confusions and incidental contingencies in surface relations with the other lands in the British Isles. English parliamentarians were fighting for practices and principles relating to the most vital conditions of their lives.

Perhaps we can regard Lake's attempt to eradicate the idea of cause as a deliberate exaggeration to further distance himself from the notion of the long-term. For if we admit to any kind of consecutive cause, it must necessarily open up the possibility of the long term, since there can be no fixed cutoff point before which one historical circumstance becomes incapable of causing another. We can offer an example of a specific causal link between the late 1620s and the early 1640s, which carries the implication of preceding causes. It is clear that the decision of Charles I to rule without parliament during the 1630s was a direct cause of the initiative taken as a priority by the Long Parliament to ensure that such an "intermission" of parliaments could never happen again. The connection is manifest, and it points us further back in time, for the determination to ensure regular assemblies arose not simply because absence had made the heart grow fonder. The public demand for more parliaments and more parliamentary influence, not less, was being expressed explicitly in the Commons by 1628. And the pressure of these parliamentary ambitions goes far to explain why Charles decided to rule without them in the 1630s. So we are drawn yet further back. Why was it that people had come to feel that parliament should be given a greater degree of input in governmental affairs? Clearly there must have been good reasons, and so we are driven ever further back.

Chronological form works in a continuum. In an age that seems oddly content to do without a concept of consecutive relationship, where can we look for a guiding precept that recognises the real nature of history as movement through time? Perhaps it might appear inadvertently. Jacques Derrida may seem an unlikely ally in the quest. He is usually seen as the high priest of the autonomy of language—the author of the most quoted axiom that there is no determinable truth existing beyond the text. More specifically, he devised the concept of "the trace", to convey the idea that no stable, settled point of meaning or "self-presence" can ever be established, because everything always contains the trace of "the other". He went part of the way with structuralism in as far as it reflected the "abandonment of all reference to a centre, to a subject, to an origin". Derrida became concerned, however, by the danger that the autonomous structure might itself be taken for a centred point of knowledge. It was therefore useful for him to extend the concept of the trace into the historical field, so that he could disallow the existence of independent structures, like Foucault's supposition of historical periods defined within the limits of their own discourse. No, said Derrida, no historical era can ever be simply of itself, it must always contain the trace if what precedes and follows.[27] The idea of "the trace", taken out of the realm of linguistic theory and applied to the reality of historical time, gives us an appropriate definition or necessary pattern of historical development. And in the parliamentary demand for more constant and more influential assembly there is the trace of the reasons for which this was desired.

What represents at once the great omission, and yet the underlying aim of the so-called *Handbook of the English Revolution*, is the absence of any treatment of the seminal socio-economic transitions in England that contemporaries regarded as the platform for the challenge to royal authority. The determination of the *Handbook* to avoid the idea of long-term explanations is further pursued by a willingness to present a truncated view of the past where events have consequences, but no causes. John Miller's article is titled, "The Long-term Consequences of the English Revolution: Social and Economic Development", as if the revolution itself was not a consequence of anything. He begins, "The impact of the revolution on England's economic and social development was considerable".[28] Possibly so, but it was little in comparison to the great socio-economic transition that occurred in the century before the Civil War, and was seen by contemporaries as a crucial contributory cause. Miller makes cursory reference to the fact that "many historians have tried to explain the origins of the Revolution in terms of social and economic change", but he mentions these attempts only to dismiss them as unsuccessful. He provides a brief survey of the hackneyed list of hostile comments on the work of R. H. Tawney and Christopher Hill, and thinks that the matter can be left there. In truth, although there have been many partial criticisms of the economic interpretations, none has seriously challenged the essential force of the developments that they identified. For the studies of Tawney and Hill were not just theories, they reflected the considered observations and opinions of the best-informed commentators at the time of the Civil War itself. Miller also chooses to ignore the fact that there has been a great deal of modern research and writing that reinforces the contemporary testimony.[29] He then seeks insurance for his evasive view by supposing that in any case, the new emphasis on "embracing the three kingdoms" means that explanations in purely English terms are no longer sufficient.[30] To the present author this rather confirms that the "British" dimension was conceived specifically as a means of diverting attention from the reality of the powerful, long-term socio-economic causes which were distinctive to the English kingdom.

So to recover the economic context of the English Civil War and Revolution is also to recover the most powerful testimonies of the time. What kind of public demand did Lucy Hutchinson perceive that led her to feel that following their "extraordinary progress" in socio-economic terms, the people were left "only to expect an opportunity to resume their power"?[31] And what exactly did James Harrington mean when he said that the economic rise of the people and the weakening of the force of the nobility undermined the position of the crown, to the effect that "the dissolution of this government caused the war, not the war the dissolution of this government"?[32]

Notes

1. C. Hill, "James Harrington and the People", in *Puritanism and Revolution,* (London 1968), pp. 291–3
2. L. Hutchinson, *Memoirs of the Life of Colonel Hutchinson*, ed. J. Hutchinson, (London 1846), p. 75
3. T. B. Macaulay, *The History of England,* (first published 1848), Everyman edition, (London 1906), vol. I, p. 71
4. Ibid, p. 85
5. S. R. Gardiner, *History of the Great Civil War,* (London 1893), I, pp. 34, 308
6. C. Hill, *The Century of Revolution,* (London 1961), p. 121
7. G. M. Trevelyan, *England Under the Stuarts,* (London 1904), pp. 30–1, 162
8. J. E. Neale, *The Elizabethan House of Commons,* (London 1949), p. 140
9. W. Notestein, *The House of Commons 1604–1610,* (New Haven 1971), p. 106
10. E. H. Carr, *What Is History?* (London 1961), pp. 96–8
11. R. H. Tawney, *The Agrarian Problem in the Sixteenth Century,* (London 1912)
12. R. H. Tawney, *Religion and the Rise of Capitalism,* (London 1926)
13. R. H. Tawney, "The Rise of the Gentry 1558–1640", *Economic History Review 11* (1941), pp. 1–38
14. Hill, *The Century of Revolution*, pp. 121–5; *Society and Puritanism in Pre-Revolutionary England,* (London 1964), pp. 124–33
15. M. Poster, *Foucault, Marxism and History,* (London 1994)
16. Early exercises in the revisionist/empiricist tendency were G. R. Elton, "A High Road to Civil War?" in *From the Renaissance to the Counter-Reformation*, ed. C. H. Carter, (London 1966); C. Russell, "Parliamentary History in Perspective 1604–1629", *History 61*, pp. 1–27
17. G. R. Elton, *The Practice of History,* (London 1969), pp. 84–6

18. A. J. Ayer, *Language, Truth and Logic,* (Harmondsworth 1971), pp. 25, 135
19. R. Barthes, "The Discourse of History", in *Post-Structuralism and the Question of History*, ed. D. Attridge, (London 1987), p. 3
20. D. Underdown, *Revel, Riot and Rebellion,* (Oxford 1985)
21. Underdown, *Revel, Riot and Rebellion*, p. vii; J. Morrill, "The Ecology of Allegiance", and Underdown's rejoinder: JBS 26, pp. 451–73
22. J. Corbet, "A True and Impartial Account of the Military Government of the City of Gloucester", in *Collection of Scarce and Valuable Tracts,* ed. W. Scott, (London 1809), V, pp. 303–7
23. *The Oxford Handbook of the English Revolution,* (Oxford 2016)
24. Ibid, pp. 4, 21
25. This critique of the "British" dimension is extended in the chapters ahead as appropriate, and will be brought together in a forthcoming article
26. Ibid, p. 34
27. J. Derrida, *Writing and Difference*, trans. A. Bass, (London 1979), p. 286; M. Foucault, *The Archaeology of Knowledge*, trans. A. Sheridan-Smith, (London 2002), pp. 5–9, 146; J. Derrida, *Positions*, ed. A. Bass, (Chicago 1981), pp. 57–8
28. *The Oxford Handbook of the English Revolution*, p. 501
29. For instance: J. Whittle, *The Development of Agrarian Capitalism,* (Oxford 2000); R. Allen, *Enclosure and the Yeoman,* (Oxford 1992); J. P. Somerville, *Politics and Ideology in England 1603–1640,* (London 1986); G. Yerby, *The English Revolution and the Roots of Environmental Change,* (Abingdon 2016)
30. *The Oxford Handbook of the English Revolution*, p. 502
31. Hutchinson, *Memoirs of the Life of Colonel Hutchinson*, p. 75
32. J. Harrington, *The Commonwealth of Oceana*, ed. H. Morley, (London 1887), p. 60

1 The Basis of Change

The Early Breach of the Manorial Stasis in England; the Coming of the Commercial Yeoman Farmer; and the Increase of Opportunity—"The Exceeding Lucre They See Grow"[1]

Lucy Hutchinson noted that the interest of the people "had been many years growing". James Harrington pinpointed some of the reasons behind this development. He cited three statutes from the reign of Henry VII whereby the prospects of the middling sort had been improved. The best known was the Statute of Retainers, which was the first significant step in the extended campaign of the Tudor monarchs to reduce the independent regional power of the great magnates, and it did indeed result in the devolution of local authority towards the middle ranks of society. The Statute of Alienations tended in the same direction, loosening the exclusive grip of the landlords by providing a freedom to sell or entail land. But perhaps most interesting is Harrington's view of the Statute of Population. Tudor governments are usually thought to have failed in their regular attempts to resist the enclosure of the common lands, and the depopulation that it was believed to cause. But Harrington perceived that the provisions of this and other statutes for protecting the integrity of smallholdings with over 20 acres, tended to promote the survival, and often the extension of the larger copyhold farms. In some cases at least it helped the dweller to avoid the status of a mere cottager and become "a man of some substance that might keep hinds [or wage labourers] and servants". In effect, this encouraged the creation of commercial units. It placed "a great part of the lands to the hold or possession of the yeomanry or middle people, who living not in a servile or indigent fashion were much unlinked from dependence on their lords".[2] Tudor laws and courts may not have done much to stop the erosion of rights on the common lands, but they did assist some of the more substantial copyholders to transcend it.

Perhaps the single most important platform of change, however, was the development recorded in another early seventeenth-century text—the history of the Berkeley family compiled by their steward John Smyth. He described and explained the widespread alienation of manorial lands to tenants, which became a distinctive feature of the English scene in the early fifteenth century. The collapse of the population level in the fourteenth century had led to a decline in the demand for tenant land, an acute shortage of labour, and a fall in the market price for arable produce. The first response of landlords was to exploit their customary rights over tenants more rigorously, because the relative value of the dues and services that they owed was now higher.[3] But the accumulated resentment at this oppressive stance was a significant cause of the Peasant's Revolt of 1381, which in turn produced a change of policy. In effect, landlords sought a more secure way of maintaining their income. John Smyth recalled that it was "much occasioned by the insurrection of Wat Tyler, and generally by all the commons in the land" that the family began to lease out their estate. "Then instead of manuring the demesnes with his own servants . . . this lord began to . . . tack in other men's cattle onto his pasture . . . and to sell his meadow grounds . . . let out by the year still more and more . . . sometimes at racked improved rents".[4] It became general in fifteenth century England for lords to sell, or lease out their demesne lands. This broke the link of obligation and restraint between the manor and the village that had maintained an essential stasis in medieval society. The working character of both the lord's estate and the tenant's land was radically altered. Their relationship came to be determined by commercial rather than feudal considerations. The farmer depended on the market rather than the manor. The land was necessarily leased out at market value, that is to say the level at which it would be profitable to the farmer. Since it had been the lord's land it had no dues or services upon it, and it tended to be physically of a more coherent shape than could readily be made of the scattered strips in the open fields. In essence, this created a new class of independent, commercialising farmers, which played a crucial part in putting English history on a markedly different course from that of other neighbouring kingdoms. An important aspect of the change was that to some extent the form of tenure ceased to matter—the decisive factor was simply whether a farmer could acquire the use of enough workable land to make a substantial profit in the market. A good example was the background of the mid-sixteenth-century churchman Hugh Latimer. He described his father as "a yeoman, and held no land of his own . . . tilled as much as kept half a dozen men. He had a walk for a hundred sheep".[5]

Smyth's commentary also puts the Peasants' Revolt in a new perspective. It has sometimes been regarded as inconsequential because the uprising was suppressed, and the promised commutation of dues and services was subsequently forgotten. But it seems that in fact there were indirect, long-term consequences that could scarcely have been more significant. Although the revolt failed, the scale and force of it, in an unusually compact kingdom, was a severe shock to the political establishment. At both manorial and central government level there was a transition towards a more circumspect approach to labour relations. The ill-judged initiative of the poll tax was not repeated. There was no further attempt to load the burden of taxation onto the shoulders of the general body of husbandmen smallholders. The English peasantry thereby escaped the fate that was overtaking their continental counterparts. The policy being pursued by other European monarchs at the time was to establish a standing army to support a system of collecting tax arbitrarily from the poorer classes, while the nobility was left largely exempt. The classic example of this kind of development was France.[6] In England, by contrast, the principal general tax, the parliamentary subsidy, fell mainly on the landowning class that could afford to pay it. This had several crucial effects. It allowed the commoners and smallholders a special and beneficial degree of freedom from fiscal burdens. It has been calculated that in some places in England in the sixteenth century, only one person in every twelve was paying tax of any kind. Equally important, this "progressive" distribution of financial obligation gave the English gentry a powerful vested interest in sustaining and extending both the practice and the principle of a right to consent to the provisions of public finance. In this way too, England was embarked on a distinctive course, and most of the classes in English society were acquiring a stake in a specific kind of economic liberty.

A recent study of landholding patterns in fifteenth- and sixteenth-century Norfolk has confirmed the consequences of the changing balance in creating a new class of independent, commercialising village farmers.

> The significance of the period between 1440 and 1580 . . . lies in the freedom, prosperity and . . . the lack of landlordly interference experienced by the rural population, and in the fact that an economy generated by small landholders unburdened with heavy exactions by state or landlord could promote the development of capitalism.[7]

Since the alienation of manorial land took place in a nationwide perspective, the net effect on the country's economic performance was considerable. Robert Allen has found that it was the emergence and success of a distinctive class of yeoman farmers that laid the basis for the doubling of crop yields that was the measurable product of the agricultural revolution that took place in early modern England.[8]

The Growth of Opportunity and Profit in an Integrated Economy: How the Rise of the Cloth Trade Encouraged Sheep Farming and Made "Notable Rich Men by the Doing Thereof in Brief Time"

The spread of farms of sufficient size and compactness to be put on a commercial basis was the main vehicle of agricultural advance. But the vital accompaniment of this transition, and in a sense the pre-condition, was a raised level of market opportunity, which enabled the yeoman farmers to make full use of their position and their freedom. In fact, it is possible to pinpoint the character of the development that constituted the principal incentive and provided the initial substance for what Lucy Hutchinson called the "extraordinary progress" of the people. There was a qualitative change in the nature and scale of economic activity in the late fifteenth and early sixteenth centuries.

In general terms this took the form of an extension of regional trading links, transcending the localised limits of medieval markets. In the words of Jan de Vries, the crucial change involved "a specialisation pattern when the English and the Dutch in particular began to trade bulk products over longer distances".[9] In England the leading example of regional specialisation and exchange came with the emergence of the cloth trade in the later decades of the fifteenth century. This was the kingdom's first manufactured export, and its rise was dramatic. By 1513 the Venetian Ambassador could hail English kerseys as "one of the most important foundations of trade in the world".[10] The cloth trade maintained a period of strong expansion through to the middle of the sixteenth century, and it brought a new dimension to the economy as a whole. The manufacturing and agricultural sectors now developed in mutual reinforcement on a national basis. There was a very substantial extension of sheep farming, which had all the more effect because it was taken up by the tenants as well as by the landlords. As Brailsford said, the new leaseholders who were farming the old demesne lands "were often graziers, who possessed some capital, and belonged to the new age of commercial agriculture".[11] They were indeed men like Hugh Latimer's yeoman father, who "held no land of his own" yet "had a walk for a hundred sheep".[12]

Contemporaries were very aware of the exceptional profits that were to be made from sheep farming. This may have provided the impetus for agricultural "improvement" in more ways than one. For instance, it probably lay behind the emergence of agricultural literature, focusing on the means by which the advantages could be maximised. It was at the height of the expansion of the cloth trade that Fitzherbert produced his pioneering books of husbandry and surveying. His farming advice was very comprehensive—he believed that it was essential to combine arable and pasture. But he recognised that sheep were "the most profitable cattle a man can have", and concentrated on how to improve the methods of sheep rearing. One definite recommendation was to provide them with enclosed pastures.

The first systematic analysis of the economy in general, *A Discourse of the Commonweal*, published in 1549, also regarded it as axiomatic that sheep farming offered an exceptional means of high profit. Men were attracted to it because of "the exceeding lucre that they see grow". It was, moreover, quite special in this regard. "They see that there is more advantage in grazing and breeding than in husbandry by a great deal . . . what should better encourage them thereto than to see them that do it become notable rich men by doing thereof in brief time?"[13] In fact, the *Discourse* understood the new power of the profit motive, and was the first text to recommended that the way forward was to channel and accommodate it. Sheep farming had all the attributes for maximising profit margins. It was lightly taxed, and unlike the corn trade, it was not subject to export restraints when prices reached a certain level. It was associated with an area of rising production—a steadily growing cloth market that created manufacturing capacity as it went along. Grazing was in general a less precarious exercise than arable husbandry, and it required only a minimum of labour, at a time when labour costs were still relatively high. The *Discourse* summed up these comprehensive advantages with the thought that the products of grazing involved "small charge and small labour" and had "free vent to be sold both on this side and beyond the sea at the highest penny".[14] The benefits of these freedoms were found to be so clear that they should be extended to other fields. So the way to "cherish" the production of corn was not to artificially control or protect the market, but to give it the same freedoms, or "allurements and rewards" that were enjoyed by the pastoral farmers. To "make the profit of the plough to be as good rate for rate as the profit of the grazier".[15]

The Great Tudor Inflation: The Beneficial Balance of the General Increase in Opportunity, Population and Prices; and the Basis of Agricultural Improvement

Arable farming was in fact to become a very profitable exercise in its own right in the course of the sixteenth century, but not through the lifting of restrictions as the *Discourse* had proposed. It was not until the early seventeenth century that central authorities began to consider lifting the age-old price controls and export restraints on the corn trade. Nevertheless, farming of all kinds entered into a generally flourishing state in the sixteenth century, mainly because, in contrast to the long periods of stability that preceded and followed it, the period between 1520 and 1640 witnessed a strong and sustained rise in the levels of population and prices. So the century and a quarter before the Civil War, sometimes called the long sixteenth century, was distinguished by a continuous inflationary trend of a kind that had not been seen since the thirteenth century, and would not be seen again until the eighteenth century. This created a steady and dependable seller's market, offering substantial profits to those with enough land to generate a regular surplus. In fact, in the agricultural world, the capacity for high profits had a fairly clear definition in terms of the amount of land required. It seems that there was a threshold of 60 to 70 acres, above which a farmer could produce a regular surplus for market, which enabled him to profit even in years of poor harvests. These conditions had a downside for the smallholder with less than 40 acres and no significant surplus, because in a bad year he would have to buy in dear, and might be in danger of losing his holding.

But this again served the interests of his more substantial neighbours who were ready to expand further.

Our knowledge of the trend in population levels rests on the work of the Cambridge Group for the History of Population, and their exhaustive "aggregative analysis" of the vital events—marriages, births and burials—of the 404 best-kept parish registers.[16] It can now be stated with confidence that the population of England and Wales roughly doubled between the 1520s and the 1640s. Over the same period there was an equally distinctive long-term rise in prices. Phelips, Brown and Hopkins compiled an index of price movements between 1264 and 1954 and concluded that, "the most marked feature . . . is the extent and persistence of the Tudor inflation".[17] And agricultural prices rose fastest of all.

The steadily rising level of population is usually, and no doubt rightly, taken as the platform or at least the necessary condition of the continuing rise in prices. As contemporaries noted, the fact that the high price of food could be met without an interruption to the upward trend in population seemed to indicate that there was plenty of money around. To identify one of the reasons, we can turn to the interesting question of what produced the increase in population. In terms of simple mortality rates it is clear that the sixteenth century offered a favourable contrast with what had gone before. In the preceding centuries Europe had been ravaged by the bubonic plague, and it was not until the turn of the sixteenth century that the incidence of the epidemic declined. The earlier centuries had also suffered to a greater extent from the recurrence of bad weather and poor harvests. To add to the problems, fifteenth-century England had experienced an unusually high level of internecine warfare, which was, in general terms, ended by the arrival of the Tudors. Thus by the early 1580s, Richard Hakluyt could observe that, "through our long peace and seldom sickness . . . we are grown more populous than ever before".[18] More recent calculations confirm the good fortune of Elizabethan England in this respect. By the general standards of early modern Europe, life expectancy in England was "exceptionally high between 1566 and 1621". And in the best years, between 1566 and 1586 "mortality was lower than it was again to be until after 1815".[19]

But the rise of population in the sixteenth century was not simply the result of a falling death rate. It is generally agreed that it was more the result of rising fertility, and most crucially a consequence of the fact that the balance of the interaction between mortality rates and fertility rates was changing. In the preceding two centuries, lower mortality rates would have been met and cancelled out by a corresponding *fall* in fertility, because at a time of finite resources and inelastic economies, the longer survival of one generation would mean less scope for the next, who might therefore delay marrying and having children. What appears to have been different in the sixteenth century, and what at least technically generated the rise in population, was the fact that lower mortality was not cancelled out by a fall in fertility, but was on the contrary, reinforced by rising or sustained fertility. It seems that in the sixteenth century there was a distinctive tendency towards younger marriages, and thus towards having children earlier and in greater numbers. The result was a steady rise in population.

This was the mechanism through which change occurred. But behind it, if less easy to demonstrate, were the economic factors that encouraged earlier marriage. There was an increasing number and range of opportunities emerging in sixteenth-century England. The younger generation did not necessarily have to delay setting up a household until the traditional source of income from an inherited smallholding became available to them. It is not difficult to identify the additional possibilities that were coming on stream. Agricultural activity was becoming more commercialised, intensive and diverse, and often in association with this there were arising new opportunities in crafts, manufactures and trade. In other words, the distinctive feature of the sixteenth century economy was the creation or discovery of extra capacities and a greater range of employments.

Much hinged on the arrival and expansion of the cloth trade, which brought with it a new dimension of manufacturing activity. The effect was reinforced by the fact that the cloth-making industry operated through the domestic system of production, whereby cloth merchants put out work to individual households in the villages, where employment could be most usefully provided. Joan Thirsk was among the first to draw attention to the phenomenon of rural industry, and the growth of semi-farming, semi-industrial communities supplying national and international markets with textiles".[20] A common feature was that rural industries arose in areas with abundant supplies of labour but limited agricultural potential, and was often a by-employment for labourers or smallholders who were glad to supplement the income that they made from the land.

H. Medick outlined the basis of the connection between extra opportunities and a rise in fertility. In a peasant household without additional potential in the market, the time of marriage of the succeeding generation was delayed until the parent died or gave up the farm. So the mean age at first marriage remained high and fertility was low. But the introduction of cottage industry created more scope, and freed the younger generation to consider early marriage. Medick's suggestion finds detailed confirmation in studies quantifying the demographic implications of rural industry. Particularly striking was David Levine's work on a pair of Leicestershire villages. In Shepshod the smallholders seized the opportunity of taking in framework knitting for London merchants. This generated a sharp drop in the mean age of first marriage, and a corresponding rise in the fertility rate. In nearby Bottesford, by contrast, there were no opportunities beyond the agricultural, and in consequence there was a rise in age at first marriage, which produced a decline in the level of population.[21] Thus, as L. A. Clarkson has said, from the sixteenth century onwards, "it seems clear that general economic expansion—including the development of rural industry—was accompanied by some slight fall in the age at first marriage, and by an increase in fertility".[22]

In this way, a steadily rising population level was economically sustained throughout the years between the 1520s and the 1640s. The 1550s saw the only five-year interval when this population rise was briefly halted by widespread famine conditions. This indicates that the period was in general one of significant advance in the kingdom's capacity to sustain the physical wellbeing of its people. That this could be achieved while agricultural prices and profits were at a continuing high was a doubly seminal change. Increasing levels of food production were the necessary basis. The remarkable statistic of a pre-industrial peak in life expectancy in the 1580s seems to underline the efficiency of the agrarian economy, in particular in the late Tudor period. If this has not received due recognition in recent historiography it is in part because of the tendency among modern historians to try to tone down the traditional lustre of Elizabeth's reign. It may also be because Eric Kerridge originally seemed to overstate the case by talking of an "agricultural revolution" between 1550 and 1650. Historians of the more recent generation tend to avoid the idea of revolution unless it is absolutely explicit, and they have been more inclined to give the name to the period after 1650, when the adoption of new crops and methods began to be systematically recorded. But it is misleading to restrict our judgements to the most obvious sources, when other general evidence may actually be more instructive. The distortion is persistent. Mark Overton, for instance, makes little of the real achievement of Elizabethan agriculture in his overall assessment, even though his statistics seem to show that there was indeed a strong upward trend in agricultural productivity between 1550 and 1650, after which it tailed away again. And most strikingly, the years from 1590 to 1630 saw a sharper rise in wheat yields than in any period until the 1830s.[23] Similarly, it is hard to see why Robert Allen puts so much stress on the seventeenth century, when his figures indicate that two-thirds of the overall improvement in corn yields occurred between 1550 and 1650.[24] These findings underline the very notable levels of life expectancy achieved in mid-Elizabethan England.

So we need to assert the distinctive significance of the period up to 1650 in agrarian and demographic advance. And in truth the agricultural achievement is not hard to explain. The expansion of pasture in the sixteenth century was so general that it is too easy to overlook. From the late fifteenth century on, there was a vast increase in sheep farming to supply the cloth trade, the kingdom's first manufactured export. It was often associated with enclosure, and the closer management of the flock, which was known to improve output. It is thought that when land was enclosed for agriculture its annual value increased by 31%, and that the value of land enclosed for pasture exceeded that of land enclosed for arable by 27%.[25] It should not be forgotten that the rise in sheep farming constituted in itself a very important field of agricultural improvement, both in respect of method and productivity.

It also provided a good basis for advance in other areas of farming. Even if there was a decline in the extent of land used for arable, this could induce other arable farmers to raise their game in order to meet the new market opportunity. And in some important ways the extension of pasture gave them the means to do it. The great expansion in the numbers of sheep produced a general rise in stock density, which was a good indicator of improvement. The availability of more animals, and more manure, corrected the shortage of dung that had been a major problem in medieval times. This allowed an extension of the arable and generated higher yields. It became axiomatic among the agriculturalists that farmers should be combining pasture and arable. "And not the one without the other" said Fitzherbert firmly.[26] He understood how the increase in stock density and the provision of enclosed fields could be used to return advantage to the arable, and raise the value of the land by half as much again—"by reason of the composting and dunging of the cattle that shall go and lie upon it both day and night".[27] The beneficial effect of sheep dung on arable fields is so marked that it is still employed by farmers today as the best way of maintaining fertility. This took force in the sixteenth century. It did not need a specific invention or discovery, but just the realisation that the vast increase in the numbers of sheep on the land made it possible to improve the productivity of the arable.

In effect the rise of pastoral farming led to a pattern of diversity and interaction, which created a more efficient balance, and enhanced the agricultural product overall. The process of conversion and enclosure did much to inaugurate the concept of improvement, as well as the idea of manipulating the land for profit. Since grain prices were rising faster than wool prices for most of the second half of the century, there was a tendency to capitalise by reconverting land to tillage. The advantages in terms of yield were substantial. The ploughing in of pasture was an effective way of creating nitrogenous fertilizer, the shortage of which had been the main limiting factor in medieval agriculture. So by various means the increase in pasture could actually work to improve arable output.

The gain could be sustained by a pattern of farming that regularly combined pasture and arable. This was what Eric Kerridge referred to as convertible husbandry and took as one of the pillars of what he perceived as the late sixteenth century agricultural revolution. If, as seems to be the case, this practice began in the sixteenth century, it was no doubt because of the marked increase in the numbers of stock available at that time. Critics have noted that it was only recorded in a formal sense in parts of the Midlands. But even if this was a true reflection of its incidence this would not necessarily limit the general effect. The late fifteenth and sixteenth centuries saw the emergence of a new economic dynamic—a pattern of regional marketing, whereby a particular region would specialise in a favoured product in order to engage in a long-distance trade with other regions. The resulting benefits have been estimated at much the same level as those of enclosure. That is to say, the process of specialisation and exchange in specific crops or commodities would increase interregional productivity by half as much again. In this way, the restriction of an agricultural improvement to selected regions could work to the general advantage.

But there is, in any case, no justification for assuming that convertible husbandry was not generalised because it was only mentioned explicitly in certain areas. The whole context of the agrarian economy led farmers towards the practice at some level. The greater availability of stock put mixed farming at a premium. Convertible husbandry was taking place piecemeal, at most times and in most places, during the period. In Sussex in the early seventeenth century, Sir Thomas Pelham was looking to "maximise his returns" by denshiring and ploughing in areas of grass, which would in itself serve to add nitrogenous nutrients to the ground.[28] The widespread conversion to pasture in the late fifteenth and early sixteenth centuries had engendered a pattern of diversity, flexibility and interaction, which meant that at any stage the land could be used in a way that maximised the productivity and the profit that was to be achieved.

Diversification thus offered various means by which the fertility of arable land could be increased. But there was another particularly important kind of fertiliser that has not been given full recognition, even by Kerridge, perhaps because it was less structural in form. This was the more targeted and widespread use of lime. It might not seem a sufficiently substantial change in method to be at the heart of a revolution, but that was probably its power. The vital effect of lime was to reduce the acidity of the soil, and free the nitrogenous nutrients to be taken up. This again addressed the shortage of nitrogen food that was the main technical handicap of medieval farming. Tudor farmers may not have understood the scientific links, but with the intensified search for improvements in the sixteenth century, the practical benefits and value of liming became clear. Fitzherbert believed that the essential ingredients for improving the arable were dung and lime. In Dorset, the process of enclosure "was accompanied by other improvements in land use. Lime was liberally used as a fertilizer".[29] The same was true in Somerset, Wiltshire and Gloucestershire. In Devon and Cornwall too, the provision of enclosure was followed by the wider use of lime and other fertilisers.[30] The liming of acid soils in Devon appears to have begun in the last quarter of the sixteenth century. The change in Cornwall was especially striking, because by the end of Elizabeth's reign, a region that had once struggled to produce enough corn to feed itself was now in a position to export the commodity. Liming was also used to great effect by "good husbands" in Wales.[31] On the other side of the island, in Sussex, when Sir Thomas Pelham "strove to maximise his returns" by ploughing in areas of grass: "Lime was spread at the same time".[32] Liming must thus be regarded as a genuine and highly significant innovation of the age. In fact it was recognised as such by contemporaries, and was the factor most often mentioned in explaining the rise in yields. In 1616 it was noted that "the husbandry of liming the ground for corn was first practiced within the memory" of living generations.[33] In 1578 the general effect was summarised thus: "in later years since the knowledge and use of liming was found there groweth more plenty of corn".[34] In the 1630s Gabriel Plattes gave it full credit: "He that found a way of fertilising land with lime (though by accident) did a more charitable deed . . . than if he had built all the capital hospitals in England". [35]

The benefits were such that farmers were prepared to put a great deal of effort and money into producing the lime. In 1618 John Norden noted that:

> In Shropshire, Denbighshire, Flintshire, and now lately in some parts of Sussex, the industrious people are at a more extraordinary charge and toil. For the poor husbandmen and farmers do buy, dig and fetch the limestone, two, three, four miles off, and in their fields build limekilns, burn it and cast it on their fields, to their great advantage.[36]

This captures the real basis of change. There was a new economic balance, of expanding opportunities, generating an unprecedented and sustained rise in population and prices, which encouraged even the "poor husbandmen" to invest in improvements, in the expectation of substantial profits. For the middling yeoman farmer it was a golden age. Those with something in excess of 70 acres could do well enough to transform their status, and swell the ranks of the gentry, joining them in the broadening processes of national administration and law making. It was also a context that engendered a desire for maximum economic freedom, which was eventually asserted in association with political aims.

Notes

1. *A Discourse of the Commonweal,* (London 1549), ed. M. Dewar, (Virginia 1969), p. 118
2. J. Harrington, *The Commonwealth of Oceana,* (London 1656), ed. Henry Morley, (London 1887), p. 59
3. M. Keen, *English Society in the Later Middle Ages,* (Harmondsworth 1990), pp. 40–4
4. John Smyth of Nibley, *The Lives of the Berkeleys,* (London 1618), ed. J, Maclean, 3 vols., (Gloucester 1883–6), vol. II, pp. 5–6

5. Hugh Latimer, "The First Sermon Preached Before King Edward", 1 March 1549, *Works of Hugh Latimer*, ed. G. Corrie, (Cambridge 1844–45), vol. I, p. 101
6. See D. Parker, *The Making of French Absolutism,* (London 1983); D. Parker, *State and Class in Ancien Regime France*, (London 1996)
7. J. Whittle, *The Development of Agrarian Capitalism,* (Oxford 2000), p. 315
8. R. C. Allen, *Enclosure and the Yeoman,* (Oxford 1992), pp. 13, 137
9. J. De Vries, *The Dutch Rural Economy in the Golden Age, 1500–1700,* (Yale 1974), pp. 1–3
10. Venetian State Archives, cited in F. Braudel, *The Mediterranean,* (London 1972), vol. I, p. 213
11. H. N. Brailsford, *The Levellers and the English Revolution,* (Nottingham 1983), p. 438
12. See above, p. 15
13. *A Discourse of the Commonweal*, pp. 53–4
14. Ibid, p. 119
15. Ibid, 57–9, 90, 117–19
16. E. A. Wrigley and R. S. Schofield, *The Population History of England 1541–1871,* (Arnold 1981)
17. C. Palliser, *The Age of Elizabeth,* (London 1983), p. 130
18. R. Hakluyt, *A Discourse of Western Planting*, ed. E. Taylor, (Hakluyt Society 1935), p. 234
19. Palliser, *The Age of Elizabeth*, p. 46
20. J. Thirsk, "Industries in the Countryside", in *Essays in the Economic History of Tudor and Stuart England in Honour of R. H. Tawney,* ed. F. J. Fisher, (Cambridge 1961), p. 86
21. D. Levine, *Family Formation in an Age of Nascent Capitalism* (1977); H. Medick, "The Proto-Industrial Family Economy", *Social History 1* (1976)
22. L. A Clarkson, *Proto-Industrialisation,* (Basingstoke 1985), pp. 42, 46
23. M. Overton, *The Agricultural Revolution in England,* (Cambridge 1996), p. 87
24. Allen, *Enclosure and the Yeoman*, p. 207
25. J. D. Mackie, *The Earlier Tudors,* (Oxford 1966), p. 450
26. A. Fitzherbert, *Book of Husbandry* (1523), ed. W. Skeat, (London 1882), p. 9
27. Ibid, pp. 9, 22
28. A. Fletcher, *A County Community in Peace and War,* (London 1975), p. 15
29. J. Thirsk, "The Farming Regions of England", in *The Agrarian History of England and Wales*, ed. J. Thirsk, (Cambridge 1967), IV, p. 67
30. Ibid, p. 75
31. Ibid, pp. 117–18
32. Fletcher, *A County Community in Peace and War*, p. 15
33. Thirsk, "Farming Regions of England", pp. 133–4
34. Palliser, *The Age of Elizabeth*, p. 197
35. Gabriel Plattes, *A Discovery of Infinite Treasure,* (London 1639), cited in G. E. Fussell, *The Old English Farming Books,* (London 1947), p. 38
36. J. Norden, *The Surveyors Dialogue,* (London 1618), p. 180

2 Dynamics of Change

The New Shape of Interregional Trading; the Mutual Benefits of Specialisation and Exchange; and the Growth of a National Land-market

The growth of opportunities was general and structured. The scope and character of trade underwent a qualitative transformation from the late fifteenth century. The period is rightly famous as the age of discovery, when the European kingdoms extended their imperial and trading power across the oceans. But it is crucial to understand that the broadening of horizons was local as well as global. The new way of business consisted essentially in the development of regional specialisation and exchange. This created a dynamic for integration within the English kingdom, as well as an enhanced profile for exports overseas. The spread of broad, commercialised marketing came to overlay the more circumscribed context of medieval times, which had been characterised by a multitude of undifferentiated local markets, each providing the same basic range of products for a relatively small area. The new extended market system would also come to be associated with another kind of departure from traditional economic assumptions. With the growing potential of trade, there arose a demand that merchants should be allowed on principle to operate free of impositions and restrictions.

The expansion of the scope of trade can be measured on the ground in terms of the number and range of markets. Mark Overton notes the "density" of markets at the beginning of the sixteenth century, when they were still at their greatest in number and most limited in reach. He estimates that most medieval markets served an area of about ten miles radius, with little traded outside.[1] W. G. Hoskins was even less generous, suggesting that "in general people found all their earthly needs met within an area of three or four miles at most, within sight of their own church spires".[2] Though perhaps over-restrictive, this captures the essential character of the medieval economy.

During the sixteenth and early seventeenth centuries there was an important change, of which Alan Everitt produced a structured analysis. He established that "economic concentration is one of the salient themes of inland trade during this period". Everywhere, agricultural traffic was being drawn away from the smaller markets and focused on larger provincial centres like Maidstone, Canterbury, Reading, Newcastle and King's Lynn. These expanded markets became the points of distribution for regional specialisations. At the beginning of the sixteenth century, "most towns still served a purely local area, and specialised in no particular commodity". But during the course of the century, "a broad pattern of specialisation becomes clear". By this time about half of the eight hundred market towns in England were specialising in the marketing of some particular product. The trend to specialisation "was clearly marked by the fourth quarter of the sixteenth century, and some of its principal features were already emerging by the 1530s".[3]

This constituted a seminal transition in the dimensions of trade and marketing, as each town and region began to concentrate on the more intensive exploitation of the most favoured products and resources of its area, to serve markets and regions further afield than before. Certain regional marketing characteristics became apparent. The markets of the Eastern counties specialised mainly in corn. In the Midlands the predominant speciality was livestock. The West Country offered another variation, specialising in wool, yarn and cloth. Northern counties showed the highest proportion of concentrated marketing, because two specialisations were on offer—livestock and cloth. London was a transcendent commercial centre, boasting a wide range of manufactures, and a uniquely broad base of consumption, while maintaining a particular importance as the dominant outlet for the nation's principal export of cloth. It drew the threads of regional specialities together into a national and international market system.

Market forces became at once more distant, but more focused and coordinated. Commercially minded farmers were thoroughly conversant with the strengths of each regional market, knowing what high-quality goods it offered, and when they were at their best.[4] Buyers and sellers travelled long distances to avail themselves of the benefits of regional exchange. The wool market at Doncaster was one of the largest in the kingdom and attracted buyers from more than half a dozen counties, and from towns fifty miles away. By Elizabeth's reign, the markets for textiles and livestock served a radius that was generally over twenty miles and not infrequently more than forty. People travelled as far as seventy miles to the great sheep marts of the Midlands and the North. Rotherham market brought sellers from Ellerburn in the Vale of Pickering, seventy miles away, and the sheep fair at Worcester drew sellers from equally distant Camarthenshire.[5] One particular example illustrates the new scope of marketing, and the essential impetus behind it. A Westmoreland packhorse man carried cloths from Kendal to Southampton every year from 1492 to 1546.[6] This coincided with the period of maximum expansion of the cloth trade. The regular trip to market, covering almost the entire length of the kingdom, encapsulates how the land was being turned into a commercial unit, and shows again how the assurance of good profits was intensifying economic activity.

One of the ways in which regional specialisation served to increase the range and the benefits of commerce was by enabling each area to concentrate on the production of those commodities to which it was especially well suited, but might not previously have been free to exploit effectively. This would raise productivity almost by definition, and Mark Overton managed to put a figure on the level of absolute advantage gained when two regions began to focus on maximising their production of the crops or items for which they naturally enjoyed the highest yields. The result was a further increase in overall output of more than half across the two regions.[7] This was much the same, we note, as contemporary estimates of the benefit achieved by enclosure. The coordinated market brought a sustained growth of opportunity.

The previous chapter touched on the diversification and extended productivity generated by the leading example of regional specialisation and exchange—the combined growth of sheep farming and cloth manufacture. Since the making of cloth was carried out largely as a cottage industry in the countryside, it could tap underused resources of labour and environment, and bring valuable by-employment to areas that were not best suited to productive farming. This, for instance, was the basis on which the people of the West Riding of Yorkshire were able to alleviate the disadvantages of poor soils and an over-wet climate, and develop a strong economic identity by the rapid expansion of cloth production. In the area around Halifax, which was "planted in the great wastes and moors where the fertility of the ground is not apt to bring forth any corn or good grass" it was said that the people "altogether do live by cloth making".[8] A further consequence of the new focus was that the manufacturers began to source their wool not as traditionally from the most local market, but from more distant, specialist suppliers. In fact, the people of the West Riding flourished sufficiently by the making of cloth to enable them to import all their other basic needs from the appropriate specialising regions elsewhere: their corn from Lincolnshire, their cheese from Cheshire and Warwickshire, and their black cattle from Lancashire.[9]

An interesting example of a regional speciality is the iron industry in the Sussex Weald. Iron was the largest metal industry, and it was sited mainly in the Weald. The area was not best suited to arable farming, but it was well equipped for harnessing waterpower, and it boasted a plentiful supply of wood for charcoal. The new technology of the blast furnace reached the Weald from France at the end of the fifteenth century. It was a true industrial advance, which increased productivity fivefold. The number of furnaces and the level of output rose rapidly during the course of the sixteenth century. By the 1570s there were at least sixty-seven blast furnaces in operation, and fifty-two of them were in the Weald. It was the principal source of many of the necessities of the Elizabethan consumer society, from ploughshares, to fire-backs, to cannon and shot. It was a good example of how the restriction of an activity to one region did not limit but actually encouraged the overall expansion of the economy.

The mining industry was an obvious candidate for intensified production in regions less well suited to arable farming. Lead mining was another field that saw a dramatic increase in output during the sixteenth century. It rose from 625 tons in 1500, to 3,300 tons in 1580, to 12,400 tons by 1600.[10] It became a specialised product, for instance, in some of the less agriculturally favoured areas of Derbyshire. The extended market in coal was also an important element in the development of interregional trade. The southwest corner of Nottinghamshire provides a good example of how this kind of activity could convert a local economy from subsistence to export mode. The area was not blessed with rich agricultural land, but it did possess a resource of convenient coal reserves, and during the sixteenth century it began to exploit them on a substantial basis. By the beginning of the seventeenth century, coal production in the hinterland of Nottingham had reached a level at which the local authorities were happy that they could rely on coal exports to solve any shortage of basic foodstuffs, by means of an annual exchange with Lincolnshire for the grain in which that county was able to specialise.[11]

J. E. Nef estimated that coal output increased fourteenfold between 1550 and 1680, as the most significant factor in the first "industrial revolution". The prime region of coal production, the northeast, generated a flourishing export trade through Newcastle. Much of this was shipped down the coast to the ports of East Anglia, which sent in return their own specialised commodity of grain. The bourgeoning market of London was another major customer. It is also notable that by the second half of the sixteenth century there was a substantial export trade in coal to France, usually in return for salt. By 1640, on the basis of this multi-dimensional trade, England was producing three times as much coal as the rest of Europe put together.[12] Coal from Newcastle was even finding its way to the more distant reaches of the Mediterranean. English ships were returning to those waters on the basis of a much broader, yet more connected pattern of trade than had obtained in medieval times.

So the development of regional specialisation and exchange had a crucial international context. In medieval times, long distance trade was mainly in luxuries, and it was very one-dimensional, as well described by R. H. Tawney: "With the Mediterranean as its immemorial pivot, expansion had hardly begun. Tapping the wealth of the East by way of the Levant, it resembled, in the rigidity of the limits placed on its commercial strategy, a giant fed through the chink of a wall".[13] In the sixteenth century these limits were transcended by a flexible, expanding European-wide trading network. Jan De Vries concluded that, "medieval commerce did little to alter local self-sufficiency because it remained dominated by long-distance luxury trade". The critical change occurred with the "specialisation pattern", through which the Dutch and the English in particular began to trade basic commodities between regional markets.[14] The cloth trade was England's main contribution, and a national speciality. In 1513 it was hailed as "one of the most important foundations of trade in the world". Fernand Braudel saw the development of the textile trade as the clearest indicator of the emergence of a capitalist marketing context, displaying "division of labour, rationalisation and specialisation . . . there grew up a textile industry on capitalist lines and connected to distant markets, which was of decisive importance".[15] In the sixteenth and seventeenth centuries, England was becoming a trading nation in a more definitive and coordinated sense than had previously been the case.

The development of internal and interregional exchange in England was encouraged by the fact that inland trade proceeded in a context of exceptional freedom, when compared to other European kingdoms. Unusually, England boasted no large urban centres except London, the uniqueness of which as a coordinating market tended to encourage rather than restrict economic integration. Nor were there any semi-independent provinces. As a result, in contrast to France and Germany, there were few internal tolls or customs barriers between regions in England.

> Internal trade went largely untaxed in the period 1500–1700 . . . one of the principal strengths of the network of internal trading . . . was the relative lightness of passage tolls, pontages and other duties on domestic trade which created in much of Western Europe a fairly rigid series of customs unions.[16]

Even the tolls that had once existed in English town markets had largely fallen into disuse by the sixteenth century. An increasing amount of business was in any case being done outside the confines of the towns, often at inns. These trends towards private marketing "seem to have developed very substantially in this period, as functions of the spread of the major interregional trades in agricultural commodities".[17]

The Development of a National Land-Market

As land became more valuable, and more readily exploitable for profit, so the demand for it increased, and it came to be bought and sold more often and more widely. By the second half of the sixteenth century there had arisen a national land-market of a recognisably modern type. In medieval times land was held under a different set of assumptions, and its transfer was less normative. The shape of landholding and occupation may be characterised as open, dispersed and limited in nature. The lines of possession and division were not as definite as the absolute property rights of today. Land was granted for use rather than sold. All land was held of the king on certain obligations. The bounds of the kingdom were also relatively open. There were no fixed state borders. It has been rightly said that the term "the medieval state" is a misnomer. The king's claims could extend into other realms, but were also subject to challenge within his immediate territory. The absence of discrete state boundaries was manifest in the position of the universal church, which was a body with independent political status, whose vast properties stretched out across the whole of Christendom. Local lords held their lands of the king, and let them on to their tenants, with a variety of tenures, obligations and services due. An equally important constraint was that property was not supposed to be used for the maximisation of individual profit, but in line with the common good, as God intended, for ultimately it was held as a trust from him.

The lands of the lord, and the disposition of the manors, both within and without, also tended to be dispersed in form. And the common lands worked by the tenants and villagers were the ultimate expression of fragmentation and dispersal. The smallholding of each village farmer would be composed of a large number of small strips, scattered across the open fields, and in the words of one contemporary "interlaced" with those of neighbours, with no formal barriers between them. It was not until the middle of the sixteenth century that surveyors began to seek ways of rendering the entirety of each smallholder's strips in one collected entry, so that for the first time it became possible to know "the parcels of land that belong to every messuage".[18] In the medieval context there had apparently been no perceived need or inclination to record a discrete individual holding in any respect. This was a society that did not treat land as an itemised commodity. The "lands" or strips were dispersed yet fixed, and it was sufficient that each farmer or household knew which were theirs to work. The essential stability of the scene is well captured by Peter Bigmore, in his description of medieval Bedfordshire. "Through the medieval period the size of the holdings, and their scattered disposition among the open fields remained remarkably static". But in the first half of the sixteenth century "there is abundant evidence that piecemeal enclosure was occurring in the open fields".[19]

A great change was in train, whereby land ceased to be the fixed foundation of regulated livelihoods, and became a commercial item. J. D. Mackie's summary of this process bears referring to at length. New concepts were arising in respect of the meaning and use of land. "No longer was it regarded solely as the stable basis of an ordered society; it was becoming a commodity to be exchanged and used for gain". Land had changed hands often enough in the middle ages, but this did not as a rule affect the economy of an estate, "or the lives of an agricultural community. Quite different was the effect of this new traffic in land. A land-market was coming into being, and people who made purchases . . . did so in the belief that the transaction would be profitable to themselves".

The land-market, and the new spirit of enterprise that inspired it "created conditions that presaged the end of the medieval world".[20]

The most conspicuous of the great changes in the balance of landholding in sixteenth century England was the lay expropriation of the properties of the church, which are said to have amounted to about a quarter of the kingdom. But it is important to be aware that a fully-fledged land-market had already begun to develop before the abbey lands came on stream. The initial impetus was the expansion of economic opportunity, profitable farming, and increasing land values from the late fifteenth century. So a modern land-market, shown in the rise of cash transactions, was already arising when the availability of the church lands provided the final fillip. Indeed, the high commercial value of land goes far to account for the strength of demand for church property. R. B. Smith captured the sequence of effect with some precision in his study of the West Riding of Yorkshire in the reign of Henry VIII, putting some interesting figures on the way that the re-distribution of the church lands constituted the final stage in the creation of a fully fledged land-market. He noted that a land-market had already appeared in embryo at the beginning of the sixteenth century, marked by the arrival of cash transactions, though "the land law had not been devised to allow for such transactions, and consequently the legal formulae available to record changes of this kind were clumsy adaptations of feudal forms".[21] Smith found that the volume of land exchanges began to increase significantly in the thirty years after 1510, with cash transactions multiplying much faster than feudal "enfeoffments for use". In the first five-year period, from 1510 to 1514, there were just nineteen transactions, of which eleven were for cash. The volume then began to rise sharply, mainly due to the increase in cash deals. By 1539, while the number of enfeoffments had roughly doubled, the number of cash deals had increased tenfold. It was at this point that the church lands came onto the market. And during the 1540s, with the powerful boost to the supply, cash transactions soared, while enfeoffments declined to insignificance. In the five years between 1545 and 1549 there were two hundred and twenty-three transactions, three of which were enfeoffments, and two hundred and twenty were for cash.[22] It is a powerful illustration of the way that, with the incentive of the rising commercial value of farming, land began to be exchanged at a faster and faster rate, increasingly and in the end almost exclusively for cash, until the buying and selling of land became normative, as it had never previously been.

It was, however, the availability of the abbey lands that normalised the force of the land-market, and made it into a truly national phenomenon. Church lands were everywhere. Medieval kings had been under the impression that the more you gave the church, the greater was your assurance of a successful reign, and the easier was your path to heaven. But by the middle of the sixteenth century, such considerations had been pushed aside by the forces of property and profit. The appetite for seizing the abbey lands was unashamed and undisguised. It was widely understood that the prospect of the properties of the church being brought within the reach of the laity would guarantee the success of Henry VIII's Break with Rome. As early as 1529, long before any ecclesiastical breach was contemplated, the French Ambassador noted that the lay appropriation of the church lands was high on the agenda of the gentry, and that once Wolsey was dead, "these lords . . . intend to impeach the state of the church and take all their goods, which is hardly needful for me to write in cipher for they proclaim it openly".[23] In June 1534 the Spanish Ambassador reported that the king was being advised to distribute the revenues of the church among the gentry, "that he may thereby gain the hearts and affections of his subjects".[24]

It must have been reassuring for Henry and his minister Thomas Cromwell to know that there would be little significant opposition to the break with Rome, as long as the abbey lands were made available to the English laity. The readiness of the government to satisfy these desires is well illustrated by an episode arising from the importunity of one Worcestershire farmer. He had tried and failed to persuade the local abbot to bow to the prevailing wind and surrender his holding voluntarily. Not to be deterred by the abbot's obstinacy, the farmer then applied direct to Cromwell to have the abbey suppressed at once, pointing out that there was a degree of urgency in the matter, since the harvest was at hand. Cromwell obliged within ten days.[25] The king's pragmatic first minister knew what was required to keep the English landowning classes on his side, and he understood the special level of economic incentive that was at stake. The lay appropriation of church property tends to be thought of as a "plundering" of static wealth, but the special motivation was the exceptionally high agricultural profit that land was now capable of producing.

From the 1540s onwards, a steady flow of ex-church property came onto the market, and the initiative in the transactions tended to come from the purchaser. Again, recognising the nature of the demand, the government seems to have made little attempt to dictate the shape of the property to be bought, which was in effect determined by the customers themselves. They would have particular lands in view, that were "lying commodious for them".[26] The criteria were usually whether the lands presented an opportunity to add to an existing farm or estate, or to create a new one out of several adjacent manors. Thus one important consequence was that the process of accumulation "made for more compactness in the geographical pattern of landownership".[27] The redistribution thereby contributed to the period's most significant change in the structural form of landholding—that is, the consolidation of discrete, gathered properties in individual hands.

An equally important development, but easier to overlook, is that the laicisation of the church lands contributed further to a consolidated, individualist idea of property by giving a coherent, autonomous shape to "the land" as a whole. This was not just a technical switch of ownership from the spiritual to the secular sphere. The expulsion of the universal church and the redistribution of its lands among the laity meant that the concept of landholding acquired a unitary character that it had previously lacked. In the medieval context, a large proportion of the kingdom had been held by a detached and self-governing church that had its base beyond the borders of the realm, and whose position extended in the same manner through all the realms of Christendom. That pervasive presence had now been expelled from England, and all landowners within the newly independent political body referred solely to the internal authority of the kingdom, operating within the omni-competent legislative sovereignty of the emergent nation-state, and the assumptions of absolute property that it reflected and protected. The effect was reinforced by the fact that most of the abbey lands ended up in the hands of a broad national class of gentry and yeomanry. Local studies, from Devon and Cornwall to Lincolnshire and Norfolk, have shown a consistent picture: "it was the gentry, old and new, who gained by far the most land".[28] In Devon, the typical purchasers were "local squires . . . rounding off their existing estates with a convenient monastic manor, or else younger sons with official connections building up new but moderate estates".[29] The process is well quantified in the figures that T. H. Swales produced for Tudor Norfolk, showing that as early as 1555, two-thirds of the old monastic lands had come into the hands of the gentry, with the remaining third shared between the crown, the nobility and the church.[30]

The new gentry included a significant sprinkling of rising lawyers and successful merchants. It was indeed from the ranks of the younger sons, the yeomanry, the legal fraternity and the world of commerce that the greatly augmented class of gentry was emerging. Their proliferation throughout the land was consolidated by a defining place in the development of a uniform, kingdom-wide framework of administration, at the heart of which were the gentry, supported by the rising local authority of the yeomanry. The same combinations of the gentry, the freeholders of the countryside and the freemen of the towns were the active agents in a system of parliamentary representation with a uniquely coordinated force. Through these channels they were able to put their property concerns in a national perspective, especially in the emergence of a dominant English passion of anti-papal xenophobia, asserting the independence of the new state against the threat that the old church might seek to take back its property. In the brief and partial restoration of papal authority in the reign of Mary Tudor, the gentry, through the forum of the House of Commons, were prepared to accept the revival of the Catholic liturgy but absolutely refused to countenance the return of the abbey lands.

So by Elizabeth's reign, the broad administrative class of gentry and yeomanry dominated a modern land-market, trading consolidated landholdings in a general framework of absolute property rights, guaranteed by the provisions of common law and sovereign representative statute. The balance of landed property was shifting decisively from the once all-pervasive regimes of church and nobility, and coming to rest in the hands of a centred, national class of middling gentry. Between 1436 and 1690 the share of land held by the great nobility remained stable at between 15 and 20%, while the proportion held by the gentry doubled from 25% to 50%. In fact, by the later decades of the seventeenth century, the gentry and the yeomanry together held three-quarters of the land of England.[31]

This was not just a reversal in the quantity of land held by the respective classes—it marked a change in the shape of landholding. A national land-market in gathered, individual properties had replaced the open, dispersed, yet settled patterns of the medieval world. The transition from "feudal" to "modern" was reflected in the specific form of transactions through which the abbey lands were conveyed. It has been called the largest transfer of land since Domesday, but it was made under different provisions. Less than two and a half percent of the church lands were simply granted by the crown in the traditional feudal fashion. All the rest, the great bulk of church property was sold for cash, usually at a market price of twenty years' purchase. The monetary nature of the process brought a fundamental change in the drivers of economic activity. Individualist property rights were also set free in another sense. The ubiquitous presence of the universal church had been the corporeal expression of the idea that property was a trust from God, and was held on obligations for the benefit of the common good. But the supervising gaze of the abbeys had now disappeared. The life of Christ had been the model of conduct, and the Body of Christ the only singular unity. But the physical manifestation of that oneness was gone. The human individual was given the psychological freedom to buy, hold and use his property without restraint. Mackie was justified in thinking that the arrival of a land-market "created conditions that presaged the end of the medieval world".[32]

Notes

1. M. Overton, *The Agricultural Revolution in England,* (Cambridge 1996), pp. 22, 45, 133
2. W. G. Hoskins, *The Age of Plunder,* (London 1976), p. 10
3. A. Everitt, "The Open Market", in *Agrarian History of England and Wales 1500–1640,* ed. J. Thirsk, (Cambridge 1967), pp. 490, 496, 500
4. Ibid, p. 501
5. Ibid, p. 499; C. Palliser, *The Age of Elizabeth,* (London 1984), p. 275
6. B. C. Jones, "Westmoreland Packhorse Men in Southampton", *Trans. Cumberland and Westmoreland Antiquarian Society, LIX* (1960)
7. Overton, *The Agricultural Revolution*, p. 103

8. *Statutes of the Realm*, IV, 2&3 Philip and Mary, cap 13
9. Daniel Defoe, *A Tour Through the Whole Island of Great Britain*, (Harmondsworth 1971), p. 496
10. D. Palliser, *The Age of Elizabeth*, (London 1983), p. 253
11. *CSP Domestic 1619–23*, p. 130, 1631–3, p. 18
12. C. Hill, *The Century of Revolution*, (London 1961), p. 20
13. R. H. Tawney, *Religion and the Rise of Capitalism*, (Harmondsworth 1966), pp. 77–8
14. J. De Vries, *The Dutch Rural Economy in the Golden Age 1500–1700*, (Yale 1974), pp. 1–3
15. F. Braudel, *The Mediterranean*, (London 1972), p. 213
16. J. Chartres, *Internal Trade in England 1500–1700*, (London 1977), p. 13.
17. Ibid. p. 49; A. Everitt, "The Marketing of Agricultural Produce", in *The Agrarian History of England and Wales*, IV, pp. 506–52
18. Valentine Leigh, *The Most Profitable and Commendable Science of Surveying*, (London 1577), BL 967. k. 15, un-paginated, but as counted, p. 61
19. P. Bigmore, *The Bedfordshire and Huntingdonshire Landscape*, (London 1979), pp. 154–5
20. J. D. Mackie, *The Earlier Tudors*, (Oxford 1966), p. 448
21. R. B. Smith, *Land and Politics in the Reign of Henry VIII*, (Oxford 1970), p. 218
22. Ibid, pp. 218–19
23. *Letters and Papers of Henry VIII*, *3*, no. 6011, (17 October 1629)
24. *CSP Spanish*, V, I, p. 256
25. J. Youings, *The Dissolution of the Monasteries*, (London 1971), p. 69
26. *A Discourse of the Commonweal* (1549), ed M. Dewar, (Virginia 1969), p. 84
27. J. Youings, "The Disposal of Monastic Lands", in *The Agrarian History of England and Wales 1500–1640*, IV, p. 340
28. Hoskins, *The Age of Plunder*, p. 136
29. Ibid, citing J. Youings, ed., *Devon Monastic Lands: Calendar of Particulars for Grants 1536–55*, *Devon and Cornwall Record Society*, New Series, I (1955)
30. T. H. Swales, "The Re-Distribution of Monastic Lands in Norfolk", *Norfolk Archaeology XXXIV* (1966), pt. I, pp. 14–44
31. Overton, *The Agricultural Revolution in England*, p. 167
32. Mackie, *The Earlier Tudors*, p. 448

3 The Structures of Change

The Displacement of the Open Patterns of Occupation on the Common Lands; the Timing and Effects of Enclosure; the Significance of Consolidation Without Enclosure

The seminal change in the socio-economic balance was accompanied, and to a large extent facilitated by an equally dramatic transition in the patterns and relationships of landholding and agricultural activity. In summary it can be characterised as a switch from a communal and customary context of husbandry, to one of individualist and commercially proactive farming. This was less a case of changing structures, than the *introduction* of structure; for in a sense the open fields had none. A distinctive feature of common land agriculture was the relative absence of manmade structures. The multitude of strips that composed each farmer's holding would be scattered across the great open fields, and as one contemporary said, "interlaced" with those of neighbours, with no formal barriers between.[1] On the common pastures, the allocations would be marked by what one historian has called "imaginary lines", often just trodden out between two natural features.[2] At the risk of over-romanticising the scene, the only structures on the common lands would be those of the plants and the trees as they grew. The farming process was not yet measured and directed in enclosed fields, but defined simply by the patterns of working activity.

The culture of the open fields and commons was not universal, but it was the most characteristic system of agriculture in northwest Europe, especially in the great arable heartlands, throughout the medieval period. In England, the open fields constituted the typical pattern of farming for something close to a millennium. They are first heard of in Wessex in the seventh century, and were probably established in the Midlands by the same period. They also seem to have been present in east Yorkshire and Lincolnshire before the ninth century.[3] They survived in a prevalent and classic form until the beginning of the sixteenth century, when "England was still medieval in every important sense . . . around possibly half the villages in England stretched the great open fields, that had hardly changed except in detail for hundreds of years".[4] They occupied a wide swathe of country down the centre of the kingdom, from Yorkshire to Nottinghamshire and Lincolnshire, stretching broadly across the South Midlands and the Thames Valley, and down into Hampshire, Dorset and

Sussex. In fact, the extent of the open field system roughly coincided with the principal corn growing areas of the kingdom. It was the basis of grain production, the most vital function of medieval agriculture.

A typical common land village was itself relatively inconspicuous in the landscape, with low-slung cottages clustered together in the middle of three great open fields, each extending for several hundred acres, with the commons, woods and wastes stretching away beyond. The usual habit was for the farmers to leave the village each morning in procession, and fan out across the open fields. Processional was a familiar way in which they moved around the landscape, again marking their place invisibly within it, often with the aim of bringing their endeavours to the attention of heavenly forces, and seeking their support. So in their devotions, as in their working practice, the farmers occupied the land not by the fixed lines of fence and bounded property, but simply by their active presence in the fields. This is not just a retrospective impression. The character of unstructured occupation on the common lands was perfectly captured in the observation of a late sixteenth century Member of Parliament. Henry Jackman was speaking in defence of the process of enclosure. As a cloth merchant he doubtless had a vested interest in the development that best guaranteed an increased supply of wool. He asserted that the spread of enclosure had not led to a reduction in the output of grain. Such shortages had been more prevalent in earlier periods, "when the whole land lay in open fields, subject only to the hand of the husbandman".[5]

The shape of occupation was as open as the fields themselves. Life on the common lands was characterised by a form of tenure very different from modern absolute property rights. Land was thought of not as individually owned, but as held and occupied in common. It carried not only obligations to a landlord, but also a general duty to God that it must only be used for the good of all, as he intended. It is no accident that the common land system was specific to the medieval period, for it fitted the distinctive spirit of that age as it would have done no other. It was the grounded reflection of a philosophy that subordinated the individual to the communal being. "The denial of the individual in favour of the corporate reality of society is a commonplace of medieval thought".[6] The medieval period saw the world not in terms of particulars, as we do, but rather of universal ideas, which were held to be the objective reality. "If the medieval world wants to know the nature of a thing, it neither looks into it to analyse its stricture, nor behind it to inquire into its origin, but looks up to heaven where it shines as an idea".[7] In practice this meant that things were "known" as given. So to modify or manipulate the land was in some degree to flout the will of God. "Improvement" was a moral concept, of drawing nearer to Christ. Piers the Ploughman worked on behalf of others as well as himself: "following the plough for poor men's sakes. I'll give them food myself . . . bear ye one another's burdens and so ye shall fulfil the law of Christ".[8] The ideal was to sustain what Gerrard Winstanley called a oneness on the land. The same was reflected in the general socio-economic relations of medieval times. Society was conceived as "a chain of incomplete corporations".[9] The only singular unity was the Body of Christ. All else worked in a continuum, with no conceptual distinction between temporal and spiritual, or between intellectual and physical effects. To improve your chances in the fields you looked not to science, but to the Saints, each of whom had a special skill that they might exercise on your behalf. "Medieval thought frequently yielded to the inclination to pass from pure idealism to a sort of magic ideal, in which the abstract tends to become concrete".[10] St. Loy would look after the horses, and St. Anthony the hogs. At Bury there were relics over which you could give supplication "for avoidance of weeds growing in corn".[11] The two great imperatives of the farm and the faith ran together, and everything militated against a particularist view of the world. "The individual's relationship with society is transposed to the higher plane of man's relationship with God, and it is inconceivable that that the individual should claim rights and privileges of his own at the expense of society".[12]

So it is not too surprising that in terms of both principle and practice there seems to have been no inclination in the medieval period to try to record the holding of a particular farmer in a collected form. The exercise was not only difficult, but also unnecessary in a context where it was accepted that each farmer "had his lands not in one gobbet of every field, but interlaced with his neighbours lands".[13] It was sufficient that there was common knowledge of how the strips were disposed. R. H. Davis provides a good description that helps us to envisage these arrangements and understand their essential rationale. With a typical holding of 30 acres, each farmer would have 10 acres in each field. But it would not be in one block. It would be composed of ten one-acre strips, scattered across the field. The original purpose was to give everyone a fair share of the conditions, good and bad. The strips would be disposed "some on the better land, some on the worse, some among the first to be ploughed and some among the last".[14] The strips were usually referred to as "lands", and were units of work, rather than ownership. They extended to about a furlong, as much as could be ploughed in one exercise. The width of a "land" would vary, up to about twenty yards, according to the nature of the soil and how often drainage furrows were required. The furrows marked the divisions between the strips. In the absence of structural borders, the delineation of the strips was determined only by the undulations of the ground, and the aim of running the drainage furrows down a slope. There were important practical benefits in keeping the fields open without formal barriers between the holdings. The arrangement made it easier for the villagers to share vital but expensive resources like the oxen, and the heavy plough, and it enabled the village flock to be freely grazed on the stubble after harvest.

The illustrations at the end of the chapter offer a direct insight into the character of life and work on the open fields, through rare survivals and some ghostly re-appearances. Figure 3.1 comes courtesy of the drought of 2011, when the reservoirs at Wilstone in Nottinghamshire dried out, and the ancient open-field strip system (once worked by the author's ancestors) was revealed. It is easy to picture the villagers moving along their "lands", and occupying the land just by their working presence. We can also note the contrast with the modern landscape in the background, which displays a world dominated by the hard lines of the hedges. Figure 3.2 was produced by the opposite effect, when the flooding of the fields at Marston, near Oxford highlighted the ancient ridge and furrow. It shows how the furrows worked to keep the ploughed ridges above the water level, and there is a sense of the way that the open field system maintained a natural balance of things. Figure 3.3 tells the same story. Chailey Common in East Sussex is protected and kept in its original state. Sheep graze the pasture and keep the brambles at bay. The trees are managed and coppiced in their natural growth patterns as they would have been by the commoners, who used these resources as renewable, and lived in equilibrium with their environment for many centuries. Figure 3.4 is of the surviving open field system at Laxton in Nottinghamshire. The sense of openness is palpable, broken only by the different colours of the crops. Here indeed was a land subject only to the hand of the husbandman.

Just as the true, original culture of the open fields was distinctive and specific to the medieval period, so its displacement would constitute a major transformation in the character of farming in England. Work in the fields was about to take a different, almost opposite course. The continuum would be broken. The sense of restraint and the balance to be held between all things would be lost, as would the notion that the individual was not at liberty to seek his private gain against the common good. The instinctive tendency to work with the land as given would also disappear.

The Timing and Effects of Enclosure

It was from the latter decades of the fifteenth century that the prevalence of the communal pattern of farming, and, crucially, the force of the ethical restraints that it involved, began to be supplanted. The principal sign was the increasing incidence of the enclosure of the commons and open fields, especially for sheep runs to serve the rising demand of the cloth trade. By the late 1480s enclosure had reached a level that provoked the first attempts of the Tudor government to legislate to try to control the process and the effect that it was having on the position of the smallholders. 1516 saw the writing of Sir Thomas More's *Utopia*, the most famous polemical attack on enclosure, which he believed to be depriving the commoners of their livelihoods and depopulating whole villages. Whatever the precise scale of the change, it is clear that by the mid-sixteenth century the open fields were being steadily displaced by the enclosure and consolidation of individual farms, and the fully-fledged commercial license that this assumed.

Enclosure has traditionally been taken as the necessary structure of individualised commercial farming, and the principal basis for increasing agricultural productivity and profits. The association is understandable, and to a great extent justified. It was certainly the unequivocal view of contemporaries. Agriculturalists and surveyors from Fitzherbert to John Norden strongly recommended enclosure as the best way for farmers "to increase their abilities, for one acre enclosed is worth one and a half in common".[15] The benefit was substantiated by the effect that enclosure had on land values. A modern estimate has concluded "that when land was enclosed for agriculture its annual value increased by 31%, and that the annual value of land enclosed for pasture exceeded that of enclosed arable land by 27%".[16] It is also testament to the advantages of enclosure to note that it was expensive, and not to be undertaken lightly. But as Fitzherbert assured his readers, within a few years the outlay would be recouped, and the farm put into substantial profit.[17]

There can be little doubt that in the circumstances of the sixteenth and seventeenth centuries, enclosure was indeed the most effective way to improve the economic performance of farmland. This was manifest in particular in the advance of sheep grazing, which can fairly be seen as the beginning of the age of profitable agriculture, both in itself, and in the increased capability for fertilising the land that it brought. As Fitzherbert suggested, the great benefit of enclosure was to improve the quality of pasture, which enabled the farmer to "put the ram to the ewe anytime", while those on the common fields or heaths were obliged to wait for certain moments of the year when the grass became generally sufficient. Thus the farmer with enclosed fields could wean lambs much earlier, quicker and more frequently than his neighbours on the commons.[18] The great increase in the numbers of sheep was in turn an essential basis for improving the fertility of the arable.

Enclosure was certainly of special importance as the principal and most conspicuous vehicle of "improvement" in the early stages of the agricultural revolution in England, and in fact it can be regarded as inaugurating the process. To this extent, recent historians have been misguided in trying to demote its significance. Some have sought to suggest that enclosure was not a necessary part of the development at all, and that an open field system could perform almost equally well. Robert Allen thought that by 1800 some open field farms were recording 86% of the improvement in yields made by those with enclosed fields.[19] The notion that the open field system may have been as productive as any other has considerable appeal at a sentimental level, but it must be said that this is a somewhat artificial comparison, which tends to obscure the real balance of importance of enclosure. Much might have changed in the centuries up to 1800. It is doubtful whether many of the surviving "open fields" would have kept the distinctive character of their original manifestation intact. And although there is no reason to suppose that the open fields were ever "impervious" to change, as once asserted by Lord Ernle, it must nevertheless be acknowledged that in their truest, initial form, they did not encourage innovation. As originally conceived, they worked, by definition, along customary lines. Enclosure, on the other hand, was aimed specifically at facilitating a process of intensification and improvement. This put it at a high premium in the circumstances of the sixteenth and seventeenth centuries.

There are then, important questions of definition when making these comparisons. We cannot assume that the "open fields" remained the same undifferentiated phenomenon over the whole period from 1500 to 1800. A true open field system was not simply one that remained technically unenclosed, but one that continued to work on the original "interlaced" and communal pattern; and standing still in that fashion might not have been an option in the face of the powerful winds of economic change that were blowing through the early modern period in general. By 1800, even where fields had not been formally enclosed, they might nevertheless have become significantly more commercial than communal, and it will be seen ahead that there were in fact various ways in which this was indeed the case. In particular, it was possible to create a consolidated individual farming unit without a formal process of enclosure. And this was the crux of the matter. The real essence of the change in the structure of farming was the *consolidation* of individual, commercialised units, and this could take place with or without enclosure. It is only in recognising this that we gain a full and true assessment of the timing, the incidence and the implications of the transformation in the practices and principles of farming.

The changing perspectives can be traced in the surveying literature that emerged during the sixteenth century. The assumption of a greater degree of power and conceptual control over the land was reflected in the force of the surveying impulse, as well as in the emergence of the more consolidated and individualised view of landholding that it entailed and illustrated. The earliest proto-surveying studies revealed how the dispersed, disassembled pattern of communal occupation militated against any kind of focused command of the land and the farming exercise. Here again, we might take the liberty of removing one of Jacques Derrida's concepts from the nebulous realms of linguistic theory and apply it as a useful description of a real historical phenomenon. Derrida sometimes complained indeed that his term "deconstruction" was generally misconstrued and popularly taken to mean a process of dismantling, or reducing to pieces. The settled state of dispersal and fragmentation on the open fields comes closer to illustrating what he seems to have had in mind, which was a condition of "never forming".

In Fitzherbert's pioneering book of surveying, which appeared as the companion to his book of husbandry in the 1520s, there seemed at first to be little place or potential for a consolidated mathematical measurement of how the land was occupied and used. The best that could be done in terms of showing the disposition of holdings on the open fields was the process to which he gave the name of "butting and bounding". This sounded quite complex and sophisticated, but in fact it involved simply proceeding across the fields and noting in due order whose strips lay next to whose, at each side and each end. The land itself was not being measured at all. What resulted was just a list of the occupiers of the strips.

> To begin at the east side next to the highway . . . the parson has two lands, the lord three lands, L.B. one land, E. G. two lands . . . the parson one land, R. X. two lands, the prior three lands, the lord two lands, L. H. one land. . . .[20]

It was not a survey of land, but a simple enumeration of "lands". And because the lands were so widely dispersed, no systematic geometrical assessment of an individual holding could be made.

The "butting and bounding" of the strips was the natural reflection of an area occupied just by the communal, physical presence of the villagers. The arrangement was not conducive to division into individual farming units, or to a formal descriptive record. It relied for evidence on the immediate personal experience of the farmers, just as each holding was worked according to their custom and understanding. This pattern of occupation did not lend itself to a central overview of farm management. Nor did it provide a basis for an interventionist approach to land use. It was a context in which the farmers related to the land as given.

But Fitzherbert was in the business of identifying ways in which land could be used in a more controlled and profitable manner. For this purpose he put forward many detailed suggestions in respect of the method, balance and timing of farming practice. And he had one, specific structural recommendation to make—enclose your lands.

> Then let it be known how many acres of arable land every men hath in tillage, and of the same acres in every field to change with his neighbours, and to lay them together, and to make him one several close in every field for his arable lands. And also another several close for his portion of the common pasture, and also his portion of the meadows in a several close by itself, and all kept in several in winter and summer.[21]

At one level this sounded very logical. Yet the suggested process of amalgamation also points up the advantages that the existing system of open dispersal held for the farmers. With enclosure, they would lose the assurance that they were getting a fair share of the best land and conditions. They would also lose the vital facility of grazing the village flock freely across the stubble after harvest.

The logical provisions of the communal pattern need to be emphasised. It should not be supposed that medieval farmers had failed to organise themselves in a rational manner. It was more that in the context of communal and customary activity there was no requirement for a focused overview of farming practice. This is well illustrated in a book of surveying produced by Valentine Leigh in the 1570s, half a century on from Fitzherbert. The communal habit was not easy to overturn, but Leigh's work provided an early sign of how things were beginning to change. He acknowledged a debt to Fitzherbert's method of "butting and bounding", which remained essential in the task of establishing the disposition of holdings on the ground. Despite those constraints, however, Leigh noted a significant advance that had been made towards a more coordinated record. It was becoming usual to bring together on the page the sum of each farmer's holdings, whereas previously each strip had been recorded separately, isolated, and in effect lost in the context of the field.

Now:

> In the same entry, all in one, they do particularly enter every man's arable land, also his meadows, closes and pastures, belonging to every man of the same several tenements altogether. By which means it is possible to know at a glance the parcels of land that belong to every messuage, where before they had to be sought out in the generality of the whole survey of the field.[22]

So even where the strips remained dispersed they could now be conceived as making up a single landholding. Of greatest interest is what this change tells us about the un-monitored, un-centralised character of the old medieval context, where there had clearly been no perceived need to record a discrete individual holding in any respect. What it tells us further is that the will to individualisation had arrived.

Henry Best's description of his Yorkshire farm in 1641 provides a good example of an individualist agricultural unit being consolidated and separated out of the common lands. It gives a very instructive illustration of the fundamental change that was taking place in both the practices and principles of farming life. Best was a successful yeoman farmer, and the principal features of his enterprise were much as we might expect. He had a detailed knowledge of the specialist regional markets, and used them in a closely targeted fashion. In line with the growing divide in agrarian society between larger employers and landless wage labourers, he hired skilled workers from outside on a seasonal basis, for harvesting and for shearing. And he employed women with rakes to gather in the stray corn from the furrows after harvest, when traditionally it would have been left for the commoners to glean. Most of his fields were enclosed. In fact, he gave powerful testament to the benefits of enclosure, noting that since he had brought his meadow lands under that regime their rental value was three times what it had been in his father's day.

But the job of dividing his interests from the customary communal assumptions of the villagers was not quite complete. He had to resist demands to contribute to the common stock of hay, which was traditionally put aside to feed the flocks in protected quarters when the snow was on the ground. He complained that, "by this means our hay would have been spent in feeding other men's animals". In similar vein, at the beginning of May, when the villagers began to put their cattle and oxen out to graze the open fields, he went to great lengths to ensure that none were turned out onto his own land, as they would once have been. This involved constructing very elaborate gate blocks, and carrying out checks in the middle of the night.[23] The old communal ways were engrained among the villagers, but they belonged to a world that was passing, and in the market conditions of the sixteenth and early seventeenth centuries, there could only be one winner.

The two contrasting ways of working and thinking came into conflict not only in the fields, but also in the general context of village life. The old patterns of open, unbroken connection and mobility were further disrupted by the proliferation of enclosures and other physical restrictions on the freedom with which the villages had traditionally moved around the neighbourhood. During the reigns of Elizabeth I and James I, there were widespread local confrontations provoked by the interposition of hedges and barriers that blocked the time-honoured route of the parish perambulation. Processional had been the very fabric of village life, reflecting the interrelationships of the community, and the essential link between the worlds of the farm and the faith. The perambulation was one of the few customary processions that had survived the forceful assault of the Reformists in the 1530s and 40s. And as Keith Thomas was the first to note, if it was coming under threat now, this was not due to Reformist rationalism, but rather to economic individualism. The perambulation was running into trouble "because of the social changes that broke up the old community, and physically impeded anything so cumbersome as a perambulation". The old rituals were well suited to "open field country, but enclosures and cultivation led to the destruction of the old landmarks and blocked the rights of way".[24] There were literally hundreds of disputes. And complaints against the perambulation as idolatrous were rare. It was almost always "because of squabbles between the minister and the parish elite, because the route had been blocked by a new wall, hedge or ditch, or because of lack of interest". Those living near the route had "blocked it with enclosures, or refused to provide customary hospitality to the walkers".[25] It is not exactly true to say that village life was being restructured, because hard divisions had been few and far between in the old open context. But those communal patterns were being torn asunder by structures that had not been prominent before.

The high incidence of these disputes in the reigns of Elizabeth I and James I clarifies the timing and sequence of the crucial phases of enclosure. The first main phase from 1470 to 1550 was associated with the spread of sheep farming and was sufficient in scale to be seen as an existential threat to the common field smallholders. The controversies over the perambulation coincided with the second substantial phase, from 1570 to 1650, when enclosure was general enough to be visibly breaking up the open topography of many villages. This displayed the change in its essential character, displacing the traditional way of communal mobility and mutuality. It was a critical transformation, which had developed through the sixteenth century and was processed through the revolutionary decades of the mid-seventeenth. The medieval concept of moral economy and conditional property had been dedicated to maintaining the given balance of things. There was now arising a different, opposite set of priorities, which licensed the individual to separate out his interests and manipulate things to his advantage. Recognising the special significance of the period from 1470 to 1650 highlights the alteration of moral values that was the heart of the matter.

The first inclination of historians was to assume that the years between the late fifteenth century and the early seventeenth were indeed the most significant time in the advance of the enclosure movement, since this was the period when the process provoked the greatest controversy, not only in terms of land-use protests, but also in the consistent opposition of the political and ecclesiastical establishments. In the best-known version of the traditional view, R. H. Tawney took the contemporary outcry at face value and characterised the agrarian changes as the expropriation of peasant smallholders by powerful landlords.[26] But although there were indeed "thousands of disputes and lawsuits between landlords and tenants in the sixteenth century", this did not necessarily reflect the general state of affairs.[27] So a later generation of academics took exception to Tawney's "picture of early capitalism as cruel and greedy".[28] Mildred Campbell concluded that, "we no longer regard it as an historical calamity visited on the poor by the rich".[29] Hence the recent tendency has been to treat the popular and political resistance as an extreme reaction, and to try to minimise the scale and significance of enclosure in the long sixteenth century. But the sceptical trend is itself an over-reaction, which rests on various misconceptions. It has been accompanied by a readiness to exploit an imbalance in the nature of the records, by supposing that the lack of systematic data in the early period reflects a low level of enclosure, and assuming that the comprehensively recorded parliamentary enclosures of the eighteenth century show that more was taking place then.[30] This is an unjustified assumption. Furthermore, although we need not regard the process as a conscious assault of the rich upon the poor, it is nevertheless apparent that the market conditions of the sixteenth and early seventeenth centuries strongly favoured the interests of the better-off farmers, and threatened the prospects of the less well placed.

The attempt to minimise the significance of enclosure in the earlier period also reflects a failure to maintain a clear balance of definitions. To iron out the chronology of the enclosure movement involves an uncritical assumption that it remained essentially the same kind of process over several centuries of economic change. To baldly measure the incidence of enclosure in the sixteenth century against that of the eighteenth is not comparing like with like. In fact it obliterates the distinction between the age when enclosure was controversial, and the age when it was not. It confuses the period when it posed a challenge to the conventional economic balance, with the period when this was no longer the case. The process of enclosure was not one and the same undifferentiated phenomenon over the four centuries between 1450 and 1850. To suppose this obscures the defining essence of the change, which was the displacement of the communal ethic of the open fields, by an individualist and commercial norm. This did not wait upon the formality of the final stages of the enclosure movement in the early nineteenth century. The new balance in favour of consolidated individual farming already held the stage by the second half of the seventeenth century, both in practice and in principle.

It is vital then to recognise the significance of the Interregnum decades as marking a transformation in the status of enclosure, and the economic ethos with which it was associated. At one level the moment of transition is quite clear. From the 1480s to the 1630s, the enclosure movement was sustained by the powerful, ungoverned forces of the gentry and the market, but it faced the consistent opposition of the political and ecclesiastical authorities. Moralists and churchmen from Thomas More and Hugh Latimer in the early sixteenth century to William Laud in the 1630s condemned the process as an ungodly transgression of the rights of the poor. And successive Tudor governments sought to legislate against it to defend the position of the smallholders on the commons and open fields. In essence it was treated as subversive of the existing socio-economic balance. But the 1650s were, as Brailsford said, "a turning point in the history of enclosure".[31] The public profile of the enclosure movement was in effect reversed. The last anti-enclosure bill was introduced into the Commons in 1656, and thrown out without a second reading. In rejecting the bill, MPs took the opportunity to proclaim the new market orthodoxy that endorsed the process of enclosure. Master of the Rolls William Lenthall said, "he never liked any bill that touched upon property", and Edmund Fowell called it, "the most mischievous bill that ever was offered to the House".[32] They would not find themselves provoked by any further attempts to restrain enclosure. Henceforth, parliament would legislate only to encourage the practice. The moral protests of the clergy were also coming to an end. The last clerical diatribes condemning the practice as irreligious and anti-social were the pamphlets of John Moore in the mid-1650s. In reply, another cleric Joseph Lee demonstrated again that enclosure was now embraced by the new market norm. He said that it was natural for men's actions to be determined by the calculation of their own profit and advantage, and he knew of no law, divine or otherwise that would deny them that right.[33] The freedom of the individual to profit to the full would not be challenged again in England. "After mid-century . . . the affirmation of a moral order where economic activities were means to social ends—God's and man's—fell from public view, [but] the individual's right to look after his own acquired a moral base through the emphasis placed on personal freedom".[34] In the new phase of farming literature, enclosure was officially hailed as the principal basis of improvement. "Any hindrance to enclosure was allocated to the world of backwardness".[35] In fact, after the 1650s, enclosure was a different kind of process. It had ceased to be subversive, and become normative.

In that respect it is clear that the revolutionary decades of the mid-seventeenth century were of seminal importance as the watershed from which a new model of commercial economics emerged. But it was not simply that the dominant climate of opinion was now established in favour of enclosure. Consistent with this was the fact that it now also represented the standard form of agricultural activity on the ground. This can be demonstrated in two main aspects. One is to underline the fallacy of trying to minimise the incidence of formal enclosure in the pre-1650 period, which was certainly greater than suggested by many recent historians. The second further consideration is that enclosure was not the only form in which an individualist, commercial farming unit could take shape. Enclosure was one manifestation of a broader and less formal development that was working in exactly the same direction. The essential basis of the change, and of the new economic balance, was the *consolidation* of larger individual farms, and this could take place with or without the technical enclosure of the fields. This also serves to underline the force of commercialisation as the leading trend in changes in the use and occupation of the land during this period, for the achievement of a substantial marketable surplus was the incentive to consolidate, and it did not always require the considerable expense of hedging.

But enclosure was the paradigm, and it should be made clear that it had indeed become a general and prominent feature of the landscape by 1650. The minimisation of the incidence of enclosure between the late fifteenth and the early seventeenth centuries depends on exploiting the inadequacy of the statistical data. Whereas the record of the parliamentary-endorsed enclosures of the eighteenth and nineteenth centuries is necessarily comprehensive, no such enumeration exists for the earlier period. The enclosures that took place in the years between the second half of the fifteenth century and the first half of the seventeenth generated widespread controversy, but no systematic record. Such sporadic attempts as were made to monitor the process were partial in every respect. From Wolsey's commission of 1517, for instance, "The surviving returns . . . are so incomplete that no conclusions about the extent of enclosure or engrossing can be built upon them".[36] The returns were, in any case, thoroughly unreliable. The juries could be easily intimidated, or packed with the servants of the culprits, and jurors might have good pragmatic reasons of their own not to cross or incriminate the local lord. One jury in Leicestershire declared that William Ashby had enclosed one hundred and twenty acres, whereas in fact it is known that he had enclosed more than a thousand acres and depopulated the entire manor.[37] There was every incentive and opportunity for subterfuge. Given the circumstances of the time, and the balance of forces in the enclosure contest, it is not surprising that much of it went under the counter. There are certainly enclosures that are known to have taken place, but which eluded the commissions or any other kind of public record. The enclosure of the fields of Tetchwick in Buckinghamshire in 1519 escaped official notice.[38] And Peter Brandon talks of the "silent revolution" by which most of the open fields of Sussex were enclosed during the sixteenth and early seventeenth centuries: "un-chronicled in surviving documents. Fortunately the landscape itself has much to tell".[39] It is clear that in this period, "enclosure could take place on a huge scale, without leaving much trace in the public records".[40]

So attempts to minimise the significance of enclosure in and around the sixteenth century do not represent the true balance of the evidence. But some more objective views are available. Robert Allen's study of the South Midlands reinstates the importance of the first marked phase of enclosure from the late fifteenth century to the mid-sixteenth century. "Between 1450 and 1525 about one tenth of the villages in the South Midlands were destroyed . . . as lords seized peasant land".[41] And the consequences were much as the Tudor moralists claimed.

> Enclosure before the mid-sixteenth century had a dramatic—negative—impact on population. Circa 1550, the average population density of villages already enclosed was only half the density of those still open . . . the Tudor conviction that enclosure caused depopulation was fact, not fancy. Enclosure before 1550 played a greater role in destroying the English peasantry than historians have been prepared to admit.[42]

These, the more balanced of recent studies, reinforce the observations of the most authoritative of contemporary sources, the *Discourse of the Commonweal*, which was a broad and judicious survey of the economic condition of the kingdom in 1549. It takes a rounded view of the enclosure movement, absolving it from being the cause of high prices and food shortages, but nevertheless asserting categorically that a dangerous amount of expropriating enclosure had indeed taken place in the decades before 1550. And "if that kind of enclosure do as much increase in twenty years to come as it has done twenty years past it comes to the great desolation and weakening of the strength if this realm".[43]

The intensive phase of enclosure identified by the *Discourse* had coincided with the most vigorous period of expansion in the cloth trade, when the profits to be made from a focused approach to sheep rearing were at their peak. This illustrates the economic reason for supposing that enclosure was extensive in the years between the sixteenth and early seventeenth centuries, which were generally characterised by a distinctive and steady rise in agricultural prices. Peter Bowden rehearsed the state of the market that worked in favour of the consolidating yeoman, and against the mere smallholder. "It was somewhere between 60 and 100 acres when general crop failure meant an increase in net income to the producer" because he had "a proportionately greater market surplus". Thus the "chief farmer" could wait his time and sell at the highest price. The smallholder, on the other hand, might have a small surplus in a good year, but would have to sell it cheap while in a bad year he would have to buy in dear. Bowden recorded the result dispassionately. "Several bad harvests could hardly fail to bring ruin to these small cultivators".[44]

These were the market conditions that encouraged and facilitated the enclosure and consolidation of individual farming units. The fears of the *Discourse* may, however, have been eased to some extent because there seems to have been a lull in the spread of enclosure for at least a decade after 1550. This was not surprising since the incentives were, for the moment, somewhat reduced. The long expansion of the cloth trade had come to a pause, and there was not so much scope for the extension of sheep farming. Furthermore, the later 1550s saw the only five-year period in the Tudor century when the steady rise in population received a setback. Demand fell away in consequence, and for a time, neither arable nor pasture held the same promise of profit. By the 1570s, however, population was again on the increase and the agricultural market was recovering strongly. The trend towards enclosure and consolidation resumed in earnest.

Margaret Spufford confirmed the nature and chronology of the process in her study of Cambridgeshire. In the years between 1560 and 1636, the farms that were secure and not reduced in size or number were the larger copyholds of 60 acres or more. Farmers with less than 45 acres, aiming essentially at self-sufficiency, were most likely to disappear. It seemed that the typical medieval smallholding was no longer a viable unit in the inflationary conditions of the sixteenth century. The trend towards the engrossing of farms accelerated in the late sixteenth and early seventeenth centuries. In one parish "it was possible to show with precision that the last half-yardland unit disappeared in exactly those years of dearth when prices were the highest so far recorded". Spufford identified the "arch engrosser", the farmer who had managed to incorporate the farms of fifteen others, largely through forfeited copyholds.[45]

One of the devices for minimising the early enclosures has been to divide the period arbitrarily into separate centuries, and assert that more took place in the seventeenth than in the sixteenth.[46] But clearly if we avoid this artificial distinction, and apply the more substantial and relevant measure of changes in the long-term trends of population and prices, it emerges that the highest incidence of enclosure bridged the centuries, from the late fifteenth to the early sixteenth, and from the late sixteenth to the early seventeenth. In the South Midlands, over the period 1450–1750, the really peak years of enclosure were between 1575 and 1650, when 60% of it took place.[47] It tailed away in the second half of the seventeenth century, when the trends of population and prices were generally static. The picture was the same in Leicestershire, in the great heartland of English arable, from where the best evidence is available. There, 36% of enclosure took place between 1485 and 1550, 5% between 1550 and 1600, 40% between 1600 and 1650, and only 17% after 1650.[48] Again in Bedfordshire, "through the medieval period the size of the holdings, and their scattered disposition among the open fields remained remarkably static. But by the middle of the 16th century the situation was transformed . . . over some fifty years there is abundant evidence that piecemeal enclosure was occurring in the open fields".[49] We have already noted Peter Brandon's identification of the "silent revolution" by which the southern flank of open field country in Sussex was enclosed in the late sixteenth century. At the other end of the kingdom, Bill Shannon has found that the great majority of the lowland wastes of Lancashire were enclosed or partitioned in the sixteenth century and the early decades of the seventeenth, prompting the conclusion that the incidence of waste enclosure in the early period has also been greatly underestimated. The process was actually being completed "just before the time of the Civil War".[50] The picture can be rounded out with reference to the interesting example of the open fields at Marston, near Oxford. Their history underlines the force of the two developments that frame the chronology of agrarian change in the early modern period. The demesne lands had been alienated into the hands of commercialising tenants by the beginning of the sixteenth century, and as a characteristic consequence of that trend, the common fields were enclosed in the decades before 1650.[51]

Enclosure was obviously extensive in the period up to 1650, which is just as expected, considering that it was the long-term upward trend in population and prices that created the opportunities and possibilities for investment during that time. The process of enclosure, and the associated practice of the engrossing or consolidation of individual farms, were certainly occurring on a sufficient scale to explain the persistent protests that came both from the people affected in the localities, and the central authorities of church and state. After 1650 the public status of the movement was transformed. The revolutionary decades saw the triumph of absolute property rights, and established a new climate of opinion that gave a fair wind to enclosure. The critical voices, and the legislative opposition died away. In fact, the process of consolidation had advanced so far that common field agricultural no longer reflected the orthodox economic philosophy, or the dominant shape of farming on the ground. By the second half of the seventeenth century England was witnessing the disappearance of the independent husbandman, and the rural scene was increasingly characterised by a distinctive polarisation between substantial commercial farmers on the one hand, and wage labourers on the other. The decisive change had already occurred before the end of the seventeenth century. It can be measured in terms of the rising proportion of landless people. It is estimated that in the mid-sixteenth century only 12% had no land. By the later sixteenth century it had risen to over 20%, and by the 1680s it was almost 70%. The gentry and the yeomanry now occupied three-quarters of the land of England.[52] It was a transformation in agrarian society, which Maurice Keen has captured to perfection: "The squire, the yeoman and Hodge the farm labourer, are clean different figures from the lord, the reeve, and the quarter virgater".[53]

The Significance of Individual Farm Consolidation Without, or Prior to Enclosure

So the technical enclosure of the open fields was widespread in the early period, and was of critical importance both in itself, and as sign and symbol of the change that was taking place. But it was not the real basis of the development of individualist commercial farming, nor was it the only form in which this could take shape. The core of the process was the *consolidation* of larger holdings, which could and did occur without a formal structure of enclosure. Recognising this helps us to understand the importance of the period before 1650 in changing the balance of landholding.

It also further underlines the fallacy of simplistic comparisons between the incidence of enclosure in the earlier and later phases. As suggested previously, after 1650 enclosure became a different kind of process. This was in part because it operated in a transformed, and indeed opposite climate of opinion, which made the interests of absolute property and commercial freedom normative. In that respect the triumph of enclosure was already complete, since the moral foundations that had sustained the communal system were fatally undermined by the middle of the seventeenth century. It can be emphasised again that the open fields proper were an *ethical* rather than just a physical concept. So although some fields may have remained technically unenclosed after 1650, they did not necessarily remain "open" in the true, original, communal sense of the word. After 1650 they were surviving in a world where individualist, free market economics had become axiomatic, and this had to be accommodated to some extent. By the second half of the seventeenth century the communal ethic no longer carried force in the context of the economy as a whole.

In fact, what might be called creeping commercialisation took definite shape in the way that the consolidation of individualist holdings could precede the formal process of enclosure. The change in the balance of occupation and land use, and the replacement of the communal pattern by the commercial, could occur without the technicality of enclosing the fields. And this is another substantial reason not to assume that the process of "enclosure" represented one and the same undifferentiated phenomenon across the four centuries. The level of effect of the later enclosures after 1650 was diminished in the crucial sense that many of them took place in a context where the essential development of the consolidation of larger individual properties had already occurred, without requiring the formal enclosure of the fields. It seems that the later enclosures were often just a tidying up of loose ends. So an assessment of the comparative incidence of enclosure in the later period needs to take account of the fact that it often constituted a confirmation rather than a real change.

The following pages outline the position on a group of manors in West Hertfordshire, where the transition to a new pattern dominated by consolidated individual farms appears to have occurred before, and probably long before the common lands were formally enclosed, under parliamentary legislation, at the end of the eighteenth century. The balance of tenure on the open fields of these manors had changed radically, even while they remained technically unenclosed. When we look at the disposition of holdings on these fields before the act of enclosure, we find that they had already lost the character of a true, open, communal system. There was little evidence of the essentially even-handed and equitable distribution of smallholdings that they would have displayed in their original, medieval shape. The commons were no longer recognisable in that form. In all these cases, there had already been a polarisation into larger commercial farms on the one hand, and smaller, uneconomic allotments on the other. So the essential process of the consolidation of substantial individual properties had already come into force, before the formality of enclosure provided the final endorsement.

On the common lands of the manor of Puttenham, for instance, there had been individual consolidation and a marked polarisation between rich and poor, some considerable time before enclosure took place in 1813.[54] There were already four very substantial farms of between 80 and 300 acres. We recall that 60–70 acres seems to have been the minimum required to ensure the capacity to profit from the market conditions of the sixteenth and early seventeenth centuries. Only the four farms mentioned above had attained that level or anything like it. There were no smallholdings of the 30–40-acre dimension that would have been the most usual, independently viable provision on the open fields in their original state. There were six holdings of between 10 and 16 acres, which was below the 16–20 mark that was regarded as the bare minimum to provide subsistence in medieval times. These holdings would only have been economically viable given a supplementary income from other sources, such as wage labour on the larger commercial farms, or work on the construction of the rapidly developing transport systems. And at Puttenham, there were many commoners, a majority indeed, who were left with even less land, and were in effect entirely dependent on finding outside work for wages. There were no less than 20 holdings of between 0 and 5 acres. From these the commoner would have struggled to bring forth anything worthwhile at all. These were unviable, token fragments of the holdings that had once existed, and as will become clear, other common rights could not be enjoyed when a smallholding was reduced to this level. So apart from the proprietors of the four large commercial farms, all the other tenants on the open fields now depended, either in whole or in part on employment as labourers for their livelihoods. It is apparent that on this manor of Puttenham, the consolidation of a minority of substantial farms and the dispossession of the majority of traditional smallholders had already taken place before enclosure.

There were other indications of the kind of rights that all these holdings had once carried, but which were no longer active, and had been in effect converted to the use of the large commercial farms. Several of the small allotment holders, some with no more than a cottage and a garden, made claim to a standard right of common pasture, for two cows, one bullock, and six sheep. But a holding of a few acres or less was apparently not a sufficiently productive unit to enable them to take advantage of these pastoral facilities, and some of the claims were challenged on the basis that the stated rights were actually no longer exercised. What had occurred in fact was that the use of these rights had been appropriated by a few substantial farmers, like Edward Barker, who had assembled a farm of 106 acres, along with the common rights to pasture ninety-two sheep and sixteen cows. It is interesting to note that Barker is on record as being opposed to the enclosure act of 1813. He clearly had no need for it, since he, or his predecessors had managed to set up a fully consolidated farming enterprise without it. The construction of hedges and fences was expensive, and in this case it was obviously not regarded as necessary. Barker is the personification of the important truth that the fundamental process of the consolidation of a commercial farm could take effect without the assistance of enclosure. It is also a further illustration of how the extension of individual sheep farms had played a crucial part in the development. The common rights of pasture on this manor had obviously ceased to be common long before they were formally enclosed.

The common rights of open field arable had gone the same way. Thomas Cadell now occupied 300 acres, 250 of which were described as "common field arable". This land too was clearly not common any more. It had been appropriated and consolidated out of the open fields. Cadell, or his forebears appear to have engrossed the arable lands of at least fifteen open field smallholders into their own hands. His farm was now ten times as large as the most typical smallholding on the original open fields. The four other arable holdings mentioned at Puttenham before enclosure were between 11 and 16 acres. These were the stragglers, the last partial survivors of the old open field system. Robert Gibbs held 13.1 acres of common field arable, and the disposition of his land is noted. It was scattered around the open fields as twenty-two separate "lands" of an acre or one third of an acre each. Gibbs had managed to cling onto the remnants of what would once have been a typical open field holding, but it was now significantly smaller than the 16–20 acres that had been regarded as the bare minimum for subsistence in the original medieval context. This would not of itself have provided an adequate income for him and his family, as would have been expected from an open field holding in its first, true, form and purpose. These households were now obliged to ensure their livelihoods in other ways. The patterns and principles of communalism no longer applied.

At Puttenham then, the basis of the development of agrarian capitalism—the consolidation of a few commercial farms and the reduction of the remaining smallholders to dependence on wage labour—had already taken place long before the formality of enclosure in 1813. This helps to correct the recent over-emphasis on the extent of the later enclosures, and tells us that they had a much less substantial effect on the socio-economic balance than the enclosures of the earlier period up to 1650. The fact that, with or without enclosure, the essential process of consolidation was clearly continuous, also suggests an adjustment to the recently prevailing view that the most significant trend in land holding patterns after 1660 was the assembling of large estates by the nobility and greater gentry.[55] It is clear that what was happening at Puttenham was basically the consolidation of commercial, yeoman-sized farms out of the common lands, and this was of more seminal importance in the reshaping of English agrarian society than the activities of the nobility in creaming off the top. There is an interesting example at Puttenham of how the construction of a medium sized farm or estate could underpin the broader accumulations of the nobility. One of the entries on the list of claims was a 160-acre farm held by the Earl of Bridgewater, who was indeed acquiring large estates across the region, but his farm in Puttenham had been put together over a long period by Edward Lucy Meacher and his forebears, who had assembled the 160 acres from no less than seventy separate pockets of land. Bridgewater had simply purchased the resulting package from him, in a sort of agrarian takeover bid.

The consolidation of commercial farms was in every sense the most crucial factor in the new disposition of landholding, and Puttenham was far being from an isolated case. The same process had occurred in just the same way on the commons and open fields of the adjacent manor of Slapton.[56] Here too, the original pattern of dispersed but intentionally equal and independent smallholdings had disappeared, and long before enclosure arrived in 1810 there was already a polarisation between a minority of substantial individual farms on the one hand, and a majority of uneconomic allotments on the other. The divide was not yet quite as stark or complete as at Puttenham, which in a sense makes the course of events easier to visualise. There were a number of consolidated farms still being formed, and some recognisably communal-sized holdings still hanging on. At the top end of the scale there was one estate of 400 acres, and four other fully formed substantial farms of between 117 and 190 acres. There were also four other farms that were reaching the stage of successful consolidation, with 60 to 70 acres each. And there was still some scope for appropriation. There were just two smallholdings that would have been recognised as typical on the original open fields, with 20 and 24 acres respectively. This was a common size of holding in medieval times, but it had ceased to be economically viable in the inflationary conditions of the sixteenth century. There were seven holdings of between 7 and 14 acres, which was some way below what had been regarded as the bare minimum for subsistence in medieval times. These were holdings that had already lost ground to the consolidating farms and now relied on the supplementation of outside labouring work. There were also eleven mere allotments of 4 acres or less, the occupants of which would have been mainly dependent on labouring employment for their survival.

So at Slapton too the polarization into a context defined by large commercial farms and wage dependent labourers had already occurred before actual enclosure took place. And once again the process can be seen to have taken shape largely as the appropriation of the rights of common pasture by the larger farms as they were put together. Cottagers with a holding of just a few acres claimed a nominal right of "commons agreeable to the custom of commonage in the parish". But it would appear that, as at Puttenham, these rights were no longer exercised, or at least, not in their original tenancies. The rights of common pasture had been taken over by the commercialising farmers as they constructed their enterprises by the acquisition of smaller holdings. Thomas Buckmaster now had 70 acres, and the right to pasture fifty-two sheep on the commons. John Buckmaster had 117 acres, with rights for one hundred sixteen sheep. Richard Broome had 135 acres, and the right to pasture the same number of sheep. Joseph Tilcott was accredited with 96 acres of arable, and the right to pasture ninety-six sheep. Early sixteenth-century commentators believed that the main incentive for enclosure was to form controlled areas for sheep runs. No doubt this was often the case. But it is important to recognise that the consolidation of commercial sheep farms could be achieved without formal enclosure. Even while the common lands remained technically open, their equitable provisions could be comprehensively overturned, and converted by piecemeal acquisition to the uses of a coordinated individual farm.

At nearby Ivinghoe the scale of the transfer of the balance of occupation was most graphic.[57] This was a larger manor both in area and population, which simply produced the result that the consolidated farms and estates were the most extensive, and the list of the dispossessed was the longest. Here was the greatest proportion of those who still claimed some kind of place on the common lands, but whose holdings had been reduced to an uneconomic level. Out of sixty-five claimants, there were forty households occupying three acres or less, and another five with between 4 and 5 acres. This meant that almost three-quarters of the commoners were already effectively landless before the formal enclosure arrived in 1820. Almost all of these asserted a customary right to "the commons, wastes and commonable grounds" of the manor. In practice it seems likely that the right to gather fuel from the wastes remained in general operation, but the rights of common pasture were now rarely exercised by the cottagers who asserted it. In only three cases was a specific usage indicated. Will Costin had 1 acre of arable, and claimed rights of common pasture for two cows and six sheep. George Garrett also held 1 acre of arable, and claimed pasture rights for two cows and a general right for sheep. Joseph Luck held 3 acres and emphasised a right of sheep commons. These men were clinging onto the rights of common pasture that were supposed to be associated with a holding on the open fields. For the great majority of the cottagers, however, it would appear that their holdings of one or two acres on the arable were now insufficiently productive to enable them to sustain a presence on the common pastures.

Once again, there was a noticeable gap where the most usual independent smallholding of 30 acres would once have been on the original open fields. There were five holdings that had managed to grow to just above that level, at between 40 and 55 acres, and were getting towards commercial security. These were borderline economic, probably with some degree of supplementation from other sources of income. But this size of holding was also noticeably vulnerable to being bought out by the larger farms and estates that already existed. Aston Ivinghoe held 400 acres, part of which he had recently purchased as 42 acres of pieces in the open fields from Thomas Younger. The Earl of Bridgewater held well over a thousand acres. Some of it had been acquired as consolidated land, and some of it as smaller strips and allotments. The Earl too had recently purchased a 42-acre holding, this time from Richard Warren. There were also three examples of what had constituted the most significant underlying change in the balance of landholding—that is to say the consolidation of medium sized commercial farms. There was one of 74 acres, one of 97 acres, and one of 104 acres. These had been put together as successful individualised farming units over the years, and were in place long before the coming of enclosure.

The formal enclosure of common land is clearly not the definitive measure of the process by which the traditional balances of communal farming were undermined through the development of individualised commercial holdings. The essence of the matter was the *consolidation* of larger individual farms, and this could occur without the technical enclosure of the open fields. On the arable land, groups of strips could be brought together and worked as a coherent unit without any imperative need for enclosure. On the common pastures the same effect could be achieved by the simple practice of monopolisation by the more substantial farmers. This was what had occurred on the group of manors in West Hertfordshire as just described, where the stark polarisation between a minority of large commercial farms and a majority of dispossessed smallholders had already occurred before they were formally enclosed at the beginning of the nineteenth century. In fact, the process was probably well in train by the second half of the seventeenth century, when the general evidence shows that the distinctive divide in English agrarian society between yeoman farmers on the one hand, and wage labourers on the other was already essentially in place. This underlines once again the fallacy of putting too much significance on the quantity of later enclosure, which was often just a confirmation of the socio-economic polarisation, rather than a cause. The basis of the great transition, in its essential nature as a reversal of the morality as well as the structure of land occupation, had occurred by the later seventeenth century, and it had been channelled through the watershed of the mid-seventeenth century revolution.

A survey of Putney in Surrey, in 1636, offers an interesting example of a manor which was in fact never formally enclosed, but where the process of the individual consolidation of larger farms out of the common fields can be seen to have occurred, and been largely completed, before the revolutionary decades.[58] The map gives a striking picture of a divide between a minority of large, consolidated farms on one side of the manor, and a majority of tiny residual smallholdings scattered among the surviving strips on the other. The manor was smaller than most in area, but its situation near the Thames and the capital gave it exceptional value. The lord of the manor, Sir Abraham Dawes, had just over 200 acres. It was composed of about fifty separately identifiable fields or strips. But they were mostly of a commercial size, and in a consolidated and collected group occupying the southern section of the manor. The two men next to him in social status and in the survey table were Mr. Henry White and Mr. William Womanfoulds. Neither of them had a consolidated farm, but both were substantial landlords, with at least eight cottages or houses each in the town centre. Next on the survey table came the most successful yeoman farmer, Edward Powell, with over 70 acres. Like Dawes' estate, Powell's holding was composed of thirty separately identifiable strips, but they were also consolidated and collected, forming a block of land in the western sector of the manor. Next in precedence was John Campion, whose farm was approaching a similarly substantial size. He occupied more than 50 acres. The land was not as closely collected as that of Dawes and Powell, and more of it was held among the central area of surviving open field strips. But Campion's holding was distinguished by the fact that he held ten times as much land as any of the lesser commoners, and also by the fact that some of his separately identifiable fields were considerably larger than the general size of the original scattered strips. He had a series of fields of between four and eight acres, which put them on a comparable scale to those held by Dawes and Powell. They were no doubt a result of the past appropriation and consolidation of several smaller strips. And once these more substantial fields had been formed, they became the viable working units of a commercial farm.

So Dawes, Powell and Campion held the three farms that were of a commercial size. The rest of the list consisted of eleven other residual open field smallholders, occupying the remaining, tiny, scattered strips that were crowded into the agriculturally less propitious northern sector close to the river. None of them held anything like the original most common independent provision of 30 acres, or even the 16–20 acres that was regarded as the bare minimum necessary for subsistence in medieval times. Six of them had no significant acreage at all, holding just a garden, or something akin to a modern-day allotment. Five of them had 4 or 6 acres each, but these were still dispersed as narrow strips of an acre or less, and not consolidated as commercial units. These were just token fragments of tenancies that had once existed as balanced smallholdings sustaining a family on the open fields. It is likely that these cottagers retained the right of gathering fuel on the Heath and Common, which remained open, but their arable strips were not economically viable, either in size or shape. Nor were they a sufficient basis for maintaining a presence on the common pastures. The smallholders had in effect been dispossessed, and reduced to dependence, either in total or in part, on working for wages elsewhere.

Figure 3.1 Open Field Strips Exposed by Drought at Wilstone.

Source: Courtesy of Chris Reynolds.

Figure 3.2 Ridge and Furrow Revealed by Floods at Marston.

Source: Courtesy of Oxfordshire History Centre.

Figure 3.3 Surviving Commons at Chailey, Sussex.

Source: Photo by author.

Figure 3.4 Surviving Open Fields at Laxton, Nottinghamshire.

Source: Photo by author.

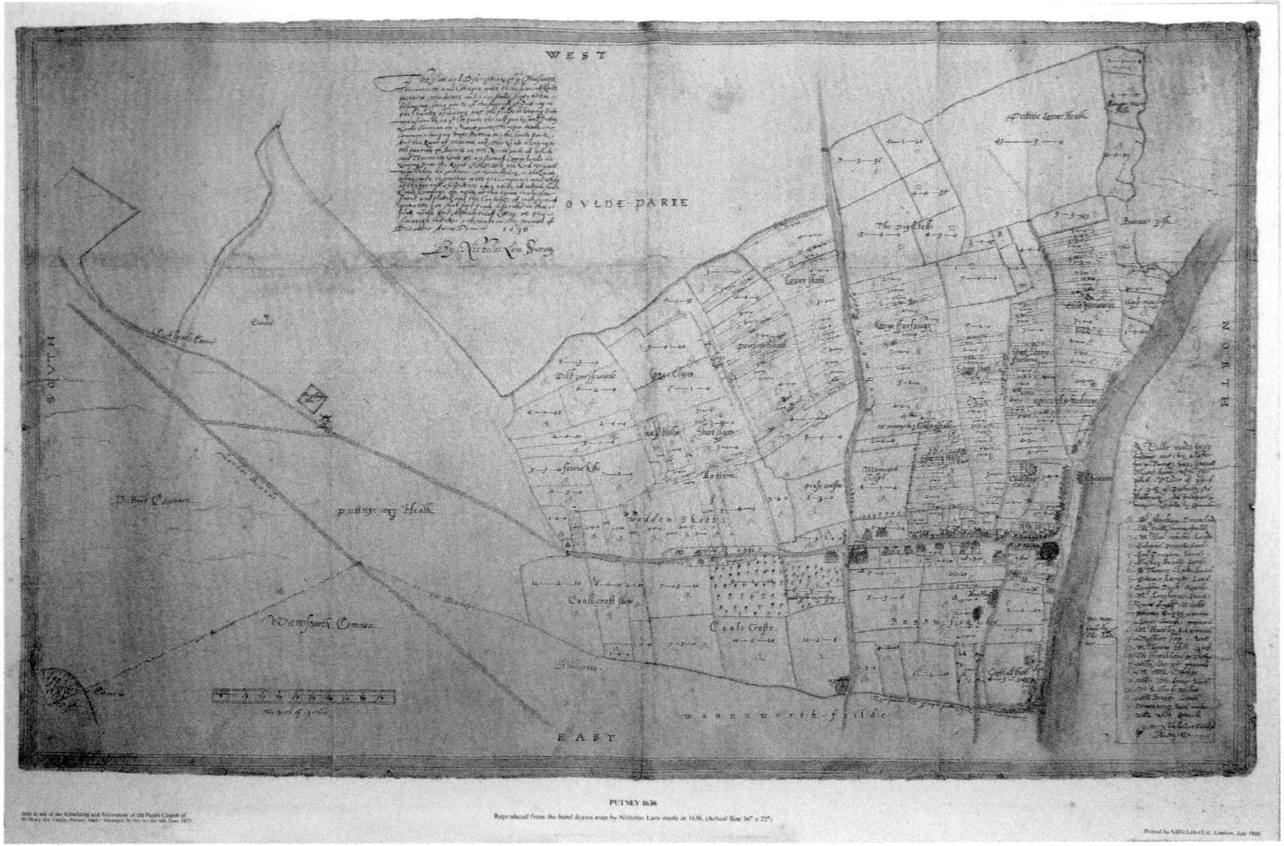

Figure 3.5 Survey Map of Putney in 1636, by Nicholas Lane.

Source: © by kind permission of St Mary's Church, Putney.

Notes

1. *A Discourse of the Commonweal* (1549), ed. M. Dewar, (Virginia 1969), p. 121
2. W. E. Tate, *The English Village Community and the Enclosure Movement*, (London 1967), p. 32
3. F. Stenton, *Anglo-Saxon England*, (Oxford 1947) p. 277
4. W. G. Hoskins, *The Age of Plunder*, (London 1976), p. 1
5. Cited in J. E. Neale, *Elizabeth I and Her Parliaments*, (London 1957), vol. II, p. 342
6. M. Wilks, *The Problem of Sovereignty in the Later Middle Ages*, (Cambridge 1963), p. 25
7. J. Huizinga, *The Waning of the Middle Ages*, (Harmondsworth1976), p. 206
8. William Langland, *Piers the Ploughman*, ed. J. Goodridge, (Harmondsworth 1966), pp. 81, 84, 87
9. Wilks, *The Problem of Sovereignty in the Later Middle Ages*, p. 30
10. Huizinga, *Waning of the Middle Ages*, p. 210
11. E. Duffy, *The Stripping of the Altars*, (Yale 1992), p. 384
12. Wilks, *The Problem of Sovereignty in the Later Middle Ages*, pp. 24–5
13. *Discourse of the Commonweal* (1549), ed. M. Dewar, (Virginia 1969), p. 121
14. R. H. Davis, *A History of Medieval Europe*, (London 1970), p. 197
15. J. Norden, *The Surveyor's Dialogue* (1618), ed. M. Netzloff, (Ashgate 2010), p. 90
16. J. D. Mackie, *The Earlier Tudors*, (Oxford 1966), p. 450
17. Fitzherbert, *Book of Husbandry* (1523), 1534 Printing, ed. W. Skeat, (London 1882), p. 77
18. Ibid, p. 42
19. R. Allen, *Enclosure and the Yeoman*, (Oxford 1992), pp. 207–8
20. Fitzherbert, *Surveying* (1523), in *Certain Ancient Tracts*, ed. R. Vansittart, (London 1762), p. 70
21. Ibid, p. 96
22. Valentine Leigh, *The Most Profitable and Commendable Science of Surveying*, (London 1577), BL, 967. k. 15, un-paginated, but as counted, pp. 61–3
23. Henry Best, "Rural Economy in Yorkshire in 1641", *Surtees Society XXXIII* (1857), pp. 9, 18, 21, 59, 74, 100, 118, 129
24. K. Thomas, *Religion and the Decline of Magic*, (Harmondsworth 1971), p. 74
25. R. Hutton, *The Rise and Fall of Merry England*, (Oxford 1994), pp. 142–3, 175
26. R. H. Tawney, *The Agrarian Problem in the Sixteenth Century*, (London 1912)
27. Hoskins, *The Age of Plunder*, p. 62
28. E. Kerridge, *Agrarian Problems in the Sixteenth Century and After*, (London 1969), p. 15
29. M. Campbell, *The English Yeoman*, (London 1960), p. 86
30. M. Overton, *The Agricultural Revolution in England*, p. 148
31. H. Brailsford, *The Levellers and the English Revolution*, (Nottingham 1983), p. 426
32. *The Parliamentary Diary of Thomas Burton*, ed. J. T. Rutt, (Colburn 1828), I, pp. 175–6
33. Joseph Lee, *A Vindication of a Regulated Enclosure*, (London 1656), pp. 7–9
34. J. Appleby, *Economic Thought and Ideology in Seventeenth-Century England*, (Princeton 1978), p. 70

35. P. Warde, "The Idea of Improvement", in *Custom, Improvement and the Landscape,* ed. R. Hoyle(Farnham 2011), p. 142
36. J. Thirsk, *Agrarian History of England and Wales*, ed. J. Thirsk, (Cambridge 1967), IV, p. 241
37. Hoskins, *The Age of Plunder*, p. 69
38. M. Reed, *The Buckinghamshire Landscape,* (London 1979), p. 152
39. P. Brandon, *The Sussex Landscape,* (London 1974), p. 148
40. R. Hoyle, *Custom, Improvement and the Landscape,* (Farnham 2011), pp. 14–15
41. Allen, *Enclosure and the Yeoman*, pp. 13–14
42. Ibid, pp. 42, 48
43. *Discourse of the Commonweal*, p. 49
44. P. Bowden, "Agricultural Prices, Farm Profits and Rents", in *The Agrarian History of England and Wales, 1500–1640,* ed. J. Thirsk, (Cambridge 1967), IV, p. 659
45. M. Spufford, *Contrasting Communities,* (Stroud 2000), pp. 80–1, 90–2, 118–19, 165
46. Overton, *The Agricultural Revolution in England*, p. 148
47. Allen, *Enclosure and the Yeoman*, pp. 28–9
48. Overton, *The Agricultural Revolution in England*, p. 149
49. P. Bigmore, *The Bedfordshire and Huntingdonshire Landscape,* (London 1979), pp. 154–5
50. W. Shannon, "Approvement and Improvement in the Lowland Wastes of early modern Lancashire", in *Custom, Improvement and the Landscape,* pp. 191, 201
51. G. N. Clark, "Open Fields and Enclosure at Marston, Oxfordshire", *Oxfordshire Record Society, VI* (1925), pp. 1–21
52. Overton, *The Agricultural Revolution*, p. 179
53. M. Keen, *English Society in the Later Middle Ages,* (Harmondsworth 1990), p. 76
54. Hertfordshire Archives, Puttenham Enclosure Claims, D/Els/036
55. H. J. Habakkuk, "The Rise and Fall of English Landowning Families 1660–1800", *Transactions of the Royal Historical Society,* (1979–1981), pp. 29, 30 and 31
56. Hertfordshire Archives, Slapton Enclosure Claims, D/Els/055
57. Hertfordshire Archives, Ivinghoe Enclosure Claims, D/Els/047
58. Map of the manor of Putney in 1636, by the surveyor Nicholas Lane. Reproduced by kind permission of St Mary's Church, Parish of Putney

4 New Patterns of Work

From Smallholders to Wage Labourers; and the Role of Industrial Activity in Undermining the Commons

Thus the consolidation of individual commercial farms by a minority, and the consequent dispossession of the majority of smallholders, could take place without the formal imposition of enclosure. This makes it easier to understand how the original balance of occupation on the commons and open fields had been overturned by the second half of the seventeenth century. Similarly, the dramatic increase that had occurred in the proportion of landless in agrarian society becomes more comprehensible. We have already quoted the figures quantifying the reversal of status that had been visited on the greater part of the rural workforce. In the early sixteenth century only about 10% of agricultural workers were landless wage labourers. The majority were independent smallholders on the open fields. But by the later seventeenth century, the position was reversed, and about 50% had become wholly dependent on wage labour, and another 20% dependent in part. The force of the change is also reflected in the fact that by the end of the seventeenth century, the gentry and the yeomanry occupied 75% of the land of England.[1] The final confirmation of the importance of the period up to 1680 is that in the next 150 year period, which included the Industrial Revolution, the proportion of landless labourers only increased by another 5%.

Once again, the primary importance of the period between the early sixteenth and the later seventeenth centuries is underlined. By then the distinctive polarisation in land tenure and agrarian society in England was already essentially in place, if not yet quite complete. Keith Wrightson provided the best-known overview of the transition.[2] But it is a development that most historians would acknowledge. The common field smallholder no longer defined the rural scene. Most villages were now characterised by a sharp divide between substantial commercial farmers on the one hand, and agricultural wage labourers on the other. It was a fundamental change. Maurice Keen's word picture bears repeating. "The squire, the yeoman and Hodge the farm labourer are clean different figures from the lord, the reeve and the quarter virgater".[3] The conditions and the character of labour were transformed. The independent status of the smallholders was overturned. The general farm worker no longer produced his own livelihood direct from his own holding. He lived on the wages earned by labouring for someone else.

In effect, by the end of the seventeenth century, England had acquired an agrarian proletariat. And in recognising that the concept of wage labour became generalised in a rural rather than an urban context, we can begin to perceive another dimension of the change. It had environmental implications, breaking the balance of relationship between people and the land. In the original disposition on the common fields, all stood in equal and direct contact with the land, which they accepted and worked in unmediated fashion, in its given character. In the new commercial dispensation, the gentry and the yeoman farmers commanded the land more absolutely, but from a distance, as something to be measured and manipulated for advantage, maximised by the employment of outside wage labour. For the labourer, the immediacy of contact with the land was lost. He no longer occupied it by his free physical presence, on his own behalf. He was there only at the direction of an employer. As Marx might have put it, the product of his labour "confronts him as hostile and alien".[4]

This reflects the structural significance of the change that was taking place. It was not only a fundamental alteration in economic relations, whereby the greater number of farm workers lost their independence and were obliged to rely on wage labour, it was also a reversal of the workers' relationship with the physical world, whereby most agricultural workers were divided from the product of their labour, and distanced from the essential closeness to the environment that they had once enjoyed. In this respect it is not too surprising that the denial of the husbandman's natural expectation of a direct connection with the basis of his livelihood, generated one of the most remarkable protest movements in English history—that of the Diggers, who as their name suggests were motivated essentially by the desire to maintain an immediate contact with the land.

The advent of the Diggers and their writings was a product of two aspects of revolutionary change: one was the depth of the transformation that was displacing the common field smallholders and turning them into wage labourers; the other was the open, libertarian context of the Civil War years, which allowed the sufferers to make their voices heard. The Diggers appeared at the pivotal point of the great transition, in the revolutionary decades of the mid-seventeenth century. Their message was a unique and single-minded expression of distaste at the oncoming generalisation of wage labour. The first manifestation of the Digger tendency was in the northern regiments of the New Model Army. In December 1648, the soldiers took advantage of the unusual facility of petitioning rights to issue a cry of anguish at the processes that were reducing their situation and their status to that of wage labourers, for which the northern term was "hinds". They complained that the raising of rents had made their customary holdings untenable, "utterly disabling them from all good nurture in learning or trades, and forcing them from generation to generation to be hinds, half-hinds, quarter-hinds, shepherds and herdsmen".[5] They clearly objected to any form of work that involved being a wage labourer for others. Their priority in life was to maintain or recover their status as independent husbandmen on the open fields. They feared that they were not merely being deprived of their holdings, but also of their true, natural relationship with the earth that they worked. The reference to being disabled from "all good nurture in learning or trades" is of great interest, because it shows how deeply they felt the loss of the right to exercise their own knowledge and skills on their own behalf through an unmediated contact with the land.

As a means of restoring their desired situation and status, these soldiers demanded that their lands should be made freehold, and that all enclosed lands should be returned to the use of the community. Further south, other Digger writings were working towards a more radical solution. A series of pamphlets from groups in Buckinghamshire began to voice the idea that the institution of wage labour was not merely unjust, but actually illegitimate. The rich were appropriating the land, and living on other men's labour. When a wealthy farmer "sweats not at all, yet makes this man pay tribute out of his labour. . . . It is theft".[6] From Iver, came another pamphlet, with the same sentiment. "We cannot enjoy the benefit of our labour ourselves, but for the maintenance of idle persons".[7] This clearly expresses once again the high value that these men placed on maintaining a direct contact with the land, and working it for themselves.

Still further south, back in Surrey, Gerrard Winstanley was producing the most extended series of Digger writings, and employing these same sentiments in a more complete, political proposal so radical that it would not really become familiar until two centuries later. The heartland of the Digger movement was in Cobham. This was not far from Putney, and it was in much the same situation regarding the balance of tenure on its common fields. In 1650 when Winstanley was writing, Cobham had not yet been enclosed, yet there had already been a polarisation of landholding between a minority of substantial farmers, and a majority of husbandmen on reduced livings. A survey of 1598 showed that as many as 80% of the tenants held less than 20 acres, and that in fact most of them were restricted to tiny allotments, "with the most common size of holdings being between 1 and 5 acres".[8] There is no reason to suppose that the old balance was restored in the half century up to 1650, and good reason to think that if anything it was further undermined. The process of polarisation was in any case far enough advanced to provide an appropriate background for Winstanley's protest.

Winstanley's writings may in fact be seen as a summation of the great transition in the balance of tenure on the land that had taken place over the preceding century. His books comprise a long and bitter complaint against the extension of enclosures, and the creation of a class of wage labour as the most general form of work on the land. Like the Buckinghamshire Diggers, he saw the imposition of wage labour as essentially illegitimate. He shared the perception that the fruits of their labour were being diverted into other pockets, and he formalised this into what came to be called the labour theory of value—the idea that the value of a product derived from the labour put into it, and that this rightly belonged only to the labourer. "The rich by their covetous wit got the poor to work for small wages, and by their labour get a great increase, for the poor by their labour lift up tyrants to rule over them".[9] All rich men live at ease, feeding and clothing themselves by the labour of other men, not by their own . . . rich men receive all they have from the labourer's hands".[10] It is not surprising that the Diggers hit upon the labour theory of value, for they were experiencing the force of it in a most explicit and unqualified form. They knew of a time when most people had possessed direct control over the product and value of their labour, but they had become aware of a great change, which brought the generalisation of wage labour, and channelled an unprecedented degree of wealth into the hands of employers.

Winstanley perceived, importantly, that the problem lay in the freedom of the market, which was the vehicle and mechanism through which appropriation and dispossession was achieved: "for when men have a law to buy and sell, then as I have said before, the cunning cheaters get great estates by other men's labours".[11] In this way too, Winstanley was reflecting the essential force of the great economic transition of the previous century, for the ability of yeomen farmers to accumulate land was undoubtedly based on the qualitative change in the scope of marketing, and the unprecedented level of profits that were to be made, which went together with the weakening of restraints, and the developing demand for freedom of trade. In the face of this somewhat overwhelming trend, Winstanley proposed a solution that would eliminate the power of buying and selling, and preclude the possibility of wage labour. He advocated the common ownership of the land. This might sound like the proposition that was to be put forward by the socialist movements that rose to prominence in the much later modern era. But it is wrong to see Winstanley's ideas as an unexplained "throw-forward". In fact, he was attempting to reclaim and reinforce the balances that had existed on the commons and open fields, which had worked on the basis of providing an independent place for all, and restraining the freedom of the market in favour of the common good. The establishment of "the commonwealth's land" was to be achieved by the recovery of the rights that had been withheld or taken from the commoners over the years.[12] The balance that had existed on the commons and open fields would be restored: "Not enclosing any part into any particular hand, but all as one man working together". It was indeed Winstanley who found the phrase that best sums up the ideal purpose of life on the open fields; to "unite every creature together into a oneness, and every creature to be an upholder of his fellows, and so everyone is an assistant to preserve the whole".[13]

So in effect, Winstanley's theory of common ownership was conceived as a way to revive and guarantee the equitable balance between the farmers, and the unmediated relationship between them and the land that had existed in previous ages. It was to restore people to what they truly were—that is to say, part of the land: "that everyone that is born in the land may be fed by the earth, his mother that brought him forth, according to the reason that rules in the creation". [14] His core justification for the institution of common ownership was not derived from any political theory or biblical precept, but from a straightforward corporeal logic. People were entitled to the freedom of immediate contact with the land because it was the essence of their being, since they were actually composed of the earth, and the properties associated with it.

> Man is compounded of the four materials of creation, fire, water, earth and air; so is he preserved of the compounded bodies of these four, which are the fruits of the earth, and he cannot live without them . . . surely then, oppressing lords of manors, exacting land-lords and tithe-takers, may as well say their brethren shall not breathe in the air, nor enjoy warmth in their bodies, nor have the moist waters to fall upon them in showers, unless they will pay them rent for it; as to say their brethren shall not work upon the earth unless they will hire that liberty of them.[15]

The land was what they were, and to deny them the freedom of a direct relationship with it, was to deprive them of the truth of their existence. Winstanley was seeking to rescue the working farmer from the servitude of wage labour, and reinstate the intimate connection with the land. By the same token, he was underlining the significance of the change that was taking place in the structure of working life, whereby the majority of traditional smallholders were losing their independent status, and becoming reliant either in whole or in part on employment as wage labourers on the consolidated commercial farms.

The Role of Industrial Activity in Undermining the Commons

The medieval context, almost by definition, involved a concept of sustainability. Things were known and accepted in their given nature. The maintenance of inherent balances, both between the village farmers and between the people and the land, was the guiding principle of economic activity. The pattern of restraint was reflected in the way that the husbandman smallholders occupied the fields communally, by an unstructured and unmediated physical presence. Life on the commons was not characterised by an inclination to assert individualist control over the land. The village farmers held and worked their "lands" by custom, and took the earth essentially as it was.

These rules of conduct were engrained in the lives of the traditional commoners, yet as illustrated earlier with reference to the farm of Henry Best, they were being specifically displaced by a different, even opposite set of assumptions, as the land and its increasing profits came to be concentrated in the hands of a few successful individuals.[16] The new class of substantial commercialising farmers were more willing and able to manipulate the character of the land in order to maximise its output. Under this regime the earth became vulnerable to exploitation and misuse, as it had never been before. The process of enclosure was the first sign of an inclination to tailor or modify the land to suit. And there were other, deeper ways in which, already by the early decades of the seventeenth century, the circumstances of the economic transition, and the force of commercialisation could be observed as a cause of environmental imbalance, and non-sustainable practices. It would be a century or more before the capacity of capitalist industry to actually change the climate became fully evident. But even in the decades leading up to the mid-seventeenth-century revolution, there were industrial activities that were disrupting the condition of the land and its uses.

A previous chapter suggested that it is important to recognise that the generalisation of wage labour occurred in a rural and agrarian context, if we are to fully understand the environmental implications of the change. But this did not preclude an industrial element in the mix. The general effect of commercialisation was to license a more manipulative approach to the land, and there were, even at the turn of the seventeenth century, genuine industrial developments that gave an even more graphic illustration of that trend. The individual consolidation of commercial farms was not the only force that was disrupting the communal context of the commons and open fields in the first half of the seventeenth century. There were many localities in which the balance of land use was also being overturned by the early appearance of the mining industry.

Lead mining output increased rapidly over the course of the sixteenth century, from 625 tons in 1500, to 12, 400 tons in 1600. Iron mining output increased from 3,300 tons to 11,860 tons in the same period.[17] Iron production and refining was the most important metal industry. It was also a good example of the force of regional specialisation, and an illustration of how intensified industrial activity was altering the balance of work patterns, and infringing the traditional communal practices of the commons. The Sussex Weald was the dominant centre of iron production. The region was far from ideal for arable farming, but it had good water flows for powering the hammers, and a ready supply of timber to provide the charcoal for the furnaces. The industry was revolutionised by the invention of the blast furnace at the end of the fifteenth century. The new technology enabled a fivefold rise in productivity, and output increased rapidly through the sixteenth century. By the end of the century there were more than fifty blast furnaces in the Weald, which greatly exceeded the number in all other iron producing areas combined The Weald was notoriously difficult to traverse, but by 1600 it was impossible to go far without encountering an ironworks. It had become an industrial region. The attraction was the profit that it generated. Most of the ironmasters in the Weald were from the yeoman class, and they built houses that were said to surpass those of the gentry. Many others too found work in the industry. There were iron founders, and forge and furnace masters. There was also a call for many miners, labourers, carters and other craftspeople. Small villages or hamlets were created to house the workers. There was a great deal of money to be made, and it was shared quite broadly. The downside was that the industry had a significant adverse effect on traditional communal lifestyles. There was a heavy draw on timber resources, on a scale never previously known, and consequently there was some "abrupt and widespread depletion of the tree cover". Most damagingly in social terms (but which we shall nevertheless find repeated in other contexts) the ironworks were usually sited in the open forests and commons. "John Norden lists 10 localities, mainly commons, where the woods had been devoured by an orgy of speculation by 1607". This not only threatened to reduce the facilities of pasture and timber on which the commoners relied, it also undermined the time-honoured balance of their relationship with the land. We cannot do better that the summary offered by Peter Brandon. "Hitherto, Wealden society had lived in harmony with its landscape, and the peasant economy was dependent on the continuation of the woods and grasses".[18]

Probably the most substantial advance of all occurred in the mining of coal. As J. U. Nef made clear, it was in the late sixteenth century that coal first became a significant and measurable factor in the national, and indeed the exporting economy.[19] Nef took it as the most important feature in what he called the first industrial revolution. Some have regarded this term as an overstatement of the case, but the dramatic rise of King Coal to prominence cannot be denied. Charles Wilson endorsed Nef's assessment that the output of coal expanded some fourteenfold between the middle of the sixteenth century and the middle of the seventeenth. It was in effect the beginning of the coal industry, and it established the place of coal as a central coordinating link in English life and trade. It was "the factor in the early seventeenth century most favourable to expansion . . . a reciprocating action thus began between the emergent coal industry, especially in the northeast and the midlands, and the growing aggregation of people in the towns, and certain industries that catered for them".[20] Most instructively, coal became a crucial element in the extended network of regional trading that developed between the nations of the northwest European seaboard during the sixteenth century, when "the Dutch and the English in particular began to engage in the long-distance trade of bulk commodities".[21] Coal was an obvious example of the kind of additional resource that provided a basis for regional specialisation in areas that were not ideally suited to high farming. Through the networks of interregional trade the coal producing counties built up exchange relationships based on the growing long-distance commerce in bulk agricultural products. The northeast region around Newcastle traded coal to East Anglia in return for corn, and to France in return for salt. But there was another, less constructive way in which coal mining came into contact with the agricultural world—it involved the commandeering of substantial areas of land, which were given over to the mining enterprise.

One of the places thus affected was western Nottinghamshire, just to the north and west of the county town of Nottingham. Here, in effect, was the geographical centre of the English coalfield, where in the early seventeenth century the mining process was relatively simple. Consequently, a very intensive development of coalmining activity was concentrated in quite a small space. It was an area, like western Hertfordshire, where much of the common land would not be technically enclosed until a later date. But already in the first half of the seventeenth century the traditional patterns and balances of common field occupation were being disrupted and displaced not only by the piecemeal consolidation of individual commercial farms, but also by the introduction of industrial scale mining,

Nef took due note of the development in western Nottinghamshire at this time, which was in effect the first substantial establishment of coalmining activity in the area. He identified fourteen working pits in 1610, and estimated that coal production from the Nottinghamshire field tripled during the seventeenth century.[22] R. S. Smith thought that Nef overestimated the scale of mining that was taking place. Smith noted that the well-publicised ventures of Huntingdon Beaumont at Wollaton and Strelley came to an end around 1620, and he assumed a downturn thereafter.[23] But when account is taken of less obvious kinds of evidence, it is clear that in fact a significant number of relatively undocumented mines were coming into production, and the coalmining enterprise was actually developing and spreading quite rapidly. The most illuminating general evidence comes from the parliamentary records showing the number of pits or mining villages that were supplying coal to the parliamentarian garrison at Nottingham during the Civil War. Smith noted only four, and did not include Wollaton in the number. But the parliamentary accounts tell a different story. They show that in the mid-1640s the garrison was receiving coal from as many as twenty-four separate localities, including Wollaton.[24] There had clearly been a substantial expansion of coalmining activity in the decades before the Civil War. One carter, William James was paid for delivering 280 loads of coal to the garrison between January 1644 and March 1645. In the same month another carter, Christopher Hardy, was paid for delivering 140 loads.[25] These figures underline the impressive capacity of the coal enterprise in the area of western Nottinghamshire at this time, both in terms of the level of production and distributive capabilities.

The emergence of an extended and integrated network of marketing, based on regional specialisation and exchange, changed the scope of economic activity in every area and at every level. A new kind of market had emerged with a coordinated regional, national and international range. This both encouraged and in a sense demanded a change in focus to exporting mode. The process of adjustment, involving specialisation and redirection for export, could also change the balance of a local economy. Western Nottinghamshire is a case in point. By the 1620s the capacity of the town and its hinterland to export coal out of the county had developed to a stage where it freed the area from the fear of corn shortages with which it might otherwise have been afflicted. Every summer, carts appeared from major specialist arable farming counties like Lincolnshire, bringing corn to exchange for Nottingham's coal. Thus, even at times of general grain shortage like 1619–23, the town's magistrates could confidently assure the Privy Council that their supply of coal to export in exchange for grain made emergency measures of corn storage unnecessary.[26] Regional specialisation had lifted the economy of Western Nottinghamshire out of the traditional limitations of local subsistence, and given it a new perspective based on export and import.

The consequences were not, however, universally beneficial. Concentrated commercial exploitation deprived many smallholders of their independence. It also changed the character of land use. It altered the balance of relationship between people and the earth, and the environmental consequences were immediately apparent. Mining was the basis of a thriving export trade, but the first place to be physically affected by the ready availability of coal was Nottingham itself. Coal became the fuel of choice, both for domestic use in the town, and for the growing manufacturing enterprises of Nottingham and its surrounding district. Some could welcome this as an exceptional benefit.

> He who goes to bed and has not a hod full of fuel, may the next morning in the shortest day in winter have coal brought to his door to dress his dinner with—a blessing that few towns of the kingdom may boast of.[27]

This was further testament to the capacity of the region to maintain a plentiful supply of coal, and to distribute it via an impressively reliable delivery system, when and where required. Less conveniently, the use of coal on such a wide and intensive scale was creating a noticeable and unwanted deterioration in air quality. Nottingham was becoming a proto "coke town". It was continually wreathed in smoke and stench to a degree that brought expressions of distaste from visitors who liked to travel in the fresh air.[28] In this, Nottingham was a microcosm of London, much the biggest user of coal for its growing population and manufacturers. William Cavert has written that by 1600 the capital had become a fossil-fuelled city, subject to similar complaints about the smoke-filled air.[29] It is another sign of the force of economic development at the turn of seventeenth century that environmental problems were already apparent.

Given the advantage of hindsight, we can also note that the toxicity in the air around Nottingham was not the only indicator of the environmental tensions that were arising there. Another, associated kind of imbalance was developing in the coalfields themselves, through the diversion and exploitation of the resources of the commons. For, in the many localities where coal was now being mined on a serious basis in western Nottinghamshire, and indeed in the adjacent coalfields just across the border in Derbyshire, the grounds that were routinely commandeered for the coalmining operation were the common lands. It was usually "the commons, woods and wastes" of the villages concerned that were being taken over for coal production, and this could distort and restrict their traditional usage over quite a wide area. It has already become clear that the process of enclosure was not a necessary condition of the individualist commercialisation of farms, which could take place very effectively without it. Coal mining is another example of an enterprise that could be carried out in a fully coordinated and efficient manner, without the technical enclosure of the land. Manorial lords could simply resume their residual rights in the common lands, either for their own purposes or for conveying them to a commercial interest, and a convenient area of the "commons, woods and wastes" could be appropriated and turned into a coalfield.

The degree to which this could detract from the facilities of the commons and destabilise the balance of use and occupation, is well illustrated by the rights that were assumed by the mining enterprise at Heanor, on the Derbyshire border. Heanor, with the associated villages of Langley, Micklehay, Loscoe and Codnor had been part of the manor that the Zouche family had received as a grant from Henry VIII. But by the 1640s, through a sequence of events that usually involved exploiting the indebtedness of the original family, the mining rights were falling into the hands of a successful yeoman sheep farmer, Nicholas Charlton. His own lands were at Chilwell, a mining village just to the west of Nottingham, and his awareness of the productivity of the mining enterprise already in place there had no doubt aroused his interest in acquiring the rights at Heanor. By 1642, Charlton was in the process of assuming overall control, with a lease that gave him rights to "all the coals, and mines of coal being on or under the moors, wastes and common grounds . . . in Heanor, Lamgley, Micklehay, Loscoe and Codnor", from "Derby Common . . . and so over Loscoe Common, and on to Codnor Field".[30] The mining was conceived as a substantial, long-term proposition, which would impinge on the other traditional activities of the common lands for the foreseeable future, so the necessary amenities for the venture had to be guaranteed. The process of distribution was one priority. The weight of the coal and the regularity with which it was currently being traded would put an extra burden on the lanes and the roads, which was something that the local farmers would not readily appreciate. So there was an assurance of "a half share of all the ways, passages, privileges and liberties for conveying the coal away".[31] Most interesting, and another indication of the intrusive physical significance of the enterprise, was a stated right to create what amounted to a mining village on the commons. Charlton was empowered to

> build cottages and to take the grounds for this, and to take grounds for gardens for them, in any places convenient in the same woods, wastes and commons, and hold and keep them for ever for the colliers or other workmen to be employed about the getting of the coals, or upon the premises, or any other work about the same.[32]

In effect, the mining interests were placed in a position to take over as much of the area, resources and facilities of the commons as they required. Charlton made a fortune from the coal mines. But once again, the customary usages and balances that had guided life on the common lands for centuries were being elbowed aside, by the assumption of a license to exploit a residual right of property and commandeer their use for commercial profit.

The right to exploit "the commons, woods and wastes", in which Charlton's lease gave him a free hand, was always specified when an area was conveyed to a commercial interest for coal mining. It was then the customary use of common pasture, and the facility to gather more traditional kinds of fuel like timber, that were being displaced to make way for the extraction of the coal. Along with Wollaton, one of the earliest substantial mining enterprises was at nearby Bramcote, which was also just a few miles outside Nottingham. In 1609 the lord of the manor asserted his residual right as landlord, and made out a lease in favour of the most prominent entrepreneur in the area Sir Percival Willoughby, giving him title to " all the coals, coal mines, and vents and delphs of coals lying and being on the wastes, woods and common grounds" of Bramcote.[33]

Another associated early mining centre was at Strelley, a few miles to the north and west. Strelley is especially instructive, because the village still exists today on the same small scale and in much the same undeveloped state as in the seventeenth century. As a result, it boasts a substantial set of visible remains of the mining operation, which was in vigorous employment at the time. The survival of the mine casts has depended on escaping not only the advancing concrete tide of the city, but also the less blatantly destructive force of the plough. In one of the few fields in the village to have remained unploughed over the ages, the markings of some of the sixteenth and seventeenth century coal pits can be seen. The residue takes the form of broad mounds of earth around hollowed centres. These were the bell-pits that played an important part in the beginning of the industry, and can be regarded as the first significant and systematic method of deep coal extraction. They are referred to as bell-pits because they were begun from a narrow opening, and then widened out into a bell shape as they were dug, sometimes to a depth of forty feet.

At the time of viewing, there were nine bell-pit remains that were still visible, and another seven which existed in an adjacent field, and which survive in the memory of local farmers, though they have been physically erased by recent ploughing. The general disposition of the fields of Strelley at this time is relevant to our themes in more ways than one. The field with the visible coal mines was once part of a much larger medieval open field. The same was true of other similarly sized fields further on. This is to say that they were all once an undifferentiated part of the great open fields that were originally attached to the village in a typical medieval common land context. These fields had been consolidated out of an open field system. The strange circumstance, though it is becoming less strange as further examples appear, is that by this Strelley had not yet been formally enclosed. In other words, it seems to reflect the same picture that has emerged in many other places—the context of open field strips had already been broken up and reassembled into more consolidated individual units long before the village was technically enclosed.

The common land context was being overturned in other ways too. Strelley Common itself still held its medieval shape, except that in the first half of the seventeenth century it had been substantially encroached upon by the coalmining enterprise. The seven recollected coal mine sites in the field adjacent to the visible remains were all situated in what was, in medieval times, Strelley Common. It is clear that the common had been substantially encroached upon by the mining enterprise. And it is most unlikely that the known bell-pits were the only encroachment. It must also be probable that there were further mines on the other side of the common, which has since been obliterated by the building of a modern road. All in all, this was a coalfield worthy of the name, and by the seventeenth century it had come to dominate an extensive area of Strelley Common.

It should also be remembered that the mines themselves would not have constituted the entire coalfield. A lot of space was required for support facilities, the housing of the colliers, and the storage and transport of the coal. In fact the field with the pit residues also contains the remains of a raised track-way, which stretched away across the fields of Strelley and beyond. A special facility of this sort was certainly required if the coal was to be produced and distributed on a substantial and regular basis. The use of existing roads and lanes would not have been efficient, nor would it have been acceptable to the local farming interests. In the context of the time, the laying of the track-way was an enormous investment, and its existence is testament to the scale and value of the coalmining operation. This finds further confirmation in the fact that the track-way did not serve Strelley alone. In one direction in ran across the common towards Wollaton and the Trent, linking up with what is has been called England's first rails, and in the other direction it is known to have continued on towards Awsworth, Cossall and Kimberley, which were all centres of early coal production, and were named as such in the parliamentary records. It becomes easier to understand the facility with which coal was being supplied to the parliamentarian garrison at Nottingham when we recognise that the villages in the area to the north west of the town now formed a coordinated network for its production and delivery. Thus by the seventeenth century, an area which might still be thought of as essentially rural, had in fact come to be largely devoted to the mining of coal on an industrial level. The coalmining context of Strelley is illustrated ahead (p. 325).

A further indication of the transformed economic focus was the pressure on the timber supply, a problem already noted in respect of the iron industry in the Susses Weald. The coalmining exercise in Strelley not only commandeered land that would once have been available for the gathering of surface fuel but it also drew heavily on other areas of the commons, woods and wastes that were attached to the village. The timber requirement for the track-way alone would have created a quite unprecedented demand. And in fact, in the 1630s, legal challenges were brought against the entrepreneurs for over-exploiting the timber resources of the manor in order to provide for the needs of the coalfield. It was stated that the value of the mines was already more than twice that of the herbage, without further depredations being made on the latter.[34]

Thus the coalmining enterprise had become the dominant economic force in a network of villages to the north and west of Nottingham, and it encroached most heavily on land and resources that had once been available to the village as commons, woods and wastes. One critical effect was to change the balance and character of fuel acquisition. For something like seven centuries, the commons, woods and wastes had acted as a surface fuel supply for the villagers. It was an easily gathered and wholly renewable source. They would gather waste wood, and cut out dead wood, helping the tree to grow on. The trees would reproduce themselves freely as saplings. Some trees could be regularly coppiced, and encouraged to regenerate. Turfs might be cut as an alternative fuel, and the grass grew again. The commoners could also harvest fast growing gorse and bracken, and use it to produce a fierce heat in their ovens.

It is, moreover, a fair assumption that the quality of the air remained equable, and sustainable, because the trees drew as much carbon out of the atmosphere as the fires emitted. This was not just a happy accident. It was a natural result of using these resources in concert with the way that they lived and grew. Thus the common lands had provided the village with fuel, and indeed with the materials for tools and building, since time immemorial, and would no doubt have continued to do so indefinitely. Suddenly these facilities were being displaced and diverted, to service a coal mining enterprise that produced high profits, but restricted the free use of the commons for fuel gathering, and created a new pattern of fuel extraction that was not renewable, or compatible with the given character of the environment.

As with the rise of commercial farming, the impetus came from the level of profit available, which was indeed very striking. The figures substantiate and explain the vigour of the enterprise, and the determination with which men like Nicholas Charlton sought to acquire an interest. The price that could be got, and the income that could be generated from it, seems to have increased steadily as the seventeenth century progressed. In some years in the 1630s a clear profit of £600 appears to have been made from the Strelley mines, with coal being sold at 6/- a load.[35] This was more than double the price that might have been expected in the earlier years of the century. It continued to rise. In the 1640s the parliamentarian garrison was careful to keep its leading supporters sweet by ensuring that the supply of coal that it required was not simply requisitioned, but often paid for at market price, which was ten or eleven shillings a load. Coal was a rapidly increasing asset, and a very attractive option for those who were making money and wished to make more. Nicholas Charlton was one, and Ralph Edge at Strelley was another in the same category. He was a successful lawyer in Nottingham. His takeover of the mining interest was long drawn out, and based on the same process of exploiting the difficulties and deficiencies of the established manorial family. He was already wealthy, and this, in conjunction with his professional expertise, enabled him to use the law to his advantage. By the 1650s the manor and the mines were under his control. Edge was able to maximise the output from the mines, and he made a fortune, which lifted the family into the higher echelons of the gentry. The mining accounts show how this was achieved. In October 1656, Edge made no less than £1,280, "for coals out of Strelley coal mines this last summer".[36]

It was a powerful incentive, which illustrates the levels of profit that were driving and encouraging the changes in the socio-economic order. And great as were the fortunes made by Edge and Charlton, we should not suppose that they were the only gainers. There will be ample evidence ahead that these enterprises were generating sufficient profits to provide a considerable number of miners, carriers, clerks, agents and carpenters, with financial rewards that they could not have expected from any other source. In March 1645, the carter Christopher Hardy was paid twenty-three shillings for delivering 140 loads of coal at two pence a load.[37] These were rich pickings. The negative consequence of commercialisation, and the changing structure of agrarian life in the sixteenth and early seventeenth centuries, was that it all seemed to tend towards the disruption or dismemberment of the communal working patterns of the open fields and common lands.

Notes

1. M. Overton, *The Agricultural Revolution in England,* (Cambridge 1996), p. 179
2. K. Wrightson, *English Society 1580–1680,* (London 1982)
3. M. Keen, *English Society in the Later Middle Ages,* (Harmondsworth 1990), p. 76
4. K. Marx, "Economic and Philosophical Manuscripts", in *Early Writings,* (Harmondsworth 1975) p. 324
5. The Humble Representation of the Desires of the Officers and Soldiers of the Regiments of Horse for Northumberland, 5 December 1648. Cited in H. N. Brailsford, *The Levellers and the English Revolution,* (Nottingham 1983), p. 447
6. More Light Shining in Buckinghamshire, cited in Brailsford, *The Levellers and the English Revolution*, p. 445
7. K. Thomas, ed., "Another Digger Broadside", *Past and Present* 42 (1969)
8. J, Gurney, *Brave Community,* (Manchester 2007), p. 3
9. "The True Levellers Standard Unfurled", in *Winstanley: The Law of Freedom and Other Writings*, ed. C. Hill, (Cambridge 1983), p. 85
10. Gerrard Winstanley, "The Law of Freedom in a Platform", in *Winstanley: The Law of Freedom*, ed. C. Hill, (Cambridge 1983), p. 287
11. Ibid, p. 371
12. Ibid, p. 340
13. Gerrard Winstanley, "The True Leveller's Standard Advanced", in *Winstanley: The Law of Freedom*, ed C. Hill, (Cambridge 1983), p. 84; "Truth Lifting Up Its Head Above Scandals" (1648), Cited in L. H. Berens, *The Digger Movement in the Days of the Commonwealth,* (Merlin 2007), p. 47
14. Winstanley, "The True Leveller's Standard Advanced", p. 84
15. Winstanley, "The Law of Freedom", in *Winstanley The Law of Freedom*, p. 295
16. See above, pp. 44–5
17. C. Palliser, *The Age of Elizabeth,* (London 1983), p. 253
18. P. Brandon, *The Sussex Landscape,* (London 1974), pp. 155–6
19. J. U. Nef, *The Rise of the British Coal Industry,* (London 1932), pp. 58–68
20. C. Wilson, *England's Apprenticeship, 1603–1763,* (London 1965), pp. 79–88
21. J. De Vries, *The Dutch Rural Economy in the Golden Age, 1500–1700,* (Yale 1974), pp. 1–3
22. Nef, *The Rise of the British Coal Industry*, pp. 58–60, 67–8
23. R. S. Smith, *Early Coal Mining Around Nottingham,* (Nottingham 1989), pp. 84–7
24. TNA, SP28/240, 241-February 1644 and June 1646, the villages providing coal were Beeston, Lenton, Chilwell, Stapleford, Arnold, Basford, Shortwood, Trowell, Awsworth, Bilborough, Kimberley, Bramcote, Snenton, Toton, Cossall, Selston, Eastwood, Wollaton, Nuthall, Strelley, Watnall, Bulwell, Sutton-in-Ashfield and Kirby-in-Ashfield

25. TNA, SP28/240/429
26. *CSP Domestic 1619–23*, p. 130
27. "A Manuscript Account of Nottingham in 1641", *Trans. Thoroton Society II* (1898), p. 50
28. Ibid
29. W. H. Cavert, *The Smoke of London*, (Cambridge 2016)
30. Nottinghamshire Archives, Charlton Papers, DD/CH35/2, pp. 1–2
31. Ibid, p. 3
32. Ibid, pp. 9–10
33. *H. M. C. Middleton*, pp. 171–5
34. Nottinghamshire Archives, DDE/5/8, 25
35. Ibid, DDE/5/8
36. Nottinghamshire Archives. DDE/5/34
37. TNA, SP28/240/429, 21st March 1645

5 The Higher Profile of Architectural Form

The mining enterprises reflected structural change in two important ways. Coal extraction usually involved the displacement of the traditional, open working patterns of the commons, by a more intensive and intrusive use of the land. And the profits that this generated contributed to a notable development in building styles. Towards the end of the seventeenth century, Ralph Edge used some of his fortune to build Strelley Hall. It was designed in a style that had first appeared in the middle years of the reign of Elizabeth I, and had spread rapidly to become the universal shape of the manor houses of the gentry. Strelley Hall was an awe-inspiring edifice, rising high and wide above the landscape. It dwarfed the other buildings in the village, and overshadowed the countryside for miles around. It had an aura of power that not only encompassed the locality, but also, in its general force, reached to the administrative centre of the kingdom. But its weight was relieved, at least aesthetically, by the sympathetic balance of architectural proportion. The perpendicular windows of the broad frontage were ranged in perfectly symmetrical form, above and on either side of the central doorway. This self-consciously complete facade was also the reflection of socio-economic and political transition.

So we should not close our view of the structures of change without noting the development that might be regarded as its most positive aspect, at least in aesthetic terms. There is no doubt that there was, especially from mid-Elizabethan times, a remarkable flowering of secular architecture. Nor was this just a coincidence. On the contrary, it constitutes the most transparent physical evidence of the great socio-economic transformation that was taking place. There is no clearer manifestation of the increasing status of the yeoman farmers, and the advance of the middling gentry to a new position of power in the land, than the unprecedented and conspicuous styling of the houses with which they now provided themselves. Contemporaries called it the great bravery of building that marvellously beautified the realm. It was notable because the affluence, and influence, of the laity had never been projected in this way before.

It reflected a different balance of lifestyles and systems of belief. The medieval world had put most of its artistic energies, and indeed its financial resources, into ecclesiastical buildings. Church architecture had thus commanded the leading public aesthetic, as befitted a society that was conceived *as* a church. The vernacular buildings of the countryside, and the late medieval town houses were not without character and charm. But this was largely because their conception was spontaneous and their design impromptu—that is to say, they did not display a coordinated, distinguishable style in the same sense as the ecclesiastical houses. So at the beginning of the sixteenth century it was still the church that was attracting the largest share of architectural talent and investment, and dominating the building scene. Consequently, it was the splendour and visual quality of the churches, abbeys, priories and cathedrals that caught the eye of observers.

At the beginning of the sixteenth century, secular building remained without a prominent or coordinated style. There were, however, some interesting tendencies appearing in the background. After 1450 there was a noticeable increase in house building by the landowning classes, facilitated by the wider availability of bricks, which were more convenient to use than stone.[1] This might be regarded as the dawning of a new architectural consciousness, encouraged by a growing socio-economic confidence, though it was no more than a beginning. The trend sometimes featured castellated rooflines, which hardly constituted a style, but did indicate a desire for pattern and relief. Perhaps it can be seen as a domestication of the traditional military role of the gentry, and a first step away from the crude style-less structures of the castles, to include this back reference in an essentially civilian building. It was a halfway house towards a more administrative function.

At the same time, the underlying economic platform for the advance of secular forms can be seen in the timber-framed fifteenth-century Wealden house of the successful farmers, clothiers and ironmasters of Kent and Sussex. They still began from the typical medieval structure, which was usually little more than a crude block shape, sitting low to the ground, and conceived around the simple concept of a central hall, often open to the roof. But significant additions were now appearing. There might be a jetty built above the servants' quarters at either end of the hall, offering the elements of a second storey, and embryo wings. It is interesting to note that this opened up the possibility of a broad but balanced frontage, which was to become the characteristic basis of the new styling of the houses of the landed classes in Elizabethan times. By the end of the fifteenth century the Wealden house was acquiring a higher profile. It was extended into a structure framed as two stories throughout, and the hall was floored over, involving a necessary provision of staircases and chimneys.

The signs of architectural ambition reflected the increasing substance and affluence of a self-conscious lay society. Their appetite for land and property would in turn provide an underlying guarantee for a successful challenge to the power of the medieval church in the 1530s. And the dispossession of the church would then clear the way for a fulfilment of secular style. The impetus was not just economic and aesthetic—it had a further political aspect. The conspicuous prominence of the land-owning laity in the countryside was facilitated not merely by the physical scope created by the disappearance of the monasteries, and the concentration of wealth and land in yeoman and gentry hands, but also by the position that these rising classes now held in the judicial and administrative structures which formed the framework of public authority in the independent, sovereign state that emerged in England during the Reformation period.

The aspect of the new secular style that was most apparent to contemporaries was what modern historians refer to as the Great Rebuilding. By this they seek to highlight the process by which, from the 1570s onwards, the houses of the smaller gentry and the yeoman farmers were being notably extended and enhanced.[2] The economic success of these classes has figured prominently in the foregoing pages of this study. They were better placed than any to take advantage of the rising agricultural market. And the extension and refurbishment of their houses was the most conspicuous form in which they affirmed their new affluence. Their rise was already under way in the second half of the fifteenth century, but it was in the 1570s that the access of wealth and the trend to architectural display was becoming so clear and so general that it could be perceived as a transformation.

Structurally, the changes usually involved the addition of an extra floor, and more rooms. This meant that the central hall or communal living area was no longer the be all and end all of the concept. The basic character of the building was transformed. Simple hall areas that had once been low to the ground and open to the roof were provided with ceilings, and surrounded by a larger number of separate rooms. So the typical house now had two floors, and an interior that was composed of parlours and chambers. The extra floor also necessitated more attention to the provision of formal staircases, and of course, chimneys.[3] Smoke could no longer be allowed to simply drift out through a hole in the roof of the main living area, as had often been the case before. Now chimneys ushered the smoke invisibly away, and at the same time epitomised the higher profile of the houses.

The change was not just "modernisation", involving the arrival of the kind of internal structure that we would recognise today. It also implied a different relationship with the exterior. In the old concept, the houses appeared closer to the ground, and the division from the physical world outside was less marked, especially as there were usually no solid windows, and the most valuable farm animals often slept within the walls. In this way too the new houses offered a transformation of lifestyle. There was greater privacy within, due to the routine provision of separate rooms, and there was better insulation from the outside, with the introduction of glass windows, curtains and wall hangings. The changes were facilitated by another productive aspect of the Tudor economy, the rapidly expanding manufacture of building materials, like brick, tiles and glass.

Contemporary observers regarded the rebuilding process as having begun in the southeast, perhaps the most affluent area, due to the opportunities for farmers to specialise and commercialise their products in response to the ever-burgeoning market of the capital. The Elizabethan commentator William Harrison recorded his perceptions of the transformation in his local region of Essex. The multitude of chimneys lately erected was, by its generality and its nature, the most obvious change. The introduction of glazed windows into the houses of the yeomanry was another noticeable addition. These, like chimneys, had once been the preserve of the richer nobility and urban elite. They were now making their first general appearance in the villages. Harrison duly recorded the important implication that there had been a substantial adjustment in the balance between lifestyle and social status. The widespread use of brick and stone in place of timber in the housing of the broad class of independent landholder meant that in this respect he now "rivals what a prince was once". The same could be said of the wider acquisition of costly furnishings and dining vessels, which were now becoming available, "even unto inferior artificers and many farmers".[4] Harrison's observations are a good measure of the exceptionally broad base of the consumer society that had arisen by Elizabethan times, on the back of the interregional markets.

Harrison thought that in some respects the improvements took a while to percolate northward. He noted for instance that the institution of feather beds in place of straw pallets had yet to reach Bedfordshire. This was perhaps the cause of some personal disappointment and discomfort. But in general terms it seems that the changes were echoed, with striking rapidity, far across the country, and down the social scale—a reflection of the widespread success of commercial farming, and of the socio-economic, political, and indeed physical homogeneity of Elizabethan England. William Smith, writing of Cheshire in the 1580s, noted the transformation in the lifestyle of the farmers. They had once "had their fire in the midst of the house against a hob of clay, and their oxen under the same roof. But within these forty years it is altogether altered, so that they had built chimneys and furnished other parts of their houses accordingly".[5] Carew observed the same transition in Cornwall, at much the same time. The houses of the farmers had once had "walls of earth, low thatched roofs, few partitions, no glass windows, and scarcely any chimneys, other than a hole to let out the smoke. But now all these customs are universally banished, and the Cornish husbandman conforms himself with a better supplied civility to the Eastern pattern".[6]

In the Great Rebuilding, the group that had benefited most from the conditions of the Tudor economy, the middle sort of yeoman farmers, announced their arrival as people of socio-economic substance and local-political consequence. And the rise of the yeomanry contributed in turn to the rise of the gentry, certainly in numbers, and doubtless with the injection of wealth. One effect of the increasing affluence of the chief farmers was to augment the gentry as a class. The strata of English society were not unbridgeable. The status of gentleman did not rest entirely on inherited dignity. The qualifications were typically pragmatic, and as William Harrison said, could be met by any who "can live without manual labour, and thereto is able to bear the port, charge and countenance of a gentleman".[7] Many yeomen were attaining a new level of wealth, and entering the ranks of the gentry. On that basis, together with their own economic success, the elevation of younger sons, and an influx of rich lawyers and merchants, the gentry had increased enormously in numbers. Lawrence Stone suggested that over the course of the sixteenth century they were multiplying about twice as fast as the general population. This was an area of social inflation that the parsimonious Elizabeth was apparently unable to control. She had no direct power over "the unprecedented torrent of claims for arms" during her reign. The overall consequence "was a dramatic increase in the number of the gentry".[8] It is a conclusion confirmed more recently by Mark Overton. "It seems clear the gentry did increase considerably in numbers from the mid-sixteenth century".[9]

One of the most striking illustrations comes from Shropshire, where there were forty-eight gentry families in 1433, and four hundred and seventy in 1623. This helps us to envisage the effect of the proliferation of the gentry on the ground. And the massing of the gentry took place all over the kingdom. There were at least four hundred gentry families in Norfolk by the 1580s, and no less than a thousand in Kent by 1600. J. T. Cliffe estimated about the same number in Yorkshire in 1603. They were becoming the unavoidable focal points of social and political power in the countryside. In the sixteenth century "the country-house civilisation was just beginning to emerge, beginning its four hundred year dominance of English society".[10] The old nucleated villages were being diminished or dispersed, as the common fields were partitioned and enclosed, and the consolidated estates and farms were set up, often at a distance, around larger, detached houses. The social power of the squires, together with their ubiquity, gave them the basis of a collective force beyond the locality. They had come to represent power over *the land* as a political state, and not just as a physical area.

Thus emerged the classic context of English rural society—each village with its squire, its tenant farmers, its labourers and its enclosed fields. The squires had not always been so plentiful. It has been estimated that at the end of the fifteenth century no more than one village in every four or five boasted a resident squire.[11] This altered dramatically during the course of the sixteenth century. W. G. Hoskins underlined the fact that at the beginning of that century, the knights and squires were "comparatively rare on the ground". The evidence for the beginning of the reign of Henry VIII indicates a total of about one thousand squires. "But if Thomas Wilson's figure of 16,000 at the end of the century is anywhere near the truth, then the Elizabethan village must have shown an entirely different picture".[12]

So it did, and the difference was clear not only because the houses of the gentry had become an unavoidable presence, but also because they had acquired a new and more imposing face. If the great rebuilding of the farmhouses was impressive, the new generation of manor house asserted itself at a different level again. It possessed qualities of architectural projection and self-confidence that had not previously been displayed in the genre. There was a transcendent sense of style, where previously there had been very little. The manor houses of the early medieval period were often quite basic in form, and just as inelegant as the farmhouses, despite the socio-economic status of the manors and the fact that they functioned as the administrative and judicial centres of wide areas of country. The manor house might be distinguished by being constructed of stone, like the church, which set it apart from most of the surrounding timber cottages and farmhouses in the village. But the stone was used very crudely, and almost entirely without a sense of styling. In their original conception the manor houses of early medieval times rarely seem to have transcended a heavy, rectangular, and unrelieved block-like shape.

The one claim to graciousness in the early medieval manor house was that it was conceived around the idea of the lord's hall. There was sometimes a large bay window at the end of the hall behind the judicial dais. This was supposed to emphasise the semi-divine status of lordship, but it did nothing to enhance the proportions of the building. In a sense the building simply *was* the hall. It was usually single storey and open to the roof. It served as the living quarters and sleeping chamber for the family, as well as the manorial courthouse. The kitchen and servants' quarters might be timber structures tacked on behind, and there would often be an undercroft serving for a storehouse. As with the early farmhouses, there was only a limited sense of division from the outside world. The windows were unglazed, and even in the manor house the most valuable animals were often stalled within the walls. All in all, these houses reflected the distinctive continuum, openness and physical roughness of medieval life.

In time, the medieval manor house took on a less crude and more picturesque aspect, but rarely attained a self-possessed distinctiveness of styling. Sections were added, but not so as to produce any kind of matching aesthetic balance. There was more feature and decoration, especially with regard to the windows, but no structural regularity. These houses displayed what has been called a "relaxed informality".[13] They were spontaneous rather than self-conscious. This could endow them with great charm, as is apparent at Bradley, from fifteenth-century Devon, with its multi-roofed façade like a row of individual cottages. The late medieval manor house presented a friendlier face than its cruder predecessors, and even perhaps than its successors, but it remained stylistically naïve. The fifteenth century sometimes saw the addition of a Great Chamber above the Great Hall. But the houses still gave the impression of being low to the ground, and piecemeal in conception, rarely transcending a kind of random functionalism. In terms of what was to follow, what they lacked most of all was a concept of clear-cut, self-contained symmetry.

Although the signs of ambition towards a secular style had been appearing since the later fifteenth century, it was the mid-sixteenth century that saw the crucial qualitative change in the architectural profile of the gentry. William Camden and William Harrison both noted that it was at this time that a new class of manor house came into view. They were conspicuously costly, and "remarkable for their elegance", and they arrived in the reign of Elizabeth I. Modern assessments have confirmed the chronology. A broad survey of Derbyshire, Shropshire, Essex and Somerset showed that, "the amount of country house building in the fifty years between 1570 and 1620 far exceeded that of any subsequent half century".[14] The expansion was driven in part by the inspiration of a new concept of manor house. Architectural practice had changed markedly in the course of the sixteenth century. At the beginning of the century it became usual for houses to be actually conceived as a two-storey structure, with all that this entailed for a raised presence. It brought the crucial potential for lifting a building above the sphere of the neighbouring cottages, and even above the tree line, making it more prominent in the landscape. The effect was assisted by the application of the principles of "English Perpendicular" to the profile of the windows. At the same time, the influence of the Renaissance began to take effect. It was reflected to some extent in the use of classical and Italianate detail, but above all in the adoption of symmetry.

The transition was comprehensive and can be illustrated across widely dispersed regions. Devon provides good examples of the medieval forms that were being displaced. Dartington Hall (Figure 5.1), from 1390, was one of the grandest of medieval hall blocks, overawing by its scale and weight, but almost specifically unrelieved by style. Bradley (Figure 5.2), from the 1490s, with its segmented frontage and undulating roofline, was the ultimate in late medieval informality. But by the end of the sixteenth century, Devon manor houses were typically symmetrical. The house at Cadhay, east of Exeter, is thought to have been begun before 1587, and encapsulates the trend. It is built as a square around a courtyard, and attempts to provide every aspect and every elevation with a symmetrical facade.[15] The manor house at Lower Bockhampton (Figure 5.8) in nearby Dorset was built in the 1590s, and has been described as the perfect Elizabethan "E" house. The perfection lay in the beautifully delineated symmetry. On the eastern side of the south coast, Sussex boasted some of the earliest instances of symmetrical tendency. Glynde Place (Figure 5.4), begun in 1569, was one of the first, and also one of the loveliest. The balance of the curved bays seems to round out the symmetry. At Parham (Figure 5.5), begun in 1577, an overall structural symmetry is breached by a variation in window sizes on either side of the entrance. By the 1580s all such deviations had been cast aside, and a perfect regularity of style was being echoed with striking rapidity all across the kingdom, in another manifestation of the exceptional homogeneity of Elizabethan society. In Derbyshire in the middle of the sixteenth century, distinctly medieval shapes had still been appearing. Thus Hazelbadge Hall (Figure 5.3) from 1549 was earth-bound and block-like, with barn attached, and no hint of symmetrical pretensions. But by later Elizabethan times, symmetry was the order of the day, as displayed in Barlborough Hall (Figure 5.6) from the 1580s, and the most iconic and familiar of Elizabethan houses, Hardwick Hall, from the 1590s, which needs no illustration. Perfect symmetry can also be seen emerging in Norfolk in the same period, with Heydon Hall (Figure 5.7) from the 1580s.

In fact, symmetry had become the basis of manor house styling, and would remain so through the succeeding centuries. It provided the homes of the gentry with a formal aesthetic character that they had previously lacked. The change has been summed-up as a combination of "symmetrical facades inspired by Italy . . . and grid windows in native Perpendicular style".[16] The use of the latter illustrates the supplanting of the architectural dominance of the church. "The building of large Perpendicular churches more or less came to a halt by the 1540s, but the tradition mingled with continental influences to produce a new and vigorous secular architecture".[17] This also illustrates the overturning of the social hegemony of the medieval church. The alliance of the symmetrical and the Perpendicular was not an accident. Both forms proclaim the elevation of the gentry.

Above all, these houses displayed a sense of perfect balance and completion, with scarcely a hint of medieval earthiness or openness remaining. The face of the manor houses of the middle ages had never transcended a kind of basic functionalism. They gave the impression of being built for the immediate purpose, with no cohesive stylistic reference, and they always appeared somehow close to the ground. But the new manor houses had, with a sudden single flourish, taken wing. They manifested a self-conscious, coordinated sense of styling to which their predecessors had never aspired. Style had not previously been much of a consideration, but now it was everything. When we look at these houses in their controlled, self-contained symmetry, we are not really aware of the natural, physical world at all.

But to note that the new styling transcended functionalism is not to say that it had no function, for it certainly did, on a very significant scale. The broader references and relationships are the most interesting, but not always recognised. A modern study by Nicholas Cooper talks of the transition in manor house styles as an indication of changes in domestic and estate relations, suggesting that by the new elevated and symmetrical shapes a gentry family could assert a more detached superiority over its dependents, and that by contrast the medieval hall structure had reflected a more homogeneous context. There were certainly important elements of continuum in the medieval lifestyle, but the specific contrast that Cooper makes is perhaps not entirely convincing.[18]

We can probably gather more about what these houses meant by focusing on how they appeared and related to the outside world. What the new style amounted to was a way of imparting complete distinction to a house. It represented detachment at various levels. Its outward connections were less immediate and sensate than the unbroken link that the medieval houses had maintained with the agrarian world. In part, the completed symmetry expressed the idea of absolute individual property. But it also signified control of the land in another way—that is to say, in the manner in which it was used. Symmetry was a Renaissance form, and it is useful to consider Renaissance principles in terms of what they implied for attitudes to the natural environment. The new manor houses reflected a relationship to the land that was at once more detached, and more manipulative than had been characteristic of medieval times, when the general inclination was to live in unmediated contact with the earth, and to work with it as given. As Huizinga said, "when the medieval mind wants to know the nature or the reason of a thing, it neither looks into it to analyse its structure, nor behind it to inquire into its origin, but looks up to heaven, where it shines as an idea".[19] Renaissance culture, by contrast, was not content to accept and know the world as given. It *did* seek to investigate and pin down the particular form of things by structural analysis and precise depiction, to bring them more closely under command. It was probably no accident that men like the seventeenth century diarist John Evelyn were preoccupied with Renaissance art forms, as well as with the advance of agricultural improvement, in areas such as forest management. He emphasised the importance of methods of mensuration, and opening up nature to reveal its inner workings, to make it "subservient to humane life".[20] The gentry were assuming complete power over the land in all its dimensions, and when we recognise that a sense of control was inherent in Renaissance forms, it helps to explain why they favoured perfect symmetry in the design of their houses. Evelyn rebuilt his house at Sayes Court in a symmetrical style.

The force of symmetry as containment and control also reflected the exercise of power over *the land* in another perspective, relating to the emergence of the nation-state in sixteenth century England. The state as an integrated, self-contained political unit was again defined in contrast to the open and fluid territorial relationships of medieval Christendom. The distinctive internal dynamic of the new, unitary form is captured in Richard Hooker's concept of the "entire society", the consent of which had become the necessary basis of sovereign law in England. "The lawful power of making laws to command whole societies of men belongs so properly unto the same entire societies".[21] The leading agents in the representative processes through which those laws were made were the gentry. By the reign of Elizabeth they were also the most crucial instruments by which the laws were implemented, through their dominating presence on the Commissions of the Peace. So the completed symmetrical style of their houses proclaimed a plenitude of power, but of a different sort from the personal and military force represented by the regional grip of the medieval magnates and the crude bulk of the castles. The controlled regularity of the manor house face was the expression of general socio-economic command and administrative authority, contained in architectural form. The speed with which the style was taken up throughout the kingdom was itself a reflection of the *national* reach of the gentry that occupied the houses. The ubiquity of the gentry in the villages underpinned their emergence as a national force. They were the agency of a uniform, kingdom-wide system of administration, representation and lawmaking. The self-conscious styling of their houses was the architectural face of the coordinated social and political prestige that the gentry had attained. It raised and distinguished them from the mundane, and referred to a broader culture of high fashion beyond, with a nod to the ultimate supremacy of classical form and imperial pretension. They now commanded the leading public aesthetic, formerly the preserve of the church. The controlled symmetry of the manor houses asserted the growing status of the gentry as a new kind of national public authority.

This brings into focus a neglected, but crucial aspect of structural change in sixteenth century England—the emerging shape of the nation-state. This was a fundamental alteration that deserves more concentrated attention than it has usually received, and it will reappear in various aspects at different stages of this volume. It was a structural change so general, and in a sense external, that it is too easy to take for granted. Yet it took very definite form. Like the houses themselves, it can be seen as a process of completion. The state was a separated and autonomous unit emerging from the undifferentiated, open patterns of territorial and political occupation that characterised the medieval world. It has been well said that until the sixteenth century there was no concept of a state as a political unit. The idea was precluded most obviously by the power of the universal church, which held place as an independent body, dominant landholder, and alternative focus of loyalty across all the kingdoms of Christendom. The expulsion of the Roman church established the outline of the English state, and the manner in which this was achieved created the most crucial internal dynamic. The independent judicial power of the church was supplanted by the sole sovereignty of representative statute. The Break with Rome also did much to create a series of self-defining national interests, and a national land-market that directed three quarters of England into the occupation of the gentry and yeomanry. It can be suggested that the unitary state was the macrocosm of the developing concept of autonomous occupation that was manifest in the individualised properties of the landed classes. This connection had important ramifications. The political challenge to the English crown in the mid-seventeenth century was fuelled largely by the economic advances and continued aspirations of the gentry and yeomanry, and it was much conditioned by their relationship to the emerging state form.

Figure 5.1 Dartington Hall, Devon, 1390.

Source: Copyright: Hugo Butterworth.

Figure 5.2 Bradley Manor, Devon, 1495.

Source: Copyright: Hugo Butterworth.

Figure 5.3 Hazelbadge Hall, Derbyshire, 1549.

Source: Copyright: Hugo Butterworth.

Figure 5.4 Glynde Place, Sussex, 1569.

Source: Copyright Hugo Butterworth.

Figure 5.5 Parham, Sussex, 1577.

Source: Copyright: Hugo Butterworth.

Figure 5.6 Barlborough Hall, Derbyshire, 1580s.

Source: Copyright: Hugo Butterworth.

Figure 5.7 Heydon Hall, Norfolk, 1580s.

Source: Copyright Hugo Butterworth.

Figure 5.8 Lower Bockhampton, Dorset, 1590s.

Source: Copyright: Hugo Butterworth.

Notes

1. I am grateful to Colin Richmond for the identification and dating of these early developments
2. W. G. Hoskins placed the process mainly in the period from 1570–1640. The reassessment by R. Machin, (*Past and Present* 77, 1977), suggested, quite rightly, that the Great Rebuilding continued after the Civil War period, but agreed the starting date of 1570, and the peaks of activity from 1570–1589 and 1620–1639. Again, my thanks to Colin Richmond for pointing out that the signs were already there in the earlier sixteenth century
3. C. Palliser, *The Age of Elizabeth*, (London 1983), p. 110
4. W. Harrison, *A Description of England*, (1577–87), in *Tudor Economic Documents*, ed. R. Tawney and E. Power, (London 1951), vol. III, pp. 68–70
5. Ibid, p. 111
6. Ibid
7. W. Harrison's, *Description of England*, ed. F. J. Furnivall, *New Shakespeare Society*, 6 Series, I, (London 1877), pt I, chap. 5
8. L. Stone, *The Crisis of the Aristocracy*, (Oxford 1965), p. 67
9. M. Overton, *The Agricultural Revolution*, (Cambridge 1996), p. 169
10. W. G. Hoskins, *The Age of Plunder*, (London 1976), p. 3
11. J. R. Lander, *Government and Community: England 1450–1509*, (London 1980), pp. 42–3
12. Hoskins, *The Age of Plunder*, p. 55
13. J. Steel and M. Wright, *The English House*, (Woodbridge 2007), p. 50
14. Stone, *The Crisis of the Aristocracy*, p. 551
15. Bridget Cherry and Nikolaus Pevsner, *Devon*, (Harmondsworth 1989), Cadhay is illustrated as plate 64
16. Palliser, *The Age of Elizabeth*, p. 369
17. Ibid, p. 368
18. N. Cooper, *The Houses of the Gentry 1480–1680*, (Yale 1999)
19. J. Huizinga, *The Waning of the Middle Ages*, (Harmondsworth 1976), p. 206
20. M. Hunter, *Science and Society in Restoration England*, (Cambridge 2014), p. 93; *The Image of Restoration Science: The Frontispiece to Thomas Sprat's 'History of The Royal Society'* (1667), (with a chapter on the instruments by Jim Bennett), (London and New York 2017), pp. 29–30
21. Richard Hooker, *Of the Laws of Ecclesiastical Polity*, ed. C. Morris, (London 1969), vol. I, bk. I, pt. X, p. 194

6 A Changing Ethos

From Conditional to Absolute Property; the Rise of Individualism and a Self-Sustaining Market; and the Growing Demand for a Right of Freedom of Trade from Arbitrary Restraints

There is a general recognition that there was a significant change in the rules of conduct of economic life during the sixteenth and early seventeenth centuries in England. Most historians would accept for instance that by the beginning of the seventeenth century there had emerged a concept of "absolute" property rights. Marc Bloch saw this indeed as the "one really striking transformation" in the agrarian history of early modern Europe, and noted that it occurred in England but not elsewhere.[1] But there is no clear perception of how this arose, and little acknowledgement of the specific and important consequences that followed.[2] Similarly, there is a rather vague and unfocused awareness that there was a new market-orientated perspective taking shape, and gaining strength as the period progressed. But there is no fully elaborated view of the change in the guidelines of economic activity that this involved, or how it related to the political sphere. The rise of a new, market economy tends to be mentioned in passing, as part of the background to the scene.[3] The present chapter attempts a more coordinated view of these developments, tracing their origins, and illustrating their force as a transforming economic ethos, which had important political ramifications.

The most systematic attempt at a connected treatment of the topic remains *Religion and the Rise of Capitalism*, by R. H. Tawney. First published in the 1930s, the thesis still carries much force. His argument is powerful when focusing on the rise of economic individualism.[4] But he attempts to associate this with Puritan belief systems, the relevance of which is not clear, and this weakens his case overall. Both Joyce Appleby and C. B. Macpherson added much to our understanding of individualist forms, but they tended to assess change on the basis of socio-economic models, which some found less than convincing, and which were perhaps too rigid to capture a sense of motive force.[5] Historical geographers like Peter Brandon and Joan Thirsk have, as a generalisation, affirmed that the processes of enclosure and consolidation involved a change from a communal to an individualist concept of farming.[6] But some historians have preferred to obscure these distinctions. Alan Macfarlane erased the chronology of change by purporting to discover an individualist world in a medieval period when in truth the most characteristic tendency was specifically to subordinate individual rights.[7] More recent studies have also veered away from the ethical perspective. John Bohmstedt, for example, acknowledges that an integrated and commercialised marketing system had arisen by late Tudor times, and he makes the valid point that the productive force of the market could offer compensations to the poor and deprived. But he seeks to treat this as a purely pragmatic consideration, which tends to obscure the place that ethical codes had once held in public provision.[8] It is necessary to recognise the normative moral framework of medieval agriculture, if we are to obtain a clear picture of the change that was brought about by the rise of an individualist economy.

We can identify connecting threads through the various aspects of change—whether economic, moral, philosophical or political. It is possible, for instance, to trace the transition from the "conditional" view of property that characterised the medieval mind-set, to the assertion that property should be regarded as "absolute", a claim that emerged into the political arena at the beginning of the seventeenth century. This was part and parcel of the switch from a "moral" to a "market" economy, and it had specific implications in terms of the preferred methods of public finance. In the medieval dispensation, property was seen as conditional in every respect—both technically and in principle. In an essentially feudal context, property was not fully "owned" as we would think of it today. It was granted by an overlord, and held for use. In the fifteenth century the great majority of village husbandmen occupied their strips by "copyhold". Most of these tenures had originally been variable at the will of the lord, though they had acquired a degree of formal status by being copied into the manorial court roll. A small minority of farmers held their lands "freehold". Even this did not constitute absolute property as such, but it was granted on fixed dues that gave effective security of tenure.

In the medieval world, all property was held upon obligations of some kind, not merely entailing dues and services, but most distinctively and importantly, carrying moral restraints on the way that it should be used. It was thought of as a trust or stewardship from God, and was to be devoted to the purpose for which God had made and intended it—that is to say, the maintenance of the common good. So the principles of conditional property, which were normative in the medieval period, were directly reflected in the communal practices of the open fields and commons. This was in tune with the general mind-set of the Middle Ages, which saw reality in terms of universal ideas rather than particular forms, and subordinated the claims of the individual to the rights of community. All things were created by God, and defined as an idea in the mind of God.[9] Thus everything had a common essence, and was integral to everything else, in a continuum without conceptual distinctions. The only singular entity was the Body of Christ, which embraced all, and all were expected to work in the light of Christ's charity. Piers the Ploughman said that he was "following the plough for poor men's sakes . . . bear ye one another's burdens and so ye shall fulfil the law of Christ".[10] Practice followed principle. The open, dispersed and undifferentiated pattern of the strip system was designed to give everyone a fair share of the best conditions, and the worst. It was also intended to facilitate the communal grazing of the stubble after harvest, and the sharing of expensive items like the teams of oxen and the heavy plough. In the same way, every household contributed to a common stock of hay to ensure that everybody's animals had the same chance of surviving a hard winter. And as we saw, the absence of an individualist perspective was reflected in the fact that there was no perceived need to record a particular holding in any completed or coordinated form.[11]

Since communal farming was the grounded reflection of medieval universalism, the most obvious threat to the principles of conditional property was the practice that became prevalent at the end of the fifteenth century whereby landlords began to assume an absolute property in their land and infringe the customary rights of the tenants by taking over sections of the commons and open fields for sheep runs. In 1515, in the first great diatribe against the commandeering of the common lands, Thomas More protested that the acquisitive lords and farmers were breaking the balance observed by their forefathers, who had not shown the same urge or requirement for increasing their profits. He found the new generation of sheep farmers to be guilty of excessive profiteering:

> not contenting themselves with the yearly revenues and profits that were wont to grow to their forefathers and predecessors of their lands, nor being content that they live in rest and peace, nothing profiting. . . . They enclose all into pastures, they throw down houses . . . the husbandmen be thrown out of . . . their known and accustomed houses.[12]

More was describing the medieval ideal where all was dedicated to the preservation of existing customary balances, and no one was considered free to use his property in a way that undermined the position of others. More perceived that the new imperatives of the profit motive entailed an assumption of absolute property that had not previously carried force. "Where possessions be private, where money beareth all the stroke, it is hard and almost impossible that there the weal-public may justly be governed and prosperously flourish".[13] It is interesting that he was observing the same consequence as noted by Gerrard Winstanley—that the unrestrained power of money, and the unlimited freedom of buying and selling land as private property, led to injustices and deprivation: "where everyone calleth that he hath gotten his own proper and private goods . . . and know from another man's what he calleth his own", there was endless contention.[14] His condemnation of the assertion of absolute property may be difficult for us to take on board, from the perspective of a modern world in which it is taken for granted. But in medieval times, most obviously on the common lands, people were not assumed to have an independent right in their property that licensed them to employ it irrespective of the interests of others.

The clearest picture of the principles of conditional property, and of moral economy as spiritual wholeness, is found in the works of Robert Crowley, writing in the middle of the sixteenth century. He was a churchman, and like Sir Thomas More, an outspoken critic of the "greedy cormorants" who "enclosed from the poor their commons". He denounced the landlords and commercial farmers for breaking the God-given balance of agrarian society. He reminded them that their possessions were a trust from God, who "makes them the stewards of their possessions . . . and decrees us not to hold from others the things that they have need of". Like More, he perceived and condemned the growing assumption of absolute property rights. It was ungodly for landlords to say, "It is mine own, who shall warn me to do with mine own as me self listeth?" Crowley answered that the warning came from God. Nothing so clearly underlines the moral imperatives of these traditional assumptions than Crowley's assertion that they would only have the right to do what they liked with their property in a world where God did not exist. "If there were no God, then I would think it lawful for men to use their possessions as they listeth". Currently, the farmers, graziers, rich butchers and gentlemen were acting "as if there were no God at all". By the same token they were departing from their God-given place in the socio-economic order. Nothing so clearly illustrates the new force of the profit motive than Crowley's complaint that the commercialising farmers were men with no proper recognisable vocation, because "they are doers in all things that any gain hangeth on".[15]

More and Crowley should not be seen as paranoid moralists urging their fellows to spiritual improvement. The change in the basis of economic conduct that they so disliked and condemned found confirmation of a more positive sort in the well-balanced text of the *Discourse of the Commonweal*. This dates from 1549, which was much the same time as Crowley was writing, but it assesses the development from a significantly different angle. The *Discourse* underlined the fact that the principal driver of change was an exceptional level of profit that had not previously been available. It was not that men had suddenly become greedier—it was just that an unprecedented opportunity had arisen to increase their profits and extend their lands. The *Discourse* recognised an irresistible temptation: "the exceeding lucre that men see grow".[16] You needed perhaps to be already among the more substantial of the common field tenants, and in addition to have benefited from the general leasing of the lords' demesne. Given this, you were in a good position to emulate Hugh Latimer's yeoman father, who "held no lands of his own . . . but had a walk for a hundred sheep".[17] As the *Discourse* concluded, there could be no greater incentive than the assurance that they would become "notable rich men by the doing thereof in brief time".[18] The *Discourse* understood that in view of the force of this there was nothing to be gained from trying to restrain it. Economic pragmatism indicated indeed that it was the generator of rising productivity as well as rising profits, and that it should therefore be accommodated. So, rather than try to halt the extension of sheep runs, government should accord the arable husbandmen the same freedom to profit that was the basis of the advance of pastoral farming.

The *Discourse* recognised that the plates were shifting in the economic world, and profit was becoming the principal foundation of increased economic activity. It may be difficult for us to comprehend the full force of the change that had taken place from the old context of communal agriculture and conditional property, but we are not without a specific, and graphic illustration of the power that the traditional arrangements had once carried, and the existential threat that they now faced. A previous chapter described the situation on the farm of the Yorkshire yeoman Henry Best, in terms of the imposition of enclosed structures on the common lands. It also provides a clear picture of the residual habits of communalism, as it resisted being pushed aside by the interventions of enclosure and absolute rights.

Most of Best's lands were enclosed. In fact, he recorded that since he had enclosed his pastures, their value had risen fourfold above the level attained in his father's time. This is in itself a good indication of how "the exceeding lucre that men see grow" was structured. But the villagers were disinclined to accept the assertion of sole personal property that it involved. They continued to believe that they had the right to graze the village flock freely over the whole area of arable fields after harvest, including the fields enclosed by Best. To deter them, he created elaborate gate blocks, which he went out to check in the middle of the night. By the same token, the villagers still expected him to contribute to the common stock of hay to feed the flock when the snow was on the ground. He declined because he did not wish his hay to be used "in feeding other men's animals".[19] He used outside labour for his harvests, and employed women with rakes to gather the stray corm that would once have been left for the poor to glean. Here were two very different outlooks on economic life, and they were at complete cross-purposes. The villagers were attempting to sustain the conditional view of property that had guided farming practice on the open fields through the Middle Ages, when there was a moral, and practical obligation to use the land in a way that served the common good. Henry Best, however, had developed a paramount individual interest in rejecting that communality.

How are we to rationalise the stark polarity of views in sixteenth and early seventeenth century society? Men like Thomas More, Robert Crowley, William Laud and others regarded it as not merely antisocial, but actually ungodly for the landlords and consolidating farmers to pursue their own profit to a degree that threatened the livelihoods of the commoners. On this view, profit was defined as necessarily inimical to the common good. On the other hand, men like Henry Best, Fitzherbert and the author of the *Discourse*, were happy to normalise the profit motive and focus in un-problematic fashion on seeking ways to maximise its effect. It hardly seems sufficient to observe that the former were moralists and the latter were economists, and they had differing perspectives on the priorities of life. The truth of the matter is that More and Crowley were speaking from a different world entirely, where there *was* no "economy" in the modern sense of an integrated general market, with measurable potentialities. The medieval world had economic affairs, and economic relations, but its overall context was social and spiritual. It was an age that measured itself in terms of the maintenance of socio-economic balances. Best, Fitzherbert and the *Discourse* had entered a new world, where the force of economic growth, and the freedom of the individual to pursue it, took precedence.

In their impassioned defence of the common lands under attack More and Crowley had identified the central premise of conditional property that was normative under the moral dictates of the medieval period. Its basis was that landed property was held as a trust or stewardship from God, and was only to be employed for God's purposes, which were to sustain the common good. This imposed the crucial restraint that the individual was not at liberty to use his property in whatever way he chose, if it might be to the detriment of others. More and Crowley also noted another principal constraint that the conditional view of property imposed on the individual. People were obliged to pay the king whatever taxes he demanded, for he was the sole judge of the overall public interest. More said that "A King . . . can do nothing unjustly, for all that men have . . . be all his".[20] Crowley concurred, because, "It is not for thee to define what great charges the king is at".[21] So in this way too, one's property was not entirely one's own in the medieval period. More and Crowley had in fact identified the twin pillars of the conditional concept of property, and it was quite specifically in the overturning of these two precepts that the idea of "absolute" property was to be established in England.

A Self-Sustaining Market and the Origins of Freedom of Trade

The essence of the challenge to conditional property and moral economy was the growing assumption of a right of each individual to hold and use land and goods with complete freedom, in contradiction of the strictures of More and Crowley, and indeed of the standard practices of government. The assertion of license appeared in some form across the whole economic field, and in these pages it is characterised as a general demand for freedom of trade. It took its genesis from two distinctive but associated developments. One was the emergence of enterprises offering exceptional levels of profit, which created the desire for liberty to exploit these opportunities freely. The other was a new kind of market which itself appeared to operate, almost necessarily, in a context of freedom. The symbiotic connection between the extension of sheep farming and the rise of the cloth trade from the end of the fifteenth century was a crucial factor in both respects. The rearing of sheep became the leading example of an enterprise that generated "the exceeding lucre that men see grow", because "there was more advantage in grazing and breeding than in husbandry by a great deal".[22] There was a potential for high profits that had never previously been available from general economic activity, and this goes far to explain why the constraints of communal agriculture were cast aside by many landlords and commercial yeoman farmers. At the same time, it became apparent that the unprecedented level of profit to be made from pastoral farming and its associated trades depended largely on the unusual degree of practical and fiscal freedom in which they were allowed to operate, at least in the formative stages. Grazing could be done with less outlay, less labour and less risk than arable farming, and wool and cloth were not subject to the same kind of export restraints by which the authorities traditionally sought to manage the domestic price and maintain the supply of grain. As one contemporary noted, the products of grazing involved "small charge and small labour" and had "free vent to be sold both on this side and beyond the sea at the highest penny".[23]

The mutually reinforcing expansion of sheep farming and the cloth trade was also the lead factor in the emergence of a broad but integrated market system. Almost of itself, the sheep-cloth connection created a coordinated national market. The agricultural and manufacturing sectors became interdependent, growing together, and generating other trading links as they went. Previous chapters have described the structural framework of the processes of interregional marketing that grew up in the sixteenth century. In summary, each region would specialise in those products to which it was best suited then export them to other regions that were doing the same with their own most favoured items of production. Areas that did not boast the most fertile soils, or the greatest potential for agriculture, were able to exploit other particular resources, such as mining or spare labour for manufacture. Many districts were thus set free to diversify and find their own most productive economic character. One result was a rise in combined productivity. Another consequence was that many local economies were refocused from an essentially "subsistence" to an "export-import" mode. This was an important factor in the development of a new pattern of marketing, which was more distant and detached in range, yet at the same time coordinated in structure.

The most conspicuous sign of the emergence of the interregional system was a change in the scope of markets. Everywhere, agricultural trade was drawn away from the smaller markets and focused on larger provincial centres like Maidstone, Canterbury, Doncaster, Worcester, Newcastle, Reading and King's Lynn. These were the points of distribution for the products in which their region specialised. At the beginning of the sixteenth century, "most towns still served a purely local area, and specialised in no particular commodity". But during the course of the century, "a broad pattern of specialisation becomes clear". The trend had become noticeable by the last quarter of the sixteenth century, when about half of the eight hundred market towns in England were specialising in the marketing of some favoured product.[24] What had developed was in effect a regional and national market, in which bulk products were traded over greater distances, yet in a more coordinated manner.

A significant facilitator of the arrival of a free, integrated market was the unusual absence of trading barriers within the English kingdom. England had no great cities except London, whose strength as a great central mart actually encouraged the general freedom of exchange. Nor were there any semi-independent provinces within the kingdom to interrupt the flow with their own customs barriers. Even the tolls imposed by market towns seem to have fallen into disuse by the sixteenth century. Interregional trade in agricultural commodities also encouraged a trend towards private marketing, with business being done at inns beyond the supervision of the towns. This practice developed substantially during the sixteenth century. As a consequence of these many-sided freedoms,

> Internal trade went largely untaxed in the period 1500 to 1700 . . . . One of the principal strengths of the network of internal trading . . . was the lightness of passage tolls, pontages and other duties on domestic trade, which created in much of Western Europe a fairly rigid series of customs unions.[25]

This practical freedom, and the fact that it seemed to work quite well in generating commercial activity, encouraged the idea that freedom of trade should be applied as a principle.

At the same time, the coordinated force of the market was pushing aside the traditional moral restraints, by which the authorities, central and local, had sought to ensure that supplies and prices were kept within the reach of every pocket. The concept of the "just price" was vital to the balance of the medieval world, restricting the profits of the individual in the general interest of the community. Tawney described it well as the determination to "try every transaction by a rule of right . . . independent of the fortuitous combinations of economic circumstances . . . no man must ask more than the price fixed, either by the public authorities, or, failing that, by common estimation".[26] But the moral perspective was now losing its normative force. As the processes of marketing became wider and freer, and yet more intensified, the capacity for restraint was reduced in a practical as well as a psychological sense. Under the pressure of the sharp increase in free market activity, "regulation gradually broke down".[27] By the later decades of the sixteenth century the force of the profit motive had become too powerful to resist. "The Elizabethan government came to accept that the grain market was driven by the desire for private gain".[28]

Some people certainly regretted the passing of the old moral economy. In a tract written in 1578, Nicholas Henning was still expounding the principle of the just price, and castigating the current tendency to circumvent it, a practice that he thought was simply avarice.[29] Another contemporary, William Harrison is best known for his description of the changes in housing and lifestyles that were the product of an integrated and expanding economy, but he took a less than sanguine view of the free market conditions that underpinned these developments. He still seemed to hanker for the restraints and balances of the regulated, moral economy. He was critical of the fact that sellers travelled great distances to particular markets "to seek the highest prices". No doubt he felt that they should proceed in the traditional manner and sell them locally at a lower price. He condemned the general failure to apply the assize of bread, which was supposed to set the quality and price of that basic commodity. And he bemoaned the fact that in most markets, the quality of the goods was "not any whit looked unto, but each one suffered to sell or set up whatever he himself listeth".[30]

These complaints showed how powerful the traditional moral assumptions had been, and Harrison had indeed captured the essence of the change. A core component of the concept of conditional property, as defined by Thomas More and Robert Crowley, was that people were *not* at liberty to do whatever they "listeth" with their land and goods. But this principle was now being overtaken by a different, even opposite belief, that in fact all should be allowed complete freedom in this respect. There were long-standing laws, still in place, that forbad farmers to store or buy up grain in order to sell it later at a higher price. By the beginning of the seventeenth century, that rule no longer ran, and a successful yeoman farmer like Robert Loder could brazenly proclaim that his standard practice was to "keep or sell accordingly as I shall think it likely to fall out most for my profit".[31] The notion of the just price was becoming a thing of the past.

As the traditions of spontaneous communal provision and local control retreated, the government sought other ways of regulating and securing the corn supply, at least at times of extreme dearth. The best-known expedient was to issue a Book of Orders, which carried instructions for ascertaining the real, total amount of grain available, and ensuring that some was directed to where it was most needed. In this, they had reasonable success, but these were emergency measures, which in a sense underlined the fact that the customary systems of restraint were no longer operative or dependable. And even while a Book of Orders served its immediate purpose, it could still be regarded as detrimental overall. It interrupted the reciprocal movement of the market, and disrupted what was becoming the necessary dynamic of economic activity. Alan Everitt pinpointed this anomaly, and its significant effects, in a passage that is worth quoting at length.

> In a period where agricultural trade was rapidly ceasing to be primarily local and becoming largely national and international, restraint in some respects only aggravated the difficulty . . . upset the system of regular deliveries . . . early Stuart policy was out of touch with a number of fundamental changes in the English rural economy. It failed to recognise that an increasing proportion of agricultural output was produced with distant markets, and not the local town or village in view.

Consequently, the early Stuart kings failed to understand the irreducible collective force of the economic groups that they chose to challenge: "that the men whose acquisitive propensities they set out to restrain . . . were no longer . . . isolated individuals, but a distinct and self-conscious community . . . by alienating that community the Stuarts made some of their most implacable enemies".[32] Perhaps "community" is not the best word to describe the new integrated network, but it captures the idea of the market as an independent entity, and it is certainly true that the Stuarts faced an increasingly insistent demand that it should be left to work in freedom.

Sales now took place not so much in a multitude of markets, but rather in a single market that was developing a life of its own. A market was no longer just a passive forum of simple transactions where you brought your product to a town square and sold it to a known local customer. The new trades were routinely carried on in bulk goods, which would be transported to a more distant mart, from where they would be duly redistributed. The market had become a network of exchange relations, interconnected over long distances—unseen, but understood. And it became apparent that each part moved in response to the next. Tawney noted that influential commentators were beginning to characterise the force of this in terms of clockwork. Thus Gerard De Malynes wrote that, "We see how one thing drives or enforces another, like as in a clock where there are many wheels, the first one driveth the next, and that the third, and so forth".[33] The first voice to identify this characteristic of a "modern" economy was, as in so many other ways, the *Discourse of the*

Commonweal written in the middle of the sixteenth century. The *Discourse* noted that market relations were now to a large extent automatic. "As in a press . . . the foremost is driven by him that is next to him, and the next by him that follows him . . . as in a clock".[34]

The *Discourse* is rightly regarded as the first exercise in "modern" economics in another sense, eschewing the idea of judgements made on moral grounds, and instead embracing the notion that profit was the dictating factor in economic affairs. It is probable indeed that the growing sense of the market as an independent force, working by its own dynamic, did much to engender the thought that the profit motive would have to be accommodated. The *Discourse* was written at much the same time as the works of Robert Crowley, around the middle of the sixteenth century. But, as we have seen, it takes a very different line. In contrast to Crowley's principled resistance, the *Discourse* proposed that the profit motive should be recognised and accepted as the most effective means of economic motivation. It takes a carefully balanced view of the vexed question of the incidence and effects of enclosure. The appropriation of the open fields is not held to blame for the inexorable rise in grain prices, which was laid at its door by uninformed opinion. But the *Discourse* does acknowledge that it was often carried out by force, and in this respect it did undermine the position of the independent husbandman. "If that kind of enclosure do as much increase in twenty years to come as it has done twenty years past, it comes much to the desolation and weakness of this realm". The *Discourse* observed that successive governments had legislated to restrict or reverse the process of enclosure. The fact that they failed seemed to underline the exceptional power of the trend, and of the profit motive. It appeared to be irresistible, and this was what the *Discourse* recognised. "Small remedy found therefore that took effect".[35] So the *Discourse* proposed a different solution. The application of the profit motive should not be resisted, but accommodated. The conditions of profiting in freedom enjoyed by pastoral farmers should not be curtailed, but actually extended to other fields of production. Arable products should be given the same facilities of exchange license and market inducement that had encouraged the pastoral side to expand and thrive: "that the husbandman might have as much liberty at all times to sell his corn either within the realm or without as the grazier hath to sell his".[36] This would "make the profit of the plough to be as good rate for rate as the profit of the grazier and sheepmaster".[37]

It was a new way of balancing the economy, devised for a changing world where there was a presumption of continuing growth, where the level of profit available had made it an irresistible motive, where "everyman will seek where more advantage lies", and where the market had become an independent, self-sustaining force working to that dynamic. In the medieval context the provision of vital commodities had been secured by local and central restraint of the markets, the artificial control of prices, and the restriction of exports. But in the changed circumstances of the sixteenth century the *Discourse of the Commonweal* had come to conclude that the new economic logic was to leave the market to its own devices, and to maintain output and supply by allowing every trade the right to engage freely with it and profit to the full.

The Emerging Demand for a Principled Right of Freedom of Trade

The growth of a self-perpetuating market was the context in which the most seminal transformations in the ethos of economic life took shape. It was the structure through which commercialisation acquired an irresistible determining force, undermining the equitable balance that had existed between the village smallholders, and between them and the land. An integrated, independent market, working to its own necessary dynamic, was also crucial to the genesis of what may be regarded as the more constructive aspect of the change, and what became in effect the defining economic principle of the age. This was the concept of "freedom of trade", which was in large part a response to the growing sense that there was now a general market that functioned best when left to its own devices.

Freedom of trade is not a phrase coined in retrospect. The term was used by a leading proponent of the concept, Sir Edward Coke, who, in the face of economic depression in the 1620s, called for, "freedom of trade . . . not burdened by impositions . . . or undone by monopolies".[38] Coke had a talent for finding the phrase that summed up the dominant inclination of the time, and illuminated its essential force. Freedom of trade is indeed the best overall characterisation of the growing demand for a principled liberty from arbitrary exaction or restraint. It was first put forward in independent economic commentaries in the middle of the sixteenth century, and by the end of that century it had emerged as a dominant public ambition. It was maintained in contradiction of the position of the royal government, which persistently sought to tax and regulate trade by prerogative levies and privileges, as had been the practice in the past. But given the economic logic and popular sentiment behind freedom of trade, establishment obduracy only served to radicalise the general preference. By the early seventeenth century, this divergence had sharpened to the point where it generated a political challenge to the crown.

It was, needless to say, in the *Discourse of the Commonweal*, of 1549, that freedom of trade was first advanced as a general prescription. To a generation determined to "seek where more advantage lies", arbitrary impositions had become a powerful disincentive, wherever and whenever they were enforced. So the *Discourse* proposed that grain production should be ensured, not by trying to halt the incursions of the graziers onto agricultural land, but by freeing the arable husbandman from levies and restraints. And once the freedom to profit had been embraced as a solution, logic dictated that it should be applied in all areas. What had caused the recent depression in the cloth trade? The error, said the *Discourse*, had been to raise and extend the custom on cloth, "which was the very highway to make the clothiers give up their occupation".[39] The *Discourse* had identified the new rule of liberal economics, which was that productivity and its benefits were best secured and distributed by the "allurements" of profit, rather than by taxation and control. "Take these rewards from them, and go about to compel them by law thereto, what man will plough or dig the ground? Or who will venture overseas for any merchandise?"[40] This was the consistent justification of freedom of trade, asserting that the liberty to profit to the full was what made an enterprise productive and worthwhile, and that in its absence trade would cease.

This rationale was established in a series of letters and memos to the Privy Council from commercially minded gentry in the years following the *Discourse*. The tract *Piers Ploughman's Exhortation*, published at the same time as the *Discourse* repeated the prescription—to raise the level of incentive for arable farming by setting the corn trade free. "To suffer all manner of corn to be freely transported over the seas as well as any other kind of merchandise". Piers also recommended that the removal of impositions in general would be "a great cause that the more tin, lead and cloth shall be wrought".[41] These propositions immediately found echo in respect of other trades in further letters to the Privy Council from influential gentlemen with an interest in commerce. In December 1550 Sir John Mason wrote protesting against the restrictions being placed on the export of cheese and butter. He pointed out that such restraints did not make things cheaper—they simply depressed production. "For who will keep a cow that cannot sell the milk for as much as the merchant and he will agree upon?"[42] The concept of freedom of trade was finding broad reception throughout the growing national economy. In the following year Cecil received a letter from William Lane, another prominent voice in economic matters, extending exactly the same advice in respect of the rather different but increasingly important products of the mining industry.[43]

In March 1559 the experienced voice of John Hales joined the chorus, with a plea on behalf of the most important of English exports—woollen cloth. He reiterated the freedom of trade rationale. Wealth production was ensured by the liberty to profit. Restrictions and arbitrary exactions were counter-productive. The proposed imposition on cloth was not the way to increase royal income, "but rather a means to make no English merchants". It would undermine the kingdom's most essential trade and manufacture. A more efficient balance in economic affairs would be achieved by allowing the maximum freedom to profit in the market. "For merchants trade for gain, and when it ceases, they trade no more".[44] Most of these pleas recognised that their advice ran counter to the official view, and was unlikely to be heeded. It did indeed remain the government's standard procedure to regulate trade by restrictions and impositions, and grants of privilege. Eventually, the developing assumptions of freedom of trade came into direct confrontation with the policies of the crown and led to the first formal challenges to aspects of the royal prerogative.

At the beginning of her reign Elizabeth I appears to have taken care not to impose too much on the purses of her subjects. In 1563, the MP Robert Atkinson could express his gratitude that "never Prince since the conquest (I speak it without flattery) hath . . . reigned over us in a quieter peace, with more love and less exaction".[45] At the same time, the economy was recovering after a period of depression and higher taxation in the 1550s. This may have reinforced the general idea that lower taxation fostered productivity. By the middle of Elizabeth's reign, however, the costs of war were obliging the government to seek additional means of finance, and there was a growing tension with the public perception that trade needed to be free of impositions and restraints. Some of the earliest assertions of freedom of trade as an inherited right came as a reaction to the government's increasing tendency to grant patents of monopoly, largely as a means of raising ready cash. The system of monopolies had begun life, innocently enough, as a way of protecting the integrity of new inventions, and encouraging the "projects" that were characteristic of the Elizabethan age. The practice became more controversial in the 1580s, when monopoly patents were widely extended as a way of regulating and taxing the trade in established commodities, such as salt, starch, paper and many other staple items. In this form, monopolies became a contradiction of the new rules of commercial economics. In the integrated network, a producer needed to be able to measure the level of his output in relation to the free conditions of the market, in order to ensure his returns. These patterns of relationship were severely disrupted by patents of monopoly, which imposed arbitrary levies and interventions.

So in 1586 the Boston salt traders protested against the salt monopoly. They found it unacceptable that "a foreigner should be privileged in a free borough in such manner and the inhabitants restrained, and that men should not convert their salt pits and salt coteries being their inheritance to the best use". Like traders in many other fields they were coming to regard it as a necessary liberty to be able to exchange their commodities free of arbitrary restrictions, to gain the full benefit of their trade. It was the strength of this desire that led them to condemn monopoly powers as "contrary to the laws of this realm".[46] This was wishful thinking. It was in fact a prerogative right of the crown to issue patents of monopoly. But this was precisely why the nation's traders and representatives were beginning to assert an "inherited", or independent right to be free of such things. The cause of the Boston traders was duly taken up in the House of Commons. The salt monopoly would "walk in the forefront of abuses" when parliament came to address the grievance of monopolies in 1597 and 1601. It was said to be costing the ports of Boston, Lynn and Hull £3,000 a year.[47] This kind of unwanted burden on trade was no longer to be tolerated.

The ports along the east coast were engaged in a varied and thriving coastal and cross-channel trade, each of them serving a broad inland country, at the heart of the network of regional specialisation and exchange. Coal came down from the northeast region to East Anglia, which sent back its own specialised export of grain. Sheep farming and cloth manufacture flourished in combination. Salt arrived from France and Spain in return for coal and corn. Any kind of monopoly interruption was not just a tax or restriction on the assumed trading liberties of the particular "subject", but also a threat to the reciprocal workings of the market as a whole. The integrated market had developed through the exceptionally free flow of goods. So any arbitrary costs placed on trading routes now contradicted the character of economic activity. It was in this context that a study of Norfolk in the Elizabethan period found there were strong objections in the county to the administrative patents that empowered private individuals to levy rates for road and pier repairs. And it was in reaction to these impositions that the Norfolk gentry began to look at things in a constitutional perspective, and place a new stress on the power of parliament as the most promising means of asserting their desire to be free of monopoly patents.[48] This marks an important phase in the growth of political consciousness. It was seminal to the ambition to consolidate and extend the rights of consent, when MPs and their constituents turned to parliament to secure them against arbitrary exactions, and to promote a right to freedom of trade.

The radical force of the emerging principle was strikingly illustrated in a prudently anonymous tract of the late 1580s, asserting a general right of freedom of trade. This in effect transferred the protest of the Boston traders onto a national stage. It took exception to the whole concept of corporations, which it regarded as tending inevitably towards monopoly. The writer condemned all monopolies on the basis that they constituted the engrossing of trade into the hands of one or a few, "which ought to be free and common to all the citizens of the said commonwealth". This was the cutting edge of freedom of trade, allowing no privileges and no exceptions. No corporation should be allowed to exclude everyone else from a trade. The idea that any privileged body or individual should be granted a monopoly of trade obstructing the interests of the rest of the kingdom was "against common right and the law, under which we are born, and is our inheritance".[49] The right of freedom of trade was being advanced as a universal requirement and a generalised belief.

With tracts like this in circulation, and an independent right of freedom of trade being widely asserted, the great monopoly companies began to feel a little insecure in their privileges. In fact, the first sign of a momentum building up behind a free trade movement was the appearance in print of attempts to pre-empt it, written by apologists of the privileged companies. Thus in 1601, John Wheeler produced an extended defence of the record and status of the Merchant Adventurers. It did not help the credibility of his case, however, that he happened to be secretary of the said Merchant Adventurers. The timing and content of the piece confirm that the strength of the demand for freedom of trade had become very apparent by the end of the sixteenth century. Wheeler deplored the notion of a freedom where all were "left to their own greedy appetites", and declared that the "governed and well ordered trade of the Merchant Adventurers is far to be preferred before a dispersed, straggling and promiscuous trade".

The weakness of Wheeler's case was that he said nothing to indicate exactly why this "well ordered" trade was in the general public interest, and nothing to counter the growing conviction that the best overall economic benefit lay in freedom. By pointing the finger at "greedy appetites" he simply highlighted the free traders' perception of their right to due profits. Each line of argument only confirmed that the real beneficiary of a "governed" trade was the government, and that the monopoly was there to command the trade and its rewards in that interest. To those who complained that they could find no market outlet for their cloth, Wheeler said that the company was "sufficient and able" to buy up all the cloth that was produced. He claimed that this did not constitute a monopoly because the powers were proportioned among the members of the company. This merely reinforced the grievance of the generality of merchants who believed that the trade should be "proportioned" freely among them all. Wheeler was obliged to acknowledge that many regarded the Merchant Adventurers as an unacceptable restraint on "the cloth market at home" and that this objection had developed to a point where "Some men hold this to be against the liberty of the subject".[50] But he was unable to say anything that was likely to reverse the now-settled trend of public sentiment.

Wheeler was obviously aware of the growing strength of opinion in favour of freedom of trade, and he had anticipated the threat that it posed to the position of the Merchant Adventurers. His fears were borne out when the "free trade" movement appeared in full flow in the parliamentary session of 1604. In mid-April, a bill to promote "free liberty to trade into all countries" was introduced into the Commons by Sir Edwin Sandys. The intention was to break the restrictive monopoly powers of the Merchant Adventurers, and for good measure the powers exercised by the Russia, Eastland, East India and Turkey Companies in their respective trading spheres. The bill sought to make it lawful for any of the king's subjects to have free passage and trade into any country, and declared that any grant of a privilege that tended to create a monopoly should be void. It is something of an understatement to say that this was "to some degree an assault on the government, which had favoured the great companies".[51] Tudor governments had indeed given strong support to the Merchant Adventurers, not least because the company provided an essential and substantial source of loans and cash flow for the royal coffers. But the threat from the free trade movement was not just an isolated technical hitch—it called into question the whole basis of the crown's financial support systems. The bill queried the validity of the king's power to create monopolies. In fact, it incorporated the assertion of a general liberty from imposed restrictions, and this was the platform from which a series of challenges to the prerogatives of the crown would be launched.

It was notable that the initiative appeared to come from the general body of merchants themselves. The Venetian Ambassador recorded that, "the Lower House, in a petition complaining of monopolies signed by many merchants, has dissolved all companies".[52] That might indeed have been the effect if the bill had taken its proposed course. It reflected the view of the radical free trade pamphlet of the 1580s that privileges always inclined towards monopoly and should therefore be rejected per se. This uncompromising position was now revealed as a commitment shared by the broad body of merchants. The further suggestion that any grant tending in that direction should be held void was a direct challenge to the powers of the crown. It was indicative of the economic force behind the movement, and the political implications that it carried, that the merchants were now prepared to assert a right of freedom of trade in contradiction of the royal government.

And of course it was not just the merchants. To pass the Commons the measure needed to have wide support among the gentry who now composed the great majority of the House, and in this it was certainly not lacking. In fact the bill had gained not only the acceptance but also the enthusiastic commitment of most MPs. It was passed "by a sweeping vote".[53] Sir Henry Beaumont, who represented Plympton and spoke consistently in favour of individual freedoms, wondered that any should wish to speak against it.[54] It may indeed be said that freedom of trade was now displayed as the economic "policy" of the House of Commons. And, as will be seen ahead, it remained so throughout the early Stuart period. The fact that it was fully embraced by the Commons makes it clear that the campaign was broadly representative of public opinion. And this is one of many reasons to question the tendency of modern historians to characterise "free trade" sentiment as just a sectional interest, reflecting the resentment of the out-ports against the power of London. London was in any case only one port, and not as dominant in its proportion of trade as is sometimes assumed. W. G. Hoskins found that in the middle of Elizabeth's reign the combined trade of the East Anglian ports was greater than that of London. Furthermore, the out-ports stretched in some number around the entire coast of the kingdom, servicing the coastal or overseas trade of every region. Their shared opposition to monopoly powers was far more than sectional. There was in fact a general movement of the broad body of merchants against the restraints imposed by monopoly privileges. It seems indeed that free trade sentiment was even the majority view among the merchants of the capital. When Sandys reported back from the committee on 21 May, he told the House that the protests against monopoly restrictions had come not only from the out-ports, but also from the general body of the merchants of London, three-quarters of whom were said to be in favour of the bill.[55]

But the single most important indication of the universal force of the idea of "free trade" within the kingdom was that it had developed in association with a general principle. It manifested the emerging psychology of freedom of trade, not only among merchants, but also among manufacturers and artisans, and indeed among landowners and farmers. It was a freedom that was being assumed and applied in all economic fields. Its broad significance was such that it was now being demanded as a right of the subject. The bill was inevitably unacceptable to the government, but it retains great significance as the first indication that the merchants and their representatives in the Commons were prepared to challenge the position of the crown in the name of freedom of trade. It underlines the fact that the subjects' claim to the absolute property of their possessions was advanced in the context of trading rights. The expressed justification for the bill was the first public statement of that principle, and it was announced with ringing force. "All subjects are born inheritable, as to their lands, so also to the exercise of their industry in those trades . . . it is against the natural right and liberty of the subjects of England to restrict it to some few".[56]

Notes

1. M. Bloch, *Land and Work in Medieval Europe*, trans. J. F. Andrew, (London 1967), p. 49
2. These are limitations for example in the analysis offered by J. P. Somerville, *Politics and Ideology in England, 1605 to 1640*, (London 1986), esp. chap. 5
3. See, for instance, D. Underdown, *Revel, Riot and Rebellion*, (Oxford 1987), pp. 19–20
4. R. H. Tawney, *Religion and the Rise of Capitalism*, (Harmondsworth 1966), pp. 179–96
5. J. Appleby, *Economic Thought and Ideology in Seventeenth Century England*, (Princeton 1978); C. B. Macpherson, *The Political Theory of Possessive Indibidualism*, (Oxford 1962)
6. J. Thirsk, *The Agrarian History of England and Wales 1500–1640*, (Cambridge 1967), pp. 205–6; P. Brandon, *The Sussex Landscape*, (London 1974), pp. 146–8; "The Common Lands and Wastes of Sussex", PhD. thesis, (London 1963), pp. 307–10
7. A. Macfarlane, *The Origins of English Individualism*, (Oxford 1972)
8. J. Bohstedt, *The Politics of Provision*, (Farnham 2010)

9. M. Wilks, *The Problem of Sovereignty in the Later Middle Ages*, (Cambridge 1967), pp. 27–31; J. Huizinga, *The Waning of the Middle Ages*, (Harmondsworth 1976), pp. 206–7; and see above, pp. 37–39, for a fuller picture of communalism on the open fields
10. William Langland, *Piers the Ploughman*, ed. J. Goodridge, (Harmondsworth 1966), pp. 81, 84, 87
11. See above, p. 44
12. Thomas More, *Utopia*, ed. J. Warrington, (London 1978), pp. 26–7
13. Ibid, p. 50
14. Ibid
15. Robert Crowley, "The Way to Wealth and An Information", in *The Select Works of Robert Crowley*, EETS, e series, XV, (London 1872), pp. 132, 142–4, 157
16. *A Discourse of the Commonweal* (1549), ed. M. Dewar, (Virginia 1969), p. 53
17. Hugh Latimer, "First Sermon Preached Before Edward VI", I March 1549, *The Works of Hugh Latimer*, ed. G. E. Corrie, *Parker Society*, (Cambridge 1844–5), I, p. 101
18. *A Discourse of the Commonweal*, p. 53
19. Henry Best, "Rural Economy in Yorkshire 1641", *Surtees Society XXXIII* (1857), pp. 74, 118
20. More, *Utopia*, p. 44
21. Robert Crowley, "Epigrams", in *The Select Works of Robert Crowley*, EETS, e series, XV, p. 67
22. *A Discourse of the Commonweal*, pp. 53, 119
23. Ibid, p. 119
24. A. Everitt, "The Open Market", in *Agrarian History of England and Wales: 1500–1640*, ed. J Thirsk, (Cambridge 1967), pp. 490, 496, 500
25. J. Chartres, *Internal Trade in England 1500–1700*, (London 1977), p. 13
26. Tawney, *Religion and the Rise of Capitalism*, p. 52
27. M. Overton, *Agricultural Revolution*, (Cambridge 1996), p. 133
28. Bohstedt, *The Politics of Provision*, p. 68
29. N. Henning, *A Godly Treatise Concerning the Lawful Use of Riches*, (London 1578), p. 6
30. William Harrison, "Of Fairs and Markets", in *Tudor Economic Documents*, eds. R. H. Tawney and E. Power, (London 1951), III, p. 73
31. Robert Loder, cited in Overton, *The Agricultural Revolution*, pp. 18–19
32. A. Everitt, "The Market for Agricultural Produce", in *Agrarian History of England and Wales*, ed. J. Thirsk, (Cambridge 1967), IV, p. 586
33. *Lex Mercatoria* (1622), cited Tawney, *Religion and the Rise of Capitalism*, p. 181
34. *A Discourse of the Commonweal*, p. 96
35. Ibid, p. 117
36. Ibid, p. 119
37. Ibid, pp. 54–5
38. *Commons Debates 1621*, ed. W. Notestein, (New Haven 1935), V, p. 93
39. *A Discourse of the Commonweal*, p. 90
40. Ibid, p. 59
41. Piers Ploughman's Exhortation, (circa 1550), BL 1653/8, un-paginated, but as counted, pp. 3,7
42. *Tudor Economic Documents*, eds. R. Tawney and E. Power, (London 1951), II, p. 188
43. Ibid, p. 185

44. Ibid, pp. 223–5
45. J. E. Neale, *Elizabeth I and Her Parliaments,* (London 1953), I, p. 118
46. Ibid
47. J. E. Neale, *Elizabeth I and Her Parliaments,* (London 1954), II, p. 378
48. A Hassell-Smith, *Government and Politics in Norfolk 1558–1603,* (Oxford 1974), pp. 282–92, 338
49. *A Discourse of Corporations,* (1587–9), in *Tudor Economic Documents,* (London 1951), III, pp. 266–7
50. J. Wheeler, *A Treatise of Commerce,* (London 1601), in *Tudor Economic Documents,* ed Tawney and Power, (London 1924), III, p. 293
51. W. Notestein, *The House of Commons 1604–10,* (Yale 1971), p. 106
52. Molin to the Doge, June 23, 1604, *CSP Venetian, 1603–7*, pp. 161–3
53. Notestein, *The House of Commons 1604–10*, p. 108
54. Ibid., pp. 14, 117
55. Ibid., pp. 112–13
56. *Commons Journal*, I, p. 218

7 Economic Roots of Political Change

The Merchant-Gentry Alliance Against Prerogative Customs Dues; the Central, Long-Term Challenge to the Crown—"To Have a Certainty"[1]

The claim of absolute property grew from the assumption of a right of freedom of trade in the general context of economic activity, rather than in the defence of landed property as such. The conceptual link between freedom of trade and absolute property found clear expression in the dispute over prerogative impositions, and the great constitutional debate in parliament in 1610. This was the first time that the idea of absolute property was explicitly advanced. It produced a fully-fledged confrontation between representative rights and the royal prerogative. It was the first occasion that the discretionary powers of the crown were challenged by the House of Commons on the basis of a general right of consent. This was an active demonstration of the symbiotic link between the two factors previously identified as crucial to the distinctive development of an absolute property right in England. One was the exceptional context of trading freedom, and the growing desire to make it a principle of liberty. The other was the special status attained by the concept of representative consent, which offered the most suitable and effective means to assert such freedoms.

The impositions controversy followed hard on the heels of the disputes over monopolies, and was in fact closely connected with those earlier confrontations, and with the popular demands and political tensions to which they had led. These interconnections should be underlined. The tendency of recent historiography has been to misrepresent monopolies and impositions as separate issues, or isolated occurrences, resulting from temporary pragmatic problems that flared up, then went away, with no on-going political momentum.[2] This supposition served the purposes of a revisionist generation whose principal aim was to deny the coherent force of parliamentary ambitions. But the picture of dispersal did not reflect the reality. In truth, the campaigns against monopolies and impositions had a shared genesis, and the combined and continuing political force of this was clear and significant. The same essential rationale and motivation was present in each case, deriving from a general desire to be allowed to trade in conditions of freedom from arbitrary restrictions and exactions. This was the common ground that generated a broad and coordinated challenge to the royal prerogative in the fields of public finance and regulation, throughout the early decades of the seventeenth century.

So, in keeping with its name, the impositions dispute was about trading rights, and it was initiated and played out in that context. It has sometimes been suggested that the Commons made a stand on the issue because they saw impositions as a threat to the right of consent to taxation on landed property.[3] But in fact the parliamentary argument took the opposite line. In the debate of 1610 the right of consent to land taxes was not regarded as in doubt, or in need of defence, it was simply taken as read. The positive and specific aim of the parliamentary side was to extend that already established principle of consent, and have it applied to the customs dues as well As William Hakewill said, since land taxes "which come but seldom were brought to certainty, then much more custom might, which hapneth daily".[4] They were aiming to correct this and turn the matter in their favour on exactly the same principle as first enunciated in the free trade bill of 1604, and reiterated in 1610 by Nicholas Fuller, asserting the same "right and liberty of the subjects in their lawful and free trades, mysteries and manual occupations as in their lands and goods".[5]

The dispute had begun in 1606, when the London merchant John Bate refused to pay the imposition on imported currants. He was not a lone voice. The initiative was widely supported by merchants in the capital.[6] It is interesting to ask why the protest came at that particular moment, when similar impositions had been paid without demur over many decades in the past. In fact, the timing is useful evidence of the real character of the demand. It was a further manifestation of the growing assertion of a right of freedom of trade that had recently come to the fore in other ways, too. It was no coincidence that the radical free trade bill had been introduced just two years earlier, also with the support of most of the merchants of London. And in 1606 the free traders had brought in another, more limited measure, providing for free trade to France and Spain, which they actually managed, with great satisfaction and not a little surprise, to get onto the statute book. The attack on impositions was thus part of a broadly held ambition to assert a principled right of freedom from arbitrary exactions and restrictions across various fields of activity, and this was coming into the open in the first decade of the seventeenth century.

Once again, the initiative in the protest against impositions came from the merchants, as it had with the free trade bill of 1604. But just as then, it also had the support and commitment of the gentry as represented in the Commons. Parliament was already directly concerned with the issue before the specific dispute arose. The impositions on currants and other commodities, together with complaints against the raising of customs generally, and objections to a wide range of monopolies, were the main items on the Commons' list of grievances, when the case of John Bate was added to them. There was a sense that this might be particularly challenging. There were royal apologists in the House who were ready to assert the rights of the prerogative, and the weight of constitutional convention was behind them. They suggested in effect that the crown had no case to answer, and that Bate was simply guilty of transgressing the known and accepted rule. But the House also contained strong-willed oppositionists like Nicholas Fuller, who were prepared to assert a right of freedom of trade in the face of any obstruction. With such voices to embolden them, the majority in the Commons followed their instincts and determined that the merchants should be heard. As before, the merchants themselves stated their case vociferously. One threatened indeed "to leave all rather than this shall stand—go beyond seas".[7] This was the core freedom of trade argument, to which John Hales had given early expression in 1559. Impositions were, "a mean to make no English merchants".[8] Radical freedom of trade was an uncompromising stance, and a body of opinion among merchants and MPs had decided that it was now of sufficient practical importance that it must be brought to an issue. This would produce the most persistent and contentious political difference with the king.

The House resolved that the articles should be added to the list of grievances, which was in fact largely dominated by questions of trade—including objections to the impositions on currants and tobacco, the increase of customs dues generally, and the ever-widening range of patents of monopoly.[9] This held fire because of the recess, which gave the government the chance to pre-empt what was potentially an unacceptable challenge. The king referred the matter to the Court of Exchequer, which unanimously confirmed that he had the right to levy customs by prerogative. Chief Baron Fleming added the fateful gloss that the monarch did this by virtue of the discretionary authority that he was free to exercise as guardian of the general public good. This, said Fleming, was most conspicuously the case in respect of relations with foreign states, one aspect of which was the regulation of trade, and the king would be unable to carry out those responsibilities without the prerogative right to levy impositions at his discretion. This assessment was very sound both as reason of state and as constitutional doctrine. Leading lawyers in the House of Commons, like William Hakewill and Sir Edward Coke, at first found nothing in the judgement to which they could object. The question of impositions remained on the Commons' list of grievances, but when it was finally presented, in the autumn of 1606, the king could respond peremptorily that his right to levy prerogative impositions had been endorsed by the law lords, and no more need be said.

Robert Cecil, who had taken on the unenviable task of managing the treasury, felt it safe to exploit the Exchequer decision, and imposed duties on a wide range of commodities. The principle of freedom of trade, far from being advanced as the merchants intended, had suffered a substantial setback. Impositions had become more systematic and extensive. Worse still, Fleming's statement threatened to place the customs dues in a realm of "absolute" power, outside the representative sphere. This was the opposite of parliamentary and mercantile purposes, which was to bring trading freedoms under the control of rights of consent, as they said in 1604, "so to their lands, so also to the exercise of their industry in those trades". It is a measure of the importance, and indeed the necessity that they attached to the principle, that their response was to redouble their determination to assert it, and to look for ways in which the Exchequer judgement might be challenged. So when the House reassembled in 1610 there ensued the first outright constitutional clash between king and Commons—the impositions dispute.

In theory, the agenda for the session was dominated by a possible bargain over the king's feudal rights, focusing on questions of tenure and wardship. But an indication of the further reach of the Commons' ambition came in Lord Treasurer Salisbury's opening contributions to the session. He clearly had some apprehension of a developing challenge to the royal power of impositions, for he found it necessary to state that there was no room for movement in that respect, since "in some things the prerogative was inherent and inseparable, as in impositions".[10] On the other hand, although the rights of wardship were also part of the prerogative, they were not, apparently, an inseparable part. The provision of wardship might be made less onerous, or even abolished altogether, if the Commons were to offer the crown a permanent income instead.[11] In other words, wardship might be up for negotiation, but the king's power of impositions was not. The Commons' response confirmed where their priority lay. An end to wardship was certainly sought by many landed gentlemen, but the benefit to the broader constituencies would be small, and the incentive was not sufficient to get the deal done. The Commons' main ambition was of a more general, public nature. It was to extend the range of rights of consent across the field of government finance, in this instance by launching a full-scale attack on the king's prerogative of impositions, though they had been told, categorically, that this was out of bounds. It is clear that the determination to undermine the power of impositions was an imperative for them. In common with the broad classes of merchants and yeoman freeholders whose interests they represented, MPs were primarily concerned to establish the principle of freedom of trade, by denying the right of the king to set customs dues by discretion. So as already suggested, the development of an "absolute" property right was less about changes in tenure than about the assertion of a freedom to trade and use property without arbitrary restrictions and exactions. It was in this context that the claim of absolute property was now explicitly advanced.

The issue was brought into the main political arena at the beginning of May 1610, just before the negotiations over the proposed deal on tenures reached another impasse. The starting gun was fired when Sir Edwin Sandys reported from the committee charged with formulating the petition of grievances. They had come, he said, to the question of impositions. The king's stance, already stated, was that there was no basis on which they could address the matter. But Sandys asked the House to authorise a search for precedents, which was in effect an attempt to discover some grounds on which they could challenge the decision in Bate's case. The king attempted to nip this in the bud with an instruction that they should not presume to query his prerogative, or propose laws against it. It was not their place he said, "to question what a king may do".[12] Perhaps James would have done better to leave them to their own devices, and simply dismiss whatever they came up with. But he knew that their conclusion was bound to involve a challenge to his prerogatives, and he obviously wanted to pre-empt this by disallowing any such thing in advance. James understood that the essence of a discretionary power lay precisely in being beyond question.

The Commons queried the provenance of the message, apparently not wanting to believe that the king was trying to prevent them from dealing with a matter that they considered so vital. On the twenty-first of May James came in person to remove any doubts. He reiterated his position—saying that it was not lawful for them to question what a king may do, such as his right to impose. It was a power that English kings had always possessed, and which had been exercised in living memory by Mary and Elizabeth. He had heard that there were precedents showing that English kings had sometimes waived certain impositions, but what monarchs had done as temporary concessions was not a measure of what they could do if they wished. He repeated that the Commons did not have the right to dispute the power as such, but only to complain of any particular inconveniences that might have arisen. He said that he would consult them about future levies, but could not promise to follow their advice. The power would always be his. There were many things that he might choose to do with parliament, but could do without them if he wished.[13]

The tone of the speech was measured, and reflected the true and existing balance of rights in the matter, yet the Commons received it as if it was a greatly exaggerated view of the royal power. John Chamberlain said that it was "so little to their satisfaction that I hear it bred generally much discomfort, to see our monarchical power and regal prerogative strained so high".[14] This seemed, by any standards, a rather extreme and overstated reaction. In one sense it showed how settled and determined they had become in their desire that the power of impositions should be brought under the control of representative consent. But most importantly, it also indicated that they now ascribed the representative concept specific constitutional force. James's assertion that there were many things that he chose to do with parliament, but could do without them if he wished, ran counter to the growing popular assumption that sovereign powers should only be exercised in parliament, on the model of legislative sovereignty. It was becoming the settled belief of MPs that all such erstwhile discretionary acts should henceforth only be performed with parliamentary consent, and that it was no longer acceptable for the king to do these things alone. This critical difference of opinion had emerged into the light of day in 1604, when a suggestion in the Canons that the king could give church regulations the force of law induced a Commons' statement that James was "misinformed" if he thought that he could enforce such orders other than "by consent in parliament", as with the statutes.[15] It seems that in the view of MPs, all binding general levies and regulations were now to be interpreted as law, and only made in parliament. It was in this context that the king's assertion of a residual personal sovereignty might be seen as the "regal prerogative strained so high".

So the Commons' stance in the impositions dispute was to reassert the idea that sovereign legislation could only be made in parliament, and exploit the force of this by extending it to cover the customs dues. James Whitelocke expressed the assurance with which the concept of representative sovereignty was now held. He said that their liberties rested on two principles. One was that the subjects' property could not be taken without consent. The other was that the law could not be made without the consent of parliament. So the edict of a prince was not a law.[16] Whitelocke was now asserting this in contradiction of the king. His first proposition was only half true—the right of consent had long applied to landed property, but not to customs on trade. It was only since 1604 that the MPs and the merchants had been seeking to extend it in that direction. The second proposition was, however, absolutely true. In England, since the mid-sixteenth century, it had become the unique and accepted constitutional position that sovereign law could only be made in parliament. This did not of itself show that the king had no right to impose customs dues, but it did create a general presumption that "the edict of a prince was not a law", and this could be used to undermine the prerogative of impositions.

As I have written at greater length elsewhere, these radical implications were embedded in the distinctive concept of representative sovereign law that developed in England in the mid-sixteenth century.[17] It derived from the circumstances of the Break with Rome in the 1530s, which was achieved by the destruction of the independent legislative authority of the universal church, and the elevation of parliamentary statute into the one, omni-competent, overriding sovereign law of the land. Henry VIII, or at least his minister Thomas Cromwell, had found that the moral authority of the Church of Christendom could only be displaced by the moral force of parliament as embodying the beliefs and desires of the whole kingdom, since, in the words of the theory's leading advocate, the lawyer Christopher St German: "it could not be thought that the deed of the king, the Lords and all the Commons could declare a thing against the truth".[18] This was the basis on which there emerged in England a distinctive form of sovereign law that took its binding authority from the capacity of parliament to reflect the will of what Richard Hooker called the "entire society": "The lawful power of making laws to command whole societies belongs so properly unto the same entire societies". And it was Hooker who most clearly outlined the radical thrust entailed in the idea that the king could not make sovereign law of his own volition. "For any prince or potentate of any kind whatsoever on earth to exercise the same of himself . . . is no better than mere tyranny . . . laws are they not therefore which public approbation hath not made so".[19] This was a precept that lent itself to general application should the entire society come to find itself seriously inconvenienced by other prerogative powers, like the king's right of imposing the customs dues.

In view of what was involved, James really had no choice but to try to pre-empt the attack, but in the event his initiative proved counterproductive, for it gave the Commons a pretext to assert that their liberty of free speech was being denied. The king had strengthened their hand, for although they had no legal warrant for disputing the prerogative of impositions, they did in certain respects have a right of free speech, and this was, by its very nature, open to extension. In the past, their privilege of free speech had been held by grace of the crown. In effect, it was limited to matters that the monarch was happy for them to discuss, such as their particular, practical concerns; and in any case they had no real basis for discussing anything else. But in the second half of the sixteenth century, as the Commons became involved in legislating for all causes, great and small, the range of their direct interests increased. It was in their concern about the succession, and the marital plans of the Tudor Queens, that they began to push out the boundaries of free speech. In 1576, Peter Wentworth gave the first airing to the claim that it was an inherited, or independent right, which entitled them to discuss anything.[20]

In 1610, the Commons were taking a further, and more threatening step, by redefining their private or local interests as a collective, national requirement. There ensued a heated discussion about exactly what the Commons had the right to discuss. It sounded like an exercise in hair-splitting, as each side glossed the issue according to political preference. But the difference reflected an important development. The Solicitor General, Sir Francis Bacon, said that they should restrict themselves to practical and individual grievances, for they were entitled to discuss "the right or interest of any subject or the commonwealth". He was using the term commonwealth in its older sense of the welfare of the populace, and trying to limit the Commons to their traditional sphere of the pragmatic and particular, unconnected with general issues of authority or political principle. MPs pointed out, however, that the power of impositions was now seen as affecting everyone's rights.

> If it be true as Mr Solicitor confessed that the parliament may not be inhibited to debate of anything which concerns the rights of particular subjects, much less may they be inhibited in this matter of impositions, which concerns the rights and interests of all the subjects in general in those things which they enjoy.[21]

In part, this reflected the arrival of a coordinated national market, which engendered a general awareness of the economic conditions that were most efficient and desirable. Freedom of trade had become a common imperative. The argument highlighted a critical moment of change. The issues that the Commons addressed were ceasing to be just a multitude of local interests, and coming to be perceived, in their eyes at least, as overall public priorities. In the second half of the sixteenth century, there had emerged a series of freestanding, or self-defining national interests, that is to say general public concerns that could be identified without necessary reference to the wishes of the crown, and which were, in the event, often asserted in contradiction of royal policy. The popular commitment to freedom of trade, now in contention with the prerogative of impositions, was the most important domestic example.

The new perspective clearly reflected the transition that had taken place in the scope of economic activity during the sixteenth century. At the end of the fifteenth century, economic interests had still been essentially local and pragmatic, even when they had involved sensitive general issues, like a shortage of work or grain. But by the end of the sixteenth century, there was a new context—an integrated national market that worked to reciprocal patterns of regional specialisation and exchange, in a climate of exceptional trading freedoms and substantial profits. Every aspect of the new market tended to engender a belief that freedom of trade was a natural and necessary aspect of successful economic life. In 1604 this emerged as the claim of a principled right to liberty from arbitrary restrictions and exactions on the product of "their industry in those trades". It was on the same principle that in 1610 the royal prerogative of impositions on trade was taken to affect "the rights and interests of all the subjects in general in the things that they enjoy".

In the circumstances the king would probably have been wise to adhere to his original intention not to allow the House to pursue the matter. But while mounting their high horse of free speech, the Commons had, with a degree of low cunning, played to James's weaknesses, in particular the continuing inadequacy of his financial situation. They said that their intention was not to dispute the king's power, but only to understand its basis, and they took care to hint that if they were given permission to discuss it, this would encourage them to loosen the parliamentary purse strings. The statement was well judged, if entirely disingenuous. The king relented and allowed a debate, while underlining the shortsightedness of this decision by reiterating that they did not have the right to question the power of impositions as such, but only its particular practical inconveniences. What ensued was the first great encounter over the balance of political sovereignty in England, the initial confrontation between the royal prerogative and the assertion of representative rights.

At the end of June and the beginning of July 1610, the great impositions debate took place. The question before the House was quite clear: Did the king have a right to raise customs dues by prerogative? The answer in law was also quite clear, and it told in favour of the king. Impositions were an anciently held and recently confirmed right of the crown, which had been exercised with particular vigour over the past half century. But the force of the position in law was contradicted by the great weight of sentiment in the Commons. Most MPs wished, simply and specifically, to bring the setting of the customs dues within the sphere of representative consent. So a long series of parliamentary speakers stepped forward to declare that it was unlawful for the king to raise customs dues by imposition, and that they should only be levied by consent in parliament. The Commons were doing what James had forbidden them to do, and indeed what no subjects of an English king had ever presumed to do before, that is to say they were challenging the validity of one of his most essential prerogatives.

It was difficult for them to make a case in terms of the content of the law. They could cite medieval precedents that for certain times and purposes kings had agreed that customs should be raised by consent. But this had never become a general principle, and it did not alter the orthodox constitutional position that the king could raise taxes by prerogative when he judged it necessary for the public safety, as recently affirmed by the Barons of the Exchequer. The real strength of the Commons' case was political. It lay partly in the force of their determination, as representatives of the kingdom, to establish a comprehensive right of consent in the raising of the customs. It also lay in the fact that parliament did now possess a sovereign *legislative* authority that gave them a rationale for asserting that the king should not be permitted to exercise such powers alone.

The opening speaker on the parliamentary side was Nicholas Fuller, who was one of the most uncompromising of free traders, and was often first into the lists. He set out the parliamentarian agenda very clearly. Their aim was no less than to displace the royal power of impositions, by extending the right of consent to cover the raising of the customs dues:

> That by the laws of England the subjects have such property in their lands and goods as that without their consent the king can take no part thereof from them lawfully, by any kind of imposition or

> otherwise without an act of parliament . . . that the laws of England do as tenderly preserve the right and liberty of the subjects in their lawful and free trades, mysteries and manual occupations as in their lands and goods.[22]

This was in essence the same principle that they had first enunciated in 1604. But it was rather more explicit in its claim of an absolute property right, which was thus being asserted specifically in the context of an attempt to extend the right of consent to cover the raising of dues on trades and manufactures. As already suggested, the emergence of a distinctive notion of absolute property in early seventeenth-century England occurred not primarily in relation to the land, but rather in the general context of freedom of trade.

The principal means by which this was to be asserted was by taking their unfounded claim to freedom from impositions and attaching it to their well-founded claim of freedom from prerogative law. This platform was set out at the beginning of Nicholas Fuller's speech. He offered a logical syllogism. The major premise was that in England the laws could not be made or altered without consent. The minor premise was that freedom from impositions had once been a law. The conclusion was that the freedom could not be taken away without consent, and that therefore the king did not possess the power to set impositions by prerogative.[23] Fuller declared that "by this form of argument, all objections that have been made or can be made and although it be a judgement for the king by the Barons of the Exchequer, are easily answered and avoided". In one sense Fuller had overrated his achievement. The inner force of the proposition was not secure. The weakness was in the minor premise, which referred to the ancient statutes in which the king had waived some impositions in certain commodities at certain times. But this did not show that the law had ever provided a general freedom from impositions. The statutes were more reasonably glossed as qualified concessions of the royal grace. They did nothing to undermine the accepted constitutional principle that the monarch possessed a discretionary right in the setting of customs dues.

Nevertheless, Fuller's confidence was not entirely misplaced. There was a more powerful logic contained in his syllogism, based on the nature of the legislative process, rather than the content of the law. However limited the force of the medieval statutes might be, the setting of impositions could be construed as overriding them in some respect. For the Commons to interpret this as "changing the law" was a sleight of hand, but it successfully transposed the debate into a question of the nature of sovereign power. The idea that the law could only be made or changed by consent created a presumption that the king did not by his own patent possess the kind of sovereign power that could bind his subjects. It might be said to follow that the king could not legitimately set impositions on trade. In this way Fuller had associated the raising of customs with the right of consent in its most fundamental and influential form. He had based a presumptive right of representative customs on the undoubted right of representative laws. If the most sovereign power of lawmaking could only be exercised in parliament, was it not logical to suppose that the sovereign power of setting the customs dues should also be subject to representative consent? In this way the parliamentarians could win the political argument even if they could not win the legal case.

The force of this was such that royal apologists felt the need to attack the premise of the syllogism because they feared being wrong-footed by Fuller's attempt to direct the issue away from the content of the law, and towards the form in which it was made. They had a reasonable point when they accused Fuller of sidestepping the legal facts. But another prominent parliamentary speaker, James Whitelocke, came to his support, putting the emphasis back on the power of legislation, in a way that made it clear that Fuller was expressing what leading parliamentarians regarded as the authentic strength of their case.

> It hath been alleged that those which in this case have enforced their reasons from this maxim of ours 'that the king cannot alter the law' have diverted the question. I say under favour they have not; for that in effect is the very question in hand; for if he alone out of parliament may impose, he altereth the law of England. So in this point the question is, whether the King's patent hath the power of the law, or not, for if it be not maintained that he hath, it can never be concluded that he can transfer the property of his subjects' goods to himself, without the assent of them.[24]

The argument was strained, yet powerful. It was really just another way of expressing their desire to be rid of prerogative customs dues, but they were putting it in a context of general legitimacy by exploiting the dictum that the king could not make sovereign law alone. Fuller and Whitelocke were taking the fact that the king could not legislate by patent, and extending it into the idea that he could not take any kind of property without consent. In effect they were saying that if the king raised customs by prerogative it was *as if* he was making law by patent, and since in England the king's patent no longer carried the force of law, this could not possibly be valid.

The same argument underlay Whitelocke's more famous contribution to the debate, in which he outlined the idea that the king had two levels of power—one that he exercised by his own authority, and another that he could only exercise by consent, in parliament. The killer punch was that since it was only in parliament that the king could perform the sovereign functions of making law and raising taxes, it was therefore the second power that was "the greater of the two and doth rule and control the other".[25] Here was the explicit invocation of the radical potential entailed in the theory of sovereign representative law—the notion that the "absolute" power of lawmaking could only be exercised by parliamentary consent, and not by the king alone. In the light of this it could surely be concluded that he did not possess the right to raise money by patent either. In 1610, Fuller and Whitelocke were employing this principle to undermine the king's prerogative in the raising of the customs dues. So the crux of the issue was indeed "whether the king's patent hath the force and power of the law". In their desire to be rid of impositions, Fuller and Whitelocke, and many others in the House, had come to the conclusion that the king's patent did not have the power of law in any field. All such sovereign functions, they suggested, should now be done by consent in parliament. Thus the central agenda of the parliamentarian movement was taking shape—it was to extend the concept of representative rights to cover all aspects of the raising of public monies, and the regulation of economic affairs.

So the claim of absolute property was first explicitly advanced in the context of extending representative rights to the raising of the customs. The essence of this development, and its political implications, was captured by the foremost political theorist of the time. Thomas Hobbes identified a new economic ethic, arising particularly among the citizens and traders of market towns, and entailing the belief that each man was, "so much master of whatsoever he possessed, that it could not be taken from him upon any pretence of common safety without his own consent".[26] This was a precise description of the claim that had actually been advanced in the impositions debate. It overturned the basic principles of "conditional" property, which were that the individual did not possess his property in complete freedom from the interests of the commons, or the demands of the king. A speech by Sir Heneage Finch showed exactly how the "conditional" concept had been supplanted by a theory of "absolute" property. "Every man hath a property in his goods against the king as against all other men . . . and any man that would take away any man's goods must show his reason for it".[27]

The parliamentarian aim of establishing representative control of public finance became clear in the impositions debate of 1610, but we should be careful not to regard this as the genesis of the idea. It is important to recall that the two main principles on which the parliamentary case turned were both set out in 1604. One was contained in the justification of the radical free trade bill, which was in effect the first public statement of a right of freedom of trade: "all subjects are born inheritable, as to their lands, so to the exercise of their industry in those trades. It is against the right and liberty of the subjects of England to restrict it to some few".[28] The other was in the Commons' reaction to a suggestion in the Canons that the king could give church regulations the force of law by his act alone. The Commons asserted that on the contrary, James was "misinformed" if he supposed that he could enforce such orders other than "by consent in parliament", as with the statutes.[29] From those two tenets flowed the proposition that the king could not set customs dues by his own patent, and they must only be raised in parliament. It seems that this claim was developing, at least in its core components, by 1604.

The Merchant-Gentry Combination

The parliamentary agenda in 1610 was specifically to incorporate the levying of the customs dues within the sphere of representative consent. One of the most distorting misconceptions of recent historiography has been the suggestion that the battle against impositions was undertaken as a surrogate defence of the principle of consent in land taxation.[30] This was, very importantly, not the case. Generalised apprehensions that "if the king may impose, what need he call a parliament?" derived from an anxiety that the services of parliament, and especially the legislative function, might be curtailed. This did not reflect a concern to defend the principle of consent to land taxes as such. The parliamentarians took the opposite approach. In the debate, and in all associated Commons' statements, the right of consent to land taxes was taken as read. The express aim in 1610 was to extend that right to the customs dues. This was stated just as plainly as it had been in respect of the Free Trade bill in 1604. The assertion was that people were "inheritable" in the property of their trades, just as in the property of their land. Fuller's summary was unequivocal: "the laws of England do as tenderly preserve the right and liberty of the subjects in their lawful and free trades, mysteries, and manual occupations as in their lands and goods".[31]

Fuller waxed lyrical about the value of commercial practice. "For no trade in England ought more to be cherished than the trade of merchandise, which doth greatly uphold the wealth, strength and credit of the land, and doth vent whatsoever the fruitful labour of any subject doth yield".[32] This reflected an awareness of the growing scale, substance and potential of the nation's trading activity, which undoubtedly concentrated minds on the importance of ensuring that the rewards were distributed in an appropriate manner. Fuller concluded that the law should "more tenderly preserve the subject's freedom of his trade (since by trades and occupations commonwealths are upholden) than the inheritance of his lands".[33]

Thomas Hobbes did not approve of the trend that he observed whereby each man was coming to consider himself "so much master of whatsoever he possessed, that it could not be taken from him upon any pretence of common safety without his own consent".[34] Hobbes regarded this as an infringement of the crown's necessary prerogatives, and he noted with distaste the commercial obsessions that were leading the merchants, traders and farmers to challenge the king's rights. He thought that they had become "mortal enemies" to taxation, "their only glory being to grow excessively rich by the wisdom of buying and selling".[35] The parliamentary view was indeed obsessive, but they placed it in a very positive light. A contribution to the debate from William Hakewill illustrated clearly how the claim of absolute property arose as a demand for trading freedoms in a rising market, and he showed precisely what the merchants would gain from an end to impositions. Trade now went on in every dimension, all the time. Hakewill observed that if subsidies "which came but seldom were brought to certainty, then much more custom might, which hapneth daily".[36] The desire to "have a certainty" conveys the real benefit that would come from an end to arbitrary levies. In a coordinated market of regional specialisation and exchange, the merchants needed to know that the conditions of trade would be subject to no interventions and exactions other than those agreed in parliament.

Just as historians have been reluctant to acknowledge that the impositions dispute was, as its name implied, actually *about* trading freedoms, so they have failed to recognise the powerful alliance of merchants and gentry that was driving the agenda. MPs' enthusiastic espousal of the merchants' cause illustrates the point made earlier that the rise of a claim of absolute property in England rested on two factors—the developing demand for a right of freedom of trade, and the growing status of the concept of consent as embodied in parliament. This was already in evidence in 1604, but the full force of it became apparent in 1610. The close association of merchants and gentry is reflected in the fact that most of the detail of the impositions debate referred to above comes from a set of records preserved by the merchants of Dartmouth. They had forged a relationship with the leading Commons free trader, the gentleman lawyer Nicholas Fuller. He had been a promoter of the radical free trade bill of 1604, and the limited but successful free trade act of 1606, which West Country merchants hailed as the only advance made so far towards the conditions of complete freedom in which they wished to trade. They were fully committed to the idea that the customs dues should only be set by consent in parliament, and in 1610, they were able to acquire drafts of Fuller's powerful oppositionist speeches asserting that principle.[37]

The Dartmouth representatives also compiled a set of rough notes of their own, recording other speeches that challenged the royal prerogative of impositions. One was that of William Jones, MP for Beaumaris, who shared the core commitment to freedom of trade, asserting that mercantile activity should in essence be free of restraints and impositions. He repeated a point made by Fuller and others, that although the king had the right to restrain trade in the event of national emergencies, even then he did not have the right to set impositions on the trade that was allowed. The parliamentary case was typified throughout by an absolute conviction that there should never be a right to take money arbitrarily. Jones asserted, somewhat optimistically, that it was enshrined in statute that "every merchant may freely pass and re-pass with his goods . . . none shall meddle with the goods of merchants". His conclusion was that "the king either by Common Law of Magna Carta cannot impose but by consent of parliament".[38] This was an earnest expression of desire rather than a discovery of fact, and it showed once again how far the MPs and merchants had convinced themselves of the principle that trade should be free of arbitrary impositions, and of the general idea that all sovereign powers should be exercised in parliament. Sir Heneage Finch, who spoke on 2nd July, made the even wilder assertion that parliaments were the original source of customs dues. It is not clear what he meant by this in historical terms, but it was another demonstration that in the eyes of these MPs and merchants, trading freedoms had become dependent on an elevated view of parliament's powers and the rights of representative consent. More practically Finch offered support for some kind of measure to enforce an injunction against impositions, calling for "an act of parliament to tie the king".[39] This was confronting political realities. Such an act would certainly be required to end the practice of impositions. But the king would never accept it, or treat the proposal as anything but anti-monarchical. It would be another three decades before James's successor found himself helpless in the hands of parliament, and MPs were able to put the necessary measure into place.

The merchants were taking a strong constitutional interest in parliament as the best hope of promoting the vital principle of freedom of trade, encouraged by the fact that the majority of MPs were also fully committed to the idea, with the focus on the shared and central aim of bringing the customs dues under representative control. The combination of merchants and gentry appears to have been distinctive to the English context, just like the exceptional force of the concept of consent, and the general demand for freedom of trade itself.[40] The king referred to the Commons as "merchant like".[41] This was not intended as a compliment. But nor was it likely to give them pause. The label reflected an important truth about the economic aspirations of the gentry. This was one of the many aspects of the Commons' activities that they pursued with positive determination, but which the king regarded as unorthodox or subversive. James had a much clearer perception than most modern historians of the distinctive character and aims of the English parliament, and the challenges that it posed to the position of the crown.

The parliamentary gentry were indeed merchant-like, and this was a very significant factor in the distinctive path along which the English polity was moving. The unique character and structure of the English House of Commons derived largely from the fact that the gentry had taken over the borough seats. In other European kingdoms, the Commons chamber was still constituted as originally conceived, that is to say it was composed essentially of the merchants and urban representatives. The English Commons had taken a different direction in part because of the existence of an unusually uniform nationwide network of administrative shires, which made the inclusion of county MPs useful for authorising general taxation. In its initial form the House contained just one gentleman to every four merchants. But the gentry were of greater social prominence, and their interest in parliament increased as their administrative role developed, and indeed as the Commons acquired another power denied to the European chambers—becoming active and equal participants with the king and the Lords in the process of legislation. So as the numbers and political horizons of the gentry expanded, they sought to enlarge their presence in the House by appropriating the borough seats. By the end of the sixteenth century the original balance had been reversed, and in a greatly enlarged House of Commons, there were four gentlemen MPs to every townsman.

Crucially, this did not diminish the influence of the mercantile sphere, which tended on the contrary to benefit from the change. The gentry took on board the main concerns of the towns and traders, not just because they had acquired representative responsibility for them, but also because they were inherently committed to the same essential interests and aims. In fact, they were actively involved in the activities and necessities of trade. The unusually high degree of participation of the English gentry in commercial affairs was noted in an important, though now neglected study by Theodore Rabb.[42] He set out to explain why a prominent member of the gentry, Sir Edwin Sandys, seemed to devote most of his time and energy to matters of trade. As the king had observed, this was not the kind of focus expected of a gentlemen. But Rabb discovered, like James himself, that Sandys was far from alone in this unusual tendency. In fact, a close interest in trade was a distinctive pre-occupation of the Elizabethan and early Stuart gentry in general. There were various factors that explain why the gentry became so involved in the trading sphere. At the broadest level, oceanic expansion and the founding of a trading empire was now the pre-eminent national project, displacing military ambitions, and the gentry had become a national representative class, with a defining sense of such public priorities. They had an equally significant involvement in the working of the domestic economy, which was now characterised by a coordinated market that generated economic relations between all commodities and classes. The new patterns of interregional exchange applied first and foremost to the products of the land, traded in bulk. And in absolute terms the gentry were the greatest gainers from the extended and intensified trading systems, which also gave them a direct concern with the prospects of the all-important cloth trade. As Joyce Appleby said, "with their entrepreneurial outlook and social leverage, members of the English landed class had forged a crucial link between market incentives and farming practices".[43] In every respect, freedom of trade from exactions and restraints had become the required condition of economic activity, for both merchants and gentry, whether in the assumption of a license to enclose the land, or the determination to displace the prerogative of impositions.

If the gentry's commitment to trade has been neglected, the capacity for radicalism among the merchants has been greatly underrated by historians of all persuasions. The modern tendency has been to emphasise the local and formal aspects of urban life, which might be interpreted in a conservative light. This overlooks the radical potential of their economic imperatives, and belies the distinctive fact that the market towns gave general and staunch support to parliament during the Civil War. Anthony Fletcher may be seen as exemplifying a pattern of avoidance. He noted the need to explain the enthusiasm with which many towns mobilised for parliament; then he offered reasons that hardly reflected the range and spontaneity of the phenomenon. He suggested that they viewed the king's forces as aggressors, and saw parliament as the guarantor of their local security.[44] In truth, if most of the market centres in England saw the king as an aggressor, it was not as an aggressor against their parochial position, but as an aggressor against the national provisions of parliament, on which the towns now placed a high value.

A recent article by Phil Withington perpetuates the tendency to restrict the urban outlook to a local dimension and avoid the significance of their economic character. Although he seems concerned that, unlike Civil War contemporaries, modern historians have not regarded the towns as notable participants in the mid-seventeenth-century struggles, Withington does not consider that this may be a failure to recognise the radicalism of the merchants' economic imperatives.[45] He is justifiably sceptical of Robert Brenner's view that the townsmen were more at odds with each other than with the policies of the royal government.[46] Yet he takes a not-dissimilar line himself. He starts from a memo of Samuel Hartlib's—encouraging the towns to maintain their military preparedness in the parliamentary cause. Hartlib puts this in a national perspective, but Withington turns it in upon itself. He postulates an idea of citizenship with a militaristic outlook inculcated by institutional rivalries within the town: "a field of conflict . . . constituted by configurations of civil institutions".[47] This is obscure and theoretical, and it is difficult to see what it could mean either in terms of the towns' working lives, or their motives in volunteering for parliament. Withington's picture bears no relation to the public preoccupations of the urban centres that figure in the present volume. The Dartmouth merchants had a dominant concern with freedom of trade, as manifested in their direct involvement in the parliamentary attack on impositions in 1610.[48] The same imperative appeared again in the 1620s, when in conjunction with the merchants of Plymouth they sought legislation to free them from a monopoly recently placed on the Newfoundland cod fishing. The bill had no chance of royal approval, but in 1624 the Commons issued an order unilaterally declaring free trade in the area and seeking on their own authority to nullify the restraints of the monopoly. The Plymouth merchants declared, with pointed intent, that they were preserving a copy of the order in their town chest. The merchants of Totnes had no part in the cod fishing, but were equally committed to freedom of trade, and hailed the act of 1606 for free trade into France and Spain as the most beneficial factor in the town's life "by wisdom of the state in parliament".[49] The disputes that occurred within the towns tended to be between the corporation and elements such as the church authorities, over facilities like almshouses and schools, as in Totnes in 1606 and Exeter in 1624. A significant feature was that they looked primarily to parliamentary legislation to resolve the issues.[50]

The situation of the English towns told against a defensive, inward frame of mind. Trade in England was distinguished by the relative absence of internal barriers and deterrents. In a widening interregional market of specialisation and exchange, the towns were naturally, and necessarily outward looking. Their most conspicuous concern was to enhance their prospects further by having any remaining levies and restraints removed. The coordinated market required maximum freedom, and it was most effectively serviced by the national provisions of statute law, which the towns regarded as much their best recourse. In one sense, Withington's definitions are specifically misleading, for the kind of citizenship that was developing in sixteenth- and seventeenth-century England was not an introverted urban bellicosity—it was the citizenship of the emerging state, with an exceptionally well-integrated national market.

Withington does mention in passing some aspects of the economic transition that was taking place. He notes that from 1571, "urban economies not only expanded but became more capitalistically structured".[51] This gets nearer to the defining factors in urban life, but still following the predisposition to deny the force of economic causes, Withington makes nothing of it in his overall analysis. And although he is suggesting a stage in the development of capitalism, the familiar fixation with structure, rather than essence, limits the usefulness of the observation. No doubt there were capitalistic systems taking shape in the towns, but this was of less general force than the crucial developments in the relations of exchange, and the growing insistence on economic freedoms in sixteenth- and seventeenth-century England. So the most powerful motivations came from what the townspeople believed to be required for them to make a living and to thrive. Their paramount concern was with the conditions of trade, and they had concluded that a context of freedom was the best platform for success, and its necessary guarantor was parliament.

An over-preoccupation with status structures and the position of the elites has diverted many historians away from an analysis of the active force of the economic concerns of the merchant class as a whole. Thus a study of Bristol concluded that notwithstanding their worldwide trading interests, the merchant elite was an exclusive group with a hierarchical concept of authority, and the impression is left that this defined the politics of the merchant body.[52] But the focus on an elite and privileged minority group does not necessarily reflect the position of the generality of merchants. In fact, the activism of the towns in emphasising and advancing the rights of parliament was often aimed against the great company monopolies. Merchants at large had come to feel that such arbitrary powers and restraints were neither necessary nor acceptable. The middle sort of Bristol were probably most concerned by the crown's incorrigible resort to fiscal impositions and monopolies, which for instance posed a threat to the city's important specialisation in soap manufacture.

The focus on formal status structures has been pervasive among historians. Even some Marxists have been reluctant to acknowledge the powerful dimension of liberal freedoms generated by the development of commercialised interregional marketing. Maurice Dobb regarded the mercantile elites as being in collaboration with the old feudal order.[53] Similarly, Robert Brenner has suggested that in the first four decades of the seventeenth century, the London merchant community was passive in its relationship with the royal government.[54] Even for the late 1620s, when the mercantile protests were too loud to ignore, Brenner supposes that the real opposition was coming from a radicalised Commons, turning "the merchants' simple economic grievances into a constitutional issue".[55] In truth, the evidence of the parliamentary involvement of the Dartmouth merchants and their fellows shows that already by 1610 they were placing their economic interests in a strongly constitutional light, on their own initiative. And in fact it is quite clear that at crucial moments in 1604 and 1606, the merchants generally were shaping the attack on monopolies and impositions. Again, as regards the mid-1620s, Brenner seems to be contradicted by his own evidence, which indicates that it was the merchants who were taking the lead in reviving the full force of the challenge to prerogative impositions.[56]

The foremost political theorist of the age, Thomas Hobbes, was in no doubt that life in the early seventeenth century English market town was characterised by an especially intense economic drive: "their profession is private gain . . . their only glory being to grow excessively rich by the wisdom of buying and selling". This gave them an obsessive resistance to taxation, and made them liable to be persuaded by parliamentarian propaganda that "pretended the people's ease from taxes".[57] This was the political shape of the demand for freedom of trade. The desire to live and work in liberty from arbitrary impositions, and refer all to the right of consent, was the crux of the matter in the first great constitutional clash in 1610, just as it would be in the more decisive confrontation in 1640.

The foregoing pages have illustrated the basis and substance of merchant radicalism in the assertion of that principle. It was manifest in the extensive body of records preserved by the merchants of Dartmouth from the impositions debate, showing them fully and actively supportive of the attempt to displace the royal prerogative and bring the setting of the customs dues under the control of parliamentary consent. We will say more ahead of the similar initiative taken by the corporation of Plymouth in 1624, expressly stating that they were preserving in their town chest the order of the Commons Committee of Grievances declaring that the monopoly in the Newfoundland cod fishing was to be regarded as suspended, and its provisions for restraint and imposition void. Like their Dartmouth fellows, the Plymouth merchants were ready and willing to regard parliament as the public authority in these matters, and the necessary guarantor of the vital imperatives of freedom of trade. Here was the reality of merchant radicalism in the early seventeenth century.

Previous chapters have suggested how the demand for economic freedoms emerged in contrast to the moral and psychological restraints of the medieval world. And the confidence to trade successfully if left at liberty was accompanied by a propensity to challenge authority in general. John Corbet noted that the radicalism of the middle sort of traders and craftsmen in Gloucester was reinforced by their readiness to ask questions of everything.[58] This tendency was sometimes defined as the assertion of a right to exercise "natural reason", and found to be especially evident in London.[59] In modern times, Christopher Hill is one of the few commentators who has managed to capture how the self-confidence of the merchants in controlling their economic and physical context went hand in hand with a general rejection of dependence on given authority, challenging the ethical and social constraints of the medieval past. Hill observed that writers like Raleigh and Bacon "summed up the ways in which traditional authority was being undermined . . . caught the optimism of the merchants and artisans, confident in their new found ability to control their environment, including the social and political environment, and their contempt for the old scholasticism".[60]

The Continuing Drive Against Prerogative Impositions

The desire to displace the prerogative of impositions, and subject the raising of customs dues to representative consent, had emerged as the Commons' dominant ambition in 1610. They were not inclined to desist, despite plain statements from the king and his ministers that the power was beyond question. Following the full-blown constitutional confrontation of 1610, the Commons' determination to overturn the right of prerogative customs dues remained their most central and consistent aim. Their unequivocal reassertion of this in 1614 provoked a complete breakdown of relations with the king. Sir Edwin Sandys reiterated the basis of their case, which was to establish freedom of trade as absolute property. "Every man hath a propriety in his goods, which will not suffer that to be transferred to others without his own consent . . . we have no propriety in our goods as long as the king's prerogative is to impose as much upon us as he pleaseth".[61] The challenge to the rights of the crown was very clear. By undermining the prerogative of impositions, the Commons would in effect be denying the king any right of raising money by discretion.

But the royal government had learned an important lesson in 1610—to allow the ambition to be aired was to encourage it, and this strategic error was not repeated. In the Lords, the Bishop of Lincoln reverted to James's much sounder initial position and declared that it was seditious to question the royal prerogative in this way. The Commons confirmed the imperative nature of their own agenda by seeking to make their vote of subsidies conditional on the ending of impositions. The king responded by bringing the Addled Parliament to an end. There was a significant aftermath, which again illustrated the depth of the divide that was opening up between crown and Commons, or "patent" and "parliament". In the wake of the assembly the king oversaw the burning of the written arguments that the Commons' leaders had intended to use to make their case against impositions in the Lords.[62] This was a further demonstration of James's view that the Commons' demands were too subversive even to be allowed expression. But the act highlighted the force of the challenge that was developing. The fact that the king could take satisfaction in the destruction of the earnest thoughts of the nation's representatives on their most vital concerns makes a revealing contrast to the care and commitment with which the merchants of Dartmouth had preserved exactly the same kind of record.

Although there appeared to be no way forward in attacking the king's jealously guarded rights with a simple assertion of their own claims, it remained the most significant and settled purpose of the Commons to put an end to impositions. In 1621 the chastening effect of a crisis in foreign affairs concentrated thoughts on the need for a display of unity, and with that in mind the question of impositions was something to be avoided as far as possible. There was a general realisation in the House that this was not the most appropriate time to address the matter, which would inevitably lead to confrontation. Not all accepted the injunction meekly. To the merchants of the West Country, committed free traders, the case against impositions was too important to pass without mention. Sir Edward Giles, MP for Totnes, attempted to raise it, but the suggestion was apparently not taken up.[63]

The issue did, however, appear in other forms. There was a close association between impositions and monopolies, for the ending of the latter practice was another important plank of the freedom of trade agenda. In fact, impositions and monopolies were related targets of the same economic and constitutional drive—the desire to secure a principle of liberty from all arbitrary restraints and exactions. Looking ahead to the meeting of parliament, John Chamberlain bracketed impositions and monopolies together as the things most likely to cause irresolvable controversy: "for impositions and patents are grown so grievous that of necessity they must be spoken of, and the prerogative on the other side is become so tender that it cannot endure to be touched".[64] In 1621, it was useful for the royal government to be able to divert its constitutional critics towards the monopolies side of the question. For although in one sense the demand was the same, and the Commons wanted to end the practice of monopoly patents, in another the field of monopolies offered greater scope for the pursuit of the most detested "inconveniences", and the Commons could feel a degree of satisfaction. In the wake of the chase, they could also proceed quietly with their long-term objective of a bill to outlaw the granting of monopolies in principle, which would have been a major advance for the freedom of trade lobby.

Furthermore, even while avoiding direct provocation over the question of impositions, MPs were quite prepared to raise it in connection with the decay of trade. William Nyell of Dartmouth, another prominent free trader, and not much inclined to diplomatic silences, spoke against the pretermitted customs on cloth, which were another instance of dues levied without formal representative consent. Nyell provided an informed estimate of the burden that these customs placed on clothing interests in Devon and concluded that every major cloth producing area in England must be suffering to the same extent. MPs from Yorkshire and Berkshire confirmed that this was the case.[65] Thomas Wentworth agreed that impositions, such as the pretermitted customs, were a major cause of the decay of trade.[66] John Delbridge from Barnstaple, and Edward Alford from Sussex also expressed the view that impositions were an unacceptable and depressive restriction on the market. And Sir Edward Coke was happy to bracket two evils together and aver that, "Freedom of trade is the reason that the Low Countries so prosper. They are not burdened with impositions to burden trade, nor monopolies to restrain it".[67] So even if the Commons were suppressing their instinct to out-rightly condemn the setting of impositions, they were underlining the basis of that indictment—that is to say the belief that arbitrary impositions were an unsustainable inhibition on trade. This had been the basic proposition of freedom of trade psychology since the mid-sixteenth century—impositions were "a means to make no English merchants".

When parliament met again in 1624, the crisis in foreign and military affairs still dominated the political scene, but the balance of domestic forces had changed. Prince Charles and the Duke of Buckingham had put together a grand alliance of peers and Commons to try to persuade King James to abandon his pro-Spanish policy and embrace the opposite definition of the national interest favoured by parliament. In pursuit of this consensus the leading figures in the Commons were expected once again to deflect the House away from the most contentious issue of impositions, and by comparison with earlier assemblies they showed restraint. King James, however, was aware that the issue had not gone away, and he was still inclined to take steps to assert his prerogative against the underlying and continuing challenge that he knew it faced. The legal officers of the crown seem to have been instructed once again to make a pre-emptive statement on the question of prerogative customs dues. But

James could no longer command the situation as he did in 1614, so when Sergeant Hitcham attempted to justify the levying of impositions, "he was interrupted by a general mislike of the House". The Commons were refraining from an outright assault on the power of impositions, but they would not hear it defended. On Wentworth's motion, Hitcham's speech was erased from the clerk's book.[68] It was the kind of dismissive gesture that James himself had indulged in, from the other side of the argument, when he was more the master in his own house. It exposed a settled and insuperable line of division. James was determined to sustain the prerogative of impositions, while the Commons were equally determined to be rid of it.

The obsession was displayed once again in the part that the Commons played in the attack on Lionel Cranfield. The latter was in the unfortunate position of being almost the only powerful figure excluded from the grand alliance. This was not entirely due to the prejudice of his enemies. Cranfield had been staunch in his support of James's view of foreign affairs, and he shared the old king's fears that to allow parliament to take an active role in the making of foreign policy was to encourage another dangerous encroachment on the prerogative rights of the crown. In consequence, Cranfield's only influential supporter was James. On the other side, the Prince, the Favourite, the Lords and the Commons were happy to combine to bring the Treasurer down.

Buckingham's main charge against Cranfield concerned corruption in the management of the Court of Wards. The contribution of the Commons revealed a different sense of priorities—they condemned him for recommending the levying of impositions, especially on wines and groceries. Of this Cranfield was apparently guilty, if that is the right word, for he was simply advising the king on a specific use of an undoubted monarchical right. But the Commons no longer wished that right to exist, and they had therefore convinced themselves that it was not legitimate. Sir Edwin Sandys introduced the charge when reporting from the Committee of Trade on 2 April. In defence, Cranfield pointed out that the policy was not his alone. But Sir Robert Phelips deflected claims that the responsibility lay with the Privy Council collectively. He thought that they must deal with the source of the recommendation, and this, he believed, was Cranfield.

> In reformation of grievances, we ought to consider as well the persons who give princes ill advice as the effects which succeed from that advice. Therefore it will be well if the committee deal with the referees. And if it shall appear that any man, to raise his own fortune, has given the king advice against the rights of the subject, let us not spare him.[69]

Their case against Cranfield could scarcely have been more contrived. He stood accused of a collective decision taken in the normal run of

Privy Council business to exercise a power that the highest court in the land (saving parliament) had endorsed as perfectly legal. The Commons were taking advantage of Cranfield's weakness to put forward once again their own highly subversive view that impositions transgressed the rights of the subject. Tying this in with the case against Cranfield was actually quite an effective way of reinforcing a general presumption against the power of impositions. On 12 April, Phelips consolidated the attack by associating it with the fiscal principle that they were seeking to establish across the board—he placed it in the context of a general right that all public money raising should be subject to representative consent. He identified Cranfield as not only the "projector" of the new impositions, but also the inspiration behind other attempts to evade the process of parliamentary consent, like the raising of benevolences, the "unwarrantable course of benevolence against the king's honour and the liberty of the Commonwealth".[70]

This underlined the radical breadth of the Commons' long-term, central agenda. They were seeking to bring the setting of the customs dues under their own control, and establish a general right of consent to the raising of all public monies. In the process they would be destroying the king's fundamental power of prerogative impositions. The citizens and representatives of the merchant communities, like John Delbridge MP for Barnstaple, William Nyell for Dartmouth, John Guy for Bristol, and Robert Bateman for London, all stepped up to add their voices to the condemnation of the Treasurer, showing themselves again in the forefront of the movement for freedom of trade. The powerful alliance of merchants and gentry was alive to every opportunity to undermine the prerogative of impositions.

Freedom of trade was just as relevant to the internal market as to the international, and was indeed the natural ethos of a fully coordinated system. So it was Richard Spencer, MP for the inland borough of Northampton who summed up the guiding principle at stake. His speech is sometimes misconstrued, as if he was defending the traditional concept of property in land.[71] But in fact his words encapsulated the demand for a principled right of freedom of trade that lay at the heart of the dispute. Impositions were "against the essence of a free man and subject . . . which provides for freedom in buying and traffic. It overthrows the freedom of the subject and makes him a slave in that it deprives him of the property of his goods". [72] This illustrates again how the concept of absolute property emerged as an active freedom, and was applied not just to landed property, but rather to the economic field as a whole. It was in essence the assumption of a right to work and trade free of arbitrary restrictions and impositions.

It might have been supposed that in 1625, with the crisis in foreign affairs becoming ever more controversial and all-consuming, the issue of impositions would have slipped down the list of priorities, but in fact it retained its place as central to the parliamentarian agenda, and a critical continuing bar to a working relationship between king and Commons. Indeed, the Commons took the opportunity of the beginning of the reign of Charles I to add a new dimension to their campaign against prerogative customs dues. In the first assembly of Charles's reign in 1625, the alliance between Prince and parliament of 1624 was not renewed, and there was no projected foreign policy consensus to encourage mediation or disguise division. So the issue of prerogative customs was immediately raised by the influential figure of Sir Robert Phelips and given a prominent place among the Commons' grievances.[73] Once again, the assumed right to be free of impositions was being placed in the context of a general determination to bring all matters of public finance under parliamentary supervision. Phelips' other major initiative was the proposal to withhold supply until the crown embraced the foreign policy preferred by the Commons. In both cases there was the same political and constitutional ambition at work—that is to say, a specific intention to extend the range and force of rights of consent. The continued centrality of the issue of impositions was demonstrated when Sir Nathaniel Rich summed up the main conditions on which the House would be prepared to cooperate on the matter of supply. There were five principal stipulations, which contained not only the most current demands for a change in the course and leadership of foreign and military affairs, but also the on-going demand for a response to their grievance of impositions.[74]

Furthermore, the Commons took the opportunity of the accession of Charles I to put in place a structured policy by which they hoped to prise that prerogative away. It was a slightly more subtle approach than simply declaring it illegal and demanding that it be brought to an end. Charles expected, in this first parliament of his reign, to receive confirmation of the traditional grant of tonnage and poundage, which had become a customary right of the crown. By convention, parliament made this grant to the king for life at the beginning of each reign. This had been done for over two hundred years, and for every monarch since Henry V, including all the Yorkists, all the Tudors, and the first Stuart. It had become a formality. In 1625, however, the Commons decided to exploit the theory of their grant, and use it as leverage in their desire to undermine the prerogative of impositions. They determined that until they had received satisfaction in that regard, they would offer the grant of tonnage and poundage for one year only.

Sir Robert Phelips flagged this up, proposing a saving clause be included in the bill of tonnage and poundage, to ensure "that nothing in this act may be passed against us for the maintenance of impositions".[75] This was the cue for the Commons to institute what became their established policy of making tonnage and poundage dependent on the ending of the power of impositions, in pursuit of which they had decided to restrict their offer of tonnage and poundage to just one year. It has been called "an insulting proposal".[76] Indeed it was, but it should not be interpreted as a sign of animosity against Charles himself. He was rather unfortunate to arrive on the throne at a time when the Commons were, as a priority, seeking ways and means to dislodge the prerogative of impositions. In the light of this fixed determination, it is surprising that some historians have sought to downplay the radical force of the Commons' position. The possibility that Phelips and Coke were prepared to offer a retrospective endorsement of existing impositions if Charles gave up the right of setting them in future has sometimes been misconstrued as non-confrontational.[77] This reflects the predisposition of revisionist historians to see the Commons' aims as just pragmatic. It was, on the contrary, another form of leverage to achieve the constitutional change that they desired—that is, for the king to surrender the power of imposing the customs. The Commons would have gained their essential aim of eliminating the prerogative of impositions and establishing the right of consent in that field.

The full context of the desire to generalise the principle and practice of rights of consent was displayed when the matter of tonnage and poundage was discussed in a committee of the whole House on 5 July 1625. MPs linked their limitation of the grant directly to their desire to displace the right of prerogative customs across the board. They wanted to address "the exactions of the officers and the customs they require". The general solution was that parliament itself should assume the responsibility for composing the book of rates, relieving the royal officials of that duty. This was the logical conclusion of their ambitions, and was recommended by Sir Edward Coke. But it was not very realistic in current circumstances. It could not "be prepared in so short a time and sitting". And the king showed no inclination to allow them the scope to assume this authority. So the grant of tonnage and poundage was held back, while the general situation regarding the rights of the customs dues remained in question. MPs went through the lists of prerogative customs, all of which they simply wanted to bring to an end. Some "alleged the pretermitted customs, grounded upon the misconstruction of that law . . . others to this added the question of impositions in general, and craved a special care not to have that excluded".[78]

This policy had little or no chance of success, but it was probably nevertheless the best that the Commons could do towards achieving their central ambition. It also served the important purpose of bearing permanent testament to what they wanted the situation to be. As James had understood, the freedom to make their point was in the circumstances a considerable reinforcement of their case. So the offer of the grant of tonnage and poundage in return for the surrender of the right of impositions remained their consistent stance of the Commons through to the final breakdown of relations with the king in 1629. It was really a kind of blackmail, with the Commons offering the further inducement that the king's income from the customs would be set on an acceptable basis, and might actually increase, if he would give them the power to set the book of rates.

In 1626, crown and Commons became locked in further confrontation, over parliament's pursuit of the Duke of Buckingham for what was considered to be the misconduct of military affairs. But even while preoccupied with dealing in the highest matters of state, the Commons did not lose sight of their most consistent and central ambition—the desire to undermine the royal prerogative in the field of the customs dues. And in 1626 the merchant community continued to play its essential role, with initiatives bringing forward the issue of impositions, and keeping it high on the agenda. Unlike another more recent grand domestic alliance, the merchant-gentry league was still in full force, so the Commons needed no second bidding to assert that the taking of tonnage and poundage without consent was a grievance, and the taking of impositions "a great grievance".[79] And even while Dr Turner was inaugurating the attack on the Duke of Buckingham, the House was also taking the first steps to try to enforce its position on tonnage and poundage, asserting that in the absence of a parliamentary grant, the king had no right to raise the levy. They were holding firmly to the line that they would only agree to the grant in full if the king agreed in turn to surrender the prerogative of impositions. Thus in 1626 Sir Nathaniel Rich assured Charles that "the subject would keep up his revenues according to the book of rates" if the king "would undertake that he be quieted from further impositions".[80] Otherwise the Commons could not see their way clear to confirming tonnage and poundage. They clung to this as their one real form of leverage, the only way that they could give some practical substance to their central purpose of bringing the customs dues under the control of representative consent. Not surprisingly, however, the king still displayed no inclination to surrender his right of prerogative impositions in order to recover his right of tonnage and poundage.

In the parliament of 1628, Charles's increasingly dire need to obtain financial and public support for his military policy obliged him to make at least a show of acceptance of the Petition of Right. In this, the Commons condemned as unlawful the king's recently exercised emergency powers of arbitrary imprisonment, forced billeting, and discretionary taxation. The king responded only in the most vague and general terms that the laws and customs of the realm should be upheld.[81] But the Commons having, as they fondly supposed, established the principle that no money should be raised without parliamentary consent, now hoped that they could go on to settle that right in terms of the customs dues, their persistent radical ambition since 1610. In the wake of the agreement over the Petition in 1628, MPs reiterated their view that impositions were illegal and that the system of prerogative customs dues should be ended.[82] The proposed deal was the one that had been put forward by Commons' leaders like Sir Edward Coke and Sir Nathaniel Rich since 1625. They would confirm a grant of tonnage and poundage, if the king would surrender his right of impositions and allow them to compile the book of rates on their own authority. They asked for an adjournment so that they could consult their constituents.

Charles preferred to prorogue the assembly. He would certainly have liked his right in tonnage and poundage to be endorsed, but not on the terms that were being offered. His consistent position on the matter was that he simply wanted the grant confirmed as it had been for his predecessors. There was no time allowed for MPs to establish the desired levels for the customs, and for this the king was held to blame. Sir Nathaniel Rich protested that, "in this straight of time we have no way left . . . when if it had pleased the king to have adjourned we might have taken a different course . . . had his full revenue and the subject well contented".[83] Sir John Eliot expressed the same sense of frustration and resentment. As so often they were reduced to entrusting their demands to a remonstrance, declaring "tonnage and poundage and other impositions not granted by parliament . . . a breach of the fundamental liberties of the kingdom, and contrary to . . . the Petition of Right".[84]

Charles had the power, and an urgent practical need to continue collecting tonnage and poundage notwithstanding the absence of parliamentary endorsement. In fact he had closed the 1628 session with a speech stating his intention to do so as of right. Afterwards he called in the *Commons Journal* and unilaterally enrolled the speech, underlining his view of the matter. To Charles, tonnage and poundage was an undoubted right, which the Commons were seeking to deny him. So the 1629 parliament was called with the simple aim of getting the grant confirmed as it had been for his predecessors. The continued withholding of parliamentary approval had caused him some inconvenience, both financial and personal. Many merchants had responded to parliament's incitement to refuse the levy, in what has been called a "general strike". Furthermore, the king's reputation was suffering. The Tuscan ambassador was heard to observe "the sailors refuse to pay the usual duties, insisting that parliament did not grant them to the king as they did to his father".[85] Charles had powerful motives to try once more to get the monarch's traditional right to tonnage and poundage reinstated.

He prepared the ground by adding another gloss to his position, saying that he had only presumed to collect tonnage and poundage by necessity, not of right. This was an indication of what he proposed now, to give parliament another chance to make the customary grant. If the Commons would pass the bill as it had done for his predecessors, he would acknowledge that he raised tonnage and poundage by right of this grant, and not by prerogative.[86] In other words, he simply wanted the levy regularised on the conventional basis. This took no account of what the Commons had been trying to achieve by withholding their approval since 1625. They gained nothing by the king denying that he had a prerogative right in tonnage and poundage. What they wanted was for him to deny his prerogative right of impositions.

So although some members were happy to set the tonnage and poundage bill in motion as the royal government wished, the dominant group in the House, led by Sir John Eliot, chose to defer it, while they focused on the new challenge to their liberties arising from recent controversies.[87] There was an obvious concern that the measure should not be driven through before the question of impositions had been dealt with. Secretary of State Sir John Coke was told precisely this when he tried to bring in the tonnage and poundage bill on 26 January.[88] Eliot noted that the bill in its present form left the power of impositions unchallenged. He also recalled that they might have resolved these matters in the previous session, if the king had allowed them the time.[89] This confirmed the one condition upon which they would have been happy to make the grant of tonnage and poundage—that is, if the king had been prepared to permit them to bring the customs dues in general under representative control. In the absence of this, the tonnage and poundage bill did not receive a reading. So if the proceedings of the 1629 assembly appeared somewhat unfocused, it was because the king and the Commons were completely at odds over this central issue, and neither could make progress with it. The Commons occupied their time with tangential matters of privilege and religion. To the king, these debates were "no more than a distasteful preliminary to a possible vote of tonnage and poundage".[90] Eventually, Charles concluded that such a vote would never take place, and brought the session to an end. What the king had desired from the assembly was shown by his declaration following the dissolution, describing at some length how the grant of tonnage and poundage had always been taken as read by his predecessors.[91]

Thereafter, the king determined to rule without parliament. The decision could be rationalised at various levels. There was the general reason that the assembly had given him much more in the way of political aggravation than financial supply. The traditional relationship whereby parliament provided fiscal support for public policy as made by the crown had broken down. But there was also the specific reason that Charles had failed, after a prolonged attempt, to induce the Commons to give him what he now wanted most—that is to say, the restoration of his rights in tonnage and poundage. And on the other side of the argument, he had also failed to deflect them from what *they* wanted most—the elimination of his right of impositions. There was little reason for Charles to call a parliament when it would only produce another round in that irresolvable dispute.

Notes

1. Henry Ireton, *Puritanism and Liberty*, ed. A. S. P. Woodhouse, (London 1938), p. 72
2. The line taken for instance by C. Russell, *Parliaments and English Politics 1621–1629,* (Oxford 1979); D. Hirst, *Authority and Conflict,* (London 1986)

3. See, D. Hirst, *Authority and Conflict,* (Arnold 1986), p. 103; B. Coward, *The Stuart Age,* (London 1994), p. 140; J. P. Somerville, *Politics and Ideology in England 1603–1640,* (London 1986), p. 152
4. W. Cobbett and T. B. Howell, *A Complete Collection of State Trials*, (London 1809–28), II, p. 407
5. Devon Record Office, Dartmouth Borough Archive, DD67721, f. 7; *Proceedings in Parliament 1610*, ed. E. Foster, (Yale 1966), II, p. 152. The wording in 1604 had been that "all subjects are born inheritable, as to their lands, so also to the exercise of their industry in those trades". *Commons Journal*, I. p. 218
6. R. Brenner, *Merchants and Revolution 1550–1663,* (Cambridge 1993), p 206
7. W. Notestein, *The House of Commons 1604–10,* (Yale 1971), p. 171
8. *Tudor Economic Documents*, eds. R. Tawney and E. Power, (London 1951), II, pp. 223–5
9. Notestein, *The House of Commons 1604–10*, pp. 175–6
10. Ibid, p. 258
11. Ibid, pp. 265–6; S. R. Gardiner, *History of England 1603–1642,* (London 1886–89), II. p. 68
12. *Proceedings in Parliament 1610*, II, pp. 100–6
13. Notestein, *House of Commons 1604–10*, p. 324
14. *Letters of John Chamberlain*, ed., N. E. McClure, (Philadelphia 1939), I, p. 301
15. W. K. Jordan, *The Development of Religious Toleration in England,* (London 1936), II, p. 24; Notestein, *The House of Commons 1604–10*, p. 133
16. Notestein, *The House of Commons 1604–10*, p. 327; and above p . . . for the statement of 1604
17. G. Yerby, *People and Parliament: Representative Rights and the English Revolution,* (Basingstoke 2008), pp. 29–34; G. Yerby, *The English Revolution and the Roots of Environmental Change,* (Abingdon 2016), chap. 10
18. Christopher St. German, *Doctor and Student,* (London 1523), p. 300
19. Richard Hooker, *Of the Laws of Ecclesiastical Polity,* (London 1593), ed. C. Morris, (London 1969), vol. I, bk. 1, pt X, p. 194
20. J. E. Neale, *Elizabeth I and Her Parliaments,* (London 1953), I, p. 321
21. *Parliamentary Debates of 1610*, ed. S. R. Gardiner, Camden Society Old Series, lxxxii, p. 39
22. *Proceedings in Parliament 1610*, II, p. 152
23. Devon Record Office, Dartmouth Borough Archive, DD67721, f.1
24. Cobbett and Howell, *Complete Collection of State Trials*, II, pp. 483–6
25. Ibid.
26. Thomas Hobbes, *Behemoth*, ed. F. Tonnies, (London 1889), p. 4
27. Devon Record Office, Dartmouth Borough Archive, Ms. DD7723; *Proceedings in Parliament 1610*, II, pp. 226–7
28. *Commons Journal*, I, p. 218
29. Jordan, *The Development of Religious Toleration in England*, II, p. 24; Notestein, *The House of Commons 1604–1610*, p. 133
30. Somerville, *Politics and Ideology in England 1603–1640*, pp. 51–3; B. Coward, *The Stuart Age,* (London 1984), p. 140; Brenner, *Merchants and Revolution*, p. 205
31. Devon Record Office, Dartmouth Borough Archive, DD67721, f. 1
32. Ibid, f. 5
33. Ibid, f. 7
34. Hobbes, *Behemoth*, p. 4
35. Ibid, p. 126
36. Cobbett and Howell, *Complete Collection of State Trials*, II, p. 407

37. Devon Record Office, Dartmouth Borough Archive, Mss. DD67721, DD67723
38. Devon Record Office, Dartmouth Borough Ms DD67723
39. Ibid
40. For further aspects of these connections, and a transcript of the Dartmouth Parliamentary Diary see Yerby, *People and Parliament*, chapters 2 and 3, and Appendix 2
41. Notestein, *The House of Commons 1604–10*, p. 323
42. T. K. Rabb, *Enterprise and Empire: Merchant and Gentry Investment in the Expansion of England 1575–1630,* (Harvard 1967)
43. J. Appleby, *Economic Thought and Ideology in Seventeenth Century England,* (Princeton 1978), p. 55
44. A. Fletcher, *The Outbreak of the English Civil War,* (London 1981), pp. 355–6
45. P. Withington, "Urban Citizens and England's Civil Wars", in *The Oxford Handbook of the English Revolution,* (Oxford 2016), p. 313
46. Ibid, p. 319
47. Ibid, p. 320
48. See above, pp. 135–6
49. Devon Record Office, Totnes Borough Archive, 1579A/16/35; West Devon Record Office, Plymouth Borough Archive, W48, f. 92
50. Devon Record Office, Totnes Borough, 1579/16/17 and CJ, I, P. 277; Exeter Corporation Letter Book, 60d, L243
51. Michael J. Braddick, *Handbook of the English Revolution*, (Oxford 2016), pp. 314, 317
52. D. Sacks, "The Corporate Town in the English State", *Past and Present 110* (1986), pp. 69–105
53. M. Dobbs, *Studies in the Development of Capitalism,* (London 1963)
54. Brenner, *Merchants and Revolution*, p. 205
55. Ibid, p. 222
56. Ibid, pp. 219–20
57. Hobbes, *Behemoth*, pp. 2, 126
58. J. Corbet, *A True and Impartial History of the Military Government of the City of Gloucester*, in *A Collection of Scarce and Valuable Tracts*, ed. Sir Walter Scott, (London 1809–15), V, pp. 303–4, 307
59. *Salus Populi Solus Rex,* (October 1648), BL, E467, (39), p. 12
60. C. Hill, *Intellectual Origins of the English Revolution,* (London 1972), p. 289
61. *Commons Journal*, I, pp. 472, 484
62. Gardiner, *History of England*, II, p. 249
63. *Commons Debates in 1621*, eds. Wallace Notesetin, Frances Helen Relf and Hartley Simpson, (New Haven 1935), II, p. 55
64. John Chamberlain, 28 October 1620, *The Chamberlain Letters*, ed. E. Thompson, (London 1966), p. 249
65. *Commons Debates 1621*, II, p. 78; *Commons Journal*, I, p. 521a
66. Ibid, I, p. 520
67. *Commons Debates 1621*, V, p. 93
68. R. Ruigh, *The Parliament of 1624,* (Cambridge, MA 1971), p. 50
69. The Parliamentary Diary of John Pym 1624, Northamptonshire Record Office, Finch-Hatton Ms. 50, f. 46v
70. The Diary of Sir Walter Earle 1624, BL Add. Ms. 18,597, fol. 135; Sir William Spring, Diary of Proceedings in the House of Commons 1624, Harvard, Houghton Library, MS English 980, ff. 209–10; The Diary of Sir Thomas Holland 1624, Oxford, Bodleian Library, Rawlinson Ms. D1100, fol. 12–12v
71. Somerville, *Politics and Ideology1603–1640*, p. 155

72. Diary of Sir William Spring 1624, f. 194; *Commons Journal*, I, pp. 759–60
73. *Commons Debates 1625*, pp. 31–2; C. Thompson, "Court Politics and Parliamentary Conflict in 1625", in *Conflict in Early Stuart England*, eds. R. Cust and A. Hughes, (London 1989), p. 175
74. *Proceedings in Parliament 1625*, eds. M. Jansson and W. Bidwell, (New Haven 1987), pp. 414, 417–419
75. *Commons Journal*, I, p. 813
76. Hirst, *Authority and Conflict*, p. 140
77. Ibid
78. *Proceedings in Parliament 1625*, pp. 510–11
79. *Commons Journal*, I, pp. 863, 868
80. The Diary of Bulstrode Whitelocke 1626, Cambridge University Library, Dd, 12–20, 21,22, 27 March 1626, f. 234
81. *Constitutional Documents of the Puritan Revolution*, ed. S. R. Gardiner, (Oxford 1968), pp. 66–70
82. *Commons Debates 1628*, eds. R. C. Johnson et al., (New Haven 1977), III, p. 595
83. Ibid, IV, pp. 449, 458
84. Ibid, pp. 388–95
85. Brenner, *Merchants and Revolution*, pp. 232–3
86. J. Rushworth, *Historical Collections*, (London 1659–1701), I, p. 642; *Commons Debates 1629*, eds. W. Notestein and F. H. Relf, (Minneapolis 1921), p. 11
87. *Commons Debates 1629*, pp. 6, 113
88. Gardiner, *History of England*, VI, pp. 34–5
89. *Commons Debates 1629*, pp. 108–9
90. Russell, *Parliaments and English Politics*, p. 412
91. *Constitutional Documents of the Puritan Revolution*, p. 83

8 New Definitions of Good Government

"Parliament" versus "Patent"; the Opposition to Monopolies; Freedom of Trade as the Economic Policy of the Commons; and the Unsatisfied Demand for Parliamentary Legislation

The long and persistent desire to eliminate prerogative customs dues was the central, radical ambition of the House of Commons. But the freedom of trade agenda also informed a less conspicuous, yet fundamental division of opinion about what constituted good government in general. In fact, this was a concept that MPs and their constituents were beginning to redefine, in terms of new imperatives and more effective means of addressing them. This posed an equally powerful challenge to the crown, and indeed most clearly reflected the nature of the dichotomy between the principles and practices of "parliament" and "patent".

The campaigns against monopolies and impositions were intimately connected with the movement for free trade. They all reflected the same desire to be allowed to live and work in freedom from arbitrary restrictions and exactions, and they had a common enemy in the various forms of government and administration by patent that were favoured by the crown. As a consequence, the freedom of trade perspective was asserted broadly and continuously, and almost always in contradiction of the policies and preferences of the royal government. Modern historiography has tended to leave the false impression that monopolies and impositions were separate matters, and that resistance to them was restricted to isolated moments of stress when it flared briefly and then disappeared. It is true that the Commons might focus on different aspects at different times, according to which form of restraint or imposition was currently most threatening. And the government might harden or soften its line according to its own priorities, and the level of its need for parliamentary support. But the same antithesis between arbitrary practices and the desire for representative consent was always present. There thus developed what I have characterised here and elsewhere as a generalised polarity between the claims of "parliament" and "patent". This reflected two sharply contrasting perspectives about the most acceptable and effective methods of public finance and administration, and the tension was constantly in play.

Following the bitter clashes over impositions in 1610 and 1614, James avoided calling parliament again for seven years, and the exercise of government by patent was given full rein. But the freedom of trade agenda had not gone away. In 1615, John Kayll published a very challenging book called *The Trades Increase*. Like the radical tract of the 1580s and the free trade bill of 1604, Kayll would also have "dissolved all companies", on the principle of an inherited right of freedom of trade for all. He began from the observation that trade was not in a very flourishing state. Much of the book is devoted to a somewhat rambling complaint about the perceived reduction in the nation's shipping, bemoaning the restrictions and discouragements placed on it, and concluding that "we find most of our sea trades either decaying or at a stay". Although this may have sounded vague and impressionistic, it was actually quite prophetic, for the "decay of trade" was indeed just around the corner.

But the most forceful and coherent section of the tract is the final half dozen pages, which contain Kayll's suggested solution. "Let me, without offence, propose the consideration of a remedy thereto, even by a freedom of traffic for all his majesties subjects to all places".[1] Kayll was aware that this was a contradiction of the official stance. He was advancing an uncompromising vision of absolute freedom of trade, which was in a direct line of descent from the radical pamphlet of the late 1580s, and the Commons' very assertive, not to say iconoclastic free trade bill of 1604. Like them, Kayll proposed that there should be an end to all privileged companies, to let

> the whole corporation of merchants reap comfort, in that they may communicate with all adventures, and the universal body of the subjects of the land content in that they may become merchants . . . whereas now otherwise merchandise, sorted and settled in companies, confineth merchants into those limits that private orders tie them to.

He reinforced this with a powerful and challenging definition of this freedom as a general right and liberty of the kingdom. Company restrictions were unacceptable

> to fellow subjects and equal citizens in this great monarchy, to be so serviceably tied and subject one to the other, and the rather for that those privileges, by the indulgence of the Prince being granted as a reward to some . . . are strictly used to the eternal benefit of a few and the wrong of all the residue.[2]

This illustrates how closely the demand for freedom of trade was bound up with the developing assertion of an "absolute" right of the individual not to be subject to arbitrary impositions and restraints from any other quarter—in this instance from the king and those privileged parties to whom he had granted monopoly powers.

Kayll regarded all the major companies as examples of restrictive practices. The way forward, he thought, was to emulate the act for "free liberty" of trade to France and Spain, which the merchants and the Commons had managed to get onto the statute book in 1606. His one concession to the concept of patents was that privileges might be justified for the protection of a genuine discovery in the very early stages, but not "to keep others out for ever, unless they pay, and subject to their orders".[3] In effect Kayll was condemning the royal government for using grants of monopoly as a form of patronage, which enriched a few, but disadvantaged all the rest of the king's subjects. Furthermore, he held this to be a contravention of the subjects' assumed right of freedom of trade. Kayll was confronting the position of the crown at every level, ultimately by the same assertion of an inherited freedom from arbitrary restraints and exactions that had been claimed in the impositions debate. It is not too surprising that the tract was suppressed by the Archbishop of Canterbury, and Kayll was sent to reconsider his thoughts in prison. He had not merely complained of monopoly patents as an inconvenience, he had declared them to be invalid, as a transgression of the independent rights of the subject. This was the assumption that King James always found most threatening, and with good reason. Kayll was putting forward a general principle of freedom of trade, which was the basis of an attack taking shape against the whole concept of administration by patent.

This fundamental divergence of approach became set. The early Stuart government never freed itself of dependence on grants of monopoly as a convenient form of regulation, taxation and patronage. Between 1614 and 1620, with parliament in abeyance, the king and court indulged in what can fairly be described as an unrestricted binge of patents of monopoly, the incidence of which more than quadrupled. "The world doth even groan under the burden of these perpetual patents, which are become so frequent that, whereas at the king's coming in there were complaints of some eight or nine monopolies in being . . . these are now said to have multiplied by many scores".[4] In fact, when ministers stirred themselves into taking something like an accurate tally, there were found to be more than forty monopoly patents in being. Quite apart from the damage done to specific economic interests, monopolies were exposed as a practice that was out of control in every sense. It was an abdication of responsibility rather than a tool of administration, and it undermined the governmental reputation of the crown.

The force of public opposition meant that James could only pursue this policy with impunity in the absence of parliament. He evaded the assembly for seven years, until he was obliged to turn to it again because of a major crisis in foreign affairs. When the Habsburg powers annexed the Palatinate inheritance of his daughter and son-in-law in 1620, James could no longer avoid seeking the moral support and financial backing of his people. But there was a realisation in court circles that the use and abuse of monopoly patents had become an insupportable general grievance, and this would have to be addressed in some degree, if parliament was to be made amenable to voting the required subsidies. In advance of the assembly, the Lord Chancellor Sir Francis Bacon, no doubt foreseeing an attack on himself as one of the referees who had approved the patents, suggested lancing the boil with a cull of those monopolies that were known to be especially unpopular. But the most that the king was prepared to do was to acknowledge in his opening speech that in some of the grants he may have harmed himself and his subjects, and that he would listen to specific grievances against particular monopolies.

Many modern historians, in their determination to minimise the assertiveness of parliament, have allowed the impression to grow that the government was somehow taking the initiative in the attack on monopolies and had suddenly swung into opposition against its own standard policy. This is a misinterpretation that conceals the essential fact that the contrasting views of the crown and the Commons about the validity of the concept of monopolies remained unaltered. It is true that some figures in the Privy Council chose at certain stages to divert blame or undermine court rivals by joining the popular agitation. But this was never for reasons that indicated a change in the general predilection of early Stuart regimes to favour and indeed depend upon monopolies as an instrument of government. And if Privy Councillors like Coke and Cranfield became involved in the pursuit of the referees, it was partly because they both hated Lord Chancellor Bacon, and partly because in this instance they were actually opposed to the position of the crown, and felt some degree of personal sympathy with the Commons' view that patents of monopoly were not acceptable in principle or efficient in practice.

The basic dichotomy remained clear. The king regarded grants of monopoly as a right of prerogative, and he had shown himself to be literally addicted to their use. The Commons, on the other hand, were seeking to bring the practice to an end in its current form, as an unacceptable breach of the assumed liberty of freedom of trade, and indeed as an unsustainable arbitrary interference with the natural flow of economic relations. The difference was not easy to reconcile. An interesting development of these years is the appearance in print of some leading merchants who had been advisers of the government, and had now taken on the task of a reasoned attempt to deflect the powerful drive for free trade into more orderly channels, and to justify the concept of monopolies. But at the same time they found it difficult to ignore the real commercial problems that the system was creating. Gerard de Malynes, for instance, acknowledged that there did at times arise a problem of monopoly powers being exploited for private advantage, but he did not accept the uncompromising view that all company privileges tended to degenerate in that way. He stressed that company regulations were essential for the stability of trade. He certainly managed to convey the challenging radical threat posed by the free traders. He took issue with the sentiment that was abroad among MPs and the general body of merchants that

> would have all things at large in the course of traffic, and that there should be no society of merchants for any places of trade (terming them monopolies) . . . these men have no regard that innovations are as dangerous as to remove the cornerstone of a building . . . neither do they observe a momentary difference between the end of a monopoly . . . and the government of a democracy that is popular.[5]

He thus noted the principle of liberty on which the movement turned, and suggested that the free traders brought disorder at a political as well as an economic level.

In reality, however, neither of these charges was true. The attempt to slur the free traders with the charge of being "democratic" did reflect a specific tendency in the movement. Freedom of trade had a liberal thrust, which clearly related to the emergence of economic individualism, and the idea that people had an equal and independent right to the free use of their trade and property. So the label of "democracy" was not entirely misplaced, but nor was it likely to give the free traders pause lest disorder run rife, for this was an exclusive kind of democracy that worked in favour of those with property, rather than those without. This was a freedom that the merchants, the gentlemen MPs and the yeoman farmers could embrace without qualms, especially as they knew very well that it did not bring commercial disorder either, since market forces were self-regulating. And in fact, even while underlining the inherent radicalism of the free trade movement, De Malynes could not avoid identifying the powerful economic case against the government's use of monopolies. The most revealing section of the book is an outright attack on the monopoly of the Merchant Adventurers, the government's most indispensable bankers, and the most widely abominated target of the free traders. De Malynes joined in the castigation. It was "a general prejudice to the whole kingdom . . . this engrossing of trade into a few men's hands has caused our home trades to decay, our manufactures to decrease, and our commodities to lay upon our hands unsold".[6]

So it was with a fair degree of righteousness that the free traders determined that the system of monopolies was not to be borne. As S. R. Gardiner said, the parliamentary position in 1621 was that "such grants were held to be illegal, as encroaching upon the rights of the subject in the exercise of his trade".[7] Accordingly, the general bill to outlaw monopolies was seen as the most widely desired of the many bills that were brought forward by the House in 1621. It was, said Sir Nathaniel Rich, the measure on which the heart of the country was set.[8] The aim was to wrest control of monopoly patents from the sphere of the prerogative. It should be clear that this was a continuing, and not a new ambition. In fact, it directly reflected the intent of an original legislative proposal on the matter that the Commons had floated twenty years earlier at the beginning of the controversy.

One of the most significant occurrences in 1621 was the arrival of Sir Edward Coke on the parliamentary side as a champion of freedom of trade. Although he was nominally still a Privy Councillor, his emergence in opposition to the principle of monopolies did not indicate that the royal government was making the same journey. On the contrary, his intervention not only reinforced the radicalism of the free trade stance, it also revealed other ways in which the assumptions of good government and the "state" interest were being appropriated by the House of Commons. Coke was not speaking for the government—he was actually in the process of leaving the government, and taking on the role for which he became famous, as the most authoritative voice in the promotion of English liberty against arbitrary exaction and restraint.

Coke entered the lists on 19 February, when he seconded William Noy's motion for an enquiry into the monopolies and their referees. Crucially, he did not restrict himself to condemning the monopolies as abuses perpetrated by particular individuals, which was the indictment that the king was prepared to hear. Coke averred that monopolies were inherently illegitimate.[9] In effect, he suggested that the very concept was an infringement of the liberties of the subject. In response to Coke's intervention, Edward Alford expressed a feeling of satisfaction, and said that this was the first time that he had seen Councillors of State have such care of the state. The terminology was significant. It indicated that there were public imperatives that the Commons were defining as necessities of "state", but for which the royal government could not usually be relied upon to take order. In similar vein, the representatives of Totnes Corporation could note that the one successful free trade bill, for trade to France and Spain, pushed through by the Commons in 1606, had been achieved by "the wisdom of the state in parliament".[10] Such phrases identify an important moment of change. The making of statute law was coming to be seen as the natural and necessary means of providing for a series of independently defined "state" interests, and the critical development was that these matters were in effect becoming the preserve of the House of Commons.

In 1620, James complained that people were now turning to parliament for solutions to all their problems. "Before parliament met, my subjects whenever they had a favour to ask used to come to me or to Buckingham. But now, as if we had both ceased to exist, they go to parliament".[11] James would have been well advised to consider not just the slight, but also the reasons for it. In sober truth, he was not in tune with the vital, common priorities of his people, which parliament now reflected. Nor was he in sympathy with the practice that his subjects now regarded as the most effective means of meeting their needs—the provision of parliamentary legislation. It was a major weakness of the early Stuart regimes that they showed neither the capacity nor the inclination to act upon an objectively conceived state interest, or to use the processes of statute law that were best suited to serving it. In the absence of monarchical initiative in this regard, the grasp of a developing "state" perspective, and the definition of good government in the public interest, passed to the House of Commons. Alford praised Coke for acting "like a parliament-man in Queen Elizabeth's time".[12] That was indeed the moment when the concept of the state interest had begun to take shape. The difference then was that Elizabeth and her Councillors had put themselves at the head of the most important, independently definable national priorities. In order to do the same, Coke had to detach himself from the position of the early Stuart crown.

Coke continued to expound a root and branch approach to the problem of monopolies. Dealing with the patent for alehouses, he said "if we had branded this in the execution only, the commission might have start up again in a short time, therefore we brand the very institution of it".[13] This encapsulated the parliamentary case. They did not want merely to address particular abuses, and leave open the possibility that they might readily recur. This would mean after all that the damage to trading freedoms would already be done before they could address the matter. They wanted to prevent it from happening, or in effect to ensure that trade would be left its necessary liberty. Coke was not able to offer any specific precedent that would show monopolies to be illegal. The best he could do was to take as his starting point the Commons statement in 1604 that the practice was a denial of the liberties of the subjects in their trades, and derive the somewhat circular conclusion that it was therefore a breach of Magna Charta.[14] The real advantage of Coke's support to the opposition was that, as the leading expert in English law, he believed that monopolies *ought* to be regarded as against the subjects' liberty. And the basis of this belief was economic. "Freedom of trade", said Coke, "is the reason that the Low Countries so prosper. They are not burdened with impositions to burden trade, nor monopolies to restrain it".[15] This drew all the threads together—freedom of trade had come to be regarded as a general administrative necessity.

To secure it, a radical new law would be required. The monopolies bill was brought in on 5 March 1621, and introduced by Sir Dudley Digges and Sir John Walter. It was, said Sir Nathaniel Rich, the measure on which the heart of the country was set.[16] Sir John Walter summed up its purpose. "Let all patents be called in and suppressed, and have none granted hereafter. Let all projectors henceforth incur praemunire for preferring suits".[17] Adjudication was to be "by the ordinary courts of Common Law".[18] Grants of monopoly were no longer to be a royal prerogative. Walter suggested that if they could get this through it would solve the problem in perpetuity, and they could avoid provoking James by the further pursuit of ministers. S. R. Gardiner noted the wisdom of this: "It was of greater importance to define the law . . . if they could convert into law the bill before them, it would never again be in the power of any minister, however high in favour, to divert disputes relating to the commercial privileges from the ordinary courts".[19] The problem was that the bill was actually more threatening to the position of the king than was the pursuit of abuses. It would have been a new law, removing the king's power to sustain the system of monopoly patents. In fact, it would have been "the first statutory invasion of the royal prerogative".[20] In view of this it failed to clear the House of Lords. The radical and unconstitutional thrust of the monopolies bill was very clear. It was equally significant that this illustrated the growing difference of opinion between crown and Commons about what comprised the basic requirements of good government, and fair and efficient regulation, especially regarding their respective and contrasting judgements about the value of sovereign representative statute in providing it.

Freedom of Trade as the Economic Policy of the Commons

The monopolies bill was the most generally desired measure on the legislative programme in 1621, reflecting the most clearly defined public requirement. It would in itself have done much to create a climate or context of freedom of trade. But there were also many other legislative initiatives brought forward, and many of these were aimed in the same direction. Their provenance, and their fate, further demonstrated the deeply contrasting attitudes of crown and people to the value of parliamentary legislation, and the needs of good government.

In some ways, the difference of approach is not difficult to understand. The very distinctive concept of representative sovereign law that had developed in England gave parliament a defining share in legislative sovereignty. This was not really compatible with James's view that in a free monarchy the crown was the source of sovereign legislative power. And since he regarded himself as the sufficient judge of the public interest, he did not see parliamentary law as an essential function of government. It is probable indeed that he was more inclined to view it as disruptive, both in principle and in practice. To parliament and its constituents, on the other hand, the attractions of statute law were unique and irresistible. Parliament could directly reflect public needs and preferences, both local and general, and could address them with nationally definitive legal solutions. This was another critical area where parliament, rather than the crown, was appropriating the concept of good government, and the developing structures of "state" provision.

The first parliament of James I, from 1604 to 1610, had been very productive in terms of public legislation, the great bulk of it being done by the initiative of the MPs and their constituents, while the royal government had at least refrained from impeding them overmuch. But by 1614 the relationship between king and Commons had been soured by the impositions dispute, and no opportunity was given for legislation in the Addled Parliament. The assembly of 1621 met with at least the intent of maintaining a more harmonious climate, and an extensive programme of legislation was envisaged. There was a backlog of vital concerns to be addressed. Furthermore, a particularly pressing general problem had appeared on the agenda. The state of the commonwealth was less flourishing than it had been for more than sixty years. Various sections of the economy were in downturn. The "decay of trade" had set in, and remedial measures were required.

The depression was manifest most obviously in the decline of the kingdom's most substantial trade in cloth. Business had been good following the peace with Spain in 1604, and in the decade up to 1614 the export of cloth from London rose by about a quarter. Thereafter, there was a general slowdown. It was exacerbated by the ill-fated Cockayne Project, which aimed to break into the valuable market for dyed cloth, but only succeeded in provoking reprisals from the Dutch, who had an established position and a greater capability in this field. The consequent withdrawal of Dutch goodwill led to a sharp reduction in the overall demand for English cloth. This was compounded by disruption in some other markets that had been particularly important to English exports. Between 1617 and 1623 a number of German, Polish and Baltic princes sought to raise money by manipulating their currencies, which tended to increase the price of English goods. Finally, there was the outbreak of another European-wide war in 1618, and these traditional markets became permanently dislocated. By 1622 the volume of cloth exports from London had fallen to little more than half the level of 1614.

The problems were understood to be fundamental, and the severity of the slump generated an inquest into possible causes and solutions. Recognised experts in mercantile affairs, like Gerard de Malynes and Edward Misselden, made valiant but inconclusive attempts to explain the decay of trade in terms of variations in currency values. Thomas Mun led the way to a more concrete assessment by looking at the matter the other way round, and suggesting that the leading factor was the balance of trade itself. "In those countries . . . which send us more of their wares in value than we convey to them . . . there our monies are undervalued, and in other countries where the opposite is performed, there our money is overvalued".[21] This indicated a solution, based on the positive promotion of the nation's trade. In the long-term this would be provided partly in the form of diversification and innovation, and partly in the systematic support of English trading capacity, including the encouragement of growing trades like coal and fishing, and the development of seafaring and ship building skills. Ultimately, it would require the consistent and well-coordinated exercise of state provision to create a favourable context. This would be achieved above all by the Navigation Acts of 1651, consolidated by further legislation in 1660. By this means "the general enforcement of trade and maritime policy was transferred . . . from the companies to the state".[22]

The response in 1621 was considerably less coherent and efficient. Early Stuart government was not naturally inclined to think in terms of an objectively defined state interest. Their notion of political organisation was personal and dynastic, and they continued to view trade as a fragmented rather than a coordinated function, structured and regulated only by the powers of the great companies. By the same token, they did not conceive that the problems needed to be addressed by employing the most powerful judicial dynamic of the developing state—the processes of sovereign representative legislation. James had an exalted and protective view of the monarch's role, as displayed in his displeasure at the redirection of public petitioning towards parliament. He did not regard parliamentary legislation as the most necessary or authoritative instrument of government, and he was to some extent unwilling to allow it to consolidate that reputation. He therefore felt no compunction about limiting its use. The kind of legislation that James seemed prepared to encourage was principally to deal with technical issues of law, such as measures against Informers and the Abuse of Supersedeas, and for Limitation of Suits. There was no indication that he shared the view of the Commons that the legislative process was the appropriate and most effective means of addressing the vital economic concerns of the kingdom. So the early Stuart kings never managed to transcend their dependence on the grant of monopoly privileges to regulate the commercial activities of their subjects.

The parliamentary approach was opposite in every respect. MPs believed that the system of administration by monopolies was invalid, and that it did much more harm than good. As an alternative, the Commons and their constituents had an unequivocal commitment to the force and function of representative statute law as the proper and efficient method of providing for the economic priorities of the kingdom. Once again, this meant that parliament rather than the king was assuming responsibility for meeting the general public interest with the appropriate "state" provisions. And in fact they did manage to formulate a policy with a genuine national reach, the consequence of which would have been to take trade out of the restrictive control of the great companies.

Freedom of trade was parliament's economic policy in 1621, as indeed it was throughout the early Stuart period. They regarded it as a public priority in itself, and it was their principal response to the critical problem of the "decay" of trade. In essence it was certainly seen as a means of offering positive encouragement to English trade, which was where the eventual solution would lie, though as yet they were not able to focus on the provision of administrative infrastructure that would also be required. John Kayll had foreseen that a chronic trading depression was setting in, and the general solution proposed by the House of Commons echoed what Kayll himself had recommended—to encourage free trade wherever possible. Sir Edwin Sandys suggested that the best cure would be to set up seven committees to challenge the seven great monopoly companies of London. This neatly symmetrical proposal illustrated the force of the Commons' desire to eradicate monopolies across the board, in order to free up trade and alleviate the depression. What they could do in practice was to propose a programme of free trade measures for that purpose. As so often it was Sir Edward Coke who summed up the rationale. "Freedom of trade is the cause that the Low Countries so prosper. They are not burdened with impositions to burden trade, nor monopolies to restrain it".[23]

Coke was speaking in the context of the central bill against monopolies, which would in itself have encouraged a climate of freedom of trade. The Commons also brought forward a raft of other measures seeking to promote the practice of free trade, in particular and in general. This was the main hope for improving the economic condition of the kingdom. Sir Nathaniel Rich, a leading protagonist of freedom of trade, said that "their state was a decaying state" but they "were preparing remedies".[24] Accordingly, a series of bills were proposed with the aim of establishing commercial freedom in every aspect of the vital cloth trade. There was an early move to address the downturn in the trade by a bill for "free liberty of the buying and selling of wools". It was noted that less than half the amount of cloth was being produced as formerly, and many clothiers and cloth makers were out of work. It was thought that the monopoly of the Merchant Adventurers was restricting the market, and they should be deprived of the power to determine which cloth should be sold, and who had the right to sell it. The proposed solution was a bill for free trade.[25] This was later reinforced by another bill, which addressed the matter from the opposite direction and affirmed the right of currently excluded merchants to participate in the trade, thus "restoring the free trade of the merchants of the staple for the export of cloth into parts beyond the seas".[26] Again, this was aimed at undermining the monopoly of the Merchant Adventurers, and empowering other traders to export cloth independently from the out-ports. There is no doubt that MPs and their constituents believed that a major cause of the depression in the nation's crucial commerce in cloth was the artificial restraints placed upon it, and that the answer was to create conditions of free trade from every angle.

There was also an attempt to deal with a specific problem hampering the Welsh cloth trade, which was believed to have flourished in conditions of freedom, but was now suffering restraints in some English markets. A bill was proposed for "the free trade and traffic of Welsh cloths, cottons, linens, etc., through the kingdom of England". Other measures were also aimed at providing free trading rights for the principality. A week later came a bill for "free trade in Welsh butter".[27] It is clear that the free trade programme had a national reach, reflecting the kingdom-wide representative network through which it was being advanced. The northeast of England was not neglected. Another bill that was brought forward early in the session was "for the free traffic of sea-coals in and out of the counties of Durham and Northumberland".[28] This was intended to give encouragement to the developing and increasingly significant trade in coal, which was an important element in the networks of specialisation and exchange.

Conditions of free trade were thereby sought for all the principal items of production and manufacture throughout England and Wales, and for export beyond the seas. There were also more general measures to promote the freedom of overseas trade by area. The bill against monopolies was not the only one that would have had the effect of creating a broad context in which trade could flow freely. On 2 March, just over a week before the monopolies bill, there was brought forward a bill "for liberty of trade into all countries".[29] There was also a bill for "free trade into the kingdom of France". It was the same demand and the same solution in respect of every region and every industry. MPs were proposing to construct and reinforce a complete, coordinated network of freedom of trade. The breadth of the programme displayed not only the coherent thrust of the Commons' policy, but also the power of parliamentary law as a central dynamic of provision.

It should indeed be noted that the freedom of trade perspective incorporated the agrarian sphere as well. It was not simply that many of the free trade bills concerned agricultural products or items manufactured from them, but more specifically that this parliament took an important step in changing the relationship between legislation and the process of enclosure. There was a significant break with the past. From 1487 to 1597, the persistent habit had been for governments to legislate to try to restrict the enclosure movement. The unexpected dearth of corn in 1597 had induced the same response, but this was to be the last attempt to proscribe enclosure as the cause of high prices and depopulation. Thereafter, the flow of legislative initiative gradually switched direction towards a favourable view of the process. In 1607 there was a widespread revolt against enclosure in the Midlands. But there were nevertheless opinions expressed that the practice was a necessary means of increasing productivity to feed the growing population, and 1608 saw the first limited pro-enclosure measure. By 1621 the balance of opinion in the Commons was firmly set in favour of free scope for the enclosure movement, and with the House left largely to its own devices in formulating legislation, there appeared the first general enclosure bill with the aim of facilitating the practice. In 1624, the existing statutes against enclosure would be repealed.[30] The turning of the legislative tide in favour of enclosure was an integral part of the growing assertion of freedom of trade. It was another aspect of the core demand that each individual should be free to enjoy and employ his property without arbitrary restraint. It was the view of the majority of MPs that the gentry, the freeholders and the commercial farmers should have absolute control over their lands, even if this meant displacing the customary common rights of others. This is also a reminder that the rise of capitalist marketing in the sixteenth and seventeenth centuries had a significant agrarian aspect, for the principal purpose of enclosure was profit.

There was also another free trade measure concerning foodstuffs, which provides an interesting demonstration that the freedom of trade perspective extended to the furthest reaches of the nation's trade. And it is a particularly good example of the contending forces of "patent" and "parliament". This was the bill for free fishing off the coasts of America. It was an instance of a free trade measure that was consistently favoured by popular opinion in the Commons, but which faced the specific obstacle of the royal government's preference for regulation by monopoly patent. It was a very forceful challenge to the government's approach, and was orchestrated by the merchants of the West Country, who were prominent and vocal in the interests of free trade. It was brought forward in every parliament of the 1620s, usually by the merchants of Dartmouth or Plymouth, the ports with the largest stake in the Newfoundland cod fishing enterprise. This had previously flourished in a context of freedom of trade, which the merchants and fishermen had come to regard as vital to their prospects and prosperity.

The free-fishing bill sought to remove the restrictions and charges that had recently been applied under a royal patent issued to Sir Ferdinando Gorges in November 1620, on the eve of the 1621 parliament, in the final flurry of the king's notorious binge of monopoly grants. The patent had authorised Gorges to regulate and tax the fishing in Newfoundland, ostensibly in the interests of the New England colonists. The relevance of this was not immediately obvious, and the West Country fishermen believed that, like other monopolies, Gorges' patent had no regulative validity or usefulness, but was merely a pretext to divert hard earned money from their own pockets and deliver it into the coffers of the royal government and the favoured monopolist.

In this they had the notable support of Sir Edwin Sandys, who represented the Cinque Ports. Neither he nor his constituency had a direct interest in the cod fishing, but they both had a very definite commitment to the general struggle for freedom of trade. Drawing on his own knowledge and experience of the colonial sphere, Sandys assured the House that other ventures like the Virginia Company had no need of this kind of privileged protection—the fishing should be free for all.[31] The bill had the strong and consistent backing of the House, but the government continued to seek restrictions with equal determination, and insisted that the colonists must be guaranteed priority position on the fishing grounds. The Dartmouth representative William Nyell, one of the most uncompromising free traders, declared that the colonists could "take the first place now, if they can get it".[32] This sounded like a reasonable offer, since the colonists held a geographical advantage. Nyell was speaking as a genuine free trader, in full command of the conditions of the enterprise, and confident in his ability to thrive and profit, if given the maximum liberty to do so. But the government still adhered to a different pattern of economy, where the role of the crown was to preserve a balance in favour of interests that appeared to need protection, and it expected, by the by, to gain some fiscal return for its trouble. On this view, Nyell's bullishness, and his objection to any kind of restriction or regulative levy, simply underlined the need for restraints. Secretary of State Sir Edward Calvert insisted that it was necessary to control the fishermen, who were "wonderful unruly".[33] Nyell's kind of economic individualism threatened to take matters out of the reach of government supervision. So the free-fishing bill was unlikely to receive the royal assent.

Nor, however, did the government's antagonism stand much chance of diminishing or discouraging the general demand for freedom of trade, which continued deep and broad. The representatives of the West Country merchants later repaid Sir Edwin Sandys for his support over the free-fishing bill by giving their vocal backing to the protest of the Cinque Ports against the most powerful and increasingly disliked of all monopolies, that of the Merchant Adventurers in the cloth trade. William Nyell moved that the business of dealing with the Cinque Port's petition "should precede all others". Nyell's neighbouring MP, Sir Edward Giles from Totnes, declared that this was a grievance shared by every other port in the kingdom.[34] The fishermen of Dartmouth and Plymouth had no major interest in the cloth trade, or any particular grievance against the Merchant Adventurers, but they did have an unyielding commitment to the practice, and principle of freedom of trade. In the same vein, Sandys also had the support of the most eminent of free traders, Sir Edward Coke, who thought that there was "no greater cause in all this parliament" than the Cinque Ports petition against the Merchant Adventurers.[35]

It was a demonstration of the national reach of the demand for freedom of trade, and the defining force that it had acquired among MPs, merchants and commercialising farmers. Historians have sought to diminish the significance of the movement for free trade in the early seventeenth century on the basis that it was a sectional protest of the merchants of the out-ports against the London monopolies, rather than the fully-fledged, generalised concept that emerged in the later eighteenth century. This conceals the truly radical and national appeal of early seventeenth-century freedom of trade. The combined animosity of the out ports against the privileged elites of London constituted a national perspective, not only because of their number and kingdom-wide distribution, but also because the collective volume of their trade was far greater. And in fact the wider body of merchants in the capital itself was also committed to the furtherance of freedom of trade against arbitrary restrictions and impositions. Above all, this was a principled stance shared by merchants, gentlemen landowners and commercialising farmers alike. These close, but broad connections are reflected in the ascendancy that the free trade movement held in the economic policy of the House of Commons from 1600 to 1640.

To the royal government the demand for freedom of trade merely produced unwanted initiatives that threatened to undermine the king's ability to regulate and tax the mercantile sphere in the traditional manner. In fact, such measures challenged the position of the crown at various levels, and this was one reason why James I ceased to take a sympathetic interest in the legislative process. We will never know what effect the programme of free trade measures of 1621 might have had in alleviating the depression, because the king chose to dismiss the assembly before any of them could reach the statute book. Sir Nathaniel Rich, a leading proponent of the bill against monopolies, was distraught at the loss. "Our estate is a decaying estate. We were preparing remedies. We are taken off and intercepted . . . this is a grief to be testified".[36]

It was an important moment in various respects. It implied a challenge to the king's right to end the assembly, because the Commons regarded the work on which they had been engaged as simply indispensable. It was a critical stage in the transfer of public trust and governmental credit from "patent" to "parliament". MPs believed that they had been addressing the most urgent and vital needs of the country, by the most effective means available. Their view of the legislative programme as the best that could be done was plausible. The attempt to create a general context of freedom of trade showed an awareness of the requirements of the integrated, interregional market. And by seeking to employ the function of sovereign representative law to bring this about, they were implementing a state provision of unprecedented force. The early Stuart kings had no purchase on any of this, and so their subjects were drawing away from them, into a new political and economic world, where the services of monarchy were ceasing to be the most practical necessity.

The essential relevance of the Commons' stance in terms of economic policy is displayed most interestingly in the publications of leading economic authorities who had taken on the task of defusing the radical thrust of the free trade movement, but in fact found themselves echoing some of its core propositions. Gerard de Malynes was a sometime adviser to the royal government on economic affairs. He is most often noted for a general analysis connecting the decay of trade with the vagaries of the exchange rate, and he would normally be regarded as advocating the need for an orderly trading context, as against the uncompromising assumption of complete individual freedom. Yet his book *The Maintenance of Free Trade* is by no means just an attempt to contain the concept within regulated bounds. A residual sympathy with the free trading position breaks through at some crucial points. The most striking passage in the book is an extended tirade against the monopoly of the Merchant Adventurers. One of the main causes of the depression, he said, was the restrictive practice of the privileged companies. Like Sir Edwin Sandys in the Commons, he pointed the finger at the great companies of London, such as the Eastland Company, the Russia Company, and especially the Merchant Adventurers. "Having engrossed into their hands . . . the sole power of exporting all white cloths, all coloured cloths, kersies, bays, says, serges . . . hath abated the trade".[37] Their privileges suppressed and undermined the activities of other merchants "from all the staple ports at London, Westminster, Bristol, Southampton, Royston and Newcastle that heretofore exported either cloth or wool or both, which now they may not". All trade was "in the power of the Merchant Adventurers only, and it is come to be managed by 40 or 50 persons of that company . . . nay, one man alone has compassed into his hands the whole trade of coloured cloths and kersies".[38] This monopoly was "a general prejudice to the whole kingdom . . . this engrossing of trade into few men's hands has caused our home trades to decay, our manufactures to decrease, and our commodities to lie upon our hands unsold".[39] It seems that the defence of orderly trade was not necessarily the most powerful factor in his calculations. His instinct was to hold monopoly practices largely to blame for the decay of trade, and to bring them to book in a tone that was difficult to distinguish from the free trading voices in the House of Commons. By the same token he was happy to rehearse the basic principle of freedom of trade, which asserted that liberty from arbitrary restrictions and exactions was a right of the subject. "Shall this be proclaimed a free trade, when we ourselves are in bondage? Let every man judge".[40] This seemed to dilute his earlier castigation of unrestrained free trade, and he had actually concluded by highlighting the economic justice of the free traders' case. It makes the royal government appear rather isolated. The king was tending to convey more and more power and privilege into the hands of particular companies and monopolists, very largely to create new sources of ready money for the crown. On the other hand, it was becoming the settled opinion among commercial interests at large that traders had both the necessity and the right to work in freedom from arbitrary restrictions and impositions.

In a sense it was quite logical to suppose that the decline in trade might be reversed by bringing restrictive privileges to an end, and opening up the market to everyone, and this was clearly a view that extended beyond the committed free trade lobby in the Commons. Edward Misselden was another authoritative economic commentator who made valiant attempts to unravel the mysteries of currency exchange rates, and was associated with defending the idea of an orderly trading context. Yet once again, in offering a practical explanation for the depression, he had harsh words for the privileged companies like the Merchant Adventurers, and especially for the fiscal demands that they made. He thought that they did great harm

> by over-lading the cloth trade, either with a general or special charge . . . as the chief weight of the cloth trade lieth to the Merchant Adventurers, so also is the burden of charge most felt under that trade, for impositions and imprest money by them laid upon the trade, for defraying the charge of their government, and payment of their debts hath driven many good merchants out of the trade.[41]

The perception that commerce was made unproductive by the burden of arbitrary levies had been the underlying premise of the freedom of trade concept since its inception in the mid-sixteenth century: impositions were "a mean to make no English merchants".

It seems then that Misselden also tended towards the belief that as a general principle, trade should be left free. It was wrong "that others of his majesty's subjects should be deprived of the liberty thereof, but that upon equal and reasonable terms . . . without that ill tincture of monopoly, the king's highway of trade should be open to all".[42] He did not go so far as to agree with the "many" who held it as the liberty of the subject that anyone should be free to trade in anything without qualification. Nor did he think that all restrictive patents should always be condemned as an infringement of that liberty. And naturally he blamed the monopolists for abusing the patents, rather than the king for misusing his prerogative by scattering them around like confetti. Nevertheless, Misselden was unable to avoid the conclusion that in point of fact these grants had tended to turn into the worst kind of monopolies, as particular patentees engrossed the trade in a commodity and fixed the price of it. Hence "those catalogues of crying monopolies" that had been exposed in 1621.[43] His general remedy again echoed the principles of free trade: "rooting out the name and use of monopolies from amongst this nation . . . and to free and open the course of trade . . . to the encouragement of subjects, and the benefit of the public".[44]

Such analyses cannot have brought much comfort to the ears of the king. They were actually more an indictment of the policies of the crown than of the demands of the free traders. The problem of monopolies had become chronic because they were the chosen resort of royal government, which had thereby ceased to work for "the benefit of the public". The call to maintain an orderly trade and not to define all restrictive patents as opprobrious appears as something of a token gesture in view of Misselden's overall conclusion that the concept of monopolies should be rooted out, in favour of encouraging a trading context characterised by the principle and practice of freedom from arbitrary restraints and impositions. It shows again that the demand for a right of freedom of trade that had first been voiced by the House of Commons in 1604 had now become generalised among the body of merchants and traders at large.

The Unsatisfied, But Continuing Demand for the Legislative Service—the Basis of a New Concept of Good Government

MPs had a clear perception of the remedies that they could offer to alleviate the depression, but in 1621 they were frustrated in their aim of applying their prescription of a programme of free trade legislation. The king had never been party to this agenda, and was unlikely to assent to a series of measures that put statutory restrictions on his right to tax and regulate trade by prerogative patent. Furthermore, although the parliament had begun in a spirit of relative cooperation, and some of the "inconveniences" of monopoly practice had been brought to book, the mood of conciliation was gradually dissipated as serious tensions emerged over questions of finance, freedom of speech and foreign policy. In consequence, the assembly was dismissed before its very substantial programme of remedial legislation could be passed. The great raft of free trade bills, covering generally and severally every significant aspect of commerce and manufacture in the kingdom, with the aim of easing the depression, were none of them to reach fruition.

The disappointment was severe, and it had important political implications. This lay partly in the fact that the process of parliamentary legislation was coming to be seen as the most necessary and efficient provision of good government, in the eyes of MPs and their constituents. The Commons struggled to decide whether they should try to get a few bills through in the short space of time that the king had allowed them. Sir Edwin Sandys, at the head of the free trade lobby, thought that, "the eyes of all the kingdom are upon us. They stand expecting, and gazing after the good that we will bring them". But he feared that the bills they could complete in the time left would not satisfy the constituencies.[45] John Delbridge of Barnstaple dreaded the disappointment of the country so much that he would, "rather never have gone home than to go home in this manner". William Nyell thought that it was vital to have something to take back. "The matter of trade stands in a miserable state, though we cannot do what we would, let us do what we can for the country's good".[46] The impediment was that none of the free trade bills was in a sufficient state of readiness to get through. Conrad Russell thought that the Commons were at fault for, "their own failure to complete any satisfactory programme of legislation", and that they should have cleared as much as they could in the week that the king had allowed them.[47] This was exceptional generosity on James's part. But Russell's suggestion missed the point of what the Commons were trying to achieve. He failed to understand the significance of the programme of economic legislation, which constituted the essential, coordinated priority of the House. Of the one hundred or more bills that were at some stage of the legislative process, there were seventeen at most that could have been completed; in effect those that had already passed both Houses. These were mainly adjustments to legal practices, and were the kind of acts that James would probably have approved. But they did not include any of the free trade measures that were most urgently required by the Commons. MPs could not really be blamed for failing to take the opportunity to deal with a few side issues, which were of little general interest, when what they needed was the scope to apply their remedies for the fundamental problems of the kingdom.

The authoritative voice of Sir Nathaniel Rich concurred with the view that it would be better to defer the passing of legislation until these major national economic measures could be obtained, and that the country would not be satisfied with token gestures. Rich and his fellow MPs were in effect taking on the responsibility of trying to provide for the vital common interests of the kingdom. It is clear that they, and their constituents, were convinced of the benefit of a free trade context, and confident of their ability to put it in place through the lawmaking function, if allowed. Rich was already a figure of some standing in the House, and he gave expression to the high value that was placed on the legislative process as the necessary instrument of reform. In the face of the king's dismissal he moved that all the bills should be brought in from the committees and itemised so that nothing would be lost.[48]

Most significantly for the future, the king had put himself in the position of appearing to frustrate the processes of good government. Some critical repercussions were entailed in Rich's complaint about the king's decision to dismiss them. Rich raised the issue of whether the calling of the recess should itself be presented as a grievance: " to be suddenly taken off our business is a grievance to be testified".[49] This was in effect to imply that the king's hitherto undoubted prerogative of determining the life of parliaments might be opened to question. It was apparently too radical a suggestion for some MPs to hear, for at this point Rich was interrupted. But he appealed to the House as a whole to decide whether he should be allowed to continue, and general opinion must have been favourable, since he went on to amplify his argument at some length: "our estate is a decaying estate in England . . . we were preparing remedies and are taken off and intercepted".[50]

Rich was taking a position that would have momentous consequences, if maintained. He saw the legislative programme not as a series of local requirements that might be met in other ways but as an overall public necessity, especially in its proposals for addressing the decay of trade. This revealed a House of Commons that was becoming more and more settled in its assumption of a right to define the priorities of the nation, and increasingly confident of its capacity to serve that interest with definitive statutory provisions. The king, however, seemed not to recognise the national perspective, or the unique force of sovereign representative law, or if he did, it was probably with displeasure. So he had no compunction about "intercepting" the process when parliament had ceased to serve his own dynastic ends. If the royal regime continued to contradict the perceived needs of the country and the requirements of good government, the king's power to obstruct parliament would appear less and less acceptable. In fact, Rich's stand in 1621 was to become the confirmed stance of the House, and by 1628, the "often abortion of parliament" had been formally installed at the top of the Commons' list of grievances.[51]

Revisionist historians have endeavoured to present the legislative function as a matter of "little businesses", or a non-controversial miscellany of local concerns, with no national-political import. The truth is very different, as was clearly demonstrated in 1621. The legislative programme of over one hundred bills was intended centrally to address the most serious economic depression that the kingdom had faced for seventy years. The Commons were responding to a national crisis by seeking to apply the most powerful remedy available—the nationally definitive force of statute law. The fact that it was parliament attempting this exercise, while the king seemed more inclined to offer obstruction than assistance, did not enhance the professional reputation of the monarchy. Conrad Russell once offered the somewhat myopic suggestion that since the king had ceased to want to legislate, therefore parliament's legislative capacity was deprived of political significance.[52] This is the partial view of an historian looking at the world just in terms of the edifice of power, and ignoring the underlying forces and foundations on which it is built. In truth, the very fact that the crown had, for various reasons, lost sympathy with the legislative function, greatly increased the political force of the Commons' growing commitment to the process. It bears repeating that the programme of legislation of 1621 attempted to construct a coordinated, kingdom-wide context of freedom of trade, which the country's representatives understood to be the necessary basis of prosperity. This demonstrated a growing confidence in the efficacy of commercial freedoms, and in the force of sovereign representative law as the core regulative dynamic of the emerging national economy. That the crown had no share in these perspectives goes far to explain the rational basis and underlying strength of parliamentarian ambition. As the Commons assumed the capacity and responsibility for good government in the national interest, only to be persistently frustrated by the king, the feeling would develop that the necessary legislative provision could only be guaranteed by displacing the king's power to restrict the meeting of the assembly.

One of the misapprehensions of modern revisionist history has been to suppose that parliament was not a constant feature in people's minds because it was more an event than an institution, and was only called into being intermittently. This overlooks the fact that since the most essential concerns of the constituencies *were* continuous, both individually and collectively, and parliamentary law had come to be seen as the best and necessary way to meet them, parliament actually *was* a permanent part of the public agenda. MPs and constituencies ended each assembly looking ahead to the next. They brought forward their most pressing bills again and again, to each successive meeting, in the belief that this was the most efficient and often the only way that their problems could be solved. The free-fishing bill, for instance, was presented in every parliament of the 1620s, despite the unlikelihood of its ever receiving the royal assent. The merchants persisted with it simply because it was a provision that they believed to be absolutely right and necessary, and which could only be realised in parliament. It was through the House of Commons alone that they had any chance of establishing what they regarded as the most crucial condition of their principal trade and livelihood.

And in 1624, despite the fact that the king and Lords continued to obstruct the free-fishing bill, the merchants did gain some reward for their faith in the good offices of the House of Commons. In the 1624 assembly, Prince Charles and the Duke of Buckingham entered into a league with the parliamentary leaders to try to convert King James to parliament's national, that is to say anti-Spanish, view of foreign affairs. In consequence, the Commons were given an unusual degree of freedom to assert their position on various issues. The powerful Committee of Grievances, chaired by Sir Edward Coke, with a continuing brief to expose the "inconveniences" of monopoly powers, pressed the principal patentee Sir Ferdinando Gorges into accepting that notwithstanding the powers of restraint in his grant of monopoly, he would hereafter allow the fishermen to "freely visit the coasts of Newfoundland and fish there without any interruptions". Having forced this concession, the Commons seized the moment, and declared free trade in the area. The merchants of Plymouth gratefully preserved a copy of the resolution:

> Thereupon it is resolved by the same House of Commons that the fishermen of England shall have free liberty of fishing on the said coasts of New England, with all the incidents necessary of drying their nets and salting and packing their fish. And it is secondly resolved that in the opinion of this House the clause in the said patent of confiscation of the ships and goods is void and against law.

The Plymouth representative pointedly added the note: "which said order is remaining in the town chest".[53] They obviously valued the resolution as a statement of the legitimacy of the conditions of freedom that they regarded as crucially important to their trade. In effect, they were happy to regard parliament as the arbiter of the law in this field, even though it might be contradicting the position of the crown. It was a striking illustration of the way that parliamentary regulation was coming to be regarded as the authoritative voice of good government. The Plymouth merchants were keeping this order for exactly the same reason that the merchants of Dartmouth had preserved their record of the impositions debate—it was a statement of what they would accept as the legal position. In fact it shows that the real imperatives in the lives of these merchants could only be guaranteed by parliament, and this revealed a basis on which they might be ready to endorse an enhanced constitutional status for the representative assembly.

So the vital economic concerns of the merchants were continuous, as was their perception that parliament was the only place where they could obtain assurances of the conditions in which they wished to trade. They therefore brought their most necessary bills forward again and again. The royal government was not always in direct opposition to their aims, but even when the measures in question were less contentious to the crown than the free-fishing bill, they failed because the king still seemed disinclined to provide the time for them to reach the statute book. A good example is the Exeter cloth bill, which was first presented in 1621. It was in essence about what is now called quality control. This was a crucial factor in maintaining the viability and value of the kingdom's most substantial export. It had often been the subject of parliamentary legislation, which was much the most effective means of enforcing standards of production in all cloth making areas. In fact, the availability of a nationally definitive statute law had been an important factor in establishing the high reputation of English cloth. Exeter had turned to parliament for this service throughout the Elizabethan period, as had all the towns and areas concerned in the manufacture and export of cloth.

The bill of 1621 was brought forward by the Exeter MP John Prowse, who had successfully supervised legislation for the town in the parliament of 1604–1610. It was presented as of general benefit to the commonwealth as a whole, and especially "to any city or market town where such serges and perpetuanos shall be sold". The particular examples given were Taunton, Norwich, Colchester and Canterbury. It was in every respect a measure with national scope. Its purpose was "for the better making of serges and perpetuanos". It was concerned with a new type of cloth. The traditional product of the Exeter clothiers had been the Devonshire Kersey, and the legislative provisions regulating its manufacture had proved sufficient and satisfactory. But by 1621 the pre-eminence of the kersey was being challenged by the emergence of the serge or perpetuano, a lighter but hardwearing cloth, which was proving popular in the French market. The Exeter merchants needed an authoritative regulation to ensure the quality of the new cloth being produced outside the town. The growth of rural industry was vital to the expansion of the cloth trade, but so was the maintenance of manufacturing standards. The merchants had been expressing concern about the problem since 1609, but parliamentary legislation was the only effective way of dealing with it, and 1621 was the first opportunity to attempt to get a law in place.

The Exeter merchants had cause to be optimistic. The 1604–1610 assembly had passed two of their bills, and they possessed an expert and experienced MP in John Prowse. The city also had influential patrons, and there was no reason for the royal government to be antipathetic to the bill, as it was to the free trade measures. Furthermore, for the first session at least, the undercurrent of dissension over foreign policy had not yet broken surface to sour the relationship between crown and Commons. Things seemed to be set fair. But the bill was nevertheless to fail. When Prowse wrote to the mayor he was becoming aware that there might not be sufficient time allowed to get the measure through. He said that he could not give assurance of the king's intentions, "only that we labour heartily to prepare our bills for the king's assent, hoping that we shall bring some home though not all that we desire".[54] He was preparing the mayor for a disappointment, though it is of positive interest that he was thinking in terms of a legislative programme, and hoping that they could bring home some laws that would be welcome as of general benefit, even if not their own much needed cloth bill. The city's other MP, Ignatious Jourdain was also in the business of consolation, saying that they hoped to pass some bills, and to preserve the rest for a future session.[55]

It is clear what great store they set by these initiatives, and indeed by the legislative programme as a whole. These were not optional extras, they were matters of necessity, and the fact that the king seemed not to give them any such priority, or even to give them much consideration, contributed to the growing discrepancy between the attitude of the crown and the perceived requirements of good government. It is not clear why James called the recess and brought the great legislative programme to a shuddering halt in May 1621. Samuel Gardiner suggested that it was because he had received no response to his request for a second subsidy grant. This reaction would certainly have been in line with what became the standard practice of both James and Charles I—that is to say, dispensing with parliament as soon as their financial demands had either been satisfied, or conclusively refused.[56] One thing can be said with certainty—if the royal government continued to show such a lack of regard for a legislative function that the Commons now saw as a public necessity, then in a simple practical sense, MPs would become conditioned to Sir Nathaniel Rich's motion that it was really not acceptable for them to be "intercepted" in this way.

By 1621, even the less prominent Members were expressing an awareness of the gulf that was opening up between the vital public interest of the legislative programme, and a king who seemed to be oblivious to it.

The Ilchester MP, Richard Wyn, was from Gwydir in North Wales, but he shared the perspectives of English MPs. When he wrote to his father he spoke of the bill for free trade in Welsh cottons, and the bill to repeal the clauses in Henry VIII's Act of Union that had allowed the king to legislate for Wales by prerogative.[57] Wyn also stressed the importance of the legislative programme in general. He noted that, "many good businesses are set on foot, but nothing yet finished: there was never parliament of so good hope".[58] But at the calling of the recess he had to record that these hopes had been dashed, and the whole legislative programme aborted. "I make no doubt you have heard how unexpectedly the parliament was adjourned, without the effecting any of our businesses, which as I am informed the king repents him of".[59] If the early Stuart kings ever did repent of their dismissive attitude to the legislative process, it was not apparent from their future actions. James and Charles fell into a standard procedure of dispensing with parliaments as soon as their own fiscal demands had been either granted or denied, routinely leaving the legislative ambitions of their subjects unfulfilled.

There was, however, one constituency that had reason to be grateful to the king for halting the legislative programme of 1621. It saved the merchants and cloth-makers of Bridgewater from an unwelcome new regulation on their own special product. The Exeter bill was not the only measure of quality control to be brought forward in 1621. There was also a bill introduced in the first session to supplement the statute of 1606 "for the true making of cloth". The 1606 act had comprised a comprehensive attempt to establish standard sizes and qualities for every traditional variety of cloth manufacture in the kingdom. The follow-up bill before the House in 1621 declared that the 1606 measure had been a success, and had done much to substantiate the reputation of English cloth, but that there were certain particulars in which it could usefully be extended. One of its provisions had been that certain inferior types of wool should only be used for short cloths of twelve yards in length. It was now proposed that "noiles", a kind of residual wool, should be added to the restricted list. This made the bill a direct threat to the trade of Bridgewater. Noiles, or in West Country parlance "pinnions", were a principal component of the type of kersey with which the town was traditionally associated, and kerseys were normally eighteen yards long.[60] The town's MPs had arrived at Westminster in 1621 to be confronted by a legislative proposal that would undermine their time-honoured manufacturing practices. They returned for the second session armed with their only effective line of defence—a bill of their own to protect their concerns. On 13 November 1621 the Bridgewater receiver's accounts recorded a payment to the MP Roger Warre "for drawing the books for a bill to be exhibited in the parliament for the long casey".[61] They were seeking to gain exemption for their particular style of kersey manufacture from the proposed additional quality controls. They would have had a good chance of success. Parliament had often shown itself capable of accommodating special cases. On this occasion the king's negligent treatment of the legislative process saved them all the trouble. But it showed once again the force and efficiency of the governmental tool that James was setting aside. Parliamentary law was both nationally comprehensive and closely targeted. The merchants of Bridgewater would have been unable to avoid the regulations and restrictions of the new cloth bill, unless they had managed to get a statutory exemption of their own. This was why the legislative function had become a crucial and constant factor in constituency calculations. It was widely recognised as the most effective guarantee of economic interests, local and general, and the sense of loss was very sharp when it was allowed to fall into disuse, especially at a time of crisis.

The economic necessities behind the legislative proposals of the constituencies did not go away—they were too important to the livelihoods of the communities concerned. Their cloth bill, for instance, remained vital to the trade of Exeter, and indeed to that of other towns and cities with the same interests. Accordingly, John Prowse carried it up to parliament again in 1624. This assembly saw a systematic attempt at cooperation between parliament and king in the field of foreign policy. It seemed a more favourable climate in which legislation could proceed. It was also facilitated by the fact that many of the details had already been covered, in 1621. All the important measures brought forward in 1624 were revivals of bills from 1621 or earlier, and they were reintroduced by constituency MPs rather than by the royal government.[62]

So on 24 April, just over two months after the opening of the 1624 parliament, John Prowse was able to write to the mayor of Exeter saying that he had got the cloth bill through two readings and into committee. Included on the committee were the MPs for Norfolk, Suffolk, Essex, Hampshire, Devon and Cornwall. The measure had wide relevance to cloth manufacturers and markets right across the south and east of the kingdom, and was something on which all clothiers could agree as a general guarantee of the trading viability of the product. There seemed to be nothing to prevent the passage of the bill. But Prowse was nevertheless pessimistic—the problem of time was arising once more. "I doubt that our stay will be so long as to make it a law this session, but it must sleep with many other good bills until a new meeting".[63] A further letter three days later spelled out the position in detail. The bill was being considered by the committee and would then be given its third reading. But it would fall short at the final stage: "the next step is engrossing, and so to be presented to the Lords, which I fear will hardly pass this session of parliament".[64] The merchants of Exeter had come within an ace of getting this vital measure through, but the king had now secured his subsidy, and parliament was being brought to a close.

A limited programme of legislation did get through in 1624, for the only time between 1610 and 1640. With King James on the back foot, the freedom of trade agenda scored some successes. The general bill against monopolies, and the bill for free trade in Welsh cloth both reached the statute book. But even in the relatively favourable circumstances of 1624 the great bulk of constituency initiatives fell by the wayside. In fact, Exeter had another proposal to bring forward in 1624, concerning the provision of educational facilities in the town, but the city was advised by its MP Nicholas Duck that there was no point in pursuing it. The pressure of demand was such that "if every day were a week there would be little enough time to determine them, and many will come short of their expectations".[65] This highlighted a fundamental fault line in the governance of England in the early Stuart period. The provision of parliamentary legislation had established a singular pre-eminence in the public mind as the indispensable answer to their problems, and the necessary basis of good government, yet the king never seemed prepared to allow them the time to bring a programme to fruition.

James was not without specific information on the matter. His own favourite and first minister the Duke of Buckingham produced some of the clearest evidence of the way that the responsibility for the practice of good government was coming to be relocated in parliament, and the king was no longer seen as the provider of that service. In 1624, with a display of good judgement above his reputation, Buckingham set out to ascertain the issues that most concerned the Commons, and what concessions by the king were most likely to loosen the subjects' purse strings. He duly noted that a repudiation of the widely hated Spanish alliance would be much appreciated. But more instructively, he was led to understand that the parliamentary coffers would be opened wider if they were given guarantees that their legislative programme would be allowed to proceed.

> Because it is feared, that when your turns are served, you will not call them together again to reform abuses, grievances, and for the making of laws for the good government of the country. [66]

The dissociation of the king from "the good government of the country" would eventually begin to undermine the reputation of the monarchy, and a new balance of political initiative would be indicated.

The county of Nottinghamshire provides a local echo of this growing dichotomy. When Charles I was denied sufficient parliamentary funding at the beginning of his reign he turned to discretionary methods of finance. The people of Nottinghamshire resisted the Benevolence of 1626: "the generality . . . refusing to give other than by parliament, the ordinary and usual way, as they alleged". The same problem arose with the Forced Loan the following year. Government pressure was more systematic on this occasion, but the Nottinghamshire subsidy men still had to be cajoled into payment by the assurance that their cooperation would induce the king to allow more parliaments, and not limit them to his own purposes.[67] It was becoming a glaring omission in the agendas of royal government that the king's "turns" did not include the provision of parliamentary legislation, though his subjects now regarded it as the indispensable means of sustaining the most vital public interests.

The 1624 parliament was the only occasion between 1610 and 1640 when any kind of legislative programme was allowed. It was limited in substance compared to the demand, and even then Buckingham had to pressurise the king to give the MPs a week's grace so that the measures in train could be completed. The Devon diarist Walter Yonge had his own complaint to make against the government's negligence, from a yet more telling angle. He condemned the Lords for their failure to make a significant contribution to the measures that had been passed.

> In this parliament there was not one public bill sent to the Lower House by them. See what care they have for the commonwealth, who were wont to be the chief statesmen and should be the pillars of the commonwealth.[68]

This was an implied criticism of the king and Privy Council, for any initiatives made by the crown would have come via the Lords. The force of Yonge's indictment of establishment inactivity is very striking. It is another illustration of how the process of legislation was coming to be seen as the essence of good government, and how the king's regime was increasingly regarded as defaulting on that responsibility.

After 1624, the opportunities for producing an effective programme of legislation virtually disappeared. Exeter's vital cloth bill was never to get further than the third reading of that year. The town's most experienced legislator John Prowse died in 1625, no doubt in some disappointment that his care and skill had not enabled him to get the measure through. Even in 1624 the House had to plead for enough time to get some laws onto the statute book, and the great bulk of proposals were still left unsatisfied: "if every day were a week there would be little enough time to determine them, and many will come short of their expectations".[69] It would not be surprising if Prowse looked back to his successful legislation in the prolific first parliament of the reign as the model of what could be achieved, and wondered why it had been allowed to fall by the wayside,

In the parliaments of Charles I there was little attempt at a climate of conciliation, and no scope offered for a programme of legislation. The most important requirements of the constituencies were left in limbo, and the legislative service fell into abeyance while the early Stuarts remained in power. Charles I followed the pattern set by his father of treating parliament as merely a possible source of money. Each assembly became a fiscal battleground, with the king seeking unconditional supply, and the Commons insisting that their grievances should be redressed, and their policy preferences accepted, before they would vote subsidies. When his financial demands had been either granted or rejected, the king would dismiss the assembly as being of no further use in the government of his people. It should be added that the Commons' position on matters of general political concern, such as the conduct of foreign policy, often amounted to an alternative definition of the public interest, and therefore comprised a challenge to the authority and the prerogatives of the crown. This did not encourage Charles to keep the assembly in being longer than necessary. But these disputes in themselves tended to underline the increasingly sharp divergence of crown and Commons about the value of the legislative function and the basis of good government.

1628: The Culminating Clash Between Patent and Parliament

The parliament of 1628 has always stood out in the history of the 1620s. Although every assembly of the decade was characterised to some degree by divisions over the rights and purposes of government, it was 1628 that saw the first full-blown constitutional confrontation since 1610. Ironically, it was also the only parliament from which Charles managed to obtain substantial supply. But in return he was obliged to let the Commons condemn every aspect of the discretionary powers that he had been exercising to sustain the military effort since 1626, including un-parliamentary taxation, arbitrary imprisonment, martial law and billeting.

The Commons were attacking the king's prerogative powers on a broad front, and the significance of this should be underlined. Recent historians have tended to portray the aims of the Commons in 1628 as just restorative. But this is to be misled by the surface of conventional references to precedent and "ancient liberty". The contemporary critics who condemned the programme as anti-monarchical came closer to pinpointing the force of the Commons' proposals. Sir Nathaniel Rich felt obliged to deny the charge of subverting the monarchy, and protested that they wished to continue to live under a king. He was protesting a little too much, for this would be a king deprived of the entire range of discretionary rights with which he had originally been empowered to enable him to guarantee the public safety in times of emergency. The Commons now sought to bring all such matters under parliamentary control. This would be a change in the constitutional balance, subjecting the prerogatives of the crown to the exercise of representative consent. Equally important, it was also a further graphic illustration of the contending concepts of government. It was in many ways a culminating clash between "patent" and "parliament".

One reason that the radical thrust of the parliamentarian position has been underestimated is that historians have failed to recognise the importance of the differing concepts of good government. Derek Hirst, for instance, persists in the revisionist supposition that the Commons' programme was just restorative, then rather contradicts himself by noting that in fact they were not relying on existing law: "they appeared to insist that there ought to be a statutory warrant for every executive action".[70] To be surprised by this is to fail to understand the full significance of the Commons' belief in the force of representative law, both in terms of the principles of sovereignty, and the practice of government.

The apparent contradiction between the perspectives of discretionary power on the one hand, and representative rights on the other, encapsulates the subversive force of what the Commons were attempting—they wanted to subject the king's emergency prerogative to parliamentary control. Their willingness to entertain such a challenging and disruptive ambition derived in part from what I have identified as the political paradox created by the distinctive development of sovereign statute law in England, which made the most unlimited or "absolute" power of legislation dependent on the express consent of the "entire society".[71] This gave parliament a defining share in legislative sovereignty, and elevated the authority of representative rights as an acceptable basis of administrative provision. It led further to a presumption that this was the form that all sovereign exercises should take. A previous chapter described the unqualified self-confidence with which MPs extended the concept to cover the raising of the customs dues, and in the process to displace the king's right of impositions. They were now doing the same in the context of his discretionary powers in general. The fact that this not only subjected the king's prerogatives to the consent of parliament, but also denied his real contingency needs at times of crisis, underlined the force of the paradox. The Commons' belief that the representative basis of legislative sovereignty should be extended to cover all areas of "unlimited" government was in this instance being taken to an extreme.

Sir Nathaniel Rich wanted the king's activities to be outlawed by the authority of a statute. Charles, on this occasion, showed sound political judgement, and firmly rejected the idea, which would, after all, have been the Commons using their most sovereign power to undermine his own. Charles said that they must trust him to observe their liberties. He was happy to have Magna Charta and other relevant statutes confirmed, knowing no doubt that they were open to interpretation, but he could not allow the Commons to expand the statutes to specifically outlaw his recent activities. Rich found this response quite inadequate: "unless they be confirmed as we have expounded them, they are but shells . . . he will take order for soldiers, let him say it is against the law; so for loans, privy seals, imprisonment and the like".[72] The strength and breadth of public support for the Commons' demands, and the clarity of their requirement for statutory control, is well illustrated in an exchange of letters between the MP Thomas Smyth and his mother Elizabeth. Smyth wrote when the bill was being finalised in the Commons for presentation to the Lords, in the expectation, or at least the hope of acceptance. Elizabeth had received less encouraging reports from other quarters, and was glad that her son could reassure her that "the freedom" was being secured: "I was told of a trust that was commanded, but they could not tell the reason for it. Such an escape as hath been deserves thanksgiving".[73] But her earlier information was to prove more accurate. The bill would fail, like many others, and on this occasion the king had very good reason to reject it.

The Petition of Right was a compromise. Charles would acknowledge their concerns, but it would not comprise new legislation as such. The king took the opportunity to reiterate that he was really offering nothing more than his original promise to obey the law as it stood. The true wishes of MPs were still being denied, and their disappointment was palpable. There was a long silence in the House. Then Rich proposed a Remonstrance, stating that the king was being misled by evil influences. This suggestion was seconded by Sir Edward Giles, MP for Totnes: "We sit here as men daunted. Let us put on the spirits of Englishmen and speak to the purpose. Let us follow the motion made".[74] Rich accordingly drew up a long list of items for the Remonstrance, headed by "Often abortions of parliament" and "Neglect of the counsels of parliament".[75] The king was minded to respond in customary fashion, and dissolve the assembly. But the Lords advised restraint, and urged that there must be some agreement in the interests of the kingdom. Charles was persuaded to make a more specific acknowledgement of the Commons' concerns. This still fell far short of declaring his powers unlawful, and he asserted again that it really amounted to no more than his original commitment to observe their liberties. The Commons, now desperate for any concession, grasped the offer with relief. But it was Charles who had reason to feel the more satisfied. He had evaded the Commons' determination to bring his discretionary powers under the control of parliamentary law. At the end of the session he felt free to call in the Petition and record once again that he had only committed himself in general terms not to breach their liberties. He declared specifically that his prerogative rights could not be subject to parliamentary statute.[76] This highlighted the central issue, and Charles had got the best of it. The Petition of Right was significant for what the Commons had wanted to do, not for what they actually achieved. But the king had done enough to get his subsidy, which now went through the House quickly.

And having obtained a substantial vote of supply, he had no further reason to keep the assembly in being. He was thus in a position to deny MPs the opportunity to fulfil their most important long-term ambition, which was to establish control over the customs dues. In the wake of the "agreement" over the Petition and the subsidy, the Commons felt that the time was ripe to bring this crucial purpose to fruition. The ending of impositions seemed indeed a logical implication of the principle outlined in the Petition of Right that no public money should be raised without parliamentary consent. MPs stood up to reiterate their belief that impositions were illegal.[77] They asked for an adjournment to give them time to consult with their constituents about the most acceptable forms and levels of customs on trade.

The Commons were still offering the inducement that, suitably encouraged they would ratify the king's collection of tonnage and poundage, but Charles had never shown much interest in surrendering his right of impositions in order to get his right of tonnage and poundage restored. Everything he said on the issue indicated that he simply wanted the grant made as it had been for his predecessors, without conditions. So rather than allow parliament to take command of the customs dues, the king prorogued the assembly. The Commons were again reduced to entrusting their feelings to a remonstrance, declaring "tonnage and poundage and other impositions not granted by parliament . . . a breach of the fundamental liberties of the kingdom, and contrary to . . . the Petition of Right". Aware by now that words were not enough, the Commons applied the only sanction available to them, and enjoined the merchants to refuse payment of tonnage and poundage.[78] MPs could at least feel vindicated by the fact that this incitement to fiscal disobedience was very effective. There ensued what has been called a "general strike" against any kind of un-parliamentary levy.[79] A significant aspect of the dispute overall was the strength of public support for parliament's radical ambitions.

They had failed, however, to achieve a statutory guarantee to control the king's discretionary powers. They had also failed to progress their most constructive aim—a programme of legislation for "the good government of the country". In face of the dissolution, Rich did his best to keep the idea of such a programme alive. He called on, "those gentlemen that have any bill pending, that they may deliver them to the clerk, to be in readiness against the next meeting".[80] He led the way by outlining an initiative that he had in mind himself, namely a bill to promote trade via the West Indies, which he promised to "study and fit against the next session", apparently receiving a great cheer in the House. This was not just in gratitude for the idea that there would be a "next session". The issue of the West Indies carried a considerable significance of its own, which may not be obvious on the surface. The promotion of English trade and naval activity in that arena was a notable example of an independently defined public priority for which the Commons were eager to take order, even if the royal government was not.

The Kingdom "Bereaved" of the Legislative Power in the 1630s

There was in fact to be one more parliament. A previous chapter dealt in detail with the circumstances of the 1629 assembly. The king called it in a final attempt to get the Commons to confirm his right to tonnage and poundage. The assembly was ended when it became clear that the House had no intention of making that grant unless the king agreed to give up his prerogative of impositions. Thereafter, the king chose to govern without parliaments, and the 1630s were the decade of Personal Rule. But the vital economic concerns of MPs and their constituents did not disappear with the absence of parliaments. What vanished was the chance to resolve their problems by the most desirable and effective instrument of sovereign statute law. Yet at the same time the importance of that facility was underlined. The unique advantages offered by parliamentary legislation are illustrated by the difficulties that the Exeter merchants faced in trying to secure the regulation of cloth production by other means. It remained crucial to the trading prospects of Exeter, and many other towns, to be able to ensure reliable standards and quality in the manufacture of the new types of cloth. This would have been secured with promptness and efficiency if the cloth bill presented to parliament in 1621 and 1624 had been given time to reach the statute book. In the absence of this best option, other avenues were tried in an attempt to deal with the problem, but none were successful. In 1625 the royal government proposed a scheme to regulate cloth production through county corporations, but it came to nothing.[81] In the later 1630s, with no prospect of a parliament, the Exeter merchants began to take soundings in the Privy Council with a view to obtaining orders for regulatory powers. The government favoured regulation in principle, and in May 1638 Exeter sent a representative to pursue the question. Discussions were held but again nothing was achieved.[82] These failures, and the fragmentary and limited nature of the alternative proposals show just why parliamentary law was an unrivalled provision. In one single, coordinating statute, it was possible to establish a rule that was precisely targeted and nationally binding. Nothing else carried the same certainty. This was of particular value in economic affairs. Not only was statute the ultimate guarantor of property rights, it also provided a perfect judicial framework for the developing commercial sphere. Like the integrated market itself, parliamentary law worked in a context of completion and continuity. It was directly responsive to the imperative needs of the trading community, through sympathetic representatives in the national parliament. It was embedded in the day-to-day life of society. It was comprehensive, definitive and stable in operation, yet open to systematic review. Only sovereign representative law could offer this level of provision.

This illustrates again the force of statute law as the principal inner dynamic of a developing "state" concept, binding the country into a judicio-political unit, as it bound every community and individual to its provisions. The recognition of this as a state function explains the very elevated view of parliament's legislative service voiced by John Pym early in 1641, when the Long Parliament found itself in a position to ensure that the representative body would never again be denied the opportunity to exercise its law-making power. In his indictment of William Laud,

Pym claimed that the Archbishop had counseled the king to avoid calling parliaments and thereby conspired to "bereave this kingdom of the legislative power, which can only be used in parliaments . . . and which is the only means to restore it from distempers and decays".[83] The legislative function was now seen as more than just a particularly desirable method of administration. Pym articulated its value in the strongest possible terms, as the very structure of good government, and in effect the basis of a "state" concept. It was, he said, "that which makes and constitutes a kingdom". The phrase was portentous, for it revealed the coordinating dynamic of statute law as one of the principal factors that were turning the kingdom into a different kind of polity—that is to say, a nation-state with independently definable structures and interests. It added greatly to the strength and ambition of the parliamentarian movement that they, rather than the crown, were embracing that perspective.

Notes

1. J. Kayll, *The Trades' Increase,* (London 1615), BL 1138. b. 10, p. 50
2. Ibid, pp. 51–2
3. Ibid, p. 55
4. Chamberlain to Carleton, 8 July 1620, *SP Domestic*, CXVI, 13
5. Gerard de Malynes, *The Maintenance of Free Trade,* (London 1622), BL 712. c. 30, pp. 67–9
6. Ibid, pp. 49–50
7. S. R. Gardiner, *History of England 1603–1642,* (London 1886–9), IV, p. 7
8. Edward Nicholas, *Proceedings and Debates in the House of Commons, 1621,* (Oxford 1766), II, p. 303
9. *Commons Debates 1621*, ed. W. Notestein, (New Haven 1935), IV, pp. 79–80; VI, pp. 249–51; V, pp. 475–6
10. Devon Record Office, Totnes Borough Archive, 1579A/16/35
11. Gardiner, *History of England*, IV, p. 49
12. *Commons Journal*, p. 514; *Commons Debates 1621*, IV, p. 54, n.2
13. *Commons Debates 1621*, II, p. 118
14. C. Hill, *Intellectual Origins of the English Revolution*, (Oxford 1966), p. 233; D. O. Wagner, "Coke and the Rise of Economic Liberalism", *Economic History Review VI*, pp. 30–44
15. *Commons Debates 1621*, V, p. 93
16. Ibid, II, p. 303
17. *Commons Journal*, I, p. 539; *Commons Debates 1621*, II, p. 169, V, p. 272, VI, p. 31
18. *Commons Debates 1621*, IV, p. 197
19. Gardiner, *History of England*, IV, p. 55
20. C. H. McIlvain, *Constitutionalsm, Ancient and Modern,* (Ithaca 1940), p. 138
21. Mun's memo of 1623, cited in C. Wilson, *England's Apprenticeship,* (London 1965), p. 60
22. Wilson, *England's Apprenticeship*, p. 135
23. *Commons Debates 1621*, V, p. 93
24. Ibid, III, p. 361
25. *Commons Journal*, I, p. 520
26. Ibid, p. 592

27. Ibid, pp. 526, 537
28. Ibid, p. 529
29. Ibid, p. 534
30. C. Hill, *Reformation to Industrial Revolution,* (Harmondsworth 1969), p. 69
31. *Commons Journal*, I, p. 591b
32. Ibid, p. 654a
33. Ibid, 591b; *Commons Debates 1621*, III, p. 82
34. *Commons Journal*, I, p. 620
35. Ibid
36. *Commons Debates 1621*, II, p. 544; III, 361; IV, p. 384
37. Malynes, *The Maintenance of Free Trade*, pp. 49–50
38. Ibid, p. 51
39. Ibid., pp. 52–4
40. Ibid, p. 53
41. E. Misselden, *Free Trade: Or the Means to Make Trade Flourish,* (London 1622), BL 712. c. 2, p. 50
42. Ibid, p. 55
43. Ibid, p. 71
44. Ibid, p. 133
45. *Commons Debates 1621*, IV, 391–7; III, 348–9; 374; VI, 178
46. Ibid, II, p. 345
47. C. Russell, *Parliaments and English Politics,* (Oxford 1979), pp. 118–19
48. *Commons Debates 1621*, II, p. 544; IV, p. 384
49. Ibid
50. Ibid, III, 361
51. *Commons Debates 1628*, IV, pp. 169–70
52. Russell, *Parliaments and English Politics*, p. 36
53. West Devon RO, Plymouth Corporation Archive, W48, f.92
54. Devon RO, Exeter Corporation Letter Book, 60c, L206, L209
55. Ibid, L210
56. Gardiner, *History of England*, IV, p. 126
57. National Library of Wales, Wyn of Gwydir Ms. 9058E/1096A
58. Ibid, 9057E/943
59. Ibid, 9057E/959
60. E. Kerridge, *Textile Manufacture in Early Modern England,* (Manchester 1985), pp. 26–7
61. Somerset RO, Bridgewater Borough Archive, D/B/bw 1609
62. R. Ruigh, *The Parliament of 1624,* (Harvard 1971), p. 50
63. Devon RO, Exeter Corporation Letter Book, 60d, L268
64. Ibid, L243
65. Ibid
66 BL Harleian Ms. 6987, ff. 200–1. Buckingham's letter to James, discussed in Ruigh, *Parliament of 1624*, pp. 214–15
67. TNA, SP16/33/126; SP16/36/34; SP16/55/1
68. *Diary of Walter Yonge*, ed. G. Roberts, *Camden Society 41*, (London 1848), p. 76
69. Devon RO, Exeter Corporation Letter Book, 60d, L243
70. D. Hirst, *Authority and Conflict*, (Arnold 1986), p. 152
71. G. Yerby, *People and Parliament*, chaps. 2, 6 and 8; *The English Revolution and the Roots of Environmental Change*, chap. 10
72. *Common Debates 1628*, ed. R. C. Johnson et al. (New Haven 1977), III, pp. 275, 281
73. Bristol Record Office, Smyth of Long Aston Ms. AC/C48/6, 12
74. *Commons Debates* 1628, IV, pp. 114, 123

75. Ibid, pp. 169–70
76. Gardiner, *History of England*, VII, p. 30; Russell, *Parliaments and English Politics*, pp. 399–401
77. *Commons Debates 1628*, III, 595
78. Ibid, IV, pp. 388–95
79. R. Brenner, *Merchants and Revolution,* (London 1993), pp. 232–3
80. *Commons Debates 1628*, IV, p. 473
81. *CSP Domestic 1623–5*, pp. 484–5
82. Devon RO, Exeter Corporation Act Book, 1/8, ff. 20, 35, 71
83. J. Rushworth, *Historical Collections*, (London 1659–1701), IV, pp. 201–2

9 Economic Aims of Parliament's Foreign Policy

Elizabeth I as the Embodiment of the National Enterprise; the Dynastic Preference of James I for the National Enemy

The developing nation-state concept also had an outward dimension. This too came to be occupied by parliament rather than the crown. Few would deny that the frequent and extended foreign affairs disputes of the 1620s had an important economic aspect, at least in respect of how the military efforts of the kingdom were, or were not, to be financed. It is not sufficiently recognised, however, that the root cause of the dissension, and the dysfunction in England's external relations, was parliament's insistence that it would only fund a policy that was in line with its own perception of where the best interests of the kingdom lay. The parliamentary view was defined at core by a particular, yet universal economic project. This priority was significantly different, and often directly opposite to those of the crown, and the stance of the representative assembly therefore became in effect an attempt to seize the initiative in a field of activity that had always been the most jealously guarded preserve of the monarch.

In the late sixteenth and early seventeenth centuries, the House of Commons and its constituencies, and indeed a significant element in the House of Lords, had a clear and consistent view of what England's long-term aim in the international arena should be. The prospect was both all embracing and specific, and it can thus be summarised quite simply as the pursuit of a sea-borne trading empire, to be created by the extension of maritime power and enterprise across the oceans of the globe. There was also a clear perception of the identity of the rival that needed to be displaced in order for this ambition to be realised. And it was in the light of these imperatives that the outward perspectives of the nation-state were forged.

That parliament came to appropriate the outward as well as the inward dynamic of the new nation-state owed much to the particular circumstances in which the English imperial enterprise was conceived and structured. It did not follow the Spanish model, which was inspired essentially by the ambitions of the Castilian crown and focused on military power and monetary plunder. The English version was not dissimilar to the Dutch, which was driven essentially by the aspirations of the mercantile community and focused on trade. Even more than the Dutch, however, the English project was "national" in form, because it engaged all the economically powerful sections of society. It was in effect the furthest extension of the unusual combination of merchants, gentry and yeoman farmers, which has been highlighted in previous chapters, coordinating the pursuit of a distinctive context of freedom for English trade, whether internal or international.

The enthusiastic participation of gentlemen landowners in the commercial sphere seems to have been peculiar to the English scene. Dutch trade revolved around a group of substantial mercantile towns, and the contribution of the landowning class was not so conspicuous. This was the usual pattern across most of Europe. A previous chapter described the surprise of Theodore Rabb when he found that the prominent English gentleman Sir Edwin Sandys appeared to spend a great deal of his time and energy on matters of trade. Rabb then embarked on an important study and discovered the equally surprising explanation—that in fact Sandys was not out of line in the English context, because a large number of MPs in Elizabethan and early Stuart times had a direct involvement in the expansion of trade and empire.[1] This appears as less of an anomaly when we recall the other distinctive features of the position of the gentry in England—that is to say, their participation in the commercialisation of farming; their appropriation of the borough seats in what would normally have been the mercantile chamber of the Commons; and their acquisition of a powerful vested interest in the principle of representative consent. All these factors combined to place the gentry side by side with the merchants and commercial farmers in pressing the demand for a right of freedom of trade, and an end to arbitrary customs dues. In similar vein, it was as a genuinely collective vision that a national-imperial, trade-driven foreign policy found its natural voice in parliament, the representative of all those associated interests.

The English project, and the parliamentarian approach, was also exceptionally cogent and consistent in that for almost the first century of the enterprise its fire was concentrated on one particular rival. This too can be perceived in part as another contrast with the Dutch pattern of empire. The latter, being focused mainly towards Africa and the East, was not in direct competition with the Spanish. The principal aspirations of the English empire, on the other hand, were directed towards the West, where Spain was already in occupation. So for the English to realise their ambitions in this favoured area, the Spanish grip would have to be loosened, or better still, broken. There were other reasons too why the English came to harbour a special antipathy towards Spain, associating it with militant Catholicism, a proclivity for religious persecution, and a tendency to absolutist government. But English and Spanish interests came into conflict most constantly and directly on the Western Seas, and this gave parliamentarian foreign policy a specific form.

The special inclination of the English for oceanic trading enterprise became apparent in the mid-sixteenth century, like so many other crucial developments in the emergence of the English nation-state. It was during the Edwardian Protectorates that the great overseas enterprise was first conceived. General explanations for the timing can be suggested. This was in various respects a moment of liberation, when the spontaneous inclinations of the political nation at large could find expression. In the economic field, the cloth trade had reached a peak in its traditional form and was displaying some limitations, and the process of lay investment in the church lands was largely complete. The expansive economic energies of the gentry, merchants and yeomen of the growing nation sought other avenues. The oceans beckoned, and the third great national project was put in hand.

It was not inhibited by disruptions in the agrarian world. The structure of agricultural activity was changing, as the old communal pattern of farming was gradually displaced by the consolidation of commercial units. The 1550s saw depression, bad harvests and a struggling population, but given the rising market, some gentlemen landowners and yeoman farmers were now in a position to make money even in hard times. So there was still capital available for manufacture and trade. The merchants of the rapidly growing port of London were able to help the government service its debts, "and when, in 1552, the government repaid its obligation by cancelling the privileges of the Steelyard, the entrepreneurs of England were ready to exploit the opportunity".[2] The Edwardian Councils had a lively interest in exploration, and gave support to Sebastian Cabot's proposed search for a northeast passage. The merchant community raised substantial funding, and in 1555 three ships under Sir Hugh Willougby and Richard Chancellor set of "for the discovery of the Northern part of the world". The ultimate purpose was the development of commerce, and the initiative bore fruit in the setting up of the first joint-stock company, to trade with Russia. This may fairly be regarded as setting the tone of the English enterprise.

The assault on the imperial power of Spain would display similar levels of vigour and resolve. This held fire during the reign of Mary Tudor, when Spanish interests came under the protection of the crown, and parliament was more exercised in preventing the introduction of Spanish influences into the English realm. In the process, however, the peculiar antipathy of the English people to all things Spanish became evident, most notably in the unprecedented impertinence of the parliamentary petition asking the Queen not to take a Spanish prince for her husband. The English public showed considerable distaste for Mary's campaign of religious persecution, and associated it with the Spanish presence. In the disastrous French war at the end of the reign, the English navy was obliged to operate in support of Spain. The lesson was drawn for the future that this must not happen again.

Elizabeth I did not immediately hasten to satisfy the general view among her subjects that Spain was the natural enemy. She had more pressing problems with France and Scotland, and there were good pragmatic reasons not to rush to antagonise the Spanish, who possessed the most efficient military force that Europe had seen for centuries and controlled the main route of the cloth trade, through Antwerp. Elizabeth did, however, give a clear indication that she would not reprise Mary's generally deplored policy of allying herself with the Spanish crown.[3] In her first parliament, her deputy, the Lord Keeper drew a contrast in "guarded but unmistakable words" between the unfortunate policies of the late Queen and such a princess as they now had, " to whom, nothing—what nothing? no, no worldly thing under the sun is so dear as the hearty love and good will of her nobles and subjects".[4] The commitment to apply herself objectively to the interests and desires of her subjects was often repeated, and it was not an empty promise. In general terms it was fulfilled, and this had specific implications for the making of policy, and for the balance of interests in foreign affairs.

Elizabeth's official attitude towards Spain hardened gradually as the reasons for maintaining Spanish friendship came to be outweighed by the reasons for resisting Spanish power. But almost at the beginning of the reign the stage was set for the more general, if at first unofficial, confrontation on the high seas. In 1561, Secretary of State William Cecil issued a declaration of intent by repudiating the Spanish claim to a monopoly of trade in the New World, as originally granted to them by the Pope. Thus liberated, in 1562, John Hawkins set forth to carve out a share in the lucrative commerce in African slaves to the West Indies. At first the Spanish settlers welcomed the new source of supply, and high profits accrued for all, including, by the second voyage, Queen Elizabeth. By the third voyage, however, the Spanish authorities were fully alert to the intrusion, and the venture concluded with a pitched battle. Such conflicts were now likely to arise anywhere and at anytime. As a consequence: "It was impossible any longer to disguise the fact that although England and Spain were nominally at peace in Europe, a state of war prevailed beyond the line".[5]

The traditional rationale for maintaining good relations with Spain was the need to ensure that the main trade route through the Low Countries remained open, but at the end of the 1560s this balance of interests was being undermined. Elizabeth, perhaps not entirely by choice, had become the de facto champion of Protestantism in northern Europe. Spain, on the other hand, was mobilising forces to suppress the revolt of the Dutch United Provinces, which were Protestant. The Spanish had thus become a threatening military presence just across the channel. The various elements of increased tension began to knit together into a broad pattern following an episode in 1568, when some ships carrying money to pay the Spanish troops in the Netherlands were attacked by Huguenot pirates and obliged to seek refuge in Southampton and Plymouth. The English hosts were unable to resist the temptation to do what they usually did and commandeer the money. The Spanish authorities were understandably incensed, and English property in Spain and the Netherlands was seized. A trade war ensued, which severed normal relations for five years, and the central, traditional route of the cloth trade through Antwerp never really recovered. The Spanish crown had rightly calculated that the English would be most damaged by the obstruction of their trade, but had perhaps not realised that the naval impulse and the momentum for expansion was now so strong that they would simply turn elsewhere.

In fact, the stopping of the flow of trade through Antwerp proved to be the final incentive for English ships to range far and wide across the globe in search of new outlets. "With the collapse of the Antwerp market in 1568–73, the English cloth trade was freed from dependence on the House of Burgundy. The merchants had to seek out new marts all around the coast of the continent".[6] This they did, escorted by Her Majesty's Navy. One of the most instructive examples of this combination in action occurred on the other side of the world, in the North Atlantic. As the reasons for maintaining friendship with Spain disappeared, the availability of the Royal Navy for disrupting Spanish trade increased. In the early 1580s, naval forces swept the Newfoundland waters clear of Spanish shipping, and the West Country cod fishing venture thrived mightily from then on. This effect, repeated on a global scale, was the essence of the enterprise.

It was in the 1580s that the central force and character of the project was defined and confirmed. The threat from Spain in Europe had become significantly greater. Victory in the great sea battle of Lepanto had freed the Spanish from the challenge of the Turks in the Mediterranean.[7] The flow of silver increased, and the Duke of Parma appeared to be engaged on a systematic re-conquest of the rebellious provinces in the Netherlands. Elizabeth was obliged to aid the United Provinces in a more substantial and direct manner. The king of Spain in turn became convinced that England would have to be taken out of the equation if the Netherlands were to be re-conquered. Plotting against Elizabeth intensified, with undoubted Spanish involvement. The recovery of both England and Scotland by a Habsburg/Guise alliance was seriously projected. In 1584 this took shape in the Throckmorton plot to murder the Queen, in which the Spanish were again closely implicated. There was an obvious need for some kind of pre-emptive action.

In October 1584, Elizabeth and her Privy Council finally determined on a declaration of war. An expeditionary force would be sent to help the independent Dutch provinces, and there would be a systematic naval attack on the Spanish West Indies. As Wallace MacCaffrey has said, by this decision royal policy was catching up with the dominant trend of public opinion in the kingdom. But this was not just the technical supplanting of one foreign policy by another. It marked a qualitative change in the way that foreign policy was formed, and the basis on which it was defined. In his very important article, MacCaffrey identified this as the moment of transition from a "dynastic" to a "national" concept of foreign affairs in England. The war aim no longer revolved simply around the subjective interests and wishes of the king, issuing the traditional appeal to feudal loyalty to come to his assistance in the defence of his rights. It was now the collective concerns and desires of the kingdom at large that were at stake. Accordingly, the policy and the war aims were formulated and presented in concert with the House of Commons, to guarantee that it had their moral, and financial commitment. "In these pre-war parliaments one sees the fulfilment of the shift which had been taking place for decades past, away from a policy built on a dynastic view of foreign relations to one orientated on national interests".[8] It is difficult to overestimate the significance of the change. The crucial difference, with critical implications for the future, was that foreign policy was being conceived not on the personal objectives of the crown, but on a balanced view of the outward priorities of the nation as a whole. An area of dispute would arise if and when a monarch failed to recognise this new responsibility.

The selected national project was driven by a strong and clear vision of the future, reinforced by the course of events. In 1588, the core proposition of the enterprise found dramatic shape and vindication in the defeat of the mighty armada of one hundred thirty ships sent by Philip of Spain to escort an army of invasion across the English Channel. This act of aggression could well be taken to confirm the justice of the English view of Spain as an agent of arbitrary and overweening power that needed to be resisted and reduced. The question now was whether a successful resistance could be mounted in the face of the concentrated force of Spanish arms. The answer turned out to be quite positive.

Most schools and generations of historians have rather underestimated the significance that the Armada's defeat had in confirming the viability of England's chosen national project. Traditional historians were too prone to look at the matter in terms of a national tradition of defying the big bully across the channel. The defeat of the Armada was taken as the first instance of this characteristic stance, to be followed by similar triumphs against Louis XIV, Napoleon and Hitler. The recent generation of historians have, understandably, been more inclined to question assumptions of national glory, and have suggested that, in any case, the defeat of the Invincible Armada was not a great triumph of arms—it owed at least as much to the timely intervention of the weather as to the effectiveness of English naval action. On this basis there has been a general tendency to describe the successes of the Elizabethan stand as "mythical". Even an historian open to the idea of a popular foreign policy, Tom Cogswell, is happy to suppose that James I was in the shadow of the "myth" of his predecessor's triumphs, and that in actuality the war with Spain "had not proved an outstanding success". Cogswell then proceeds to contradict himself by adding, "admittedly she secured the independence of the new Dutch Republic and the French monarchy".[9] When we recall that she also secured the independence of her own realm against the greatest military threat since the Norman Conquest, and stabilised the position of the Protestant religion in Europe for a generation to come, we may conclude that in truth there was nothing "outstanding" left for her to do.

Historians have been misled by their own restrictive focus on measuring the issue as a feat of arms, when in fact this was not the essence of the matter. The defeat of Spain, however achieved, was not the endgame—it was a task that had to be performed to clear the way for the great enterprise, and in this aim it was actually quite a success. Geography and climate undeniably played a part in the discomforting of the Invincible Armada, but this was not just fortuitous—it had a positive significance in underlining the viability of the national project. In an important sense, the island had proved capable of defending itself, and it was thereby established as a secure platform for commercial advance. And the Elizabethan seamen had done what they needed to do to maintain the natural fortress. The important thing about the wind was not that it was Protestant, but that the advanced design of the English ships enabled them to sail closer to it. The Royal Navy might have failed to destroy the Spanish fleet in some grand Nelsonian encounter, but the sailors, with their more "weatherly" ships, had displayed an exceptional command of oceanic conditions, which left them in no doubt as to where the future lay.

In practical terms, as John Guy concluded, "Elizabeth's navy had extended her control over the coastline of the British Isles and the waters of northwest Europe".[10] This completed the picture of the defensible island and the serviceable surrounding sea. It was not just a "moat defensive to the house", it was also—and here was the beauty of the vision—a free way out to gather wealth from across the oceans. The year after the Armada campaign, Drake instigated a counter attack that once again revealed the true purpose of the exercise. He proposed, with the help of Norris and his men, to attack Lisbon, with the aim of inspiring regime change in Portugal. This would further weaken the position of the Spanish crown, and most importantly, it would open up the Portuguese Empire to English merchants. This proved to be a little over-ambitious at the time, but it displayed the real nature and the full range and force of the English national project.

Also in the year that followed the defeat of the Armada, the project found its celebratory text in Richard Hakluyt's work *The Principal Navigations, Voyages, Traffics and Discoveries of the English Nation*. He recorded past achievements and looked ahead towards an even more glittering future, with the thought that in Elizabeth's reign, the English people had shown themselves to be peculiarly destined for this mission. In the dedication to the first edition in 1589, he declared that Elizabeth's subjects, "in searching the most opposite corners and quarters of the world, and compassing the vast globe more than once, have excelled all the nations and peoples of the world".[11] Hakluyt was able to put a lot of detail on the claim. It was a vast book, describing ventures to all parts of the earth.

> Which of the kings of this land before Her Majesty had their banners ever seen in the Caspian Sea? Which of them hath ever dealt with the Emperor of Persia . . . and obtained for her merchants large and loving privileges? Who ever found English consuls and agents at Tripolis in Syria, at Aleppo, at Babylon, at Balsara, and which is more, who ever heard of Englishmen at Goa before now?[12]

What he was describing was a growing empire of commerce. "His interest lay in the extension of markets, in the development of trade, in the utilisation of products of new territories for the benefit of the home market".[13] Hakluyt spelled this out in the dedication to Cecil that introduced the second edition. "Our chief desire is to find out ample vent for our woollen cloth".[14] The great project was very homely at heart. It was all about increasing trade and bringing back wealth. Hakluyt sought to promote the exploration and exploitation of the Americas as especially profitable. The fact that this was also where the power of Spain comprised the biggest obstacle was not a deterrent. On the contrary, it presented the target that focused the motive force of the enterprise.

So James I was not in the shadow of a myth, he was in the shadow of an established national project, which could hardly have been less mythical. It was a very material proposition, in its nature, in its essential viability, and in the fact that it commanded the coordinated commitment of the English people. This was why James created problems for himself when he chose, quite specifically, to contradict the galvanising premise of the enterprise, the thrust of which was to oppose and disable the power of Spain. Putting himself at odds with the strength of English opinion might appear perverse in terms of his own interests. Why would he wilfully limit the force of his foreign policy by setting it on a course that ran counter to the known traditions and inclinations of his subjects? In one sense, the paradox is not difficult to explain. Quite simply, James did not recognise the validity of the new national, or state perspective. He had no concept of defining a policy on an objective view of the active interests of the nation as a whole. His aims were purely dynastic. He pursued matches and alliances that would bring prestige to the Stuart line, and reinforce the authority of monarchical rule in general. A popular determination of foreign affairs struck him as subversive. But it should not be supposed that in rejecting the national view he was neglecting an established royal commitment. It had long been normal practice for foreign relations to be conceived around the personal and dynastic needs of the crown, with no national obligation assumed. As Mary Tudor had pointed out when parliament had tried to influence her choice of spouse, they would never have taken such a liberty with any previous monarch. The fact that they were seeking to prevent her from marrying a Spanish prince illustrated the national imperatives that were arising within the body of the kingdom. When James I showed himself similarly oblivious to national sentiment by following the same policy as Mary, it was not a dereliction of duty, but it did put him at odds with the newly established outward priorities of his people.

James was not in the shadow of a myth, but he was placed in an unsympathetic light by the fact that his immediate predecessor Elizabeth had adapted her rule to suit the independent outward perspectives of the kingdom. One of the reasons that the national definition of foreign affairs had been established in the reign of Elizabeth I was that the Queen was, perhaps uniquely, willing and able to accommodate it. There were various special factors in Elizabeth's position that made her more effective as the vehicle rather than the driver of policy. It might be said indeed that the reign of her half-sister Mary had engendered a sense that for monarchical rule to be fully successful in England, it would now need to take greater account of the dominant views of the kingdom at large. Mary's rule was associated with a time of famine and disease, bad harvests and high taxes, religious conflicts induced by the hated influence of Spain, and a disastrous foreign policy. Much of this had been done in opposition to the known inclinations of her people. There was a perception that this was an imbalance that would need to be rectified.

There is no doubt that Elizabeth consciously determined to take a different route from her sister. In her first exchanges with parliament she was anxious to provide assurances that her greatest study would be the wishes of her people, and that there would be no repetition of the worst scenario of a Spanish match. The perception that Mary had been in error in failing to recognise popular sentiment is clear in the words of the Lord Keeper at the opening of the assembly, contrasting the memory of the late queen with the promise of the princess that they now had, "to whom nothing—what nothing?—no, no worldly thing under the sun is so dear as the hearty love and good will of her nobles and subjects".[15] The phraseology is striking, and clearly intended to assure her audience that her first consideration would be their needs and desires. The contrast with her half-sister could be extended. In a picture of the family of Henry VIII, painted just over a decade into her reign, Elizabeth is placed to one side of her father, hand in hand with Edward and the images of peace and plenty, while on the other side are Mary and Philip of Spain, associated with war and division. This was not propaganda—it was a statement of policy that was already in the process of delivery. In 1563 the MP Robert Atkinson could express gratitude for the Queen's middle way in matters of religion, and he went on to hail the general advantages of

Elizabeth's approach: "I ween never prince since the Conquest, (I speak it without flattery), hath . . . reigned over us in a quieter peace, with more love and less exaction".[16] Elizabeth was fortunate in that her instinct for not dictating to her subjects coincided with spontaneous advances in the national economy. It was during her reign that the developments of an interregional market, a consumer society, and improved methods of commercial farming began to take effect to the noticeable benefit of her subjects. The statistical evidence of rising grain yields, exceptionally low levels of mortality, and high life expectancy has already been noted.[17] By the 1580s it could be said that the kingdom was "never better in worldly peace, in health and body, in abundance of victuals".[18] Strains developed at the end of the reign, largely due to the burdens of a continuing war. In the famous Golden Speech to parliament she had to defuse the anger of her subjects at the spread of monopolies, which was no easy task. She did it by renewing the vows of a loving and successful partnership:

> this I count the glory of my crown, that I have reigned with your loves . . . neither do I wish to live longer days than I may see your prosperity, and that is my only desire . . . And though you have had and may have many princes more mighty and wise sitting in this seat, yet you never had nor shall have any that shall be more careful and loving.[19]

The disclaimer of mightiness and wisdom was not entirely disingenuous, for although Elizabeth had actually displayed those qualities in abundance, this had depended largely on reigning "with their loves", which was thus indeed the "glory" of her crown. The fact that she claimed a special capacity to be "careful and loving" shows how specific and significant this stance had been. The consequences were momentous. We need not suppose that Elizabeth was deliberately setting out to switch the focus from a dynastic to a national perspective, but this was the effect of her approach in the circumstances of the time.

Her personal situation was also of central significance in enabling her to embody the character of the national enterprise. The cult of her virginity is most familiar, and it did become of great importance, though a modern study suggests that it was not in place at the beginning of the reign.[20] Her reluctance to select a husband and thus settle the succession was famously of great concern to her parliaments in the early years of her rule. Recent interpretations are probably right to say that although she was happy to consider marriage, she was equally prepared to rule alone, and that in the end "the choice of a husband involved so many contingencies" that she never felt justified in making it.[21] We might add that with the problematic case of her half-sister in mind, she wanted no undue influences to divert her wish to govern with the love of her people. This seemed indeed to be the drift of her opening assurance that "nothing—what nothing?—no, no worldly thing" was so important as retaining their goodwill. She eventually settled for the rationale of being married to *them*, and they in turn became very contented with the match.

As the years went by, the chances of her concluding a fruitful marriage receded. But at the same time it began to seem less important, as the sense increased that her personal government was not only stable and successful, but exceptionally so. A different model presented itself. In the most common allusion she was celebrated as Astraea, the just virgin, described by Virgil in the Fourth *Eclogue*. Astraea was the last of the immortals. She had abandoned the earth because of the wickedness of mankind, and inhabited the heavens as the constellation Virgo. Her return to earth was foretold, and would inaugurate a golden age, bringing peace, plenty and eternal springtime.[22] The analogy seemed quite close. The prosperity of Elizabeth's realm was undoubted, at least for those with property interests. It was not quite eternal springtime, but her reign registered a level of life expectancy that would not be seen again for two centuries. The relative peacefulness of her kingdom was conspicuous, and her even-handed justice marked her out. She was indeed distinctive as the Virgin Queen, which might well be considered a necessary freedom to enable her to exercise her beneficial powers. She loved only her people. She was not encumbered by the claims of a husband, or by the traditional princely pursuit of personal military glory. Her commitment was to the powerful aspirations of her subjects. As luck would have it, Astraea was also synonymous with the moon, one of the properties of which was to govern the tides. This became a popular metaphor, disseminated by leading sailors and politicians like Sir Walter Raleigh, who wished to foster the idea of Elizabeth as mistress of an empire of the sea.[23]

In effect, Elizabeth offered a clean sheet on which the nation could sketch in the vision that had opened up before it. It became standard practice to present her in this role quite early in the reign, and it was depicted with remarkable power and precision. In a portrait by Massys the Younger, from 1579, she carried a sieve in reference to the Vestal Virgin Tuccia, whose purity enabled her to carry water in that unlikely receptacle. On a pillar behind Elizabeth was carved the story of Aeneas, who had forsaken Dido and founded Rome, as Elizabeth must avoid entanglements, leaving her sailors and traders free to roam the seas in search of empire. In the background was a globe, on which, from a sunlit England, ships were setting out towards the west. The significance of this image becomes clearer when it is contrasted with the standard pose of the male prince, who was typically pictured on a prancing horse, in armour, with sword at the ready. He is off somewhere in pursuit of personal glory, or the assertion of dynastic rights. Elizabeth was not best suited by such a role. She would probably not sit too well on a warhorse, and armour might not sit too well on her. But she had a kind of steady, all-embracing poise when portrayed standing atop a globe of the world. Although it may discomfort the feminists among her modern admirers, she needed to do nothing but remain still. In a portrait by Marcus Gheerhaerts the Younger, from 1591, she stood upon, and metaphorically secured the island, as a sound and solid base, from which her people could advance across the oceans. The vision peaked in the Armada portrait. The great "invincible" fleet had arrived in all its pomp on one side of the Queen, and been dispatched in ruin and disarray on the other. Again, Elizabeth stood for the physical integrity of the island. The Virgin Queen reflected the inviolability of her realm. She was the rock against which the Armada had broken. The Spanish threat had been dispelled, and the surrounding seas were clear. She rested her hand on the globe, and the oceans of the world were presented to her people. It was a rather different process from the traditional way of things, where the triumphant feudal lord granted territories to his lieutenants.[24]

The Dynastic Preference of James I for the National Enemy

So it became a problem for the king, and indeed for the people, when James I failed to accept the new balance of initiative. Elizabeth had provided a general platform for the furtherance of the national enterprise, through its chosen route of displacing the power of Spain. This had appeared as an endorsement, and a validation, of a popular or national definition of foreign affairs. It involved a seminal change in the way that policy was made. But Elizabeth's position and her approach were distinctive. An unwanted degree of tension might arise in the not unlikely situation that a future monarch failed to follow suit.

James I was as well fitted to the older dynastic perspective as Elizabeth had been to her love affair with the people. It bears repeating that James's divergent choice in foreign policy is explained by the fact that he had no concept of an objectively defined national interest. His aims were those of a personal monarch. He pursued alliances that brought the greatest degree of prestige to the Stuart house, and which underlined the authority and legitimacy of royal government in general. All the particular factors in his background and his outlook on the world inclined him to a somewhat exaggerated view of the traditional balance of initiative, where the unitary interests and outward relations of the kingdom were defined essentially by the monarch, on the basis of his own preferences and concerns. James had not shared in the affirmation of English national consciousness that emerged from the life and death struggle with the Spanish Armada, and he had no real reason to follow where that led. Nor did his rule in Scotland provide him with any concept or experience of a national perspective. The political condition of his northern kingdom remained medieval. His most vital task had been to maintain his own position in the face of a disorderly, overbearing nobility and a self-important Kirk that entertained theories of a right of popular resistance to ungodly kings. James wrote books to assert the inviolable rights of "free" monarchies, and warn against the threat of Puritanism and "popularity".[25] He was left with a horror of anything that savoured of rebellion, and this was always the underlying influence on his approach.

James was therefore more likely to dismiss the idea of a popular concept of foreign relations than to accommodate it pragmatically. In fact, both in practice and in principle, he sustained the traditional view that the making of foreign policy was the sole preserve of the monarch. He clung firmly to this right, often in the face of a House of Common that was seeking to deprive him of it. And all these circumstances inclined James to make a friend of Spain, rather than to confront it as the national enemy. In terms of dynastic prestige, a Spanish match was the best in Europe. Furthermore, from James's point of view it would associate him with the very model of a "free", not to say "absolute" monarchy—one that certainly did not have to tolerate over-assertive representative assemblies, and was so rich that it might help him to avoid the troublesome House of Commons that he had found in England. The dowry of a Spanish princess would be greater than anything that he might, or might not, get from parliament. So, as Tom Cogswell has said, a Spanish match "allowed James to contemplate life without parliamentary subsidies".[26] In fact, James's foreign policy was calculated to address his domestic challenges, quite as much as those that he faced abroad, and from his own point of view, he was actually more successful on the home front.

The sharp divergence of approach between king and kingdom was masked for a while, in part because it was somewhat difficult to make a marital treaty with a militant Catholic power that would ultimately insist on conversion to that faith, and in part because the first decade and a half of James's reign was a time of general peace in western Europe. The contending kingdoms were in a state of military and financial exhaustion, and James was able to play his self-appointed role of peacemaker with some semblance of reality. Nor was peace necessarily without benefit to the great enterprise of a trading empire. Commerce with the Indies, at least with those areas not already in Spanish occupation, was allowed, though it was not exactly encouraged. And trade in general reaped some benefit from more stable international relations. Cloth exports were in a healthy balance until 1614. The national project did not require that England should always be at war, only that when there was a war it should be aimed primarily against Spanish sea power.

Despite the lull in hostilities, there were early signs that James's choices in foreign policy were going to be provocatively different from those of his people. He gave no indication of taking popular opinion into account. A Spanish match was always his preferred option for his sons, and was attempted first for Henry, then for Charles. This would be reprising the dynastic connection that had been so vigorously denounced in the reign of Mary Tudor, and great events since then had served to make such an alliance seem even less appropriate now, at least in the eyes of the political nation. When, in 1617, James published his intention to seek a Spanish wife for Charles, parliament was not present to voice an opinion, and not likely to be called upon. But the commissioners who were detailed to consider the treaty proposals gave a reply that "veiled a repugnance to the proposed marriage". The king, however, "did not take the hint".[27]

At this time James was flattering himself that he had arranged a "settled repose" among the kingdoms of Western Europe, but this illusion was dispelled in 1618 when the crisis over the crown of Bohemia brought the first conflicts of the Thirty Years War. This general and almost interminable military contest was characterised at first by the Habsburg attempt to recover northwest Europe for the Catholic Church, and latterly by the struggle between France and Spain for hegemony on the continent. England was involved, at least theoretically, because the first specific dispute arose when James's son-in-law Frederick of the Palatinate accepted an offer from the popular, Protestant movement in Bohemia to take the crown, in contention with the claims of the Habsburgs. This did not deter James from his chosen allegiance to Spain. As usual, his responses were determined primarily by his horror of anything that seemed to usurp monarchical rights. "From a war in support of revolt or usurpation he shrank as from the plague".[28] This dominating phobia outweighed any thought that the cause of his son-in-law and the Bohemian people might possibly have been a good one. He expended his diplomatic energies "officially denying to every sovereign in Europe that he had countenanced or even known of the project".[29] In fact it is clear that James "never approved of what he called Frederick's usurpation of the de facto Habsburg rights in Bohemia".[30] James was persuaded by the Spanish to attempt a peace initiative, which played to his self-image, though it was never a serious proposition. The suggestion was a ploy to "divert him from taking any action", while the Habsburgs recovered their position in Bohemia.[31]

The result of Frederick's actions was to present the Habsburgs with a pretext for attacking the Palatinate, which was of particular strategic value as a staging post between northern Italy and the Netherlands. Few in Europe were surprised when the Spanish and Imperial armies were launched against Frederick's homeland. This made James's stance more awkward, because the Habsburgs were now undoubtedly the usurpers, yet he was not swayed from his conviction that Spain should be adhered to as the model of legitimate monarchical power. He allowed himself to be persuaded by the Spanish argument that Frederick's aggression in Bohemia had been the root of the trouble, and that the Habsburg action in the Palatinate would apply the necessary pressure to restore good order. James duly toed the line—"His reaction to the invasion of the Rhineland was to put pressure on Frederick to renounce the Bohemian throne".[32] James's obeisance to Spanish power led him, both emotionally and pragmatically to the conclusion that whatever part they had played in causing the problem, retaining their friendship remained the best chance of resolving it. The crisis thus "served only to wed James more firmly to the idea of a Spanish match".[33] On the eve of the invasion he was at pains to assure Ambassador Gondomar of his fidelity to Spain. "I give you my word as a king, as a gentleman, as a Christian, and as an honest man, that I wish to marry my son to no one but your master's daughter, and that I desire no alliance but with Spain".[34]

James's position was settled and clear to all. The difficulty in trying to maintain this as national policy was that the predominant view among his people ran on precisely the opposite lines—they wished to fight no one but Spain. This became a practical problem for James because the severity of the crisis obliged him to look for the moral and financial support of parliament, and there was little doubt that the stance of the representative body would be very different from his own. Even before the assembly met, the taverns, streets and markets were alive with condemnation of Spanish and Catholic militancy. The difference of opinion between James and his kingdom was clearly reflected in the pamphlet "Vox Populi", by the Norwich divine Thomas Scot. This offered a strikingly graphic description of a king who was completely at odds with his kingdom over the appropriate course of foreign policy. Scot depicted an English court that "gaped wide for Spanish gold", with a king that "extremely hunts after peace . . . as that for it he will suffer anything". Scot suggested that the national cause would be espoused and promoted by a parliament, but that "the king will never endure parliament again but will suffer absolute want, rather than receive conditional aid from his subjects".[35]

But James had perforce to endure parliament again, and face the problem that any substantial aid that they might give would indeed be conditional, and in the event actually made dependent on the pursuit of their policies rather than his. It seems that in truth James did not have a war policy at all. His intention was to avoid war if he possibly could. In his opening speech to parliament he said that he needed to be prepared for war in order to strengthen his hand in the peace negotiations. This was not a strategy that inspired confidence in James's resolve, and he duly went on to betray the fact that the Spanish match was his only policy. His assurances that the marriage would not entail concessions to Catholicism showed that he was still putting his faith in an entente with Spain. It also indicated that he lacked a realistic view of the uncompromising nature of Spanish aims.[36] The Commons' perception of Spanish militancy was sounder, and they wished to fight fire with fire. But since there was no evidence that James was about to lead them forth, they decided to vote just two subsidies to cover the king's regular contingencies, rather than as a provision for war. James was said to be delighted with the advance, having received supply without conditions. But the gesture foretold great problems for the crown in the future. It was the first sign of what would become the settled stance of the Commons—they would only give substantial supply if they were getting precisely the foreign policy that they required.

When the king asked for a further subsidy, with no war policy in place, the Commons failed to respond. Gardiner thought, no doubt correctly, that this was the reason that James dismissed them early in June, with their legislative programme uncompleted.[37] This was a sign of things to come. Just as it became the routine position of the Commons only to pay for their specific chosen policy, so it became the standard reaction of the king only to keep the House in being while they might offer supply. MPs were distraught at the aborted session. A previous chapter described Richard Wyn's dismay at their untimely dismissal: "without the effecting of any of our businesses". They had also expected the king to take a bolder initiative in the military field: "All the princes in Christendom are arming, yet we are not moved with all this. I pray God keep us, for we were never more in need of his help".[38]

Before departure, however, the Commons did manage to produce a Declaration, which confirmed their position, and gave the king some inducement to recall them. They said that if perchance James's peace negotiations for the return of the Palatinate should prove unfruitful, and the king were to decide on a more forceful approach, the House would be ready to assist him with supply. The Declaration was well received in the constituencies by such as the Devon diarist Walter Yonge, who hailed it as the best chance of instigating a forward policy and hoped that it was similarly approved by the king. But James was very unlikely to allow parliament to dictate his policy, or to follow the line that was being suggested. Yonge's concept of foreign affairs was based on two main considerations, one was his Puritanism, and the other was his commercial interest as a merchant. Both indicated a single target. Most noticeably from 1610 onwards, Yonge's diary displayed a constant antipathy to the power and ambitions of Spain. When the crisis came in the 1620s he echoed Richard Wyn's plea for a more determined policy, and applied it specifically to the need to challenge Spain at sea. "All the talk is of a Spanish fleet, and doubted it is for England, and yet we make no preparation to resist them".[39] He was articulating the dominant view in parliament and the political nation, that England's military effort should be channelled principally into a sea war against Spain.

During the summer it became clear that James's peace initiative had been worse than useless—it had allowed the Habsburg armies to complete the conquest of the Palatinate without serious challenge. The king now had no choice but to make at least some gesture towards a more forceful response, and parliament was recalled to provide support. There still remained, however, the same basic difference of opinion between king and Commons as to what the appropriate action should be. The

House would have to be allowed to debate the matter if they were to advance supply, but their view, if freely stated, would certainly contradict that of the king. To pre-empt this, James suggested that they should restrict their discussion to the question of *how* they were to supply him, rather than why. He stressed that there must be no invective against particular targets, since this kind of freedom of opinion was not acceptable to him.[40] James was fully aware of who the particular target of the Commons would be. They would call for a sea war against Spain, whereas for his own part the king had by no means abandoned his plan for a Spanish alliance.

It was testament to the strength and clarity of the parliamentary view that the Commons showed no intention of restricting themselves within the traditional boundaries that the king had underlined. They believed that they knew where the vital interests of the nation lay, and in the absence of any appropriate leadership, it seemed to be up to them to point the way. James had given no indication of any projected course of action of his own, and he chose to be away at Newmarket on the day of the debate. If he expected that the discussion would be a formality, and that MPs would passively toe the uncontroversial line that he had set out, he was to be disappointed. On 26 November 1621, the House of Commons settled down for the first time to identify the foreign policy that they understood to accord with the real strengths and requirements of the nation that they represented.

What they had to say was powerful and consistent, reflecting the clarity and strength of the perceived national interest. Almost every recorded speaker advocated positively that the war effort should be directed against Spain. Sir Edward Giles exemplified the sentiment, declaring that their preparations should not be focused just on the recovery of the Palatinate, but rather on resuming the essential confrontation with Spain on the oceans. He issued the authentic and proven battle cry, to "take Elizabeth's course . . . find his Indies".[41] Thomas Crew, who was a leading figure in debate in these affairs, echoed Giles's emphasis on "opening" the Indies, and summed up the mood of the House. "We all see which way we incline".[42] The stress on opening the Indies was not just a general umbrella term for challenging Spanish interests—it was a specific, selected line of attack. This was what the Commons' understanding of naval and trading interests had identified as offering the best chance of profit and success. John Pym later referred to it as "the most facile and hopeful way for this kingdom to prevail against the Spaniard". This was where the financial outlay was least and the economic benefit greatest, and Pym condemned royal policy for failing to take that course.[43] This was the general perspective that explains why, in 1628, when any hope of the government embracing the design had gone, Sir Nathaniel Rich would receive a great cheer in the House for his initiative to bring forward a bill for the West Indies. This then, was the policy that the Commons sought to establish from the beginning, and held to throughout the 1620s. In 1621, Thomas Crew outlined in detail the projected form of a war aimed at disabling Spanish power in the West Indies, and described how it could be fought and maintained. The aim was pragmatic as well as passionate. The debate "reached its crescendo in a violent speech by Coke, who throwing off all restraint, poured forth vituperation against Spain and Catholicism".[44] Coke reflected the settled feeling in the political nation that Spain was the natural, national enemy, and he would later give definitive voice to the main reason. War against Spain was "England's best prosperity".[45]

Merchant MPs of lesser status, who were not recorded in debate in 1621, nevertheless expressed the same clear and powerful views. John Prowse and Ignatious Jourdain of Exeter wrote letters to their constituencies, excoriating Spain as the "invertirable enemy" and taking hope from the arrival of some Dutch envoys, though they could not be certain as to how or whether the king had received them.[46] At the close of the debate, the House proposed specifically to have Spain named as the enemy, and when the Treasurer of the Duchy of Lancaster tried to obstruct the move, "he was quickly crossed" by William Nyell of Dartmouth, "resorting to the former question against whom we should fight". Nyell warned that Spain was seeking world domination, which must be resisted on a broad front at sea. He said his constituents would support such a war.[47] His assurance was based on experience. In the 1580s, English naval action had swept the Newfoundland waters clear of Spanish shipping and opened the way to the success of West Country cod fishing, which had thereby become the most important trade of Dartmouth.

The result of the Commons' deliberations reflected the fear that the king did not share their vision. They voted just one subsidy now, pending some assurance of the projected course of action. This became the settled stance of the Commons—they would only give full supply for the kind of war that they could fully approve. Thus, Sir Nathaniel Rich confirmed that their commitment to extra supply in the Declaration had been made on the condition that the king followed their advice.[48] To make their position crystal clear they penned a petition, asking for Spain to be named as the enemy, and the prince to be married to a Protestant, that is to say, not to a Spanish princess. James was simply and understandably enraged. In effect the Commons were trying to impose their view on the course of foreign policy, even though it ran counter to the known preference of the king. This was to usurp the crown's most jealously guarded preserve of determining the outward relations of the kingdom. As James said, "what have you left un-attempted in the highest point of sovereignty in that petition of yours?"[49] The fundamental challenge to the prerogative of the crown lay not just in the Commons' attempt to extend their right of free speech to encompass such sovereign matters, but rather in the simple fact that they were seeking to direct the foreign and military policy of the kingdom by refusing to pay for anything that was not exactly what they wanted. Their assumption that they knew what was required, and that they had a right to enforce it, was another aspect of parliament's appropriation of the new dimension of the nation-state.

Parliament was dismissed, and James was left without the means to attempt a military solution, even if he had so desired. This mattered less because he was also left free to pursue his own single, chosen line of policy, which was an alliance, preferably by marriage, with Spain. Negotiations proved difficult, as they were bound to do, given that the Spanish probably had no real intention of ever agreeing a marriage to a Protestant. In this respect, the traditional assessment seems justified—the Spanish were "merely temporising, to forestall any English military action".[50] In February 1623, Prince Charles and the Duke of Buckingham set off for Spain, to try to resolve the matter in person. The journey may be variously interpreted as the desperate and futile pursuit of a wholly misconceived policy, or a politic initiative to bring things to a head. It is probable that the most important touchstone for James and Charles was whether the Spanish were prepared to make an undertaking on the restoration of the Palatinate. The early Stuarts may not have had much grasp of a national concept of foreign policy, but they did have the consistent dynastic aim of recovering the rights of their family in the Palatinate. Their mistake was to suppose that an alliance with Spain was a realistic means to that end. It was never likely that the Spanish would or could simply arrange the restoration of the Palatinate. In fact they preferred to treat it as a matter to be resolved between the Stuarts and the Emperor. Brendan Purcell is no doubt right to suppose that it was when the Spanish first minister Olivares specifically rejected an agreement to restore the Palatinate that Charles decided that there was no further point in the negotiations.[51]

Ironically, by failing, despite the most strenuous efforts, to acquire a Spanish bride, Charles had quite by accident made himself a hero to the English. His return, on 23 October, was greeted by an unprecedented outpouring of "universal joy . . . even in small towns the festivities were extraordinary".[52] William Laud, who was not a man to overrate popular initiatives, described it as "the greatest expression of joy by all sorts of people that ever I saw".[53] It was in fact another striking demonstration of the depth and unanimity of the anti-Spanish perspective among the English people. Spain was, quite simply, the natural enemy against which the new nation banded together and measured its position in the world.

Charles and Buckingham now had their own, albeit more private grievance against Spain, and they determined to seize the moment and put themselves at the head of popular feeling. Ruigh described it as "Buckingham's identification with the will of the nation".[54] It is doubtful, however, whether he and Charles ever saw it in a truly national light, and it was not certain that they could persuade James to make the switch in any case. Only James could take the final decisions on foreign affairs, and only James could authorise the summoning of a parliament, and even the two people to whom he was most prepared to listen would not find it easy to convince the old king of the need to reverse the pro-Spanish policy to which he was dedicated. Charles and Buckingham did manage to contrive an unusually united front among the peers and the Privy Council, which on the 20 December 1623 voted for a parliament. James agreed to call the assembly, but it was another matter to get him to agree to follow the line that parliament would demand.

On this occasion they were actually invited to give their advice, though James seems to have managed to convey the feeling that the gesture was made with distaste and without commitment. The Venetian ambassador thought that the king "said more than he meant, as he spoke as if he were carried away . . . the speech shone more by contrast with the one delivered to the last parliament, as they then called felony what is now submitted to the free discussion of the present assembly".[55] In practice, James clung firmly to the fallback position that although he was prepared to countenance parliament giving the advice, he was not obliged to take notice of it. For the Commons, however, the invitation seemed to vindicate their assumed right to define the foreign policy of the nation, and they pursued their agenda with increased determination.

There was little doubt what parliament's advice would be in regard to the negotiations with Spain. "Without a dissenting voice, the Commons resolved to recommend the dissolution of the treaties".[56] It was not entirely unhelpful to James that parliament should take responsibility for ending the treaties, which had become unworkable in their current form. The more significant consideration was whether the king could be prevailed upon to actually reverse his policy, and adopt parliament's consistently recommended war aim, naming Spain as the enemy. This resolved itself into the question of what means could be found to tie James to do what the Commons required. The best that could be achieved as an agreed set of war aims was four undertakings so vague as to be virtually meaningless. The government was to agree to the defence of England, the securing of Ireland, the assisting of the Low Countries and the setting forth of the Royal Navy. This was all open to interpretation. What the Commons meant by setting forth the Royal Navy was the instigation of a sea war against Spain, which to their mind was the natural occupation of the English navy, but it was most unlikely that the king would see things in the same light. In fact, James insisted throughout that the war should be aimed at the recovery of the Palatinate, and that this should be done without confronting Spain.

A sea war to undermine the imperial power of Spain was the parliamentary proposal, and it reflected the dominant and persistent anti-Spanish sentiment in the country. It is misleading to judge the merits of this by asking, as many historians have, whether it had any more chance of achieving the recovery of the Palatinate than James's policy of conciliating Spain. To measure the matter in that way is to fail to take account of the fact that recovering the Palatinate was never parliament's chosen war aim in any case. In 1621 and indeed earlier, MPs would no doubt have supported a serious attempt to recover the Palatinate if it had been undertaken when it had some chance of success. But the essential advocacy of a sea war against Spain was not conceived primarily as a means of achieving that end. War against Spain was always an end in itself. The concept of attacking Spanish naval, financial and colonial power, and as a corollary providing assistance to the Dutch, was seen quite simply as the best way of sustaining and advancing England's interests and position in the world. This was a positive priority to be undertaken for its own sake. And Sir Edward Coke expressed the rationale to perfection. "War . . . with Spain is England's best prosperity".[57] This was the galvanising force of the national project. Economic success was to be gathered from across the oceans, in the founding of a commercial empire, forged in the struggle against Spain.

So the policy put forward in the Commons represented the continuing pursuit of a clear and powerful vision, not the backward looking idealisation of an Elizabethan "myth". It was a settled agenda, and it was not unrealistic, either in terms of advancing those stated national ambitions, or even of addressing the immediate situation on the continent. Although a sea war against Spain was not proposed essentially as a way of recovering the Palatinate, it probably had as much chance of achieving that end as any other approach. In 1624 MPs recognised specifically that direct military action for that purpose was no longer a serious option. Sir Francis Seymour wanted the enemy and the war aim to be made explicit, taking account of the fact that a Palatinate campaign was beyond their resources, and "far from our thoughts". He said that what they could usefully sustain was a sea war against Spain, and the provision of aid to the Low Countries. [58] Sir Benjamin Rudyerd recommended the same formula, and said that they should be prepared to dig deep to finance assistance to the Dutch and the equipping of the fleet.[59] Sir Edward Coke confirmed that a war at sea combined with assistance to the Low Countries was indeed the most effective policy, and the most acceptable to the constituencies. The Palatinate was beyond their reach, he said, but not so the Americas. He hoped to "live to see the king of Spain lose his Indies".[60] Here again was the beauty of the vision—the Americas were much further away, but somehow more accessible. "Let us remember", said Sir John Eliot, "that the war with Spain is our Indies, that there we shall fetch wealth and happiness".[61] William Nyell of Dartmouth looked forward to the Spanish navy being "swept from the sea". This sounded somewhat grandiose, but Nyell had direct experience of just such an effect. As already noted, in 1584, English naval action had cleared the Newfoundland waters of Spanish shipping, and the West Country fishing fleets had thrived thereafter. This, repeated on a global scale, was the idea behind the national enterprise. The basis of the Commons' firm and consistent advocacy of a sea war against Spain was that they knew that it worked to the furtherance of the nation's economic success.

They knew exactly what they wanted. The problem was how to get the king to take it on board. Expedients like the parliamentary appropriation of supply were constitutional innovations, but would give them no control over what James actually did. As Sir John Savile said, allowing parliament's commissioners to account for the expenditure was only to the purpose if the money was being used for the desired ends. Sir Edward Coke attempted to assert a new constitutional doctrine that if the king was seeking their aid, he must also follow their advice.[62] The insistence that their supply would be conditional on the adoption of their chosen policy was echoed by prominent speakers such as Sir Edwin Sandys, Sir Robert Harley, Sir Henry Mildmay, Sir Robert Phelips and Sir Henry Vane, between the 11th and the 19th of March. This was the real constitutional challenge to the royal prerogative—they were attempting to subvert the king's policy in favour of their own, by refusing to pay for anything else.

The king recognised no obligation to do as the Commons desired. In fact, he duly confirmed that the final decision must always rest with him, and that it was unlikely to follow the course that they had suggested. "Whether I shall send 20,000 or 10,000, whether by sea or land, east or west, by diversion, or otherwise by invasion upon the Bavarian or Emperor, you must leave that to your king".[63] He made it clear that his concern was limited to the Palatinate, and that he held the Emperor to blame for the problem there. He "saw no cause as yet to make the Spaniard the capital enemy".[64] By the same token, at this time he was assuring the Spanish envoys that he had no intention of going to war against Spain, and that he still looked to Philip to assist constructively in the restoration of the Palatinate to his son-in-law. There were apparently no circumstances in which James would ever give up his one consistent policy, of pursuing friendly relations with Spain.

Having made it clear that he reserved the right to do as he saw fit, and that his decision was not likely to accord with the Commons' desire for a sea war against Spain, James attempted to get his own priority firmly on the record by demanding that the subsidy bill be altered to include a fifth point, stating that the central aim was to be the recovery of the Palatinate. This provoked an uncompromising response from the Commons, which confirmed that they were indeed engaged in a very radical initiative to wrest control of foreign affairs from the hands of the king and redirect it along the opposite course that they favoured. James's request to focus policy on the Palatinate was rejected as "clean contrary to the intent of the House".[65] It had been their purpose throughout to demote the issue of the Palatinate, and they were not to be cornered into reinstating it now. The bill passed in its original form, without the king's proposed amendment. But the last word remained with James, as he had asserted, and when, on 29 May, he indicated his acceptance of the money, he continued to reject the Commons' definition of its purpose. "He insisted particularly and largely on the recovery of the Palatinate, although that be not specified in the act".[66]

In a similar vein, James sent word to Madrid to assure the Spanish that they need not pay too much heed to parliament's aggressive threats against them, because his prerogative powers in the matter remained undiminished, and the decision would be his alone: "His majesty is bound no further than to advise with them but not to rest upon their advice, except their advice concur with his majesty's wisdom and piety to guide all things to the greatest reason for the public good".[67] This was in effect a restatement of the basic principle of a "free" monarchy—that the king was the sole judge of the unitary public interest, and the general opinion of the people had no definitive status. James had managed, with a display of considerable guile and resilience, to sustain that position, in the face of the Commons' attempts to subvert it. But by the same token it had become clear that the monarchy was facing a fundamental challenge. The political nation, as represented in parliament, had reached a very definite view of where its outward interests lay, and was assuming a right to apply that judgement. The net result was likely to be an increasing doubt as to whether the personal monarch could any longer be relied upon to ensure the public safety, and this might lead in turn to a feeling that parliament might need to seek other ways of making its opinion count.

The course of events that followed did nothing to restore faith in the king's capacities. Needless to say, no sea war materialised. The only military action that James saw fit to allow was an expensive and disastrous gesture towards the Palatinate. Twelve thousand recruits were sent to serve under Count Mansfield, who was seriously over-matched in the contest against the Habsburg armies. The condition of the English contingent only compounded the problem. The soldiers were not properly prepared, and something like half their number died of disease. Many of the remainder deserted to the Spanish commander Spinola. This had a peculiar kind of logic considering the direction of James's own sympathies. Most frustratingly, there was another mission on which the English force could have been more meaningfully employed. The Dutch were in need of assistance in their struggle against the Spanish at Breda, and some of the English commanders favoured going to their aid. But James insisted firmly and repeatedly that they should not go to the relief of Breda, but direct their efforts just at the Palatinate.[68] James's policy was irredeemably distorted by a blinkered dynastic viewpoint, a blind refusal to countenance any movement that might be termed rebellious, and a deep attachment to Spain as the leading model of monarchical authority, amounting to hero worship.

Domestically, in the "negotiations" with parliament in 1624, James had fought his corner with some success. He had extracted a substantial amount of supply from the Commons by allowing Charles and Buckingham to convey the impression that the anti-Spanish line demanded by parliament would be followed. Then he had simply reasserted his traditional prerogative to take sole command in the field and ignored their advice. He had thereby managed to resist the Commons' persistent attempt to subvert his own policy and replace it with theirs. In James's own terms this outcome was not unsatisfactory. He had made a gesture towards furthering his dynastic interests abroad, and he had won a battle to maintain monarchical rights on the home front. The victory was, however, bought at a cost that put the monarchy in greater danger of losing the domestic war as well. The consensus forged by Charles and Buckingham had reinforced the Commons' belief that they had a natural capacity to define the outward interests of the nation, and that they had a right to expect their views to be followed. But James, acting alone, and exercising his traditional power as king, had specifically overturned these expectations. This can only have added to the Commons' accumulating list of reasons for thinking that the prerogatives of the crown could usefully and justifiably be limited.

Notes

1. T. Rabb, *Enterprise and Empire: Merchant and Gentry Investment in the Expansion of England,* (Harvard 1967)
2. J. D. Mackie, *The Earlier Tudors,* (Oxford 1966), p. 507
3. J. E. Neale, *Elizabeth I and Her Parliaments,* (London 1953), I, pp. 42–3, 50
4. Ibid, pp. 42–3
5. J. B. Black, *The Reign of Elizabeth,* (Oxford 1965), pp. 123–5
6. G. D. Ramsay, "The Foreign Policy of Elizabeth I", in *The Reign of Elizabeth,* ed. C. Haigh, (London 1984), p. 167
7. F. Braudel, *The Mediterranean,* (London 1973), II, pp. 1184–5
8. W. MacCaffrey, "Parliament and Foreign Policy", in *The Parliaments of Elizabethan England*, eds. D. Dean and N. Jones, (Oxford 1990), p. 80
9. T. Cogswell, *The Blessed Revolution,* (Cambridge 1989), pp. 12–14
10. J. Guy, *Tudor England,* (Oxford 1988), p. 342
11. Dedication to Walsingham, 1st edition, (London 1589)
12. R. Hakluyt, *The Principal Voyages, Navigations, Traffics and Discoveries of the English Nation*, 2nd edition, (London 1599), Everyman Edition, (London 1907), vol. I, p. 3
13. Black, *The Reign of Elizabeth*, p. 319
14. Hakluyt, *Principal Voyages*, dedication of the second edition, (London 1599)
15. Neale, *Elizabeth I and Her Parliaments*, I, pp. 42–3, 50
16. Ibid, p. 118
17. See above, pp. 19, 21
18. Bishop of Salisbury, cited-S. Schama, *History of Britain,* (London 2000), p. 369
19. J. E. Neale, *Elizabeth I and Her Parliaments*, II, pp. 389–91
20. S. Doran, *Monarchy and Matrimony: The Courtship of Elizabeth I*, (London 1996)

21. Ilona Bell, *Elizabeth the First: The Voice of a Monarch,* (Basingstoke 2010), p. 5
22. R. Strong, *The Cult of Elizabeth,* (London 1977), pp. 16, 114
23. A. Somerset, *Elizabeth I,* (London 1991), pp. 354–5
24. The Massys the Younger, and the Marcus Gheerherts the Younger can be viewed in Somerset, *Elizabeth I*, pp. 372–3; The Armada Portrait is in Schama, *History of Britain*, p. 331
25. *Basilikon Doron*, and *The True Law of Free Monarchies*
26. Cogswell, *The Blessed Revolution*, p. 16
27. S. R. Gardiner, *History of England 1603–1642,* (London 1886–9), III, p. 61
28. D. H. Wilson, *James VI and I,* (London 1966), p. 411
29. C. V. Wedgwood, *The Thirty Years War,* (Harmondsworth 1957), p. 99
30. G. Redworth, "Of Pimps and Princes: Unpublished Letters of James I and the Prince of Wales", *Historical Journal 37* (1994), p. 403
31. Gritti to the Doge, 6 September 1618, *CSP Venetian XV*, p. 306
32. Redworth, "Of Pimps and Princes", p. 403
33. Cogswell, *The Blessed Revolution*, p. 19
34. Gondomar to Philip II, 15 March 1620, cited, Gardiner, *History of England*, III, p. 338
35. Thomas Scot, "Vox Populi", in *Somers' Tracts,* (London 1809), II, pp. 508–24
36. Gardiner, *History of England*, IV, pp. 25–6
37. Ibid, IV, p. 126
38. National Library of Wales, Wyn of Gwydir Ms. 9057E/959
39. *Diary of Walter Yonge*, ed. G, Roberts, *Camden Society 41*, (London 1848), pp. 33, 41, 58
40. Wilson, *James VI and I*, p. 421
41. *Commons Debates 1621*, ed. W. Notestein, (New Haven 1935), III, p. 460
42. Ibid
43. *Constitutional Documents of the Puritan Revolution*, ed. S. R. Gardiner, (Oxford 1966), p. 208
44. Wilson, *James VI and I*, p. 421
45. R. Ruigh, *The Parliament of 1624,* (Harvard 1971), p. 205
46. Devon RO, Exeter Corporation Letter Books, 60c, L206, L210
47. *Commons Debates 1621*, II, p. 452; III p. 460; IV pp. 200, 441; V p. 215
48. Ibid, III, p. 470
49. Wilson, *James VI and I*, p. 422
50. D. Hirst, *Authority and Conflict,* (London 1986), p. 133
51. B. Purcell, *The Winter King: Frederick V of the Palatinate and the Coming of the Thirty Years War,* (Farnham 2002), p. 204
52. Cogswell, *The Blessed Revolution*, p. 9
53. Diary of William Laud, 6 October 1623, *The Works of William Laud*, eds. W Scott and J. Bliss, (Oxford 1847–60), III, p. 143
54. Ruigh, *The Parliament of 1624*, p. 15
55. Valoresso to the Doge, *CSP Venetian*, XVIII, pp. 231–4
56. Ruigh, *Parliament of 1624*, p. 183
57. Sir William Spring, Diary of Proceedings in the House of Commons, February to May 1624, Harvard, Houghton Library, Ms English 980, f. 105; Ruigh, *Parliament of 1624*, p. 205
58. *Commons Journal*, I, p. 741; Edward Nicholas, Diary of Proceedings in the House of Commons 1624, TNA SP14/166, f.91v; Diary of John Holles, BL Harleian Ms 6383, f. 104v; Diary of Sir Walter Earle BL Add Ms, 18, 597, f. 95v
59. Ruigh, *Parliament of 1624*, p. 204
60. Nicholas Diary, f. 97v; Earle Diary, f. 99v; Holles Diary, f. 109

61. *Commons Journal*, I, p. 740; Spring Diary, 124; Earle Diary, f. 94; Holles Diary, f, 103v
62. Nicholas Diary, f. 97v; Earle Diary, f. 99v; Holles Diary, f. 109
63. J. Rushworth, *Historical Collections,* (London 1659–1701), I, p. 140
64. Earle Diary, f. 89
65. Ibid, ff. 184–184v; Dudley Carlton, (junior) to Sir Dudley Carlton, 17 May 1624, TNA SP14/164/81
66. Sir Simonds D'Ewes, Diary of Proceedings in the House of Commons, February to May 1624, BL Harleian Ms. 159, f. 130; Sir Francis Nethersole to Sir Dudley Carlton, 2 June 1624, TNA SP14/167/10
67. Sir Edward Conway to Sir William Aston, TNA SP Foreign, (Spanish), 94/30, f. 180
68. Gardiner, *History of England*, V, pp. 287–90

10 The Religious War of Charles I Against his Scottish Kingdom; and the People of England "Left Now Only to Expect an Opportunity"[1]

It might have been supposed that when Charles came to the throne in 1625 he would have taken steps to repair the damage caused by James's failure to fulfil the promises made to parliament in 1624. It might have seemed a golden opportunity to act on the consensus that Charles and Buckingham had encouraged. Charles had certainly not forgotten the attempt. In his opening speech he reminded the House of the efforts that he had made, if unsuccessfully, towards that end: "I laboured all I could to bring my father to assent thereto".[2] But for some reason Charles decided not to resume that initiative, even though there was now nothing to impede its success. He chose not to reassemble the coalition, or to embrace the policy around which it had been formed. "No attempt seems to have been made to reengage the allies of 1624".[3] The good will that had been fostered with such difficulty and determination was allowed to dissipate. Part of the explanation maybe that Charles's own position appears to have changed significantly in the intervening months. In fact, he at once put policy on a different basis from the one that he and Buckingham had previously agreed with parliament. It is not always sufficiently recognised, but the new king reintroduced the restoration of the Palatinate as the central war aim. He asserted that parliament had engaged James and himself "in a war for the recovery of the Palatinate".[4] Whether the phrase was being employed loosely as a generalisation, or deliberately measured, it amounted to a direct misrepresentation of the clearly stated view of the Commons. This was the war aim for which they had specifically *not* engaged. This was the definition of policy that they had expressly refused to allow James to insert into the subsidy bill, and which they had declared to be "clean contrary to the intent of the House".

Charles had thus contrived to begin his reign by specifically misconstruing the Commons' position. He had offered a definition of foreign policy that sounded like the one that had been asserted by his father in direct defiance of what the Commons had expected in return for their subsidy. This was the war aim that MPs had already, and very explicitly, rejected. By his misconstruction of the Commons' clearly stated intent, he had compounded his father's evasion, and broken his own promise. Why did Charles apparently choose, from the very start, to put himself at odds with the strongly held views of his parliament and his people, of whose sentiments he was very well aware and had appeared to be in sympathy? It may be that since, despite all overtures, the recovery of the Palatinate was the military policy that James had actually put in place, Charles felt that this must be respected. But it seems all the more strange because events would show that action against Spain was not excluded from his options. The most likely explanation is that now he had assumed responsibility for the dynastic interest, and the maintenance of royal authority in general, he had come to share his father's disinclination to accept a popular or national perspective in foreign affairs. It needs to be recalled that Charles's grievance against Spain was personal, not universal like that of the Commons. Now that his dealings with parliament were final, Charles may have felt the force of his father's view that the Commons could not be allowed to stipulate the national enemy, not if the royal prerogative in the making of foreign policy was to be kept intact.

The position of the Commons remained what it had always been—they believed that a sea war against Spain reflected the conspicuous strengths and interests of the nation, and was, as Sir Edward Coke proclaimed, "England's best prosperity". This was how they wanted the war defined. This was the war aim for which they would provide maximum supply, in the confident expectation that their money was being put to the best use, with the surest hope of future gain. This was definitive as national policy in the view of the Commons, and it was not negotiable. Since Charles appeared to have withdrawn his support for this as the central line of attack, and adopted his father's specific alternative in preference, MPs felt they had no option but to reiterate their position, and to resist cooperation with the king's revised war aims. Edward Alford reaffirmed the expressed consensus in the Commons: "We are not engaged for the recovery of the Palatinate, for when it was in the act of parliament as first penned, it was struck out by order of the House".[5] Sir Robert Phelips advocated that they return to their previous expedient of giving no more than the minimum supply, and denied that they were obliged to give more, since their chosen enemy had not been named.[6] It was once again Sir Edward Coke who found the most revealing phrase, asserting that the engagement of the House "was no other but if the king would turn his weapon against the right enemy, we would supply him".[7] This encapsulates the real force of the foreign policy issue in the 1620s. As far as the Commons were concerned there was only one "right enemy", and in the imperative clarity of that perception they were determined to pay for nothing that was not aimed towards that target. They made strenuous attempts to impose this approach on the crown, but the early Stuarts were unable or unwilling to embrace a popularly selected national perspective in foreign affairs, so the outward relations of the English kingdom became dysfunctional.

Revisionist historians have gone to great lengths to suggest that there were less directly contentious reasons for the deep and intractable division between crown and parliament over the foreign and military policy of the kingdom in the 1620s. The most determined of deniers was Conrad Russell, who contrived to ignore the fact that the Commons expressed a strong desire to pursue "the right enemy", as indicated by the imperative needs and sentiments of the country. Russell sought instead to explain the divide on the basis that the principal concern of MPs was to protect the financial interests of their localities, and that they avoided responsibility for matters of war and foreign affairs.[8] This could hardly have been further from the truth. The polarisation between king and Commons derived from the fact that MPs had a powerful collective vision of where the dominant outward interests of the nation lay, and they would not give approval or substantial support for anything that did not address that priority. Once again, the "state" perspective was being espoused by parliament, not the crown.

So the Commons continued to press for a declaration of war against Spain, and the king persistently declined to make it. Charles's unwillingness to accommodate a parliamentary definition of the enemy was sustained despite the fact that he was prepared to instigate some kind of attack on Spanish interests. Such a move was indeed entailed in the alternative treaty of alliance that he had now made with France. It is probably significant that Charles's grievance against the Spanish was not based on a settled national antipathy, but rather on a feeling of resentment that they had rejected his earnestly proffered hand of friendship. The practical motive for action against Spain was to encourage the French to assist with his real aim of recovering the Palatinate. It was not a sound strategy. The enterprise attempted was an attack on Cadiz. It had the hallmark of a token gesture. It was undertaken too hastily and without adequate preparation, and it resulted in another ignominious failure. Ironically, this was not in any case the kind of approach that parliament considered to be the most desirable, and potentially profitable, at the time. In this sense, it was Charles and Buckingham who were slavishly reprising the tradition of Elizabethan days, when the sacking of Cadiz had been a regular exploit. The parliamentarian agenda had moved on. It was still of course the same essential project—that is to say, extending English interests across the oceans, mainly by dint of displacing Spain. In Elizabeth's time there had been a necessary preoccupation with weakening Spanish power and naval capacity around the coasts of northwest Europe. The parliamentary focus was now turned more positively towards the ultimate purpose of dislodging Spain from the West Indies. This would establish the central platform of the trading empire, and it was the specific war aim advocated by the Commons.

Since Spanish interests were still dominant and entrenched in the area, it was clear that the project would benefit from the assistance of the Royal Navy. This combination had been shown to work in practice, and had received recognition in print from Sir Francis Bacon. In his essays on policy, written as the enterprise evolved, Bacon had extolled the advantages of sea power, "which is one of the principal dowries of this kingdom". He pointed out that it was the natural strength of a realm bordered by the sea, and it gave them a unique opportunity to fight the kind of war that served the balance of their interests. "He that commands the sea is at great liberty, and can take as much or as little of the war as he will". Ultimately, the assertion of sea power guaranteed the extension of trade, and cleared the way for future prosperity. "The wealth of both Indies seems in great part but an accessory to the command of the seas".[9] Bacon had captured all the very powerful reasons for favouring a sea war, and it is not surprising that the Commons and their constituents had imbibed this doctrine word for word. On this view, the instigation of such a war against Spain appeared to be the only worthwhile proposition. It could be sustained with less financial strain and less risk than most military exercises, and it could be kept at a distance. It could be expected, furthermore, to result directly in the generation of wealth. In this light the Commons showed sound judgement in demanding that the war effort be focused on the West Indies.

This was a consistent imperative, and for that reason the failure of the Stuart crown to embrace it was recalled when John Pym drew up the list of parliament's long-term grievances in the Grand Remonstrance in 1641. In fact, the first charge against Charles I was the betrayal of the Commons' anticipated war policy in 1625: "the diverting of his majesty's course of wars from the West Indies, which was the most facile and hopeful way for this kingdom to prevail against the Spaniard". The king had instead made "an expenseful and successless attempt upon Cadiz, which was so ordered as if it had been rather intended to make us weary of war than to prosper by it".[10] The words are revealing of the frustration felt in parliament at the breaking of the king's promises and the denial of their hopes. Pym was also pinpointing the reason that a campaign focused on the West Indies was their central and persistent demand—it epitomised a kind of war of which they did not have to be "weary", because it involved the least strain, and they expected to "prosper by it".

Charles could not see his way clear to satisfying parliament's dominant ambition, so his foreign policy staggered on without the support of his people, and with no consistent aim of his own other than the vain search for a means of recovering the Palatinate for his family. The French alliance predictably failed to produce the desired initiative towards that end. Its most conspicuous result was another "diverting" of the war effort from the manifest national interest. In the treaty negotiations, James and Buckingham had recklessly agreed to provide the French king with naval assistance against a Huguenot uprising led by the Duke of Soubise. James endorsed this most short-sighted policy with his habitual blind horror of rebellion. "If Soubise or anyone else takes upon himself to commit such follies in your majesty's dominions, I will give every assistance against him, in men, in ships, and in any way in my power . . . if those rascally Huguenots mean to make a rebellion, I will go in person to exterminate them".[11] The Huguenots could remain sanguine at the prospect of James coming to exterminate them, but the English navy was a different proposition. One to one, the Rochelais fleet had been more than equal to the French, but with the introduction of the English they were over-matched. So in the catalogue of national disasters Pym was obliged to record:

> the loss of the Rochel fleet, by the help of our shipping, delivered and sent over to the French, in opposition to the advice of Parliament, which left that town without defence by sea, and made way, not only to the loss of that important place, but likewise . . . of all the strength and security of the Protestant religion in France.[12]

This was no exaggeration. The navy, which could have been gainfully employed against the power of Spain in the West Indies, had instead been used to undermine Protestantism in France.

Not that the parliamentarians approved of the war with Richelieu into which Charles and Buckingham lurched in an attempt to atone for the previous error. As Pym concluded, war with France was not seen as advantageous: "the interests and counsels of that state being not so contrary to the good of religion and the prosperity of this kingdom as those of Spain".[13] He was expressing a strong and clear strategic perspective. The parliamentarians believed that a continuing contest with Spain benefited, and in a sense defined the national interest, and the national enterprise. The early Stuart kings preferred not to embrace that vision, and stumbled from one inappropriate foreign adventure to another, until all had failed, and Buckingham had been assassinated, and parliament banished, and the pursuit of an active military policy became almost impossible.

During the Personal Rule of the 1630s such gestures that Charles was able to make towards foreign affairs had echoes of his father's approach. There was still an all-consuming focus on recovering the Palatinate. Gardiner noted judiciously that in the context of the climactic Thirty Years War on the continent, Charles really had no policy at all. "The one thing for which he cared was the re-establishment of his sister in the Palatinate. His object was purely dynastic. How it would affect Germany, even how it would affect England, were questions he never thought of proposing to himself".[14] Since his aim was purely dynastic, Charles could consider any alliance that might help him towards it. But most often things took the form of projected treaties (usually secret) with Spain. There were detailed negotiations to this end in 1631, 1634, and 1636. The main proposition was that Charles would assist in the destruction and partition of the United Provinces, while Spain would help him to recover the Palatinate.[15]

This design not only flouted the objective national interest, it would, if carried out, have shamed the kingdom forever. England and Holland were spared its implementation because Charles's potential allies knew that he had neither the means nor the will to offer a substantial military contribution. But Spanish troops and supplies were ushered up the channel, exchange facilities were provided for the payment of the Spanish army, and in 1639 Spanish soldiers were allowed to march over English soil to enable them to evade the attentions of the Dutch. Meanwhile, the battle for the West Indies was carried on by independent companies and English sea captains acting on their own initiative, and often obliged to sail under foreign flags.

The only active military campaign that Charles undertook outside his English kingdom in the 1630s arose unexpectedly as a consequence of his attempt to impose a new order of worship on the church of his other kingdom of Scotland. This affronted the clear and powerful religious preferences of the Scottish people, and also met with condemnation from his English subjects, who perceived that it contradicted their national interest by fomenting a gratuitous conflict between the two kingdoms. Paradoxically, this needless provocation of his peoples on both fronts arose from Charles's dominant desire to reinforce the principles of hierarchy. It resulted in another humiliating reversal, which demonstrated in graphic fashion the fundamental weakness of a monarchy that was unwilling or unable to attach itself to the collective strengths of its English kingdom, or to make a balanced assessment of the public interest in either land.

One of the most distorting aspects of the recent historiography of the seventeenth century has been the misrepresentation of the position of Scotland in relation to the English Civil War, in an attempt to construct an essential connection between the two struggles, and transpose the dispute into an imaginary "British" dimension. This would serve the revisionist purpose of concealing the distinctive momentum for economic and political change that existed within the English kingdom. In a series of articles from the 1980s, Conrad Russell contrived a so-called "British Problem", suggesting that Charles was driven by a pragmatic need for a more unified structure of power in his realms.[16] This was not a convincing explanation for the king's Scottish mishap. Charles's Episcopal campaign in Scotland was what might today be called a vanity project. It was a private crusade supported only by some English bishops, and it threatened the settled and united character of the Kirk. Politically, Scotland was much easier to govern than England, even from a distance, and in this respect it was better left as a separate entity, free from infection by the radical habits of the English parliament. By postulating a "British" problem of unity, Russell was diverting attention from the real problems of unity that Charles faced within the English kingdom, where parliament had been challenging his prerogatives on a broad front, until banished in the 1630s. In this respect it is instructive to recall the respective approaches of crown and Commons to the idea of state development as such. The early Stuart kings do not seem to have possessed a concept of a "state" entity. They did not recognise the existence or legitimacy of a political unit bound together by its own self-conscious dynamic. The worldview of James and Charles was dynastic and hierarchical—they believed that each of their kingdoms took its identity from them. It was the English parliamentarians who were adopting the structures and perspectives of a state.

These essential differences were clearly illustrated very early in James's reign. The only proposal for turning Scotland and England into a unitary state came from the parliamentarians in 1606, with the suggestion of a "perfect union" of laws. This would have incorporated Scotland into the English parliamentary system of sovereign representative law, based on the principle enunciated by Sir Edwin Sandys: "it is fit and just that every man do join in making that which will bind and govern him, and because every man cannot be present, a representative body is used to perform the same".[17] This would indeed have brought the two kingdoms together in a genuine "state" dynamic. The idea was not, however, acceptable to James I. He was always suspicious of the implications of English representative law, which might be, and indeed was seen as constituting an alternative to his own belief that ultimate legislative sovereignty lay with the monarch alone. He declined the parliamentary offer, pointing out that they already had a perfect union—himself, and he could resolve any anomalies, on the basis that "rex est lex". This reflected not only two contrasting concepts of legislative authority, but also the fact that the early Stuarts's notion of the structures of power was defined by the idea of dynastic hierarchy.

Charles I was his father's son. He and Archbishop Laud did not assault the peaceful and efficient workings of the Scottish Kirk in order to create a more unified state. Their motivations derived from the most dominant and consistent concern of the early Stuart crown, which was to reinforce the principles of hierarchy. As Claire Cross once pointed out, Charles had embraced the programme of William Laud in the late 1620s, because it offered him a "concept of order".[18] They came together specifically to form a front of hierarchical authority against an English parliament that they perceived, not without reason, to be leading a popular challenge to the prerogatives of the crown.[19] In political terms, in England, the reassertion of royal authority could only be achieved by banishing parliament from the scene, as Charles did, with Laud's encouragement, in 1629. In the ecclesiastical field, however, Laud could offer a more positive solution, at least in the English context. Here, the proponents of radical Protestantism were operating as an irregular minority, finding space for independent, non-conformist practice in the interstices of the somewhat loose arrangements of the Elizabethan church settlement. Laud could bring the Puritans to heel, or at least to kneel, simply by restoring the strict patterns of ceremonial, and the structures of orderly ritual in the churches, thereby closing off the scope for dissenting schemes of worship. The campaign of Charles and Laud in Scotland was a reckless extension of that same programme for reinstating the ecclesiastical forms of hierarchy. In Scotland, the imposition of Episcopal ceremony was a far more difficult task, because radical Protestantism was not a minority movement, it was itself the established order, and the Kirk was sufficiently powerful and united to defend its settled character against the king, the archbishop, and anyone else who might care to offer. So the Caroline campaign to reinforce the traditional values of hierarchy was thrown into reverse, ecclesiastically in Scotland, and politically in England.

The king and his archbishop William Laud had embarked on a private crusade to impose a stricter Episcopal and ceremonial order on the Kirk. This proved to be completely unacceptable to the well-coordinated and largely Presbyterian system that prevailed in Scotland. In the churches, the congregations refused to listen to the new Prayer Book. Collectively, the Scots formed a national Covenanting movement to resist the unwanted intervention, by force of arms if necessary. Far from being a basis of unity, the High Ceremonialist ambitions of Charles and Laud had created a rebellion in Scotland, and were also deplored by the leading trend of opinion among his English subjects. In the southern kingdom, even those who were not creedal Calvinists tended to favour a degree of tolerance and latitude for those who were. On all sides the campaign against the Kirk was regarded as inappropriate and uncalled for. As John Pym said in the Grand Remonstrance, it had fomented "a most dangerous division and chargeable preparation for war betwixt your kingdoms of England and Scotland".[20] In fact the parliamentarians regarded it as another flagrant breach of the English national interest. There would have been little purpose in Charles summoning the English parliament to help finance his military response to the Covenanters, since the Commons would have been no more sympathetic to this cause than to the others into which he had attempted to draw them in the past.

With no standing army, or even a hard core of seasoned troops, Charles attempted to raise a force from the trainbands of the northern counties. They reached the meadows of the Tweed completely untrained, ill prepared and poorly provisioned. They faced a Covenanting army led with fervour by the feudal chiefs of each Scottish locality, stiffened by veterans who had served the cause of Protestantism in the Swedish and Dutch armies in the Thirty Years War, and galvanised by a degree of discipline and commitment which would have been the envy of any commander. The English nobles were not keen to engage in battle, and the Covenanters perceived that they had no need to fight. Charles's "army" dispersed back into England. When Strafford was given charge of affairs, a more rigorous approach was expected. His simple task was to raise a viable army. His first advice was to call a parliament, which might have been effective had there been any basis of agreement about the balance of rights in the raising of public finance. No parliamentary subsidy was forthcoming, and the resumption of discretionary levies like Ship Money, Coat and Conduct Money and a projected Forced Loan, only served to further entrench the public disinclination to pay. This did not bode well for the prospects of recruitment. The net was cast wider across the southern counties, which produced a force that was greater in number, but still more inclined to desert than to fight. Again, it was an apology for an army that marched north. The Scots felt free to cross the border. They cut through the vanguard of the king's troops at Newburn, and occupied Durham and Northumberland, realising that all they had to do now was to sit tight and negotiate favourable terms.

From the absence of effective opposition, the Covenanters gathered that the king's ill-judged initiative had little or no support in his southern kingdom. For their part, the English were confirmed in their view that the attack on the Kirk was gratuitous, and that the Scots were justified in defending themselves against it. But we should not suppose that sympathy with the Scots was the real basis of English opposition to the king. It is true that Charles was now in such a desperate position in the north that his regime could no longer be sustained without parliamentary backing, and he would therefore be obliged to succumb to parliamentary demands. To this extent, the king's Scottish debacle may be taken as providing the *occasion* for the English Revolution of the 1640s. But it should be apparent that this effect was merely contingent. One of the fundamental misconstructions of recent historiography has been to suggest that the crisis in Scotland was actually causative, or intrinsic to the English Revolution. This is clearly not the case. What the parliamentarians would demand when they met was the establishment of representative rights in the political and economic fields, ambitions that were distinctive to the English kingdom, and which the English parliament had been seeking to put in place for several decades. As the MP Harbottle Grimston said in 1640, although an invasion of the country by the Scots would certainly be unfortunate, the first priority of parliament was to secure the liberties of England within.[21]

By the same token, the opposition movements in England and Scotland were qualitatively different, in their characters and their essential aims, as in their causes. Recent historiography has been characterised by a misleading tendency to merge or mix up the two developments, as if they were interchangeable, or composed of one and the same occurrence, to create the impression that each had an equal part to play in a kind of multiple civil war. This uncritical conflation of separate events and circumstances is illustrated in graphic fashion in the lately published *Oxford Handbook of the English Revolution*, which is largely devoted to an attempt to deny the distinctively English shape of the mid-seventeenth century revolution, and conceal it under a superimposed "British" dimension. Given this brief, Julian Goodare, in his article *The Rise of The Covenanters*, feels obliged to exaggerate the political context of the Prayer Book Revolt, to try to bring it into line with developments in England. The essentially ecclesiastical basis of the Scottish Covenanting drive is obscured. Instead, Goodare inflates the idea of pre-existing political grievances in the Scottish context, relating to the Scottish parliament and the General Assembly.[22] It is not surprising to find that the Scottish assembly expressed grievances of some sort, but this does not mean that they had the same magnitude or effect as the English parliament's long-running assault on a range of royal prerogatives. The Scottish parliament understandably shared in the general objection to monopoly privileges. But crucially, it never displayed the rooted animosity that developed in the English parliament to any sort of prerogative levy, or any kind of money raising without explicit representative consent. The Scottish assembly advanced subsidies every four years without conditions, most recently in 1633, when the English parliament had been banished from the scene, as giving nothing but trouble.

The Scottish parliament was then, a much more amenable instrument of royal authority. David Stevenson, and more recently David Smith have described the "Lords of the Articles" whereby the king selected a committee, which in turn selected the representatives of the shires. This enabled the king to direct the business of parliament along the lines that he desired.[23] James had actually tried to enhance the role of the Scottish parliament, to counteract the unruly nobility and an independent-minded Kirk, which were his real problems in Scotland.[24] In England, the church and the nobility were firmly under royal control, but parliament was not, so James sought to limit its use. In comparison with the English system, the Scottish parliament lacked a true or substantial representative capacity, so it never established the kind of participatory hold on legislative sovereignty that contributed so much to the independent strength and ambition of the English assembly. Conversely, the precepts of Civil Law, which held the ruler to be the essential basis of legislative power, still carried full weight in Scotland. It is therefore not too surprising that Sir Edwin Sandys was anxious that the coordinated force of English representative statute should not be impaired or overlaid by the simple addition of Scottish judicial practice. Nor is it surprising that James I did not wish to see the pro-monarchical bias of Scottish law overtaken by the English representative network in a "perfect union". The political consequence of these differences was that the Scottish parliament did not possess, in practice or in principle, a basis for the drive to extend the application of representative rights on which the English parliament had been embarked since the beginning of the seventeenth century.

The Covenanters' demands for a "free" parliament, and a "free" General Assembly were defensive expedients to preserve the Kirk against a king who could not be swayed from a fixed determination to impose the new Prayer Book. It is wrong to suggest, as Goodare appears to do, that the Scots had the same inherent parliamentarian ambitions that existed in England. At a time of clearer vision and more discriminating judgement, before the fog of the "British" dimension descended over academia, David Stevenson pointed out that "Scotland had no strong national myth of free parliaments like England", and at the inception of the Prayer Book revolt, there was "no sign that those leading the revolt thought of holding a parliament as a necessary part of the settlement".[25] We can add further that Scotland had not experienced the great transitions that radically changed the socio-economic balance within the English kingdom in the decades prior to the English Revolution. In Scotland, there had been no rise of the gentry to a dominant national class, no emergence of a distinctive and broad body of commercial yeoman farmers, no galvanising development of an interregional market, and no politicised demand for a right of freedom of trade that bound all this together.

In the same volume, R. Scott Spurlock also appears to have been briefed to drag a political aspect of the Scottish revolt into the light. He notes that the Covenanting side of the movement has often been celebrated, at the expense of the politics. We might suggest, however, that this is not so much an omission as a true measure of the different levels of significance that attached to the two fields, and that the attempt to give equal weight to political aims denies the proper balance of the evidence. In fact, Scott Spurlock finds it impossible to escape the conclusion that the Scottish opposition was not essentially political in character—its shape was determined by the Covenanting imperative. "The position of the ruling elders in the Kirk and in parliament ensured that the movement dominated politics . . . the Covenanters' dominance of Scotland equated to a theocracy". There was no development of a specifically political state, as was emerging, distinctively, in England. Allowing the "British" dimension to fade further into the distance, Scott Spurlock observes that in Scotland there was no platform for establishing the balance of the public interest, the process around which the political nation was coalescing in England. In Scotland, by contrast, the course of debate was orchestrated from the pulpits, and efficiently turned in the direction that served the Covenanters' aims. "Scotland did not develop an open forum for public discourse like that in England".[26]

So the Scottish priority in the mid-seventeenth century disputes was, and would remain the defence and furtherance of the true Kirk. It bears repeating that at the inception of the Prayer Book Revolt, there was "no sign that those leading the agitation thought of holding a parliament as a necessary part of the settlement![27] The later demands for a free General Assembly and a free parliament were pursued because it was known that they would support the opposition to the new Prayer Book. In England, by contrast, the aim of installing and sustaining the representative assembly at the centre of affairs was the essence of the revolution, and it derived from a long-standing determination in the English parliament to extend the force of representative rights, often at the expense of the prerogatives of the crown. In Scotland, there was no pre-existing political opposition remotely commensurate with what Charles was trying to face down in England. And such political development as now occurred in Scotland was a function of the Covenanting movement, equating, as Scott Spurlock said, to a theocracy.

This was reflected in the limited and tangential part that the Scots played in the English Civil War. Their specific and constant aim was to assert the principles of the Kirk. Beyond this, they had no particular interest in the central, political dispute between the king and the English parliament. John Morrill, blinded by the "British" illusion, rehearses the evidence that should logically have led him to a different view. He acknowledges that once the Covenanters had re-established the autonomy of the Kirk and the General Assembly from royal control and political interference, they were disinclined to engage in the contest in England for any other reason.[28] When they finally did so, at the invitation of a militarily challenged English parliament, it was to consolidate the authority of the Kirk by making it the basis of the English church settlement. They withdrew when it became clear that the English parliamentarians were actually inclined in the opposite direction, towards a laicised settlement of the church. And when the Scots came to feel that they had more chance of getting their confessional programme adopted by a desperate king, they switched allegiance. When they sought a place at the settlement table, it was to try to stop the political revolution. The Scots fought alternately for either side, in pursuit of a religious objective that was truly characteristic of neither. The Scottish contribution does not show that there was a British dimension to the English Civil War—it demonstrates conclusively that there was not.

The "British" idea has nothing to offer in the way of coherent sequence or reasoned association. It rests simply on assembling all references to Scottish or Irish participation, however incidental or contingent, and presenting this as the "British" dimension, as if mentioning them in the same breath automatically turns them into a single event. The only "premise" appears to be that since Charles I was ruler in all three lands of the British Isles, therefore there must have been a British dynamic to the Civil War. The fallacy of this is exposed in a stark contradiction at the beginning of Morrill's article. He starts by noting that the revolution, at its climax, appeared as a purely English event. The king was executed in the name of the English state, for denying the authority of the English parliament, which had come to regard itself as the embodiment of the state. The act looked forward to the acceptance of the "good people of this nation of England". No other perspective was included, and none was relevant. Charles's crimes were said to have been against "this nation".

The Scottish and Irish forces that he had induced to fight for him were "foreigners". Which all seemed to confirm that the revolution took place in the specific and distinctive context of the emergent English nation-state. How is it possible to get from there to the "British" dimension? Because, avers Morrill, "Charles *was* also king of Scotland".[29] Few historical propositions can have been so lacking in logical force. The fact that Charles I *was* also King of Scotland is not an acceptable basis for assuming that a Scottish element was intrinsic to the English Civil War.

The "British" dimension is an aberrant historical theory. No such thing has normally been given credence or causative significance, either by informed commentators at the time of the Civil War, or traditionally by later historians. James Harrington, writing in the 1650s, regarded Scotland as a separate context, and attributed the Civil War to distinctive developments within the English kingdom.[30] S. R. Gardiner, writing his magisterial study in the 1880s, gave full attention to the events in Scotland and Ireland that influenced the course and timing of the English Revolution, but he did not misrepresent them as a cause.[31] The "British" dimension was the invention of Conrad Russell, who spent his career trying to explain the Civil War in ways that did not involve recognising the force of the great socio-economic changes and radical political trends that characterised the English scene in the preceding decades.[32] The "British" idea served that same agenda, and would, if allowed, produce a fundamental distortion of the proper balance of English history, not to mention the real histories of Ireland and Scotland.

The uncritical exaggeration of Scottish and Irish events to an equal part in the making of the English Civil War was intended to conceal the great socio-economic transitions of the time that were distinctive to the English kingdom. The preceding chapters of the present volume have described the multi-faceted transformation that revisionist historians were seeking to disguise and deny. There was the liberation, peculiar to England, of the more substantial tenants from manorial control, creating a distinctive, broad body of commercialising yeoman farmers. There was the enclosure or consolidation of individual holdings out of the open fields and commons, and the decline of the moral restraints that had guided the communal system. There was the displacement of the idea that property was held conditionally on obligations to the common good, and the growing assumption that property was owned absolutely and could be used however one saw fit. There was the underlying change in the way that people related to the land, no longer in its given form, but to be used and "improved" for profit. There was the development of a new network of interregional exchange, where bulk products were traded over longer distances, though in a more integrated market system. There was the exceptional liberty from internal customs barriers that came to prevail in England, and the emerging demand for a principled right of "freedom of trade" against any kind of arbitrary restriction or exaction. There was the growing assertion of "freedom of trade" as the defining basis of a long series of challenges to the royal prerogative, by a distinctive nationwide alliance of gentry, merchant traders, and yeoman farmers. There was the remarkable proliferation of the gentry into a national governing class, holding landed authority in every locality. There was the consequent installation of the gentry as the principal agents in the making and enforcing of sovereign law, the leading protagonists for the extension of representative rights, and the dominant voice in the identification of the national project and the objective national interest. None of these crucial developments occurred anywhere but in England, and it was all supposed to disappear in the stultifying illusion of the "British" dimension.

If that dimension had been sustained we would have lost sight and knowledge of the most seminal and influential economic and political changes in English history. We would also have been deprived of an understanding of the nature of state development. The nation-state first arose in the sixteenth and early seventeenth centuries, and it was forged distinctively from collective principles and processes taking hold within the English kingdom. Preceding chapters have stressed the significance of the fact that the parliamentarians, rather than the crown, were appropriating the elements of a state perspective. The early Stuarts did not possess a concept of a unitary nation-state, nor did they have an urgent need to create one out of their two kingdoms. It was only in England, through the English political nation, that the state was coming into existence. The *Handbook* talks of each of the three lands in terms of a state structure, in order once again to equip them all with the same capacity to participate in a supposed multiple civil war(s). But in fact the notion of a state had no meaningful application in Ireland or Scotland at the time. The comprehensively dispersed and disparate range of political and religious authorities in Ireland defied any idea or possibility of a unitary state. And although Scotland had only one king, the exercise of authority on the ground still rested on the personal and feudal power of nobles and lairds, coordinated only by the general influence of the Kirk. There were none of the dynamics of unity and integration that underpinned the development of the English state, in which Scotland was shortly to be enveloped.

The Civil War in England took place, specifically, in the context of an emergent nation-state that was distinctive to the English kingdom. Unfortunately for the early Stuarts, the new structure of the state had coalesced around the English parliament. Charles's problem was not that he needed to construct a united state out of his two kingdoms, but that he had to cope with the one that had already been forged out of popular developments in England. It was the parliamentarians who valued and sought to employ the principal internal framework of the emergent state in England—that is to say, the process of sovereign, representative law, which bound the people together just as it bound them by their consent in the making of its statutes, while to the Stuart kings the function of parliamentary legislation came to be seen as a threat rather than an aid to their power. Similarly, it was the parliamentarians who grasped the vision of a trading empire as the national enterprise, and the galvanising force of a consolidated national identity, which defined England's outward relation to the world. So it was the parliamentarians who became the representatives and guardians of the independently conceived national interest, supplanting the personal and dynastic priorities of the crown. Not the least of the disservices rendered by the so-called "British" dimension to the cause of constructive historical truth is the concealment of the real process of state formation that was taking place precociously and distinctively in sixteenth- and seventeenth-century England.

So the English Civil War and Revolution was not the product of an identity of circumstances and aims across the three lands. The anti-colonial rebellion in Ireland in 1641, and the anti-Prayer Book Revolt in Scotland were not among the real causes of the political opposition to Charles I in England. Nor were the Scots equal players in a supposed multiple civil war(s). They were concerned essentially with religion. Charles's Scottish disaster was a contingent occasion that gave the English parliament the chance to implement ways of ensuring the continuous exercise of parliamentary functions and representative rights, which it had been seeking to apply since 1610. In one of the more logical contributions to the *Handbook*, Joseph Cope offers a balanced historical perspective. He finds that the Irish Rebellion was indeed an anti-imperial revolt, stemming principally from "the simmering resentment caused by the New English in the late 16th and early 17th centuries". He concludes, "As with the English Civil War and Revolution generally, historians must account for the long-term tensions that come to the surface during the conflict, and the short term contingent factors that lead to the outbreak of hostilities".[33] And sometimes there was a sense of an undercurrent so strong that it must eventually break through. It is in this light that we should read Lucy Hutchinson's comment that, following their "extraordinary progress" the people of England were "left now only to expect an opportunity".[34]

Notes

1. L. Hutchinson, *Memoirs of the Life of Colonel Hutchinson*, ed. J. Hutchinson, (London 1846), p. 75
2. *Proceedings in Parliament 1625*, eds. M Jansson and W. D. Bidwell, (Yale 1987), p. 191
3. C. Thompson, "Court Politics and Parliamentary Conflict in 1625", in *Conflict in Early Stuart England*, eds. R. Cust and A. Hughes, (London 1989), pp. 171–2
4. *Proceedings in Parliament 1625*, pp. 191–3
5. Ibid, p. 407
6. Thompson, "Court Politics and Parliamentary Conflict", p. 175

7. *Proceedings in Parliament 1625*, p. 403
8. C. Russell, *Parliaments and English Politics 1621–29*, (Oxford 1979), pp. 426–7
9. Sir Francis Bacon, "Of the True Greatness of Kingdoms and Estates", in *Bacon's Essays, (1597 to 1625)*, ed. J. McNeill, (London 1959), p. 91
10. *Constitutional Documents of the Puritan Revolution*, ed. S. R. Gardiner, (Oxford 1968), p. 208
11. S. R. Gardiner, *History of England 1603–1642*, (London 1886–9), V, pp. 305–6
12. *Constitutional Documents of the Puritan Revolution*, p. 208
13. Ibid
14. Gardiner, *History of England*, VII, p. 169
15. Ibid, pp. 173–5, 367
16. C. Russell, "The British Problem and the English Civil War", *History 72* (1987), pp. 395–415
17. *Parliamentary Diary of Robert Bowyer 1606–7*, ed. D. H. Wilson, (New York 1971), pp. 258–9
18. C. Cross, *Church and People 1450–1660*, (London 1976), pp. 176–7
19. R. Cust, "Charles I, The Privy Council, and the Forced Loan", *JBS 25* (1982), pp. 205–35
20. *Constitutional Documents of the Puritan Revolution*, p. 204
21. J. Rushworth, *Historical Collections*, (London 1659–1701), III, p. 1128
22. J. Goodare, "The Rise of the Covenanters", in *The Oxford Handbook of the English Revolution*, (Oxford 2016), p. 46
23. D. Stevenson, *The Scottish Revolution 1637–1644*, (Newton Abbot 1973), p. 169
24. J. Wormald, *Court, Kirk and Community in Scotland 1475–1625*, (London 1981), pp. 155–8
25. D. Stevenson, *The Scottish Revolution 1637–44*, (Newton Abbot 1971), p. 169
26. R. Scott, Spurlock "State, Politics and Society in Scotland 1637–1660", in *The Oxford Handbook of the English Revolution*, (Oxford 2016), pp. 363–8
27. Stevenson, *The Scottish Revolution 1637–1644*, p. 169
28. J. Morrill, "The Revolution in the British Context and Irish Context", *Oxford Handbook of the English Revolution*, (Oxford 2016), pp. 556–7
29. Ibid, p. 556
30. James Harrington, *Oceana*, ed. H. Morley, (London 1887), pp. 59–60
31. Gardiner, *History of England 1603–1642*
32. C. Russell, "The British Problem and the English Civil War", pp. 395–415
33. J. Cope, "The Irish Rising", *The Oxford Handbook of the English Revolution*, (Oxford 2016), pp. 79–82
34. Hutchinson, *Memoirs of the Life of Colonel Hutchinson*, p. 75

11 The First Revolutionary Measure of the Long Parliament

The Triennial Act of February 1641—a "Course as May Not Be Eluded";[1] and the Relevance of the Rise of the Gentry

When parliament reconvened in April 1640, its eleven years' absence during the king's Personal Rule had not induced a mood of regret and reconciliation, or narrowed the political divide. King and Commons met with the same contradictory purposes, and the same conflicting expectations that had caused their estrangement in 1629. In fact, in one specific and important respect, the line of division had hardened. It was in 1628 that the often abortions of parliament had risen to the top of the Commons' list of grievances. By 1640 this complaint was magnified, and the intermission of parliaments had become the grievance of grievances.

The other most intractable and specific point of contention was also at exactly the same impasse as in 1629. King and Commons remained completely at odds over the rights of tonnage and poundage and impositions. A tonnage and poundage bill was at once brought forward by the crown. This confirmed what had been the king's sole purpose in calling the 1629 assembly—that is, to have his right to the levy of tonnage and poundage freely endorsed by parliament in the traditional way. But parliament's position on the matter was also unchanged. Since 1625 the Commons had made their endorsement of tonnage and poundage conditional on the king surrendering his right to set customs dues by imposition. In fact, the displacement of this prerogative had been the central, radical ambition of the Commons since 1610. It remained so in 1640.

So the king and the Commons began this parliament in exactly the same stalemate that had ended the last. The king made no concession to the fact that parliament now, routinely, sought the redress of grievances before advancing a subsidy. The Lord Keeper's opening speech demanded immediate supply to meet the king's urgent needs, while grievances might be addressed in due course. The elephant in the chamber was the fact that many MPs had more sympathy with the Scots than with the king. In an early speech, Harbottle Grimston made this point as clearly as it was possible to do in the circumstances. He suggested that although the idea of a Scottish invasion was to be deplored, the denial of the liberties of the subject in England was the greater danger, and should be remedied as the first priority.[2] Petitions came in from across the kingdom, pressing grievances of every description. At court it was said that this gave comfort to the Scots, as no doubt it did.

Some modern historians have supposed that parliament met in April 1640 with no particular anti-government agenda but in a mood to cooperate, and that it was only the premature dissolution after a few weeks that provoked the angry mood of the following assembly in November.[3] This is to turn the logic and the facts of the situation on their head. The king's need for money was desperate. Why would he have dismissed the assembly if it was ready to help him? The Short Parliament was dissolved precisely because it was *not* ready to cooperate. In fact, it is clear that this parliament displayed the same strategic oppositional tendencies that had produced the clashes of the 1620s. Furthermore, the grievances and demands of the Commons were couched in terms that directly prefigured the radical changes that were put in place in the opening months of its successor.

It was in the Short Parliament that John Pym took the floor to compile the catalogue of their grievances, old and new, in the first version of what would become the official parliamentarian assessment of national affairs. Pym rejected the idea of supply before grievances just as brusquely as the king had demanded it. The general dislike of the king's campaign against the Kirk was implied in Pym's assessment of religious affairs. This analysis was also significant because it revealed the basic parliamentarian stance on the church as tolerant rather than dogmatic. He deplored the "over rigid prosecution" of those who had scruples about engaging in some of the official practices of the Anglican church, which were of course the same practices that Charles and Laud had attempted to enforce upon the Scots. Pym sought no additional proscription of Catholics, but objected to them in as far as they tried to impose upon others.[4] It was a latitudinarian message, with which the dangerous obsessions of the king and the archbishop were completely out of step.

The list of secular grievances, headed liberty and property, was a long one. But Pym began, as he was to end, by identifying "the grievance of grievances"—that is to say, the long intermission of parliaments. This framed his argument and was emphasised with intent. The absence of parliaments was the grievance of grievances not simply because it was the greatest of them, but more significantly because it gave license to the many other transgressions. This was a clue to what the central solution would be. The priority of the Long Parliament when it met a few months later was a very radical measure to make absolutely sure that there could be no such intermissions in the future.

The catalogue of specific complaints began with those of greatest significance and longest standing. First in line came the king's continued collection of imposed customs dues, and tonnage and poundage, without parliamentary consent. These two issues remained interdependent, as they had been ever since 1625. The Commons were exploiting their formal right of granting tonnage and poundage and using it as leverage to try to establish a new right of subjecting all the customs dues to the control of parliamentary consent. There would be no endorsement of tonnage and poundage until the Commons' long-term aim of establishing representative command of the setting of the customs dues in general had been achieved. Pym highlighted the latter as the central, and most particular parliamentarian purpose, as indeed it had been since 1610. He also condemned the king's continued use of the granting of monopolies, in contravention of the Commons' attempts to bring the practice to an end. This was a campaign of similar longevity to the drive against impositions, and was also an intrinsic part of the freedom of trade agenda, which was the coordinating principle of the Commons' overall ambitions in the field of public finance.

Then Pym moved on to the more recent issues, especially the various fiscal expedients to which the government had resorted during the decade of personal rule—like the compositions for knighthoods, the extension of ship money, the stretching of the bounds of the forest laws, and the recent military levies like coat and conduct money taken without remuneration. It should be said that none of this was actually against the law. In fact the Caroline government gave every indication of trying to stay within the accepted limits of law and convention. The real basis of these grievances was that they came within the overall target of the Commons' desire to end the practice of raising money by prerogative. It had long been acknowledged that the crown had discretionary rights in that area, to fulfil its responsibility for public safety. But the parliamentarians now wished to bring all such matters under the control of representative consent.

For the king to rule alone, without reference to the representative assembly, was also perfectly legal. There had been gaps of eight and six years between some of Henry VIII's parliaments. Elizabethan parliaments had tended to meet every few years, but there was once a gap of five. James I had once allowed a period of seven years to elapse between assemblies. In any event, parliaments met at the discretion of the monarch, and it was not true as Pym asserted that the abrupt dissolution of assemblies without redress of grievances was "against law and custom". Such claims only underlined the belief in the Commons that parliament ought *now* to be placed in a position where it could not be dispensed with. So Pym returned to "the grievance of grievances", the long "intermission" of parliaments. The stress that he placed upon it gave a fair indication that if the chance arose the parliamentarian priority would be to find some way of ensuring that it could never happen again. A further sign of this intent, and a clear psychological justification for enhancing the position of parliament, was Pym's elevation of the representative assembly as the seat of "reason" in the kingdom. He suggested that the powers of parliament were to the body politic "as the rational faculties of the soul to a man".

As Gardiner rightly said, "The whole spirit of the coming revolution, at least on the political side, was to be found in these words".[5] Parliament was now to be taken as expressing the mind of the nation and elevated accordingly. The radical force of Pym's concept, as Gardiner also pointed out, lay in the fact that it contradicted the traditional notion, which was certainly still maintained by Charles and Laud, that the king himself was the soul of the body politic.[6] Pym's inversion of this was not just rhetoric. It reflected a substantial and significant process of transference whereby parliament was displacing the king as the essential determinant of the unitary public interest. The change finds further elucidation in the work of Thomas Hobbes who also noted, though in his case with dismay, that in the decades before the Civil War the king was losing his ancient role as the central representative of the kingdom—"the name without contradiction passing for the title of those men who at his command were sent up by the people to carry their petitions".[7]

So Pym was not just presenting the full list of grievances—he was laying the foundation for a solution that would prevent them from recurring. As Gardiner suggested, the essence of the speech lay in its deliberation. It was a far-reaching programme, formulated with great care and in persuasive detail. It is difficult to see on what basis some historians have supposed that the Commons failed to take their cue from him.[8] It was a speech of exceptional length, lasting two hours, far beyond the usual attention span of MPs. But on this occasion they listened patiently, no doubt aware that it marked a significant moment, and "at the end of it all cried out "A good oration!"[9] In truth, it seems quite clear that in general terms they followed the course that Pym set out. The keynote speech, restrained, yet commanding, "carried the House with it", and "laid down the lines upon which, under altered conditions, the Long Parliament afterwards moved".[10]

Their grievances were fundamental, especially in the central demand for control over public finance. In that light it is not entirely surprising that the king sought to avoid the issue, and with the support of the Lords and Convocation, spent some weeks trying to simply browbeat the Commons into advancing supply without redress. The MPs stood firm, as Pym had recommended, and on 23 April they resolved that, "till the liberties of the House and the kingdom are cleared they know not whether they have anything to give or no".[11] Under further pressure to respond to the king's demand for immediate supply, they conceded that they might defer their claim for redress concerning religion and parliamentary privilege, but they remained adamant that they would give nothing until the principal grievance of the kingdom concerning public finance had been met. In effect they wanted a concrete and definitive endorsement of the principle that money should only be raised by parliamentary consent.[12] Strafford, recognising that their agenda was even more uncompromising than his own, advised the king to allow the Ship Money judgement to be taken before the Lords on a writ of error, when it would duly be reversed. Charles finally agreed to this on condition of a vote of twelve subsidies. Richard Cust suggested that the king's offer was "too little too late".[13] But it is likely that no concession that the king could make would ever have been enough. Some MPs were prepared to consider giving six subsidies in return for a favourable judgement on Ship Money, but others were more concerned about other kinds of fiscal imposition—so the feint prospect of a settlement receded again. This simply reflected the fact that the Commons wanted *all* aspects of the raising of public money to be brought under the control of parliamentary consent. In effect, they were no longer prepared to tolerate any kind of arbitrary exaction. This really left no room for compromise, and it was not too surprising that Henry Vane came to the conclusion, and offered as advice to the Privy Council, that in his opinion the Commons would never give one penny. That they felt free to adopt this stance owed something to the fact that their sympathies lay mainly with the king's opponents in Scotland, and this eventually came to the surface. The House, again guided by Pym, was preparing to invite the Scots to make their case and proposing to ask the king to come to an accommodation with them. This would have been a personal humiliation for Charles. The assembly had shown itself uncooperative in every respect and was duly dismissed.

During the summer, however, the king suffered further setbacks in his increasingly hopeless military confrontation with the Scots. He was now in desperate need of money just to sustain the physical integrity of his rule and his English kingdom. There were no sources of supply that did not rest, or insist on the recall of parliament. It convened on the 3rd of November 1640. It was to prove a momentous gathering. What made the Long Parliament different, and what indeed made it the Long Parliament, was the fact that Charles's military and political situation was now completely untenable without parliamentary support, and the usual resort of dissolving an intransigent assembly was no longer available to him.

By the same token, the parliamentarians now had a chance to realise the ambitions that they had displayed consistently over the preceding decades—that is, to extend the force of representative rights, often at the expense of the royal prerogative, across most of the fields of government, finance and administration. They grasped the opportunity at once and to the full, by bringing forward a measure that would elevate parliament to an independent and permanent place at the centre of the polity and ensure the continuous, general application of representative consent in national affairs. This was done by the Triennial Act, which was the first piece of legislation produced by the Long Parliament, and was pushed through as a priority in February 1641. In effect, it deprived the king of his prerogative of deciding when and whether parliament should meet. It provided instead that parliament would assemble automatically, of its own accord, if the king had failed to call it after a three-year period. In the bill as first presented, on 24 December 1640, the proposed interval was just one year. It was introduced by Oliver Cromwell and William Strode. The latter was a veteran of the dramatic action of 1629, when the Speaker had been held down in his chair so that the assembly could be kept in being until it had put on record its case in respect of the customs dues. Strode now presented the bill of 1640 as "somewhat to comfort the people".[14] This implied that it was going to be a quid pro quo for the vote of a subsidy that the people might be expected to pay. And this was indeed to be the case. The interesting corollary is that the desire to equip parliament with an automatic place and permanent influence at the centre of affairs was now so great that "the people" would be happy to countenance the removal of the king's ancient prerogative to determine its meetings himself.

For a clear and balanced statement of the force of the act we have to turn to Thomas Bailey, a nineteenth-century historian who was in touch with the traditions of the Nottinghamshire MPs who had been instrumental in its promotion. Bailey was aware that there was earlier legislation from the reign of Edward III proposing that there ought to be a parliament every year. But this was from a time when the Lords, rather than the representative Commons, had been the active agency of parliament. In that period, lordly and personal power still reigned supreme, and the provisions were "thought of merely as general declarations, dispensed with at the pleasure of the crown". Both before and since, the assembly had always in fact been summoned and dismissed entirely at the will of the monarch. The Triennial Act of 1641 therefore struck at the root of the king's "hitherto acknowledged prerogative . . . in the maintenance of that power over the proceedings of parliament in which the safety of the monarchy had been supposed to consist". It was indeed "so great an innovation in the constitution as to form in itself a revolution of no ordinary degree of importance".[15]

Bailey's assessment was precise and appropriate in every respect. But he was writing at a time when historians were not frightened of recognising the signs of change. Most historians of the recent generation have preferred to turn a blind eye to the force of the Triennial Act, in their determination to deny the radical intent of the Long Parliament. The tendency has been either to simply ignore the measure, or to gloss over its significance, and quietly forget it. The most flagrant subterfuge was indulged in by John Morrill, who noted that the Triennial Act was an early measure, but then defined his terms so as to exclude it from parliament's proposals for remedial legislation, leaving the impression that their programme consisted simply of the later measures of the summer of 1641, condemning the various "abuses" of power practiced by Charles during the Personal Rule. These expedients had consisted mainly in the over-rigorous application of existing law, and the king was prepared to renounce the methods that were thought to have gone beyond the bounds.

So by restricting the focus to parliament's somewhat leisurely indictment of these practices, and leaving aside the urgent, priority change introduced by the Triennial Act, Morrill felt able to conclude that the aim of the Long Parliament was "just an unhurried and uncontroversial programme of remedial legislation . . . consciously intended to restore a lost balance . . . no will to remodel the constitution".[16]

Morrill's suggestion appears as a wilful avoidance of the true balance of the evidence, and it is disturbing that the vested interests of an academic system can sustain such misrepresentations. The illusion that the programme of the Long Parliament was just restorative has persisted. Recently, Rachel Foxley, while including the Triennial Act as part of the parliamentary programme, does so only to reduce it to one of the reforms that "returned England to its proper equilibrium".[17] In truth, this was precisely what the Triennial Act did not do. It specifically broke the traditional balance of political initiative. The "proper" constitutional equilibrium when parliament met on 3rd November 1640 was that only the king could give life to the assembly, as indeed he had just done. But with the passage of the Triennial Act of 16 February 1641, parliament gave itself an independent and permanent existence at the centre of political life, whether the king liked it or not.

It was, as Bailey said, "a revolution of no ordinary degree of importance". And it was not just part of the parliamentary programme—it was the crucial, core proposition that would give full and final effect to all the rest. It was not merely restorative. It was intended, specifically, to change the political balance, not just to stop the unwanted practices, but also to ensure that they could never start again. Edmund Ludlow and Clement Walker both recalled that the Commons' priority in 1640 was to prevent another "discontinuance of parliaments".[18] In the House, John Pym reiterated his diagnosis that "the intermission of parliaments . . . is the main cause of all these and other mischiefs". Lord Digby agreed that the absence of parliaments was "the cause causarum of all the mischiefs and distempers", building up to the proposition that the regular presence of parliament must be guaranteed by "some such course as may not be eluded".[19] Edward Bagshaw prepared the ground further with a graphic description of the salutary effect that parliaments had on political wrong-doers: "now during parliament, like frozen snakes, their poison dries up, but let the parliament dissolve, their poison melts and scatters abroad".[20] Sir Benjamin Rudyerd echoed Pym's assessment of the positive rationale—parliament and its facilities were now regarded by the political nation as the indispensable basis of good government: "Frequent Parliaments only are the Fountain of pure government".[21]

The man who became Charles's principal counsellor, Edward Hyde, later Earl of Clarendon, was of the conviction that nothing harmed the king's cause so much as the continual dismissal and disuse of parliament. The damage done by the sidelining of the assembly was indeed so great, and the benefits that would accrue from its regular employment so manifest, that it was now to be made impossible for the king to exclude it from the political scene. Its frequency and continuous influence had to be guaranteed. This was the work of the Triennial Act. The rationale was stated in full, and with great clarity and force, by Lord Digby in his set-piece oration on the third reading of the bill. He began with the very useful advice that they should not allow themselves to be deflected by the fact that this highly desirable provision could not be achieved without some injury to current constitutional practice.

> I rise now not with any intent to speak to the frame and structure of the bill, nor much by way of answers to objections that may be made. I hope there will be no occasion of that but that we shall all concur unanimously in what concerneth all so universally. That we may not be discouraged in this great work by difficulties that may appear in the way of it, I shall deliver to you my apprehensions in general of the vast importance and necessity that we should go through with it.[22]

The idea that the provision of automatic parliaments was a "great work" encapsulated the force of the expected benefit, and indeed the necessity that was motivating them to override the existing constitutional position.

> Let us rightly consider the nature of our sufferings . . . and there can be no cause inventible whereas to attribute them but the intermission of parliaments . . . as the deficience of parliaments has been the cause causarum of all the mischiefs and distempers, so the frequency of them is the sole antidote that can preserve and secure the future from the like danger. Unless for the frequency of parliaments there can be some such course settled as may not be eluded, neither the people can be prosperous and secure, nor the king himself solidly happy.

Here was the radical essence of the provision. They were not just asking the king to call parliament more frequently and hoping that he would gratify their wishes, they were taking steps to enforce it by "some such course as may not be eluded". In the process, they would be voting themselves a newly independent and permanent status in the political life of the nation.

Digby concluded by underlining the very clear, general argument for making parliaments automatic—that is to say, it was a provision that would not merely bring the current misdemeanours to an end, but would also make sure that no more would arise in the future. The radical force of the Triennial bill struck at the root of their troubles.

> If there be not a way found to keep them good, the mischiefs will all grow again . . . it is the opportunity of being ill that we must take away . . . which can never be done but by the frequency of

> parliaments . . . in chasing ministers we do but dissipate clouds that may gather again, is passing this bill we shall contribute so much as in our power to the perpetuation of our sun . . . no state can be confident of a public minister continuing good longer than the rod is over him.[23]

Here was the practical justification for the act—only the certainty of frequent parliaments would guarantee that the unwanted policies and practices would not recur. And Digby's words carried an important further implication. The Triennial Act was expected to *keep* ministers "good"—that is to say, in line with parliament's requirements. In other words, it would not just provide the assembly with a regular opportunity to present grievances—it would give parliament a continuous guiding hand over the executive decisions of government. It is often assumed that the Commons' leaders did not begin to demand a veto over the king's choice of ministers until the winter of 1641, and that this was a new initiative provoked by the pressure of critical events like the rebellion in Ireland. But Digby's statement of the aims of the Triennial Act shows clearly that the desire to ensure a systematic, on-going parliamentary influence over the character and course of the executive was already an inherent part of the original agenda in the winter of 1640. This was a further revolutionary effect of the measure. And it reflects the crucial fact that parliament, and the political nation that it reflected had developed an independent and definitive notion of the public priorities that they required the government to follow.

The Triennial Act was a deeply radical measure in form and intention, and it was put through, as it needed to be, with single-minded determination, on the basis of absolute practical necessity. Digby was obviously aware that there were strong constitutional objections to the course that they were taking, but chose not to dwell on the "difficulties that may appear in the way of . . . this great work". The difficulties were not in the House itself. Digby expected and assumed something like complete unanimity among MPs, and there is no doubt that in general terms this was forthcoming. There were some who may have been carried along with the tide and perhaps regretted it later. Edward Hyde noted in retrospect that the bill contained "some clauses very derogatory to monarchic principles, as giving the people authority to assemble together if the king failed to call them".[24] But there is no sign that he made any objection at the time. The only voice known to have been raised in opposition to the bill was that of Sir Simonds D'Ewes, the Commons' principal stickler for constitutional rectitude. It was once suggested that D'Ewes only opposed the bill because of the practical problems that would be raised by self-assembly.[25] But this is a misrepresentation that does D'Ewes a great injustice. It is clear that in fact he opposed the bill on principle, because it proposed to overturn the current constitutional practice. He identified the essential thrust of the bill as the provision that parliament would assemble on its own authority "though the king did not assemble it by writ". He perceived that this would encroach on "fundamental rights of the crown", and "promote a remedy worse than the disease". His basic premise was that only the king could possess the authority to initiate the political process. "All we did here had no light or force but by the king's allowing of it". D'Ewes was describing the constitutional and psychological orthodoxy of sole political initiative that underpinned the sovereignty of the crown. But the Commons were about to subvert it. So he declined to sit on the committee for the bill. "I stood up myself and showed that because I had spoken against the body of the bill I could not be of the committee".[26] He stood no chance of deflecting the House from passing the bill, so the best he could do was to disassociate from it. The only consequence of his stand was to underline the radical force of the measure.

The main "difficulty in the way of it" was of course the king, who was being deprived of his right to sole political initiative. As Gilbert Burnet said, the act was "obtained with so much difficulty . . . seemed to transfer the power from the crown to the people".[27] The king made no secret of his objections. Three days after the third reading he assembled the Houses to explain to them "the state of my affairs, my own clear intentions, and the rocks I wish you to eschew".[28] He began by reproaching them for their delay in providing the money to deal with the military emergency. He then indicated that to satisfy them he was prepared to allow the "reformation of all innovations both in church and commonwealth". He accepted that the courts of justice should be reformed "according to law", and any illegal or burdensome fiscal expedients should be discontinued. But he then went on to define a "difference between reformation and alteration of government"—a distinction that he thought was in danger of being overlooked by the Commons. He pointed out two unconstitutional demands or "rocks" on which he feared constructive agreement on finance and reform might founder. One was the proposal to exclude bishops from the House of Lords. The other was the triennial bill:

> The thing I like well, to have frequent parliaments, but to give power to sheriffs and constables, and I know not what whom to use my authority, that I cannot yield unto.

He said that he would agree to the measure only if it was amended "so that it trench neither against my honour, nor against the Ancient Prerogative of the Crown concerning Parliaments".[29] As William Clarke noted in his diary, Charles had clearly indicated that in its essential form, giving parliament the right of self-assembly, "he would no ways consent to it".[30]

Some historians have nevertheless managed to convince themselves that Charles was amenable to the bill. Conrad Russell, seeking as ever to conceal the reality of parliamentary radicalism, inverted the force of the provisions and interpreted the king's statements as if he was accepting the measure in principle and only objecting to some of the details.[31] Russell seemed to be suggesting that when Charles said he "liked" the idea of frequent parliaments, he was agreeing to the essential thrust of the bill, and his demur at the idea of losing his ancient sole prerogative to decide when and whether parliament should meet was but a minor quibble. In truth, history had shown that Charles, with good reason, did not like parliaments very much at all, and the whole purpose of the Triennial bill from the Commons' point of view was to ensure that the king's pleasure was no longer the decisive factor in their right of assembly. Charles had stated clearly, and understandably, that he saw the bill as an attempt to override his constitutional authority, and it was therefore not acceptable to him.

Further evidence, if needed, of the king's opposition to the measure can be found in the Venetian Ambassador's description of subsequent events. He noted that the Commons, undaunted by Charles's reprimand, had sent a petition asking him to satisfy them without delay regarding the triennial bill.

> The king, moved by this action, the effect of which would be to ruin his authority entirely, became very angry and displayed very little inclination to consent. He sent back the Members with a severe message. When the Members made their report, Parliament was seriously moved. Throwing aside all restraint they loudly threatened the most extreme designs and that they would suspend all business until they obtain this satisfaction, unjust as it is.[32]

For the Commons, the bill was non-negotiable, and it remained unaltered. The king was in an unenviable position. If he did not consent to the bill he faced complete disaster and humiliation in respect of his position in the north. A parliamentary subsidy was the only thing that could provide the financial security against which the king's military needs and obligations could be met, and the Commons were making their cooperation dependent on his acceptance of the triennial bill. The Venetian Ambassador again provides the most cogent guide to the determining factor in the king's stance. "The king was informed of everything . . . and after he had carefully considered for many hours the ruinous effects that a longer resistance would produce, he yielded to necessity and decided to comply".[33]

A false assumption long held by historians is that the Triennial Act was conceived as a device to provide security for loans.[34] This is an unjustified conflation of the act with the later Act Against Dissolving the Current Assembly. The latter may have been regarded as a means of guaranteeing financial security, but there is no indication that the Triennial Bill was thought of in that way.[35] It had an essential and very radical political purpose, which made it the vital basis of the parliamentary programme, and this had nothing to do with loan security. It did, in the event, underpin the advance of parliamentary supply. But since the Commons were not prepared to pass a subsidy bill until the king had agreed to the Triennial bill, the latter should rather be seen as the greatest threat to the financial security of the government.

The sequence of priorities is made very apparent by the precision with which they attached the subsidy bill to the passing of the Triennial Act. The first step, on 15 February, was a deputation to the House of Lords, "to desire them to intimate to his Majesty their desire and ours that his majesty would be pleased to give his assent to the bill of Triennial Parliaments when he gives his assent to the bill of subsidies".[36] The Lords duly picked up the implication that "the bill of subsidies might receive some prejudice", if the triennial bill were not passed.[37] When, later that afternoon, the expectation that he should pass the two bills simultaneously was put to the king, the response was not exactly reassuring. "He answered surlily that they should have his answer the following day".[38]

The Commons were understandably wary when they attended on the sixteenth. The king had told them that this was a constitutional innovation, which he could not approve. They had no explicit assurance that he would give way. All they could do was to literally hold on to their money until they were sure of getting what they wanted. So they kept a firm physical grip on the subsidy bill until the king had confirmed that he intended, there and then, to consent to the Triennial bill. Even while acceding to their wishes, Charles reiterated the reasons why he might not have agreed. He reminded them that the Triennial bill was one of the unconstitutional rocks that he had asked them to eschew, but since they had not seen fit to avoid it, he was obliged to remove it from the path himself by consenting to their demands. At the same time, he wished them to be fully aware of the damage that they were doing to the constitution. This was not to reproach them he said, "but to show you the state of things as they are: you have taken the government all in pieces; and I may say it is almost off the hinges".[39] He nevertheless confirmed that he was prepared to "yield up one of the fairest flowers in his garland, for he intended to give his royal assent to the passing of the act for the holding of a parliament every three years. He therefore hoped that we having received such large testimonies of his goodness to us . . . would therefore begin to think of him. After this speech, our speaker . . . delivered up the subsidy bill, which he had held all the time before in his hand, to one of the Lords . . . then his majesty first passed the bill for Triennial Parliaments, and afterwards the bill for subsidies".[40] Returning to their own House the Commons rejoiced at the success, and asked the Lord Keeper "to give his majesty humble thanks in the name of ourselves and the whole kingdom, which is of singular comfort and security".[41] Clarendon recalled that the measure was passed, "so much to the seeming joy of the

House that they pretended to have sufficiently provided for the indemnity of the commonwealth".[42] It certainly gave parliament a capacity for exerting a continuous influence that they had not previously enjoyed.

The Triennial Act thus comprised a fundamental alteration in the balance of power between crown and Commons, and was understandably resisted by the king. But it was the crucial, core proposition of parliament's political programme, and they pushed it through with all the determination and financial leverage at their disposal. What were the precise effects and benefits that they expected automatic parliaments to bring? Sir Benjamin Rudyerd hailed the act with the thought that "things were now put into such a state that we could not well receive hurt but from ourselves".[43] In other words, they believed that automatic parliaments would exert an effective influence over what was actually done by the king and his ministers. The knowledge that there was always a parliament coming would incline ministers to avoid doing anything that MPs might hold against them when the next scheduled assembly arrived. This, as Lord Digby had put it, was the only way to be certain that ministers would remain "good". In pursuing ministers after the fault had been committed they were just dissipating clouds "that may gather again". But the Triennial Act would ensure "the perpetuation of our sun".[44] So the guaranteed frequency of parliaments was expected to have a real effect on the policies and practices of the executive. Later, Rudyerd offered a specific example, regarding the bishops. He noted that over the last decade the church leaders had been acting in an arbitrary and extreme fashion. But he felt nevertheless that the Commons could now afford to take a moderate line when considering the future of Episcopacy. They need not go to the lengths of abolishing the bishops. They could simply lay down stricter guidelines about the balance that ought to be held in church affairs. After all, they now had a guarantee that the bishops would not overstep the mark—they had "the absolute certainty of Triennial Parliaments".[45] This was the radical effect that the Triennial Act was expected to have in practice, which in turn makes it clear that the desire to control the conduct of ministers was inherent in the original intentions of the Long Parliament when it met. MPs would no longer have to rely on being summoned in emergencies to try to cure "distempers" that had already set in. The Triennial Act would enable them to exert a systematic and continuous influence over executive decisions at the point of formulation.

There was also another, very significant way in which the "absolute certainty of Triennial Parliaments" would change the balance and character of government activity. It concerned a different aspect of government, but one that had acquired an equal, and indeed more general importance in the minds of MPs and their constituents. A crucial and specific purpose of regular, automatic parliaments was that they would guarantee the continuous use of that most comprehensive and powerful facility that the political nation had come to regard as the prime provision of good government—that is to say, the delivery of parliamentary law. The benefits of this function, and the principles behind it, counted in fact as the most important conceptual and practical basis for the implementation of the Triennial Act.

The link between the Act and the legislative function was explicit in Pym's speech on 26 February, ten days after the bill had reached the statute book. He was listing the charges against Archbishop Laud, one of which was that he had advised the king to avoid parliaments. Pym said that he had thereby conspired to divide the king from his people, and specifically "to bereave this kingdom of the legislative power, which can only be used in parliaments . . . and is the only means to restore it from distempers and decays". In fact, the idea that this was the "only means" to resolve the problems of the kingdom was not accepted by Laud or Charles, any more than it had been by James I. The early Stuarts's neglect of the legislative process was more deliberate than historians have supposed. Charles, like his father, had persistently declined to facilitate parliament's lawmaking activities, and shown no interest in using them. And in the 1630s, there are clear signs that one of the aims of the king and his party during the Personal Rule was to relegate the significance of statute law. Laud declared, for instance, that, "he would make a proclamation as available as an act of parliament".[46] Strafford in Ireland, and the law lords in the Ship Money case voiced similar denials of the sole and absolute authority of statute. Chief Justice Finch averred that "no acts of parliament make any difference" to the king's right of discretionary levies.[47] These royal apologists had come to understand that parliament's legislative role, and the high estimation in which it was popularly held, was a threat to the personal sovereignty of the crown.

Their fears were borne out by Pym's unequivocal statement that sovereign statute was "the only means" to restore the kingdom to health, and could "only be used in parliaments". This was not just a technical difference of opinion about the relative force of royal or parliamentary law. The two practices related to different forms of social, political and economic structure. The general application and broad reception of statute law had developed in the context of the consolidation of the English nation-state. Just as the exercise of universal consent bound everyone to its provisions, so it bound the nation together in all fields of activity. Its coordinated representative capacity and definitive national authority serviced the newly integrated and extended market systems. The process of its making and its implementation was in the hands of the new public administrative class constituted by the gentry and the yeomanry. It was in every way the principal internal dynamic of the emerging state structure, and Pym's eulogy to sovereign representative law reflected the fact that it was parliament rather than the crown that was embracing the new perspective. To Pym parliamentary law had come to define the very being of the state. It was "that which makes and constitutes a kingdom". He therefore hailed the Triennial Act as the basis of good government in the future.[48]

The concept of representative statute law may be regarded as the most important platform for the English Revolution, both in the imperative demand for its practical provisions in the country at large, and in the theory of political sovereignty with which it was associated. As I have written elsewhere, this was the crucial consequence of the manner in which the Break with Rome in the 1530s was brought about. In that process, the independent judicial power of the universal church was destroyed by the elevation of parliamentary statute law into the one, omni-competent, overriding law of the land. The most significant political implication was that the newly sovereign legislative authority derived its binding force, quite specifically, from the capacity of parliament to reflect the consent of the whole kingdom, or what Richard Hooker called "the entire society".[49] Parliament, and more particularly the House of Commons, had thus acquired a defining role in the sovereign legislative function. During the second half of the sixteenth century the legislative power came to be regarded as the greatest or most "unlimited" power in the state.[50] Thus in England, quite distinctively, there arose a paradox, whereby the exercise of the most "absolute" power became dependent on representative consent. This unique and contradictory, but very potent association was available for parliamentarians to reference if they ever felt the need to bring other "unlimited" or prerogative powers of the crown under representative control, and this they did, to some effect, over the issue of the king's right to impose the customs dues.[51]

The Triennial Act was a further resolution of that grand paradox. This is best illustrated in the work of the first authoritative theorist of sovereignty in the complete or modern sense of the term. Writing in the 1570s, Jean Bodin sought to devise a concept of "indivisible" power, as an antidote to the chronic civil divisions and disorders that were bedevilling the French kingdom. He conceived that the principal mark of indivisible sovereignty was the power of a ruler to enforce laws on everyone, specifically *without* their consent. This was a perfectly logical assumption in conventional terms, and Bodin seems to have been unaware that it was contradicted by the peculiar anomaly that had arisen in England, where legislation was indeed seen as the most absolute power, but it was also regarded as dependent on representative consent. Bodin knew, even in the 1570s, that the English parliament was unusually assertive and opinionated about matters of public interest. But he also understood that the force of this was limited because the assembly only met intermittently, and only at the behest of the monarch. And he assumed, again quite logically, that because it depended on the king to call it into being, this was "sufficient proof" that the English parliament did not possess a necessary or executive part in the sovereign process of lawmaking.[52] His first assumption, that parliament had no political existence without the king's summons was correct, but it did not entail the second as he supposed. For on the basis of the paradox that made the absolute power of legislation dependent on representative consent, the English parliament actually did possess an essential and defining part in the making of sovereign law. By his mistake, Bodin illustrated the political tension in the English paradox, and inadvertently indicated how it would be resolved. By the Triennial Act of February 1641, the English parliament gave itself precisely the kind of independent, automatic place at the centre of the polity that Bodin believed should be held by a body with an essential part in legislative sovereignty. This elucidates the most powerful political idea behind the English Revolution, and shows why it was indeed a revolution.

The Triennial Act was, and remained, the political basis of the English Revolution. Pym hailed the measure again as the essential guarantee of their hopes and ambitions, when he drew up the full parliamentarian programme in the Grand Remonstrance of December 1641. He itemised the reforms that had already been achieved by parliament in the past year, including the suppression of the unacceptable governmental and judicial expedients of the Personal Rule, and the indictment of the principal figures involved. But he believed that the Triennial Act, with the act against dissolving the present assembly, was the most crucial. "Which two laws well considered may be thought more advantageous than all the former, because they secure a full operation of the present remedy, and afford a perpetual spring of remedies for the future".[53]

Pym died in 1643, having done much to establish the parliamentarian movement at the centre of affairs. The Triennial Act lived on, as the primary feature of the plans of those who assumed the role of spokesmen for the revolution in its latter stages. This included the generals of the New Model Army. Oliver Cromwell had introduced the original bill in December 1640. Seven years later, when the Civil War had been won, his close associate Henry Ireton became the leading polemicist of the parliamentary cause, and took the installation of automatic parliaments as the first, basic provision of the settlement proposals that he helped to draft. The only difference was that the stipulated interval between parliaments had been shortened, and a more secure method of independent assembly was envisaged.

> That parliaments may biennially be called and meet at a certain day, with such provisions for the certainty thereof as in the late act was made for triennial parliaments; and what further or other provision shall be found needful by the Parliament to reduce it to more certainty.[54]

And in the Remonstrance of the Army, in October 1648, when the process of revolution was coming to its climax, the core proposition remained the same, except that the interval between assemblies was tightened further.

> That from the end of this, there shall be a certain succession of future parliaments, (annual or biennial), with secure provision: 1. For the certainty of their meeting, sitting, and ending. 2. For the equal distribution of elections thereunto, to render the House of Commons, as near as may be, and equal representative of the whole people electing.[55]

This incorporated the original concept on which parliament's defining share in legislative sovereignty had been based—its capacity to embody the consent of the "entire society". And this was the ultimate philosophical pretext for giving the representative assembly a permanent, automatic place at the centre of affairs, which was the core, priority provision of the parliamentarian revolution, from its inception in the winter of 1640–1 to its conclusion in the winter of 1648–1649.

Underlying these concepts were the more practical motivations. Ireton understood, as Pym had done, that a powerful drive behind the Triennial Act, and the parliamentarian movement as a whole, was the imperative need for the continuous exercise of parliament's legislative function. Ireton said that the general motivation of the parliamentary cause was that "the danger we stood in was that one man's will must be a law. The people of this kingdom have this right at least, that they should not be concluded but by the Representative of those that had the interest of the kingdom".[56] Ireton is best known as a vocal defender of property rights, and he perceived that the principal, general benefit of parliamentary law was that it provided a secure basis upon which men could acquire and consolidate property.

> And from that way I shall know a law and have a certainty. Any man that is born . . . that hath a freedom, he was capable of trading to get money, to get estates by; and therefore this man I think had a great deal of reason to build up such a foundation of interest to himself: that the will of one man shall not be a law, but that the law of this kingdom shall be by a choice of persons to represent, and that choice should be made by the generality of the kingdom. Here was a right that induced men to fight.[57]

So again, the desire to re-model the constitution and give parliament a central and automatic place in the polity was not advanced simply for its own sake—there were specific, mainly economic motives behind it. The purpose and product of parliamentary legislation can itself be regarded as having a predominantly economic aspect. Although statute law was all embracing, and was employed for important reforms in political, legal and religious affairs, its most general and characteristic application was in the socio-economic field. It was of particular value in economic affairs. Not only was it the dependable champion of property, it also brought an appropriate order to the developing commercial sphere. Like the integrated market itself, parliamentary law worked in a context of completion and continuity. It directly reflected the requirements of the trading community. It was comprehensive, definitive and stable in operation, yet open to systematic review. It offered a unique level of provision. So the identification of the legislative function as the mainspring of parliamentary ambition tells us among other things that the revolution had an underlying economic dimension.

It is often assumed that the revolution of the 1640s was reversed with the Restoration of the monarchy in 1660, and that the political nation thereby backtracked on the radical inclinations that had led to the Civil War and Interregnum. But this is not really the case. As will appear in the chapter ahead, one of most crucial, early constitutional changes relating to the customs dues remained in place. Furthermore, the Triennial Act itself stayed in force for some years. The revived royal government struggled to get parliament to remove the anti-monarchical features of the provision. They managed to defuse it only belatedly, and even then it took some political gerrymandering to achieve their purpose. It was natural that Charles II should want to restore the crown's discretion over the sitting of parliament, and seek to repeal the provisions for automatic assembly that his father had been coerced into accepting in 1641. But even in the relatively pro-monarchical atmosphere of the Cavalier Parliament, it did not prove an easy matter to turn things back. The government's first attempt to get the act amended, in 1663, failed to get through the House. The crown eventually managed to achieve its aim of "emasculating" the measure the following year, but only by rushing through an amendment at the beginning of the session before enough independent and opposition MPs had arrived at Westminster to block the move.[58]

The fact that the House of Commons had to be tricked into giving up its recently acquired right to automatic assembly underlines the revolutionary nature of the Triennial Act of February 1641, and reveals it once again as the core political proposition of the parliamentarian cause. The purpose of the act—to give parliament a continuous legislative and supervisory presence at the centre of affairs—was soon to be realised in any case, as a permanent parliamentary input became the unavoidable requirement of good government and effective public finance. The growing governmental need for the representative assembly had been understood by the Commons in the 1620s, and was a foundation of their assertiveness. The perception that parliamentary provisions of all kinds had become essential to the effective administration of the country was a principal platform of parliamentarian strength in 1640, and was intrinsic to the revolution. By the 1690s the necessity was fully recognised by the royal regimes, and parliament had become what it would remain—the permanent defining basis of government in England. And had the restored royal party not contrived a means of circumventing the intentions of the political nation and the parliamentary majority in 1664, the formal provision of automatic assembly would itself have remained in place continuously.

The Relevance of the Rise of the Gentry

It is of obvious importance to an understanding of the causes of the English Revolution to note that its first, defining, radical measure was enacted with great desire and determination by a united, and indeed virtually unanimous House of Commons, in the winter of 1640–1641. It should also be remembered that the MPs were not just acting on their own behalf. It is clear that the Triennial Act was broadly supported and indeed welcomed in the country at large. William Strode's assumption that it was "somewhat to comfort the people" was not misplaced. But the agency that actually forced it through, with such apparent satisfaction, and against the expressed wishes of the king, was the powerful majority of gentry that had come to compose the House of Commons.

The idea that there was a rise of the gentry, and a consequent decline of the aristocracy underpinning the parliamentary challenge to the crown in the 1640s is probably the most famous example of a theory of socio-economic causation in history. It gained wide currency, and its attraction is not difficult to explain. It brought many fields of activity together, and incorporated the kind of balances and connections that give an analysis objective force. It added to the depth and breadth of our picture of the period. And to those of us who find it difficult to accept that history should be just about kings and generals and institutions, the identification of a socio-economic context behind the veneer of power, seemed to relate the events of the past to the most fundamental circumstances of life.

It was an idea that could not be dismissed as pre-conceived, a criticism that is often levelled at theories of economic causation associated with Marxism. Its two principal proponents, Richard Tawney and Lawrence Stone were social historians, but not creedal Marxists. Furthermore, the theory found its genesis at the time of the Civil War itself. It took early form in the observations of many leading contemporary commentators, such as Thomas Hobbes, James Harrington and Lucy Hutchinson, who all believed that the challenge to the crown derived from a transfer of economic weight to "the people". Tawney's instinct that the gentry could be included in that category was sound. And the fact that the gentry as a class were advancing in economic strength during the course of the sixteenth and early seventeenth centuries was so plain that it was almost a truism.

More contentiously, Tawney sought to explain this development by the supposition that the lifestyle and working psychology of the gentry made them better equipped to take advantage of the Great Tudor Inflation than were the traditional aristocracy. Lawrence Stone duly supplemented this thesis by postulating a "Crisis of the Aristocracy", on much the same basis.[59] This probably underestimated the moneymaking capacities of the nobles and the fact that their outlook had much in common with that of lesser landowners. Furthermore, Tawney's associated theory that there was a new Protestant work ethic that was embraced by the middle ranks of society was also less than clear in the evidence, and constituted a weak point at which opponents who were inherently hostile to the socio-economic perspective could attack the central idea.

Some of the criticisms were, however, merely perverse, like Hugh Trevor-Roper's somewhat facetious suggestion that the Civil War was induced by the desperation of the declining gentry. In truth, there has never been a less declining class than the English gentry in the sixteenth and seventeenth centuries. Other objections were more serious but tended towards statistical pedantry. This was the case with J. H. Hexter's critique of Tawney's admittedly rather clumsy attempt to measure the rise of the gentry by the counting of manors. Tawney may have failed to establish a clear line of distinction between gentleman and noble, but Hexter's attack created the danger that the essential truth of contrasting fortunes would be lost on a technicality. Similarly, Hexter indulged in the standard revisionist gambit of defining terms in a way that concealed the true balance of circumstances. It is not difficult to deny the existence of a classic "bourgeoisie" or "middle class" in the sixteenth century.[60] But to do so is to disguise the crucial fact that there clearly was a bourgeois *context* emerging, of which the gentry were, in some important respects, an integral part. No doubt Tawney and Stone were misguided in as far as they supposed that the gentry took a uniquely business-like approach to their landed interests. But it was nevertheless quite correct to observe that there was a significant socio-economic rise of the gentry as a class.

Earlier chapters have described in detail the effects of the special circumstances of the sixteenth- and early seventeenth-century economy, which was in general terms a world of opportunity for all substantial landholders. It was distinguished by a sustained and exceptional rise in agricultural prices, which could be exploited with significant profit, and no special exertion, by any landholder who was in occupation of more than 60 acres, and who was thereby in a position to produce a surplus for a sellers' market. In theory, the more land you held, the more you could benefit, either directly or through the rise in land values and rents, and there is no reason to suppose that the aristocracy lacked either the ability or the inclination to profit. It seems that the general increase in rents outstripped the rise in prices over the period. Single examples are rarely conclusive, but we shall see ahead a good illustration of how a noble family could make itself exceedingly rich in the economic conditions of the period. By the 1620s the Earl of Kingston had become sufficiently wealthy to buy his way to the title. His younger son William Pierrepont, a prominent parliamentarian, inherited his father's business acumen, and was known as one of the richest men in the country. He seems to have had an interest in more than forty manors, and his estate records show that he made a point of reserving and exploiting the valuable timber resources on his lands.[61]

Nobles were as capable of making money as anyone. Nevertheless, the thesis put forward by Tawney and Stone holds good in relative terms, for although there is every reason to suppose that on an individual basis the aristocracy gained from the economic conditions, it is clear that in the overall balance they gained less than did the social groups below them. The middling gentry and yeomanry did proportionately better because they had lower social overheads, and they could achieve a sharper rise up the socio-economic scale. It should also be noted that when a family did get into difficulties, it tended to be the more illustrious, ancient line that failed, and a newer family that took their place. Some examples of this are described in a fuller context ahead.[62] The gentry gained above all because they were expanding markedly in numbers, as a class. Lawrence Stone spoke of "a dramatic increase in the numbers of the gentry".[63] He thought they were increasing twice as fast as the general population. More recently, Mark Overton has confirmed that Stone and Tawney were right in this respect: "it seems clear that the gentry class did grow substantially in numbers from the mid-sixteenth century".[64] They were augmented from the ranks of the affluent yeomanry, and from the advancement of younger sons. The "new men" were also successful "lawyers, government officials and merchants".[65] The actual figures are striking. In Shropshire, there were forty-eight gentry families in 1433, and four hundred and seventy by 1623. There were a similar number in Norfolk by the 1580s. There were six hundred and thirty-one in Yorkshire by 1603, and no less than one thousand in Kent by 1600. It indicated a new level of presence on the ground. They were literally filling out the land.

So there was a substantial increase in the proportion of estates owned by the gentry as a class. It is apparent that most of the church property ended up with the middling gentry: "though the nobility gained to some extent, mainly as a result of grants to a few great families . . . it was the gentry, old and new, who gained by far the most land".[66] Tawney's much maligned method of counting manors was applied in Norfolk and showed that by 1555, two-thirds of the old monastic holdings had gone to the gentry, the other third being shared between the crown, the nobility and the church.[67] Much the same picture has been found in Lincolnshire, Yorkshire, Cornwall and Devon, where "the mass of monastic lands passed to moderate sized local families".[68] It is clear that the balance of landowning strength was moving towards the gentry.

The rise of the gentry must also be measured in terms of power. They were occupying the interstices of the less consolidated patterns of authority that had characterised the medieval period. The figures for Shropshire, showing forty-eight gentry families in 1433 and four hundred and seventy in 1623, reveal the revolution in their political potential. Up to the sixteenth century the gentry had been an auxiliary element in a fluid system of military organisation that referred essentially to the personal rule of the magnates. But by the turn of the seventeenth century the gentry had expanded to provide fixed points of power in almost every locality, making them available as a new kind of administrative class. They were acquiring the position for which they became famous, as the locus of authority in every community, creating what became the classic scenario of the English countryside, with every village governed by its squire. It has been estimated that at the beginning of the sixteenth century, no more than one village in every four or five had a resident squire.[69] The transformation that then occurred is well described by W. G. Hoskins. At the beginning of the sixteenth century squires were "comparatively rare on the ground". The evidence for the start of Henry VIII's reign indicates a total of about one thousand. "But if Thomas Wilson's figure of sixteen thousand esquires by the end of the century is anywhere near the truth, the Elizabethan village must have shown an entirely different picture".[70] The fact that the gentry now had a powerful presence in almost every community in the land was the physical reflection of their new national reach. It provided them with the basic credentials for composing a more coordinated public authority, both as JPs within their counties, and collectively as the county representatives of the "entire society" in parliament.

This was a qualitatively different structure from the personal, military power of the feudal magnates, and was to some extent supplanting it. One of the most persuasive aspects of Lawrence Stone's thesis was his analysis of the changing balance of power on the ground. He established that there was indeed a diminution in the position of the great territorial magnates, the typically dominant personalities of the medieval age, who had ruled as virtual royalty in their own regions. These "over-mighty subjects" became much fewer in number, and their territorial range was significantly restricted. Thus the number of noble families holding seventy or more manors declined from eighteen out of sixty-two in 1558 to six out of one hundred twenty-one in 1641. Stone was correct to conclude that: "the top level of the English social pyramid had been substantially reduced between the accession of Elizabeth and the outbreak of the Civil War".[71] Mark Overton's more recent assessment underlines the trend. His statistics show that between 1436 and 1690 the proportion of land held by the magnates remained stable at 15% to 20%, while the proportion held by the gentry doubled from 25% to 50%. By the second half of the seventeenth century, the gentry and the yeomanry between them held three-quarters of the land of England. [72]

As the gentry acquired more weight in their localities, they were also given a more important part in government. There is no doubt that through the course of the sixteenth century, political influence devolved downwards towards the middle ranks of society. We need not suppose that the Tudors were deliberately engineering a "new" or "middle class" monarchy. But it is clear that they pursued a consistent, pragmatic line of policy that in point of fact diverted power away from the magnates and towards the broader class of gentry. Thus, "Henry VII and Henry VIII showed a marked reluctance to give control of an area to any one man. They reversed the dominant assumption—never previously questioned—that where a magnate had large lands in a particular area, he had a right to rule it".[73] The principal alternative to the essentially personal and military power of the magnates was the development of the role of the Commissions of the Peace, the main forum for the collective authority of the gentry in each county. Their status and powers began to be increased in the reign of Edward IV, but it was Henry VII who oversaw the most decisive steps by which the JPs were given ultimate responsibility for the maintenance of order and the control of the unruly aspects of the old personal regimes of the magnates. The JPs thus became "the mainstay of local government".[74] Thomas Cromwell employed this framework to great effect in implementing the major reforms of the 1530s. These processes were more amenable to overall control than might have been supposed of an arrangement that depended on county-based amateurs rather than paid bureaucrats. The government followed a practice of including Privy Councillors and church officials on the JP benches. There was also the powerful sanction that the appointments were reviewed from year to year, and no gentleman could lightly afford the ignominy of being excluded from the bench. In fact, this created an unusually efficient combination of local and central authority, especially when it was working for agreed ends. By the reign of Elizabeth the system could be seen as firmly established, and through these structures the transfer of the balance of power down towards the middle ranks was brought to something like completion. It had produced "a decisive shift to dependence on the squirearchy and gentry".[75] In counties where there were "many new gentry, like Suffolk and Northamptonshire, a substantial group of gentlemen felt confident for the first time to challenge the traditional leadership of the great families".[76] By the end of the century, "the diminution of magnate power had produced a wider diffusion of authority among provincial landowners".[77] The crucial point is that this was not just a change of personnel. Both in the counties and the overall context of the nation, the gentry were coming to constitute a new kind of *public* authority.

Every trend contributed to the establishment of the gentry as a truly national administrative and representative class. They had become a consolidated national body in a physical sense, filling out the land as the regular, public power points in the localities. This process was reinforced by the government's increasing reliance upon them for local administration, especially as JPs. Their positions as administrators and representatives were mutually reinforcing. They were elected on the basis of their standing in the county, which was then further enhanced by their status as national representatives. The fact that they were becoming the most prominent feature in almost every locality also encouraged an expansion of their electoral base. At the same time as the gentry were increasing their landed strength and consolidating their position in the villages and the counties, they were also extending the scope of their representative role in parliament. The demand from the county gentry generated a remarkable increase in the number of parliamentary seats.[78] At the beginning of the century there were two hundred ninety-six seats, while at the end there were four hundred sixty-two. John Neale called it "one of the most arresting and puzzling facts in our parliamentary history".[79] It was certainly arresting, but surely not too puzzling. At one level the increase simply reflected the growing numbers of the gentry themselves, and their new ubiquity as eminent figures in the localities. And in truth there were many obvious reasons that the gentry might seek wider opportunities to sit in parliament.

At Westminster they would take part in a Commons assembly whose significance had risen markedly, both in practice and principle, through the developments of the sixteenth century. The MPs, as the elected chamber, were now the defining element in a new concept of omni-competent sovereign law, which derived its authority specifically from the ability of parliament to embody the consent of the entire society. This also meant that they were employed in making statute law with a unique binding force as general, practical provision. Parliamentary legislation began to emerge as a genuine instrument of public, national administration under Henry VII, who used it for two specific ends—"the control of trade and industry", and "the establishment of good order" in place of the old personal and regional powers.[80] These measures "commended themselves to the knights of the shire from whom the justices of the peace were drawn". Similarly "[t]he economic legislation commended itself to the merchants and traders represented by the burgesses".[81] From the middle decades of the sixteenth century, the newly sovereign power of statute was used to reform the most vital aspects of the life of the kingdom. From the end of the century, although the government was beginning to have less use for the legislative function, the MPs and their constituents were employing it more and more, on their own initiative, as the best way of addressing their problems, particular and general. Thus, having played a central role in devising and authorising national legislation, the MPs went back to their counties to oversee its administration, and to ponder how the interests of their localities related to national affairs. A new network of public authority had arisen. It was a useful instrument for the royal government when policy was attuned to the natural inclinations of the country, but its distinctive strength was to link the local government of the counties to the sovereign legislative power and national representative force of parliament. At the heart of these developments were the gentry.

The demand for additional seats in parliament was also reflected in the gentry's continuing encroachment on the borough franchises. In the same way as the squires were establishing their dominant presence in every village, so they were putting themselves forward for election in many, and eventually most of the towns. It is difficult to establish a precise sequence among the various, diverse factors involved in the rise of the gentry. But it is of great interest that many of the most important developments seem to have had their beginning in the later decades of the fifteenth century. It was at this time that the high profits of extended sheep farming became available, to all landholders with a decent acreage. In conjunction with this emerged the new dimension of the mercantile opportunities of the rapidly growing cloth trade. It was also at this time that the House of Commons became accepted in an executive role in the process of legislation, no longer just as petitioners for the laws, but as "assenting" to them along with the Lords and the King. It was at this time too that Henry VII began the systematic advancement of the local gentry as JPs, implementing the laws that they helped to make, mainly for maintaining order and the regulation of economic affairs. The growing status of the House of Commons, and the laws that the MPs made and then enforced through the Commissions of the Peace, were powerful reasons for the gentry to extend their presence in the assembly. By the end of the sixteenth century the change in balance was almost complete. If the traditional criteria had been applied, the House of Commons in Elizabeth's later years would have contained ninety county gentry and three hundred seventy-two town burgesses. But in fact, the position was reversed: "instead of one gentleman to four townsmen, Elizabeth's later parliaments contained four gentlemen to every townsman".[82] This gave the House of Commons a significantly different character from comparable bodies in other representative assemblies in Europe. Elsewhere the Commons chamber still comprised the Third Estate, that is to say the merchants, one of the distinct orders of medieval society. In England, the gentry's takeover of the House of Commons created a chamber that transcended those limits and referred itself to a national perspective. One crucial aspect of this, not often noted, was the extent to which the gentry took on responsibility for mercantile affairs. This was not an unwelcome or unnatural task for them. They represented the towns actively, in part because they shared the merchants' most important aims—especially the central ambition of bringing the customs dues under parliamentary supervision. The status of the gentry as landowners gave them a social authority that merchants rarely possessed, but the gentlemen MPs could still be relied upon to support the mercantile interest in freedom of trade, with as much fervour as any.

The long campaign to extend parliamentary control over the customs dues and displace the royal prerogative of impositions was a central example of the gentry's overall ambition to consolidate and extend the rights of consent. This commitment derived in part from another distinctive feature of the English scene, regarding the incidence of fiscal pressure. In other European kingdoms, most notably France, the tendency from the sixteenth century onwards was to load the burden of taxation onto the shoulders of the peasantry by arbitrary collection, while the nobility were largely exempt.[83] In England, partly because of the considerable shock caused by the Peasants' Revolt, the opposite trend had taken place. The poor and the increasingly independent husbandmen were let off lightly. It has been calculated that in some places in England in the sixteenth century only one person in twelve was paying tax. The principal public levy was the parliamentary subsidy, which was a property tax that fell most heavily on the gentry. This gave then a direct and powerful interest in maintaining and consolidating rights of consent. It was also another obvious reason for them to seek to expand their numbers in the House of Commons.

So the weight of the gentry in the representative body increased at the same time as their involvement and concern with national affairs. This in itself produced a consolidation of the force of rights of consent. When the idea of consent to public taxation was established in the medieval period, it was something of a formality—an expedient by which the king could guarantee the levy that he required to finance his own concept of the interest of the kingdom. But during the second half of the sixteenth century, as MPs and constituencies developed a clear and independent notion of what they regarded as public imperatives, the right of consent acquired real application. It became possible, and then frequent for them to take a position on national affairs that was different from the monarch's. In effect they were coming to assume a capability to judge the general priorities of the kingdom for themselves. In this respect, there was an explicit link between the parliamentary attack on the king's right of discretionary taxation, and the readiness of the country's representatives to define their own version of the national interest. Earlier chapters outlined the medieval notion of "conditional" property as described by Robert Crowley. It rested on two principal pillars: that no one had the right to do whatever they wished with their property at the expense of the poor: and that everyone was obliged to pay the king what he demanded, because only he knew what was necessary for the kingdom.[84] But by the beginning of the seventeenth century, most expressly in the context of the impositions dispute, there arose a claim of "absolute" property, by which each individual did have the right to do whatever he liked with his land and goods, and to withhold them from all others, including the king, except by specific consent. Thomas Hobbes described this as a new market morality, where each man was "so much master of what he possessed, that it could not be taken from him upon any pretext of common safety without his own consent".[85] The important implication was that MPs and their constituents felt increasingly confident that *they* had the capacity, and the natural representative authority, to define the "common safety" on their own initiative.

During the first three decades of the seventeenth century the ambition of parliament to give more specific force to rights of consent began to be applied across the board, whether it be in the fixed desire to bring the setting of the customs dues under parliamentary control, or in the promotion of a principle of freedom of trade against any kind of arbitrary restrictions and exactions, or in their determination to impose their own national foreign policy on the king, or in their subsequent attempt to deprive him of the entire range of his emergency powers. In every case the Commons and the gentry were attempting to displace important aspects of the royal prerogative and subject the policies and practices of the royal government to the controls of representative consent. The fact that they failed in almost every instance was not the end of the matter, but simply an indication that in order to realise these particular objectives they might need to change the balance of political initiative between the representative assembly and the crown. So the long drive to advance the rights of consent in order to guarantee these independently defined imperatives produced, as its logical consequence, the firm intention in 1640 to give parliament an independent and automatic position at the centre of affairs.

Thus, the rise of the gentry to national significance took place largely in a parliamentary context, and revolved in great part around the developing status and potential of rights of consent. Many recent historians have denied that the socio-economic advance of the gentry took radical political force in the 1640s, saying that they did not attempt to win powers from the crown, and tended mainly towards the king's side in the Civil War itself.[86] But in truth they obviously *were* trying to change the balance of power with the crown, and to supplant important royal prerogatives by extending the force of representative rights. Furthermore, it is a false criterion to measure things by the Civil War in isolation, artificially detached from all that had gone before. In the preceding decades the gentry, in parliament, had been at the head of a broad and persistent attempt to reduce the rights of the crown, and to subject vital matters of administration and public finance to representative control. These ambitions had culminated in the winter of 1640–1641, producing a fixed determination to give the representative assembly an independent and automatic place at the centre of affairs. This was achieved by the Triennial Act of 16 February 1641, which was the central priority and core proposition of the parliamentarian revolution, and comprised a fundamental re-modelling of the constitution, ending the royal discretion over the life of parliaments, and giving the representative body an established and continuous influence over the processes of government. This highly significant constitutional change was forced through by the House of Commons, with a notable display of unity and determination, which clearly links the rise of the gentry to the inception of the English Revolution.

The gathered force of the gentry behind this first, initiating act of the revolution is clearly demonstrated in Digby's centre-piece oration on the third reading, assuring his fellow MPs that they should not dwell on the constitutional objections to the bill. "I hope there will be no occasion of that, but that we shall all concur unanimously on what concerneth all so universally". He asked them to focus collectively on "the vast importance and necessity that we should go through with it". He was expressing the sense that the dominant interests of the political nation, and the defining belief in parliament as their essential guarantor, had become so absolute that the representative body must be put in a position to exert a permanent and effective influence on affairs. "As the deficience of parliaments has been the cause causarum of all the mischiefs and distempers, so the frequency of them is the sole antidote that can preserve and secure the future from the like danger". It was no longer satisfactory to arraign ministers after the damage was done. It was "the opportunity of being ill" that they must take away, and this could never be achieved "Unless for the frequency of parliaments there can be some course settled as may not be eluded".[87]

This was the work of the Triennial Act, ending the power of the crown to dispense with parliaments. It deprived the king of the prerogative that had made parliaments dependent on his summons. In practice it meant that he would no longer be able to govern independently of the influence of the representative assembly. As Charles himself pointed out, the act had "taken the government all in pieces". It was indeed the most crucial specific measure behind James Harrington's contemporary assessment that "the dissolution of this government caused the war, not the war the dissolution of this government".[88] And it was the gentry, united in parliament, who caused the dissolution.

Notes

1. J. Rushworth, *Historical Collections*, (London 1659–1701), IV, pp. 145–9
2. Ibid, III, p. 1128
3. D. Hirst, *Authority and Conflict,* (London 1986), pp. 189–90
4. S. R. Gardiner, *History of England,* (London 1886), IX, pp. 103–4
5. Ibid, p. 102
6. Ibid, p. 106
7. Thomas Hobbes, *Leviathan*, ed. M. Oakeshott, (Oxford 1951), p. 122
8. Hirst, *Authority and Conflict*, p. 189
9. Gardiner, *History of England*, IX, p. 101
10. Ibid, p. 106
11. Ibid, p. 108
12. Ibid, p. 112
13. R. Cust, "The Collapse of Royal Power in England 1637–1642", in *The Oxford Handbook of the English Revolution,* (Oxford 2016), p. 63
14. "The Notebook of Sir John Northcote", in *Two Diaries of the Long Parliament*, ed. M. Jansson, (Yale 1984), p. 112
15. T. Bailey, *Annals of Nottinghamshire,* (London 1863), vol. II, p. 648
16. J. Morrill, "The Religious Context of the English Civil War", *Transactions of the Royal Historical Society* (1984), p. 161; *The Nature of the English Revolution,* (Oxford 1993), p. 51
17. R. Foxley, "Varieties of Parliamentarianism", in *The Oxford Handbook of the English Revolution,* (Oxford 2016), p. 416
18. C. Walker, *The History of Independency,* (London 1665), p. 6
19. Rushworth, *Historical Collections*, IV, pp. 23, 145–9
20. Ibid, pp. 26–7
21. Ibid, pp. 25–6
22. Ibid., pp. 145–9
23. Ibid
24. Edward Hyde, Earl of Clarendon, *The History of the Rebellion and Civil Wars in England,* (Oxford 1969), vol. I, p. 279
25. P. Croft, "Annual Parliaments", *Bulletin of the Institute of Historical Research 59*, p. 155
26. *The Journal of Sir Simonds D'Ewes*, ed. W. Notestein, (Yale 1923), pp. 88, 196–7
27. Gilbert Burnet, *History of His Own Time,* (London 1724) vol. I, p. 197
28. Rushworth, *Historical Collections,* IV, pp. 154–5
29. Ibid, pp. 154–5; *Lords Journal,* III, p. 142b
30. William Clarke, Diary, 23 January 1641, Clarke Papers, Worcester College Library, Oxford Ms. unfol
31. C. Russell, *The Fall of the British Monarchies,* (Oxford 1991), p. 225
32. *The English Civil War: A Contemporary Account,* (London 1996), p. 64; Gardiner, *History of England*, IX, p. 290
33. The English Civil War: A Contemporary Account, p. 64
34. For instance, Hirst, *Authority and Conflict*, pp. 195, 201
35. For further details, see G. Yerby, *People and Parliament,* (Basingstoke 2008), pp. 159–61

36. *Journal of Sir Simonds D'Ewes*, p. 360; *Two Diaries of the Long Parliament*, ed. M. Jansson, (Yale 1984), p. 86
37. *Lords Journal*, p. 162b
38. Gardiner, *History of England*, IX, p. 290
39. Rushworth, *Historical Collections*, IV, pp. 186–8
40. *Journal of Sir Simonds D'Ewes*, pp. 364–5
41. William Drake's Parliamentary Notebook, in *Two Diaries of the Long Parliament*, p. 6
42. Clarendon, *History of the Rebellion*, vol. I, p. 279
43. William Drake's Notebook, *Two Diaries of the Long Parliament*, p. 6
44. Rushworth, *Historical Collections*, IV, pp. 145–9
45. Ibid, p. 288
46. V. Morgan, "Whose Prerogative in Late Sixteenth and Early Seventeenth Century England?" in *Customs, Courts and Counsel*, eds. A. Kiralfy, M. Slatter and R. Virgoe, (London 1985), pp. 39–55
47. G. M. Trevelyan, *England Under the Stuarts*, (London 1949), p. 152
48. Rushworth, *Historical Collections*, IV, pp. 201–2
49. R. Hooker, *Of the Laws of Ecclesiastical Polity*, (1590s), ed. C. Morris, (London 1907), I, p. 194
50. Sir Thomas Smith, *De Republica Anglorum* (1583), ed. M. Dewar, (Cambridge 1982), p. 78
51. See above, Chapter 7
52. J. Bodin, *The Six Books of the Commonwealth*, ed. M. J. Tooley, (Oxford, undated), bk. 1, chap. 8, p. 32
53. *Constitutional Documents of the Puritan Revolution*, ed. S. R. Gardiner, (Oxford 1968), p. 222
54. Ibid, pp. 316–17
55. Henry Ireton, *Puritanism and Liberty*, ed. A. S. P. Woodhouse, (London 1938), p. 462
56. Ibid, p. 72
57. Ibid
58. J. R. Jones, *Country and Court*, (London 1980), pp. 25, 157-8
59. R. H. Tawney, "The Rise of the Gentry 1558–1640", *Economic History Review II* (1941), pp. 1–38; L. Stone, *The Crisis of the Aristocracy* 1558–1641, (Oxford 1965); challenged by H. Trevor-Roper, "The Gentry 1540–1640", *Economic History Review I* (1953)
60. J. H. Hexter, *Reappraisals in History*, (Northwestern University Press 1961), pp. 71–162
61. See ahead, Chapter 15
62. See ahead, pp. 323, 329
63. Stone, *Crisis of the Aristocracy*, p. 67
64. M. Overton, *Agricultural Revolution*, (Cambridge 1996), p. 169
65. W. G. Hoskins, *The Age of Plunder*, (London 1976), p. 136
66. Ibid
67. T. H. Swales, "The Redistribution of Monastic Lands in Norfolk", *Norfolk Archaeology XXXIV*, pt I (1966), pp. 14–44
68. Hoskins, *Age of Plunder*, p. 136
69. J. Lander, *Government and Community*, (London 1980), pp. 42–3
70. Hoskins, *Age of Plunder*, p. 55
71. Stone, *Crisis of the Aristocracy*, pp. 153, 264
72. Overton, *Agricultural Revolution*, p. 167
73. S. Gunn, *Early Tudor Government*, (Basingstoke 1995), pp. 42–4

74. G. R. Elton, *England Under the Tudors*, (London 1967), p. 60; J. D. Mackie, *The Earlier Tudors*, (Oxford 1966), pp. 196
75. Stone, *Crisis of the Aristocracy*, p. 256
76. C. Palliser, *Age of Elizabeth*, (London 1983), p. 82
77. P. Williams, "The Tudors and England", *History Today*, September 1985, p. 31
78. J. E. Neale, *The Elizabethan House of Commons*, (London 1949), p. 146
79. Ibid, p. 140
80. Mackie, *The Earlier Tudors*, p. 200
81. Ibid, p. 201
82. Neale, *The Elizabethan House of Commons*, p. 147
83. D. Parker, *State and Class in Ancien Regime France*, (London 2011)
84. See above pp. 105–107 for Robert Crowley
85. T. Hobbes, *Behemoth*, ed. Tonnies, (London 1889), p. 4
86. For instance, B. Coward, *The Stuart Age*, (London 1994), p. 151
87. Rushworth, *Historical Collections*, IV, pp. 145–6
88. J. Harrington, *Oceana*, ed. H. Morley, (London 1887), p. 60

12 The Triumph of Freedom of Trade

The Throwing Down of Monopolies; and the Ending of Prerogative Customs Dues

The Earl of Strafford is often assumed to have been the first specific target of the Long Parliament. His demise was certainly sought with a degree of urgency. He posed the greatest immediate danger to parliamentary plans. He was the minister most capable of organising a counter coup and reasserting the position of the monarchy. His fate was also notable because it became controversial within the House of Commons itself. It was over Strafford that the first cracks began to appear in the initial consensus among MPs. The pursuit of Strafford produced the noisy intervention of the London populace in the contest, and this became a cause of concern to the more socially conservative figures in parliament. Lord Digby, for instance, had personified the unanimity of the Commons in forcing through the Triennial Act, but he took his first steps towards Royalism in reaction to the hounding of Strafford. Similarly in the country, in Essex, the brother of the MP Humphrey Mildmay had expressed delight on receiving "the joyful news of the Triennial Act", but the spectacle of direct action on the streets turned him from an opponent of Strafford into a sympathiser.[1]

But although the question of Strafford was important in various ways, he was not in fact the first particular target of the parliamentarians. That honour was reserved for the agents of a much older grievance, which may indeed be regarded as the issue over which a radical parliamentary movement had first emerged, at the turn of the seventeenth century, and the controversy that it engendered at that time produced the first instance of the populace pressing on the parliament for action. This was the question of monopolies. It soon came to the fore again in 1640. The contemporary observer Lucy Hutchinson, who was in close contact with MPs and parliamentary affairs, said: "They began with throwing down monopolies, and then impeached the Earl of Strafford".[2] S. R. Gardiner also noted that monopolies were the first issue to be addressed.[3] This was not surprising, since monopolies had figured prominently in Pym's first, authoritative survey of the Commons' concerns in the Short Parliament, on 17 April 1640. In that list, as Gardiner said, the grievances of longest standing "which had been the subject of contention in previous parliaments" were "naturally placed first".[4] These were the crucial, and central freedom of trade issues, like impositions, un-parliamentary tonnage and poundage, and monopolies. These were the areas in which, over the last few decades, the Commons had consistently sought to displace the prerogatives of the crown, and by the same token they were obvious parliamentarian priorities in 1640. It is important to note that they were also matters over which the Commons were completely unanimous, just as they had been with regard to the radical initiative of the Triennial Act.

In relation to the king's traditional right of impositions, Pym had confirmed that they now required quite simply that this prerogative be ended, and that all the customs dues be subject to a parliamentary grant. He had said, generously, that there was no wish to diminish the king's profits, but only to establish the right of setting the customs in parliament. He failed to mention that even if this arrangement did, as was quite possible, serve to maintain the king's income, it would have the disadvantage from Charles's point of view of sharply diminishing his prerogatives, and giving parliament the ultimate authority over his finances. In the same vein Pym condemned the government for increasing the level of the customs by a new book of rates, another power traditionally exercised by the king, but which parliament had wished, at least since 1610, to bring under its own control.

Then Pym moved on to condemn another long-deplored practice—the continuing use of monopolies. He mentioned the monopolies in soap, salt, sea-coal, wine, leather, and added that there were also many others, some of which had arisen from the king's persistent granting of privileges in the 1630s: "the particulars whereof are fit for the committee of grievances". It is interesting that Pym lodged a strong, and bitter objection to the interruption and diversion of shipping, of which the monopolist authorities had apparently been guilty. An earlier chapter illustrated the powerful free trade perspectives of the West Country cod fishing enterprise. It was a vital aspect of their commerce that the merchants and sailors should be able to go where they liked, when they liked. Their livelihoods had come to depend on the right to use the conditions, and the market freely. The new way of trade could not cope with arbitrary restraints. It is important to recognise that the stopping or disruption of shipping not only obstructed individual interests, it also broke up the free, reciprocal flow of the market in general.

In the same spirit of liberal economics, Pym protested against the revival of the campaign against enclosures, and the heavy fines against depopulators, which, as he later complained, had "driven many millions out of the subjects' purses".[5] He also objected of course to the exploitation of ship money, and the extension of the bounds of the forests for the resurrection of obsolete forest fines, and the unacceptable military charges—"impositions upon counties by letters patent from the Council Table".[6] But he returned again and again to the subject of monopolies.

One of the charges against the prerogative courts was that they "countenance the oppressions, as I may instance in the courts of Star Chamber advancing and countenancing of monopolies". The Privy Councillors ought to be the lights of the realm, but if they "plot projects and monopolies, what shall we think of it: this is a great grievance". The power of the king was transcendent, but "that this power should be applied to countenance monopolies . . . is without precedent". Pym apologised that "I have by this time wearied you as well as myself", but he had still not quite finished with monopolies. "In monopolies and such like, the third part comes not to his majesties coffers, as to instance in that of wines—where the king gets £30,000 out of £230,000. The same proportion holds in all other monopolies, wherein it appears how much the subject is damnified, and how little the King gains".[7]

In the summary that appeared in the *Commons Journal* for the Short Parliament in April 1640, the grievances were placed under the same three headings as proposed in Pym's formulation. There was the grievance of the so-called "innovations" in religion. There was also the protest against the supposed attack on the liberties of parliament. Then, most substantially, and at the core of active parliamentary motivations, was the "propriety of goods". It was significant that the category of "goods" was always sufficiently broad to encompass trade, as well as landed property. Monopolies were again a standout feature, and this time they were condemned quite specifically as the "restraint of trade". Then there was a further item protesting against the imprisonment and vexation of those who had refused to submit to monopolies, or to pay "unwarrantable taxes".[8] Upon close inspection the grievances of 1640 were not so much a protest against arbitrary government, but more an assertion of the freedom of trade and property against any kind of restriction, exaction or imposition.

These problems were naturally to the fore in the parliamentarian plan of action, when the Long Parliament convened on 3 November 1640. "They began with throwing down monopolies".[9] Monopolies were mentioned in all the petitions of grievances, but they emerged with particular significance from Lord Digby's report from Dorset, on 9th November, highlighting the "multitude of monopolies". Sir John Culpepper, speaking for Kent, picked up and extended the complaint. The category of monopolies, he said, "compriseth many" grievances.

> It is a nest of wasps, a swarm of vermin, which have overcrept the land, I mean the monopolers. These men, like the frogs of Egypt, have gotten possession of our dwellings, and we have scarce a room free from them. They sup in our cup, they dip in our dish, they sit by our fire; we find them in the dye vat, washbowl, and powdering tub; they share with the butler in his box; they have marked and sealed us from head to foot. Mr Speaker, they will not bate us a pin. We may not buy our own cloths without their brokage.

This illustrated not only the wide incidence of monopolies in every area of life, but also how they were thought to infringe the privacy and freedoms of the individual. Culpepper then described how the monopolists had managed to evade the defences that parliament had sought to put in place in 1624. "They have a vizard to hide the brand made by that good law in the last parliament of King James. They shelter themselves under the name of a corporation. They make bye-laws that serve their turns to squeeze us, and fill their purses".[10] This exposed what was in every sense a great weakness of the Caroline government—it had continued to rely upon monopolies as a form of finance, regulation and patronage, and enabled them to operate under thin disguises, evading the restrictions that parliament had attempted to impose in 1624. The practice had in fact been extended to many everyday items, flouting the privacy of the subjects as well their assumed right of freedom of trade.

So, the first grievance to be acted upon, and the first significant order of the Commons, on 9 November, was that all monopolists should be excluded from the House.

> The House, bearing in mind Sir John Culpepper's speech, against the swarm of projectors and monopolists, fell into debate thereof, whereupon it was resolved to exclude all projectors and monopolists whatsoever, or that have any share in monopolies, or that do receive any benefit from any monopoly, or that have procured any warrant or command for the restraint or molesting of any that have refused to conform themselves.

This was "resolved upon the question by one unanimous vote".[11] It was quite fitting that the first target of the House of Commons in November 1640 should be monopolies. This had after all been the very first issue to cause a political confrontation between crown and parliament some decades before, in the assembly of 1597, and also the first to induce the populace to engage in some forceful lobbying in the streets of Westminster. The strength and breadth of the opposition to the practice remained striking. Monopolies seemed to provoke the anger of all sections of society, from the gentry, though the general body of merchants, to the most radical groups in the 1640s. It was the main substantial grievance in all Leveller petitions, and was indeed one of the concerns that connected them to the mainstream parliamentarian movement.

That monopolies persisted as a powerful general grievance for so long was not, however, entirely due to the crown's continued dependence on the practice as a means of finance, regulation and patronage. Although parliamentarians might wholly disapprove of monopolies in principle, there were real difficulties in dispensing with them altogether. New inventions, and new mercantile ventures had a legitimate need for protection, and this would always leave loopholes that could be exploited. By such routes the Caroline regime had been able to evade the intentions of the

Monopolies Act of 1624. It was indicative of the obstacles to a root and branch solution that in 1640 parliament had to continue to rely on that "good law" to restrain the practice. At least they could count on the fact that the statute would no longer be flagrantly abused. But nor could monopolies be entirely eradicated. In the mid-1640s the Levellers were complaining that although many of the most provocative monopolies had been ended, the worst and greatest of all, that of the Merchant Adventurers, was still in place. Even when Oliver Cromwell arrived in government, he could not immediately do away with the privileged powers of the great trading companies, though he did inaugurate the series of Navigation Acts by which the state eventually took over the regulation of maritime affairs.[12] Only then did the trade of England come to be supported in a national perspective, and in ways that did not restrict the commercial freedoms of the individual. Thereby, the long running public grievance against monopolies was finally relieved.

The Ending of Prerogative Customs Dues

The problem of monopolies did not lend itself to a simple solution. There was, however, decisive statutory action early in 1641 regarding the other principal plank of the freedom of trade agenda—the drive against discretionary customs dues. In the long-term dispute over impositions the crown had clung doggedly to its prerogatives, and the Commons had made no progress at all. In 1640, however, the king was no longer in a position to resist, and the Commons could take immediate advantage, and give the matter their radical attention. The preceding chapter showed that the first priority of the parliamentary programme was not the series of measures in July 1641 outlawing the "arbitrary" practices of the 1630s, but rather the Triennial Act passed in February 1641, which aimed to give parliament an automatic and regular place at the centre of affairs and thus ensure a continuous representative influence on the course of government. And not long after this, there was another statutory enactment that predated and was of higher priority and greater radical force than the July measures. This was the ending of the royal prerogative to set impositions on trade. The destruction of this particular aspect of the traditional powers of the crown had been the central ambition of parliament since 1610. In 1640 they were finally in a position to bring it to pass.

It was enshrined in the act of tonnage and poundage in May 1641. Since the beginning of Charles's reign in 1625, the Commons had made their grant of tonnage and poundage dependent on the king surrendering his prerogative of impositions. The connection encapsulated their dominant desire to bring all the customs dues under the control of representative consent. The act of May 1641 in effect enforced the proposition that the Commons had put in place in 1625. They would agree the grant of tonnage and poundage for a conditional period, if the king would surrender the prerogative of impositions. At that time, quite understandably, the king had shown no interest in such a deal. In the intervening period he had continued to collect both tonnage and poundage and impositions without consent. He had the right and the power to do so. This was what the House of Commons had sought to challenge, and were now about to outlaw. The act claimed that the customs' officials "have taken divers great sums of money of his majesties subjects . . . by the name of a subsidy of tonnage and poundage and by colour of divers other impositions laid upon merchandise".[13] The act declared that this had been done against the law of the land, since these sums of money and impositions were not granted by common consent in parliament. Needless to say, this interpretation did not truly reflect the traditional constitutional position. The law as it existed did not endorse the idea that customs should always be raised by representative consent. The Commons were outlining the law as they believed it ought to be, not as it was. In previous reigns, parliament's grant of tonnage and poundage for the life of the monarch had been a formality, a confirming gesture of loyalty at the accession of each monarch. Similarly, the prerogative of impositions on trade was an ancient and undoubted right of the crown, confirmed by the Law Lords in 1606. In 1610 it had been declared by Sir Francis Bacon to be inseparable from the royal prerogative. But in May 1641 the Commons were about to separate it. They were not applying the law of the land, but their own determination, which had been manifest since 1610, to bring all customs dues under the control of parliament. It is worth remembering, however, that although levies like impositions were not illegal, there was nevertheless an element of truth in the idea that the law was what parliament said it was. Parliament had become the defining authority in the concept of sovereign legislation, and this helps to explain the self-assurance with which they were prepared to declare the law as they wanted it to be. This was a further extension of the assumption that had grown up on the model of legislative sovereignty, that all such "unlimited" powers should in fact be subject to representative consent.

Bringing tonnage and poundage under parliamentary control did not preclude it from being raised in the name of the king. The Commons were well aware of the need to finance a fleet to guard the seas, and since the king was still, at least nominally, in command of the government, they were ready to give him a grant of tonnage and poundage accordingly. But they would grant it only from 25 May 1641 to the 15 July next ensuing, thereafter to be renewed for similar periods at their own discretion. This made their offer to grant tonnage and poundage for a year in 1625 seem positively generous. But it confirms that the basic intention of that earlier initiative was just the same, it was part of an attempt to prise the customs dues out of the king's discretionary control, and to ensure that they were raised, and used in a manner that parliament could approve.

The Commons had even then been attempting to convert a formality of representative consent into a reality. They were now bringing that project to a conclusion. Tonnage and poundage would henceforth be subject to the active exercise of representative consent, as part of the aim of bringing all the customs dues under parliamentary control.

This and its long-desired corollary, the ending of prerogative impositions, amounted to another notable shift in the balance of the constitution. The customs, which had formerly been the crown's principal independent source of public finance, were now being brought under the control of parliament. The act of May 1641 established this position unequivocally. "It is hereby declared and enacted . . . that it is and hath been the ancient right of the subject of this realm that no subsidy, custom, imposition or other charge whatsoever ought not to be laid or imposed upon any merchants . . . without common consent in parliament". Of course, the assumption of representative command of the customs did not truly derive from the ancient rights of the subject. The ancient rights in the matter were entirely on the side of the crown. The Commons were describing the situation not as it had been in the past, but as they wanted, and now had the power to make it. They were usurping the control of the customs dues on the principle of freedom of trade—a concept that had begun to emerge in the mid-sixteenth century and had been first asserted in the House in 1610. The direct challenge to the king's prerogative of impositions in the great debate of that year had been the first indication of the intent in the House of Commons to extend the force of representative rights by bringing all the customs dues under the control of parliamentary consent. In the succeeding decades this had been their most persistent radical ambition, which was now being realised in appropriate fashion. As Gardiner concluded, "By this bill, Charles surrendered forever his claim to levy customs dues of any kind without a parliamentary grant".[14]

There were further important implications to the overturning of the royal prerogative in the customs dues. Unlike the subsidies on landed property, the customs related to a continuously *active* sphere. The trading sector was more about using property than just retaining it. And the customs were normally thought of as being directed towards specific purposes. So when this central plank of public finance was taken under parliamentary control it consolidated the transition of the concept of consent into a more concrete shape. A nominal right of consent to land taxes had been in place since the fourteenth century, but it had always been something of a formality. Through the fifteenth and most of the sixteenth centuries, it remained essentially a convenience of the crown, a formula by which the king could raise tribute from the body of the kingdom, and lessen his dependence on the magnates. It did not amount to *active* consent—that is to say it was not taken to involve any positive input or approval of the assenter to the actual usage of the money. This began to change in the reign of Elizabeth, when the active consent of the kingdom at large was clearly implied in the presentation of foreign policy. In the 1620s it moved into another phase, when the House of Commons began consistently to decline to contribute to a foreign policy of which they did not approve.

The part played by the freedom of trade perspective in the further consolidation of active consent was displayed in another enactment of the Long Parliament, in September 1641. This was, "An act for the relief of the captives taken by Turkish, Moorish and other pirates, and to prevent the taking of others in time to come".[15] The inability of the government to guard the seas and protect merchant shipping had been a persistent cause of complaint, especially since the 1620s. In the parliamentary summary of the supposed explanation of this failure, we see the developing notion of the benefits of active consent.

> Your majesty's subjects have ever since your majesty's access to the crown been charged with the payment of great sums of money under the name of custom and without the consent of parliament, which had they been legally taken ought to have been chiefly employed upon the safeguard of the seas and preservation of your good subjects in their trade of merchandise . . . but have been exhausted by evil ministers and not employed to their proper use.[16]

Whether this had in fact been the problem, or whether the direct exercise of parliamentary consent would have improved the situation was a moot point; but it was not the essence of the matter. The essential logic of parliament's case was that the on-going application of representative consent, made unavoidable by the Triennial Act and the Tonnage and Poundage Act, was, by definition, the most effective way of ensuring that the money would be used for approved purposes. Similarly, if all customs were laid, as they said, "according to the rates set by parliament", it would be as close as possible to an assurance that the charges were only such as the traders thought reasonable and viable, and not an insupportable burden. The significance of the freedom of trade perspective to the development of the right of consent was to place it in the active context of the conditions in which people wished to work and trade. In this field, the exercise of consent had to be applied not just occasionally, but continuously. As William Hakewill had asserted in the great impositions debate in 1610: if subsidies, "which came but seldom, were brought to certainty, then much more custom might, which hapneth daily".[17]

So the crucial priorities and essential aims of the Long Parliament when it met in 1641 were not the July acts condemning the various "arbitrary" policies of the 1630s. This could be done at leisure because the Commons believed that their first radical provisions ensured that these practices could never be repeated. Thus, the central force of the parliamentarian programme lay in the earlier measures, as outlined in this and the preceding chapter. The first was the Triennial Act of February 1641, which supplanted the crown's prerogative in the calling of parliament and established the representative body with an automatic and regular place at the centre of affairs. The second was the Tonnage and Poundage Act of May 1641, which established full representative control of the customs, as of all other fiscal charges, and thus displaced the king's most vital, independent source of public finance.

The Tonnage and Poundage Act effectively completed the re-modelling of the constitution, which the Triennial Act had begun. By these two enactments the king was rendered incapable of ruling independently of parliament. Once these measures took force, Charles would be unable to avoid the presence of the representative assembly, which would convene on its own authority and on a regular basis. It would thus be able to provide the legislative service that was now regarded as essential to the good government of the kingdom, and to ensure that parliament was in a position to exert an effective, and continuous influence over the conduct of royal ministers. Automatic and frequent assemblies would also enable parliament to exercise the comprehensive control over public finance that it had established under the Tonnage and Poundage Act. Henceforth, all public monies would be subject to the active control of parliamentary consent and would be specifically directed to the uses approved by parliament. These were the actual mechanics of the change in the balance of power that underlay the view expressed by such as James Harrington that, "the dissolution of this government caused the war, and not the war the dissolution of this government".[18] Thus the two radical measures of early 1641, the Triennial Act of February, and the Tonnage and Poundage Act of May, mark the real inception of the English Revolution. By these constitutional changes, Charles I had lost his position as an independent monarch and would need to use force of some kind if he were to recover it.

The discretionary control of the customs dues had been crucial to the independent authority of the royal government. But in the political nation at large, it had come to be regarded as an unacceptable burden and restriction on the economic lives of the king's subjects. It contradicted the context of freedom in which they wished to work and trade, and which they now believed to be their right. The parliamentarians therefore sought to displace the prerogative of impositions and bring the setting of the customs under the command of representative consent. These imperative desires go far to explain the radicalism of the early initiatives of the Long parliament. Modern historians have made the mistake of treating parliament's political demands in a vacuum, and have found it difficult to understand why the people, or their representatives, should have suddenly decided that they wanted to limit the powers of the crown. But parliament's demand for change becomes easier to comprehend when we recognise that the reduction of the king's authority was not pursued simply for its own sake, but in order to address some real, practical needs, of which the extension of representative rights was felt to be the essential guarantee. Foremost among these vital interests was freedom of trade, which defined the most important application of the principle of representative consent.

By the same token, historians have failed to recognise the defining importance of the concept of freedom of trade, in part because they tend to look at questions of liberty in the abstract form of political theory, rather than in terms of the working significance of freedoms on the ground. Fortunately, contemporaries who were actually involved in the Civil War contest did not take such a restrictive view. There are writings from the period that do treat of economic aspirations in terms of principles of liberty. The central force of the freedom of trade dimension in parliamentarian motivations is shown not only in the place that it held as one of the two crucial constitutional changes enacted as priorities by the Long Parliament, but also in the way that it was conceptualised as the most specific definition of freedom to emerge in the course of the dispute.

In 1642, for instance, was published a tract examining the nature of tyranny. The pamphlet was in effect an attempt to justify the governmental re-modelling on which parliament had embarked. "Tyranny" seemed a rather harsh characterisation of Charles's essentially lawful Personal Rule, but in fact the tract condemned the practice of tyranny not in conventional political terms as the unlawful imposition of self-will, but rather as a contradiction of freedom of trade. Here, tyranny was defined principally on the basis that it denied the benefit that was now most aimed for—the right to profit freely by one's goods and property. "Tyranny may justly be condemned as the greatest calamity because it is in opposition to the greatest felicity, which lies in liberty and the free disposition of that which God and our industry has made ours".[19] The concept of liberty in early modern England tends to be seen today in rather vague terms, as a generalised alternative to autocratic power. But in truth, it had become something quite specific and substantial. In a general political sense it was about the assertion of rights of consent. But in its most active manifestation, it was about consent in the economic sphere—the freedom of trade. The elevation of freedom of trade into a philosophical principle is a measure of the importance that the concept had acquired in seventeenth century England. It was the essential condition in which people wanted to carry on their trades and live their lives. The pamphlet echoed the basic rationale of freedom of trade as it had developed since the 1550s—that the necessary motivation for a viable and prosperous economic life was the liberty to profit to the full. A king could expect the greatest resource of financial support in a commonwealth governed consensually, where men had "the strong engines of private interest to move them".[20] Although in a tyranny the ruler had all men's wealth at his command, the potential income was not so great, "the uncertainty of keeping hindering for the most part the desire of gain".[21] Thus the freedom to profit without arbitrary restriction or exaction came to be perceived as the essence of liberty.

Freedom of trade was accorded the same kind of political and philosophical status, even more explicitly, in Gerrard Winstanley's study of the nature, or law of freedom, written about a decade later, in the wake of the revolution. Winstanley noted that now the king and Lords had been disposed of, and the scope for the implementation of liberty created, people were debating what the principal focus of freedom should be. Now that they were in a position to set up a free commonwealth, and most seemed to agree that freedom was the desirable end, what form should it take? What was true freedom? Winstanley himself had a rather idiosyncratic notion of freedom as the common ownership of the land, but he also had a clear perception of the rather different kind of freedoms that had been sought by the parliamentarian movement as a whole. And first on the list of freedoms that Winstanley observed to be generally desired was freedom of trade. Many, he perceived, saw freedom as "the free use of trading, and to have all patents, licenses and restraints removed".[22] There could hardly be a more precise, or comprehensive description of the concept of freedom of trade that has been traced in this volume, developing from the mid-sixteenth century onwards, and culminating, as Winstanley perceived, as a powerful driving force of the mid-seventeenth century revolution. And closely associated with freedom of trade was the absolute freedom of property, the claim of the freeholder to be "landlord of the earth", to the exclusion of the claims of the king, and indeed of the commons.[23]

These were what Winstanley identified as the principal active elements of the freedom that the gentry, yeomanry and merchants had sought to establish through the struggles of the 1640s. He recognised that these were genuine freedoms, but only for some, because they also involved subsidiary aspects of domination, leaving others un-free. Winstanley himself believed that "true foundation freedom" lay in "the free enjoyment of the earth" as a common treasury.[24] This was in one sense very different, but there was nevertheless some significant common ground between Winstanley's foundation freedom and the freedoms pursued through the mainstream parliamentarian movement. Freedom of trade, freedom of property and freedom of the earth were all *active* freedoms. The general force of the concept of freedom in the Civil War period was as an active economic right.

Thus freedom of trade emerges as the most important of the economic factors that were central to Civil War motivation. It is indeed the thread that connects the various aspects of economic explanation. It further links the rise of the gentry to the instigation of the radical challenge to the crown, and it explains why the middling sort and commercial classes were predominantly parliamentarian. The crucial, actual freedom asserted by them all was the right to work, trade and hold property free of arbitrary impositions and restraints. This principle, in its various guises, had been the cause of the most bitter and persistent contentions between crown and Commons since 1600. It was duly addressed in the priority legislation and constitutional changes enacted by the Long Parliament in the early months of 1641. And it was recognised by commentators as the most substantial area of liberty at stake. If we are seeking the most efficient cause of the English Civil War and Revolution, it lay in the new imperatives of economic freedom, and the desire to guarantee them through the enhanced position of parliament.

It should be no surprise then to learn that parliamentary control of the setting of the customs dues was the crucial constitutional change that was not reversed with the restoration of the monarchy in 1660. The radical provisions of the other priority measure of early 1641, the Triennial Act, were only overturned in 1664 by a piece of government gerrymandering. The essential force of the Tonnage and Poundage Act of May 1641 was not overturned at all. The customs might once again be permitted to the king for life, but they were all now granted in parliament. As Gardiner said, Charles had surrendered his right of prerogative customs dues forever.

Notes

1. W. Hunt, *The Puritan Moment,* (Harvard 1983), p. 286
2. L. Hutchinson, *Memoirs of the Life of Colonel Hutchinson*, ed. J. Hutchinson, (London 1846), p. 91
3. S. R. Gardiner, *History of England 1603–1642,* (London 1886–9), IX, p. 238
4. Ibid, p. 104
5. S. R. Gardiner, ed., *Documents of the Puritan Revolution,* (Oxford 1968), p. 212
6. J. Rushworth, *Historical Collections,* (London 1659–1701), III, p. 21
7. Ibid, part 2, vol. 2, pp. 1121–35
8. *Commons Journal*, II, p. 11
9. Hutchinson, *Memoirs of the Life of Colonel Hutchinson*, p. 91
10. Rushworth, *Historical Collections*, IV, p. 33; *Commons Journal*, II, p. 24
11. *Commons Journal*, II, p. 24
12. C. Wilson, *England's Apprenticeship,* (London 1965), p. 135
13. 16 Car. I, cap. 8; *Statutes of the Realm,* (London 1810–1828), V, p. 104
14. Gardiner, *History of England*, IX, p. 400
15. 16 Car. I cap. XXIV; *Statutes of the Realm*, V, p. 134
16. Ibid
17. W. Cobbett and T. B. Howell, *A Complete Collection of State Trials,* (London 1809–28), II, p. 407
18. James Harrington, *Oceana*, ed. H. Morley, (London 1887), p. 62
19. *A Brief Discourse on Tyrants and Tyranny,* (November 1642), BL E127, (45), p. 1
20. Ibid, p. 2
21. Ibid, p. 4

22. Gerrard Winstanley, "The Law of Freedom in a Platform" (1652), in *Winstanley: The Law of Freedom and Other Writings*, ed. C. Hill, (Cambridge 1983), p. 294
23. Ibid
24. Ibid, p. 295

13 The Support of the Middle Sort

Parliament's Broad Base of Allegiance Among the Substantial Freeholders and the Merchants and Traders in the Commercial Centres—"Which Said Order Is Remaining in the Town Chest"[1]

Earlier chapters have shown that the two main foundations of the English Revolution—that is to say, setting up the representative assembly with a permanent and independent presence in the polity, and establishing a general right of freedom of trade by parliamentary command of the customs dues—were put in place by the gentry, acting in a united House of Commons in the early months of 1641. It is also clear that this was done with a strong base of support in the country. William Strode's presentation of the Triennial Act as "somewhat to comfort the people" indicated that the measure was not only accepted, but also actively desired in the constituencies, by the yeomen "subsidy men", and the merchants and traders with a direct interest in the representative network. These same groups were the principal beneficiaries of the implementation of a right of freedom of trade by the parliamentary control of the customs dues. And again, although it was the gentry who led the long running campaign to remove the royal prerogative of impositions, they did so with the general body of merchants as initiating and defining partners in the ambition, and with the undoubted endorsement of the commercialising farmers who were committed to the processes of interregional marketing and the freedoms that it demanded. It needs to be clearly recognised that with regard to these core radical changes, the gentleman, the merchant and the yeoman spoke with one voice.

So when the special relationship between the parliamentarian movement and the middle sort of people is noted, as it has often been, both by commentators at the time and by historians since, it is important to be aware that for some vital purposes the gentry were an integral part of the "middle sort" perspective. And they were not excluded from the definition of "the people", whose socio-economic rise over the preceding century was seen by contemporaries as underpinning the challenge to the crown in the mid-seventeenth century. The earliest version of this economic explanation of the Civil War was expounded by James Harrington in *Oceana*, in the 1650s, and referred to the broad body of "the people". This encompassed the yeomanry, and the merchants and traders, but

Harrington would also have included the middling gentry among those who had received an access of wealth and landed strength at the expense of the king and the greater nobility.[2]

The yeomanry, the merchants and traders, and the lesser gentry were the groups that collectively composed the "middle sort" at the time, and Harrington was not alone in perceiving that the scales of wealth and potential had tipped in that direction. Christopher Hill noted that the same view was taken by all "the best thinkers among his predecessors and contemporaries", including Sir Walter Raleigh, Sir Francis Bacon, James I, John Selden, Sir Henry Wotton, Sir Thomas Wilson, Spelman Bishop, Francis Quarles, Godfrey Goodman, Henry Parker, Henry Ireton, Gerrard Winstanley and Thomas Hobbes.[3] Lucy Hutchinson was also clear that the rebalancing of economic power towards "the people" provided the basic momentum behind the Civil War:

> when the nobility shrank into empty names the throne lost its supporters . . . when the full body of the people came rolling in upon it. The interest of the people, which had been many years growing, made an extraordinary progress in the days of Henry VIII, who returning the vast revenues of the church into the body of the people, cast the balance clear on their side and left them only to expect an opportunity.[4]

In this definition of "the people" the middling gentry were certainly included, for they were the group that ended up with most of the church lands. The transfer of economic strength towards the middle ranks of society has been manifest in all the trends outlined in the foregoing chapters of this volume. The rise of the yeomen farmers was a very striking and distinctive phenomenon, and the great proliferation of the numbers of the gentry was largely a consequence of the advances made by the yeomen, the merchants, the lawyers and the younger sons. The "middle sort" was a broad church. Furthermore, it was often the way that these groups were associated and connected across various fields of activity that was the basis of their economic and political significance.

But when identifying the core of parliamentarian activists in her neighbourhood, and defining the middle sort, Lucy Hutchinson put most stress "on the able substantial freeholders, and other commons".[5] This was the general view at the time. In this respect, David Underdown's summary of views is interesting. Although he sometimes avoided the idea of economic motivation for his own purposes, he acknowledged that "contemporaries were unanimously of the opinion that taking the nation as a whole, there were social differences between the two sides". And "it accords with the observable facts of the situation . . . that Parliament's strength rested on its appeal to the "middle sort", the craftsmen and small merchants in the towns, the yeomanry and substantial freeholders in the countryside, led by a minority of the aristocracy and gentry".[6]

Various aspects of the rise of the middle sort of yeoman have been covered in previous chapters in this volume. They can be brought together now, in a way that clarifies the significance of the phenomenon. The principal genesis of the advance of "the people" was the great change in the balance of manorial control in fifteenth-century England, whereby landlords adopted a policy of letting out their demesne to the more substantial tenants, on a commercial basis, which gave a significant number of small to middling farmers a new degree of socio-economic freedom. This was the development recorded in another early seventeenth century text—the history of the Berkeley family compiled by their steward John Smyth. He described and explained the widespread alienation of manorial lands to tenants, which became a distinctive feature of the English scene in the early fifteenth century. The collapse of the population level in the fourteenth century had led to a decline in the demand for tenant land, an acute shortage of labour, and a fall in the market price for arable produce. The first response of landlords was to exploit their customary rights over tenants more rigorously, because the relative value of the dues and services that they owed was now higher.[7] But the accumulated resentment at this oppressive stance was a significant cause of the Peasant's Revolt of 1381, which in turn produced a change of approach. Landlords sought a less risky way of maintaining their income. John Smyth recalled that it was "much occasioned by the insurrection of Wat Tyler, and generally by all the commons in the land" that the family began to lease out their estate. "Then instead of manuring the demesnes with his own servants . . . this lord began to . . . tack in other men's cattle onto his pasture . . . and to sell his meadow grounds . . . let out by the year still more and more . . . sometimes at racked improved rents".[8] It became general in the fifteenth century for lords to sell or lease out their demesne lands. This broke the link of obligation and restraint between the manor and the village that had maintained an essential stasis in medieval society. The working character of both the lord's estate and the tenant's holding was radically altered. Their relationship came to be determined by commercial rather than feudal conditions. The land was necessarily leased out at market value, that is to say the level at which it would be profitable to the farmer. Since it was the lord's land it had no dues or services upon it, and it tended to be physically of a more coherent shape than could usually be made of the scattered strips in the open fields. This all served to create a new class of independent commercialising farmers, which only developed to this extent in England.

An important aspect of the change was that in a sense the form of tenure ceased to matter—the decisive factor was whether you could acquire enough workable land to make a substantial profit in the market. A good example was in the family background of the mid-sixteenth-century churchman Hugh Latimer. He described his father as "a yeoman, and held no land of his own . . . tilled as much as kept half a dozen men. He had a walk for a hundred sheep".[9] The process often resulted in "a modern form of leasehold tenancy, first adopted when a lord, lacking labour, farmed out the demesne to one or more tenants . . . who paid him a competitive rent fixed only for a term of years . . . such men were often graziers who possessed some capital, and belonged to the new age of commercial agriculture".[10] This sums up the principal characteristics of the change, which saw the emergence of a new class of yeoman farmers who were free to profit and expand by a more concentrated use of the market. The most efficient vehicles of advance were sheep.

James Harrington believed that the early Tudor Statute of Population was not without effect in sustaining the yeoman farmer. The Tudor governments are usually thought to have failed in their regular attempts to resist the enclosure of the common lands, and the depopulation that it was believed to cause. But Harrington perceived that the provisions of this and other statutes that sought to protect the integrity of smallholdings with 20 acres or more did in fact do something to encourage the survival, and often the extension of the larger copyhold farms. So the dweller rose above the ranks of a cottager, and became "a man of some substance that might keep hinds [labourers] and servants". In other words, these provisions created the basis of a commercial farming unit. This placed "a great part of the lands to the hold or possession of the yeomanry or middle people, who living not in a servile or indigent fashion were much unlinked from dependence on their lords".[11]

The early arrival of an economically independent class of tenants on the English manors was also reinforced by an exceptional degree of freedom from fiscal demands. This too was in some degree a result of the Peasants' Revolt. Although the uprising was suppressed, there were important, if indirect, long-term consequences. The scale and force of the revolt, in an unusually compact kingdom, alarmed the political establishment, and in part no doubt because of this, there was a drift towards a more circumspect approach to labour relations, at both manorial and central government level. The ill-judged initiative of the poll tax was not repeated. There was no further attempt to load the burden of taxation onto the shoulders of the general body of artisans and husbandmen smallholders. The English peasantry thus escaped the fate that was overtaking their continental counterparts. The tendency of other European monarchs at the time was to establish a standing army, which was used to support a system of collecting tax arbitrarily from the poorer classes, while the nobility was largely exempt. In England, by contrast, the principal general tax, the parliamentary subsidy, fell mainly on the landowning class, and this left the commoners and smallholders relatively free of fiscal burdens. Equally important, this balance of fiscal obligation gave the English gentry a powerful vested interest in sustaining and extending both the practice and the principle of a right to consent to the provisions of public finance. In this way too, England was embarked on a different course from its European neighbours, and most of the classes in English society were acquiring a stake in a specific kind of economic freedom, which referred centrally on the idea that land could only be taxed by representative consent. A recent study of landholding patterns in fifteenth- and sixteenth-century Norfolk by Jane Whittle has confirmed that the consequence of this distinctive balance was to create a new class of independent, commercialising village farmers. She concluded that,

> the significance of the period between 1440 and 1580 . . . lies in the freedom, prosperity and . . . the lack of landlordly interference experienced by the rural population, and in the fact that an economy generated by small landholders unburdened with heavy exactions by state or landlord could promote the development of capitalism.[12]

We should add that an important factor was the context of increasing opportunities and rising profits that created the conditions in which the commercialising farmer could make the best use of his independence. The exceptional "lucre" to be made from sheep rearing, especially at the end of the fifteenth and the beginning of the sixteenth centuries, was the first instance of an enterprise which allowed farmers with a minimum of 60 to 70 acres to become "notable rich men by doing thereof in brief time".[13] And as the population continued to grow, and agricultural prices rose faster than any, arable farming also became unusually profitable.

The importance of the development can be measured in various ways. The emergence of a distinctive class of commercialising farmers occurred sufficiently widely in England to provide the basis of a significant increase in productivity, which is often regarded as an agricultural revolution. Robert Allen credited the yeoman farmers as the principal factor in the notable rise in grain yields that was achieved between 1550 and 1650.[14] The real benefits of this were reflected in the exceptionally high levels of life expectancy that were attained in mid-Elizabethan England. The substance of the advance of the yeomen was also reflected in a noticeable change in the architectural face of the villages and the countryside. This was the Great Rebuilding of farmhouses that was taking place from the 1570s onwards.[15] This process was described at length in Chapter 5 but can be summarised again in context. As a generalisation, most medieval farmhouses had been single storey, low to the ground, and dominated by one central room or hall, which was usually open to the roof. The Great Rebuilding brought a signal transformation. There was the addition of an extra floor and more rooms. The hall or communal living area was no longer the be all and end all of the structure—it was divided and surrounded by a larger number of separate rooms, parlours and chambers. The added floor demanded the provision of formal staircases, and of course, chimneys. Smoke was no longer left to drift out through a hole in the roof of the main living area. A new brick frontage, vertically enhanced, with a row of first floor windows, and chimneys climbing above, epitomised the rising profile of the buildings, and their occupants. The houses were impressive, and the apparent speed with which the new style spread over most of the kingdom, from Cornwall to Cheshire, was a sign not only of the integrated nature of the society and economy of England by Elizabeth's time, but also of the generality of the class of yeoman farmers, which helps to explain their economic effect.

Their success also had a political dimension. It was revealing that the Elizabethan commentator William Harrison thought that the advent of chimneys, brick building and glazed windows, and the acquisition of rich furnishings and dining vessels in the house of the ordinary farmer, meant that he now "rivals what a prince once was".[16] The distinguished new appearance of the buildings was not just an expression of affluence and comfort—it announced the arrival of the yeomen as people of socio-economic and local—political consequence. They were acquiring a stake and an established place in the administrative structures of the kingdom. They were the churchwardens, the constables and the jurors in the villages. Steve Hindle has studied the vigorous use that the middle sort made of the legal system and their concern with maintaining order in their localities.[17] But perhaps more indicative of their position in the land was the part that they played, for positive and constructive reasons, in the process that *made* and administered the law. They were not just using what was available. They were active in the systems that devised and implemented the governing rules of the kingdom. It was the yeoman freeholders who were usually the voters or "subsidy-men" in elections to parliament. In effect they were the physical manifestation of the developing reach of representative rights. They were the people whose actual votes went to make up the accredited consent of the entire society, which was now the authorising principle of omni-competent, nationally binding law. And they constituted that "entire society" in a surprisingly extensive way. A study by Derek Hirst suggested that the 40-shilling freeholder qualification was rendered almost meaningless by the Great Tudor Inflation. He estimated that by 1640 the electorate extended to between 27% and 40% of the adult male population.[18] This underlines the broad and completed substance of the coordinated networks of public authority of which the yeomen were now a part.

Their position was recognised at the time. In the 1560s Sir Thomas Smith published an authoritative analysis of the shape of English government, and placed the yeomanry among the parties by which England was "governed, administered and maintained". He noted that there were "three sorts of persons" charged with this responsibility. One was the prince. The second was the gentry, in which he also included the nobility. He went on, "The third is named the yeomanry: and each of these hath his part and administration in judgments, corrections of defaults, in election of officers, in appointing tributes and subsidies, and the making of laws".[19] This is a fine illustration of the force of the connected framework of administration that had developed during the Tudor period. A century earlier an analysis of government only found it necessary to mention the prince and the nobility.[20] But by the reign of Elizabeth the responsibility for "government" ran far enough down the social scale and wide enough through the towns and villages to give it a genuinely national dimension. Just as much as the gentry, the rising yeoman and the middle sort of people reflected the physical completion of the political nation. Most apposite is Smith's observation that they all had their part in "the making of laws". The formulation of sovereign representative law bound the nation together more effectively than a central bureaucracy could ever have done. To understand the causes of the Civil War it is crucial to note that the confidence of the people who stood against the king rested largely on the fact that they were part of an integrated structure of administration and economy that could operate independently. Again, it was the associations and connections between the gentry, the yeomanry and the merchants that created much of the motive force behind political change.

The importance of placing the middle sort in the context of these coordinated systems is not always recognised, even in sympathetic treatments of the political significance of the group, such as Brian Manning's study of *The English People and the English Revolution*. Manning's definition of the people embraced "the mass of land-holding peasants and self-employed craftsmen".[21] His concept of the middle sort extended into the ranks of the poor commoners, while at the other end of the spectrum, he made a clear differentiation between the middle sort and the gentry. In every sense this tended to contradict the idea of "the people" that was current at the time. When Lucy Hutchinson and James Harrington talked about "the people" in terms of the parliamentary cause, they were not naturally referring to the poor, nor were they necessarily excluding the gentry from the picture. To Civil War contemporaries the active "people" were not "the mass of land-holding peasants" subsisting outside the political world. The people, for parliamentarian purposes, were those who had already acquired a position in the administrative and judicial systems, they were the yeomen farmers, the small merchants and the subsidy-men who filled out and drew together the representative and legislative networks described earlier in this chapter. By the same token, the contemporary definition of the active "people" did not exclude the gentry. And in respect of the land-use question the parliamentary movement came down decisively in favour of those who were enclosing common land. So it was the agents of enclosure who were included in the parliamentarian version of "the people", rather than the dispossessed poor.

Recognising this more relevant line of differentiation helps to clarify the real motivations of the parliamentary side. The main thrust of Manning's argument is that the lower middle-sort as a class, clearly distinguished from the gentry, had a crucial influence on the course of the revolution. There is certainly an element of truth in the idea that popular pressure had some effect in dividing opinion among MPs. It is clear that the radical leaders in the Commons in 1640–1 were distinguished by their readiness to welcome the participation of the London populace in their cause, and that conversely the eruption of the body of the people into direct action on the streets was largely responsible for the first formation of a royalist party among the more socially conservative gentry, who felt their class interest to be threatened. Most historians would also agree that the popular movement was not just the creation of the parliamentary leaders—it had an independent force of its own.[22] But it is too much to say, as Manning does, that, "this comes close to according the mass of the people the decisive role in precipitating the Civil War". Inciting the formation of a royalist party was of real, but essentially negative importance. And it does not tell us precisely *why* people were parliamentarian. The Civil War was not fought as a deliberate attempt to overturn the gentry as a class. Even if it were true that the widespread popular risings tended to be in opposition to the royalists and worked in favour of the parliamentary side, this does not define the nature of the cause as Manning asserts.[23] A clearer picture of how the people connected to the parliament is obtained by asking why the prospect of popular activism was *not* a deterrent to the majority of MPs who stayed with the revolution after social conservatives like Digby had broken away. The more radical MPs understood that the efficient element in the demonstrations was not the mass of the poor, but more usually the artisans and cloth workers, and the small farmers with an interest in the markets. These were men who had a stake in the same economic, political and administrative networks as the leading parliamentarians. So, as Norah Carlin has said, the radical MPs had a concept of "the people" by which the broad middle ranks of yeomen and merchants were associated with them as administrators and posed no threat to the social order represented by the gentry.[24] We can add that their collective confidence owed much to the fact that the public frameworks in which they were all involved were perfectly capable of operating under their own steam. This is not to exclude the concept of class from the picture. The revolution did involve an element of class differences. But the divisions were less crude than Manning supposes, and they were not really where he places them. The more typical balance is summed up in a contemporary observation from Bristol, where the king's cause was favoured by the very rich and the very poor, "but disgusted by the middle ranks . . . the truest citizens".[25] When all is said and done, this was a bourgeois, not a "popular" revolution.

There are elements of class division in the idea that some groups had established a significant degree of independence from the traditional socio-economic hierarchies. But attempts to describe this aspect of parliamentarian allegiance have tended to be rather vague and generalised. David Underdown searched for it in the form of religio-cultural differences, but not with conspicuous success.[26] Alan Everitt suggested, more persuasively, that it was the independent lifestyle of the heaths and woods, with their relative freedom from manorial and parish controls, that explained why these areas were to the fore in providing troops for the parliamentarian armies during the Civil War.[27] Ann Hughes thought that the same effect took force through the individualism "associated with the industrial or wood-pasture areas in Derbyshire, Durham and Warwickshire".[28] Andy Wood has questioned the emphasis placed by Hughes and Jill Dias on the parliamentarian instincts of the lead miners of Derbyshire. He pointed out that a significant section of the Derbyshire miners in fact supported the king.[29] This may be regarded, however, as the exception that proves the rule, for many more miners did support parliament. The king usually struggled to find spontaneous support among the middle sort, but the allegiance of some miners might be bought for a while by a specific promise to exempt them from the duties of lot and cope that were levied on mining rights in the Duchy of Lancaster. And this leads us, by a somewhat circuitous route, to the essence of middle sort motivation. They were driven above all by the determination to bring about the fiscal conditions and freedoms that they felt to be their requirement, and which they had come to believe in as their right. In regard to this, the king had more usually been found on the other side of the argument.

So a more coherent picture begins to emerge. In fact, we can give a precise and substantial character to the operative concept of independence in two specific ways. One was the structural change by which the yeoman farmers had managed to escape the old manorial constraints. This development was marked in James Harrington's observation that "the yeomanry or middle people" had acquired a free commercial capacity, "much unlinked from their dependence on their lords".[30] By the same token Lucy Hutchinson identified the active core of parliamentarian support among "most of the middle sort, the able substantial freeholders, and the other commons, who had not their dependence on the malignant nobility and gentry".[31] It was of some importance that this class of independent individuals were emerging not just in the wood-pasture or industrial regions but also in the mainstream of agrarian society.

The second explicit aspect of independence may be described as an integrated economic and political mindset, which had come to characterise the attitudes of the middle sort in particular over the preceding decades. It was in essence the assumption of a right to commercial freedoms, expressing itself politically in the assertion of the principles of representative consent. It was encapsulated as a theory by Thomas Hobbes, observing a powerful trend of opinion whereby each man "was so much master of whatsoever he possessed, that it could not be taken from him upon any pretence of public safety without his own consent".[32] This was precisely reflected in practice in the impositions debate in 1610, when MPs challenged the king's right to levy discretionary impositions on trade, and demanded that all such levies should be subject to the control of parliamentary consent—an ambition that was equally the initiative of the merchants in the market towns. The psychology of rights of consent found an interesting echo in Lucy Hutchinson's report that parliamentary soldiers were in one sense less easy to lead, because they always insisted on having the purpose of the action explained. It was, "the fault of all the parliamentary party, that they were not very obedient to commands, except they knew and approved their employment".[33] John Corbet reported the same tendency to question authority in Gloucester. This seems to reflect the fact that in general terms parliamentarians were actively committed to the exercise of rights of consent.

The insistence on the specific right of consent was the political shape of an independent outlook, which naturally found its expression in a tendency to favour the development of representative forms. But the principal basis of this, and the most substantial manifestation of an independent lifestyle, was the demand for economic freedoms—that is to say, the emerging conviction that to earn a good living and carry on a successful trade or enterprise, it was desirable, and perhaps necessary, to be left free of arbitrary exactions and restraints. Thomas Hobbes observed that the trading communities had become "mortal enemies" to taxation, and that they favoured the parliament because it had "pretended the peoples' ease from taxes, and other specious things".[34] This common phobia was certainly played upon by the parliamentary polemicists, whose principal charge against the king was that he might introduce arbitrary forms of government and especially of taxation. The royalist leaders complained that the king's Commission of Array was resisted because the parliamentarians had infused the people with the belief that it was a vehicle for reducing their freedoms and their estates. The problem for the royalists was that Charles's record in government made this threat seem real.

The positive assertion of economic freedoms has been illustrated in various contemporary commentaries already cited above. John Corbet identified the general character of these aims in the actual course of the struggle, from the vantage point of the parliamentary garrison at Gloucester. He believed that parliamentarian motivation derived mainly from the fact that the restrictions and exactions of royal economic policy were unacceptable to: "a generation of men truly laborious and jealous of their properties . . . whose principal aim is liberty and plenty".[35] At the end of the war Gerald Winstanley spelled out how this was conceptualised as a specific notion of freedom. He noted that everybody talked about freedom, but what did they actually mean? Winstanley's assessment of the essence of the freedoms that parliamentarians were seeking is definitive and can be quoted again. First on the list of actual freedoms that he observed to have been generally desired was what has been identified in these pages as freedom of trade— "the free use of trading, and to have all licenses, patents and restraints removed". Closely associated with this was the other principal form of freedom that he thought men had been seeking—the claim of the freeholders to be "lords of the earth" to the exclusion of the rights of the king, and the commons.[36] This too was part of the freedom of trade agenda, which did indeed constitute the basic substance of parliamentarian ambition. This was the condition in which they wished to live and work. It was, in the words of the pamphlet from 1642, "the greatest felicity", so much so that any regime denying it was to be accounted a tyranny. The fact that this was hardly a fair characterisation of Charles's government underlines the force of the freedom of trade agenda with which it was contrasted. For, "Tyranny may justly be condemned as the greatest calamity because it is in opposition to the greatest felicity, which lies in liberty and the free disposition of that which God and our industry has made ours".[37]

So the parliamentarian mind-set emerges clearly enough. The middle sort of people were typically successful entrepreneurs of rising social status, who had come to believe that their profitable livelihoods depended on an essential degree of liberty from artificial or arbitrary restrictions. This was what bound the merchant and the yeoman together in the cause—they were part of a new age of open commerce, and they no longer accepted the legitimacy of the moral and fiscal restraints that had circumscribed economic activity in an earlier period. In general they were easily persuaded that the royal regime tended to restrict their freedom of action, and make unnecessary and unacceptable demands on their pockets. The parliamentarian spokesmen played on this theme because they understood the dominant passions of their middle sort constituency, and this was largely because they shared the same values. What they all required was an efficient degree of economic liberty. They wanted to be left to use the market "as they list", without arbitrary exactions or restrictions. They needed to "have a certainty" regarding the conditions of trade, and to know that they would not be burdened with arbitrary impositions or obstructed by monopolies. We have given these demands the active, overall definition of a right of freedom of trade. And the idea that the royalist forces, and the king's cause, carried an inherent threat to this freedom was not just propaganda—it had a very clear historical and political logic. The king had long insisted on his right to impose customs dues by prerogative. He had frequently resorted to discretionary taxation, and denied the exercise of parliamentary consent. In the 1630s he had exploited every kind of fiscal expedient, and continued the use of extortionate, disruptive monopolies. This had made his approach to economic regulation seem intrusive and burdensome. Parliament, on the other hand, was known and valued specifically for resisting all such practices and offering the general alternative of a right of consent.

Parliament and the Commercial Centres: "Which Said Order Is Remaining in the Town Chest"[38]

The imperative of "liberty and plenty" took the active shape defined in these pages as the demand for a principled right of freedom of trade. This emerged in the context of an exceptionally free flowing, integrated market, and was pursued as a priority by all the various economic groupings that tended to favour the parliamentary cause. Each made a characteristic contribution to the process of change. While the rise of the yeoman farmer and commercial agriculture was the most powerful and distinctive feature of capitalist advance, the towns were still the most recognisable centres of commercial activity. It was indeed largely from the merchant community that the initiative for the freedom of trade campaign and the long-running attack on prerogative impositions appears to have issued.

The specific force and character of these manifestations of radical intent among the merchants and traders has been described above, with particular reference to London, the West Country and the Cinque Ports.[39] They were far from alone in their demands. The gentry, as reflected in the House of Commons, were committed partners and representative agents in the furtherance of these ambitions, which were doubtless also supported by the yeoman farmers who had become significant figures in the villages, and in the extended interregional market network. But it was in many ways the merchant community that provided the thrust and substance of the economic agenda that developed into political activity through the freedom of trade imperative. Furthermore, the other principal practical facility that inspired the radical beginnings of the English Revolution in 1641—that is to say, parliament's legislative function—was employed most regularly and enthusiastically by the market towns, if again quite often by the gentry on their behalf.

It is no surprise then to find that it was in the towns and ports that Thomas Hobbes located a new market morality, which took the form of a determination to assert an inviolable property in one's goods, against the ancient rights of the crown in prerogative taxation. It was primarily in the towns that Hobbes found the assumption that "each was so much master of whatsoever he possessed, that it could not be taken away from him upon any pretence of public safety without his own consent".[40] This indeed was exactly how freedom of trade translated into a kind of political liberty. Hobbes was accordingly also obliged to note that the commercial towns tended to favour parliament. The assertion that the goods or property of an individual should never be taken or used without their specific approval was a very logical rationale for supporting parliament, which was, by definition, the embodiment of community assent. This is not to say that Hobbes approved of this development. On the contrary, he believed that the crown ought to retain its traditional powers of discretionary taxation for the safety of the state, and he deplored the fact that the citizenry seemed ready to give their support to a parliamentary side "that pretended the people's ease from taxes, and other specious things".[41] Hobbes had little sympathy with the trend that he identified so clearly as the determination to maximise income by freeing themselves from taxation, "to which citizens, that is merchants, whose profession is their private gain, are naturally mortal enemies; their only glory being to grow excessively rich by the wisdom of buying and selling".[42] Hobbes viewed this in a negative light. Like Archbishop Laud, he believed that the motivation of private gain was inimical to the public good. What he failed to appreciate was that the right of the individual to profit freely had been elevated into a principle of liberty. The citizenry had come to believe that since freedom of trade was essential to their livelihoods and their assurance of success, it must therefore be asserted as an inalienable right. John Corbet's characterisation of the men who sustained the parliamentary garrison at Gloucester thus encapsulated the most powerful of parliamentarian motives. The king's restrictive and burdensome economic policies were not acceptable to "a generation of men truly laborious, jealous of their properties, whose principal aim is liberty and plenty".[43]

Just as the trading perspective was central to the parliamentarian agenda, so all the great ports and market towns displayed a positive commitment to parliament. The only exceptions were London and Newcastle at the very beginning of the struggle. In both places the great monopolist elites still held sway at the start, and they maintained a loyalty to the king who had given them their privileges and was indeed the agency most likely to sustain them. In both places too, this changed as soon as the representative body of the citizenry dislodged the elites from power. Thereafter, as Hobbes observed, "parliament had the command of the purses of the City of London, and of most cities and corporate towns in England".[44] Royalist commentators like Edward Hyde, future Earl of Clarendon, and Sir Philip Warwick acknowledged that over most of the country, the larger towns, and especially the ports, were parliamentarian. Plymouth was perhaps the most famous and iconic of ports, and it has figured in earlier chapters here with reference to the faith that it displayed in the functions and the authority of parliament in the 1620s. It was also the most prominent example of a port that stayed doggedly loyal to the parliamentary cause throughout the Civil War, though the countryside around it was dominated by some of the most effective Royalist forces.[45]

So when the two sides began to resort to arms in 1642, the towns displayed a positive sympathy to parliamentarian mobilisation, while they tended to be cold or actually antipathetic to the royalists. Parliament was able to record volunteer companies formed under its authority in more than thirty important market towns right across the south and east of the kingdom.[46] In any logical, objective process of analysis the distinctive bias of the towns would be taken as an indication that in their essential character, these commercial centres had an inherent empathy with the parliamentary side. But the dominant pre-disposition of revisionist history has been to deny the causal force of economic factors, and they therefore looked for other, less appropriate reasons. Anthony Fletcher, for instance, could not help but note that the turnout of volunteers up and down the country was "heart-warming for parliament," and that, "when due account has been taken of pressure and firm leadership . . . the 'cheerfulness and ready obedience' that was so much noted remains to be explained".[47] But he then suggested motives that were hardly adequate to stand as an explanation for the effect. He thought that "the nature of the royalist war effort made the king's men appear as aggressors, whereas parliament . . . nurtured townsmen's localist aspirations by encouraging them to make defensive arrangements".[48] There seems something of a contradiction between "localist" and "aspirations", and it is surely not plausible that all the towns supported parliament for local reasons. Hobbes, and the Royalist commanders themselves, believed that the towns resisted the Commission of Array because the king was associated with the threat of arbitrary methods of government, especially in the field of taxation. This was not an issue of local safety; it was a national political issue, as evidenced by the fact that it was so widely influential. If the royalists appeared as aggressors it was in one sense because the towns had already embraced parliamentary mobilisation. In traditional terms they might have been expected to accept the king's commission, since the monarch had always been by definition the protector of local interests. So if the towns were looking to parliament to protect them from the king, it was because the balance of public trust had altered. It was not for localist reasons that parliament gained the combined and consistent support of all the market towns and commercial ports in the kingdom. If the king appeared as an aggressor, it was not as an aggressor against the local security of the towns, but as an aggressor against the national provisions and principles offered by parliament, on which the towns set so much store—such as consensual public finance, representative legislation, and freedom of trade. The towns now operated in an exceptionally open and well-coordinated interregional market, the force of which encouraged a demand for commercial freedoms, to which parliament alone was committed. Similarly, the towns placed a special value on statute law as the most effective form of regulation and guarantee of their economic interests, and only the House of Commons seemed inclined to supply that need. They turned to parliament as a public authority because it served their economic imperatives. The king, on the other hand, was seen as generally opposed or obstructive to all these requirements. This polarisation produced persistent contentions over the rights of public finance and regulation, and it reached a stage were parliament was regarded as an alternative administrative focus.

A pattern of avoidance is transparent in Fletcher's work, just as it is in David Underdown's evasion of the significance of parliamentarian support in the cloth producing centres, as already described.[49] It is a measure of the institutional prejudice against economic causation that historians continue to contradict the obvious reality by denying or diminishing the real contribution of the towns. This is illustrated by Phil Withington's recent article *Urban Citizens and the English Civil Wars*. He seems not entirely happy that, "recent historians have not taken English townsmen to be noteworthy participants in the mid-century struggles".[50] But he does not go on to note that this is particularly incongruous because at the time, the urban centres were regarded as a mainstay of the parliamentary effort. Withington persists in ignoring the economic motives of the towns that contemporary commentators took as read. He is rightly sceptical of Robert Brenner's view that townspeople were more at odds with themselves than with the king. Yet he falls into a similar misconception. He begins from a memo by Samuel Hartlib from the 1650s, suggesting that the towns should keep up their guard against reactionary elements. From this, Withington infers a concept of citizenship governed by militaristic contentions within the towns. The idea of a formal role of citizenship is in any case something of a superimposed construct that is more appropriate to a city-state than to an English market town. In fact, contemporaries appear to have used the word just as a general denomination identifying the working people of a commercial centre. "Citizens, that is merchants", said Thomas Hobbes, helpfully.[51] He for one was in no doubt that life in a seventeenth-century English town was dominated by an exceptionally powerful economic drive. Their "profession is private gain . . . their only glory being to grow excessively rich by the wisdom of buying and selling".[52] Withington's notion of citizenship as "a field of conflict . . . constituted by configurations of civil institutions" is obscure and theoretical. [53] It is difficult to envisage what this could actually have meant in terms of parliamentarian motivations, and it is not a characterisation that readily brings to mind any of the sixteenth- and seventeenth-century towns that have appeared in the pages of the present volume. The governing perspectives of those ports and market towns was not an inward-looking defensiveness, but an outward-going desire to make maximum use of the exceptionally integrated, free-flowing national market in which they now operated. Their working ambition was to exploit and extend these freedoms to the full, especially by the use of the distinctive form of nationally binding, sovereign representative law, which they took to be the most effective guarantee of their interests, including freedom of trade.

These were the collective frameworks that structured the urban outlook on the world. It is a fundamental misconception to suppose that the urban viewpoint was merely local and institutional, when all the active circumstances point in a different direction. Hartlib himself put the matter in a national perspective. The provisions that he recommended were for "the preservation of the parliament itself, and the whole land".[54] In England, towns did not bear much resemblance to the defensible, parochial urban centres that still existed elsewhere in Europe. No English town had ever been large enough to establish an independent identity, except London, whose dominance made it the hub of a coordinated commercial system. The Italian cities of the fifteenth century had shown signs of capitalist development, but their failure to transcend local limits and attain a wider territorial unity meant that this never took force as an economic system. The English towns, however, traded in a distinctively unrestricted/ free-flowing national market, through a reciprocal system of regional specialisation and exchange, which was unusually free of internal tolls and customs barriers. They also participated in a uniquely unified system of administration and representation, and they were the most regular uses of the nationally definitive provisions of statute law to serve their economic interests. The principles that bound all this together were rights of consent and freedom of trade. It is this combination of individualist claims and integrated market systems that explains why a fully-fledged form of capitalism emerged first in England.

So the English towns were not inherently geared to military engagement, either within or without. The fact that they resorted to arms with some determination in 1642 shows the imperative force of the concept of "liberty and plenty" that they were asserting. This was anything but a localist view—it referred at every point to national perspectives, whether administrative, legislative, commercial or political. They believed accordingly that the best and probably the only way to secure the principles and the practices that they required was by supporting parliament. It may indeed be suggested that in searching for a concept of citizenship within the English towns in this period, Withington is looking in the wrong place. The notion of citizenship that was developing, precociously and distinctively in sixteenth- and seventeenth-century England was the citizenship of the state.

The most frustrating aspect of Withington's article is that he does touch upon the economic perspectives that connected to the real circumstances as observed by Civil War contemporaries. He notes that from 1570, "urban economies not only expanded, but became more capitalistically structured". And again, "the characterisation of citizens as harbingers of capitalism and civic republicanism is entirely plausible".[55] Perhaps it is the pre-occupation with "structure" that prevents him from extending these comments and recognising the more general changes in the character of economic activity, and the rise of commercialising forces, which were the most significant basis of capitalist development and a better explanation of the active role of the towns. There was certainly a seminal transition to a capitalistic economy in late sixteenth- and early seventeenth-century England, but apart from the enclosure and consolidation of the open fields, it was not primarily concerned with structure. It took shape as a change in the nature of marketing and the development of commercial systems. It was essentially about relations of exchange. Markets became more extended in scope, yet more broadly integrated. They came to operate in effect as a single entity, which acquired an independent force, and helped to generate a growing perception that it needed to be left to work to its own rules. This was associated with a transition in the ethics of economic life—that is to say, a shift from a context where economic activity was guided by moral or communal restraints and regulated by government imposition, to one that indicated and demanded individual freedom of trade.

So the towns adopted the parliamentary cause not out of defensive localism, but for the very broad and positive motives that related to their essential character as commercial centres. In that vital function, and for the gaining of their livelihoods they operated in a market structure that was actively national and interregional. To make the most effective use of those opportunities they had come to believe that they required the regular service of parliamentary legislation, the right of consent to any kind of public money raising, and a general context of freedom of trade. These were the crucial freedoms that over the years since 1610 had been consistently denied by the policies and activities of the crown. Parliament, on the other hand, could reasonably be expected to provide them, according to its firm commitments, not just as promised in the present, but also as delivered in the past.

Many modern studies have viewed the towns in terms of the formal hierarchies of government, and inferred from this that their view of the world would have been conservative, a supposition that contradicts the radical freedoms of the market in which they traded, and the plain fact that they offered general support to parliament in the Civil War. In a study of Bristol, David Sacks pointed out that the economic activities that many historians treated as matters of little account were actually of transcendent, global proportions. He might then have asked what these powerful open perspectives might have meant for the urban mind-set, but instead he based his assessment of the town's political outlook on the observation that the merchant elite was an exclusive group, with a conventional and hierarchical concept of authority.[56] In truth, the elitist presumptions of the greater merchants and monopolists did not necessarily reflect the general body of opinion in a town, and might actually induce an overall tendency to radicalism. The worldwide trade of Bristol had certainly created a few merchant princes, who were not unhappy to avail themselves of the king's offer to transfer in their direction the privileges that the London merchant elite had held in the great trading companies.[57] But the wider community of merchants had usually looked to parliament to free them from monopoly domination, and the general body of townsmen in Bristol were probably most exercised by the arbitrary and intrusive economic policies of the crown in the 1630s, which had tended, for instance, to undermine Bristol's important soap manufacture. This was the most likely basis on which the king's cause was "disgusted by the middle ranks . . . the truest citizens".[58] Disgusted is a strong word, implying that there was indeed something in early Stuart policy that was seen as inimical to the general economic interest. Bristol was one of the towns that raised an impressive body of volunteers for parliament, and was a strong parliamentarian garrison, until reduced after a bitter struggle against the most successful of Royalist armies completing its occupation of the West Country.

Even some Marxist historians have been reluctant to acknowledge the new emphasis on liberal freedoms that had been generated by the powerful development of commercialised interregional marketing and the growing resentment against arbitrary exactions and restrictions. Maurice Dobb seemed happy to take the mercantile elites as his touchstone, and regarded them as being in collaboration with the old feudal order.[59] There was some truth in this, but it is not an accurate guide to the position and mindset of townsmen as a whole. The great monopolists, and the policies of the "feudal" monarchy, were at odds with the general inclination towards freedom of trade. With a similarly restricted view, Robert Brenner has suggested that in the first four decades of the seventeenth century the London merchant community was essentially passive in its relationship with the royal government. Even in respect of the late 1620s, when the merchant's protests were too loud too ignore, Brenner proposes that this was really the voice of the gentlemen of the House of Commons, turning "the merchants' simple economic grievances into a constitutional issue".[60] In truth, as has been shown in previous chapters, it is evident that at critical moments, from as early as 1604 and 1606, it was the merchants, from London, from the West Country, and generally as represented in parliament, who were shaping the attack on monopolies and impositions.[61] It was the merchants who provided the motive force behind the first major freedom of trade initiative—the radical free trade bill of 1604. And it was the London merchants who inaugurated the impositions dispute in 1606, quite specifically as a test case challenging the royal prerogative in this field. It was therefore not surprising to find that the Dartmouth merchants made and kept a substantial record of the impositions debate in parliament in 1610, highlighting their determination that all the customs dues should be brought under the control of representative consent. Crucially, this also showed how the merchant communities were coming to regard parliament as the efficient and acceptable public authority in this respect. This was demonstrated again in 1624, when the Plymouth merchants pointedly preserved a parliamentary statement unilaterally declaring free trade on the Newfoundland fishing grounds and asserting that the restrictions put in place by the king's grant of a monopoly were to be regarded as void. By the same token, it was, unsurprisingly, the merchants who took the lead in reviving the challenge to discretionary customs dues in the mid-1620s. Robert Brenner is wrong to suggest that the merchants were presenting "simple economic grievances". They had long placed their economic demands quite explicitly in a context of constitutional change. They certainly knew that they would get powerful support from the House of Commons, and that the MPs would duly formalise their protests into a political agenda. But the merchants were not just passively passing the ammunition. It had been their positive desire for some decades to see the displacement of the royal prerogative over the customs dues. It is crucial for an understanding of early seventeenth century history to recognise that although the gentry, as reflected in parliament, certainly shared the merchants' persistent demand for representative customs dues, and an established right of freedom of trade, this was not conceived primarily in the landowning interest. The drive for freedom of trade, which was in many ways the lead factor in the growth of opposition to the crown, was prompted and in a sense defined by the imperative concerns of the mercantile sector.

The positive parliamentarian allegiance of the towns and commercial centres is a remarkable phenomenon, and to conceal its significance is to misrepresent one of the most distinctive and instructive aspects of English history, and indeed of history in general. The broad parliamentary sympathies of the towns were not an accidental consequence of seeking the best means of defence in a conflict of no direct concern. Urban parliamentarianism was an explicit reflection of the essential, underlying nature of the challenge to the crown, which centred on the demand for freedom from arbitrary exactions and restraints. The foregoing pages of this volume have described two specific but connected ways in which, over a period of some decades, these towns displayed a preference for the authority of parliament as the governing force in the regulation of their most vital activities. One was the great store that they set by parliamentary legislation as an unrivalled means of providing for their needs, with its unique capacity to reflect their concerns, local and general, and cater for them with nationally definitive provisions. The towns were the most enthusiastic users of the legislative function, which could offer by far the most effective guarantee of their economic interests. Thus, the merchants of Exeter made every effort to implement a crucial bill to ensure quality control in cloth manufacture. They presented it in 1621, and again in 1624, when they were on the verge getting it through, until the king arbitrarily called time on the assembly. In the absence of legislative opportunities, the merchants continued to try to solve the problem by other means, but the suggestions made were limited and ineffectual, which underlined again the unique advantages of parliamentary statute, which alone was directly representative, closely targeted and nationally binding. A powerful reason for supporting parliament in 1642 was to ensure the continuous provision of this vital facility.

The most important general motivation, however, is reflected in the free-fishing bill, which was brought forward by the merchants of Dartmouth and Plymouth in every assembly of the 1620s. This stood little or no chance of being accepted by the royal government, but the merchants continually proposed the measure because they believed it was absolutely necessary for the success of their principal trade, and the Commons would certainly have implemented it, if they had they been given the chance. Only parliament could be expected to support the freedom of trade that the towns believed to be essential to their commercial interests, and their livelihoods. It is this above all that explains why the towns, from the beginning of the seventeenth century, developed a constitutional interest in furthering the powers of parliament. This was clear not just from the force of merchant initiatives, but also in the way that the corporation of Dartmouth treasured parliamentary records from the impositions debate of 1610, showing that they wanted to see the crown's prerogative of imposing the customs dues set aside, and that they now regarded parliament as the acceptable arbiter of the law in that area. Again, the Order of the Commons' Committee of Grievances preserved by Plymouth Corporation in 1624, unilaterally declaring an end to the cod fishing monopoly, and voiding its power of restrictions, shows that the merchants were pleased to regard parliament as the decisive and legitimate public voice in these matters, even though it was in contradiction of the intentions of the crown. This indicates most crucially that these were their imperative requirements, and they were coming to regard parliament as the natural, and most reliable means of bringing them about. Only through the process of parliamentary consent could they avoid unwanted impositions and interventions, and "have a certainty" in the conditions of their trade. So they displayed a willingness over the long-term to embrace and elevate the influence of parliament, and especially the House of Commons, and to regard it as the desired authority in respect of their most crucial demands. It is this above all that explains the distinctive allegiance of the towns in the Civil War. In the note of the Plymouth representative declaring, "which said order is remaining in the town chest" we hear encapsulated the determining force of the parliamentarian loyalties of the market towns.

Notes

1. West Devon Record Office, Plymouth Corporation Archive, W48, f. 92
2. C. Hill, "James Harrington and the People", in *Puritanism and Revolution,* (London 1968), p. 291
3. Ibid, p. 293
4. L. Hutchinson, *Memoirs of the Life of Colonel Hutchinson*, ed. J. Hutchinson, (London 1846), p. 75
5. Ibid, p. 100
6. D. Underdown, *Prides Purge,* (Oxford 1971), pp. 11–12
7. M. Keen, *English Society in the Late Middle Ages,* (Harmondsworth 1990), pp. 64–5
8. John Smyth of Nibley, *The Lives of the Berkeleys,* (London 1618), ed. J. Maclean, 3 vols., (Gloucester 1883–6), II, pp. 5–6
9. Hugh Latimer, "The First Sermon Preached Before King Edward", 1 March 1549, *Works of Hugh Latimer*, ed. G. Corrie, (Cambridge 1844–45), I, p. 101
10. H. Brailsford, *The Levellers and the English Revolution,* (Spokesman 1983), p. 438
11. Harrington, *The Commonwealth of Oceana,* (London 1656), ed. Henry Morley, (London 1887), p. 59
12. J. Whittle, *The Development of Agrarian Capitalism,* (Oxford 2001), p. 315

13. *A Discourse of the Commonweal*, ed. M. Dewar, (Virginia 1969), pp. 53–4
14. R. Allen, *Enclosure and the Yeoman,* (Oxford 1992), p. 297
15. See above, Chapter 5
16. William Harrison, "A Description of England 1577–87", in *Tudor Economic Documents*, eds. R. H. Tawney and E. Power, (London 1951), III, pp. 68–70
17. S. Hindle, *The State and Social Change in Early Modern England,* (New York 2000)
18. D. Hirst, *The Representative of the People?* (Cambridge 1975), pp. 104–5
19. Sir Thomas Smith, *De Republica Anglorum*, ed. M. Dewar, (Cambridge 1982), p. 77
20. J. Lander, *Government and Community,* (London 1980), p. 42
21. B. Manning, *The English People and the English Revolution*, 2nd edition, (London 1991), pp. 7–8
22. K. Lindley, "London and Popular Freedom in the 1640s", in *Freedom and the English Revolution,* eds. R. C. Richardson and G. M. Ridden, (Manchester 1986), p. 124; W. Hunt, *The Puritan Moment: The Coming of Revolution in an English County,* (Cambridge, MA 1982), p. 289
23. Manning, *The English People and the English Revolution*, p. 262
24. N. Carlin, *The Causes of the English Civil War,* (London 1999), pp. 121, 133
25. S. Seyer, *Memoirs Historical and Topographical of Bristol,* (Bristol 1821), II, p. 314
26. D. Underdown, *Revel, Riot and Rebellion,* (Oxford 1985)
27. A. Everitt, "Farm Labourers", in *Agrarian History of England and Wales*, ed. J. Thirsk, (Cambridge 1967), IV, p. 463
28. A. Hughes, "Local History and the Origins of the Civil War", in *Conflict in Early Stuart England*, eds. A. Hughes and R. Cust, (London 1989), p. 242
29. A. Wood, "Beyond Post-Revisionism? The Civil War Allegiances of the Miners of the Derbyshire Peak Country", *HJ 40* (1997), pp. 28–33
30. J. Harrington, *Oceana*, ed. H Morley, (London 1887), p. 59
31. Hutchinson, *Memoirs of the Life of Colonel Hutchinson*, p. 100
32. T. Hobbes, *Behemoth*, ed. F. Tonnies, (London 1889), p. 4
33. Hutchinson, *Memoirs of the Life of Colonel Hutchinson*, p. 203
34. Hobbes, *Behemoth*, p. 2
35. John Corbet, "A True and Impartial Account of the Military Government of the City of Gloucester", in *A Collection of Scarce and Valuable Tracts,* ed. Sir Walter Scott, (London 1809), V, pp. 303–7
36. G. Winstanley, *The Law of Freedom in a Platform*, (London 1652), in *Winstanley: The Law of Freedom and Other Writings*, ed. C. Hill, (Cambridge 1983), p. 294
37. *A Brief Discourse on Tyrants and Tyranny,* (November 1642), BL E127, (45), p. 1
38. West Devon Record Office, Plymouth Corporation Archive, W48, f. 92
39. See above, Chapters 7 and 8
40. Hobbes, *Behemoth*, p. 4
41. Ibid, p. 2
42. Ibid, p. 126
43. Corbet, *A True and Impartial History of the Military Government of the City of Gloucester*, V, pp. 303–4, 307
44. Hobbes, *Behemoth*, p. 2
45. E. A. Andriette, *Devon and Exeter in the Civil War,* (Newton Abbot 1971), p. 123
46. Nottingham, Lincoln, Boston, Leicester, Northampton, Coventry, King's Lyn, Shrewsbury, Bury St, Edmonds, Worcester, Cambridge, Gloucester,

Oxford, St. Albans, Hertford, Bristol, Colnbrook, Rochford, Marlborough, Basingstoke, Salisbury, Taunton, Poole, Dorchester, Winchester, Bridport, Lyme Regis, Cranbrook, Ashford, Canterbury, Rochester, Twickenham, Southwark

Lords Journal, V, 147, 156, 193, 228–9, 233, 281, 300, 309–11, 312, 318, 323, 374

Lords Journal, II, 601, 629, 648, 677, 683, 716, 719, 723–4, 727–8, 733, 735, 737, 765, 777, 793

BL E114, (15), E116, (5). *HMC Portland*, I, pp. 49–50

47. A. Fletcher, *The Outbreak of the English Civil War,* (London 1981) p. 353
48. Ibid, p. 394
49. See above, p. 7
50. P. Withington, "Urban Citizens and the English Civil Wars", *The Oxford Handbook of the English Revolution,* (Oxford 2016), p. 313
51. Hobbes, *Behemoth,* p. 126
52. Ibid
53. Withington, "Urban Citizens and the English Civil Wars", p. 320
54. Ibid, p. 312
55. Ibid, pp. 314. 317
56. D. Sacks, "The Corporate Town in the English State", *Past and Present 110* (1986), pp. 69–105
57. C. V. Wedgwood, *The King's War,* (London 1958), p. 235
58. Seyer, *Memoirs Historical and Topographical of Bristol*, II, p. 314
59. M. Dobb, *Studies in the Development of Capitalism,* (London 1963)
60. R. Brenner, *Merchants and Revolution,* (London 1993), pp. 205, 222
61. See above, Chapters 6 and 7

14 Commercial, Political and Religious Connections in Parliament's West Nottinghamshire Heartland—"To Know a Law and Have a Certainty"[1]

The importance of the freedom of trade perspective as a motivating force was that it gathered all the main economic fields together behind one central aim. It was a defining purpose for the merchant-gentry alliance against impositions, as well as for the enclosing and commercialising yeoman farmers, as also for the ports and towns that served the extended and coordinated markets, and indeed for the industrialising regions. The latter should not be forgotten. The areas that had developed an industrial base were a crucial element in an increasingly integrated economic context. Their new fields of production enabled them to contribute to the processes of specialisation and exchange that comprised the dynamic of the interregional market. And in fact, like the substantial freeholders in the countryside and the merchants and traders in the market towns, the regions of intensified industrial and manufacturing activity displayed a tendency to favour the parliamentarian cause.

There have been many studies confirming that support for parliament was characteristic of areas with a substantial degree of industrial or manufacturing activity. Some have revealed this conclusion by accident, which has in a sense served to underline the connection. Thus, David Underdown's view of popular allegiance in Somerset and Dorset attempted to shift the emphasis towards religio-cultural preferences, but his evidence showed that the one clear association was between the parliamentary cause and the cloth-making areas.[2] John Gurney has recently affirmed the same for Surrey in a more straightforward fashion.[3] Clive Holmes highlighted the precocious development of trade and industry, and the associated spread of radical ideas, as the factors that made East Anglia a reliable base of parliamentarian support.[4] Ann Hughes found that in Warwickshire, "the old forest area, with an abundance of enterprising small landholders and industrial craftsmen was typical of the area in which parliament obtained support in 1642". She suggested that this inclination derived from the individualism "associated with industrial or wood pasture areas in Derbyshire, Durham and Warwickshire".[5] Jill Dias confirmed this assessment in respect of Derbyshire, noting that there was a correlation between regional economics and choice of sides, and that it was among the numerous independent and prosperous freeholders of the lead mining and sheep rearing districts that parliament found most support.[6]

There is an important truth in the idea that the growth of individualism and socio-economic independence played a part in the development of the parliamentary cause. But the actual form that this took as a motivating force has rarely been defined with certainty or clarity. Previous chapters have attempted to fill that need, showing that the individualist drive took shape above all in the demand for rights of consent, and freedom of trade. The context of the commercial centres and industrialising regions provides further confirmation. The general significance of the industrial areas was to unlock the particular, additional potential of their localities. By so doing they added to the range of bulk commodities on the market and made a crucial contribution to the processes of regional specialisation and exchange. For these purposes they required specific commercial conditions, perhaps to an even greater extent than the established merchants and farmers. The craftsmen and workers of an industrial or manufacturing area were seeking to maximise the special resources of their locale by developing new products. To do so, they needed to be free of arbitrary taxes and restraints.

West Nottinghamshire provides a particularly useful study in this respect, in part because it is not an obvious candidate. Its market town of Nottingham was not the most prominent kind of trading centre. It was not a seaport, and it was not a major regional exchange mart. Nor was the area a substantial base of cloth production. But Nottingham was nevertheless growing in economic significance, and by Elizabethan times was it was beginning to supplant Lincoln as the most important urban centre in the East Midlands. In that sense it was becoming the commercial capital of the region. The industrial and manufacturing activities of the town and its hinterland were not yet fully formed, but they were developing strongly enough to change the balance of the local economy, and to illustrate the general nature of commercial development. The character of West Nottinghamshire as an area of new economic potential makes it an especially good indicator of the generality of economic motivation in parliamentarian support.

The main industrial specialisation of West Nottinghamshire was coal. It was not yet being produced here on the same scale as in the principal mining region of northeast England, but it was at a sufficient level to enable the West Nottinghamshire economy to advance from "subsistence" to export mode. Specifically, by the beginning of the seventeenth century, there was an annual "coal for corn" exchange between the "country of Nottingham" and the specialist arable farming regions of Lincolnshire, and this seems to have removed the traditional requirement of organising an emergency supply of corn at a time of harvest shortage.[7] This illustrates the stage that the West Nottinghamshire economy had reached, and suggests a useful definition of what can be regarded as industrialisation in the sixteenth and seventeenth centuries. Charles Wilson provided a good outline of the typical dynamic involved, which had the recognisable effects of an industrial focus, but did not require the structure of urban factories. Craft production usually remained small scale by modern standards, and it was generally organised as rural cottage industry. But certain aspects of industrialisation were emerging. The putting-out system of manufacture did involve a significant widening of the division between capital and labour. And the context was differentiated most of all from what had gone before, because the concentration on producing particular favoured items for more distant markets was displacing the old patterns of self—sufficiency. "More or less specialised industries were growing up to provide services formally provided by the consumers themselves".[8] Thus, in the pages ahead, the essential definition of industrial development is taken to be a process of specialisation that changes the balance of a local economy to export mode.

J. U. Nef once went so far as to perceive an industrial revolution in the late sixteenth and early seventeenth centuries, largely on the basis of a phenomenal rise in the level of coal production.[9] He estimated, persuasively, that it increased fourteenfold between the mid-sixteenth century and the mid-seventeenth, making it for the first time a significant element in the nation's economy and an important factor in the export trade. The idea of an industrial revolution at this time is not as much of an overstatement as later historians have sometimes supposed. The development of coal mining was notable not just for its own sake, but also as a crucial feature of the defining context of specialisation and exchange. Mining was a perfect option for maximising the resources of an area not over endowed with rich farming land. Moreover, the exploitation of coal reserves had a capacity to coordinate and encourage other industrial activities—it was no accident that by-employments proliferated most readily in pastoral areas with a good supply of coal. And Charles Wilson sums up another aspect of symbiotic exchange between coal production and the vital domestic market: coal was "the factor in the economy of the early seventeenth century most favourable to expansion . . . a reciprocating action thus began between the emergent coal industry, especially in the northeast and midlands, and the growing aggregation of people in the towns, and certain industries that catered for them".[10] The "country of Nottingham" was a perfect example of coal-based industrialisation.

Unlike the Trent Valley that ran towards the east of the county, Western Nottinghamshire was not blessed with the most fertile soils for arable farming. There seems to have been enough viable pasture for sheep rearing, which was usually the best agrarian option in these circumstances. But the greatest potential for commercial expansion lay in the convenient coal reserves of the area. This distinctive provision reflected a geological divide. If a line were drawn the length of the county, starting in the north eastern corner, running along the eastern edge of Sherwood and the western edge of the vale of Trent, and finally slicing through the middle of Nottingham town, then to the west of that line lay the more ancient Palaeozoic rock formations, while to the east of it lay the much younger crust of the Neozoic. The line would mark the point at which the newer soils, which had been the essential foundation of the medieval agricultural economy, ran shallow, but where the earth offered up a more ancient geological level for further exploitation. Here the coal outcrop of the older rock formations found its way to the surface. This was in fact the centre of the English coalfield. Here the coal was most accessible and could be got with least expense.

J. U. Nef was very aware that there was a substantial development of coal production in the West Nottinghamshire area from the late sixteenth century. He estimated that coal output tripled over the course of the next century. References to coal production in the medieval period are very sparse, and at the beginning of the sixteenth century it had still not developed to a stage where it warranted mention as an export commodity. Nef was doubtless correct to assert that the coal industry only came into being as a significant and measurable factor at the end of the sixteenth century, but it developed quickly thereafter. Nef identified fourteen working pits at work in West Nottinghamshire in 1610.[11] R. S. Smith, in a more recent study, thought that Nef overestimated the level of activity. Smith noted that Huntingdon Beaumont's well-publicised ventures at Wollaton and Strelley came to an end around 1620, and assumed a downturn thereafter.[12] But this does not necessarily follow. Coal mining was a growing industry, which could be entered into with less preparation than traditional forms of manufacture, and it is very likely that less well-documented schemes would have followed the more obvious initial ventures. In fact there is good evidence, amplified ahead, that this was the case. The clearest information comes from the parliamentary records of the number of pits that were supplying coal to the garrison at Nottingham. Smith noted only four, not including Wollaton. But the parliamentarian accounts show that in the mid-1640s, the garrison was receiving coal from as many as twenty-five separate localities, including Wollaton.[13] It seems that there had been a substantial expansion of coal producing capacity in the decades before the Civil War. One carter, William James, was paid for delivering two hundred eighty loads of coal to the garrison between January 1644 and March 1645. In the same month, Christopher Hardy was paid for delivering one hundred forty loads.[14] These figures underline the level of production, and the distributive capabilities of the coal enterprise at this time. The substance of the local coal industry facilitated the garrisoning of Nottingham. But the town had long been, in its normal day-to-day functions, a crucial factor of the rise of coal mining, both as an outlet for export to other regions, and as a domestic and industrial market in itself. "He who goes to bed and has not a hod full of fuel, may the next morning in the shortest day in winter have coal brought to his door to dress his dinner with—a blessing that few towns of the kingdom may boast of".[15] By the 1630s the craft of "scuttlemaker" had been added to the trades of Nottingham.[16]

Coal production coordinated a context of consumerism and industrialisation. The Nottingham area also had two other particular examples of manufactures emerging as genuine industries. One was stocking knitting. This was to become a characteristic and important staple of Nottingham's manufacturing base in the long-term, and it is arguable that it took its most decisive step forward in the last decades of the sixteenth century. It was responding to the incentive of strong domestic demand, which is often the lead factor in industrial development. Stockings had become standard and fashionable items of attire for an increasingly broad and wealthy Elizabethan society. Industrial production was also encouraged by a contribution from the other classic determinant of industrial advance—the introduction of new technology. In 1590, William Lee, who lived just outside Nottingham at Woodborough, invented the stocking frame, the effect of which was to make hand knitting obsolete. The stocking frame was a machine with a separate needle for each loop, enabling a complete row of stitches to be made in one exercise. This superseded the traditional method of casting the loops one by one on a single needle. The frame could make six hundred stitches a minute, as against the average of one hundred produced by the best hand knitters. It was a genuine industrial invention, which amounted to a step change in productive potential. There seem at first to have been fears that this would tend to reduce rather than increase employment opportunities. But the responsive market society of Elizabethan times offered a general basis for expansion, and the frame had great advantages in terms of the logistics of manufacturing activity at the time, because it could engage labour in the most convenient form, where it was most readily available. It did not require a central source of power and could therefore be used conveniently in a system of cottage industry. In fact, the frame was perfectly suited to the process of "putting-out", whereby clothiers and entrepreneurs in towns such as Nottingham would hire out equipment to knitters in the surrounding countryside. Stocking knitting was at once transformed into a rural industry, and the frames came rapidly into common use during the first half of the seventeenth century. The net result seems to have been a substantial increase in output and productivity, which resulted in an expansion rather than a diminution of employment opportunities. There were estimated to be at least a hundred of Lee's frames at work in the countryside around Nottingham by the mid-seventeenth century.[17] This made it second only to London in the scale of stocking manufacture, and gave it more than twice the volume of its nearest provincial rival in the trade at Leicester. It has been said that the advance of stocking knitting was "almost as spectacular n its way as that of the New Draperies".[18] By the time of the Civil War there had been a transformation in the level of production, which had indeed turned the local stocking knitting enterprise into an industry. This was underlined when the Nottingham producers appealed to the Interregnum government for official establishment. "In the space of fifty years the art was so improved and the number of workmen became so great . . . for better regulating and keeping this valuable business from spreading abroad, petitioned Cromwell to make them a corporative body".[19] The note sums up what was at issue here—the maintenance of lucrative, expanding export trades in the context of an integrated exchange network.

The new status that Nottingham was acquiring as the principal economic centre in the East Midlands was due equally to another kind of specialised manufacture. This was the making of leather goods. By the mid-seventeenth century it has been said that Nottingham was already a real "leather town", again second only to London as the most substantial base of leather production in the kingdom. By the 1660s there were at least forty-seven tanneries stretching out from Nottingham along the banks of the river Leen as it came down from Sherwood. The concentration of leather making facilities seems to have caused some environmental offence by adding further to the stench and smoke in the town, but it carried the compensation of bringing a considerable amount of wealth to the area. Between 1580 and 1620, the proportion of leather workers in Nottingham was running at just over one third, which was, for instance, twice as high as the proportion in Leicester, which was itself regarded as having an unusually high percentage. As Clarkson has said, this was a clear indication that Nottingham was engaging in a national trade in the product, serving a general and urban market as well as the usual one of small farmers.[20] This was confirmed by the fact that the proportion of glove makers in Nottingham was unusually high, for it was in gloves that the main export demand was to be found. The expanding trade also involved another familiar aspect of industrialisation—a more pronounced division of labour. Extended market opportunities meant that it was often beneficial for merchants and employers to commission work in bulk orders. In fact, it seems that the leather industry was among those that experienced a greater degree of differentiation between capital and labour at this time. Like stocking knitting, leather crafts flourished as a cottage industry. "Economies of scale were encouraged by the introduction of the putting-out system into glove making".[21]

So the "country of Nottingham" boasted a series of substantial specialisations, in the production of coal at an industrial level, and the powerful advance of the trades of stocking knitting and glove-making. This involved certain adjustments towards a more capitalist form of the division of labour. But the most significant new requirements of the local enterprises related to a different aspect of liberal economics. These ventures depended above all on the capacity to maximise the return from previously unused resources. They were focusing on particular, new products for export, and this necessitated the freedom to operate without the burdens and obstacles of arbitrary exactions and restraints. They wanted a low-tax regime and relief from unaccountable impositions and interventions. They needed to know the expected market conditions, and to "have a certainty". In fact they required the policies of freedom of trade and consensual taxation that MPs had long sought to establish. Enhancing the power of parliament might even be expected to give the constituencies some influence in sustaining such a context. In this light it is not surprising to find that the area of West Nottinghamshire appears to have been sympathetic to the parliamentary cause,

The association between intensified commercial activity and parliamentarian support is clear both in terms of the identified personnel and the geographical correlation. The industrialising region of West Nottinghamshire comprised a distinctive combination of commercialised manufacturing and mining activities, occupying a compact corner of the county, and focused on the market centre of Nottingham. Various studies of Civil War allegiance have already been cited above, suggesting that the people of such localities tended to favour parliament. This was certainly the case in West Nottinghamshire. What is most easily known about the generality of parliamentarians is their place of origin, and a study of this shows that support for parliament was geographically concentrated, and it coincided closely with the industrial areas, and the commercial town of Nottingham.

This is illustrated in the maps ahead. The first shows the correlation in its most general and fundamental form as it related to the geology of the county. The line through the centre of the county marks the divide between the ancient Palaeozoic rocks with the coal measures to the west, and the younger Neozoic crusts bearing the fertile farming land to the east. The circle represents the area of manufacturing or industrial activities: that is to say, the forty-seven or more tanneries that stretched along the banks of the Leen running out of Nottingham; the rural glove-making speciality that they served; and the one hundred or more knitting frames that sustained the expansion of stocking knitting as a cottage industry in the countryside around the town. The shaded area is the coalfield, and the broken line encompasses the parishes of concentrated parliamentarian allegiance. The great majority of parliament's supporters lived here.

The distinctive concentration of parliamentarian support is underlined when seen in comparison with the distribution of other allegiances. More than two hundred and seventy individual parliamentarians have been found, and their localities are recorded on the second map. The large squares are Nottingham, which is represented by one hundred and thirty-nine names, and Hucknall, which sustained the Broxtow garrison, and is represented by twenty-eight names. The middling squares are Eastwood, Nuthall, Strelley, Newthorpe, Bilborough, and Cotgrave, each with between four and ten names, and the small squares mark places with three names or fewer. The individual parliamentarians are listed in the Appendix with some reference to their activities, and notes on the sources.

The most marked feature is obviously the concentration of parliamentarian support in and around Nottingham, in what is identified in these pages as the industrialising area of West Nottinghamshire. It is also noticeable that the highest density of parliamentary allegiance correlates quite closely with the coalmining district, as illustrated on the third map. This shows the working centres of coal production and supply, based on the twenty-five locations that were sending coal to the parliamentary garrison in the 1640s.[22] It will become clear that the association was not just a coincidence. The links between parliamentarian activism and the coalmining project were specific.

The fourth map locates one hundred and fifty-one Royalists.[23] While the parliamentarians were concentrated in the commercial area, the Royalists were evenly spread. One reason that fewer Royalists have been identified is that many in the Newark garrison came from Lincolnshire. Another reason is that the king's support seems to have been very top heavy. He relied on the allegiance of the greater gentry, whose estates were found throughout the county, and beyond. The large circle marks the Newark garrison with thirty-two names, the medium sized circles mark Nottingham with fourteen names, and Newstead and Southwell with six each. The small circles represent places with four names or fewer. Individual Royalists are listed in the Appendix.

The fifth map locates the notable Godly groups in the first half of the seventeenth century. It uses three sources: my study of parishes with a persistent record of lay non-conformity between 1604 and 1640; R. A. Marchant's list of Puritan ministries, which often concealed non-conformist practice; and the parishes that registered more than one in ten dissenters in the archdeaconry survey of 1676. The overall impression given by this map is of a wide distribution throughout the county—a spread that is more akin to the geographical shape of Royalist support than to that of the Parliamentarians. There are more radical Godly groups in the broad eastern half of the county than in the west. Parishes and sources are listed in the Appendix.

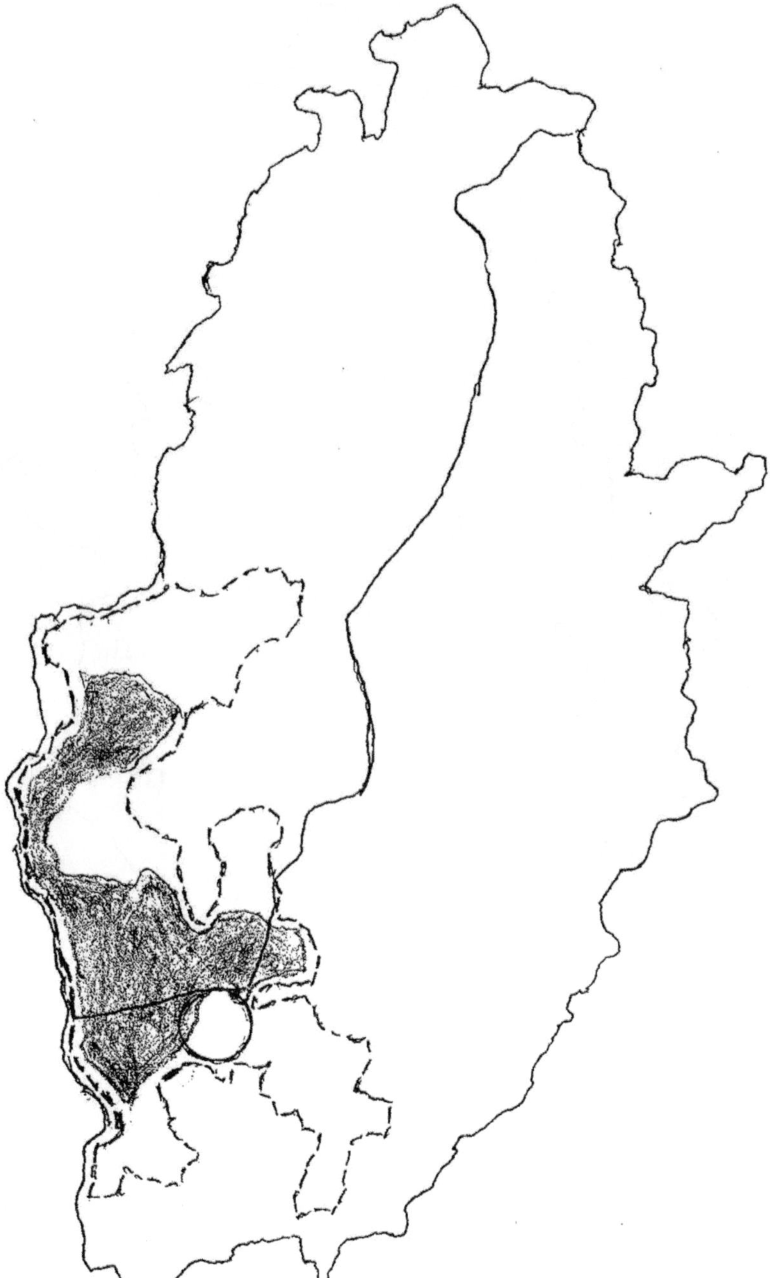

Figure 14.1 Geology and Industry in Early Seventeenth-century Nottinghamshire.
Source: Map by author.

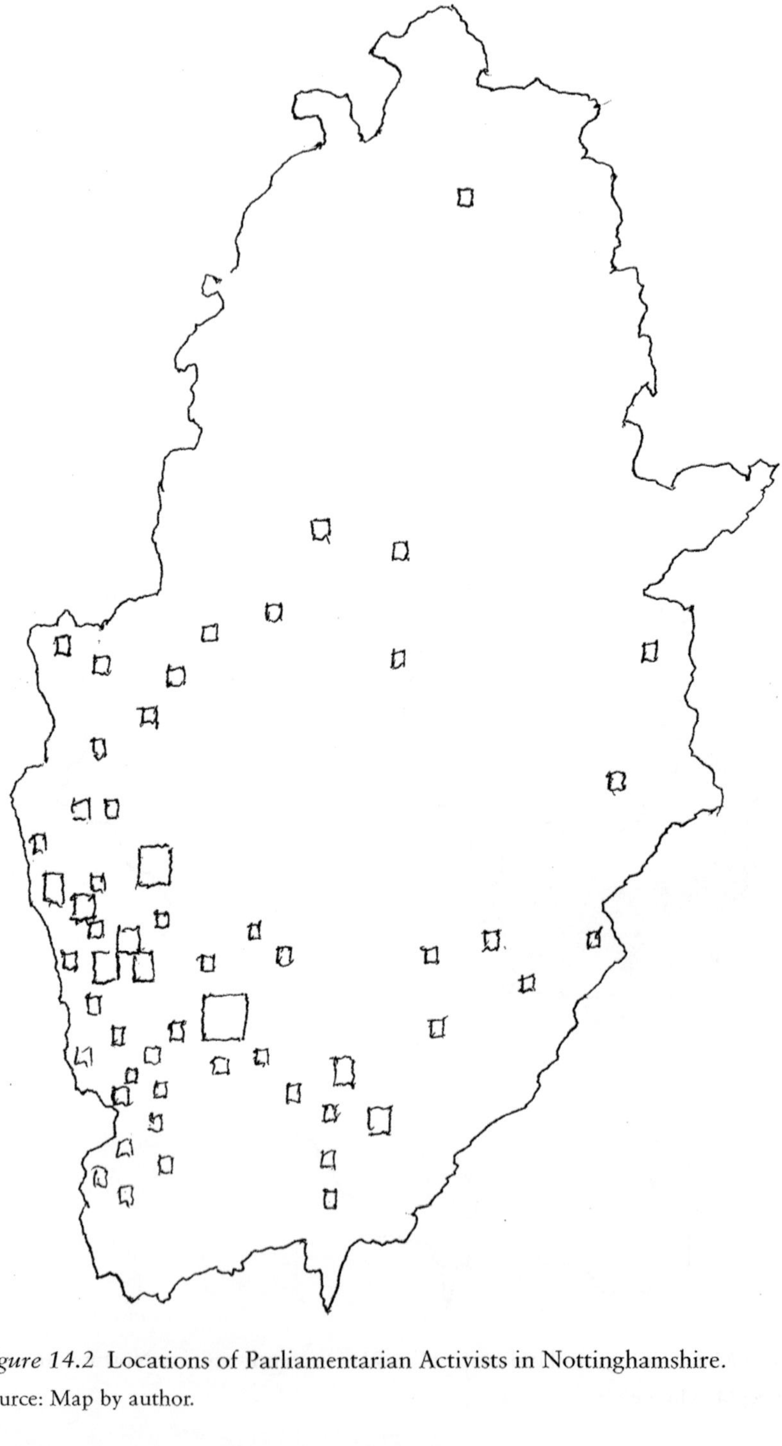

Figure 14.2 Locations of Parliamentarian Activists in Nottinghamshire.
Source: Map by author.

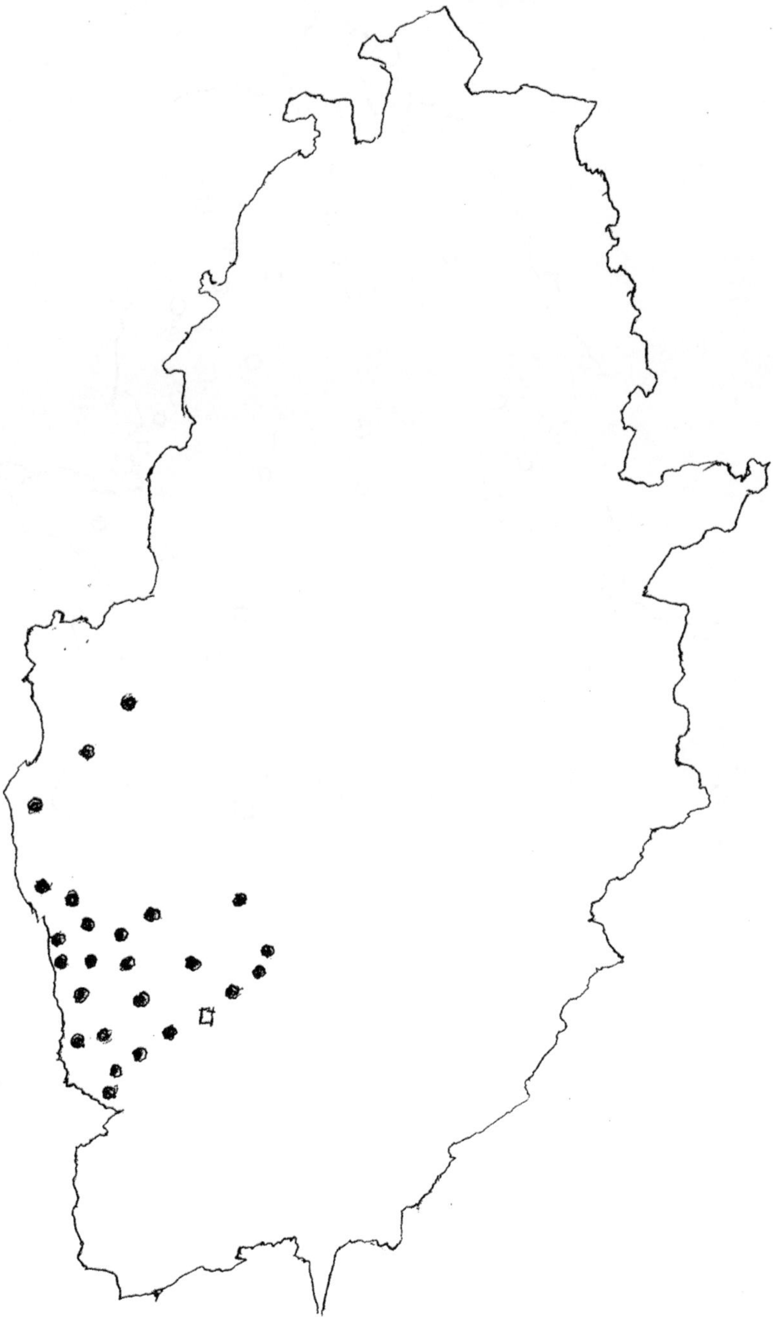

Figure 14.3 Centres of Coal Production in Early Seventeenth-century Nottinghamshire.
Source: Map by author.

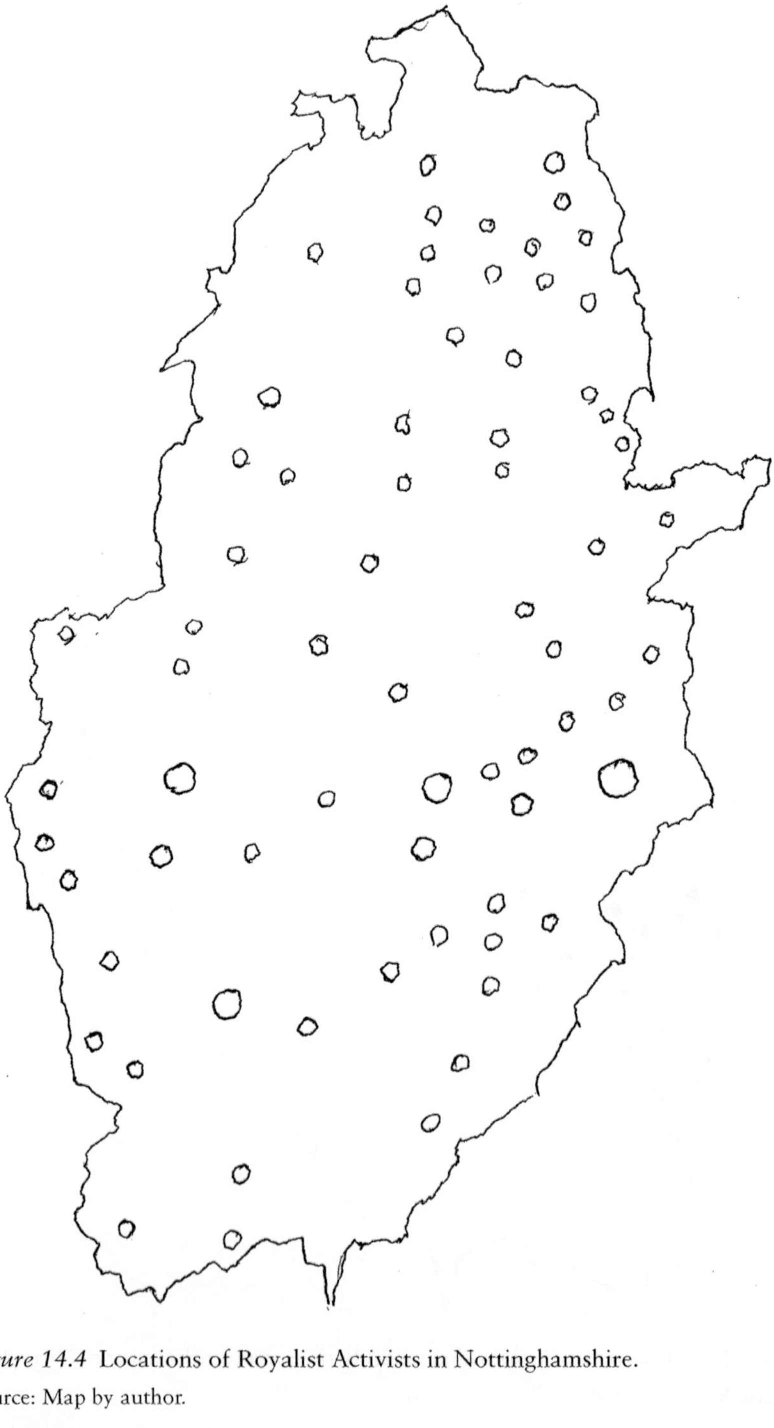

Figure 14.4 Locations of Royalist Activists in Nottinghamshire.
Source: Map by author.

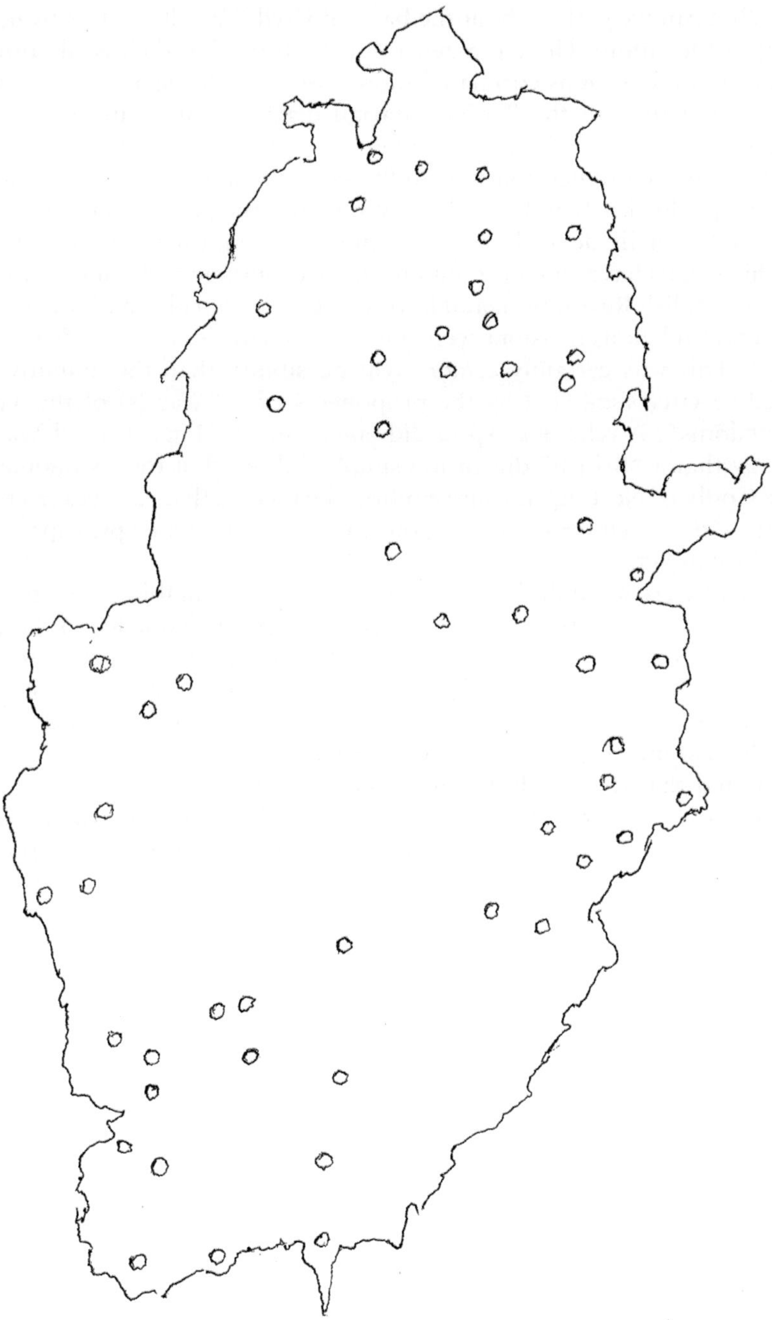

Figure 14.5 Locations of the Radical Godly in Seventeenth-century Nottinghamshire.

Source: Map by author.

What can we gather about the basis of Civil War allegiances from the maps of location? There is a general impression that the distribution of radical Godly groups correlated more closely with the area of Royalist support than with the Parliamentarian district. This is in one respect misleading, because there is a great deal of other evidence to suggest that in the national dimension the Godly tended towards Parliament. What the maps do clearly indicate, however, is that the parliamentarian cause was not actually defined by Godly aims. In recent times, many revisionist historians have sought to minimise the economic and political causes of the English Revolution, and have suggested as an alternative explanation that religious divisions were a primary factor in the Civil War struggle.[24] This was certainly a more real possibility than the unmotivated muddle later suggested by the proponents of a "War (s) of the Three Kingdoms". A religious aspect did enter into the English Civil War, in a way that a "British" dimension simply did not. But the testimonies of the Godly of Nottinghamshire confirm the picture that emerges from the maps—that even for them, religion was not the initial or principal issue of the conflict.

There were a handful of Godly groups with a notable public profile, and they were in the northeast sector, at Collingham, Kneesall, East Retford, Bawtry and Scrooby, the latter being a point of origin for the Pilgrim Fathers. These parishes were on the opposite side of the county to the area of parliamentary allegiance in the southwest, and only one of them seems to have produced a Parliamentarian. It might have been expected that these radical Puritan communities would have sent contingents to reinforce the garrison at Nottingham, as was true of areas nearer to the town, but there is no sign that this was done by the powerful Godly groups of the east. The only figure that might be regarded in that light was Henry Champion, who had connections with the Puritan parish of North Collingham on the eastern border. But he was also associated with Cotgrave, in the main parliamentarian area. He had lands there, and other prominent members of his troop also hailed from Cotgrave.

It seems that very few known Parliamentarians came from the main centres of radical non-conformity. There was, naturally enough, a significant and committed Godly element in Nottingham itself. But it was no greater that would have been expected as a function of the size and character of the town. Nottingham did not stand out in terms of Godliness in the county as a whole, either as regards the incidence of nonconformist practice, or the militant force of activity. For a long time the Puritan element in Nottingham were able to exercise their preferred scheme of worship without much inconvenience alongside the established systems. I have described in detail elsewhere the context in which, from the turn of the seventeenth century, the Godly groups in the town were able to carve out scope for dissenting practices within the somewhat lax pattern of authority created by the Elizabethan settlement of the church. First at the "great church" of St Mary's, then after 1615 at the smaller church of St Peter's, they found sympathetic ministries that offered the kind of active, independent-minded preaching that they desired, and also provided cover behind which they could evade prescribed physical rituals such as kneeling at communion.[25] In the later 1630s the Laudian regime exposed these avoidances by the simple expedient of systematically reinstating altar rails in all the churches, and imposing a strict enforcement of the rule that all communicants should kneel at them. This provoked an organised protest by the Godly group at St Peter's at Easter 1638, when forty-three of the congregation declined to leave their pews to take communion.[26] Most of the protesters were women, and there were no identifiable Parliamentarian supporters among them.[27] Of the fifteen men who took part in the protest, only two can be identified as Parliamentarians.

The perception that religious concerns were restricted to a minority, both in the parishes, and in the parliamentarian movement, is reinforced by the stated views of the local Godly themselves. To Henry Ireton the "chief subject of our contest" was "the public interest of the nation in relation to common right and freedom".[28] Religion was one of "the more particular or special interests that have occasionally fallen into the contest".[29] Ireton's overall view, as we shall see, was not inconsistent with the possibility suggested by the maps that parliamentarian allegiance had a distinctive economic dimension. He was in fact a leading proponent of what we might call the political-economic concept of the freedom of property and rights of consent.

One of the most prominent Parliamentarian families in the county, the Hutchinsons, were inclined towards Godliness, but they recognised, like Ireton, that religion was not the essential basis of the contest. They were gentry from the core Parliamentarian area just outside Nottingham, and John Hutchinson was to assume command of the parliamentary garrison there. But in 1642 as people took sides, his wife Lucy identified his motivation as political. He was "convinced in conscience of the rightness of the parliament's cause in point of civil right". Although he was aware of a threat to "the true Protestant religion, yet he did not think this so clear a ground for the war as the defence of the just English liberties".[30]

Henry Ireton was not quite in the ranks of the gentry, as Lucy Hutchinson could not resist remarking—he was rather from the broad base of parliamentarian support that she identified as "the able substantial freeholders", but he was nevertheless a close associate of her husband. Ireton also became involved with Cromwell, and in 1647 he stepped forward as the political spokesman for the New Model Army. As such he had a powerful influence on affairs in the later stages of the revolution. He is best known for his stern insistence on the rights of property in the Putney Debates. "All the main thing that I speak for is that I would have an eye to property".[31] He expected, correctly, that the Levellers too would do nothing intentionally to threaten property, for they were just as committed to the freedom of trade agenda as mainstream Parliamentarians. The assertion of absolute property rights was indeed a central parliamentarian purpose, and when Ireton came to define the political aims of the revolution it was to establish the position of the representative body as the natural guarantor of the freedom of property.

> The people of this kingdom must have this right at least, that they should not be concluded [but] by the Representative of those that had the interest of the kingdom . . . And from that way I shall know a law and have a certainty. Every man . . . that hath a freedom, he was capable of trading to get money, to get estates by; and therefore this man, I think, had a great deal of reason to build up such a foundation of interest in himself: that is, that the will of one man should not be a law, but that the law of this kingdom should be by a choice of persons to represent, and that choice to be made by the generality of the kingdom. Here was a right that induced men to fight.[32]

Godliness was clearly not the initial or principal consideration. Religion was just one of the "other more particular or special interests" that had "occasionally fallen into the contest on each part". And even then this occasional, special interest had a distinctly political aspect. What the Godly hoped to achieve for their own purposes was "freedom and enlargement to the Gospel for the increasing and spreading of light amongst men, to take away those corrupted forms of an outside religion and church government . . . by means whereof snares and chains were laid upon conscientious and zealous men, and the generality of people held in darkness, superstition, and a blind reverence of persons and outward things, fit for popery and slavery".[33]

Ireton and his family provide a good illustration of the way that this defining concept developed through the processes and necessities of non-conformist practice in Nottinghamshire in the decades before the Civil War. Lay non-conformity became a significant factor in the church court records after 1605, when the Puritans had hoped for some relaxation of the rules on surviving ceremonial, but King James and his new Archbishop Richard Bancroft determined instead on a strict enforcement. The order went out, with the king's personal blessing, that any clergyman who refused to conform should be expelled. James's apologists describe this drive for conformity as a "temporary aberration".[34] It is true that only about 1% of clergy refused to subscribe, including four in Nottinghamshire, in the northern parishes of Headon, Babworth, Bawtry and Worksop, but this was just the surface flurry of the disruption caused. A crucial but little remarked aspect of Bancroft's crackdown was a review of preaching licences between 1604 and 1606. This was a severe frustration to the Godly groups who did not regard licences as the most important qualification for preaching. In fact, it was the attack on independent preaching activity that produced the initial burst of citations for sermon gadding and related practices that were dealt with by the Nottinghamshire Archdeaconry courts in 1605. There were seventeen people from five different parishes cited—the largest number in any single year. And Henry Ireton's parents were regularly summonsed for the offences of sermon gadding and not kneeling at communion from 1609 onwards.[35]

Many modern historians have sought to diminish the Puritan commitment to preaching on the basis that this was an ambition shared by the church as a whole. A recent thesis takes this view of consensus, and suggests that it was only the Laudian attempt in the 1630s to demote preaching in favour of ceremonial that provoked the Godly to dissent.[36] But the court figures show that this was simply not the case. From 1605 to 1610 there were 40 citations for offences of sermon gadding or unlicensed preaching, the same number as in the whole decade from 1630 to 1640. In the late 1620s, some years before the Laudian drive had begun, Samuel Harsnett, a veteran scourge of the Godly in the area, conducted a major purge of those who were sermon gadding to St Peter's from parishes around Nottingham.[37]

The Puritan commitment to preaching was always non-conformist, simply because they were assuming the right to decide for themselves what kind of preaching they desired, and to get it they were prepared to break the rules of the church and seek the required service independently, outside their parish, whenever they thought it necessary or appropriate. In effect, they were asserting a right to the exercise of free and direct individual consent to scripture as the essential requirement of the faith. This led them to act very frequently beyond the rules of the church, in pursuit of the desired illumination. It also meant that they were taking it upon themselves to make the necessary judgement. The further implication was that the traditional requirement to follow the established order was no longer a priority, and might even become dispensable.

The second pillar of non-conformist practice gave the same prominence to intellectual initiative, but from the other side of the coin. Along with the necessary exercise of sermon gadding, the other imperative of the Godly scheme of worship was the need to avoid kneeling at communion. The ritual of kneeling at communion was the most explicit manifestation of "bodily" worship that had survived from the medieval Church and been retained by the Church of England as established. It was therefore the rule that the Godly sought most avidly to evade. It was not just an irksome reminder of a ceremonial system that they believed should be wholly rejected—it was an actual contradiction of the crucial principle that the Godly now embraced, that faith came through express individual consent to the words of the Bible. The process of kneeling was what Ireton meant by "a blind reverence of persons and outward things, fit for popery and slavery".[38] He and his mother were summonsed before the church courts in 1636, for refusing to come up to the rail to take communion kneeling.[39]

Again, modern historians have contrived to leave the impression that the offence of not-kneeling was a new kind of non-conformity provoked into existence by the Laudian reinstatement of ceremony and ritual in the 1630s.[40] This misrepresents both the character and the chronology of non-conformist practice. In fact, Ireton and his family were among the many Godly summonsed by the Nottinghamshire church courts for the offence of not-kneeling from as early as 1605, and regularly thereafter. Along with sermon gadding, not-kneeling was the most substantial and persistent non-conformist misdemeanour recorded throughout the decades from 1605 to 1640. There was no great change in incidence over the course of the period. There were eighteen citations for not-kneeling between 1605 and 1617 and fourteen between 1630 and 1642. In terms of the overall volume of dissenting worship it should be remembered that the court appearances represent the occasions when the cover of the Godly was blown. There were undoubtedly many other parishes where, right from the beginning of the period, the cooperation of a sympathetic minister enabled them to maintain their non-conformist practices unchallenged. The most general subterfuge was to allow them to take communion in their pews, where their posture was not open to view. This had long been the habit of the Godly protesters at St Peter's, Nottingham.[41] Another ploy was to raise the height of the pews, to further obscure the view. When the Laudian inspectors reached the churches of South Leverton and Gringley-on-the-Hill, in the northern sector of the county, they found that some of the pews had been "topped with fir boards, higher than they anciently were, by which means it cannot appear whether the people sit or kneel at time of divine service".[42] These were the camouflages behind which the Godly had sustained their own scheme of worship for many decades. In the assessment of one of Laud's agents, it had been going on for half a century. Laud's simple expedient of enforcing the rule of kneeling at the altar rails did not create a new non-conformist offence it exposed a very old one.

So the Godly rejected "outward" religion, and placed a sometimes almost exclusive emphasis on the need for free individual comprehension and acceptance of the teachings of the Bible. There has, however, been a recent tendency to downplay the radical force of this by stressing the significance of the idea of predestination in the Puritan scheme of worship. Such suggestions are often based on a simplistic reading of R. T. Kendall's study of the Calvinist concept of assured salvation.[43] Some historians have been happy to suppose that the process therefore involved little more than a passive belief on the part of the Godly.[44] But in truth, Kendall suggested a much more active procedure. The sense of election was neither automatic nor fixed—it had to be established and maintained, and the method by which this was achieved was far from passive. Kendall quoted Arthur Hildersham, a radical Puritan minister who preached in southwest Nottinghamshire, and was associated with the Ireton family. He said that the Saint had to "prove by the Word that Christ died for him". This necessitated an intense effort of individual analysis and perception, to demonstrate "a willingness to obey God in all his commands". The vital requirement then, was a specific, personal knowledge of the Bible, for salvation was based, said Hildersham, on "the assent and credit that the mind giveth to the Gospel".[45] It was a concept that naturally entailed the assumption of an individual right to determine when that level of understanding had been attained. It was the prioritising of the exercise of private judgment and the overriding need for explicit consent to the Bible that made the Godly a non-conformist element within the English Church.

Thus the main imperatives of Godly non-conformity in Nottinghamshire were to avoid a "bodily" or outward religion, and insist on a right of intellectual consent in their faith. This meant that their relationship with, and within the Parliamentarian movement was a complex affair. It was not about simple theological preferences. It was more concerned with maintaining a certain scope for individuals to establish their own balance of worship. This was what Winstanley observed as the third of the active freedoms sought. After freedom of trade came, the "freedom to have ministers to preach, and for people to hear whom they will, without being restrained or compelled from or to any form of worship".[46] Puritans and parliamentarians had a common commitment to the principles of consent. In consequence, when the Godly favoured parliament, it was usually for the assertion of the political concept of representative rights. As they made clear on their own account, the Nottinghamshire Godly supported parliament for political reasons. Moreover, the particular Godly purposes that emerged in the course of the struggle also tended to be political in character—it came to involve the issue of liberty of conscience.

So Godliness and the Parliamentarian movement occupied the same psychological territory. In Ireton's system of beliefs, the rejection of a bodily religion or the "blind reverence of persons and outward things" was on a par with the insistence that "one man's will should not be a law", and the principle that property was sacrosanct and not to be taken arbitrarily. All these positions rested ultimately on the determination not to be "concluded" except by free, individual consent. This was a mindset that gave the Godly a natural inclination towards parliament. By return, it gave parliamentarians in general a degree of sympathy with the radical Godly in the face of the Laudian attempt to proscribe their independent practices. But it also underlines the fact that the parliamentary cause was essentially secular. Henry Ireton believed as strongly in the right of consent to the making of law, as in the right of consent to the faith. The parliamentarian inclinations of the Godly underline the fact that the original and substantial basis of the parliamentary challenge to the crown was the advancement of rights of consent in the political and economic sphere.

We return then, to Ireton's succinct summary of the politico-commercial basis of parliamentarian motivation: "to know a law and have a certainty", and this brings us back to the most pronounced feature of the maps of allegiance—that is to say, the concentration of parliamentarian support in the commercialising region around Nottingham, and especially just to the northwest of the town. The most specific contemporary commentaries on the socio-economic composition of the parliamentary side also come from within that area. Lucy Hutchinson, who lived a few miles outside Nottingham, provided one of the best-known descriptions. "Most of the middle sort, the able substantial freeholders, and the other commons, who had not their dependence on the malignant nobility and gentry, adhered to the parliament".[47] It was not an impressionistic judgement. She had precise evidence on which to base her conclusions. In the spring of 1642, Nottingham produced a parliamentarian petition, which urged the king to refer himself to his parliament, and was carried to Charles at York by Lucy's husband John. It was said to contain the names of four thousand five hundred knights, gentlemen, freeholders, and the mayor, aldermen and other inhabitants of Nottingham.[48] This assessment of the position of the middle sort of people was confirmed a decade later by another figure who came from just outside the town, Edmund Whalley. As with Ireton, his service was done mainly in the national arena, but he returned to the county in the 1650s as a Major General. In 1655 he wrote to Cromwell to advise that the scope for punitive taxation was limited, "the middling-sort of men being almost all for the parliament, or neuters".[49] A revealing aspect of these views is that both Hutchinson and Whalley appear to be talking about "most" of the middle sort, not just a minority that happened to be parliamentarian but a class that tended generally in that direction. It is equally clear that they noted no significant royalist support among the middle sort. The idea of a special relationship between parliament and the middle sort has sometimes been challenged on the facile basis that there were middle sort of people on both sides. This is hardly surprising, but it does not alter the plain fact that a significant majority of the middle sort favoured parliament. This can indeed be shown by a comparison of the two allegiances in the Nottinghamshire subsidy rolls.

Royalists		*Parliamentarians*	
Sir Gervase Clifton	40		
Robert Burton	30		
George Lascells	20		
Thos Williamson	20		
Thomas Somers	20	Sir Thomas Hutchinson	20
Timothy Pusey	15		
Sir Roger Cooper	15		
Robert Sutton	15		
Robert Mellish	12		
Percival Willoughby	10		
John Burnall	10		
Richard Hacker	10	Sir Francis Molyneax	10
Sir John Byron	10	Richard Reynes	10
Gilbert Neville	10	Lady Grantham	8
William Staunton	10	Francis Thornaugh	6
Anthony Eyre	10	Gervase Pigott	6
Sir Matthew Palmer	8	Thomas Linley	5
Lord Chaworth	7	Edward Ayscough	5
Sir John Digby	5	Gilbert Millington	5
John Wood	4	Francis Hacker	4
Robert Butler	3	John Wildman	3
		Francis Heape	3
		Richard Pendock	3
		Thomas Jalland	3
		Thomas Medlum	3
		George Flower	3
		Gilbert White	3
		Henry Smith	3
		Edward Roberts	3
		John Jaques	3
		William Howett	3
		John Collishaw	3
		Nicholas Charlton	3
		Richard Toll	3
		Joseph Widmerpool	2
		John Richards	2
		Richard Brough	2
		Robert Holford	2
		Richard Brooks	2
		John Scrimshaw	1
		Luke Dolphin	1

Thus, in the subsidy rolls of 1628 and 1641 are found the names of twenty-one known Royalists and thirty-one known Parliamentarians.[50] The subsidy rolls are often regarded as an unreliable measure of wealth because the assessment was under the control of the county gentry themselves. But what is required in our case is a guide to relative social positions, and the gentry tended to be punctilious in such matters. The levels indicated can therefore be taken as a good reflection of respective standing in the locality. The diagram shows a very marked differentiation in the overall status of the two groups. In general terms, on the basis of what is known about the individuals, it appears that a rating of seven or above represents the county gentry. One obvious feature is that the great majority of the Royalists are at a level of ten or above, and this can probably be termed the upper gentry bracket. The other distinctive feature is that the great majority of the Parliamentarians are rated at two or three, the typical mark for the yeomanry and lesser gentry. Parliament did have some supporters among the middle or upper gentry, and they often made a particularly useful contribution. Sir Thomas Hutchinson was MP for the county, and had led the popular party in taking a stand against arbitrary taxation in the 1620s. The Hutchinsons and the Thornaughs raised troops in the locality. The Earl of Kingston had divided loyalties, but his son William Pierrepont was a leading parliamentarian politician in the national arena throughout the conflict, though he does not appear in the subsidy roll. Overall, however, the comparison conveys the clear message that the Royalist cause depended overwhelmingly on the upper gentry, with little commitment from the social ranks below, while the Parliamentary cause rested distinctively on the broad support of the middle sort. The contrast also gives an indication of why it was the parliamentary side that was able to develop a concentration of support in one region. The Royalist connections were looser and more dispersed, whereas the Parliamentarians, working on a wider socio-economic base, were able to establish an integrated network throughout a particular area.

There was an early demonstration of the coordinated strength that the region could muster. In August 1642, a large enough number of the parliamentarian-inclined middle sort of West Nottinghamshire were able to combine to prevent the Royalist gentry from carrying off Nottingham's munitions. This was no mean feat, because the Royalist forces, stiffened as they were by the warlike and fiercely loyal Byron clan, all professional soldiers, were not easy to deflect. Nevertheless, "the country of Nottingham came in multitudes, and lately prevented Lord Newark, the Lord Lieutenant, the sheriff and the Byrons from taking any part of their magazines, and so they were fain with their troop of horse to quit the place".[51] The phenomenon of the "country" coming "in multitudes" to support the town is a sign not just of the breadth of support in the area, but also of the common ground that existed between the yeoman farmers, the industrialising region, and the commercial interest.

Despite this discouragement, and a comparably cold reception in other Midland towns like Warwick and Coventry, Charles decided to set up his standard at Nottingham. Some of his advisers recommended York in preference, but as Alfred Wood suggested, it is likely that Charles saw Nottingham as a good strategic central point. To the north and west were areas from which he did not expect substantial opposition. To the south and east was the area that he would in effect have to re-conquer.[52] Wood saw this as reflecting a general geographical distinction in Civil War allegiance. "Though there were adherents to both sides in every shire, it is broadly true to say that the war was one between the north-western and the south eastern halves of England".[53] Some historians have denied that this represented a contrast in economic levels, and have reasonably objected to the idea that the northwest was "backward". But the distinction encapsulates an important reality. The principal exceptions to the overall line of division were the commercial towns and areas that sustained themselves as parliamentarian strongholds in the royalist north and west throughout the war. This was in itself a function of the economic substance of these parliamentary localities, and the positive commitment that they displayed to the cause. The south and east appeared as mainly parliamentarian because it was there that the administrative and marketing links were widest and deepest, revolving around the greatest commercial centre of all—the capital city of London.

Charles's decision also reflected the fact that Nottingham was on a geological border, as already described. Behind him were the more ancient and hillier landscapes of the Palaeozoic north and west. There in general terms the land was relatively wild and open, and unlikely to carry a coordinated challenge to the traditional powers of the crown. Physically, he was choosing the high ground. To the north of Nottingham ran a Carboniferous limestone ridge. This was in effect the southern tip of the Pennines, and it culminated in the great river cliff on the top of which Nottingham castle was built. This may have seemed to Charles an ideal vantage point from which to look out over those parts of his kingdom that had shown themselves to be disloyal.

The king would, however, have been less conscious of the fact that from that same Carboniferous limestone ridge, the coal measures had originally swept down, and that they now formed the basis of the coordinated economic strength of Nottingham town and its western hinterland. This did much to give the area the inclination and ability to hold Nottingham for parliament throughout the conflict, in the face of what appeared to be the overwhelming weight of traditional military forces in the county. The king, who still saw the world very much in terms of personal and hierarchical authority, could scarcely have comprehended the kind of independent force that was emerging in areas like West Nottinghamshire. He would, however, have known that in the county in general he could depend on the armed loyalty of many of the upper gentry. He would have been fully aware of the active, warlike presence of such as the Byron brothers, and he would have assumed that in the light of this, the time-honoured feudal concept of the mobilisation of a "power" around the royal banner would take effect.

Charles was soon disabused. When he tried to set up his standard at Nottingham castle on 22 August 1642, he was bitterly disappointed by the lack of "resort" to his cause. He expected to assemble the infantry force that was the necessary basis of an army, but none materialised. The only sign of positive allegiance was displayed on the parliamentary side. When, on 30 August, the people of Nottingham and its surrounding country finally came to attend their monarch, it was to present him with another petition recommending that he "return to his parliament". By mid-September, the king had left Nottingham, where, according to his principal adviser Edward Hyde, "he had received so many mortifications".[54] Charles was learning the hard way that especially in and around the towns and commercial centres, there were now middle sort groupings that were quite capable of mounting an effective resistance to the traditional feudal forces.

Nottingham was one of a large number of important market towns noted as having raised a volunteer militia for parliament in the summer of 1642, when the two sides had concluded that it was necessary to arm.[55] The crucial thing to be aware of, however, is that the process of mobilisation was a coordinated effort between the town and its "country". Since they were not entirely lacking in support among the upper gentry, the Nottinghamshire Parliamentarians were able to find three colonels from elite county families—the Thornaughs, the Hutchinsons, and the Pierreponts. Joseph Widmerpool was another from an ancient gentry line who raised a troop. The estates of all of them were close to Nottingham. Several of the citizens of Nottingham are also known to have taken it upon themselves to raise troops. So did some of the lesser gentry who resided near the town, and became prominent in the cause nationally, like Edmund Whalley and Henry Ireton. Some of their soldiers came from Nottingham itself. For instance, Ireton's cornet, Samuel Clarke, who did much of the recruiting for the troop, was a resident of the town.[56]

A particularly interesting example of a substantial force gathered from the middle sort in the country outside the town is the troop of horse raised by Charles White. He recruited from the coalmining districts just to the north and west of Nottingham, and his troop was largely concerned with patrolling that area. His family was from Greasley, on the western edge of the county where it bordered Derbyshire, and he was a good example of a rising yeoman. The family appear to have made their money as sheep farmers. Sheep, it seems, were the most viable basis for successful farming on the limited soils of West Nottinghamshire. They could make the best use of dry, rough land, and they were invaluable not only as the producers of lucrative wool, but also because the folding of sheep was the necessary requirement for enriching the soil. White had an enterprising, rather than a glittering background, and much as Lucy Hutchinson appreciated the support of the middle sort, she was scathing about his social origins and pretensions, and suggested that he had gained influence in his neighbourhood by insinuating himself among the "underling gentry", and courting "the common people". This testified to the breadth of his support, and Mrs. Hutchinson clearly resented the fact that White's mobilising capacities rivalled those of her husband. In fact, White seems to have been among the first to get a troop of horse into the field: "who armed and mounted themselves out of devotion to the parliament's cause, and being of his neighbourhood, marched forth in his conduct".[57] A troop might have numbered as many as fifty, which would have been a considerable achievement for a mere yeoman. But the phrase "underling gentry" is revealing, because the line between the yeomanry and the gentry was fluid, and one of the features of the period was the frequency with which it was crossed. White was certainly finding support among those who were recorded in the subsidy lists at the level of yeoman or lesser gentry. One of his dragoons, Thomas Medlum, was a yeoman of Bulwell. Another of White's neighbours and associates was Gilbert Millington, who was local to Greasley, and was from the class that Lucy Hutchinson belittled as the "underling gentry". Millington sat on the committee in Nottingham, but spent much time in London. He became a regicide, and a republican, though some thought that his position owed more to avarice than principle.

All these men came from the coalfield district. The particular force of parliamentarian allegiance in the region is further shown by the attempt to garrison the manor house at Broxtow, on the northwest flank of the coalmining area. This was no doubt intended to put a substantial barrier between the county royalists and the coalfield, as seemed both desirable and feasible. Charles White's troop was to the fore in the initiative. One of the tasks of his dragoon Thomas Medlum was to gather supplies for Broxtow. His accounts list more than fifty names of the middle sort from the villages in the coalmining area. They were often known supporters, who were now contributing money or provisions to sustain the garrison. The fact that there are also entries itemising collective contributions from the "inhabitants" of more than fifteen of the villages, seems to indicate that the parliamentary cause was also finding support among the poorer classes in the area, as does White's "courting" of the "common people".[58] The parliamentarians appear to have felt that, given the normal balance of socio-economic power in West Nottinghamshire, they could effectively seal off the region from royalist incursions. At the same time, they took steps to garrison another nearby industrial centre of Wollaton, which was on the southern flank of the coalfield. The approach of the main royalist field army under the Duke of Newcastle seems to have obliged the parliamentarians to withdraw all their forces at least temporarily into Nottingham. But the fact that they felt it possible and worthwhile to garrison these places testifies again to the strength and support that parliament gained from the coalmining district.

The connection was very clear in the maps showing the distribution of allegiance. Royalist and Godly groupings were widely distributed across the county, with something of a bias towards the eastern side. Parliamentarian support was, by contrast, almost exclusively focused in the southwest sector, showing a strong pattern of association between parliamentarian supporters, the industrialising area of the coalfields, and the commercial centre of the town. This was the most instructive and, in a sense, conclusive feature of the comparative charts. The generalised incidence of Royalists and Puritans underlines by contrast the distinctive correlation between parliamentarian places of residence and the commercialising area of the south-west. This was so specific that it can be taken as revealing the most substantial basis of support for parliament.

We may feel that the distinction is so clear that there is no need to look any further for the efficient foundation of the parliamentary cause. But there is nevertheless much more that can be said about the relationship between parliamentarian support and the commercialising district. The significance of the coal industry can be brought into closer focus. Individual parliamentarians can be seen participating in various respects of the coal mining enterprise. Moreover, the paramount importance of the mining ventures and their profits as a motivating and galvanising force can be demonstrated. It is possible not only to show that the connection existed, but also to indicate why.

Charles Wilson pinpointed the importance of coal as the coordinating link in a consumerist, commercialising development. It was "the factor in the economy of the early seventeenth century most favourable to expansion . . . a reciprocating action thus began between the emergent coal industry, especially in the northeast and the Midlands, and the growing aggregation of people in towns and certain industries that catered for them".[59] His assessment of where the biggest financial gain was made is particularly interesting. It was not, he thought, the great landowners with the ultimate mining rights who benefited most. "This was the age of the salesman, the middleman, the merchant, the entrepreneur. Urbanisation multiplied his opportunities. A large part of his skill lay in spreading his interests and risks".[60] This was indeed the case. Many of the "middle sort" in West Nottinghamshire seem to have been "middlemen" of some kind, servicing the coal trade, and they had an attendant need for maximum commercial freedom. It should, however, be added that although it may be true that the original families did not gain the most, yet the expansion of the coal mines offered great opportunities for rising landowners in the area.

An earlier chapter spoke of Nicholas Charlton, as an example of the rising yeomen who were so characteristic of the time, and whose commercial interests were changing the balance of land use, and the patterns of work and occupation. It can now be added that he was a staunch Parliamentarian. He was a sheep farmer from Chilwell, which was a few miles southwest of Nottingham town. He was no doubt a representative figure of what Lucy Hutchinson called the "able, substantial freeholders". In fact he was very substantial indeed. He donated heavily to the cause, and he was a leading and regular presence on the parliamentary committee in Nottingham throughout the Civil War period. He was associated with the Ireton family who lived at Attenborough, not far away. Chilwell was itself a coalmining village, but Charlton's acquisitive ambitions were focused on a mining area just to the north of Chilwell, on the border between Nottinghamshire and Derbyshire. It often appears to have been the accumulating difficulties of an older elite family that gave affluent yeomen like Charlton the chance to extend their commercial interests and take their fortunes up to another level. In this case, the potential for investment was around the village of Heanor, where there appeared to be broad scope, but the current management and tenure of the mining land was insecure. Charlton was able to advance and then exploit a series of loans and mortgages, and by 1642 he had acquired rights to "all the coals and mines of coal being on or under the moors, wastes and common grounds . . . in Heanor, Langley, Micklehay, Loscoe and Codnor" from "Derby Common . . . and so over Loscoe Common, and onto Codnor Field".[61] The profits propelled Charlton into the ranks of the gentry.

Charlton's leases give a particularly good indication of the scale of the coalmining enterprise in the area, and the industrial substance that did much to sustain the parliamentarian cause both in terms of motivation and resources. The distribution of the coal entailed a new dimension in transport facilities, and special arrangements had to be made. So the leases provided "a half share of all the ways, passages, privileges and liberties for carrying the coal away".[62] The most striking feature, however, was a specified right to create what amounted to a mining village on the commons. Charlton was authorised to

> build cottages and to take the grounds for this, and to take grounds for gardens for them, in any place convenient in the same woods, wastes and commons, and hold and keep them forever for the colliers or other workmen to be employed about the getting of the coals, or upon the premises, or any other work about the same.[63]

The provisions allocated at Heanor give a powerful sense of the dominating physical significance of the coalmining enterprises, and the exceptional level of commercial production that this implied.

Another particularly interesting location in this respect is the village of Strelley, which is about three miles west of Nottingham. It was one of the earliest mining centres to become prominent at the beginning of the seventeenth century. The context of Strelley has already been mentioned as an example of how the increasing substance of industrial activity was contributing to the early breakup of the common field system. It is described again now as a powerful reflection of the force of the coal mining enterprise and its significance in the parliamentary movement—in military provision, financial backing, and personnel. It also provides an indication of exactly how and why the various elements of the coalmining interests might have favoured the parliamentary cause. Strelley contributed eight known parliamentarians to our chart. One of them was in the process of acquiring overall control of the mining operation in the village.

Strelley is particularly useful to the historian because the village still exists today on much the same scale and in much the same shape as it was in the mid-seventeenth century. In fact, some of the mining sites remain visible. Their survival has depended on escaping not only the advancing concrete tide of the city, but also the more subtle destructive force of the plough. In one of the few fields that have remained unploughed over the ages, the markings of some of the seventeenth-century coal pits can still be seen. They take the form of mounds made by the spoil from "bell-pits", which may be regarded as the first significant form of coal extraction. The mounds are typically about ten yards wide, and about three feet above the general level of the ground, though they are sunken in the middle, where the pit has been back-filled. They are referred to as bell-pits because they were widened into a bell shape as they were dug, sometimes to a depth of forty feet.

The known locations of bell-pits in Strelley are shown on the map ahead. Surviving evidence exists of sixteen mines, either as visual traces or recollected sites. The solid black circles are the bell-pit remains that are still visible in the unploughed field today. The open black circles in the field to the east mark other bell-pit mounds that are known to have existed before they were levelled by recent ploughing.[64] It was clearly a heavy concentration of pits, occupying a large portion of the village. Not all of them would have been in constant production throughout the period. On the other hand, it is probable that there were many more adjacent pits, in fields that have been continually ploughed, and of which there is no specific memory. There are also surviving traces of raised tracks across the fields of Strelley and beyond, built for the easier transportation of the coal. They are shown on the map by broken double lines. In one direction they ran towards Wollaton and the Trent. This was in fact another industrial invention of the time—the first known railed track-ways to be constructed.[65] In the other direction is a less familiar and more interesting route. This ran parallel with Strelley village street, and thence towards Awsworth, Cossall and Kimberley—all centres of coal production for the parliamentary garrison. It was an extended network of connections that indicates how this area of West Nottinghamshire had become in effect an industrial region.

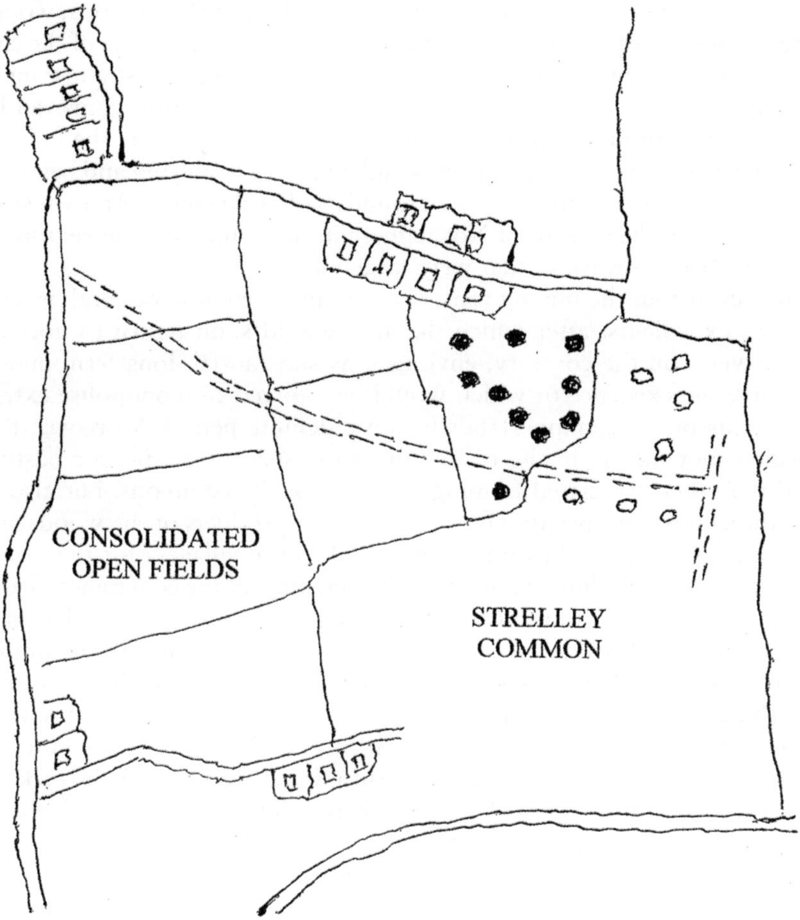

Figure 14.6 The Coalmining Context of Early Seventeenth-century Strelley.

Source: Map by author.

Reconstituting the coalmining context of Stelley and its neighbours shows how an ostensibly rural area in the early seventeenth century could come in effect to be largely devoted to the extraction and carriage of coal. Another significant feature is that the track-ways and the mines, of which there were probably many more, would have dominated a large area of Strelley Common, and occupied other fields that had once been open. We have already seen that this kind of infringement was not unusual. The same was happening in respect of the iron mining enterprise in the Sussex Weald. And the taking over of common land for the mining operation was standard practice in the West Nottinghamshire area. The rights that the lords made over to the mining interests routinely focused on the commons, and other kinds of open ground that had once been part of the common field system. The leases always specified the "commons, woods and wastes" as the areas on which coal was to be sought. One of the earliest substantial mining ventures was at Bramcote, again just a few miles outside Nottingham town. In 1609, the lord of the manor conveyed by lease to the prominent entrepreneur Sir Percival Willoughby the right to "all the coals, coal mines, and vents and delphs of coal lying and being on the wastes, woods and common grounds" of Bramcote.[66] And we shall see that when the citizens of Nottingham itself set up a mining venture, it was the "town's wastes" that were targeted.

It is clear that the mining ventures were not seen as peripheral or temporary expedients, after which the area would soon return to normal. They were, on the contrary, envisaged as substantial, long-term undertakings, the existence of which would be allowed to monopolise extensive areas of the common lands for an indefinite period. Moreover, this resulted not merely in the reduction of the space available for pasture and the other associated farming activities of the commons, but also in the direct misappropriation of other valuable products of the woods and wastes, especially timber, which was vital to the villagers for the provision of fuel and building materials. The demands of the coal mines placed an unprecedented strain on the timber supply. It was not just the bracing and boarding of the mines themselves that was involved. The timber requirements of the track-ways in particular would have been beyond anything previously experienced. The diversion of resources at such a level did not go entirely unresisted. At Strelley in the 1630s, legal challenges were brought against the resident mining interests for the reckless exploitation of the woods of the manor in order to serve the coalfield.[67]

Thus it can be noted once again that in the period before the Civil War, the despoiling of the common lands was occurring in a greater variety of ways and on a larger scale than recent historians have acknowledged. This must be recognised if we are to understand the real timing and force of the economic transition that was taking place. It was shown in earlier chapters that the consolidation of larger individual farms out of the commons and open fields was often achieved by processes that did not necessarily involve the formality of enclosure by a hedge or fence. It can now be seen in addition that the appropriation of the open fields for individualist agriculture was not the only kind of commercial enterprise that was commandeering the facilities of the common lands at this time. The annexation of the commons and wastes for coal mining was another. By the mid-seventeenth century, the supplanting of the communal patterns by the commercial trend was taking general effect.

Coal mining on an industrial level was probably only to be found in areas of the Midlands and Northeast. So the appropriation of the commons for coal extraction did not apply so broadly as the consolidation of larger individual farms, which was a kingdom-wide phenomenon. The coalmining enterprises nevertheless carried general significance as an integral part of the same commercialising trend. Just like the bulk commodities exported by the commercial farms, the products of the mines played a vital role in the pattern of regional specialisation and exchange that was the basis of the newly extended and integrated market systems. And the context in which the mining took place contributed directly to the general economic climate, in which expansion was pursued through the maximum freedom to profit. This associated both the commercial farms and the mining ventures with the principle of freedom of trade that was crucial to parliamentarian motivation.

The context of the coal mining also brings into focus a matter that is too often left out of account—that is to say, the relationship between the parliamentary cause and the new structures of occupation and commercialisation on the land. The land-use question is often looked at just in terms of the general socio-economic issue of how far the rise of individual commercial farms displaced the smallholders and husbandmen from the open fields. But it needs to be recognised and assessed more specifically in the context of its natural place in the parliamentarian movement. The determined drive of the yeomanry and the gentry towards the enclosure or consolidation of individual holdings was integral to the assumption of rights of absolute property and freedom of trade. As such, it was a fundamental element in the political and economic psychology that brought the freedom of trade agenda to a successful conclusion, with the radical provision of parliamentary control of the customs dues in early 1641.

Accordingly, the processes of consolidation acquired a new kind of public license through the revolutionary period, which has rightly been described as a watershed in the history of the enclosure movement.[68] The 1630s had seen the final episode in a long series of governmental attempts to halt or reverse the enclosure of the commons. The campaign was orchestrated by Archbishop William Laud, who condemned enclosure with the same fervour, and for the same reasons, as moralists like Robert Crowley had done a century before. To both of them, enclosure represented the undue elevation of the appetite for private gain at the expense of the community, and it transgressed the God given precepts of restraint that were supposed to guide economic activity. "If any man be so addicted to his private, that he neglect the common, state, he is devoid of the sense of piety".[69] Laud was active on the commission against enclosure, and it was the most effective of its kind. Many of the culprits were fined or imprisoned, and forced to restore enclosed land. One Northamptonshire landowner was obliged to plough up 95 acres. A Nottinghamshire farmer tried to forestall punishment with a letter to the Privy Council assuring them that he had thrown open all his enclosures, according to their instructions.[70] Between 1635 and 1638 the Council compiled a list of no less than six hundred offenders, which demonstrates both the breadth of the enclosure movement, and the strength of the government's determination to stop it. In 1639 the culprits were still being hauled up before Star Chamber. The campaign was only brought to a close by the arrival of the Long Parliament in 1640.

In the parliamentarian movement, the matter was regarded in a quite different light. In fact, the natural sympathies of the great majority of MPs were decidedly in favour of the enclosing landowners and farmers. To John Pym, compiling the official catalogue of parliamentary grievances, the royal government's anti-enclosure campaign had been an assault on the rights of property, which was now perceived as sacrosanct. The king's policy was condemned as having "driven many millions out of the subjects' purses".[71] So with parliament now effectively in power, the license to enclose was firmly and finally endorsed. The last bill that sought to limit the freedom of enclosure was introduced into the commons in 1656 and thrown out without a second reading. In rejecting it, MPs proclaimed the enthronement of the new orthodoxy of absolute property that now underpinned the process of enclosure. Master of the Rolls William Lenthall said, "he never liked any bill that touched upon property". Edmund Powell called it "the most mischievous bill that ever was offered to the House".[72] For more than one hundred and fifty years the aim of legislation had been to restrict the process of enclosure, but henceforth parliament would legislate only to encourage it. The public status of enclosure was thereby transformed through the revolutionary period. After mid-century, governmental proscription ended, and the moral condemnations of the churchmen died away.

It is important to note that the development of local coal industries was making a significant contribution to the commercial takeover of the common lands, if we are to fully understand the basis of sympathy between the coal interests and the parliamentarian movement. Parliamentarian economics, in both practical and psychological terms, gave *license* to the entrepreneurial interests that found it advantageous to override the traditional restraints on individual freedom. This does much to explain the strength of their motivations. The mining aspect of commercial advance is less familiar than others, partly because it was less general than the practice of farm consolidation, and less explicit in its displacement of the commons than the practice of enclosure. But in a sense the context of the coal mining provides the clearest illustration of the actual character of the economic drive that was now at work. It is apparent that the expansion of mining output to an export level required the super-session of traditional balances and restrictions on the land, and the exploitation of space and resources that had once been part of a subsistence based local economy. Equally important, it necessitated a different set of working precepts. Those looking to make money from the ventures included the mine owners, the coalminers, the carriers, the merchants, and the coal agents. They were all seeking to maximise the product of a previously underused resource, in order to create a viable export for the interregional markets. This required, by definition, a context of freedom from the kind of arbitrary constraints, levies and regulatory controls that had guided economic activity in previous centuries. The policies of the crown had tended in effect to perpetuate that past regime, and the early Stuarts always displayed an incorrigible determination to disrupt and impose upon the market. Parliament, on the other hand, was by nature the body most likely to guarantee commercial liberty. The entrepreneurs of the area needed, as the local yeoman Henry Ireton said, to "know a law and have a certainty".

The underlying inducement was the substance and value of the enterprise, and of this there is good, specific evidence. The coal mines of Strelley continued to be worked vigorously through the decades before the Civil War. In 1631, Nicholas Strelley leased the mining rights to one Gervase Russell. The latter was apparently determined to maximise his profits, and came under challenge for the reckless way that he was managing the pits.[73] The campaign against Russell became entangled with a dispute about the inheritance of the manor, which the powerful parliamentarian Ralph Edge, a wealthy Nottingham lawyer, was able to use to his advantage. It would emerge that Edge's ultimate objective was to get control of the mines for himself. He began by trying to undermine Russell, contending that the latter was abusing his lease by over-exploiting the timber resources of Strelley Park in order to supply the needs of the coal pits.[74] Edge made the interesting assertion that the depredations were unnecessary because even without these resources, the mines were operating at a more than sufficient profit level. He said that the herbage in the park was worth about £200 a year, while the mines were worth as much as £400, after expenses. In some years a clear profit of £600 seems to have been made from the mines, with coal being sold at 6/- a load.[75] This was more than double the price that might have been expected in the earlier years of the century. Coal was a rapidly appreciating asset, which gave Ralph Edge a powerful incentive for trying to dislodge Russell from the control of the mines. At the same time, the original Strelley family was in difficulty, facing debts, disputes and doubtful successions. Edge had the advantages of great wealth, legal expertise, and an influential status in the local parliamentarian movement. He was able to intervene in ways that gave him command of the course of events. By the 1650s, the manor and the mines were in his hands. They were to make him a great fortune, and would remain in his family for three centuries to come. They moved into the upper gentry, which is another example of a new man rising by taking advantage of the problems of an original manorial family. The value of the mining enterprise continued to increase. In October 1656, Edge received £1,280 "for coals out of Strelley coal mines this last summer".[76] These were phenomenal profit levels, which indicate very clearly why the freedom to engage to the full in such enterprises was such an important part of parliamentarian motivations.

Strelley was one of four coal production centres that coincided with the individual parishes where the highest number of parliamentarian supporters can be located.[77] It would be too much to expect more specific evidence of the connections, but there are strong indications of some of the personal links. In 1659, when there were at least four pits in production in Strelley, each was listed under the name of a particular husbandman in the village. In 1651, each of these tenants was also listed as holding a part of the Rye Field, or the New Field, in which some of the mines were located. One of the coalmine tenants was named Betteridge, a surviving representative of a prominent Strelley husbandman family known to have provided active parliamentarians from among their number. A similar association can be suggested for Huntingdon Noone, who was clerk at the coal mines in Strelley in the 1640s. The Noone family is known to have provided supplies for the parliamentarian cause.[78] This also serves to underline the suggestion that although Ralph Edge was immeasurably the greatest gainer from the mines, there was nevertheless sufficient scope in the enterprise for those at all levels of the production process to make significantly more money than would usually have been their lot.

The parliamentarian records also identify other middling-sort supporters with coal mining connections in the West Nottinghamshire area. Edward Ausborne, a yeoman, and Edward Ayscough, of the lesser gentry, both had mining interests in Nuthall, just under two miles north of Strelley. Ayscough was active on the parliamentary committee, and both men were regularly entrusted with taking money to pay the colliers in Nuthall. The details of these transactions shed a revealing light on the strength of the financial common interests that bound the parliamentary cause together. The colliers and the carriers were paid for the work that they did in producing and carting coal for the garrison. In normal times the enterprise generated increased incomes at all levels of the production process, and to a degree these benefits actually grew further in meeting the demands of the military effort. The parliamentary cause was in every respect good for business. But the actual value of the coal was sometimes discounted against the needs of the "state" or "the public service". This was not a difficult proposition to accept, because the concept of the state as it had evolved in the perceptions of the political nation had coalesced around the growing force of the coordinated national market, the requirements of open trading, and the processes of national law. If parliament could be placed in a position to influence things more consistently, it could be expected to establish the general climate of freedom from arbitrary taxation that the market required, as well as the regular availability of the legislative function that the towns always looked to employ, and which was indeed much the most efficient and acceptable instrument of regulation in the new context of economic affairs. "To know a law and have a certainty". So the diversion of a proportion of profits to ensure the success of the cause was not begrudged.

At the same time, the parliamentary authorities took care to sustain the context of enterprise and consensual economics that lay at the heart of the movement. Requisitioning seems to have been accepted, as long as it was properly authorised by the parliamentary committee of merchants and freeholders sitting in Nottingham. When this authority was not available, the market still appears to have been respected, and the garrison paid full price for the coal that it received. There were, inevitably, occasions when these understandings were not observed, but then restitution was made. Thus it was when Edward Ausborne came to complain to the committee that two carts of coal had been taken from him without a warrant. He pointed out that he and Ayscough had already delivered the four loads specifically requisitioned from Nuthall, and that the other two loads had not been earmarked for the public service, but had been brought to Nottingham to be sold for his own profit. The committee acknowledged that there had been a mistake, and recompensed him 20/- for the two loads.[79] The episode is revealing in many ways. That the mining interests could serve both the state and themselves at the same time illustrates the scale and potential of coal production. It also indicates what the parliamentary authorities were willing and able to do to keep their middling-sort supporters sweet. Perhaps most interesting of all, it shows a consensual economy at work, revolving around the kind of provisions that parliament, in general, had to offer. There was a basis of sympathy here, not only because these people were the actual backbone of the effort, but also because they were clearly representative of the economic principle on which the parliamentary cause was based—that is to say, the idea that public monies should only be raised by public consent. The agreed arrangements about coal supply in Nottingham show how the parliamentarians sought to live up to that promise in practice. The details of the payments also illustrate a powerful reason that it had become imperative to apply these consensual freedoms—the value of the coal seemed to be going up almost daily. In January 1645 the committee paid 11/6 for one load of coals for the use of a parliamentarian nurse, Mrs. Nethercoates.[80] R. S. Smith doubted Nef's suggestion that that coal was commanding a price of 10/- a load at this time, but these instances seem to confirm that it was certainly that, and it was still rising. There was much to gain if economic freedoms and rights of consent could be firmly established, and much to lose if they were not.

The town of Nottingham had a pivotal involvement in the commercialising and industrialising drive at every level. It was not merely a market and an export centre for the coal. The townsmen themselves became participants in the expanding enterprise and the spirit of initiative that it engendered. In 1630 a project was set up to "sink a pit or pits in the town's wastes, in hope (by the favour of God) to find coals there". Once again, it was the common "wastes" that were to be exploited. The investors were not certain that they would find coal, but if they did, they expected the profits to be substantial. The rule of return was laid down on the basis that the benefits would only be available to those "that shall now or before the work begins, adventure a part or proportion of money".[81] The initiators of the scheme were three aldermen who were to become most active on the parliamentary committee, William Nixe, John James and William Drury, in company with Mr. Greaves, another parliamentarian supporter from the coalmining village of Nuthall.

Men like Nixe, James, Drury, Greaves, Ausborne, Ayscough, Charlton and Edge were mainstays of the parliamentary effort in West Nottinghamshire. Here, in action, were the "able substantial freeholders" and "citizens of market towns" clearly identified by contemporaries as the backbone of the cause. The fact that they worked closely together highlights the essential character of the movement, which was based on a broad commercial impulse, operating in an exceptionally well-coordinated market. These men personified the most powerful and fundamental motivations of parliamentary allegiance. They perceived the prospect of acquiring great wealth and power in a new world of opportunity that encompassed the agricultural and industrial spheres, and they looked to parliament to provide the context of economic freedoms that would enable them to realise those ambitions to the full. If the king's cause was "disgusted" by these men, as by the middle sort of citizenry in Bristol, it was because his government had always tended to deny rather than encourage those freedoms. The citizens of Nottingham and the freeholders of its rural and industrial hinterland chose parliament because it was the natural and necessary guarantor of rights of consent, especially in the field of public finance. West Nottinghamshire thus provides a further example of the dynamic that John Corbet observed in another parliamentary garrison, at Gloucester, where the constraints and impositions of royal policy had become unacceptable to "a generation of men truly laborious, jealous of their properties, whose principal aim is liberty and plenty".[82] Liberty and plenty had become interdependent. As Gerrard Winstanley said, the principal freedoms sought by the parliamentarians were freedom of trade and absolute property.[83]

As a result, the parliamentary cause was not short of funds. The lesser gentry and yeomen lent large amounts at the start—there was £200 from Nicholas Charlton, £100 from Robert Reynes of Stanton, and £100 from Thomas Newton from the coalmining village of Sutton. Nottingham citizens bankrolled the war effort on a regular basis. Aldermen Nixe, Gregory and Hardmett each lent £10 towards the troops in 1643, in a collection totalling £215, then advanced a further £50, £34, and £30 respectively in 1645. The mercer Samuel Burrowes lent £10 in 1643, and £50 in 1644. Then in January 1645, 135 townspeople collected more than £500 to pay the garrison.[84] The accounts also show, of course, a great number of smaller donations, and no doubt there were many others that went unrecorded. It appears, moreover, that when the money was loaned, the regime was able to refund it. Nottingham and its surrounds boasted many affluent citizens who were investing heavily in a cause that gave every impression of promoting a context of commercial viability. The most eminent of West Nottinghamshire parliamentarians, William Pierrepont, who became an important political figure at the administrative centre of the war effort, noted regularly that "the people" were prepared to spend money to further the cause.[85] This was certainly true of the people of his own home neighbourhood. And they were spending in the expectation that increasing the influence of parliament would enable them to gain more, since they would "know a law and have a certainty".

Notes

1. Henry Ireton, *Puritanism and Liberty*, ed. A. S. P. Woodhouse, (London 1938), p. 72
2. D. Underdown, *Revel, Riot and Rebellion,* (Oxford 1987)
3. J. Gurney, *Brave Community,* (Manchester 2012), p. 33
4. C. Holmes, *The Eastern Association in the English Civil War,* (Cambridge 1985), esp. p. 7
5. A. Hughes, *Politics, Society and Civil War: Warwickshire 1620–1660,* (Cambridge 1987), p. 151; "Local History and the Origins of the English Civil War", in *Conflict in Early Stuart England,* eds. R. Cust and A Hughes, (London 1989), p. 242
6. J. Dias, "Lead, Society and Politics in Derbyshire Before the Civil War", *Midland History 6* (1981)
7. *CSP Domestic 1619–23*, p. 130; 1631–33, p. 18
8. C. H. Wilson, *England's Apprenticeship,* (London 1965), pp. 66–8
9. J. U. Nef, *The Rise of the British Coal Industry,* (London 1932)
10. Wilson, *England's Apprenticeship*, pp. 79–88
11. Nef, *Rise of the British Coal Industry*, pp. 58–60, 67–8
12. R. S. Smith, *Early Coal Mining Around Nottingham, 1500–1650,* (Nottingham 1989), pp. 84–7
13. TNA SP28, 240, 241, February 1644 and June 1646. Beeston, Lenton, Chilwell, Stapleford, Arnold, Basford, Carlton, Gedling, Trowell, Awsworth, Bilborough, Kimberley, Bramcote, Sneinton, Toton, Cossall, Selston, Eastwood, Wollaton, Nuthall, Strelley, Watnall, Bulwell, Sutton-in-Ashfield, Kirby-in-Ashfield
14. TNA, SP28/240/429
15. *A Manuscript Account of Nottingham in 1641*, *Transactions of the Thoroton Society II* (1898), p. 50
16. Will of William Benson, "scuttlemaker", Nottinghamshire Wills, PRNW, 26 June 1636
17. G. Henson, *A History of the Framework Knitters* (1831), (Newton Abbot 1970), p. 60
18. J. Thirsk, *Economic Policy and Projects,* (Oxford 1978), p. 5f
19. J. Thoroton, *History of Nottinghamshire*, ed. J. Thoresby, (Nottingham 1790), I, p. 47
20. L. A. Clarkson, "The Leather Crafts in Tudor and Stuart England", *Agricultural History Review 14* (1960)
21. C. Palliser, *The Age of Elizabeth,* (London 1983), p. 252
22. Beeston, Lenton, Chilwell, Stapleford, Arnold, Basford, Carlton, Gedling, Trowell, Awsworth, Bilborough, Kimberley, Bramcote, Sneinton, Toton,

Cossall, Selston, Eastwood, Wollaton, Nuthall, Strelley, Watnall, Bulwell, Sutton-inAshfield, Kirby-in-Ashfield. References above . . .

23. *HMC 1964*, "Newark on Trent, the Civil War Siegeworks", pp. 75–95; A. Wood, *Nottinghamshire in the Civil War,* (Oxford 1937), pp. 217–22
24. See for instance, John Morrill, "The Religious Context of the English Civil War", *Transactions of the Royal Historical Society* (1984), p. 161
25. G. Yerby, *People and Parliament: Representative Right and the English Revolution,* (Basingstoke 2008), chapter 7, "The Song of the Puritans of Nottingham".
26. Nottingham University Library, Archdeaconry Act Book A45, ff. 169–70
27. The pre-eminence of women was always a marked feature of the Godly group in Nottingham
28. Ireton, *Puritanism and Liberty*, p. 457
29. Ibid, p. 458
30. Lucy Hutchinson, *Memoirs of the Life of Colonel Hutchinson*, ed. J. Hutchinson, (London 1846), pp. 98–9
31. "The Putney Debates", in *Puritanism and Liberty,* ed. A. S. P Woodhouse, (London 1936), p. 57
32. Ibid, p. 72
33. "Remonstrance of the Army" (November 1648), in *Puritanism and Liberty,* ed. A. S. P. Woodhouse, (London 1936), pp. 458–9
34. B. Coward, *The Stuart* Age, (London 1994), p. 132
35. Nottinghamshire University Library, Nottinghamshire Archdeaconry Act Books, A24 January 1609: A36 July 1616; A39 June 1632
36. S. B. Jennings, "The Gathering of the Elect in 17th Century Nottinghamshire", Nottingham Trent PhD (1999), pp. 39, 74, 82–5
37. Yerby, *People and Parliament: Representative Rights and the English Revolution*, p. 195
38. "Remonstrance of the Army", p. 459
39. Nottinghamshire University Library, Nottinghamshire Archdeaconry Act Books, R6, f. 505
40. N. Tyacke, *Anti-Calvinists,* (Oxford 987); A. Foster, "Church Policies of the 1630s", in *Conflict in Early Stuart England,* eds. R. Cust and A. Hughes, (London 1989)
41. Nottingham University Library, Archdeaconry Act Book, A45, ff. 169–70
42. Nottinghamshire Archives, Archdeaconry Transcripts M462, pp. 515, 524
43. R. T. Kendall, *Calvin and English Calvinism to 1649,* (Oxford 1979)
44. P. Lake, "Calvinism and the English Church 1570–1635", *Past and Present 114* (1987), pp. 32–76
45. As quoted in Kendall, *Calvin and English Calvinism*, pp. 89–92
46. G. Winstanley, *The Law of Freedom*, in *Winstanley: The Law of Freedom and Other Writings*, ed. C. Hill, (Cambridge 1983), p. 294
47. Hutchinson, *Memoirs of the Life of Colonel Hutchinson*, p. 100
48. *Commons Journal*, II, pp. 458, 522; *HMC Cowper*, II, p. 309
49. Whalley to John Thurloe,12 December 1655, J. Thurloe, *Collection of State Papers,* (London 1742), IV, p. 308
50. TNA E179/160/293–307
51. *CSP Domestic 1641–43,* p. 368, 9 August 1642
52. Wood, *Nottinghamshire in the Civil War*, p. 20
53. Ibid
54. Clarendon, *History of the Rebellion*, ed. W. D. Macray, (Oxford 1958), vol. II, pp. 283–5, 290–3
55. A. Fletcher, *The Outbreak of the English Civil War,* (London 1981), p. 354

56. TNA SP24, H40
57. Hutchinson, *Memoirs of the Life of Colonel Hutchinson,* pp. 130–1
58. Ibid, And TNA, SP28/133/2/83–88. The villages were Kimberley, Watnall, Newthorpe, Brinsley, Selston, Bulwell, Papplewick, Linley, Arnold, Beeston, Wollaton, Stapleford, Bramcote, Toton and Chillwell. The names of the individual Broxtow donors are in the Appendix
59. Wilson, *England's Apprenticeship*, pp. 66–8
60. Ibid, pp. 79–88
61. Nottinghamshire Archives, Charlton Papers, DDCH 35/2, pp. 1–2
62. Ibid, p. 3
63. Ibid, pp. 9–10
64. I am grateful to David and Jennifer Appleyard, of Broad Oak Farm, Strelley, who provided the information about the coalfield. I was fortunate to get there at the right time to benefit from their knowledge and hospitality, and to see the bell-pit remains before any danger of further ploughing
65. R. S. Smith, "England's First Rails", *Renaissance and Modern Studies*, Series Vi, vol. 4, Nottingham University
66. *H. M. C. Middleton*, pp. 171–5
67. Nottinghamshire Archives, Edge Papers, DDE/5/8. 25
68. H. N. Brailsford, *The Levellers and the English Revolution,* (Nottingham 1983), p. 426
69. *The Works of William Laud*, eds. W. Scott and J. Bliss, (Oxford 1847–1860), vol. I, pp. 28–9; vol. VI, pt 2, p. 520
70. TNA, SP16/475/72; SP16/404/142/
71. "The Grand Remonstrance", of 1641, in *Constitutional Documents of the Puritan Revolution*, ed. S. R. Gardiner, (Oxford 1968), p. 212
72. *The Parliamentary Diary of Thomas Burton*, ed. J. T. Rutt, (Colburn 1828), I, pp. 175–6
73. Nottinghamshire Archives, DD E 5/5, 46
74. Ibid, DD E 5/25
75. Ibid, DD E 5/8
76. Ibid, DD E 5/34
77. The other three being Nuthall, Bilborough and Eastwood. This excludes the parish of Hucknall, where even more are known because there was a specific collection for the support of the garrison
78. Ibid, DD E 5/7; DD E 46/66/1–11
79. TNA SP28/240, f.338
80. TNA SP28/241, January 1645
81. *Records of the Borough of Nottingham*, eds. W. Stevenson and J. Raine, (London and Nottingham, 1889), V, p. 144
82. J. Corbet, "A True and Impartial Account of the Military Government of the City of Gloucester", in *Collection of Scarce and Valuable Tracts*, ed. Sir W. Scott, 2nd edition, (London 1809–15), V, pp. 303–4, 307
83. See above, p. 272.
84. *Records of the Borough of Nottingham*, V, pp. 210–11; TNA, SP28/174/41–44
85. Diary of Walter Yonge, BL, Add. Ms. 18, 777, f. 157

15 A Middle Sort of Aristocracy

William Pierrepont and the Course of the English Revolution

The context of West Nottinghamshire before and during the Civil War displays the economic and political force behind the parliamentary movement. Previous chapters have shown how this was reflected in the early revolutionary measures of the Long Parliament in the winter of 1640–1641. A study of the aims and beliefs of another Nottinghamshire parliamentarian illustrates how the common economic demands of the gentry and the middle sort emerged in the form of a political revolution at the centre of the state. William Pierrepont was from the ranks of the upper gentry, and his highly influential contribution to the cause shows, among other things, the fallacy of assuming that there was no substantial support for parliament from that direction. In many ways he epitomised the close connection between the rise of the gentry and the parliamentary cause. He rose as a younger son, and he had an explicit and enduring commitment to the radical priorities of the Commons and the constituencies. In general terms this focused on establishing the rights and processes of parliamentary consent with a permanent and normative influence at the centre of political life. Pierrepont's principal purposes were to gain complete representative control of public finance, to achieve the automatic and regular assembly of parliament, and to ensure the continuous provision of parliamentary legislation as the essential basis of good government.

Pierrepont came from an ancient gentry family, which had arrived on the scene with William the Conqueror, though it was not until the seventeenth century that they reached the apex of the social hierarchy in Nottinghamshire. Furthermore, they did not arrive by the channels most usually taken by the feudal nobility. Their eminence was not achieved through service as soldiers or courtiers. Pierrepont's father Robert has been noted as one of the few members of his class who owed his advancement to skilful economic management.[1] It was his great wealth that bought him the Earldom of Kingston in 1628. William inherited his father's aptitude for business, and even as a younger son he quickly became established as a rich landowner in his own right. During the 1640s and 1650s he was one of the most powerful men on the London scene, and also one of the wealthiest. He indulged in the conspicuous expenditure expected of his class, though his personal modesty was also remarked upon.[2] The family estate was just outside Nottingham, but he came to reside mainly at Thoresby in Sherwood, which was settled on him in 1633. It boasted "one of the most beautiful parks in the kingdom, an inseparable part of the old forest".[3] He drew much of his wealth from the careful harvesting of agricultural rents, but also in particular from the sale of timber, a rapidly appreciating asset, the rights to which he always reserved for himself. During the course of his life he appears to have acquired an interest in more than forty manors.[4] Previous chapters have already mentioned the family's tradition of business acumen as an illustration that being an aristocrat was no bar to making money in the rising markets of sixteenth and early seventeenth-century England.

By the late 1630s Pierrepont's marriage had given him additional property interests in Shropshire, and he was elected MP for Much Wenlock in the Long Parliament. Lucy Hutchinson noted that although he did not sit for Nottinghamshire, the reputation that he gained for wisdom and eloquence made him "an ornament" to his home county.[5] He was included among the dozen leading MPs who "made the motions, spoke to the issues and developed reports".[6] He acquired the sobriquet of Wise William, for his capacity to look for lines of rational compromise in negotiations, but the persistently radical aims that he pursued by those means underlined the central force of the parliamentarian movement as a broad challenge to the prerogatives of the crown. He was immediately active in coordinating the condemnation of the perceived failings of royal policy, and he focused particularly on the abuse of ship money. This reflected a principal defining purpose of his political life—that is to say, the determination to bring all public finance under representative control. Parliament had asserted this aim across various fields of policy and administration for several decades, most obviously and controversially in respect of their desire to take command of the setting of the customs dues and to direct the course of foreign policy. In every respect this involved a readiness to displace important aspects of the royal prerogative. By the same token, Pierrepont displayed a notable degree of enthusiasm for dislodging the king's discretionary powers from the most critical fields of government.

In taking ship money, Charles had not been acting illegally. It was an ancient right of the king to make such levies by discretion on his own assessment of public safety, and it had been endorsed as such by the law lords in rejecting the case brought by John Hampden in 1637. But Pierrepont, like parliamentarians generally, had come to feel that such powers were no longer necessary or supportable, and that they should be consigned to the past. The process of reclassifying them as illegal involved another of Pierrepont's defining political tenets—the absolute sovereignty of parliamentary law. In the House on 8th December 1640, he denounced Lord Keeper Finch for giving the opinion that the tax was so inherent in the king's prerogative that it was not within the power of parliament to declare it illegal. Pierrepont recalled that Finch had been heard to say, "that a hundred acts of parliament could not take it away".[7] The quote was accurate enough, and Pierrepont was right to regard Finch's words as a challenge. In much the same way as Archbishop Laud, Finch was himself reacting against the confirmed belief of parliamentarians like Pierrepont, and indeed the political nation at large, that statute law was the greatest sovereign power, and that just one act of parliament could take away anything.

Pierrepont led the move to impeach Sir Robert Berkeley, the judge who had defended Ship Money most vociferously. He berated Berkeley for advising the king to proceed with the collection of the levy, though he "knows the laws are to the contrary".[8] In fact, the laws were not to the contrary, and Berkeley was simply affirming the constitutional orthodoxy. Nevertheless, as already suggested in the context of the impositions dispute, there was some genuine force behind Pierrepont's confident assertion that ship money was illegal, for it was also a fact that parliament had become the defining element in a distinctive concept of sovereign, representative legislation, and in this sense the law was indeed what parliament said it was. The Commons could extend this psychological leap to cover ship money, just as they had applied it to prerogative customs dues in the preceding decades.

The contention between discretionary ship money on the one hand, and parliamentary law on the other was not random. It was another expression of the deepening polarity between the respective uses of "patent" and "parliament". And it was a further extension of the underlying logic deriving from the development of sovereign representative law. If the greatest and most "unlimited" power of legislation could only be employed by consent in parliament, should not the same obviously apply to all such sovereign exercises? Pierrepont said that "the countryman followeth the plough" in the assurance that his goods could not be taken from him without his consent. "He knows the usual payments by law, and in extraordinary causes has that care to choose such for his Knights of the Shire and Burgesses as might be mindful of the cause of payment and his estate".[9] In other words, the king was no longer to be permitted the discretion to tax at will in what he judged to be extraordinary causes. This confirms that the determination to subject all matters of public finance to the control of representative consent lay at the heart of Pierrepont's political aims, just as it did with parliamentarians generally.

The unique sovereign power of parliamentary legislation could also be extended to justify the idea that the representative body should be given a regular and automatic place at the centre of governmental affairs. As Pierrepont said:

> Unlimited power must be in some, to make and repeal laws to fit the dispositions of times and persons—nature places this in common consent only, and where all cannot conveniently meet, instructeth

> them to give their consents to some they know or believe so well of as to be bound by what they agree to. His Majesty, your Lordships and the Commons are thus met in Parliament, and so long as we are often reduced to this main foundation our King and we shall prosper.[10]

The speech encapsulates the idea of the common consent of the entire society as the only justification for "unlimited" power. It captures the force of the paradoxical link between sovereign power and representative rights and shows how it could be applied generally to encourage a demand that all public money raising should be subject to representative consent. This is clearly displayed in Pierrepont's picture of the farmer following the plough, knowing the usual payments by law, and assured of a right that in "extraordinary causes" he would be represented by an MP who could be relied upon to judge the necessity on his behalf, and understand what he could afford. It is a powerful confirmation that the parliamentary cause was motivated at core by the need of the generality of people for a guarantee of the best conditions in which to carry on their economic affairs, or as Pierrepont's neighbour Henry Ireton put it, "to know a law and have a certainty".[11]

Right from the early months of the Long Parliament, Pierrepont's distinctive contribution was promoting initiatives for transferring a significant degree of political authority from king to parliament, beginning with the measures that freed the representative body from the king's discretion over when or whether it should assemble. Lucy Hutchinson recalled that "by him was that bill promoted and carried on which passed for the continuation of this parliament".[12] The wording might seem to suggest that she was referring to the act of 10 May 1641 declaring that the present assembly "should not be adjourned, prorogued or dissolved" but by itself. It is generally supposed, however, that she actually meant the Triennial Act, the first great radical measure of February 1641, by which parliament was empowered to meet automatically in the absence of the king's summons. It is likely indeed that this was the act referred to, since it was much the most notable public initiative, and it certainly reflected Pierrepont's statement of the imperative need for regular assemblies. Wallace Notestein assumed that this was the act in question, and pointed out that this did not contradict other indications that William Strode introduced the bill, since he and Pierrepont often worked in unison.[13] Furthermore, Thomas Bailey, who was still in contact with the traditions of Nottinghamshire history, said simply, "William Pierrepont . . . at the early part of this session—brought forward and carried into law that important measure, the Triennial Bill".[14]

Bailey also understood the real constitutional change that the act brought about. He recognised that the medieval statutes desiring a parliament every year were just advisory, and were considered "merely as a general declaration dispensed with at the pleasure of the crown". They were made at a time when the influence of the Lords and the principles of nobility were pre-eminent, and they did not constitute a challenge to the sole right of the king to decide when and whether parliament should meet. The Triennial Act therefore struck at "the very root of the power of the crown . . . in its hitherto acknowledged prerogative . . . in the maintenance of that authority over the procedures of parliament in which the safety of the monarchy had been supposed to consist". The act thereby produced "so great an innovation in the constitution as to form in itself a revolution of no ordinary degree of importance".[15] This was indeed the core proposition of the English Revolution, to provide the representative assembly with an independent and automatic place at the centre of the polity, and thereby establish the full and continual exercise of rights of consent. It is a further demonstration of the public demand behind this radical change to the constitution that an earlier Nottinghamshire historian, Lucy Hutchinson, was happy to claim for her neighbour William Pierrepont a direct, leading role in bringing the measure to the statute book. And she could be unstinting in her praise because she could regard him as the social equal of her husband's family.

Events on the ground in West Nottinghamshire also reflected another of Pierrepont's radical aims—the determination to bring the military forces of the kingdom under parliamentary control. The capacity of Nottingham and its hinterland to resist the feudal power of Lord Newark and the Byrons at the outset of the struggle was a microcosm of the shifting basis of military potential. This had precise echoes in Pierrepont's activities at Westminster, especially in his drive to establish parliament's military authority. At the end of 1641, the Irish Rebellion brought some urgency, or perhaps a moment of opportunity, to the need to have the militia put into the hands of men that parliament could trust. From early January 1642, Pierrepont acted as the principal spokesman for the Commons in their attempts to persuade a hesitant House of Lords that the king should be obliged to accept the removal of Sir John Byron from his post as Lieutenant of the Tower. By the eighth of February this demand had been successfully imposed, and Byron himself recorded the speech to the Lords in which Pierrepont plainly declared the independent authority of parliament. After asserting the necessity of putting the forts "into such hands as may be confided in", Pierrepont added, "as for the extent of this power, and the continuance of it . . . both the one and the other should be left to the Parliament".[16] Byron hoped that they would not be allowed the "unlimited power" that they sought. Pierrepont was indeed engaged once again in displacing an important aspect of the royal prerogative and transferring the power to parliament, emboldened by the familiar justification that made the exercise of "unlimited" power dependent on the endorsement of parliament consent.

The extension of the concept of the "unlimited power" of parliamentary law to other fields, as required, was the basis of the parliamentarian position, both in principle and in practice. Pierrepont went on to chair the important committee, moved by Oliver Cromwell, for the overall settlement of the militia, with the controversial task of bringing it under parliamentary control. A way had to be found to authorise the appointments of the Lord Lieutenants in the counties without reference to the king, who had traditionally been regarded as the locus of military authority. The answer, as ever, was to take parliament's defining role in the making of sovereign law to a logical conclusion. On the eighteenth of January, at an open committee again chaired by Pierrepont, it was resolved "these men to be appointed by Ordinance of Parliament".[17] In effect, this was to exploit the position of the Commons as the actual representative body, in order to exclude the king from the legislative function. It was also to usurp the military command that had been the original defining character of the monarch's role. In one sense this reflected a significant degree of confidence that public estimation of the practices and principles of representative sovereignty was now so high that people generally would accept a binding regulation authorised by parliament alone. And this in fact proved to be the case. But at the most elevated social levels, it opened up a very sensitive issue on which many Royalists decided their allegiance.[18] The status of the greater gentry was after all based traditionally on a delegation of military authority from the king. For many it was a point of honour and obligation. There is an instructive letter written to the Nottinghamshire MPs in July 1642, on behalf of a group of the leading gentry who were to form the core of the Royalist cause in the county. Interestingly, they embraced the representative basis of sovereign law, with the implication that the king could not exercise that power in his own person. It was "our greatest privilege that the king could not make a law to bind us without our consent in parliament". This was the underlying principle on which a series of royal prerogatives had already been displaced, and they approved indeed of all the radical measures that parliament had taken—until the Militia Ordinance. "We shall not conceive ourselves bound to obey one or both Houses without the King . . . we never conceived your only votes would be our law . . . nor to engage us in any civil war for the maintenance of such votes".[19]

It is useful to try to clarify a line of difference. These elements of the upper gentry embraced the fact that parliament now had an indispensable place in sovereign legislative power, and they accepted the early radical measures depriving the king of his prerogatives over parliamentary assembly and the setting of the customs dues, even though Charles had assented to them only under great duress and protesting all the while against the constitutional violence that was entailed. When, however, the king acquired the capacity to try to recover his position by force, the elite of Nottinghamshire found that their personal loyalties drew them to the king's side, and dictated that they could not allow parliament to usurp his military role, or to exclude him from the legislative function. Pierrepont, on the other hand, was prepared to take parliament's defining part in sovereign representative law to a logical, if extreme conclusion, and propose that if necessary the representative body should and could assume supreme power alone.

When the struggle began, William Pierrepont's father Robert, Earl of Kingston, found himself with divided loyalties. He made a public statement to that effect. "When I take up arms with the King against the Parliament, or with the Parliament against the King, let a cannon bullet divide me between them".[20] This has sometimes been cited as reflecting the force of neutralism, but it is more usefully interpreted in a different way. It not only expressed an unwelcome dilemma, but also illustrated the real political choice that had arisen. There was now a duality of public authority where king and parliament could be given equal weight, and this tended on balance to give momentum to the parliamentary cause. The Earl's family was also divided. His eldest son Henry was an active supporter of the king. But the younger son Francis was a staunch parliamentarian like William, and he commanded a regiment under the Nottingham garrison. Lucy Hutchinson regarded him as "well affected to honest men and righteous liberty".[21]

At Westminster, William came into direct contention with his brother Henry. When summoned to the Lords as Baron Pierrepont in 1641, Henry at once joined a protest against William's efforts to bring the Lieutenant of the Tower under parliamentary control. Henry also endorsed the letter of the Nottinghamshire elite denying parliament's right to legislate on its own authority, a protest provoked in particular by the Militia Ordinance, of which William had been an instrumental proponent. The matter became very personal, since the Ordinance actually displaced Henry as Lord Lieutenant of Nottinghamshire. They were again at odds on religious issues. Henry wanted the bishops to retain their place in the Lords, and their right to be involved in temporal affairs. William, on the other hand, was at the forefront of a campaign to exclude the bishops from the upper chamber. This was in line with his consistent preference for a moderated Episcopacy, shorn of coercive powers.[22] The critical distinction seems to be that Henry joined the king's side when the parliamentary cause became a direct threat to hierarchical authority in various forms. William, however, believed that the hierarchical prerogatives of the king had become prejudicial to the prospects of the people, and should be superseded by the enhancement of popular liberty.

William Pierrepont has sometimes been regarded as a member of the "middle group" in the Long Parliament, holding the centre ground between the War Party and the Peace Party. This is accurate enough in as far as he avoided the extremes of doctrinal Puritanism and republicanism. But it is misleading if it is taken to suggest that he rowed back from the original radical purposes set in train at the beginning of the Long Parliament. He held firm to the intent to reorder the constitution in favour of the permanent influence and independence of parliament, as set out by John Pym in 1640. The consistent aims were to establish the representative assembly with a permanent and automatic place at the centre of governmental affairs, and to achieve complete representative control of public finance. He also sustained Pym's initial vision of a religious settlement based on moderating the activities of the bishops by removing their coercive powers. As Valerie Pearl once pointed out, the agenda of Pym, Pierrepont and others ascribed to the "middle group" was always to engineer a change from a "personal" to a "constitutional" monarchy.[23] Nor should it be supposed that Pierrepont was ever inclined to discontinue the military struggle before these ends had been achieved. On 17th February 1643, he opposed the suggestion of the Lords that they should cease hostilities before a treaty was negotiated. He thought that "the people" would be discouraged by the cessation of military activity, and that they would pay more readily to support the cause if they knew that it was being prosecuted with determination.[24]

Pierrepont had always been at the forefront of parliament's drive to enforce the Militia Ordinance and resist the king's attempts to raise troops by the Commission of Array.[25] Furthermore, the retention of the militia in parliamentary hands was a basic condition in all the settlement negotiations in which he took part during the course of the war—though the proposal was rejected by the king with equal consistency. Pierrepont was also prominent in advancing the military organisation that was to provide parliament with an army capable of bringing the war to a successful conclusion. He promoted the Self-Denying Ordinance, which aimed to remove the Peace Party lords Essex and Manchester from their commands. It was Pierrepont who carried the Ordinance up to the Lords in December 1644, once again finding himself in the position of trying to persuade a reluctant second chamber to accept a radical measure that aimed to secure the position of parliament by displacing the power of the ancient military elite.

The New Model Army proved to be a force capable of winning the war against the king. But it was another matter entirely to persuade Charles to accept the decision of battle and agree to terms favourable to parliament. In fact it was impossible to tie Charles to any kind of mutual agreement. The king knew that no settlement was possible without him, and waited for his opponents to acknowledge the fact. There was a Peace Party-Presbyterian alliance in parliament prepared to give way and propose an unconditional treaty with the king, and they were soon to be reinforced by a disgruntled Scottish party hovering in the wings.

Pierrepont had not been in favour of the Solemn League and Covenant with the Scots. He resisted it, and for a while withdrew himself from the leadership group in the Commons on account of it.[26] With his noted degree of wisdom he recognised that the Scottish agenda was really quite different from theirs. The Scots had no essential commitment to the central parliamentarian ambition of reordering the constitutional balance to give parliament an independent position and an on-going influence at the centre of affairs. They had one consistent aim, which lay in the religious sphere, and even this ran counter to English preferences. The Scots joined the contest in the expectation of bringing the English church into conformity with the "best Reformed" practice that they believed to be represented by their own Kirk. This was a dictatorial Presbyterian system, encouraging the pre-eminence of the clerical establishment, and in the wake of the Prayer Book Revolt the Covenanters established a command of Scottish politics that "amounted to a theocracy".[27] This, as Pierrepont understood, was almost the opposite of what the English had in mind. The central tendency of parliamentarians was towards a laicised and more latitudinarian settlement of the church. The Scots found their way obstructed by the erastian and tolerationist inclinations of the English Parliament.[28] When it became clear that this was the dominant mood in England, and that there was little chance of getting their own programme accepted, the Scots withdrew. When they returned, in the post-war arena, it was to put their weight on the side of the king. In May 1646, Charles fled to their protection.

Since Pierrepont's view of the inappropriateness of the Scottish alliance had proved prescient, he was detailed to compose a rebuttal of various Scottish claims. To their complaint that they had not been paid, he pointed out that both armies were financed by the same kind of public levy, and the reason that the assessments for the Scottish army had not been forthcoming was perhaps that they had made little contribution to "the public service". They had remained in the north "where no enemy was". To the Scottish demand for an equal part in the settlement negotiations Pierrepont replied that the League and Covenant had been made in the context of the church, and for the Scots to claim that "the king relates to both kingdoms the same" was "confounding the particular rights of the two kingdoms".[29]

There were, however, Peace Party and Presbyterian elements in parliament who were more inclined to welcome the Scottish intervention, as reinforcing their preference for an unconditional treaty with the king and a less tolerant religious settlement. To resist these moves, Pierrepont and the middle group found themselves making common cause with the Independents in the Commons, and in the Army. To a readily politicised New Model Army the idea of a sell-out treaty with the king was unacceptable. The reactionary groups in the Commons realised for their part that the army would have to be disbanded if the prospect of an unconditional treaty was to proceed in safety. But the threat of disbandment only served to complete the radicalisation of the New Model, which now formally entered the political arena. It was at this point that Henry Ireton stepped forward as the principal spokesperson for the army, as it moved to ensure that the original, central aims of the parliamentarian revolution were sustained.

As radicalisation spread through the ranks, and the army mobilised for political action in 1647, William Pierrepont was not deflected from his course. It was easier for him to hold firm because the intentions of the Independent generals were fully in line with the most central and consistent parliamentarian purposes. With the middle group in parliament, Pierrepont supported the generals and the Independents in resisting Scottish and Presbyterian demands for disbandment and an unconditional treaty with the king. He backed the Army's initiative in putting forward its own "Heads of the Proposals" as the basis for a settlement. He combined with Cromwell, Ireton, Oliver St John, Nathaniel Fiennes and Henry Vane in persuading the Commons to adopt the proposals.[30] In fact, although the terms are assumed to have been drafted principally by his Nottinghamshire neighbour Commissary-General Ireton, they bear a striking resemblance to Pierrepont's own consistent agenda of guaranteed assemblies (now to be biennial), parliamentary control of the militia, and a tolerant religious settlement retaining episcopacy without coercive powers.[31] Pierrepont and Ireton were standing by the original aims of the revolution, as outlined by John Pym in 1640—that is to say, a moderated episcopacy, the certainty of regular parliaments to ensure the availability of the legislative process as the basis of good government, and complete parliamentary control of public finance. The core proposition, as always, was, "1. That parliaments may biennially be called, and meet at a certain day, with such provision for the certainty thereof as in the late act was made for Triennial Parliaments, and what further or other provision shall be found needful by the Parliament to reduce it to more certainty".[32]

Charles, however, had not really agreed to these changes when they were forced upon him in 1641, and he was in a better position to reject them now. Ironically, time was to show that the Army's Heads of the Proposals had been his best opportunity for a settlement. At the end of 1647, parliament put forward its own proposals in Four Bills, among which were the abolition of Episcopacy, and control of the militia by parliament for twenty years. This was completely unacceptable to the king, but he believed in any case that there were other options available to him. His alliance with the Scots was now secure, though this in effect decided his fate. In the debate on the Vote of No Addresses on 3rd January 1648, Ireton said that since the king had now plainly broken his contract with the people, they could justifiably proceed to "settle the kingdom without him". Cromwell said the same, and Pierrepont also spoke in favour of the motion.[33]

Enraged by the prospect that Charles was about to resume hostilities with the active support of the Scottish army, the Independent generals could be forgiven for vowing simply to bring "that man of blood" to final account. But the balance of opinion in the Commons reacted differently to the threat of invasion and further conflict, which would be expensive in lives and money. MPs concluded that the search for a settlement must be continued. Pierrepont played a part in various attempts to contrive a set of terms that might be put forward. The generals of the New Model were dismayed to find that their defeat of the Scots in August 1648 did not end the parliamentary search for a settlement with the king. On the contrary, since Charles was, for the moment, deprived of military options, there was a greater danger that he would make himself available for a treaty, and a war weary parliament might take him back on easy terms. The army leaders decided that the parliamentary cause would have to be secured by forcefully removing reactionary elements from the House of Commons.

Pierrepont was not among those MPs who were excluded by Prides Purge in December 1648, but he strongly disapproved of the invasion of parliamentary liberties. This was the moment when the revolution departed from its original premise of establishing the ultimate authority of the Representative. It thus forfeited the outright support of William Pierrepont, who had been the personification of that purpose. He duly absented himself from the purged House. But even as the hard-line elements in the army gathered to take the revolution to its ultimate, though unintended conclusion, with the final, lethal assault on the person of the king, Pierrepont did not entirely break with the army leaders. The new regime thought it worthwhile to nominally include him in the High Court of Justice that was to bring Charles to trial. Moreover, Pierrepont was still signing warrants for the Army Committee in March 1649, a month after absented MPs were supposed to be disqualified, and two months after the king's execution.

Pierrepont did not return to the Rump Parliament, but nor did he finally abandon the cause. Cromwell stayed at his house at Thoresby on his way to defeat the Scots in 1651.[34] And when the general returned to political command in London, Pierrepont became part of his inner circle, and provided consultative support on an informal but regular basis. He was "admitted when advice is wanting".[35] He was, said Bulstrode Whitelocke, one of a handful of trusted advisers whose counsel was accepted and followed by Cromwell "in most of his greatest affairs".[36] Pierrepont was no doubt particularly exercised by questions of revenue. His first arrival on the political scene had been marked by the principal purpose of subjecting all matters of public finance to the control of representative consent. And in fact it seems that he was instrumental in persuading Cromwell to phase out the Decimation Tax.[37] He continued as a close adviser to Cromwell's son Richard, during whose brief reign Pierrepont was said to be working out a scheme to resolve the problem of debt, and reduce the tax burden of the Army. It was a middle sort frame of mind.

Pierrepont may be regarded as exemplifying the central character of the parliamentarian cause, avoiding the extremes to which it came, but holding firm to its essential radical aims from beginning to end. The institution of automatic parliaments and the control of the militia were the means of securing the independent authority of parliament. The concept of the "unlimited power" of representative sovereign law was the main rationale and justification of parliamentarian ambition. But the principal, practical aim was to subject all matters of public finance to the control of parliamentary consent. And it is this latter purpose that emerges most clearly from the career of William Pierrepont.

Pierrepont was elected to the Convention Parliament for Nottinghamshire and resisted the Restoration because he felt that the Stuarts could not be expected to observe the liberties that had been established through the revolution. He tried to intercede for some of the republicans, gaining at least a stay of execution for his Nottinghamshire neighbour John Hutchinson. Pierrepont himself received a general pardon.[38] He may have been saved from a different fate by Lucy Hutchinson's steadfast refusal in inform about his championing of Richard Cromwell.[39] Pierrepont was defeated in the election for the Cavalier Parliament, but his service to the Good Old Cause was not quite at an end. In December 1667 he took part in what has been described as the one great success of "those who opposed the court". Parliament recruited him for the Brook House committee to "examine the accounts of the money that was given in the Dutch War".[40] The king tried to halt the committee, but it proceeded nonetheless, and duly discovered widespread corruption and incompetence. The investigation reflected the central and most enduring aspect of parliamentary ambition. Just as the Commons' assumption of the power of setting the customs dues was not reversed with the Restoration, so parliament retained its original determination to make all public expenditure accountable to representative consent, for the desire to end the practices of discretionary taxation had been the general driving purpose of the parliamentarian movement.

Notes

1. L. Stone, *The Crisis of the Aristocracy 1558–1641,* (Oxford 1965), pp. 112, 190
2. *The Verney Memoirs*, ed. Francis Verney, (London 1907), I, p. 392
3. J. Rodgers, *Sherwood Forest,* (London 1908), p. 143
4. Some details of Pierrepont's landholdings and estate management can be found in BL Egerton Mss. 3516, 3536, 3562; and Nottinghamshire Archives, DDP, DD4P, DD44
5. Lucy Hutchinson, *Memoirs of the Life of Colonel Hutchinson*, ed. J. Hutchinson, (London 1846), p. 118
6. *Private Journals of the Long Parliament*, eds. V. F. Snow and A. S. Young, (New Haven 1982), vol. I, p. xxii
7. *Notebook of Sir John Northcote*, ed. A. H. Hamilton, (London 1877), p. 44
8. J. Rushworth, *Historical Collections,* (London 1659–1701), IV, p. 325
9. Ibid, p. 326
10. Ibid

11. Henry Ireton, *Puritanism and Liberty*, ed. A. S. P. Woodhouse, (London 1938), p. 72
12. Hutchinson, *Memoirs of the Life of Colonel Hutchinson*, p. 118
13. *The Journal of Sir Simonds D'Ewes*, ed. W. Notestein, (Yale 1923), pp. 188–9, (n)
14. Thomas Bailey, *Annals of Nottinghamshire*, (London 1863), vol. 2, p. 648
15. Ibid
16. *CSP Domestic 1641–3*, p. 277
17. *Private Journals of the Long Parliament*, I, p. 105
18. Clarendon, *History of the Rebellion*, ed. W. D. Macray, (Oxford 1958), I, p. 444
19. *A Letter from Divers Knights and Gentlemen of Nottinghamshire*, BL E154, (45), pp. 3–6
20. Hutchinson, *Memoirs of the Life of Colonel Hutchinson*, pp. 149–50
21. Ibid, p. 136
22. *Lords Journal*, IV, pp. 508–9; *Private Journals of the Long Parliament*, I, p. 41; *Old Parliamentary History of England*, (London 1751), IX, pp. 287, 322; *Two Journals of the Long Parliament*, ed. M. Jansson, (New York 1984), p. 47
23. V. Pearl, "The Royal Independents and the English Civil War", *Transactions of the Royal Historical Society*, 5th series, *18* (1968), pp. 69–96
24. Diary of Walter Yonge, BL Add. Ms. 18,777, f. 157
25. Ibid., ff. 4, 21; *Private Journals of the Long Parliament*, I, pp. 360, 384, II, pp. 119, 343, III, pp. 145, 284
26. *Verney Memoirs*, I, p. 305
27. See above, Chapter 10
28. D. Hirst, *Authority and Conflict*, (London 1986), p. 249
29. The Answer of the Lords and Commons to the Commissioners of Scotland, BL, E811, (2), pp. 43–4, 61–6
30. *Putney Projects*, BI, E421, (19), p. 43
31. *Constitutional Documents of the Puritan Revolution*, ed. S. R. Gardiner, (Oxford 1968), pp 316–26
32. Ibid, p. 316
33. D. Underdown, *Prides Purge*, (Oxford 1971), p. 88
34. Rodgers, *Sherwood Forest*, p. 155
35. *CSP Domestic 1655–6*, p. 80
36. Bulstrode Whitelocke, *Memorials of the English Affairs*, (London 1733), p. 656
37. *The Writings and Speeches of Oliver Cromwell*, ed. W. Abbot, (Harvard 1937), IV, p 394
38. BL Egerton Ms. 7986
39. Hutchinson, *Memoirs of the Life of Colonel Hutchinson*, pp. 419–20
40. G. Burnet, *History of His Own Time*, (London 1724), I, p. 267

16 The Socio-Economic Limits of the Revolution

Parliament, the People and the Poor; and on Whose Side Were the Levellers?

William Pierrepont was the son of an earl, and "as considerable . . . a person as any in England". He sat at the very pinnacle of the social and economic hierarchy, yet he identified closely with the cause of "the people". Lucy Hutchinson recalled how he sought to reassure her husband that the political nation would never countenance a Stuart restoration because it would be "the ruin of the people's liberty".[1] As became apparent in the previous chapter, Pierrepont was guided by a precise definition of the principal elements of that liberty. He believed that it lay essentially in establishing the sovereign authority of representative consent over the making of law, the raising of revenue, and the general course of governmental activity. He regarded this as the best guarantee of his own interests, as well as those of the public at large. But did Pierrepont, and Lucy Hutchinson who was of similar class, actually think of themselves as part of "the people"?

This is a relevant and important question because it raises the issue of exactly what was meant by the term "the people" in the early seventeenth century. We should not assume that it carried the same force or connotations then as it does in current usage. It is the kind of term that may be regarded, mistakenly, as timeless, and recent historians writing about the seventeenth century have indeed been inclined to apply it too uncritically in a modern sense. Parliamentarians invested heavily in the idea of the people, but the seventeenth century version of the concept was significantly different from that of today, and it is necessary to clarify that distinction in order to maintain a clear understanding of the relationship between "the people" and the parliamentary cause. Is it possible that a man of William Pierrepont's aristocratic birth might have found a more natural place among "the people" in the early seventeenth century than he would now?

The term "the people" has been burdened with a variety of applications, over the centuries. It is sometimes used rather vaguely, or in a "populist" sense, to convey the impression of talking about actual persons, as opposed to social trends or political institutions. In fact the present author should confess to applying it in a somewhat imprecise manner, in the title of a previous volume, *People and Parliament*. The intention was to indicate that among the general population of early seventeenth century England there had developed a homespun, or working philosophy of representative rights that could motivate a parliamentarian allegiance, without necessary reference to the formal ideologies of resistance that were current at the time.[2] There may be some doubt as to how far the phrase in the title managed to convey that idea, though perhaps it was to some extent substantiated by detailed illustration.

The term "the people" can mean literally everything, or nothing. "The people" can refer to the sum of all the actual people within a particular state; or it can refer to a fiction—that is to say, the theoretical or mythical "people" who are imagined to have been party to the original contract of government, through which the kingdom, and its balance of power, was founded. This image of a "people" engaged in the inception of the political structure was often employed to assert the rights of subjects against their king, and it was still being invoked in that sense in the sixteenth and seventeenth centuries. It had the advantage of being as difficult to disprove as it was to substantiate. It has fallen out of use since the nineteenth century, with the growing tendency to allocate natural rights to the present reality of the people. In modern times we do not regard "the people" as having had a stake in the formation of the state. For us, the political force of the people is active and current, and seen in terms of their due interests in the balance of the community now. This is reflected in the fact that our notion of the people almost always entails the real sense of a whole population. Crucially, this includes the very poor, and in fact the usage is in a sense defined by their inclusion. In other words, we now conceive "the people" from the bottom up. And it is in this respect that the seventeenth century definition displayed a very significant difference.

In time of civil strife the phrase "the people" takes on an extra balance or dimension of meaning, by which it becomes attached or arrogated to a broad political movement that is ranged against a governing elite. The "popular" party will typically present itself as acting on behalf of the people as a whole against the exercise of personal, authoritarian rule. In certain circumstances, however, a ruling autocracy, or military regime will also assert that it is holding power *for* the people. In these cases the force of "the people" is taken for granted, and may be misrepresented, though it is not actually fictionalised as it was in traditional foundation theories. Thus a political party that claims to be ruling for the people does not necessarily possess a mandate from the whole of the population, or even from a majority among them, but it will usually maintain at least a theory, or a promise of the devolution of power to a broader base.

In the case of the English Civil War and Revolution, with which this study has been particularly concerned, "the people" were associated with the parliamentarians, who used the term with great regularity and conviction. Lucy Hutchinson, for instance, regarded the Civil War as deriving in every sense from a rise of "the people", whose socio-economic advance had developed to the point where it could underpin a challenge to the power of the crown. "When the nobility shrank into empty names the throne lost its supporters . . . when the full body of the people came rolling in upon it . . . the interest of the people, which had been many years growing".[3] The Stuart monarchs, on the other hand, had little use for the concept of "the people". James I employed the word "popularity" only in a pejorative sense, as being necessarily in contention with the prerogatives of the crown. Charles I spoke of the general population as "the subjects", and would never have spoken of "the people" as an independent force in the same way as the parliamentary side. Thus, at the very inception of the revolution in February 1641, William Strode could confidently present the bill for automatic parliaments as "somewhat to comfort the people". [4] But when, under duress, the king was finally brought to accept the measure, he said, begrudgingly, that, "never bill passed here in this House of more favour to subjects than this is".[5]

So it was the parliamentary side that flew the banner of "the people", while the king's side flew his own. This is not to say that the royalist armies did not include many commoners in their ranks. On the contrary, it was a standard observation among contemporaries that the king's forces contained the higher proportion of the very poor. This was perhaps because they were often there as the retained servants or labourers recruited from the estates of the Royalist nobility. But the perception of this pattern of allegiance was quite general. In the city of Bristol, for instance, it was said that the king found support from among the very poor and the very rich, while his cause was "disgusted by the middle ranks . . . the truest citizens".[6] It is possible that the main determinant of these perceived contrasts was not so much the position of the poor themselves, but the fact that the middle sort, as a generality, inclined towards the parliamentary cause. But it may also be that the force of deference was easier to activate and enlist among the poor, whether in favour of the king himself, or his noble lieutenants, as Lucy Hutchinson suggested.

From the beginning to the end of the struggle, parliament was identified with "the people" as the alternative body in which political rights resided. Many leading parliamentarian spokesmen, including Henry Parker, John Pym and Henry Ireton, were ready to invoke the general tenet of "salus populi", that the safety of the people was the supreme law. This was useful shorthand. But in essence the parliamentarian movement had relatively little use for formal theories of resistance, though these were certainly available if required. During the second half of the sixteenth century there had arisen a powerful and influential body of political writings ascribing to the people a right to depose a tyrannical or ungodly ruler, usually on the basis of an original contract.[7] These ideas had active force in the different circumstances that prevailed in Scotland

and France, but they found little purchase in England. Some historians have noted the relative absence of formal resistance theory as an inspiration for the English Revolution, but have failed to recognise the main reason.[8] In fact such theories were surplus to requirements. As already suggested, the parliamentarians found their motivation, and their justification, in a working philosophy of representative rights that was distinctive to the English context.

So parliament's "people" were not the mythical people of the ancient constitution, though some recent historians have seemed oddly content with the notion.[9] Parliamentarians did make play with the idea of a "freeborn people", which was voiced with particular urgency on the fringes of the movement, for instance by the Levellers. John Lilburne, the first Leveller leader, was nicknamed "Freeborn John". The concept presupposed that the original England of the Anglo-Saxons had enjoyed a kind of popular liberty, which had ended with the imposition of the Norman Yoke. This derived some force from the fact that there had indeed been a Conquest by a domineering Norman nobility, but there was really nothing to show that the position of the people had been significantly better before the Normans arrived. In truth, the idea of a freeborn people throwing off the Norman Yoke was just a way of representing the fact that a constitutional difference had arisen between the present English people and their king, and that this involved a demand for freedom from certain royal powers.

The people to whom the parliamentarian cause related were not an historical myth. They were a present and active people, in keeping with the freedoms that they sought. The concepts in which the parliamentarians found inspiration were not imaginary ancient constitutions, or even the formal resistance theories of their own day. Their political confidence and ambition were based on a working philosophy of representative rights, underpinned by a belief in the sovereign power of parliament's legislative function. The essence of this is captured in Henry Ireton's summary of why people had fought for parliament.

> The people of this kingdom have this right at least, that they should not be concluded but by the Representative . . . that the will of one man should not be a law, but that the law of this kingdom should be by a choice of persons to represent, and that choice to be made by the generality of the kingdom . . . Here was a right that induced men to fight.[10]

It is also clear in William Pierrepont's condemnation of discretionary finance. "Unlimited power must be in some, to make and repeal laws to fit the disposition of times and persons—nature places this in common consent only".[11] This was not an ancient freedom. It derived from the emergence of a distinctive concept of sovereign law in mid-sixteenth-century

England, by which the most absolute power of legislation became dependent on the consent of the "entire society". Since the early seventeenth century, parliament had sought to extend that right to displace other royal prerogatives, especially regarding public finance. In 1641 this liberty was being secured by establishing the representative body at the centre of the state.

"The people" of the parliamentarian movement who were behind this change had a definite reality, but who exactly *were* the politicised "people"? We need to keep in mind that it was in one respect a specifically "national" people, not simply in the sense that the English parliament was a truly national representative body in a manner that was quite unique among European kingdoms, but also because the equally distinctive concept of sovereign representative law drew its authority, explicitly, from the idea that parliament reflected the consent of the "entire society" as Richard Hooker called it. A vital aspect of this model was that it referred itself to the inclusion of "everyman", a notion enshrined in the authoritative account of Sir Thomas Smith in the 1560s.

> The most high and absolute power of the realm of England is in the Parliament. . . . That which is done by this consent is called firm, stable and sanctum, and is taken for law. . . . For every Englishman is intended to be there present, either in person or by procuration and attornies . . . from the Prince . . . to the lowest person of England. And the consent of the Parliament is taken to be every man's consent.[12]

The figure of "everyman" was an effective symbol of the representation of the whole, but it was not applied literally, as we would use it today. "Every Englishman" did not mean *every* Englishman—it referred only to those who already possessed a degree of economic freedom, and a political voice, in England. In the actual construction of the "entire society" it was certainly important that Smith included the yeomanry, along with the prince and the gentlemen, as comprising those who governed the kingdom and made and administered the law.[13] But it was also significant that the classes below the yeomanry were *excluded*. In practice, the term "everyman" only encompassed those with a real degree of socio-economic independence. Thus Henry Ireton could regard parliament as elected "by the generality of the kingdom", while insisting that the franchise should not be extended beyond the traditional freeholder qualification.[14] Ireton could also refer to the "meanest" as having the right to vote, but it was only the "meanest" with a "local interest" or property. "Those that have the meanest local interest—that man that hath but forty shillings a year, he hath as great a voice in the election of the knight of the shire as he that hath ten thousand a year".[15] It seems that there were equal representative rights, but only above a certain socio-economic level.

Sir Thomas Smith's exclusion of the poor from the political scene is explicit.

> The fourth part or class amongst us is what the old Romans called *capite censij proletarij* . . . day labourers, poor husbandmen, yea merchants and retailers who have no free land, copyholders, all artificers. . . . These have no voice or authority in our commonwealth, and no account is made of them but only to be ruled.[16]

It is striking that Smith accords the yeomanry such a substantial, though quite recent place among the rulers, while the common people were only "to be ruled". It underlines the fact that the poor were not the effective parliamentarian people. It is, however, of some interest that their exclusion was not completely inflexible. "Yet they be not altogether neglected. For in cities and corporate towns for default of yeomen . . . And in villages they be commonly made churchwardens, alerunners, and many times constables, which toucheth more upon the commonwealth, and at first were not employed any such low and base persons".[17] This too tended to underline the sharpness of the distinction. And yet, as we shall see ahead, it was one of a variety of ways in which the administrative and representative systems could reach out to the poor, and offer them a subsidiary role, when occasion demanded.

So the parliamentarian "people" were real, but they were not all the people. The operative "people" for Henry Ireton did not include the very poor—only those who already possessed a degree of economic substance and political initiative. It was the same for another contemporary commentator, James Harrington, who gave a cogent account of the underlying rise of "the people" through the centuries leading up to the Civil War. For Harrington, "the people" included the merchants, artisans and lesser gentry, but especially the middle sort of substantial farmers, who over the years had gained their commercial freedom, and become "much unlinked from dependence on their lords".[18] He thought that over the course of the preceding century the socio-economic standing and political potential of these groups had grown significantly at the expense of the traditional establishment of crown, nobility and church. He believed that this amounted to a transfer of economic weight to "the people", and that this in turn created the platform for the parliamentary challenge to the sovereignty of the crown, culminating in the Civil War. He was obviously not talking about all the people—just the middle sort.

This was a viewpoint shared by Lucy Hutchinson, as she observed the results, on the ground, in terms of Civil War allegiance. "The interest of the people, which had been many years a growing, made an extraordinary progress in the reign of King Henry the Eighth, who returning the vast revenues of the church into the body of the people, cast the balance clear on their side".[19] Like Harrington, she did not exclude the gentry from the body of the people. It was after all the middling sort of gentry who had acquired the bulk of the church lands. She did, however, exclude the poor, who she thought had their "dependence" on the Royalist lords. Conversely: "most of the middle sort, the able substantial freeholders, and other commons . . . adhered to the parliament".[20] Here too, the parliamentarian people were those with an effective degree of socio-economic substance and independence.

The fact that these contemporary commentators could classify "the people" as a group that we might today regard as just the middle class highlights the crucial difference between that time and ours. For us, the concept of the people naturally includes the poor. This may indeed be taken as the essential feature of the way that we define the term, reflecting the fact that we do mean all the people. But in the sixteenth and seventeenth centuries, "the people" did not necessarily include the poor. More normally indeed, they were specifically *excluded*, as being without political status. It was not a contradiction for Civil War contemporaries to suppose that although the king's supporters contained the largest proportion of the very poor, yet it was the parliamentary side that could validly claim the allegiance of the body of the people, in the shape of the middle sort.

In this light, recent historiography has probably tended to deflect us from a true understanding of the association between parliament and the people. There has been in effect a tendency to apply the modern definition, and to put the question in terms of whether the poor or common people were to be found on the parliamentary side. Thus, the main debate has been about the political status of popular actions like land-use riots, or anti-enclosure protests, and whether these can be related to the principles or personnel of the parliamentary movement. Roger Manning for instance identified a large number of land-use protests in the century before the Civil War, but thought that they displayed no sign of a broader political consciousness.[21] Buchanan Sharp's study of the popular protests of the southwest also suggested that the issues were localised, and although they did involve an element of class antagonism against the gentry, there was no obvious connection with Civil War allegiances.[22] Keith Lindley thought that the Fenland riots were similarly parochial in character, though they sometimes attracted the support of parliamentarian figures. On the other hand, Steve Hindle for Buckinghamshire, and John Gurney for Surrey, have found that there were strong connections between preceding local protest movements and the broader politics of the Civil War.[23]

This is a wide range of conclusions, somewhat difficult to apply in a coherent way. A more cogent and relevant picture can be obtained by recognising that contemporaries did not associate the politicised "people" with the poor. There is also a need to clarify where the lines of socio-economic distinction lay. Steve Hindle leaves us with a rather hazy definition of the middle sort. He noted that at Caddington the voice of the very poorest cottagers was never heard, but it could be assumed that they had a vital interest in retaining their rights in the commons, woods and wastes. Some of the smaller copyholders seem to have "agreed" to the enclosure, though as Hindle rightly points out, "agreement" was often nominal, and more like a reluctant acceptance of a fait accompli. He found that the protests against enclosure appeared to be led by copyholders with smallholdings of between 10 and 40 acres. Hindle interpreted this as the middle sort making common cause with the poor, and concluded that they could face either way, according to circumstances.[24] But in truth their position was probably more consistent than this suggests. It is questionable whether these copyholders can be accurately characterised as "middle sort". A holding of 10 to 40 acres was of typical medieval scale, and did not produce the marketable surplus that was necessary to survive and thrive in the inflationary conditions of the sixteenth and early seventeenth centuries. These people might be better described as poor husbandmen, whose place on the land was under threat. The use of the common pastures was essential to them, which was a good reason to oppose the enclosure. But they were not the middle sort as described by contemporaries like Lucy Hutchinson. The parliamentarian middle sort were essentially the yeoman freeholders, with consolidated farms of more than 70 acres, ensuring commercial success in the prevailing economic climate.

To investigate the possibility of a relationship between local land-use protests and parliamentarian politics is to pose a question that would not have been considered relevant at the time. Civil War contemporaries would not have supposed that there could be any kind of natural connection between the parliamentarian movement and the poor. If we are looking for the popular basis of the parliamentarian cause, the emphasis on the position of the poor leads us, specifically, in the wrong direction. The parliamentary movement certainly had a "popular" aspect, but almost by definition this had little to do with the poor. It was the yeomen farmers, smaller merchants and traders, and even the middling gentry who were regarded as "the people" in the context of the English Civil War and Revolution. The popular dimension of the parliamentary cause revolved largely around the commercial interests and ambitions that these groups shared. In certain important ways the motivations of the middle sort, and the aims of the parliamentarians, were precisely antithetical to the position of the poor. And this was most notable in the light of their contrasting positions on the land-use issue, especially regarding the enclosure of the commons. In effect, this amounted to a general conflict of interest between parliament and the poor. The English parliament was the natural representative of those classes—the gentry, the yeomanry and the merchants—who were engaged in the enclosure and commercial consolidation of the common lands into individual properties, and who stood to gain from the expansion of the wool and cloth trades that did much to encourage the process.

The balance of forces is illustrated by the fluctuating fortunes of the enclosure movement in the decades before the Civil War. 1597 was the last occasion when conditions of dearth produced the time-honoured response of an act against enclosure. In the first parliament of James I the Commons were relatively free of official pressure, and the widespread Midland Rising against enclosure in 1607 did not bring forth a similar legislative response. In fact, 1608 saw the first, limited, pro-enclosure measure, on the rationale that the process actually tended to increase the food supply. This was the first clear indication that the natural stance of the Commons on the question of enclosure was to favour and encourage it. In the 1620s, the royal government never quite managed to impose its authority on the Commons, and was never in a position to control the anti-social aspects of parliamentarian economics. In 1621, in spite of the depression, came the first general pro-enclosure bill. In 1624, the long-standing statutes against enclosure were repealed. And in practice, the decade witnessed a renewed flurry of enclosing activity.

So in this most important area of their livelihoods, the poor husbandmen had little reason to expect assistance from the further empowerment of the representative body. They might, however, have supposed that they could count on the help of the king. If the poor were looking for one specific, practical motive for supporting Charles, it was his anti-enclosure policies of the 1630s. That decade had seen the latest in a long series of campaigns by almost all Tudor and Stuart regimes to stop or reverse the process of enclosure, and it appears to have been by far the most effective. The moral condemnations of the church combined powerfully with government action. Archbishop Laud sat on the enclosure commissions, making good his claim to be "a great hater" of enclosures, as "one of the greatest mischiefs in this kingdom". He said that it put the pursuit of private gain above the common good, and therefore constituted an act of impiety.[25] The campaign was pursued with the force of a crusade. More than six hundred culprits were identified. Many were fined—an exercise which as John Pym later protested had "driven many millions out of the subjects' purses".[26] Others were imprisoned, and landlords and substantial farmers were forced to plough up land that they had enclosed for pasture. A steady stream of transgressors was still being hauled before the courts in 1639, when the arrival of the Long Parliament brought the regime to a close. In this light, it ought to have become apparent to the poor husbandman on which side his bread was buttered. If Charles had won the Civil War, and returned to power with a standing army capable of sustaining his personal rule on a more stable basis, the anti-enclosure drive would presumably have been renewed, if only as a means of obstructing the pretensions of the commercial classes and diverting a goodly proportion of their wealth into the royal coffers. This was the best chance of securing the future of the commons on their traditional basis.

What happened in the event was that the king was defeated and beheaded, and the triumph of parliament instituted a seminal change in the guiding rules of economic activity. This established the absolute rights of individual property against both king and commons, and it brought to an end the medieval presumption that the free play of private advantage should be restrained in the common interest of the poor. The turnaround was reflected both generally and specifically in the reversal of the relationship between enclosure and the legislative process. For one hundred and fifty years, successive royal governments had legislated to try to restrict the enclosure movement, but after 1650, the only enclosure legislation would be for the purpose of encouraging the process. The revolutionary decades have thus rightly been described as a turning point in the history of enclosure.[27] A principal effect of the parliamentarian revolution was to put an end to the policies of sympathy and support for the interests of the poor on the common lands that had always been followed by the political and ecclesiastical establishments of the past.

Who Were the Real Levellers, and Whose Side Were They on?

Which side did the Levellers take in the matter? The answer is not as obvious as it might appear. The Levellers cast an interesting, and in some ways unexpected light on the land-use issue, as indeed on the general question of the balance of relationships between parliament, the people, and the poor. The Levellers presented themselves as the immediate champions of "the people", and the phrase was never far from their lips. Since they were called the Levellers, it is easy to assume that this meant all the people, and especially perhaps the poor. But this was not really the case. Notwithstanding Rainsborough's famous plea at Putney for the rights of "the poorest he", the Levellers were not the natural party of the poor. The Leveller movement had its beginnings among the artisans and small traders of Southwark and the City of London. In Christopher Hill's useful phrase, they represented the small proprietors of town and countryside. Accordingly, their central and most consistent economic concerns revolved around their opposition to monopolies and trading restraints, which they regarded as the principal barriers to success. And notwithstanding Ireton's provocative comments in the Putney Debates, the Levellers were not against property. Ireton's suggestion that their political aims were open to that charge was intended not to confront them, but to give them pause, as indeed it did, if only long enough to assert that their proposals could be carried through without any danger to the rights of property. They hoped, said Maximilian Petty, "that they may see the power of the king and Lords thrown down, and yet may live to see property preserved".[28]

Enclosure was a function of property, and the Levellers were not instinctively the defenders of the poor husbandman working the commons and the open fields. The Levellers' economic programme had little or nothing to offer to this group. By the same token, in the early years of the movement, in 1645 and 1646, their pamphlets did not treat of the land-use issue. At the beginning they were speaking for their core constituency, the trading and manufacturing classes of London and its surrounds, and their focus was on obtaining the market freedoms and legal rights that they believed would enable them to thrive. They did eventually come to display a concern with the problem faced by many of the agricultural poor in trying to sustain their use and tenure of the land. But the Levellers focused on this only belatedly, and even then their interest proved to be somewhat fleeting. The demand that the common lands should be restored was made first by Richard Overton in 1647.[29] "That all the grounds which anciently lay in common for the poor, and are now . . . enclosed . . . may forthwith, in whose hands soever they are, be . . . laid open again to the free and common use and benefit of the poor".[30] This was about two years after the Levellers had begun to set out their programme, and there is a sense that the poor are being spoken of in the third person, rather than as integral to the movement. It seems indeed that there was an accidental element in the way that the Levellers happened upon the issue. The inclusion of the item about the commons was almost certainly a product of the contacts that the Levellers had made among the soldiers of the New Model Army in the early months of 1647. It was indicative that the demand came at the end of a list of "Articles for the Good of the Commonwealth, Presented to the Consideration of his Excellency Sir Thomas Fairfax and to the Officers and Soldiers under his command".[31] There was certainly some awareness that the army, especially in the form of its rank and file, was a particularly useful recruit to the Leveller cause, since it possessed guns as well as an urge for political liberty. The adoption of the vital economic interests of the poorest soldiers was, however, not enduring. The issue became gradually less prominent in Leveller writings, and by May 1649, with the publication of the culminating statement of their aims and demands, in the Third Agreement of the People, the request for the return of the common fields had disappeared altogether.

Only the Diggers really embraced the interests of the poor husbandmen on the commons and open fields. In fact, the land-use issue is very clearly the driving force and the dominant motif of their writings. The Diggers are often thought of as just the left wing of the Leveller movement, but in fact they were pursuing a quite different economic agenda. At the core of their special concern was a resentment, not to say abhorrence, at the process that was displacing the independent husbandmen from their holdings and reducing many of them to wage labourers. One of the earliest and clearest expressions of the Digger case came in fact from within the Army, from the troopers of the Northumberland horse. They wrote "with their swords in their hands", and said that the exploitation of tenures and the enclosure of the commons had destroyed their independent holdings, "utterly disabling them from all good nurture in learning or trades, and forcing them from generation to generation to be hinds, half hinds, quarter hinds, shepherds and herdsmen".[32] "Hind" was the northern term for wage labourer, and these Diggers obviously had a rooted objection to having that role imposed upon them in any shape or form.

The essential difference between Digger and Leveller economics is illustrated by the fact that the Diggers' powerfully stated objection to the indignity and deprivation of wage labour, finds no echo in Leveller writings. Along with their general opposition to monopolies, impositions and trading restraints, the main local concern of the Leveller groups in their London heartland was with trying to assert their democratic rights within the guild structures of their trades. Brailsford saw this in terms of a class struggle between the craftsmen and the increasingly detached capitalist merchants.[33] But it is probably better regarded as a reflection of the general parliamentarian drive to establish rights of consent, which was indeed the underlying principle at work in respect of all the economic aims of the Levellers. This kind of connection is illustrated by John Wildman's rationale for the demand that all wards should have a voice in the choice of the Lord Mayor and sheriffs, "especially in this parliamentary time, wherein the parliament hath pleased to declare that the original of all just power is from the people. And how governors should derive a just power from the people but by assent of the people, I understand not".[34]

Gerrard Winstanley, who was by far the most prolific of Digger polemicists, had originally possessed a freedom and a trade in London. He had been ruined and alienated by "the thieving art of buying and selling" and had left to seek a livelihood in the country. He came to the conclusion that all should be possessed of a freedom to live from the land. When, in one brief pamphlet, he addressed the City of London again, it was to remind them that the parliamentary cause had been fought in the name of liberty for all, and that this should apply not just to the freemen of the City and the enclosing freeholders of the countryside, but also to those who sought to reassert their right to a stake on the common lands.[35]

Winstanley's voluminous writings can in fact be considered as one, long continuous tirade against the great agrarian transition of the preceding century. This period had been characterised by the gradual enclosure and displacement of the commons and open fields by the consolidation of larger individual farms and properties, which had tended to result in the deprivation of many erstwhile independent smallholders. The common field husbandmen had once comprised a majority of the rural workforce, but they were now being bought out or dispossessed, in whole or in part, and reduced to the status of wage labourers, working for the more substantial, commercially successful farmers. Consequently, by the second half of the seventeenth century, the balance had been reversed, and there was a majority of wage labourers in the countryside. This was the inversion of fortunes that Winstanley recorded. "The rich have by their covetous wit got the plain hearted poor . . . to work for them for small wages, and by their work have got a great increase". To rectify this injustice, he advocated the common ownership of the land. "Making the earth a common treasury for all, both rich and poor . . . not enclosing any part into any particular hand".[36] This would in effect have restored the communal occupation of the common fields and put it on a more secure basis. And it would have excluded the possibility of wage labour. This would have been an efficient solution from Winstanley's point of view, except that it had very little chance of finding any kind of official support. The Digger agenda was an anomaly in terms of mainstream parliamentarian economics. Nothing was ever less likely to be enacted by an English parliament than the common ownership of the land. The most important, practical purpose of the parliamentarian revolution was to establish the rights of freedom of trade and absolute property.

Yet Winstanley was a parliamentarian, both by word and action. He claimed consistently that the commoners on whose behalf he was speaking were also parliamentarians. "We amongst others of the common people that have ever been friends to the parliament . . . we did come with purse or person and underwent great hardship, and still you promised us freedom in the end".[37] His support for the enthronement of representative rights was explicit. In the *Law of Freedom*, in which he outlined his plan for the common ownership of the land, he also offered a full endorsement of the proposition that parliament should hold a permanent place of authority at the centre of affairs. As plainly as Pym, Pierrepont or Ireton, he took the provision of automatic, regular assembly as the foundation of a new balance of government, based on the same understanding of parliament's defining part in the function of sovereign legislation. "Seeing that we shall have successive parliaments every year, there will be rules made for every action a man can do". The law was "the mind and determination of the Parliament and of the people of the land, to be their rule to walk by and to be the touchstone of all actions". And seeing that the king was no more, the parliament now could step forward as the natural executive force. "A parliament is the head of power in a commonwealth, and it is their work to manage public affairs, in times of war and in times of peace".[38]

Did he really expect parliament to enact the common ownership of the land? Not in so many words. But he did say that the "work of a Parliament" should include the restoration of the commons that had been enclosed by the oppression of landlords, and that this in effect comprised "the Commonwealth's land", which should be maintained as such for the free use of the people. [39] This was, to say the least, an unrealistic expectation. The inconsistency is all the more apparent in the light of Winstanley's clear recognition that the freedoms sought by parliamentarians in general were freedom of trade and absolute property.[40] The absence of a credible working connection between Winstanley's pro-parliamentary politics and his plan for the common ownership of the land highlights the real, and very different economic aims of parliamentarians generally. The fact that he was nevertheless a forceful advocate for the power of parliament underlines the strength in depth of the parliamentary cause, and the wide reception of the representative principles that it embodied. Winstanley's reference to the contribution of "the common people" also indicates that sometimes the poor did attach themselves to the parliamentary cause and sought to advance their demands under the general banner of "liberty". But in the end, his suggestion that the freedom of the poor was to be achieved by a system of common ownership confirms the essential polarity between their economic interests and mainstream parliamentarian ambitions.

Further confirmation of these distinctions is found in the much more coherent stance of the central Leveller movement. At heart, the Levellers were not primarily concerned with the hardships and indignities that the husbandmen were suffering through the enclosure of the common lands and the imposition of wage labour. On the contrary, the Levellers were rather in favour of the assertion and extension of individual property rights. In fact, their economic requirements directly reflected the aims of parliamentarians generally. Their core, consistent grievances related to trading restraints. For instance, they believed, like other parliamentarians, that many economic ills stemmed from the insidious practice of monopolies. In his early pamphlets in 1645 John Lilburne objected in particular to the monopolies in the cloth and printing industries.[41] And in their first general statement of affairs in 1647, the Levellers applauded the fact that the creation of new patents had been halted, but protested that the most powerful monopoly of the Merchant Adventurers still persisted: "to the great abridgement of the liberty of the people, and the extreme prejudice of all such people as do depend on cloth and woollen manufacture . . . to the discouragement and disadvantage of all sorts of tradesmen and seafaring men".[42] These were words that might have been used by MPs and leading economic commentators at any stage in the long drive for freedom of trade between 1604 and 1640.

Much the same can be said as regards the political position of the Levellers. Gerald Aylmer expressed surprise that the Levellers were able to make such an impact given the hierarchical assumptions of the age.[43] But this becomes easier to understand when we perceive that the age was not nearly so hierarchically restricted as modern historians have chosen to believe. Since 1610, MPs had been engaged consistently in challenging prerogative powers of the crown, in favour of the extension of representative rights. This was a specifically non-hierarchical activity. And the Leveller movement took political force because they were in line with the basic aims of the parliamentary cause in general. The failure to recognise the substantial, radical common ground between the Levellers and mainstream parliamentarians is a fundamental flaw in recent studies of the topic.[44]

Aylmer took the work of J. Frank as the guide to the genesis of Leveller thought, and located it mainly in the rational, natural law traditions that had been brought to the fore by the Renaissance. The Levellers certainly characterised the freedoms and equalities that they were seeking as, in general terms, natural rights. But this does not capture the essence of their thinking. In fact, their political ideas had a specific and fully elaborated indigenous derivation, which related in essence to the developing principles and practice of representative rights in England. Leveller theory owed little to the nebulous suppositions of natural law, but much to the working concept of English sovereign representative law. They espoused the latter as a central, motive force, in common with mainstream parliamentarian leaders from John Pym to Henry Ireton. And in recognising this we may avoid the very misguided assumption that the dispute in the Putney Debates was between the Levellers seeking egalitarian democracy on the basis of natural rights, and the Generals defending the traditional hierarchical order. In reality, they all shared the essential, radical aim of establishing the representative assembly, and the representative principle, with a permanent, independent place at the centre of affairs.

The concept of sovereign representative law was a basic point of reference and departure in most Leveller writings, beginning with John Lilburne's first essay in asserting the political rights of the people in "England's Birthright Justified". This was written as a protest against a trumped-up charge brought by some of his Presbyterian opponents that he had been spreading scandal about the Speaker of the Commons. In his defence, Liburne did not plead the assumed and ancient right of Englishmen not to be committed without cause shown, nor did he refer himself to Magna Charta, or assert the claims of natural justice. Instead, he invoked the concept of sovereign statute law, of which, he said, his treatment had been an abuse. "All rational men" acknowledged that parliament had a sovereign power to make law. These laws were clearly defined and known, and none should be arraigned unless they had transgressed them. He then elaborated the essential premise on which the concept of sovereign representative law was based—the authority of consent. Nothing "doth bind the free-man thereof, but what is made and declared by common consent in parliament".[45] This was the fundamental principle of sovereign law by consent that underpinned the political self-confidence of the Levellers, and the parliamentarian movement as a whole.

It has sometimes been pointed out that Lilburne was not a political theorist in the formal sense. But he had no need to be. Leveller philosophy, like parliamentarian philosophy, was not an esoteric theory of resistance, but rather a working concept of the value and status of representative rights. And since the Levellers were extending the logic of this and needed to establish the platform in their own terms, they shed a special light on the underlying psychology of parliamentarian beliefs. In a postscript to "The Freeman's Freedom Vindicated", Lilburne produced a shorthand or homespun description of the origin of political rights in a form that directly reflected the active representative ideal that had emerged in England during the past century. More than most Levellers, he looked to religion as his starting point. And an insistence on individual rights of consent was indeed a crucial psychological link between Godly non-conformity and the parliamentarian cause.[46] Lilburne identified the genesis of such rights, and the nature of the connection. God, he said, "gave man the sovereignty (under himself) . . . and imbued him with a rational soul, or understanding, and thereby created him in his own image".[47] The idea of the inherent sovereignty of the individual became clearer in other Leveller writings, but Lilburne said simply that they were "all equal in power, dignity, authority and majesty, none of them having (by nature) an authority, dominion or magisterial power over another". Power could only be exercised over them by "institution or donation, that is to say by mutual agreement or consent". This was not an historical myth—it took precise form in the consent given to "their parliament-men, commissioners, trustees, deputies".[48] It was unjust "for any man whatsoever, spiritual or temporal . . . to appropriate and assume upon himself a power, authority or jurisdiction . . . over any sort of man in the world, without their free consent".[49] The formula was echoed in *London's Liberty in Chains*. God gave man reason, and reason found scope in consent. None had the right to impose upon another: "no further than by free consent". The same derivation of rights of consent is to be found in mainstream proponents of the representative principle, like Richard Hooker writing in the 1590s. Hooker was above all a rationalist, and believed that "It is not required, nor can it be exacted at our hands that we should yield unto anything other assent than such as doth answer the evidence which is to had of that which we assent unto".[50] People were creatures of reason, and the instrument through which the faculty of reason found scope and expression was the exercise of consent. In every sphere, this stood as the proposed and preferred alternative to the use of arbitrary or discretionary imposition.

The psychology that linked the rational faculties of the individual to the right of consent becomes clearer in the work of another leading Leveller polemicist, Richard Overton. His prose was more studied that Lilburne's and was relatively free of religious associations. Overton dealt essentially in logic. He felt no need to derive his argument in a sequence from the Creation—he simply proclaimed the sovereignty of the individual. "To every individual in nature is given am individual property by nature, not to be invaded or usurped by any, for everyone, as he is himself, so he hath a self-propriety, else he could not be himself, and of this no second may presume to deprive any of".[51] In his concept of a self-propriety without which "he could not be himself" Overton is in effect describing the emerging self-consciousness and self-confidence of the individual, as over the preceding decades, private realms of liberty were discovered, such as freedom of conscience, freedom of consent, freedom of trade, freedom of property, and the freedom of representative law. The sense of self-propriety was closely related to the assertion of absolute property, which was essentially the assumption by the individual of a right to hold and use his possessions freely for his own profit and purposes, without imposition. Overton captures the link between property and self-propriety with precision—"mine and thine cannot be, except this be".[52] Full property rights could only exist when each individual had an established freedom from the arbitrary claims of others. This confirms, of course, that the Levellers were not against property. On the contrary, like other parliamentarians, they were seeking to consolidate it.

Overton also shed light on the inherent connection between the absolute property of the individual, and the absolute legislative sovereignty of parliament. On the self-propriety of the individual, none could presume without consent, that is "but by deputation, commission".[53] What people conveyed by vote was the reflection of their individual sovereignty: "each of them communicated so much to you (their chosen ones) of their natural rights and powers, that you might thereby become their absolute commissioners and lawful deputies . . . their own, proper sovereign power".[54] They "empowered the Body Representative with their own absolute sovereignty". Thus parliament's general, legislative sovereignty came to be compounded of the consents of each and every self-possessed individual. Overton elucidates how the absolute representative and the absolute individual grew up together, as part and parcel of one another.

We come back again to the portentous paradox, distinctive to the English kingdom. After the triumph of parliamentary law in destroying the independent jurisdiction of the universal church in the mid-sixteenth century, the most "unlimited" power of sovereign legislation came to depend specifically on the exercise of representative consent. This created a political tension that found one form of resolution in the Triennial Act of 1641, giving parliament the kind of continuous, automatic place at the centre of the polity that in general theory was expected to belong to a body with sovereign legislative authority.[55] Overton had now described another detailed way in which the apparent contradiction between representative rights and absolute power was reconciled. The sovereign authority of parliamentary law was made up, in effect, of the combined personal sovereignties of every consenting individual. The complete self-propriety of the individual comprised the real element of the "absolute" in the process of representation.

Leveller theory thus helps to clarify the psychological developments behind the growing belief in representative forms that underpinned the parliamentarian movement, and put English history on a different course from other European kingdoms. By the same token, the central, practical proposition of the Levellers' political programme precisely reflected the core constitutional changes put in place by the MPs of the Long Parliament at the inception of the revolution in the winter of 1640–1641. The most crucial area of common ground was the insistence that there should be continual, guaranteed assemblies. The Levellers proposed, as the essential, consistent basis of their agenda that there should be automatic and successive parliaments. When voiced by the Levellers this is regarded by historians as a radical idea. Indeed it was. But one of the blind spots of recent historiography has been the failure to recognise that it was equally radical when brought forward by mainstream parliamentarian leaders like Pym, Cromwell and Pierrepont early in 1641, some years before the emergence of the Levellers. The Levellers referred themselves to the Triennial Act of 1641 as the model upon which the concept of automatic and successive parliaments was formed.[56] In fact, the Levellers' reiteration of the idea underlines the political radicalism that was inherent in the parliamentary cause from the beginning.

This was the fundamental change in the constitutional balance that was proposed by the parliamentarian leaders at the inception of the revolution, and taken up by the Levellers. The aim of them all was to give parliament an independent and continuous place at the centre of governmental affairs, enabling it to guarantee the regular provision of vital legislation, bring public finance under parliamentary control, and maintain a general supervisory influence over the executive. As Henry Ireton said during the Putney Debates—"we all agree that you should have a Representative to govern".[57] The establishment of automatic and successive assemblies remained at the core of the various settlement proposals that Ireton was involved in drafting in 1647–1648, just as it had been for John Pym in the winter of 1640–1641.[58]

"We all agree that you should have a Representative to govern". What then did they disagree about at Putney? It was, in some respects, a subsidiary question—exactly who should be regarded as qualified to elect the empowered Representative? Providing parliament with an independent and continuous place at the centre of the polity, by means of the Triennial Act, was the indispensable first step in applying the representative concept. Rights of consent only became an established political force when the king was deprived of the power to prevent the meeting of parliament. The extent of the electorate was, in that sense, a secondary issue, even for the Levellers. In fact, rather like their stance on the return of the common lands, it was only taken up belatedly. A demand that the franchise should be generally extended was not among their first priorities. In John Lilburne's early pamphlet *England's Birthright Justified*, he spoke simply of "the knights and burgesses chosen according to law, and sent to make up the parliament".[59] In *The Freeman's Freedom Vindicated*, he was at pains to assert that it was not the Lords but the elected Commons that constituted the sovereign power, but he showed no concern about who or how many should be enfranchised to vote them in.[60] The *Remonstrance of Many Thousand Citizens*, which was principally the work of Richard Overton, displayed a similar determination to deny the authority of the Lords, who did not "stand to be chosen for knights and burgesses of the people, as the gentry and other freemen of this nation do".[61] But the only recommendation for the electoral system itself was that it should be implemented more regularly. The Levellers noted the provision of the Triennial Act, which had guaranteed an assembly every three years, but they thought that this was not frequent enough—there should be a free choice of a parliament every year, to ensure that grievances and mischiefs did not develop beyond remedy.[62] Perhaps Overton knew that this reflected the original intention of the promoters of the Triennial Act, which had started out as a bill for guaranteed annual parliaments. Overton's suggestion of the mechanism for convening the automatic assembly displayed great faith in the spontaneous force of the representative process. There was to be "a meeting of the choosers of the parliament-men, to be expressed upon one certain day in November yearly . . . at the place accustomed . . . there to make choice of whom they thought good according to law". But again there was no indication that this would involve an extension of the electorate. Those expected to take part were simply "all men that have a right to be there".[63] This sounded like a straightforward acceptance of the status quo. It seems that in the context of their original programme, the Levellers were reasonably content with the existing franchise.

It needs to be understood that the Levellers were, in their original London heartland, people who already had the vote. When Overton addressed "our own House of Commons", and spoke of "our choosing you to be our parliament men", this often applied literally in the case of his Leveller associates. The urban franchise was, it is true, somewhat varied, and its exact character and scope is often difficult to establish. At the most exclusive it might be restricted to the governing body of aldermen, or at its broadest it could be vested in the whole body of the inhabitants. The technical rights are not always transparent, and even when they are known, it is not easy to be sure to what extent this was put into practice. Nevertheless, it seems clear that in Southwark and the City of London, where the Levellers took their rise, the franchise was at the wider end of the range, both in theory and actuality. London elected six MPs, and it is apparent that the general body of the inhabitants had a powerful voice in the process. The number of voters involved in elections was regularly referred to as "an immense multitude of the commons of the city". In Southwark, the franchise was sometimes defined as "scot and lot". This referred to a local rate that was typically paid by about three-quarters of the households in a borough. And sometimes it was described simply as being "in the inhabitants". There is no doubt that those at the heart of the Leveller movement were people who already possessed electoral rights, and in the run up to the Long Parliament the citizens of London were prepared to use their votes to engineer the election of MPs with an oppositionist stance on current controversies.

At the beginning then, the Levellers had no direct need, and apparently no particular desire, to demand an extension of the franchise. This still seemed to be the position in March 1647, with the publication of *The Leveller Large Petition*, which may be regarded as the first presentation of a coordinated Leveller programme. They remained concerned that the existing parliamentary system was not working more effectively in their interests, but they were content to assert the general logic that they had a right to expect it to do so. The sovereign power of parliament had "its foundation in the free choice of the people" and this assembly had been elected to "deliver the whole nation from all kinds of oppression and bondage".[64] This promise had not yet been fulfilled. The Lords were still exercising arbitrary powers, the monopoly of the Merchant Adventurers persisted to the great detriment of freedom of trade, and there were reactionary elements in the Commons. But there was still no sign that the Levellers had concluded that these problems would only be properly addressed if the franchise were extended to everyone.

The same was true of Richard Overton's *Appeal* of July 1647. He was appealing over the heads of the "Degenerate Representative Body The Commons of England" to "the Body Represented".[65] He recognised that this was a radical departure, but there was still no indication that the Body Represented would need to be substantiated by an extension of the franchise for that purpose. He took the opportunity to repeat his very powerful statement of the derivation of rights of consent: "For every one as he is himself has a self-propriety—else could he not be himself-and on this no second may presume without consent".[66] But Overton did not draw the implication that therefore everyone should have a vote. The one substantial recommendation for changing the parliamentary system was that the integrity of the Commons' sovereign power should be asserted by the elimination of non-elected elements.[67] There was an insistence that the possession of sovereignty came only from election by the people. But there was no apparent concern as to how many of the people should be involved in the electoral process. Thus, for the first two years of their polemical career the Levellers seemed to have no particular quarrel with the existing scope of the franchise.

But again as with the issue of the common lands, there came a point when their position changed, and it was probably due to the same influence. There is a clue in the fact that Overton's Appeal was addressed "in especial to his excellency Sir Thomas Fairfax . . . and all the officers and soldiers under his command". In another place he hailed the "right worthy and faithful Agitators", who were the chosen representatives of the rank and file.[68] The Levellers were now in the business of recommending themselves to the New Model Army, and particularly to the common soldiers. The ranks included a much higher proportion of the poor than the Levellers were used to dealing with in their original manufacturing and trading constituency. For the first time, they had to make a case to, and for, the poor husbandmen on the open fields. The economic problem of this class was that many of them were losing their rights and their place on the common lands. Their political disadvantage was that by definition, they did not possess the vote.

There are clear signs that the Levellers and the army radicals were in direct contact at least from the early months of 1647. A pamphlet produced on behalf of the soldiers at the end of March protested against the persecution of the Leveller leaders "who have shown themselves with us and for us" and "among whom we number ourselves".[69] Some historians wishing to deny the early politicisation of the rank and file have chosen to overlook this pamphlet, and following their own false trail rather than the evidence, have gone on to dismiss as "mistaken" the April newsletters that confirm the same development.[70] It is wrong, in any case, to see the matter just as a question of when the Levellers began to infiltrate the Army. There may have been a real sense in which the pre-existing political tendencies among the soldiers influenced the Levellers. Given that the extension of the franchise had not been a Leveller priority, it is likely enough that this ambition originated in the ranks.

It is important to remember that the New Model Army was in a sense inherently radical. It was called into being specifically to sustain the force of the parliamentarian challenge to the crown, and to circumvent the inertia of conventional noble commanders who were coming to be seen as an impediment to the cause. Many of the officers were drawn from social groups outside the elite gentry, and could, in that sense, be regarded as commoners themselves. This was certainly true of the greatest of them—Oliver Cromwell. The ordinary soldiers found themselves fighting alongside officers who were not of vastly different class, and who were very conspicuously brandishing the banner of liberty. It was probably quite difficult for the rank and file not to be politicised to some degree.

The recent tendency among historians has been to attribute army radicalism to material grievances such as arrears of pay. But this explanation fails to match up to the evidence, or to the event. As the soldiers themselves said in their *Apology*, their concern was for "our liberties ten thousand times more than our arrears".[71] In fact, the revisionist view of the matter has been rather contradictory, appearing to suggest that the problem was neither a reluctance of the Peace Party to settle the arrears, nor a concern to move against what they perceived as dangerous elements in the Army.[72] The reality is that the material grievances could certainly have been settled, if this had been the main issue. There had never been a shortage of funds to resource the Army. So, in truth, it would not have been necessary for the MPs of the Peace Party to confront the New

Model if they had not feared that it harboured a pre-disposition to political activity.

Some of the most persuasive evidence of early politicisation in the ranks is the specific and authentic character of the opinions that they were heard to express. The first, and most prominent of the polemicists to raise the alarm about the radical tendencies of the New Model was Thomas Edwards, in *Gangrena*, in late 1646. His evidence tends to be anecdotal, but it acquires substantial force in the detail of what he describes. Edwards had, for instance, been informed that on a particular day in August 1646, a captain in Hammill's regiment had been heard to say that the House of Commons was the whole of parliament, not just a part. He was told, furthermore, that this was a sentiment endorsed by the entire Army. It maybe that attributing this supposition to the whole army was an overstatement, but the idea itself carries the ring of truth. It was a very precise and topical radical position. The elimination of the unelected Lords from the parliamentary system was at the cutting edge of Leveller demands in 1646, which is another indication that they were working in concert with the soldiers by that time. For the Leveller polemicists, the idea that the Commons constituted "the whole of parliament" was based on an understanding of the concept that underpinned so much parliamentarian self-confidence, that is to say, the notion that legislative sovereignty derived specifically from representative consent. For the soldiers, it was a way of rationalising their own particular place in the movement. The House of Commons, viewed independently of non-elected elements, came to represent the common people. And from there it was but a short step to asserting that they ought to have a vote.

C. B. Macpherson suggested that the Levellers were encouraged to establish a more radical stance on the franchise because the negotiations with the generals meant that for the first time they had a prospect of getting their ideas actively considered. It must be said, however, that the absence of such opportunities in the past had not deterred them from setting out some strikingly new political positions whenever circumstances seemed to demand it. If these claims had not, up to now, included a proposal for a broader franchise, it was in all likelihood because the need for it had not been indicated or arisen. It was only when the Levellers met the soldiers of the New Model Army that the requirement for an extension of voting rights became a live issue. Furthermore, it should not be assumed that the generals engaged in the discussions just as a matter of military convenience. It was the peculiar strength of the common cause that it referred directly to representative principles, and this created the platform on which the soldiery could sit down to discuss political rights with the officers. And if there was a widespread opinion in the ranks that on the basis of the concept of representative sovereignty the House of Commons comprised the whole of parliament, then that would go a long way to explain why they wanted to talk about getting the vote.

It is wrong above all to suppose that the Leveller programme was a kind of throw forward in time to a future era, and that it had no intrinsic connection with the mainstream parliamentarian movement of its own age. In fact, it was a genuine product of the mid-seventeenth century. The political ideas of the Levellers and the parliamentary leaders had their roots in the same very specific concept of representative rights that had developed in England over the preceding century. They both referred ultimately to the distinctive notion that the "unlimited" power of sovereign legislation drew its authority from the actual consent of the entire society. The Leveller initiative for enlarging the franchise was in a sense just filling out the logic of that principle.

The initial struggles of the Leveller leaders against the judicial power of the Lords had led them to conclude at an early stage that, seeing as the elected Commons were the literal essence of the concept of representative sovereignty, the composition of parliament could fairly and usefully be rationalised by the exclusion of the Upper House. But for a long time they appeared to have harboured no particular thought that the electoral system itself should be extended in the opposite direction, that is to say towards the poor. At the beginning, they seem to have regarded the existing franchise as an adequate vehicle to carry the consent of the entire society. But as they established contact with the soldiers of the New Model Army, the Levellers were introduced to a class of copyholders and agricultural labourers who did not possess the kind of free property that conveyed a political vote, though they had been conscious of fighting for a cause that aimed to assert and consolidate the force of representative rights. So when, with the encouragement of the Levellers, they considered their position, they naturally concluded that the electorate should not be limited by property qualifications. One of them, Edward Sexby, expressed this very clearly in the debate.

> There are many of us soldiers who have ventured our lives, who have but little property in the kingdom as to our estates, yet we have had a birthright. But it seems now, except a man has a fixed estate in this kingdom, he hath no right in this kingdom. I wonder we were so much deceived. [73]

It may be open to doubt whether the soldiers had started out with the expectation of being rewarded with a formal place in the representative system. But many certainly regarded themselves as fighting, quite explicitly, in the cause of liberty, and in the present circumstances, of what should that freedom ultimately consist if not of a right to vote?

Historians have sometimes suggested that the holding of the famous debate about democracy was fortuitous, and need not really have happened at all. Ireton, it has been said, made an error in raising the issue of the franchise, because it did not figure in the document *The Agreement of the People* that the Levellers actually presented for discussion.[74] It is true that the reference to the vote being distributed "according to the number of the inhabitants" might have been more explicit, but it strongly implied a process of enlargement, and when Ireton asked what the phrase meant, the Levellers confirmed his fears. It is clear in any case that the franchise was on the agenda, since the Agreement was but an abbreviated version of a longer document that had been offered to Fairfax a few weeks earlier—*The Case of the Army Truly Stated*. This gave the full context of Leveller demands, and it certainly did raise the question of extending the electorate.

The *Case of the Army Truly Stated* has usually been regarded as the work of John Wildman, though there are now suggestions that it was by Edward Sexby. The important thing to recognise is that, whatever the precise authorship, it sets out a position based on the concept of representative sovereignty that underpinned the parliamentarian movement as a whole. It asserted that "their free choice of consent by their representative is the only original and foundation of all just government" and demanded that "the supreme power of the people's representative be forthwith declared". They were wholly at one with Ireton and Cromwell in their belief that for the maintenance of the integrity of this supreme trust, the people had a right to successive elections at regular, guaranteed intervals. They proposed:

> That therefore it be positively and resolutely insisted upon that a law paramount be made . . . that the people shall of course meet without a warrant or writ, once in every two years upon an appointed day in their respective counties for the election of their representatives in parliament.[75]

It bears repeating that the establishment of an independent and automatic political life for parliament, as inaugurated by the Triennial Act of February 1641, was the most fundamental extension of the representative concept being proposed at Putney. The mere enlargement of the numbers entitled to vote would have been a less radical break with constitutional convention than the seminal change that freed parliament from the king's discretionary command and gave it a permanent, supervisory position at the centre of the state. The primary significance of this latter proposal is confirmed by the fact that the Generals and the Levellers were in complete accord about it. As Ireton said, "We all agree that you should have a Representative to govern".

The Leveller demand for an extension of the electorate would in this sense have involved a less substantial alteration. Furthermore, even in its own context, it did not go as far as has sometimes been supposed. Contrary to some popular assumptions, the Levellers were not proposing straightforward manhood suffrage. There were important ways in which they accepted the traditional forms of limitation of the franchise. The *Case of the Army Truly Stated* suggested that those with a right to vote in the self-activated elections should be "all the free-born at the age of 21 years and upwards . . . excepting those that have or shall deprive themselves of that freedom . . . by delinquency".[76] The term "the free-born" was open to interpretation. It was certainly intended to imply an extension of the vote to those who possessed a freedom in something other than property, but this did not entirely preclude some kind of socio-economic restriction.

When Ireton sought further clarification at Putney, the leading Leveller spokesman Maximilian Petty said, "we judge that all inhabitants that have not lost their birthright should have an equal voice in elections".[77] But again, the term "inhabitants" was not beyond interpretation. It could be taken to mean just those with the status of householder. This was the assumption made by C. B. Macpherson, who was the first to address the possibility that the Levellers were not essentially committed to manhood suffrage. He suggested that in this opening statement, Petty was already implying the exclusion of servants and alms-takers from the proposed extension of the vote, and that this reflected the Levellers' generally preferred formula of a "non-servant franchise".[78] On the other hand, Keith Thomas argued that although Petty was prepared at Putney to exclude apprentices, servants and alms-takers, there was no reason to treat this as the definitive Leveller position, which was actually quite diverse, and not always transparent.[79] In a sense, however, the lack of absolute clarity underlines Macpherson's point—the Levellers were not necessarily in favour of manhood suffrage.

There is, however, no doubt that the Levellers wished to extend the vote to classes beyond the traditional freeholder restriction defended by Ireton. They wanted in effect to enfranchise the general body of copyholders and leaseholders in the counties. These were often poor people in a mainly subsistence mode of economy, and they lacked the formal freeholder status that conveyed a right to vote. But many of them did work their own holdings in relative freedom from manorial control, and some of them were of increasing socio-economic substance. They were therefore not entirely without the kind of economic independence that was the basis of the conventional qualification for political rights. And in fact the Levellers seem to have acknowledged the force of that traditional idea to some degree. There is a revealing passage where they affirm the rationale of restricting the vote to people of independent status. As Maximilian Petty made clear, "the reason why we would exclude apprentices or servants, or those that take alms, is because they depend upon the will of other men".[80] Since at this time the term "servants" covered an extensive class of live-in labourers and may even have been applied to regularly employed wage labourers from outside, it becomes clear that the Levellers were prepared to exclude a considerable proportion of the population from the extended franchise. Manhood suffrage was not their guiding principle.

In fact, Petty's statement clarifies the conventional logic of restricting the vote to those with some degree of economic independence. If representation was to be a true reflection of the general will then the individual's exercise of consent had to be free and specific, and this could not be ensured if his livelihood was in the power of others. The Levellers thus accepted the idea that personal economic freedom was the best qualification for the possession of the vote. So even in their proposals for an extended franchise they were within the parameters of mainstream parliamentarian thought. They were in line with the precepts of economic individualism, as with the concepts of representative sovereignty. It is a fundamental misunderstanding of the balance of initiative to suppose that the Levellers were engaged in an attack on property, or that the generals were defending the status quo. In truth they were all equally committed to advancing the principle of freedom of trade and "liberty and plenty", as indeed they were all in favour of establishing the representative body in a position to provide an absolute guarantee of those rights.

So when Ireton warned the Levellers that their proposals might pose a threat to property, his tone made clear that he was appealing to a common interest. "All the main thing I speak for is because I would have an eye to property. I hope we do not come to contend for a victory—but let every man consider with himself that he do not go that way to take away all property".[81] Ireton was employing this as the argument most likely to deter the Levellers from a general extension of the franchise, for he knew that they too would wish to "have an eye to property". The effect of the warning was limited, however, because the Levellers had a secure grasp of the force of the representative concept, and they knew that whatever aspects of the established order it might call into question, this would not include the rights of property. It was the natural tendency, if not the very essence of representative principles that they worked in favour of property. It was in this light that Petty could declare, "I hope that they may live to see the power of the king and Lords thrown down, that yet might live to see property preserved". He suggested that the extension of the franchise to all inhabitants would actually favour the preservation of property, for that was the whole purpose of representative rights, which were "the only means to preserve all property". The people elected representatives "that they who were chosen might preserve property . . . and therefore men agreed to come into some form of government so that they might preserve property".[82] Petty's belief that the preservation of property was the initial and central aim of government would find a precise echo in the ideas of John Locke, when, some decades later, he summarised the rationale of the parliamentarian revolution: "The great end of men's entering into society being the enjoyment of their properties in peace and safety, and the great instrument and means of that being the laws", which took their "force . . . and sanction from that legislative which the public has chosen and appointed".[83] Petty went further than Locke with his suggestion that since the House of Commons was the defining element in representative sovereignty, they could logically dispense with the services of the king and the Lords. Locke would not have regarded that as desirable or necessary, but for him too the Commons were the heart of the matter, for both of them knew that it was the representative body that existed to promote and protect property.

So the position of the Levellers helps to clarify the definition of "the people" in the Civil War context. In essence, the Levellers were to be numbered among the parliamentarian "people". They shared the "middle sort" perspective that was characteristic of the movement, with a dominant interest in freedom of trade, and the rights of individual enterprise and consent. They embraced the proposition held by the parliamentary cause in general, that these desires could only be guaranteed by establishing the representative body, and the representative concept, with a permanent and automatic place at the centre of governmental affairs. They were not truly to be counted among the unheralded "common people"—the mass of poor husbandmen and labourers prising out their living from the open fields. As already indicated, the Levellers were not primarily concerned with the plight of the poor, or their loosening grip on the common lands. Leveller interest in that matter was belated and transient. Their proposal for extending the franchise was also something of an afterthought, and they did not go so far as to demand manhood suffrage.

The only voice raised in favour of straightforward manhood suffrage was that of Gerrard Winstanley, who was also distinctive in his opposition to freeing the force of the market. It was only Winstanley who seemed to assume that "everyman" should actually mean every man. He agreed with the Levellers and Ireton about the basic provision that parliament should meet automatically every year, but when it came to the question of who should be the "choosers", he went beyond both. And he did so specifically by rejecting the qualification of independence on which the Levellers had seemed to insist. Winstanley proposed to include "even drunkards, quarrellers and fearful ignorant men, who dare not speak truth lest they anger other men . . . yet they may have a voice in the choosing".[84] This was a function of Winstanley's refusal to accept that socio-economic substance was the truest definition of liberty.

By the same token, the one group that was fully and consistently committed to the cause of the common people was the Diggers, who wrote, as they lived, outside the framework of parliamentarian economics. The many works of their most prominent spokesman, Gerrard Winstanley, were in effect a bitter and extended protest against the enclosure movement, which he believed was destroying the quality and viability of the lives of the poor husbandmen who were losing their position as independent smallholders on the commons and open fields. But he knew that the mainstream parliamentarian movement embraced the kind of economics that favoured enclosure. He highlighted the dominant parliamentary aims as freedom of trade: "the free use of trading and to have all patents, licences and restraints removed"; and the associated demand of the property owner to be "landlord of the earth", to the exclusion of the claims of the king, and of the poor.[85]

Specifically, and most revealingly, Winstanley also provided a precise description of the power of commercialisation, the trend that created opportunities for the middle sort, but threatened the customary rights of the poor. He identified the developing force of unrestrained market activity as the root of the problem. He railed persistently against "the crafty art of buying and selling".[86] It was indeed the extended range, influence and license of the "art of buying and selling" that was undermining the patterns of restraint that had guided the communal occupation of the open fields. So Winstamley opted out of the bourgeois context of the parliamentarian movement, and envisaged a different kind of revolution. His proposal of the common ownership of the land would ensure that "neither the earth, nor the fruits thereof, should be bought and sold by the inhabitants one among the other".[87] His parting shot at the parliamentarian freeholders was "wherefore are you so covetous after the world, in buying and selling, counting yourself a happy man if you be rich, and a miserable man if you be poor".[88] Thus Winstanley not only deplored the great transition that was turning the smallholders into wage labourers, he also recognised the economic developments that underlay the rise of individual property—that is to say, the emergence of an integrated, regional market, where "buying and selling" acquired new power through the processes of specialisation and exchange, often of bulk agricultural products, encouraging the consolidation of larger individual farms, but threatening the position of the smallholders.

From the opposite end of the political spectrum, in prose that was equally voluminous but rather more systematic, and in the most authoritative philosophical form, came precisely the same assessment of the critical change that had taken place in the balance of economic activity. Thomas Hobbes and Gerrard Winstanley were somewhat idiosyncratic theorists, even in the context of their own, very different, allegiances. But they reached a common conclusion in proposing a more controlled form of social order, and they made the same identification of the force that they felt to be in need of discipline. Both Hobbes and Winstanley understood that the underlying momentum of the parliamentary cause came from the assumption of a right of untrammelled economic license that was as socially disruptive as it was individually libertarian. Hobbes pinpointed the dominant parliamentarian motive as rejecting discretionary taxes, levies and restraints on their incomes: "their only glory being to grow excessively rich by the wisdom of buying and selling".[89] He described exactly how this imperative translated into a political challenge to the crown, and a demand for the establishment of representative rights in government. The propertied and trading classes had come to believe that each man was "so much master of what he possessed, that it could not be taken from him upon any pretence of common safety without his own consent".[90] This of course directly reflected Winstanley's view that the active liberties sought by parliamentarians were freedom of trade and absolute property. Interestingly, Hobbes also shared Winstanley's assessment of how the commercial drive undermined the position of the poor, by diverting the product of their labour into other pockets. The entrepreneurial farmers and merchants thrived "by making poor people sell their labour to them at their own prices".[91]

But perhaps the most instructive and unexpected commentary on Leveller, and True Leveller, economics is to be found in the writings of John Locke. His *Second Treatise of Civil Government*, often assumed to be composed in justification of the Glorious Revolution of 1688, was in fact written between 1679 and 1682, and is more appropriately regarded as a philosophical summation of the great political and economic changes that had been channelled through the original English Revolution of the mid-seventeenth century. Locke was encapsulating what had now become the orthodoxy, but his words often echo the most radical voices of the Civil War period. Just like the Leveller Maximilian Petty, Locke understood that in the course of the transformation in the conduct of economic life, men had come to believe that the very purpose of political society was to guarantee the rights of property, and the means of achieving this was representative law: "The great end of men's entering into society being the enjoyment of their properties in peace and safety, and the great instrument and means of that being the laws established in that society". The "force and obligation" of law takes "its sanction from that legislative which the public has chosen and appointed". Over that society "nobody can have a power to make laws but by their own consent".[92] Similarly, "the preservation of property being the end of government . . . the supreme power cannot take from any man any part of his property without his own consent". No power can "dispose of the estates of the subjects arbitrarily, or take any part of them at pleasure. This is not much to be feared in governments where the legislative consists in assemblies which are variable".[93] Locke was echoing Hobbes' analysis of the rise of the claim of absolute property rights in the early seventeenth century, but with satisfaction rather than dismay. Locke embraced the rise of absolute individualism, which underpinned the sovereignty of representative law. And his words therefore relate to the Leveller Richard Overton's concept of a self-propriety, upon which no other could presume without consent. In fact, says Locke, in nature "every man has a property in his own person; this nobody has any right to but himself. The labour of his body and the work of his hands we may say are properly his".[94] He goes on, in effect, to outline the basis of the transition in economic life, identified by Winstanley as the rise of the power of "buying and selling". The earth was originally given to all in common, and there was only a limited right of appropriation: "where there is enough and as good left in common for others".[95] This would have served as a description of the ideal balance of activity on the commons and open fields. "No man's labour could subdue or appropriate all, nor could his enjoyment consume all but a small part".[96] These limitations would still hold good "had not the Invention of Money, and the tacit agreement of men to put a value on it, introduced, (by Consent), larger Possessions, and a Right to them". Although money had been "invented" long before the sixteenth century, there had, in that period between 1500 and 1640 been a critical increase in the power that it exercised. It had acquired a newly dominant force in land sales, and in general through the systems of intensified regional marketing. In effect, Locke was reflecting the process of commercialisation, which, as Winstanley saw, was undermining the position of the smallholders on the common fields, even while it benefited the parliamentarian middle sort of people.

It is clear that the economics of representative consent and freedom of trade had a very broad area of reception, from the Levellers to John Locke, but like the parliamentarian concept of "the people" this tended to exclude, rather than include the poor. There was in fact an underlying contradiction between the vital interests of the poor husbandmen, and the dominant economic motives of parliament's natural supporters. Parliamentarians were concerned, specifically, to seek guarantees for the perspectives of commercial freedom and absolute property, which often tended to work to the deprivation of the commoners. In this respect, the poor had no substantial incentive to volunteer their support to parliament. There is certainly a case for supposing that in general terms the poor had little direct, positive involvement in the struggle on either side, and that the notion that they tended to favour the king was largely a false impression created by the obverse circumstance that the middle sort favoured parliament. Thomas Hobbes, who was the most acute of commentators, recognised the parliamentarian bias of the middle sort and the commercial centres, but did not allow this to prejudice his judgement of the allegiances of the poor, which was that in the overall context, they had none: "there were very few of the common people that cared much for either of the causes".[97]

This is not to deny that some "few" of the poor found reasons for backing parliament. Gerrard Winstanley indicated that this was the case among his associates, and we have seen that it was probably the same for the "common people" of West Nottinghamshire. But the benefits they could expect were generalised and indirect. Parliament gave them no specific inducement of the kind that it offered to the middle sort. There was the unintended effect that the context of the campaign for "liberty", and the climate of free expression of opinion generated by the revolutionary drive, created the scope for the airing of popular grievances that could not normally have been stated with such force or cogency. Winstanley catalogued the most prominent issues concerning the poorer elements in society. They desired that the operation of the law should be made more amenable to their situation, the impositions of the clergy both theological and fiscal should be ended, the status of the smallholder on the commons should be secured, and the burden of rents lightened.[98] But he also had to note that none of these requirements had been met. In truth, they were simply not on the parliamentary agenda, and in some respects they contradicted it. The only real satisfaction for the commoners was the chance to put their issues on record.

But one particular avenue that was opened up to the possibility of wider access was the operation of the representative system itself. It is clear that the general idea of representative authority was positively embraced by elements of the common people, even though they might not claim an active part in the electoral system. The link between the force of representation and the "entire society" may have created a presumption among some of the commoners that their demands should also be satisfied, if only by an indirect right. Everything that has been said in the earlier pages of this chapter has indicated that for the Levellers, as well as for mainstream parliamentarians, the principle of successive elections, and automatic assembly was of more fundamental importance than the question of the scope of the electorate. And when Gerrard Winstanley surveyed the opinions of his friends, followers and neighbours and asked them to enumerate the promises that they would most like to see performed, "first, say they, 'the current of succeeding parliaments is stopped, which is one of the great privileges (and people's liberties) for safety and peace' ".[99] It is possible that the desire for guaranteed regular assemblies, which was the original core proposition of the parliamentarian cause, was shared not only by Winstanley, but also by the commoners for whom, and with whom he spoke, if only on the basis that a more established place for parliament *ought* to work in their interests.

We can only speculate by what exact sequence such general aspirations could turn into the demand for a vote, as arose in the New Model Army. But perhaps it was a natural development among men who were so directly engaged in the cause. And it was not so complete a departure from standard parliamentary perspectives as it might seem. It is of some interest that when the ambition did emerge, it was resisted not by denying the poor any place at all in the parliamentary system, but by referring them to an indirect kind of participation that they could be thought to possess already. It was suggested earlier that the administrative and representative systems were capable of offering the common people a subsidiary role when occasion demanded.[100] There was another example of this during the Putney Debates. To defuse the pressure for an extended franchise, Henry Ireton invoked the idea that the general force of the representative concept carried benefits even for those who were not directly involved in the voting process. He suggested indeed that this had provided a positive motive for the un-enfranchised commoners to give their support to the parliamentary cause. Rainsborough's famous question merited a response. "I would fain know what the soldier hath fought for all this while".[101] He believed that the common soldiers had been fighting, often consciously, to advance parliamentary liberty, and what should they expect to gain from that, if not the vote? Ireton did have an answer, though it took him some moments to gather it together. He would suggest in effect that the representative concept was not dependent on one simple form of operation. He outlined a way in which a limited, property-based franchise could be sustained, while nevertheless admitting the property-less to a stake in the process, with a benefit that was worth fighting for.

> I will tell you what the soldier of the kingdom hath fought for. First, the danger that we stood in was that one man's will must be a law. The people of this kingdom must have this right at least, that they should not be concluded but by the Representative of those that had the interest of the kingdom. Some men fought in this because they were immediately concerned and engaged in it. Other men who had no other interest in the kingdom than this, that they should have the benefit of those laws made by the Representative . . . That the will of one man shall not be a law, but that the law of this kingdom should be by a choice of people to represent, and that the choice to be made by the generality of the kingdom. Here was a right that induced men to fight.[102]

This was a notable illustration of the normative status that the practice, and principle of sovereign representative law now commanded. Just as to John Pym, at the beginning of the struggle, it had been "that which makes and constitutes a kingdom", so to Henry Ireton it was the overall definition of why parliamentarians had fought.[103] Its power was further evident in the fact that although it referred itself to the authorisation of "every man", this was not a literal requirement. As long as the representative body could be taken to reflect what Ireton called a "generality", it could serve its essential purpose of disallowing any kind of arbitrary or discretionary exaction or restraint. This was what enabled Ireton to suggest that the poor could gain the general benefit of the concept, without the need to compromise the freeholder franchise that was the specific guarantee of property rights. Further on in the debate, Ireton offered his own challenge to the Levellers, recalling perhaps that their original programme had made no call for an extended franchise. Was it not just for the general force of representative rights, based on the existing electoral framework, that they had first engaged?

> I will ask that gentleman that spoke (whom I love in my heart) whether when they drew out to serve the parliament in the beginning . . . whether then they thought of any more right or interest in the kingdom than this, whether they did think that they should have as great interest in Parliament-men as freeholders had, or whether from the beginning we did not engage for the liberty of parliaments, and that we should be concluded by the laws that such did make.[104]

This was forceful in part because it was an accurate reflection of the Levellers' own initial position, which had not displayed an urgent concern with the extent of the franchise. It also carried force because it showed that the poor could be motivated by a general commitment to parliament that did not infringe the existing representative balance, which no doubt reflected the way that things had happened. Furthermore, Ireton spelled out a real benefit that the poor might expect to gain from the general rule of parliamentary law, though it was somewhat middle-sort in character, and would be obtained without breaking up the charmed circle of the freeholders. He suggested that an overall, if technically partial representative system created a platform of opportunity, even for the poor.

> They thought that it was better to be concluded by the common consent of those that were fixed men, and settled men, that had the interest of the kingdom in them. "And from that way" [said they] "I shall know a law and have a certainty". Every man that was born [in the country, that] is a denizen in it, that hath a freedom, he was capable of trading to get money, to get estates by; and therefore this man, I think, hath a great deal of reason to build up such a foundation of interest in himself: that is, that the will of one man shall not be a law, but that the law of this kingdom should be by a choice of persons to represent.[105]

This was the only practical promise that the parliamentarian cause held out to the poor. It offered them less than nothing in terms of their general interest in maintaining their position on the common lands. But the establishment of an overall representative polity, through which they would "know a law and have a certainty", would guarantee the commercial freedoms that might allow a fortunate few to escape the fate of most, and join the ranks of the middle sort.

Notes

1. Lucy Hutchinson, *The Memoirs of the Life of Colonel Hutchinson*, ed. J. Hutchinson, (London 1846), pp. 377–8
2. G. Yerby, *People and Parliament: Representative Rights and the English Revolution,* (Basingstoke 2008)
3. Hutchinson, *Memoirs of the Life of Colonel Hutchinson*, p. 75
4. Notebook of Sir John Northcote, *Two Diaries of the Long Parliament*, ed. M Jansson, (Yale 1984), p. 112
5. J. Rushworth, *Historical Collections,* (London 1659–1701), IV, p. 186
6. S. Seyer, *Memoirs Historical and Topographical of Bristol,* (Bristol 1821), II, p. 314
7. A good study of these developments is J. W. Gough, *The Social Contract,* (Oxford 1936)
8. For instance, J. P. Somerville, *Politics and Ideology in England 1603–1640,* (London 1986), p. 75
9. For instance, R. Foxley, "Varieties of Parliamentarianism", in *The Oxford Handbook of the English Revolution,* (Oxford 2016), pp. 419–20
10. From "The Putney Debates", in *Puritanism and Liberty*, ed. A. S. P. Woodhouse, (London 1938), p. 72
11. Rushworth, *Historical Collections*, IV, p. 326
12. Sir Thomas Smith, *De Republica Anglorum,* (written between 1562 and 1565, first published 1583), ed. M. Dewar, (Cambridge 1982), pp. 78–9
13. Ibid, p. 76
14. A. S. P. Woodhouse, *Puritanism and Liberty*, (London 1938), p. 72
15. Ibid, p. 54
16. Smith, *De Republica Anglorum*, p. 76
17. Ibid, 76–7
18. J. Harrington, *Oceana*, ed. H Morley, (London 1887), p. 59
19. Hutchinson, *Memoirs of the Life of Colonel Hutchinson*, p. 75
20. Ibid, p. 100
21. R. Manning, *Village Riots,* (Oxford 1988), p. 319
22. B. Sharp, *In Contempt of All Authority,* (Berkeley 1980), pp. 257–66
23. S. Hindle, "Persuasion and Protest in the Caddington Common Enclosure Dispute 1635–39", *Past and Present 158,* (February 1998), pp. 42, 61, 67; J. Gurney, *Brave Community: The Digger Movement in the English Revolution,* (Manchester 2012), pp. 31–42
24. Hindle, "Persuasion and Protest in the the Caddington Common Enclosure Dispute 1635–39", pp. 66–7
25. *The Works of William Laud*, eds. W. Scott and J. Bliss (1847), VI, pt 2, p. 520
26. "The Grand Remonstrance" (1641), in *Constitutional Documents of the Puritan Revolution*, ed. S. R. Gardiner, (Oxford 1968), p. 212
27. H. Brailsford, *The Levellers and the English Revolution,* (Nottingham 1983), p. 426
28. Woodhouse, *Puritanism and Liberty*, p. 61
29. Richard Overton, *Appeal from the Degenerate Representative Body, the Commons of England, to the Body Represented, the Free People in General . . . and in Especial, to . . . Sir Thomas Fairfaxand to All the Officers and Soldiers Under His Command,* (London 17 July 1647)
30. Woodhouse, *Puritanism and Liberty*, p. 338
31. Ibid, p. 335
32. *The Humble Representation of the Desires of the Officers and Soldiers of the Regiment of Horse for Northumberland*, (5 December 1648)

33. Brailsford, *The Levellers and the English Revolution*, pp. 102–4
34. J. Wildman, *London's Liberties*, (London 1950); Woodhouse, *Puritanism and Liberty*, pp. 369–70
35. Gerrard Winstanley, "A Watch-Word to the City of London and the Army", in *Winstanley "The Law of Freedom"*, ed. C. Hill, (Cambridge 1983), pp. 130–50
36. Gerrard Winstanley, "The True Leveller's Standard Advanced", in *Winstanley: The Law of Freedom, Winstanley*, ed. C. Hill, (Cambridge 1983), pp. 84–5
37. Gerrard Winstanley, "Appeal to the House of Commons", in *Winstanley: The Law of Freedom*, ed. C. Hill, (Cambridge 1983), pp. 111, 116–17
38. Gerrard Winstanley, "The Law of Freedom in a Platform", in *Winstanley: The Law of Freedom*, ed. C. Hill, (Cambridge 1983), pp. 335, 344–5
39. Ibid, p. 342
40. Ibid, p. 294
41. John Lilburne, *England's Birthright Justified*, (London 1645), BL 304, (17), pp. 8–10
42. *The Leveller Large Petition*, (London 1647), BL E464, (19), p. 3
43. G. Aylmer, *The Levellers and the English Revolution*, (Cornell 1975), p. 12
44. For instance, M. Mendle, ed., *The Putney Debates*, (Cambridge 2001)
45. Lilburne, *England's Birthright Justified*, BL E304, (17), pp. 2–3, 8
46. Yerby, *People and Parliament*, chapter 7, and See above, pp. 312–316
47. John Lilburne, *The Freeman's Freedom Vindicated*, (London 1646), BL E341, (12), p. 11
48. Ibid
49. Ibid, p. 12
50. R. Hooker, *Of the Law of Ecclesiastical Polity*, ed. C. Morris, (London 1909), vol. I, bk. 2, pt. 7, p. 268
51. Richard Overton, *An Arrow Against All Tyrants*, (London 1646), BL E356, (14), p. 3
52. Ibid, p. 3
53. Ibid, p. 4
54. Ibid
55. Yerby, *People and Parliament*, chapter 2; *The English Revolution and the Roots of Environmental Change*, chapter 10
56. *The Remonstrance of Many Thousand Citizens*, (London 1646), BL E343, (11), pp. 19–20
57. Woodhouse, *Puritanism and Liberty*, p. 70
58. See, "The Grand Remonstrance"; "The Heads of the Proposals" (1647), in *Constitutional Documents of the Puritan Revolution*, ed. S. R. Gardiner, (Oxford 1968), pp. 222, 316
59. Lilburne, *England's Birthright Justified*, p. 3
60. Lilburne, *The Freeman's Freedom Vindicated*, p. 9
61. *A Remonstrance of Many Thousand Citizens*, BL E343, (11), pp. 6–7
62. Ibid, pp. 19–20
63. Ibid, p. 20
64. *The Leveller Large Petition*, BL E464, (19), pp. 1–2 0
65. "An Appeal from the Degenerate Representative Body the Commons of England assembled at Westminster to the Body Represented", in *Puritanism and Liberty*, ed. A. S. P. Woodhouse, (London 1938), pp. 323–38
66. Ibid, p. 327
67. Ibid, p. 335
68. Ibid, p. 334
69. *Apology of the Soldiers to Their Officers*, BL E381, (18)

70. A. Woolrych, "The Debates from the Perspective of the Army", in *The Putney Debates of 1647*, ed. M. Mendle, (Cambridge 2001), p. 57
71. *Apology of the Soldiers to Their Officers*, BL E381, (18)
72. J. Morrill, "Mutiny and Discontent in English Provincial Armies 1645–7", *Past and Present 56* (1972); M. Kishlansky, *The Rise of the New Model Army*, (Cambridge 1979), pp. 150–6
73. "The Putney Debates", p. 69
74. A. Woolrych, in Mendle, ed., *The Putney Debates*, p. 72; J. Morrill, "The Army Revolt of 1647", in *The Nature of the English Revolution,* (London 1993), p 326
75. "The Case of the Army Truly Stated", in *Puritanism and Liberty*, ed. A. S. P. Woodhouse, (London 1938), p. 433
76. Ibid
77. "The Putney Debates", p. 53
78. C. B. Macpherson, *The Political Theory of Possessive Individualism,* (Oxford 1964), pp. 114, 122
79. K. Thomas, "The Levellers and the Franchise", in *The Interregnum,* ed. G. Aylmer (1972), pp. 66–7
80. "The Putney Debates", p. 83
81. Ibid, p. 57
82. Ibid, pp. 61–2
83. J. Locke, *Second Treatise of Government*, ed. J. W. Gough, (Oxford 1966), p. 67
84. "The Law of Freedom", in *Winstanley: The Law of Freedom and Other Writings*, ed. C. Hill, (Cambridge 1983), p. 321
85. Winstanley, "The Law of Freedom", p. 294
86. Ibid, pp. 309, 310
87. Ibid, p. 303
88. Ibid, p. 349
89. Thomas Hobbes, *Behemoth*, ed. Tonnies, (London 1889), p. 126
90. Ibid, p. 4
91. Ibid, p. 126
92. Locke, *The Second Treatise of Government*, p. 67
93. Ibid, p. 71
94. Ibid, p. 15
95. Ibid
96. Ibid, p. 19
97. Hobbes, *Behemoth*, p. 2
98. Winstanley, "The Law of Freedom", pp. 279–81
99. Ibid, p. 278
100. See above, p. 354
101. "The Putney Debates", p. 71
102. Ibid, p. 72
103. For Pym, See above, pp. 244–5
104. Woodhouse, *Puritanism and Liberty*, pp. 76–7
105. Ibid, p. 72

17 The Economy of the State—The First Fully Capitalist Society

On the tenth of March 1643, as the Civil War continued, Lieutenant General Cromwell wrote a letter of advice to Major General Crawford. "Sir" he said "the State, in choosing men to serve it, takes no note of their opinions; if they be willing faithfully to serve it—that satisfies. I advised you formerly to bear with men of different minds from yourself: if you had done it when I advised you to it, I think you would not have had so many stumbling blocks in your way".[1] The passage is well known, but usually just as an early expression of Cromwell's inclination to allow diversity of devotional opinion in the ranks. This certainly became a contentious issue, and Cromwell's stance reinforces Winstanley's suggestion that the religious aspect of Civil War motivation was essentially about the liberty of individuals to follow their own scheme of worship. But as Cromwell also made clear, religion was not at first a principal element in the contest. He believed, like his Nottinghamshire colleagues and co-religionists Henry Ireton and the Hutchinsons that the Civil War began as a struggle for political liberty. And in fact Cromwell's insistence that the only criterion for choosing men should be their willingness faithfully to serve "the State" brings into focus an important aspect of the context in which that struggle took place. The emergence of the "state" form in England provided a defining framework for the parliamentarian cause. In a sense, as Cromwell indicated, the only "opinion" of which they needed to take account was a willingness to serve parliament as the representative of the state.

So Cromwell's use of the term "the State" demands closer attention. It should not be treated as just another way of describing the parliamentary movement, when in fact it has a considerable structural significance in itself. It was, as already noted, employed in the same way, that is to say as a definition of their allegiance, by parliamentarian activists in and around Nottingham during the Civil War period. John Howlett, of Nottingham, maintained his son "in the state's service". Edward Troupe, of Nottingham, "served the state faithfully" as a work's foreman in the garrison, "setting aside his private vocation". John Sawre, a yeoman of Nottingham, died in "the state's service" in Scotland, in 1651. Thomas Medlum collected supplies to garrison Broxtow "for the state's service".[2] The usage was not casual. Cromwell, and his Nottinghamshire allies, might have referred their service to "the parliament", or "the people". But these terms would not have carried the same force. They did not so clearly identify a wholly self-contained, and independently defined political unit. Nor was this a concept coined in the heat of battle to give definitive form to the alternative polity for which they found themselves fighting. We have seen that in the early decades of the seventeenth century MPs were already expressing the idea of the state as embracing the unitary public interest that they believed ought to be followed, not necessarily in concert with the interests of the crown. Even then, the state could be linked with the parliament. Thus the representatives of the borough of Totnes could refer to the free trade act pushed through by the House of Commons in 1606 as reflecting "the wisdom of the state in parliament".[3]

It is therefore of some interest that the idea of the state appears to have been common currency among English parliamentarians, though it was a relatively new concept. Medieval Christendom had not recognised a separated or singular form of statehood. It has been well said that to talk of the medieval state is a misnomer. John Guy noted that the idea of the state as we would understand it, emerged in England, during the course of the sixteenth century. "In the fifteenth century there was no conception of England as a unitary state: regnum and sacerdotium owed allegiance to king and pope respectively". By the end of the sixteenth century, however, the term "the state" had come into being. It was used to refer to a fully independent nation, a new focus of loyalty, and a higher level of unity. This was qualitatively different from the looser, personal frameworks of the kingdom, or lordship. As Guy concluded, "the shift from "realm" to "state" is among the more interesting developments of English history".[4]

It is also one of the most significant of developments, particularly because in the English context "the state" had the potential to become an alternative to "the realm". The precocious arrival of a unitary state form in sixteenth- and seventeenth-century England has been referred to regularly in the foregoing pages, along with the important circumstance that it was parliament rather than the crown that was embracing the emerging state concepts. Thus it was the MPs and their constituents who displayed a paramount concern to employ the most powerful dynamic of inward unity—the nationally binding force of parliamentary law, which was neglected and even distrusted by the Stuart kings. By the same token, it was parliament that reflected and espoused the new perspectives of a national interest in foreign policy, defined independently, and often in opposition to royal purposes. Both the internal and outward dimensions of state unity were being appropriated by the parliament, not the king, and this added greatly to the strength and ambition of the parliamentary cause. It reflected their growing acceptance as a central authority, and underpinned their assumption of responsibility for national affairs. It also provided them with a ready-made basis of government when they took charge in 1641.

The early rise of a fully-fledged nation-state was as distinctive to England as were the great socio-economic transitions taking place at the same time, and these things were not unconnected. Along with the concentrated power of statute law, and the galvanising force of a national foreign policy, the third principal pillar of the unified state structure was a uniquely integrated economy. The shape of the autonomous nation, as defined by the expulsion of the universal church of Rome, was achieved through the exercise of sovereign representative statute, destroying the independent legislative authority of the spiritual sphere, on the basis of parliament's unique capacity to reflect the assent of the entire society. Parliamentary statute became established as the most powerful inward dynamic of the emergent nation-state, binding the land together in a self-determining legal and administrative framework, even as it bound everyone to its provisions by their own consent. Statute law was the natural restorative of an extended but exceptionally well-coordinated interregional market—it served the specific needs of the commercial interests with nationally definitive regulations. The widespread leasing of manorial demesnes in England was the basis of the rise of a broad and distinctive class of commercialising yeoman farmers who filled out the national scope of the market. As Henry Ireton said, the benefit of representative statute was to create a foundation of "known" and "certain" economic conditions within the body of the kingdom. Trade and property came to be protected by the same principle of consent that gave force to sovereign statute law. Merchants and gentry formed a highly distinctive national alliance to mount a long-term campaign for a right of freedom of trade from discretionary exactions and restrictions. Earlier chapters described the way in which the national market came to be seen as self-regulating, with a reciprocal motion that was compared to clockwork, encouraging the idea that it should be left free of restraints and impositions. The same sense of a self-sustaining commercial context reinforced the idea of the kingdom as an economic unit, and this in turn served to complete the identity of the state.

Like the coordinated representative and administrative systems, economic integration took much encouragement from the distinctive geographical character of the land. The particular convenience of English topography for coherent political organisation was demonstrated at the very foundation of the kingdom. It was the restricted scale and shape of the island that enabled the West Saxon kings to re-conquer it from the Danes as a unified realm. They achieved this by piecing together a uniform sequence of boroughs and shires, filling out the land, for the coordination of government and defence. It was often a case of turning the original, smaller Anglo-Saxon kingdoms into counties of West

Saxon England. The shire system remained in place throughout the feudal period. It was overlaid, and frequently overawed by the unbounded territorial pretensions of the great magnates or "over-mighty subjects". But it continued to offer a basis on which royal law and administration could be applied in the localities, and it served to limit the scope for the growth of independent provinces. Perhaps most crucially, it survived to serve as a framework for the development of administrative and representative networks with their own integral force and character.

A crucial aid to organisational unity was the distinctive triangular shape of the island. This meant that it could be encompassed from a central point with exceptional speed and efficiency. The Romans had left a legacy of direct roads, which radiated to all corners, and there were no major geological barriers to negotiate. There was, furthermore, the especially convenient facility of coastal transport. It was this pattern of connections that made London the focus of the early development of administrative and economic integration. The advantages of accessibility, and the absence of territorial rivals or provincial "capitals", ensured that London emerged as the only substantial urban centre. This in turn made London the principal generator of economic expansion. The most obvious indicator of the growth of the capital is the phenomenal increase in the number of residents. Unlike most other European cities of the time, the population of London was rising, strongly from 1500 to 1600, then steeply from 1600 onwards.[5] The expansion was due in part to inward migration, as London offered a new start to those displaced by agrarian change, or by the relative decline of some other towns. But it was also self-generated, because in a period of generally rising population levels, London had the widest range of the additional economic opportunities that were likely to encourage early marriage and an increase in the birth rate, in the prevailing demographic conditions of the time.

The great and growing preponderance of people in the capital made it the leading centre of manufacturing activity and demand. The first to draw attention to London's influence as an engine of conspicuous consumption was F. J. Fisher, who noted that it gave a significant boost to the craft industries and transport trades on a national scale. Fisher treated this mainly as a luxury trade serving the upper classes. But the circumstances and force of the development indicated a broader base, and Joan Thirsk has since suggested that the consumer market was most notable for its social breadth, so that by the end of the sixteenth century, goods that had once been classed as luxuries "were being made in so many different qualities and at such varied prices that they came within reach of everyone".[6] The unusual profitability of farming had ensured that many commercialising yeoman farmers now had more money to spend on accessories. This accounts for the observations of William Harrison in the 1580s that the more luxurious range of fitments and household utensils were now displayed a long way down the social scale, "even unto inferior artificers and many farmers".[7]

Equally notable, if not quite so obvious, was the effect of the London market in raising agricultural production. The ever-burgeoning population of the capital required first and foremost to be fed. In fact the gargantuan appetite of London drew forth a broad hinterland of expansive commercial farming and horticulture, attracting supplies from right across the south and east of the country and beyond. This served to inspire a general rise in productivity, and most importantly, it encouraged the development of intensive local and regional specialisation, which was the most important driver of increased capacity. So London was not just an engine of growth—it was a focus of economic integration. It acted as the principal fulcrum of interregional exchange, which was the basis of a new kind of self-reciprocating national market.

London's position as the point at which all routes, by land and sea, converged, also made it the principal outlet for exports. The nation's first significant manufactured export, woollen cloth, was marketed through London. Cloth making had its most substantial centres of production in The West Country, East Anglia and Yorkshire, and it engendered a nationwide network of regional specialisation and exchange, but the great majority of it went out from London. London's place at the hub of a precociously diversified yet unified economy encapsulates its power as a centralising force, and underlines the effect it had in promoting an exceptional degree of national integration. Quite unusually for a European city, London acted as both the administrative capital and the greatest port of the kingdom. It played both roles to the full, and in significant combination.

To this extent, the nation-state formed around London, which was at the centre of everything, political and economic. But it is important to realise that the connections were spontaneous. The growth of administrative integration tends to be underestimated, because too much emphasis is placed on developments in central government. Much more important in this respect were the uniform framework of county administration, and the uniquely powerful networks of national representation that gave authority to the force of sovereign law. It has often been supposed that these structures were less effective than a controlled bureaucracy, because they were operated largely by local gentlemen "amateurs". The truth is rather the contrary. The voluntary basis of the systems made them a natural force for integration. The downside for the royal government was that this also gave the political nation the capacity for developing an independent and coordinated perspective of its own, with a central forum in London.

The trends towards administrative, judicial and economic integration were intimately connected. The representative control of public finance, and the services of sovereign parliamentary law, came to be seen as the best, and eventually the only acceptable means of administrative and fiscal regulation. The most basic of economic facilities, the right of land occupation was determined along the same lines. The development of a national land-market was, like so much else, administered through London. It was not only that the church lands most often ended up in the hands of the national class of gentry, it was also that the sales tended to take place centrally in London, and disputes of tenure were ultimately decided in the central courts, again in London. The vast transfer of land and wealth, which in effect put the gentry and yeomanry in complete physical occupation of the newly independent country, was orchestrated, quite appropriately, through the good offices of the uniquely dominant capital city.

London was the greatest commercial centre, but it was also an equal participant in the general development of interregional trading. This was the core dynamic of economic change overall, and its emergence can be measured in the growth of specialist regional markets, at the expense of the greater number of local markets that had characterised the medieval world until the end of the fifteenth century. Mark Overton has noted the "density" of markets at the beginning of the sixteenth century, when they were still at their most numerous, but also most limited in individual reach. He estimated that the generality of markets served an area of about ten miles in radius, with little traded beyond that.[8] Alan Everitt substantiated the significant change in the balance that occurred in the sixteenth and early seventeenth centuries. He noted that everywhere, agricultural traffic was being drawn away from the local markets and concentrated on larger provincial centres, which were the points of distribution for regional specialisations. At the beginning of the sixteenth century "most towns still served a purely local area, and specialised in no particular commodity". But during the course of the century, "a broad pattern of specialisation becomes clear".[9] The most crucial difference was that although specialist products were now being traded in import-export mode at a greater distance, the marketing system as a whole was also becoming connected and coordinated, as it had never previously been. In other words, a fully integrated national market was coming into being.

The connections of the coal trade may be taken as exemplifying the pattern. As already described, the coal industry of West Nottinghamshire changed the balance of the local economy to import-export mode. But coal was above all the specialised product of the Northeast region, from where it was shipped down the coast to the ports of East Anglia, which sent in return their own specialist products of cloth and corn. Much of the coal went onto London, which was the greatest user for both industrial and domestic purposes, and was becoming something of a coke-town in the process. From London, in turn, went out a large proportion of the manufactured goods that supplied the broadening consumer market that appeared in Elizabethan times. Charles Wilson highlighted the centrality of the coal trade to the processes of economic integration. It was "the factor in the early seventeenth century economy most favourable to expansion . . . a reciprocating action thus began between the emergent coal industry, especially in the Northeast and the Midlands, and the growing aggregation of people in towns and certain industries that catered for them".[10] The other important facilitator of these developing links was that trade within the English kingdom was exceptionally free of internal barriers and customs tolls. The fact that there were no semi-independent provinces, and no dominant urban centres except London, meant that "Internal trade went largely untaxed in the period 1500–1700 . . . one of the principal strengths of the network of internal trading . . . was the relative lightness of passage tolls, pontages and other duties on domestic trade which created in much of Western Europe a fairly rigid series of customs unions".[11] So the only customs barrier that affected English trade was the one described by the sea border that encompassed the entire emergent nation-state. Inland, commercial activity was characterised by an exceptional degree of freedom and coordination.

So the fabric of the new, unitary state comes into view. By the mid-seventeenth century England was covered by an interwoven pattern of physical, economic, administrative and judicial connections, representing every aspect of the life of the country. Each system was a force for integration, stretching from one corner of the land to the other, and each related constructively to the workings of the rest. Through these combinations the entity of the nation-state drew itself together. This was naturally expressed in the form of self-awareness, and it is possible to illustrate the emergence of singular, state concepts in the public mind. Its outward perspective has been shown in earlier chapters, in the determination of parliament to countenance nothing but their own definition of the appropriate course in foreign affairs, as encapsulated in the insistence of Sir Edward Coke that there was only one "right enemy". The popular view was determined above all by the chosen national project of a trading empire, to be forged largely by dint of displacing the sea power of Spain. War with Spain, continued Sir Edward, "is England's best prosperity". Sir John Eliot agreed: "Let us remember that the war with Spain is our Indies, that there we shall fetch wealth and happiness".[12] This defined the outlook of the new state on the rest of the world. The most powerful inward dynamic of the state was reflected in the imperative popular demand for the unique service of sovereign representative law, which was appropriately hailed by John Pym as "that which makes and constitutes a kingdom".[13] A general understanding and acceptance of the authority of sovereign statute was inherent in the concept. People knew that the law was made binding through the exercise of their consent in parliament. Among other things, this made parliamentary law the best servant, and master of the integrated economy. It could meet the specific interests of the trading classes with definitive national provisions. The rights of trade and property would be protected by the same principle of consent that authorised the sovereign law itself. Freedom of trade from arbitrary exactions and restraints was duly installed as a special liberty of the English, as first proclaimed in 1604: "All subjects are born inheritable, as to their lands, so also to the exercise of their industry in those trades . . . it is against the natural right and liberty of the subjects of England to restrict it to some few".[14]

The establishment of a fully integrated and autonomous state also involved a different, and sharper definition of the country as a geographical whole. I have suggested elsewhere that the sixteenth century witnessed a significant transition in the way that the actual land was perceived.[15] This too reflected the emergence of the state as a separated entity out of the medieval context. In medieval Christendom there had been no sense of absolute separation in any sphere. People saw the land, like everything else, in an open continuum, and their relationship to it was direct and unmediated. But as the commons and open fields were broken up, many of the dispossessed smallholders came to work on the land at one remove, as wage labourers under the direction of employers on the consolidated, individual farms. The immediacy of contact was lost. Even for the employers there was a kind of withdrawal. Although they were asserting control over broader acres, they were standing back from the land, and treating it as a passive object, to be measured and manipulated. At the same time, the kingdom itself was coming to be defined as a discrete, political "land"—in some way and some degree distinguished from the actual working land. This was another aspect of the development of the state as a wholly detached unit.

There were strong links, both real and psychological, between the formation of consolidated individual properties, and the establishment of a completely autonomous state body. Both constituted a reversal of the medieval concept of land occupation. In the feudal relationships of the middle ages, all the definitions of land tenure, both legal and physical, militated against the assumption of absolute property rights. Land was not regarded as wholly "owned" and free of any other claims upon it. It was rather "granted" for use, under a series of conditions and obligations, not only to your lord, but also to your community—for land was held as a trust or stewardship from God, who had decreed that it must only be used in ways that served, and did not contradict the common good. The pattern of occupation on the open fields was the earthly reflection of a world where reality was seen not in terms of actual particulars, but of universal ideas, and the claims of the individual were always subordinate to the interests of the whole. So the copyhold farms were occupied as a multitude of strips, typically of an acre or less, scattered across the great open fields, and in the words of one contemporary "interlaced" with those of neighbours, with the original intention of giving each a fair share of the best land, and the worst. There were no fixed barriers between the strips or "lands", and they were worked cooperatively, with communal stores of hay, the open grazing of the stubble, and the sharing of expensive necessities like the oxen and the heavy plough, to sustain the livelihoods of all.

In line with these open dispensations, and like everything else in the medieval period, land was not conceived in discrete, separated forms. Earlier chapters have noted the revealing observations of the surveyor Valentine Leigh, who observed that it was only in the middle of the sixteenth century that anyone began to set down the holdings of each farmer in a collected form, "to know the parcels of land that belong to every messuage". Until then, it had been necessary to search for every strip, "in the generality of the whole survey of fields".[16] It is clear that on the common fields in medieval times, there had been no perceived need to record a complete individual holding in any respect. Even the land of the lord tended to be relatively dispersed in form, and indeed some of it might be held as strips in the open fields. And although the king was regarded as the overall landlord, by right of conquest and God's will, he had to contend with rivals within who believed the crown to be rightfully theirs, while his own claims might also extend to other realms. Last but by no means least, and infiltrating everywhere right across the continent of medieval Europe, were the vast lands of the universal church. The ecclesiastical estate was an independent authority, with its own judicial system, which it was often able to impose on everything around as a cultural norm. The fact that the church was the greatest of all landlords reflected the indeterminate character of land occupation in the medieval world, inhibiting the development of a concept of outright individual ownership.

So the expulsion of the universal church from England changed the nature as well as the personnel of land holding. The withdrawal of the ubiquitous presence of the church, and thus also of its direct influence over social mores, pulled away one of the principal props of communal practice on the open fields. At the same time as the availability of the church lands was greatly increasing the scope and inducement for property accumulation, so the disappearance of the spiritual figurehead removed the model of restraint that had exerted some degree of control over secular ambitions. Free license was given to the consolidation of larger agricultural units in individual hands, though this might mean the deprivation of the smallholders. The strictures of men like Robert Crowley that the enclosure and engrossing of common land was an ungodly activity no longer carried practical force. In a sense, Crowley's worst-case scenario that these practices would only be acceptable in a world where God did not exist had actually come to pass.

Landholding now became a uniformly secular affair, as the church lands passed rapidly into the hands of a national class of middling gentry and yeomanry. The purchases were often made for the purpose of filling out an individual holding or estate, and therefore tended to further reinforce the trend towards consolidated units. The sequence through which lay acquisition had taken place also served to solidify the sense of allegiance to the new unitary national land. The property of the church had been commandeered as an act of state, by king-in-parliament. It had then been redistributed among the general body of lay landowners. Nothing was better calculated to ensure the continued loyalty of the propertied class to the emergent nation-state. The close association between the integrity of the state and the property of the individual became apparent at once. The principal imperative of parliament from 1540 to 1560 was to sustain the autonomous powers of the new nation against any attempt by the Papacy to recover its lands in England.

So the process of the consolidation of landed properties developed under the protection of the unitary state structure. The body of the state provided a model of the "separated whole"—a concept that been quite alien to the open dispensations of the medieval world. Property rights were now established within that overall definition and preserved by the force of statute law. The assumption of state autonomy warded off any intention of the universal church to take back its property. And behind that rigid shield, the interests of individual landholdings were asserted and promoted by the force of sovereign representative law, the very concept that had displaced the independent judicial authority of the spiritual sphere. As Henry Ireton put it, to "know a law and have a certainty" was the necessary platform for trading successfully and acquiring property. Parliamentary law was seen as a state provision that naturally worked in favour of trading freedoms. Thus the West Country merchants could note that the one successful free trade bill of 1606 had been implemented by care of the House of Commons, and "the wisdom of the state in parliament".[17] Parliament championed the demand for a principled right of freedom trade against any kind of arbitrary exaction or restraint. This was an ambition shared by the gentry, the merchants and traders, and the commercialising yeoman farmers, and it was duly elevated into an assumed liberty of the English people as a whole.

The concepts of the wholly independent state, and the absolute individual property, grew hand in hand, and were to some extent interrelated. The disputes and debates of the Civil War gave rise to a good illustration of the way that the land of England came to be envisaged as a gathered, separated whole, and how this was reflected in the outlook of individual parliamentarians. Henry Ireton's impassioned defence of property in the Putney Debates is well known, though, as already noted, in this particular case he was preaching to the converted.[18] In fact, his assertion of the inherent political rights of the freeholders is notable most of all for the reference it makes to certain crucial aspects of the unitary state. Ireton shared John Pym's high estimation of statute law as the essential basis of the emergent national structure. In reply to Rainsborough's query as to what the soldiers had been fighting for, he summed up the defining aim of the parliamentary cause as the guarantee of government by representative law.

> The people of this kingdom must have this right at least, that they should not be concluded but by the Representative of those that have the interest of the kingdom . . . here was a right that induced men to fight.[19]

It was a powerful expression of the force of sovereign representative law as the principal integrating dynamic of the new political state. And representative law was above all the guarantor of property. As Maximilian Petty had affirmed, the preservation of property was precisely why men had conceived the notion of an elected representative. After all, the right of consent that gave binding authority to statute law was the same political principle around which the definition of a right of absolute property and freedom of trade had developed. All these precepts were embraced for the same reason. For Ireton, the central parliamentarian aim was to put the representative body in a position to perform its task of protecting property without gainsay.

> Some men fought in this because they were immediately concerned and engaged in it. . . . Others fought that they should have the benefit of those laws made by the Representative. . . . They thought it was better to be concluded by the common consent of those that were fixed men and settled men, that have the interest of this kingdom in them. 'And from that way I shall know a law and have a certainty'. Any man that was born is a denizen in it, that hath a freedom, he was capable of trading to get money, to get estates by.[20]

The idea of "the interest of this kingdom" carried a significance of its own. It was only since the second half of the sixteenth century that men could have spoken of the body of the freeholders having the interest of the kingdom in them. Only since then had the wholly independent state grown up, around the consolidated fabric of individual properties that composed it. Ireton was not talking of "the kingdom" in its medieval form of an open realm, in which only the king and the nobles could be said to have "an interest". He was speaking of the kingdom as the separated entity of the emergent state. In another place, indeed, he phrased it more specifically, and spoke of "those that have the interest of England in them".[21] It is worth recalling that by the second half of the seventeenth century the broad class of middling gentry and yeoman freeholders for whom Ireton spoke had physically come into possession of almost three-quarters of the land of England, which could thereby be seen as essentially composed of their individual properties, often assembled at the expense of the universal church and the open fields. This tended to encourage the idea that there was a connection between the emergence of England as a discrete unitary state, and the general definition of absolute property rights. This was the context in which individual landholdings could be taken to represent the whole, and it became possible to refer to "all those that have any personal interest in the kingdom, and who, taken together do comprehend the whole interest of the kingdom".[22]

Ireton went on to elaborate the connection. "I mean by permanent local that is not anywhere else". A freehold property "cannot be removed out of the kingdom".[23] Whereas, "if a man be an inhabitant upon a rack rent, for a year, for two years, or twenty years, you cannot think that that man hath any fixed or permanent interest . . . that man may have as much interest in another kingdom as here".[24] So it was England, as well as each freehold property within it, that was "not anywhere else". This was the necessary guarantee. The entity of England itself had to be fixed and permanent, and fully detached from the open continuum of medieval Christendom, before it was possible to regard the general body of the freeholders as having the "interest of England in them". They were released from the constraints of communal obligations, and all their properties together filled up, and were safeguarded within, the inviolate body of the state.

So Shakespeare's "other Eden . . . this fortress built by nature for herself against infection and the hand of war" was not just the Elizabethan kingdom successfully standing firm against the sea-borne might of Spain, it was the form of an autonomous state, of the modern kind, taking shape.[25] For the first time, England could now be seen as "nowhere else". The state structure was breaking up the old open, fluid patterns of moral economy and undifferentiated land occupation that had run continuously within and between the realms of medieval Europe. And behind the solid, moated walls of English statehood, the consolidation of individual property could proceed without respect to any broader interests beyond.

Thus the development of the nation-state and the process of the consolidation of individual landholdings were mutually reinforcing, and to a significant extent they grew together. They were in effect the macrocosm and microcosm of the "separated whole", a concept that had found no place in the open dispensations of medieval Christendom. The new English state was a self-sufficient political space, geared to excluding all counter-veiling claims and influences. Within it, the self-propriety of the absolute individual, as recorded by such as Richard Overton and Thomas Hobbes, went collectively and by election to make up the "unlimited" sovereignty of parliamentary law, which was the judicio-political cement of the state structure, and stood as the unrivalled champion of property. The emergence of the state was an important aspect of the context of the English Revolution. It gave definition to the parliamentary assumption of responsibility for the unitary public interest. It provided the parliamentarians with a ready-made basis for government when they displaced the royal regime in 1641. The individualist freedoms that the state structure reflected and protected were fundamental to parliamentarian motivations.

The arrival of the state also encouraged the "rise of capitalism". In fact, it may be said that the two forms grew together, and were mutually reinforcing. It is clear that the period constituted a critical, and in effect decisive stage in the development of a capitalist economy in England. In defining the shape of capitalism, emphasis has often been placed on a growing divide between merchant capital and craft labour in manufacturing. Fernand Braudel saw the changing conditions in the textile trade as the clearest indicator of capitalist advance, whereby through "division of labour, rationalisation and specialisation there grew up a textile industry on capitalist lines".[26] But division of labour was not the most important factor, and does not adequately explain the overall effect. It was only in England that a capitalist system acquired full force at this time, and it happened for reasons that were specific to England. One was the emergence of agrarian capitalism, based on the early break of manorial ties, and the subsequent spread of a new class of substantial yeomen farmers, who engaged in the consolidation of individualised commercial holdings. This only occurred on a significant scale in England.[27] It led to the displacement of many independent smallholders, who were often obliged to become wage labourers employed by their yeomen neighbours. This was a variant of the division of labour, but it was still not the critical development.

The most crucial aspect, which was equally distinctive to the English scene, and more directly instrumental to the revolutionary drive, was the assertion of a right to work and trade free of arbitrary impositions and restrictions. It was essentially about the relations of exchange. The demand for freedom of trade challenged the most vital prerogatives of the crown and sought to subject all public finance to the control of parliamentary consent. The establishment of the state structure did much to encourage and facilitate that demand. The emergent state was driven by the dynamic of sovereign representative law, and this was the context in which the principle of consent acquired broad, normative force. Economically, the discrete national unit was large enough to subsist independently, yet sufficiently integrated for a fully-fledged capitalist economy to take shape. It enabled a well-coordinated market to operate free of internal barriers and communal restraints. In place of the undifferentiated continuum of the medieval world, a new territorial concept had materialised. England was now the land of the "separated whole", which was reflected with peculiar force in the generalisation of consolidated individual property, the self-reciprocating market, and the autonomous state structure. A general process of commercialisation could proceed without fear of interruption by common interests, whether from within the realm or beyond. It only remained for the prerogatives and restrictive powers of the medieval monarchy to be brought to an end, and the continuous exercise of parliamentary law, and the representative control of public finance to be guaranteed.

The development of the nation-state in the sixteenth and early seventeenth centuries was as distinctive to England as were the great economic, judicial and political transitions that have been described in the foregoing pages. It was only in England that there emerged a national class of substantial yeomen farmers to broaden the base of commercialisation. It was only in England that the merchants and the gentry formed a powerful alliance to establish a right of freedom of trade and the parliamentary control of public finance, in contradiction of the prerogatives of the crown. It was only in England that every influential economic force was committed and contributing to a general process of intensified commercial activity, and the shape of a national market could be completed. It was only in England that there came to exist a concept of sovereign representative law that offered a paradigm for the right of consent, and a political basis upon which these individual freedoms could be asserted. Parliamentary law was the ultimate guarantor of property rights and could offer the definitive national regulations and provisions that the integrated economy required. All these things contributed to and drew upon the creation of a unitary state body, which was also peculiar to England at this time. The interrelated structures of individualist occupation and commercial integration go far to explain why a fully-fledged capitalist form of economy developed in sixteenth and seventeenth century England, and nowhere else to a significant degree.

A comparison with England's potential rivals in this respect is instructive. The United Provinces of the Netherlands presented a very different kind of unification from that which now obtained in England. They constituted an alliance of provinces that had managed to break free of Habsburg rule, and they composed a very limited form of integration. The great trading towns tended to operate independently. "The provinces preserved their separate rights and privileges . . . the governments of the main provinces, particularly Holland, were too closely aligned with particular capitalist interests for the central apparatus of the States General to take decisions that could advance their collective interest".[28] Similarly in France, there were areas of capitalist advance, but no unifying focus to draw them together. Perhaps most importantly, only England had the facility of a nationally definitive, sovereign representative law that was the basis of the completed, spontaneous integration of the state, and serviced and coordinated the commercial interests of the entire society, eradicating the claims of the old feudal dispensations as it went. The emergence of the first fully-fledged capitalist economy, and the first unitary state form were interdependent. This was why the new capitalist nation of England went from strength to strength, while the Dutch Republic went into decline.

The great socio-economic and political changes in England, which went together with the emergence of the unitary state form, were among the most critical transformations in our history. They were clearly recognised by Civil War contemporaries as a fundamental reordering, which for instance replaced the feudal and communal restraints of the past with a new class of yeoman farmers, who were "much unlinked from dependence upon their lords, and living in a free and plentiful manner". This provided a substantial platform for a parliamentary cause that depended largely on the fact that prerogative taxes and restrictions had become unacceptable to a "generation of men truly laborious and jealous of their properties, whose principal aim is liberty and plenty".[29] This was a mindset that Gerrard Winstanley elucidated more specifically in his analysis of the principal freedoms sought by the parliamentarians, which were: "the free use of trading, and to have all patents, licences and restraints removed", and the desire of the freeholders to be "landlord of the earth", to the exclusion of any outside claims, by commoners or kings.[30] The same motivation was voiced by the anonymous pamphleteer of 1642, who thought that tyranny was the greatest calamity "because it is in opposition to the greatest felicity, "which lies in liberty and the free disposition of that which God and our industry has made ours".[31] These were the actual freedoms that parliamentarians were seeking to guarantee by establishing the representative body as a permanent legislative and supervisory force at the centre of the polity.

This involved a reversal of many of the most important aspects of English life—in the rules and assumptions that governed economic activity, in the way that the land was occupied and perceived, in the frame in which the kingdom itself was defined, and in the balance of power between the prerogative and the representative. These transitions were visibly developing during the course of the late sixteenth and early seventeenth centuries in England. But it was an overturning so comprehensive that it involved a moment of inner collision and revolution. And it is in recognising the force of the revolutionary watershed of the 1640s that we comprehend the fundamental nature of the change, from the world that went before, to the world that we have now.

Notes

1. *Oliver Cromwell's Letters and Speeches*, ed. T. Carlyle, (London 1893), p. 148
2. TNA, SP28/133/2/84; 240/12, 338; 241/136
3. Devon RO, Totnes Borough Archive, 1579A/16/35
4. John Guy, *Tudor England,* (Oxford 1990), p. 352
5. Population trends from "The Significance of the Metropolis", in *London 1500–1600*, eds. A. L. Beier and R. Finlay, (London 1986), p. 3
6. F. J. Fisher, "The Development of London as a Centre of Conspicuous Consumption in the 16th and 17th Centuries", in *Essays in Economic History,* ed. E. M. Carus-Wilson, (London 1962), II, pp. 197ff; J. Thirsk, *Economic Policy and Projects: The Development of a Consumer Society in Early Modern England,* (Oxford 1978), p. 179
7. W. Harrison, "A Description of England, (1577–1587)", in *Tudor Economic Documents*, eds. R. Tawney and E. Power, (London 1951), III, pp. 68–70
8. M. Overton, *The Agricultural Revolution in England,* (Cambridge 1996), pp. 22. 45, 133
9. A. Everitt, "The Open Market", in *Agrarian History of England and Wales 1500–1640*, ed. J. Thirsk, (Cambridge 1967), pp. 490, 496, 500
10. C. Wilson, *England's Apprenticeship,* (London 1965), pp. 66–8
11. J. Chartres, *Internal Trade in England 1500–1700,* (London 1977), p. 13

12. For Coke and Eliot See above, pp. 209, 21
13. See above, pp. 244–5
14. *Commons Journal*, I, p. 218
15. G. Yerby, *The English Revolution and the Roots of Environmental Change: The Changing Concept of the Land in Early Modern England,* (Abingdon 2016)
16. Valentine Leigh, *The Most Profitable and Commendable Science of Surveying,* (London 1577), BL 967. k. 15, un-paginated, but as counted, p. 61
17. Devon Record Office, Totnes Borough Archive, 1579A/16/35
18. See above, p. 374
19. "The Putney Debates", in *Puritanism and Liberty*, ed. A. S. P. Woodhouse, (London 1938), p. 72
20. Ibid
21. Ibid, p. 70
22. Ibid, pp. 57–8
23. Ibid
24. Ibid, pp. 62–3
25. William Shakespeare, *Richard II*, Act 2, Scene 1
26. F. Braudel, *The Mediterranean,* (London 1972), p. 213
27. See above, Chapter 1
28. N. Davidson, *How Revolutionary Were the Bourgeois Revolutions*, Abridged edition, (Chicago 2017), p. 96
29. James Harrington, *The Commonwealth of Oceana* (1656), ed. H. Morley, (London 1887), p. 59; John Corbet, "A True and Impartial History of the Military Government of the City of Gloucester", in *A Collection of Scarce and Valuable Tracts . . . of the Late Lord Somers*, ed. Sir Walter Scott, (London 1809–15), V, pp. 303–4, 307
30. Gerrard Winstanley, "The Law of Freedom in a Platform", in *Winstanley: "The Law of Freedom" and Other Writings,* ed. C. Hill, (Cambridge 1983), p. 294
31. *A Brief Discourse on Tyrants and Tyranny*, November 1642, BL E127, (45), p. 1

Appendix

Locations of Civil War Allegiance in Nottinghamshire

Parliamentarians

The more eminent parliamentarian figures, such as William Pierrepont, Henry Ireton and the Hutchinsons left a strong imprint on the national records, many of which are cited in the chapters referring to them. For the generality of local supporters, the criterion for inclusion in the list is evidence of activity. This might include military or administrative service, the gift or loan of money, and the provision of supplies. The list does not include those who were named to a committee, but are not known to have been active, though it is likely that such people were thought to be parliamentary sympathisers. The personnel display some important differences from the basis of Royalist support. All the Royalists named were in the garrison at Newark, though they originate from places widely spread around the county. The Parliamentarian list, by contrast, includes many donors and activists from outside the Nottingham garrison, though they are from a much tighter area of West Nottinghamshire. Since the evidence is more extensive and varied, more can be said in detail about their activities.

The sources used are as follows. A. C. Wood, *Nottinghamshire in the Civil War*, (London 1936), pp. 127–135, 223 (for committee members). *Records of the Borough of Nottingham*, V, pp. 210–11 (for Nottingham donors). TNA, SP24/H39–H48 (for parliamentarian petitions). TNA, SP28/174/41–4 (for Nottingham donors).

TNA, SP28/133/2/83–8 (for Broxtow donors). Lucy Hutchinson, *Memoirs of the Life of Colonel Hutchinson*, ed. J. Hutchinson, pp. 136–9 (for troop commanders).

Acklom, Major, of Wiseton. Raised troop.

Aldred, Josiah, Colonel of Bilborough. Associated with the Betteridge family of Strelley.

Anton, George, Esq. of Boughton. Associated with Rowland Foster.

Ashhurst, William, of Nottingham. Donor.

Ausborne, Goodman, of Nuthall. Coal agent. Entrusted with paying colliers.

Ayscough, Edward, of Nuthall, Lesser gentry. Donor. Associated with Ireton family.

Astlyn, John, of Nottingham. Donor.

Badge, Richard, of Nottingham. Wheelright. Corporal, under Richard Dolphin.

Baker, Jerome, of Nottingham. Donor.

Baker, Robert, of Nottingham. Entrusted with payments.

Baker, Thomas, of Cotgrave. In Henry Champion's troop.

Baker, William, of Wilford. Given charge of Scottish prisoners August 1648.

Balderson, Mrs., of Nottingham. Donor.

Barker, John, of Nottingham. Recompensed as a maimed soldier.

Barnes, James, and his mother, of Nottingham. Donors.

Barrett, William, Captain. Location unknown.

Barton, Thomas, of Nottingham. Trooper. Purchased own horse and arms.

Bateman, Mr., of Nottingham. Donor.

Batty, Thomas, of Nottingham, coal-monger.

Baylie, John, of Nottingham. Donor.

Beardsley, Anthony, of Hucknall. Broxtow garrison. Donor.

Beck, Thomas, of Nottingham. Donor.

Bell, John, of Nottingham. Donor.

Bellamy, John, of Nottingham, Gent. Sequestrator.

Betteridge, Henry, of Strelley. Soldier with Gervase Lomax.

Bonnington, Anthony, of Hucknall. Broxtow garrison. Donor.

Boote, Henry, of Nottingham. Donor.

Bracknell, Lancelot, of Hucknall. Broxtow garrison. Donor.

Bradshaw, John, of Hucknall. Broxtow garrison. Donor.

Brasgirdle, (Mr.) of Stapleford. Broxtow garrison. Donor.

Briggs, Richard, of Basford. Entrusted with payments.

Brough, George, of Hucknall. Broxtow garrison. Donor.

Brough, Richard, of Hucknall, (Yeoman). Broxtow garrison. Donor.

Bruntz, Robert, of Mansfield Woodhouse. Sub-committee.

Buller, Thomas, of Newark.

Burrowes, Gervase, of Nottingham. Entrusted with large sums of money.

Burrowes, Robert, of Nottingham. Donor. Sequestrator.

Burrowes, Samuel, (Mercer) of Nottingham. Donor. Large amounts.

Butcher, John, of Hucknall, Donor.

Butler, Lancelot, of Hucknall. Broxtow garrison. Donor.

Butler, John, of Hucknall. Broxtow garrison.

Butler, William, of Kimberley. Broxtow garrison. Donor.

Chadwick, John, Barrister, of Nottingham. Original committee. Resolute.
Champion, Henry, of Cotgrave and Collingham. Raised troop of horse.
Charlton, Nicholas, of Chilwell. Yeoman and mine owner. Committee. Big donor.
Charlton, Thomas, of Chilwell and Nottingham. Donor.
Clarke, Leonard, Tailor, of Bingham. Well affected. Pride's regiment.
Clarke, Peter, elder brother of above, also in Pride's regiment.
Clarke, Samuel, of Nottingham, Cornet to Henry Ireton. Raised horse troop.
Clarke, Thomas, of Hucknall. Broxtow garrison. Donor.
Clarkson, John, of Hucknall. Broxtow garrison. Donor.
Caunt, William, of Nottingham. Donor.
Cludd, Edward, of Southwell.
Coates, Samuel, Godly cleric, of Nottingham. Raised troop.
Cock, William, of Nottingham. Lent money. Donor.
Collins, Edward, Mr., of Nottingham. Garrison engineer
Collishaw, Robert, of Nottingham. Donor.
Collishaw, Robert, of Lemton. Donor.
Collishaw, Thomas, of Bilborough. Recompensed for ill health.
Cooke, Adrian, of Nottingham. Quartermaster. Donor.
Cooke, Francis, of Nottingham. Donor.
Cooke, Nicholas, of Wilford Entrusted with payments.
Cooke, Thomas, Mr., of Nottingham. Donor.
Cooke, William, of Eastwood. Broxtow garrison.
Cooper, John, Mr., of Nottingham. Donor.
Cooper, Richard, of Nottingham. Served under Richard Dolphin.
Cooper, Thomas, of Nottingham. Donor.
Cramplin, Richard, of Nottingham. Donor.
Crooke, William, of Hucknall. Broxtow garrison. Donor.
Crosley, John, of Kirkby-in-Ashfield. Died in state's service.
Dodsley, Mr., of Nottingham.
Dolly, Widow, of Nottingham. Donor.
Dolphin, Luke, of Nottingham. Cordwainer. Gave brother Michael £15 for soldiers.
Dolphin, Michael, of Cossall. Commanded troop of horse.
Dolphin, Richard, of Nottingham. Captain of foot company. Paid for garrison coal.
Dringe, Mr., of Nottingham. Donor.
Drury, John, of Nottingham. Godly. Collector.
Drury, William, of Nottingham. Alderman and Mayor. Active committee.
Dyson, John, of Nottingham. Foot soldier for parliament. Continuing in the design.
Edge, Ralph, of Nottingham. Lawyer. Donor. Took over Strelley coal mines.

Egginton, Brownlow, of Nottingham. Lieutenant. Payment of troops.
Egginton, Robert, of Nottingham. Ensign.
Ellot, Widow, of Nottingham. Donor.
Eyre, Huntingdon, of Nottingham. Donor.
Farnsworth, Richard, of Nottingham. Trooper.
Faulconbridge, George, of Hucknall. Yeoman, Broxtow garrison. Donor.
Fellingham, Mr., of Nottingham. Donor.
Flamstead, Mr., of Nottingham. Donor.
Flower, George, of Hucknall, Donor. Mining interests. Friend of Nicholas Charlton.
Forman, Charles, of Nottingham. Donor.
Foster, Christopher, of Boughton. Yeoman.
Foster, Rowland, of Boughton, Yeoman. Advanced parliament's service since beginning.
Foxcroft, John, of Gotham. Godly minister. Joined the parliament at the beginning.
Gamble, Mary, of Nottingham. Garrison nurse.
Gamble, Corporal, of Nottingham.
Gamble, Thomas, of Nottingham, Mayor. Donor. Committee.
Garner, Adrian, of Nottingham. Donor.
Garton, (Goodwife), of Wilford. Godly. Tended wounded soldiers.
Garton, William, of Wilford, Godly. Collector. Kept sequestered beasts.
Gilman, Richard, of Hucknall, Donor. Broxtow garrison.
Grantham, Dame Lucy, of Radcliffe on Sour and Nottingham. Donor.
Greaves, (Mr.) of Nuthall. Donor. Broxtow garrison.
Greene, Richard, of Hucknall. Donor. Broxtow garrison.
Gregory, John, of Nottingham. Alderman. Donor. Active committee.
Gregory, John, of Brinsley. Collector in Brinsley, Eastwood and Strelley.
Gregory, Joseph, of Arnold. Collector in Arnold and Kirkby. Pays for garrison coal.
Gregory, Robert, of Brinsley. Nottingham garrison.
Groves. Mrs. of Nottingham. Donor.
Hacker, Francis, Colonel, of East Bridgeford. Regicide.
Hall, Henry, of Thoroton. Gent. Donor.
Hall, Richard, probably of Lowdham.
Hall, Stephen, probably of Gotham. Lieutenant. Received payments.
Hall, William, of Nottingham. Tanner. Donor.
Hall, William, of Nottingham. Vintner. Donor.
Hanford, John, of Eastwood, Cornet. Provisions for the public service.
Hanford, Robert, of Eastwood Hall. Yeoman. Donor. Broad lands around Broxtow.

Hardnett, Richard, of Nottingham. Alderman. Skinner. Donor. Original committee.
Hawkins, Richard, of Nottingham. Clerk of ammunitions.
Heape, Francis, of Gedling. Farm sequestered to him. Added to committee.
Hearden, Timothy, of Nottingham. Donor.
Helmsley, William, of Nottingham. Donor.
Henton, Thomas (Mr.), of Nottingham. Donor.
Hezellam, Elijah, of Nottingham. Donor.
Hides, Thomas, of Nottingham. Donor.
Higden, Mrs., of Nottingham. Donor.
Hill, Francis, of Bilborough. Donor. Broxtow garrison.
Hill, Joshua, of Nottingham. Donor.
Hilton, John, of Nottingham. Donor.
Holmes, Stephen, of Nottingham. Donor.
Holt, Thomas, of Nottingham. Donor.
Hood, Mr, of Nottingham. Donor.
Hooper, John, of Nottingham. Garrison engineer. Godly.
Hooton, Gervase, of Nottingham. Castle works and canoneer.
Hooton, Paul, of Nottingham. Service to the parliament.
Hough, John, of Nottingham. Notary. Committee treasurer. Donor.
Howet, William, of Eastwood. Husbandman. Lands sequestered to him. Donor.
Howlett, John, of Nottingham. Shoemaker. Maintained son in the state's service.
Hurt. Richard, Mr., of Nottingham. Donor.
Hutchinson, George, of Nottingham.
Hutchinson, John, of Basford. Colonel. Garrison governor.
Hutchinson, Lucy, of Basford. Garrison governess. Author of Hutchinson Memoirs.
Hutchinson, Thomas. Knight, of Owthorpe. Parliamentarian MP.
Ireton, Henry, of Attenborough. Raised troop. National arena. Parliamentarian publicist.
Jacques, Mr. of Toton. Donor. Broxtow garrison. Associate of Henry Ireton.
Jackson, Lawrence, of Eastwood. Donor. Broxtow garrison.
Jackson, probably Richard, of Nottingham. Linen draper. Ensign.
Jackson, Eliza, widow of above, held sequestered lands in Sneinton.
Jalland, Thomas, of Scarrington. £15 for service of parliament.
Jalland, William, of Nottingham. Donor.
James, Henry, Mr., of Nottingham. Donor.
James, John, of Nottingham. Alderman. Donor. Leading supporter.
James, Thomas, of Nottingham. Garrison wagon master.
Jervis, Widow, of Strelley, Donor. Broxtow garrison.

Kirkby, Robert, of Nottingham. Captain.

Lacock, Philip, of Nottingham, Solicitor. Committee accounts signatory. Donor.

Langford, William, of Mansfield. Given sequestered lands.

Lawson, Thomas, of Nottingham. Godly. Gave horses. Paid for pains in public service.

Lealand, William, of Nottingham. Donor.

Letton, William, of Nottingham. Surgeon. Godly. Parliamentarian petition.

Linley, Thomas, of Skegby.

Lomax, Gervase, of Thrumpton. Gentry. Captain. Fought with Cromwell and Ireton.

Ludlow, Mr. of Nottingham. Donor.

Lynn, Robert, of Nottingham. Colonel Hutchinson's troop.

Lynne, Thomas, of Annesley. Sergeant under Richard Dolphin.

Mabbutt, Edward, senior, of Nottingham. Donor.

Mabbutt, Thomas. Provided coals for public service.

Malyn, (Mr.) of Nottingham. Donor.

Martin, John, of Nottingham. Donor. Committee signatory.

Martin, Richard, of Strelley. Donor. Broxtow garrison.

Mason, John, of Nottingham. Lawyer. Captain. Added to committee. Resolute.

Meanell, Daniel, of Nottingham. Baker. Parliamentarian soldier.

Medlum, Thomas, of Bulwell. One of Charles White's dragoons. Supplies for Broxtow.

Meldrum, John, Major. Sent by parliament to command Nottinghamshire forces.

Millington, Charles, of Felley Abbey. Committee. Became active in London. Regicide.

Millner, Randle, of Nottingham. Donor.

Mitton, John, of Nottingham. Donor.

Molyneux, Francis, (Sir) of Teversal. Added to committee.

Moore, Mr., of Strelley. Donor. Broxtow.

Morris, John, location unknown. Goes to Derbyshire for charcoal.

Musson, Thomas, of Kingston-on-Soar. Carrying warrants.

Needham, Will, of Staunton. Raised troop and served on committee.

Nethercoates, Edward, of West Bridgeford. Captain.

Nethercoates, Mrs., a parliamentarian nurse. Regular payments and coal deliveries.

Newton, Mr., of Sutton-in-Ashfield. Substantial donor.

Newton, John, of Hucknall, Donor. Broxtow garrison.

Nixe, William, of Notingham. Original committee. Donor. Resolute.

Nodin, John, of Nottingham. Donor.

Noone, Widow, of Strelley.

Oldershaw, Rose, of Lenton. Regular payments for nursing sick soldiers.

Oldershaw, Mr., of Lenton, also a supporter.

Oxley, Mary and Isabel, of Nottingham. Donors.

Palmer, Lawrence, of Gedling. Parson. Raised troop. Collecting for Broxtow.

Parker, Widow, of Nottingham. Donor.

Parker, Mr. William, senior, of Nottingham. Donor.

Parker, Mr. William, junior, of Nottingham. Apothecary. Donor.

Parsons, Mr., of Nottingham, Donor.

Pendock, Barry, of Tollerton.

Pendock, Richard, of Tollerton. Lesser gentry. Committee. Resolute.

Pendock, Philip, of Tollerton. Son of Richard. Captain. Related to Nicholas Charlton.

Pierrepont, Francis, of Nottingham. 3rd son of Earl of Kingston. For righteous liberty.

Pierrepont, William, of Thoresby, 2nd son of Earl of Kingston. Leading politician.

Pigott, Gervase, of Thrumpton. Lesser gentry. Godly. Committee. Resolute.

Pinder, John, of Hucknall. Donor. Broxtow.

Plumtree, Huntingdon, of Nottingham. Doctor. Committee. Athiest. Resolute.

Pogson, Michael, of Hucknall, Donor. Broxtow.

Poulston, Mrs, of Hucknall, Donor. Broxtow garrison.

Poulton, Thomas, probably of Nottingham. Company of foot under Francis Pierrepont.

Porter, Richard, of Mansfield Woodhouse. Yeoman. Signed for committee of accounts.

Porter, William, of Eastwood. Donor. Broxtow.

Pott, Robert, of Nottingham. Donor.

Reason, Mrs., Donor.

Reckbye, William, of Strelley. Donor. Broxtow.

Reynes, Robert, of Stanton-on-the Wolds. Lesser gentry. Donor. Accounts committee.

Reynor, Thomas, of Hucknall. Donor.

Richards, Edward, of Nottingham. Donor.

Richards, John, of Newthorpe, Yeoman. Donor. Broxtow.

Richards, John, of Nottingham. Donor.

Richards, William, of Nottingham. Donor. Signed for committee. Mayor 1648–1649.

Riley, William, of Nottingham. Maltster. Sequestrator. Donor.

Ryley. Widow, of Nottingham. Donor.

Roberts, Edward, of Newthorpe. Donor. Broxtow.

Robinson, Matthew, Ensign, of Nottingham. George Hutchinson's company.

Rotheram, James, Ensign, of Nottingham.

Rowse, John, of Newark. Driven thence with his family.

Rudder, Peter, Ensign, of Clipston. Yeoman.

Russell, Edward, of Eastwood. Sequestrator and collector.

Russell, William, of Eastwood. Donor. Broxtow.

Sacheverell, Henry, of Barton-in-Fabis. Original committee. Connected with Ireton.

Salisbury, Thomas, of Nottingham. Original committee. Treasurer.

Sawre, John, of Nottingham. Yeoman. Died in state's service in Scotland in 1651.

Saxon, Robert, of Nottingham, Donor.

Scrimshaw, John, of Cotgrave. Committee of accounts. Troop of infantry.

Sergeant, Richard, of Hucknall, Donor. Broxtow.

Selby, Thomas, of Nottingham. Blacksmith. Captain. Raised company of foot.

Silvester, Robert, of Nottingham. Donor. Took money to Charles White.

Smalley, John, of Nottingham. Donor.

Smith, Henry, of Newthorpe. Donor. Broxtow.

Somersall, Robert, of Mansfield, Yeoman. Sub-committee of accounts.

Stevenson, John, and his mother, of Nottingham. Donors.

Strey, Nicholas, of Beeston. Yeoman. Sub-committee of accounts. Providing hay.

Starbucke, William, of Toton. Donor. Broxtow.

Stone, George, of Hucknall. Donor. Broxtow. Rode with Richard Dolphin.

Story, John, of Hucknall, Donor. Boxtow.

Sully, Roger, of Nottingham, Lieutenant. Collector of sequestrated rents in Eastwood.

Sumner, Mr., of Nottingham. Donor.

Swindon, John, of Greasley. Extraordinary pains organising 40 oaks from Bulwell.

Sylvester, Gregory, Mr., of Nottingham. Donor.

Sylvester, Robert, of Nottingham. Donor.

Symons, Robert, of Nottingham, Donor.

Symons, Roger, of Nottingham. Donor.

Taylor, Robert, of Nottingham. Donor.

Terrill, Arthur, Mr., of Nottingham, Collector and organiser of timber.

Thompson, Richard, of Eakring. Yeoman. Petition.

Thorpe, Anthony, of Eakring. Yeoman. Petition.

Thornaugh, Francis, of Gotham and Nottingham. Gentry. Committee. Horse troop.

Thornaugh, Sir Francis, of Fenton House. Father of above. Gentry. Committee,

Toll, Richard, of Hucknall, Yeoman. Donor. Broxtow.

Tomlin, Roger, of Nuthall. Donor. Broxtow.

Tomlyn, Mr., of Nottingham. Donor.

Troupe, Edward, of Nottingham. Petition. Served state faithfully, leaving vocation.

Trowell, James, of Nottingham. Donor.

Turpin, Mr., of Nottingham. Donor.

Vaus, Ralph, of Cotgrave. Yeoman. Wealthy. Donor. Cornet to Henry Champion.

Viccars, Henry, of Eastwood. Sergeant. Petition. Totally employed for the service.

Viccars, William, of Eastwood. Lieutenant. Employed in public service.

Wagge, Widow, of Strelley. Donor. Broxtow garrison.

Walker, John, of Nottingham. Donor.

Ward, William, of Nottingham. Donor.

Whalley, Edward, of Screveton. Raised troop but served outside.

Wilkinson, Christopher, of Hucknall. Donor. Broxtow.

Wingfield, Thomas, of Nottingham. Donor.

Woolley, Thomas, Mr., of Nottingham. Donor.

Wright, John of Nottingham. Captain. Raised troop. Donor.

Wright, John, of Hucknall, Donor. Broxtow garrison.

Wright, Thomas, of Bramcote. Raised foot company, with Henry and William Viccars.

Whitby, Richard, Mr., of Trowell. Donor. Broxtow garrison.

Whitby, Captain. Operating in Broxtow.

Whitby, Mr., of Nottingham. Donor.

White, Charles, of Newthorpe and Greasley. Yeoman. First to raise troop of horse.

White, The Lady, of Nottingham. Donor.

Whiteman, William, of Cotgrave. Original committee. Associated with Charles White.

Widdowson, Richard, of Thrumpton, Hay for the public service. Associate of Lomax.

Widmerpool, Joseph, of Widmerpool. Committee. Gentry. Raised foot company.

Wilkman, Christopher, of Hucknall. Donor. Broxtow garrison.

Wood, Thomas, of Bilborough. Donor. Broxtow garrison.

Royalists

Royalists are identified and located from the records of the Newark garrison, in *HMC* 1964, pp. 75–95, "Newark on Trent, the Civil War Siegeworks", and A. C. Wood, *Nottinghamshire in the Civil War*, Appendix 2, pp. 217–222. The Royalists are fewer in number than the Parliamentarians because a high proportion of the soldiers in Newark came from Lincolnshire. This is in stark contrast to the Parliamentary garrisons, where all the soldiers seem to have come from Nottinghamshire, and from a very specific district within the county. The Royalist cause depended heavily on the greater gentry, whose estates were spread throughout the county and beyond. The clusters of Royalists registered at places like Southwell and Newstead, reflect the extended kinship groups or affiliations of the gentry themselves. There is no obvious indication that they were raising many troops from among their tenants, though no doubt this was occurring at some level. Another reason that there are fewer Royalists in view is that the king's support appears to have been very top heavy.

Andrews, Edward, of Oxton.
Andrews, William, of Blyth.
Armstrong, Gilbert, of Rempstone.
Atkinson, Gilbert, of Newark.
Atkinson, John, of Newark.
Atkinson, Thomas, of Newark. Alderman.
Baker, William, of Newark.
Barker, John, of Southwell.
Barwick, William, of Normanton.
Bellasis, Lord John, of Holme.
Bingham, John, of Hayton.
Blackwell, Sir Thomas, of Mansfield Woodhouse. Commissioner of Array.
Bohun, Gilbert, of Normanton. Recorder of Newark.
Bowler, Edward, of Nottingham.
Brightman, Richard, of Nottingham.
Broadhead, William, of Nottingham.
Brown, Francis, of Newark.
Butler, Robert, of Southwell.
Byron, Gilbert, of Newstead. Colonel. Governor of Rutland Castle.
Byron, Lord John, of Newstead.
Byron, Philip, of Newstead.
Byron, Sir Richard, of Strelley. Governor of Newark.
Byron, Robert, of Newstead.
Byron, Sir Thomas, of Newstead.
Byron, William, of Newstead.
Cam, Henry, of Newark. Alderman.

Capel, Lord Arthur. Greasley and Selston.
Cartright, Sir Hugh, of Southwell.
Cartwright, Hugh, of Southwell.
Cartwright, John, of Wheatley.
Cartwright, William of Ossington.
Chaworth, Lord John, of Wiverton.
Chesterfield, Earl Philip, of Shelford.
Clarke, Richard, of Newark.
Clifton, Sir Gervase, of Clifton. Commissioner of Array.
Cock, Charles, of Sutton Bonnington.
Cock, William, of Brinsley.
Conde, John, of Newark.
Cooper, Michael, of Thurgarton.
Cooper, Sir Roger, of Thurgarton.
Cooper, Cecil, of Thurgarton.
Dand, Rowland, of Mansfield Woodhouse.
Digby, Sir John, of Mansfield Woodhouse. Commissioner of Array.
Draper, Richard, of Flintham.
Dugdale, John, of Worksop.
Eyre, Anthony, of Rampton.
Eyre, Sir Gervase, of Rampton.
Fields, Richard, of Nottingham.
Fitzwilliam, Oliver, of Nottingham.
Forster, Edward, of Newark.
Fox, John, of Warsop.
Garlick, John, of Hayton.
Gilbey, Anthony, of Everton. Lieutenant Colonel.
Gill, Henry, of Newark.
Glossop, Thomas, of Nottingham.
Golding, Sir Edward, of Colston Basset.
Golding, John, of Colston Basset.
Greaves, Robert, of Nottingham.
Grundy, William, of Newark.
Hacker, Rowland, of East Bridgford and Colston Basset. Colonel. Governor of Wiverton.
Hacker, Thomas, of East Bridgford and Colston Basset.
Haslam, Christopher, of Newark. Alderman.
Hays, Robert, of Newark.
Hickman, Sir Willoughby, of Gainsborough and Mattersey.
Hobman, Thomas, of Newark.
Hobman, William, of Newark.
Houlder, Thomas, of South Wheatley. Commissioner of Array.
Hynde, Burton, of Nottingham.
Jackson, Luke, of Nottingham.
Johnson, John, of Newark.

Langford, Anthony, of Upton.
Lascelles, Henry, of Beckingham.
Leake, Francis, of Houghton and Newark.
Lee, Gervase, of Norwell.
Machell, William, of Retford.
Markham, John of Dunham.
Markham, Robert, of Dunham. Commissioner of Array.
Markham, Thomas, of Ollerton. Colonel.
Marshall, Richard, of Newark.
Martin, John, of Newark.
Martin, Robert, of Newark.
Martin, William, of Newark.
Mason, Thomas, of Southwell. Captain.
Mazine, John, of Carburton.
Mellish, Robert, of Ragnall. Commissioner of Array.
Melyn, Anthony, of Nottingham.
Millington, John, of Sturton.
Molineux, Roger, of Tevershall.
Molineax, Rutland, of Little Muskham.
Moore, Sir Edward, of Kirklington.
Moore, John, of Kirklington.
Neville, Anthony, of Grove. Major.
Newark, Lord Henry (Pierrepont), of Holme Pierrepont.
Newcastle, Earl William, of Welbeck.
Newport, John, of Orchard.
Newton, Thomas, of Bole.
Norris, John, of Newark.
North, Charles, of Walkeringham.
Palmer, Sir Matthew, of Southwell.
Parkyns, Isham, of Bunny.
Paulden, William, of Newark. Captain.
Payne, Adam, of Nottingham.
Pearson, Richard, of Flintham.
Pocklington, William, of Collingham.
Porter, Richard, of Mansfield Woodhouse. In the garrison at Welbeck.
Powtrell, Henry, of Chilwell.
Pusey, Timothy, of Selston.
Queninborough, John, of Newark. Alderman.
Ridgeway, William, of Nottingham.
Rogers, Elizabeth, of Everton.
Rogers, John, of Everton.
Rolleston, Lancelot, of Watnall. Colonel. Governor of Newark.
Royston, Ralph, of Claworth.
Sanderson, Robert, of Blyth.
Sanderson, William, of Blyth.

Sandys, John, of Laneham.
Sandys, Samuel, of Lound Woods.
Sandys, William, of Askham. Colonel.
Savile, Sir William, of Rufford.
Scrope, Simon, of East Bridgeford.
Shaw, Robert, of Nottingham. In the garrison at Wiverton.
Shipman, Thomas, of Scarrington. Captain.
Smith, Sir Thomas, of Broxtowe.
Somers, Thomas, of Newark.
Spight, William, of Rolleston.
Standish, Edward, of Newark. Mayor, 1645.
Stanhope, Ferdinand, of Shelford.
Stanhope, Michael, of Shelford.
Stanhope, Philip, of Shelford.
Stanhope, William, of Arnold or Linby.
Staunton, William, of Staunton. Colonel. Commissioner of Array.
Stringer, Nicholas, of Sutton on Lound.
Sutton, Robert, of Averham. Commissioner of Array.
Tevery, John, of Stapleford.
Thompson, Joseph, of Newark.
Thompson, Lancelot, of Newark.
Thompson, William, of Newark.
Tresse, Hugh, of Newark.
Tresse, Thomas, of Newark. Alderman.
Tyrwitt, William, of Laneham.
Walker, John, of Mansfield Woodhouse. Captain.
Warren, Arthur, Sibthorpe.
Watson, William, of Newark. Alderman.
Wells, George, of Newark.
Whalley, Peniston, of Screveton.
Wharwood, John, of Mansfield.
Wildaye, Samuel, of Nottingham.
Williamson, Robert, Lound Hall and Haughton.
Williamson, Sir Thomas, of East Markham. Commissioner of Array.
Wood, George, of Newark.
Wood, Richard, of Nottingham.

Notable Non-conformist Groups by Parish

This incorporates three sources: my study of parishes with a persistent record of non-conformist offences between 1604 and 1640, in *People and Parliament* (Basingstoke 2008), chap. 7, "Politics and Religion"; R. A. Marchant's list of Puritan ministries, which could often conceal non-conformist practice, in *Puritans and the Church Courts*, (London 1960), pp. 325–6; and parishes that registered more than one in ten dissenters in the Archdeaconry survey of 1676, Nottingham University Library, Archdeaconry Misc. 258, Compton Returns.

Grove
Adboulton Girton
Annesley Hawton
Attenborough Hayton
Beeston Kneesall
Bawtry Marnham
Barnby Mansfield
Burton Joyce Nottingham
Babworth Normanton-on-Soar
Boughton Newark
Balderton Ordsall
Bramcote Ossington
Cotgrave Rempstone
Collingham, North Saunby
Carlton-in-Lindrick Skegby
Clareborough South Leverton
Clayworth Stanton-in-the-Wold
Cromwell Sneinton
Elksley Scrooby
East Retford Sutton-in-Ashfield
Eastwood Sibthorpe
Everton Thrumpton
Flintham Treswell
Farndon Winthorpe
Gotham Worksop
Greasley West Bridgeford
Gringley-on-the-Hill Willoughby

Index